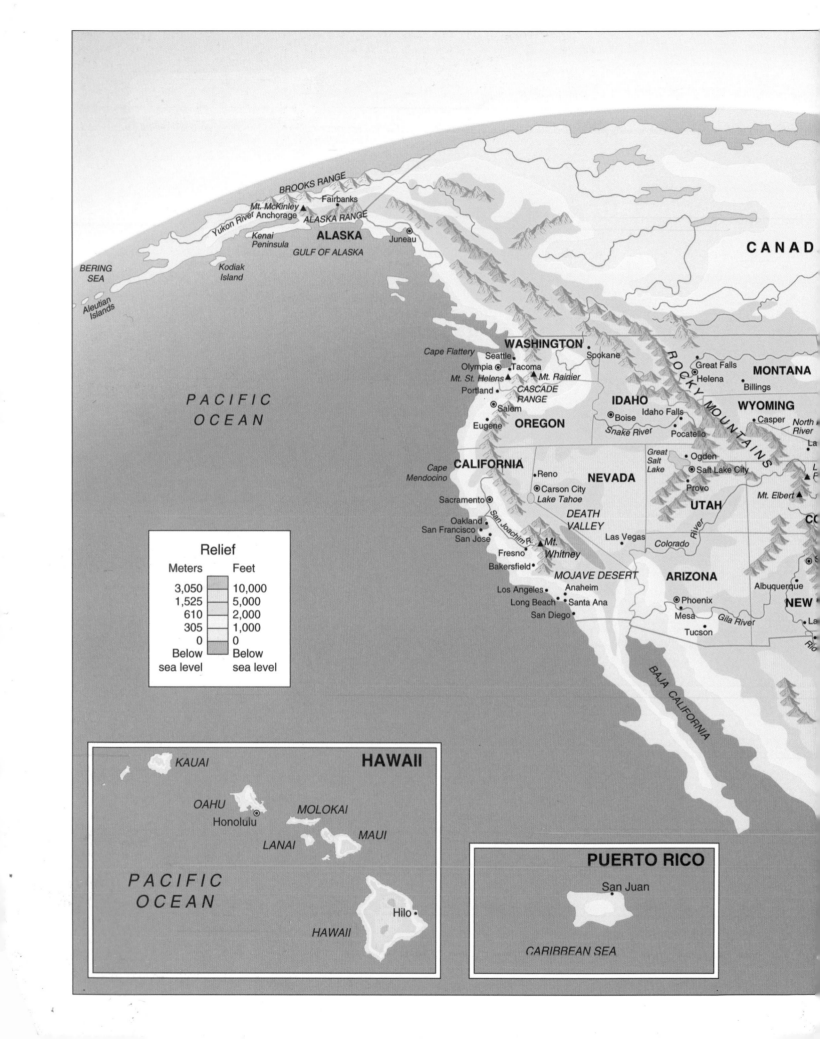

BROOKS RANGE

Fairbanks

Mt. McKinley ▲
Anchorage
ALASKA RANGE
Yukon River

Kenai
Peninsula
ALASKA

Juneau ◎

GULF OF ALASKA

**BERING
SEA**

Kodiak
Island

Aleutian
Islands

CANAD

**PACIFIC
OCEAN**

Cape Flattery
WASHINGTON
Seattle ●
Olympia ◎ ● Tacoma
Mt. St. Helens ▲   ▲ Mt. Rainier
Portland ●
**CASCADE
RANGE**
● Salem
Eugene
OREGON

Spokane

ROCKY MOUNTAINS

● Great Falls
Helena
● Billings
MONTANA

IDAHO
Boise ◎   Idaho Falls ●
Snake River   ● Pocatello

WYOMING
● Casper
North
River

La

Cape
Mendocino
CALIFORNIA
● Reno
◎ Carson City
Lake Tahoe
NEVADA

Sacramento ◎

Oakland ●
San Francisco ●
San Jose ●
San Joaquin R.
Fresno ●
▲ Mt.
Whitney
Bakersfield ●

**DEATH
VALLEY**

Las Vegas ●

Great
Salt
Lake
● Ogden
◎ ● Salt Lake City
● Provo
UTAH

Colorado
River

▲ Mt. Elbert ▲

CO

MOJAVE DESERT

Los Angeles ●   Anaheim ●
Long Beach ●   ● Santa Ana
San Diego ●

ARIZONA
● Phoenix
Mesa ●
Tucson ●
Gila River

Albuquerque ●

NEW
● La

Rio

BAJA CALIFORNIA

Relief

Meters	Feet
3,050	10,000
1,525	5,000
610	2,000
305	1,000
0	0
Below sea level	Below sea level

HAWAII

KAUAI

OAHU   MOLOKAI
Honolulu ◎
LANAI   MAUI

**PACIFIC
OCEAN**

Hilo ●

HAWAII

PUERTO RICO

San Juan ●

CARIBBEAN SEA

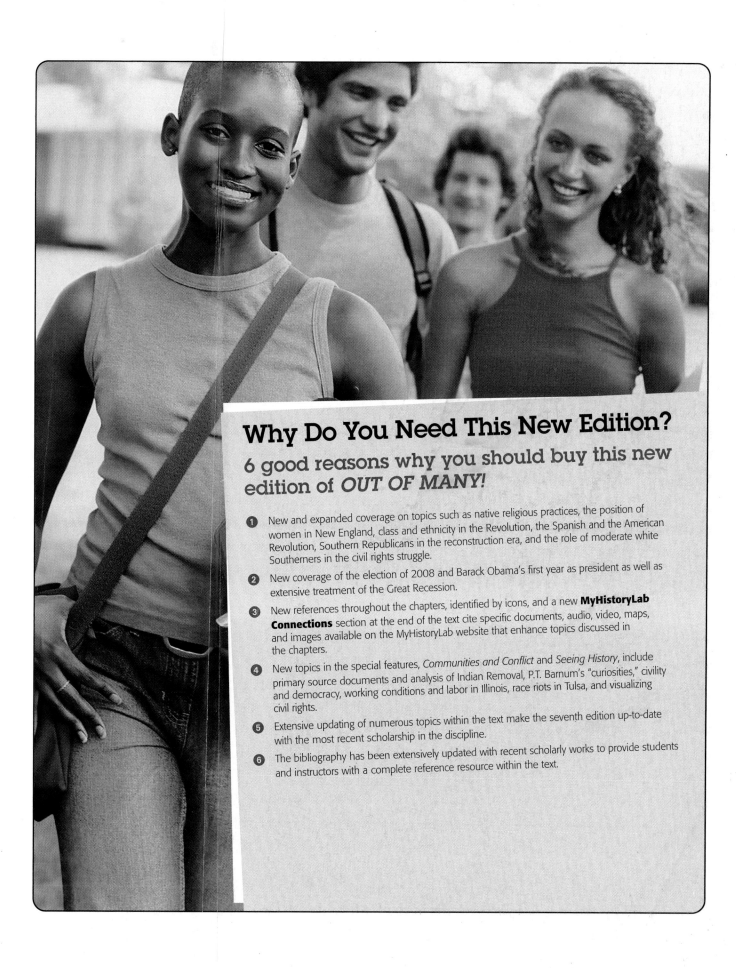

Why Do You Need This New Edition?

6 good reasons why you should buy this new edition of *OUT OF MANY!*

1. New and expanded coverage on topics such as native religious practices, the position of women in New England, class and ethnicity in the Revolution, the Spanish and the American Revolution, Southern Republicans in the reconstruction era, and the role of moderate white Southerners in the civil rights struggle.

2. New coverage of the election of 2008 and Barack Obama's first year as president as well as extensive treatment of the Great Recession.

3. New references throughout the chapters, identified by icons, and a new **MyHistoryLab Connections** section at the end of the text cite specific documents, audio, video, maps, and images available on the MyHistoryLab website that enhance topics discussed in the chapters.

4. New topics in the special features, *Communities and Conflict* and *Seeing History*, include primary source documents and analysis of Indian Removal, P.T. Barnum's "curiosities," civility and democracy, working conditions and labor in Illinois, race riots in Tulsa, and visualizing civil rights.

5. Extensive updating of numerous topics within the text make the seventh edition up-to-date with the most recent scholarship in the discipline.

6. The bibliography has been extensively updated with recent scholarly works to provide students and instructors with a complete reference resource within the text.

Out of Many

VOLUME I

Out of Many

Seventh Edition

A History of the American People

John Mack Faragher

Mari Jo Buhle
EMERITA, BROWN UNIVERSITY

Daniel Czitrom
MOUNT HOLYOKE COLLEGE

Susan H. Armitage
EMERITA, WASHINGTON STATE UNIVERSITY

Prentice Hall

Boston   Columbus   Indianapolis   New York   San Francisco   Upper Saddle River
Amsterdam   Cape Town   Dubai   London   Madrid   Milan   Munich   Paris   Montréal   Toronto
Delhi   Mexico City   São Paulo   Sydney   Hong Kong   Seoul   Singapore   Taipei   Tokyo

Editorial Director: Craig Campanella
Publisher: Charlyce Jones Owen
Editorial Assistant: Maureen Diana
Associate Editor: Emsal Hasan
Senior Manufacturing and Operations Manager for Arts & Sciences:
  Nick Sklitsis
Operations Specialist: Christina Amato
Director of Marketing: Brandy Dawson
Senior Marketing Manager: Maureen E. Prado Roberts
Marketing Assistant: Samantha Bennett
Senior Managing Editor: Ann Marie McCarthy
Senior Project Manager: Cheryl Keenan
Manager, Visual Research: Beth Brenzel

Senior Art Director: Maria Lange
Cover Art: "Native American women gathering rice in a
canoe" by Seth Eastman. Getty Images Inc.
AV Project Manager: Mirella Signoretto
Cartographer: International Mapping Associates
Director of Digital Media: Brian Hyland
Media Editor: Andrea Messineo
Full-Service Compositon and Project Management:
  GEX Publishing Services
Printer/Binder: Courier/Kendalville
Cover Printer: Lehigh-Phoenix Color
Text Font: 10.5/13 Bembo

Credits and acknowledgments borrowed from other sources and reproduced, with permission, in this textbook appear on appropriate page within text or on page C-1.

Library of Congress Cataloging-in-Publication Data
Out of many : a history of the American people / John Mack Faragher ... [et al.]. -- 7th ed.
    p. cm.
  Includes bibliographical references and index.
  ISBN-13: 978-0-205-01192-6 (combined volume)
  ISBN-10: 0-205-01192-6 (combined volume)
  ISBN-13: 978-0-205-01191-9 (v. 1)
  ISBN-10: 0-205-01191-8 (v. 1)
  ISBN-13: 978-0-205-01190-2 (v.2)
  ISBN-10: 0-205-01190-X (v.2)
  1. United States--History--Textbooks. I. Faragher, John Mack
  E178.1.O935 2012
  973--dc22   2010044582

10 9 8 7 6 5 4 3 2 1

Combined Volume
ISBN-10: 0-205-01192-6
ISBN-13: 978-0-205-01192-6

Examination Copy
ISBN-10: 0-205-01203-5
ISBN-13: 978-0-205-01203-9

Volume 1:
ISBN-10: 0-205-01191-8
ISBN-13: 978-0-205-01191-9

Volume 1 à la Carte:
ISBN-10: 0-205-01209-4
ISBN-13: 978-0-205-01209-1

Volume 2
ISBN-10: 0-205-01190-X
ISBN-13: 978-0-205-01190-2

Volume 2 à la Carte:
ISBN-10: 0-205-01219-1
ISBN-13: 978-0-205-01219-0

Prentice Hall
is an place of

PEARSON

www.pearsonhighered.com

Brief Contents

CONTENTS

1

2

3

PLANTING COLONIES IN NORTH AMERICA, 1588–1701   50

4

SLAVERY AND EMPIRE, 1441–1770   74

5

THE CULTURES OF COLONIAL NORTH AMERICA, 1700–1780

6

FROM EMPIRE TO INDEPENDENCE, 1750–1776   132

7

THE AMERICAN REVOLUTION, 1776–1786

8

THE NEW NATION, 1786–1800

9

AN EMPIRE FOR LIBERTY, 1790–1824

10

THE SOUTH AND SLAVERY, 1790s–1850s

12

13

14

THE TERRITORIAL EXPANSION OF THE UNITED STATES, 1830s–1850s 362

15

16

THE CIVIL WAR, 1861–1865   424

17

RECONSTRUCTION, 1863–1877   458

COMMUNITIES IN CONFLICT

MAPS

CHARTS, GRAPHS & TABLES

OVERVIEW TABLES

PREFACE

Out of Many: A History of the American People, seventh edition, offers a distinctive and timely approach to American history, highlighting the experiences of diverse communities of Americans in the unfolding story of our country. The stories of these communities offer a way of examining the complex historical forces shaping people's lives at various moments in our past. The debates and conflicts surrounding the most momentous issues in our national life—independence, emerging democracy, slavery, westward settlement, imperial expansion, economic depression, war, technological change—were largely worked out in the context of local communities. Through communities we focus on the persistent tensions between everyday life and those larger decisions and events that continually reshape the circumstances of local life. Each chapter opens with a description of a representative community. Some of these portraits feature American communities struggling with one another: African slaves and English masters on the rice plantations of colonial Georgia, or *Tejanos* and Americans during the Texas war of independence. Other chapters feature portraits of communities facing social change: the feminists of Seneca Falls, New York, in 1848, or the African Americans of Montgomery, Alabama, in 1955. As the story unfolds we find communities growing to include ever larger groups of Americans: the soldiers from every colony who forged the Continental Army into a patriotic national force at Valley Forge during the American Revolution, or the moviegoers who aspired to a collective dream of material prosperity and upward mobility during the 1920s.

Out of Many is also the only American history text with a truly continental perspective. With community vignettes from New England to the South, the Midwest to the far West, we encourage students to appreciate the great expanse of our nation. For example, a vignette of seventeenth century Santa Fé, New Mexico, illustrates the founding of the first European settlements in the New World. We present territorial expansion into the American West from the viewpoint of the Mandan villagers of the upper Missouri River of North Dakota. We introduce the policies of the Reconstruction era through the experience of African Americans in Hale County, Alabama. A continental perspective drives home to students that American history has never been the preserve of any particular region.

Out of Many includes extensive coverage of our diverse heritage. Our country is appropriately known as "a nation of immigrants," and the history of immigration to America, from the seventeenth to the twenty-first centuries, is fully integrated into the text. There is sustained and close attention to our place in the world, with special emphasis on our relations with the nations of the Western Hemisphere, especially our near neighbors, Canada and Mexico. The statistical data in the final chapter has been completely updated with the results of the 2000 census.

In these ways *Out of Many* breaks new ground, but without compromising its coverage of the traditional turning points that we believe are critically important to an understanding of the American past. Among these watershed events are the Revolution and the struggle over the Constitution, the Civil War and Reconstruction, and the Great Depression and World War II. In *Out of Many*, however, we seek to integrate the narrative of national history with the story of the nation's many diverse communities. The Revolutionary and Constitutional period tested the ability of local communities to forge a new unity, and success depended on their ability to build a nation without compromising local identity. The Civil War and Reconstruction formed a second great test of the balance between the national ideas of the Revolution and the power of local and sectional communities. The depression and the New Deal demonstrated the importance of local communities and the growing power of national institutions during the greatest economic challenge in our history. *Out of Many* also looks back in a new and comprehensive way—from the vantage point of the beginning of a new century and the end of the Cold War—at the salient events of the last fifty years and their impact on American communities. The community focus of *Out of Many* weaves the stories of the people and the nation into a single compelling narrative.

Out of Many, seventh edition, is completely updated with the most recent scholarship on the history of America and the United States. All the chapters have been extensively reviewed, revised, and rewritten. The final chapter details the tumultuous events of the new century, including a completely new section on the "war on terror," and concluding with the national election of 2008. Throughout the book the text and graphics are presented in a stunning new design. Moreover, this edition incorporates two important new features. The seventh edition offers two features in each chapter designed to bring history vividly alive for students: *Communities in Conflict*, featuring two primary sources that offer opposing voices on a controversial historical issue and *Seeing History*, carefully chosen images that show how visual sources can illuminate their understanding of American history.

WHAT'S NEW TO THIS EDITION

With each edition of *Out of Many* we have sought to strengthen its unique integration of the best of traditional American history with its innovative community-based focus and strong continental perspective. This new version is no exception.

- New and expanded coverage on topics such as native religious practices, the position of women in New England, class and ethnicity in the Revolution, the Spanish and the American Revolution, Southern Republicans in the reconstruction era, and the role of moderate white Southerners in the civil rights struggle.
- New coverage of the election of 2008 and Barack Obama's first year as president as well as extensive treatment of the Great Recession.
- New topics in the special features, *Communities and Conflict* and *Seeing History*, include Indian Removal, P.T. Barnum's "curiosities," civility and democracy, working conditions and labor in Illinois, race riots in Tulsa, and visualizing civil rights.
- Extensive updating of numerous topics within the text make the seventh edition up-to-date with the most recent scholarship in the discipline.
- New references identified by icons cite specific documents, audio, video, maps, and images available on the MyHistoryLab website that enhance topics discussed in the chapters. A description of MyHistorylab appears on page xxxix.
- The bibliography has been extensively updated with recent scholarly works to provide students and instructors with a complete reference resource within the text.

Chapter-by-Chapter Changes

Chapter 1 There is more discussion of native religious practices. The chapter now incorporates new theories of migration from Asia.

Chapter 2 Expanded discussions are included on the "Merchant Class and the Renaissance" and the "Columbian Exchange," and the newest material on the demographic consequences of the conquest.

Chapter 3 There is new coverage of the position of women in New England, the Salem Witch Trials, and Bacon's Rebellion.

Chapter 4 The sections on slavery in the Spanish and French colonies have been thoroughly revised.

Chapter 5 Sections within the chapter have been revised for better narrative flow, and there is increased emphasis on the importance of religion.

Chapter 6 New emphasis on the importance of the Seven Years War has been included as well as more explicit coverage of class and ethnicity in the Revolution and of soldiers in the early fighting.

Chapter 7 There are two new sections in this chapter on "The Toll of War" and "Women and the War" and new material on the Spanish and the Revolution.

Chapter 8 The discussions of American culture and on the writing and ratification of the Constitution have been extensively revised, and a new discussion of republicanism has been added.

Chapter 9 Two new historical views of the capitol building underline the point that the nation's new capital city had small and undistinguished beginnings. The updated bibliography describes the Missouri Compromise to make the point that differing views on slavery were a political danger as early as 1820.

Chapter 10 This chapter Incorporates the newest scholarship to deepen student appreciation of the human costs of the slave system.

Chapter 11 There is a new **Communities in Conflict** feature on Indian Removal and extensive updating of the chapter bibliography.

Chapter 12 A new set of maps emphasize the importance of transportation in the rapid development of the Yankee West and commercial agriculture and new detail has been added in readings on early factory conditions.

Chapter 13 A new **Seeing History** analyzes the popular appeal of PT Barnum's "curiosities."

Chapter 15 A revised **Seeing History** feature includes a new picture and poses a question about civility and democracy.

Chapter 16 There is a use of new scholarship to increase understanding of the impact of the Civil War on soldiers and civilians.

Chapter 17 The expanded discussion of Southern Republicans in the Reconstruction era emphasizes regional differences within the South.

Chapter 18 The section on "Producing for the Global Market" has been dropped, with the material integrated into "New Production Technologies," to streamline the outline.

Chapter 19 There is a new **Communities in Conflict:** Regulating the Conditions and Limiting the Hours of Labor in the State of Illinois.

Chapter 21 A new section discusses immigration from the Carriibean basin in the early twentieth century and includes a revised map of Immigration to the U.S., 1900–1920.

Chapter 22 A new **Communities in Conflict** explores the race riot in Tulsa, 1921, and the coverage of women's experiences during WW I has been revised.

Chapter 23 The coverage of the relationship between global commerce and U.S. foreign policy has been strengthened. The extensively revised bibliographies reflect a large amount of new scholarship on the 1920s.

Chapter 24 There are revised and updated statistics and analysis of "Underlying Weaknesses of the 1920s Economy."

Chapter 25 Much of the Isolationism section has been streamlined and merged into the section "Roosevelt Readies for War" to streamline the chapter outline.

Chapter 26 The section "Zeal for Democracy" is replaced by "The American Way," which is a phrase that comes up in the most recent scholarship on Cold War culture.

Chapter 27 Clarified are the major goals—and tensions within—Eisenhower's foreign policy.

Chapter 28 A new **Seeing History** explores visualizing Civil Rights. There is new material on the role of moderate white Southerners in the civil rights struggle. The extensively revised bibliographies reflect a large amount of new scholarship on the civil rights movement.

Chapter 29 The chapter outline has been streamlined by grouping the sections "Playing the China Card" and "Foreign Policy as Conspiracy" under a new section, "Nixon's Foreign Policy." The section on Johnson and the Vietnam War has been revised to reflect recent historiographical tendency to characterize Johnson as more hesitant about escalating the war than earlier scholars contended and to assign more responsibility to his advisors.

A discussion of the founding of *Ms. Magazine* has been added.

Chapter 30 The **Seeing History** feature has been revised to compare the Reagan and Carter inaugurations.

Chapter 31 A new section, "Barack Obama and the Audacity of Hope," covers the election of 2008 and Obama's first year as president. Extensive treatment of the Great Recession examines its causes and its impact on American life. The chapter has been reorganized to more fully integrate political and economic developments in the Clinton/Bush/Obama years.

SPECIAL FEATURES

Out of Many offers a wealth of special features and pedagogical aids that reinforce our narrative and helps students grasp key topics and concepts.

- **Community and Diversity.** This special introductory essay begins students' journey into the narrative history that unfolds in *Out of Many*. The essay acquaints students with the major themes of the book and provides them with a framework for understanding American History. (pp. xliii–xlvi)

- **American Communities**. Each chapter opens with a story that highlights the experiences of diverse communities of Americans as a way of examining the complex historical forces shaping people's lives at various moments in our past.

- **Communities in Conflict.** This special feature highlights two primary sources that offer opposing voices on a controversial historical issue. With introductory source notes and critical thinking questions, "Communities in Conflict" offers students and instructors the opportunity to discuss how Americans have struggled to resolve their differences at every point in our past.

- **Seeing History.** This feature helps students use visual culture for making sense of the past. These carefully chosen images, with critical thinking questions for interpretation, include a broad array of fine art, drawings, political cartoons, advertisements, and photographs. Encouraged to look at the image with an analytical eye, students will think critically about how visual sources can illuminate their understanding of American history and the important role visuals play in our knowledge of the past.

- **Focus Questions.** These critical thinking questions are located at the beginning of each chapter. They focus on the content of each main section within the chapters and allow students to consider carefully the main issues addressed in the narrative.

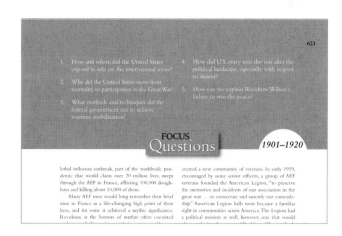

- **Overview tables.** Overview tables provide students with a summary of complex issues.

- **NEW Myhistorylab Icons.** Throughout each chapter, icons refer students to primary source documents, maps, videos, and activities from the MyHistoryLab website that relate directly to specific topics within the chapter.

- **NEW MyHistoryLab Connections.** A list of documents, images, maps, activities, and videos available online at **www.myhistorylab.com** that relate to the specific content in each chapter. For a full description of the MyHistoryLab website for *Out of Many*, see page xxxix.

- **Photos and Illustrations.** The abundant illustrations in *Out of Many* include extensive captions that treat the images as visual primary source documents from the American past, describing their source and explaining their significance. In addition, the **Seeing History** feature in each chapter highlights a stunning visual and introduces students to the importance of visual documents in the study of history.

Joseph Brant, the brilliant chief of the Mohawks who sided with Great Britain during the Revolution, in a 1786 painting by the American artist Gilbert Stuart. After the Treaty of Paris, Brant led a large faction of Iroquois people north into British Canada, where they established a separate Iroquois Confederacy.

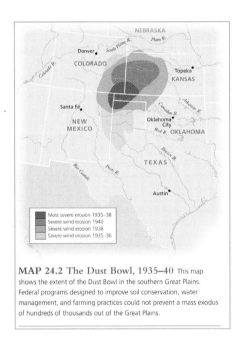

MAP 24.2 The Dust Bowl, 1935–40 This map shows the extent of the Dust Bowl in the southern Great Plains. Federal programs designed to improve soil conservation, water management, and farming practices could not prevent a mass exodus of hundreds of thousands out of the Great Plains.

- **Chronologies, Review Questions, and Recommended Readings.** A chronology at the end of each chapter helps students build a framework of key events. Review questions at the end of chapters help students review, reinforce, and retain the material in each chapter and encourage them to relate the material to broader issues in American history. The works in the short, annotated Recommended Reading list at the end of each chapter have been selected with the interested introductory student in mind.

FOR INSTRUCTORS AND STUDENTS

Supplements for Instructors	Supplements for Students
myhistorylab www.myhistorylab.com **Save TIME. Improve Results.** MyHistoryLab provides a wealth of resources geared to meet the diverse teaching and learning needs of today's instructors and students. (See page xxxix for a description of the MyHistoryLab features.)	**myhistorylab** www.myhistorylab.com **Save TIME. Improve Results.** MyHistoryLab's many accessible tools will encourage you to read your text and help you improve your grade in your course. (See page xxxix for a description of the MyHistoryLab features.)
Instructor's Resource Center www.pearsonhighered.com/irc This website provides instructors with additional text-specific resources that can be downloaded for classroom use. Resources include the Instructor's Resource Manual, PowerPoint presentations and the test item file. Register online for access to the resources for *Out of Many*.	***American Stories: Biographies in United States History*** This collection of sixty-two biographies provides insight into the lives and contributions of key figures as well as ordinary citizens to American history. Introductions, pre-reading questions, and suggested resources helps students connect the relevance of these individuals to historical events. Volume 1 **ISBN-10: 0131826549 ISBN-13: 9780131826540** Volume 2 **ISBN-10: 0131826530 ISBN-13: 9780131826533**
Instructor's Resource Manual Available at the Instructor's Resource Center for download, **www.pearsonhighered.com/irc**, the Instructor's Resource Manual contains chapter outlines, detailed chapter overviews, lecture outlines, topics for discussion, and information about audio-visual resources.	**Library of American Biography Series www.pearsonhighered .com/educator/series/Library-of-American-Biography/10493.page** Pearson's renowned series of biographies spotlighting figures who had a significant impact on American history. Included in the series are Edmund Morgan's *The Puritan Dilemma: The Story of John Winthrop*, B. Davis Edmund's *Tecumseh and the Quest for Indian Leadership*, J. William T. Youngs, *Eleanor Roosevelt: A Personal and Public Life*, and John R. M. Wilson's *Jackie Robinson and the American Dilemma*.
Test Item File Available at the Instructor's Resource Center for download, **www.pearsonhighered.com/irc**, the Test Item File contains more than 2,000 multiple-choice, identification, matching, true-false, and essay test questions.	**Penguin Valuepacks www.pearsonhighered.com/penguin** A variety of Penguin-Putnam texts is available at discounted prices when bundled with *Out of Many, 7/e*. Texts include Benjamin Franklin's *Autobiography and Other Writings*, Nathaniel Hawthorne's *The Scarlet Letter*, Thomas Jefferson's *Notes on the State of Virginia*, and George Orwell's *1984*.
PowerPoint Presentations Available at the Instructor's Resource Center for download, **www.pearsonhighered.com/irc**, the PowerPoints contain chapter outlines and full-color images of maps and art.	***A Short Guide to Writing About History, 7/e*** Written by Richard Marius, late of Harvard University, and Melvin E. Page, Eastern Tennessee State University, this engaging and practical text explores the writing and researching processes, identifies different modes of historical writing, including argument, and concludes with guidelines for improving style. **ISBN-10: 0205673708; ISBN-13: 9780205673704**
MyTest Available at **www.pearsonmytest.com**, MyTest is a powerful assessment generation program that helps instructors easily create and print quizzes and exams. Questions and tests can be authored online, allowing instructors ultimate flexibility and the ability to efficiently manage assessments anytime, anywhere! Instructors can easily access existing questions and edit, create, and store using simple drag-and-drop and Word-like controls.	***Longman American History Atlas*** This full-color historical atlas designed especially for college students is a valuable reference tool and visual guide to American history. This atlas includes maps covering the scope of American history from the lives of the Native Americans to the 1990s. Produced by a renowned cartographic firm and a team of respected historians, the Longman American History Atlas will enhance any American history survey course. **ISBN: 0321004868; ISBN-13: 9780321004864**
Retrieving the American Past Reader Program Available through the Pearson Custom Library (**www.pearsoncustom.com, keyword search I rtap**), the *Retrieving the American Past* (RTAP) program lets you create a textbook or reader that meets your needs and the needs of your course. RTAP gives you the freedom and flexibility to add chapters from several best-selling Pearson textbooks, in addition to *The American Journey, 5/e* and/or 100 topical reading units written by the History Department of Ohio State University, all under one cover. Choose the content you want to teach in depth, in the sequence you want, at the price you want your students to pay.	

PEARSON

For Instructors and Students

Save TIME. Improve Results.

MyHistoryLab is a dynamic website that provides a wealth of resources geared to meet the diverse teaching and learning needs of today's instructors and students. MyHistoryLab's many accessible tools will encourage students to read their text and help them improve their grade in their course.

Features of Myhistorylab

- **Pearson eText**—An e-book version of *Out of Many* is included in MyHistorylab. Just like the printed text, students can highlight and add their own notes as they read the book online.
- **Audio Files**—Full audio of the entire text is included to suit the varied learning styles of today's students. In addition there are audio clips of speeches, readings, and music that provide another engaging way to experience history.
- **Pre-test, Post-tests, and Chapter Reviews**—Students can take quizzes to test their knowledge of chapter content and to review for exams.
- **Text and Visual Documents**—Over 1,500 primary source documents, images, and maps available organized by chapter in the text. Primary source documents are also available in the MyHistoryLibrary and can be searched by author, title, theme, and topic. Many of these documents include critical thinking questions.
- **History Bookshelf**—Students may read, download, or print 100 of the most commonly assigned history works like Homer's *The Iliad* or Machiavelli's *The Prince*.
- **Lecture and Archival Videos**—Lectures by leading scholars on provocative topics give students a critical look at key points in history. Videos of speeches, news footage, key historical events, and other archival video take students back to the moment in history.
- **MySearchLab**—This website provides students access to a number of reliable sources for online research, as well as clear guidance on the research and writing process.
- **Gradebook**—Students can follow their own progress and instructors can monitor the work of the entire class. Automated grading of quizzes and assignments helps both instructors and students save time and monitor their results throughout the course.

NEW In-text References to MyHistorylab Resources

Read, View, See, Watch, Hear, Study, and Review Icons integrated in the text connect resources on MyHistorylab to specific topics within the chapters. The

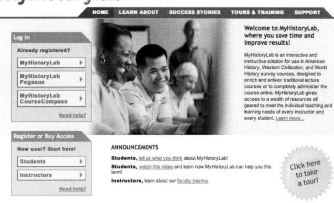

icons are not exhaustive; many more resources are available than those highlighted in the book, but the icons draw attention to some of the most high-interest resources available on MyHistorylab.

Read the **Document** Primary and secondary source documents on compelling topics such as *Brown v. Board of Education of Topeka, Kansas* and Engel, Address by a Haymarket Anarchist enhance topics discussed in each chapter.

View the **Image** Photographs, fine art, and artifacts, provide students with a visual perspective on topics within the chapters, underscoring the role of visuals in understanding the past.

See the **Map** Atlas and interactive maps present both a broad overview and a detailed examination of historical developments.

Watch the **Video** Video lectures highlight topics ranging from Columbus to Lincoln to Obama, engaging students on both historical and contemporary topics. Also included are archival videos, such as footage of Ellis Island immigrants in 1903 and the Kennedy-Nixon debate.

Hear the **Audio** For each chapter there are audio files of the text, speeches, readings, and other audio material, such as "Battle Hymn of the Republic" and "The Star Spangled Banner" that will enrich students' experience of social and cultural history.

Study and **Review** MyhistoryLab provides a wealth of practice quizzes, tests, flashcards, and other study resources available to students online.

NEW MyHistorylab Connections

At the end of each chapter, a new section, MyHistorylab Connections, provides a list of the references within the chapter and additional documents, maps, videos, or additional resources that relate to the content of the chapter.

ACKNOWLEDGMENTS

In the years it has taken to bring *Out of Many* from idea to reality and to improve it in successive editions, we have often been reminded that although writing history sometimes feels like isolated work, it actually involves a collective effort. We want to thank the dozens of people whose efforts have made the publication of this book possible.

We wish to thank our many friends at Prentice Hall for their efforts in creating the seventh edition of *Out of Many*: Yolanda de Rooy, President; Craig Campanella, Editorial Director; Charlyce Jones Owen, Publisher; Maureen Prado Roberts, Senior Marketing Manager; Brandy Dawson, Director of Marketing; Cheryl Keenan, Project Manager; Ann Marie McCarthy, Senior Managing Editor; Maria Lange, Art Director; from GEX Publishing Services: Micah Petillo, Production Editor.

Although we share joint responsibility for the entire book, the chapters were individually authored: John Mack Faragher wrote chapters 1–8; Susan Armitage wrote chapters 9–16; Mari Jo Buhle wrote chapters 18–20, 25–26, 29; and Daniel Czitrom wrote chapters 17, 21–24, 27–28. For this edition Buhle and Czitrom co-authored Chapters 30–31.

Each of us depended on a great deal of support and assistance with the research and writing that went into this book. We want to thank: Kathryn Abbott, Nan Boyd, Krista Comer, Jennifer Cote, Crista DeLuzio, Keith Edgerton, Carol Frost, Jesse Hoffnung Garskof, Pailin Gaither, Jane Gerhard, Todd Gernes, Mark Krasovic, Daniel Lanpher, Melani McAlister, Rebecca McKenna, Cristiane Mitchell, J. C. Mutchler, Keith Peterson, Alan Pinkham, Tricia Rose, Gina Rourke, Jessica Shubow, Gordon P. Utz Jr., Maura Young, Teresa Bill, Gill Frank, and Naoko Shibusawa. Our families and close friends have been supportive and ever so patient over the many years we have devoted to this project. But we want especially to thank Paul Buhle, Meryl Fingrutd, Bob Greene, and Michele Hoffnung.

REVIEWERS AND CONSULTANTS

Historians around the country greatly assisted us by reading and commenting on chapters for this and previous editions. Their many insightful suggestions, encouragement, and dedication have been a tremendous help to us and to the textbook. We want to thank each of them for the commitment of their valuable time and for sharing their experience and ideas on previous editions as well as this new seventh edition.

Seventh Edition:

Daniel M. Anderson, *Cincinnati State Technical and Community College*
TJ Boisseau, *University of Akron*
Cynthia Carter, *Florida Community College, Jacksonville*
Thomas Clarkin, *San Antonio College*
Dr. John S. Leiby, *Paradise Valley Community College*
Richard H. Owens, *West Liberty University*
Burton Peretti, *Western Connecticut State University*
Michael J. Pfeifer, *John Jay College of Criminal Justice*
Jeffrey M. Schulze, *University of Texas, Dallas*
Deborah Welch, *Longwood University*

Previous Editions:

Jeffrey. S. Adler, *University of Florida*
Jennifer L. Altenhofel, *Taft College*
Lee Annis, *Montgomery College*
Caroline Barton, *Holmes Community College*
Jon S. Blackman, *University of Oklahoma*
James Bradford, *Texas A&M University*
Fran Campbell, *College of Southern Nevada*
Frank Chartrand, *Los Angeles Pierce College*
Robert E. Cray, *Montclair State University*
Lawrence Culver, *Utah State University*
Amy Curry, *Montgomery College*
Alan Downs, *Georgia Southern University*
John T. Duke, *Alvin Community College*
Keith Edgerton, *Montana State University, Billings*
Greg Ference, *Salisbury University*
Kate Foss-Mollan, *University of Wisconsin, Milwaukee*
Jennifer Fry, *King's College*
Michael Gabriel, *Kutztown University*
Jessica Gerard, *Ozarks Technical College*
George Gerdow, *Northeastern Illinois University*
Jerry Gershenhorn, *North Carolina Central University*
Jolyon P. Girard, *Cabrini College*
Wendy Gordon, *SUNY Plattsburgh*
Kathleen Gorman, *Minnesota State University, Mankato*
W. Scott Haine, *College of San Mateo*
Gordon Harvey, *The University of Louisiana, Monroe*
Leslie Heaphy, *Kent State University*
Rebecca Hill, *CUNY, Borough of Manhattan Community College*
Don Jacobson, *Oakton Community College*
Jeff Janowick, *Lansing Community College*

Hasan Jeffries, *Ohio State University*

Jeanette Keith, *Bloomsburg University*

Kathleen Kennedy, *Western Washington University*

William Kerrigan, *Muskingum College*

Jonathan Mercantini, *Canisius College*

Peter Messer, *Mississippi State University*

James Mills, *University of Texas, Brownsville*

Joseph P. Moore III, *University of Vermont*

James Owens, *Oakton Community College*

Ken Poston, *Beaumont Independent School District*

G. David Price, *University of Florida*

Caroline Pruden, *North Carolina State University*

Carol Quirke, *SUNY Old Westbury*

Kathleen L. Riley, *Ohio Dominican University*

James R. Rohrer, *University of Nebraska, Kearney*

Joshua P. Schier, *Western Michigan University*

Melissane Schrems, *St. Lawrence University*

Jeffrey Shepherd, *University of Texas, El Paso*

Jean Stuntz, *West Texas A&M*

Karen R. Utz, *University of Alabama, Birmingham*

James Williams, *Middle Tennessee State University*

Larry Wilson, *San Jacinto College*

James Wolfinger, *DePaul University*

Jason Young, *SUNY Buffalo*

Charles A. Zappia, *San Diego Mesa College*

ABOUT THE AUTHORS

John Mack Faragher

John Mack Faragher is Arthur Unobskey Professor of American History and director of the Howard R. Lamar Center for the Study of Frontiers and Borders at Yale University. Born in Arizona and raised in southern California, he received his B.A. at the University of California, Riverside, and his Ph.D. at Yale University. He is the author of *Women and Men on the Overland Trail* (1979), *Sugar Creek: Life on the Illinois Prairie* (1986), *Daniel Boone: The Life and Legend of an American Pioneer* (1992), *The American West: A New Interpretive History* (2000), and *A Great and Noble Scheme: The Tragic Story of the Expulsion of the French Acadians from their American Homeland* (2005).

Daniel Czitrom

Daniel Czitrom is Professor of History at Mount Holyoke College. Born and raised in New York City, he received his B.A. from the State University of New York at Binghamton and his M.A. and Ph.D. from the University of Wisconsin, Madison. He is the author of *Media and the American Mind: From Morse to McLuhan* (1982), which won the First Books Award of the American Historical Association and has been translated into Spanish and Chinese. He is co-author of *Rediscovering Jacob Riis: Exposure Journalism and Photography in Turn of the Century New York* (2008). He has served as a historical consultant and featured on-camera commentator for several documentary film projects, including the PBS productions *New York: A Documentary Film; American Photography: A Century of Images*; and *The Great Transatlantic Cable*. He currently serves as a Distinguished Lecturer for the Organization of American Historians.

Mari Jo Buhle

Mari Jo Buhle is William R. Kenan, Jr. University Professor *Emerita* of American Civilization and History at Brown University, specializing in American women's history. She received her B.A. from the University of Illinois, Urbana-Champaign, and her Ph.D. from the University of Wisconsin, Madison. She is the author of *Women and American Socialism, 1870–1920* (1981) and *Feminism and Its Discontents: A Century of Struggle with Psychoanalysis* (1998). She is also coeditor of the *Encyclopedia of the American Left*, (second edition, 1998). Professor Buhle held a fellowship (1991-1996) from the John D. and Catherine T. MacArthur Foundation. She is currently an Honorary Fellow of the History Department at the University of Wisconsin, Madison.

Susan H. Armitage

Susan H. Armitage is Professor of History and Women's Studies, *Emerita*, at Washington State University, where she was a Claudius O. and Mary R. Johnson Distinguished Professor. She earned her Ph.D. from the London School of Economics and Political Science. Among her many publications on western women's history are three coedited books, *The Women's West* (1987), *So Much To Be Done: Women on the Mining and Ranching Frontier* (1991), and *Writing the Range: Race, Class, and Culture in the Women's West* (1997). She served as editor of the feminist journal *Frontiers* from 1996 to 2002. Her most recent publication, coedited with Laurie Mercier, is *Speaking History: Oral Histories of the American Past, 1865–Present* (2009).

COMMUNITY & DIVERSITY

One of the most characteristic features of our country is its astounding variety. The American people include the descendants of native Indians; colonial Europeans of British, French, and Spanish background; Africans; and migrants from virtually every country and continent. Indeed, at the beginning of the new century the United States is absorbing a flood of immigrants from Latin America and Asia that rivals the great tide of people from eastern and southern Europe one hundred years before. What's more, our country is one of the world's most spacious, sprawling across than 3.6 million square miles of territory. The struggle to meld a single nation out of our many far-flung communities is what much of American history is all about. That is the story told in this book.

Every human society is made up of communities. A community is a set of relationships linking men, women, and their families to a coherent social whole that is more than the sum of its parts. In a community people develop the capacity for unified action. In a community people learn, often through trial and error, how to transform and adapt to their environment.

The sentiment that binds the members of a community together is the mother of group consciousness and ethnic identity. In the making of history, communities are far more important than even the greatest of leaders, for the community is the institution most capable of passing a distinctive historical tradition to future generations.

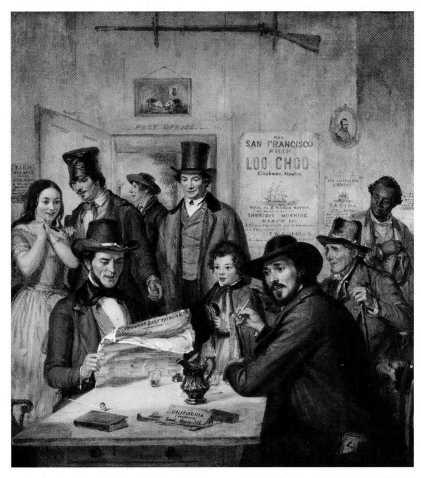

William Sidney Mount (1807–1868) *California News* 1850. Oil on canvas. The Long Island Museum of American Art, History and Carriages.

Harvey Dinnerstein, *Underground, Together* 1996, oil on canvas, 90" × 107".

Photograph courtesy of Gerold Wunderlich & Co., New York, NY.

Communities bind people together in multiple ways. They can be as small as local neighborhoods, in which people maintain face-to-face relations, or as large as the nation itself. This book examines American history from the perspective of community life—an ever-widening frame that has included larger and larger groups of Americans.

Networks of kinship and friendship, and connections across generations and among families, establish the bonds essential to community life. Shared feelings about values and history establish the basis for common identity. In communities, people find the power to act collectively in their own interest. But American communities frequently took shape as a result of serious conflicts among groups, and within communities there was often significant fighting among competing groups or classes. Thus the term *community*, as we use it here, includes conflict and discord as well as harmony and agreement.

For decades Americans have complained about the "loss of community." But community has not disappeared—it has been continuously reinvented. Until the late eighteenth century, community was defined primarily by space and local geography. But in the nineteenth century communities were reshaped by new and powerful historical forces such as the marketplace, industrialization,

the corporation, mass immigration, mass media, and the growth of the nation-state. In the twentieth century, Americans struggled to balance commitments to multiple communities. These were defined not simply by local spatial arrangements, but by categories as varied as race and ethnicity, occupation, political affiliation, and consumer preference.

The "American Communities" vignettes that open each chapter reflect these transformations. Most of the vignettes in the pre–Civil War chapters focus on geographically defined communities, such as the ancient Indian city at Cahokia, or the experiment in industrial urban planning in early nineteenth-century Lowell, Massachusetts. Post–Civil War chapters explore different and more modern kinds of communities. In the 1920s, movies and radio offered communities of identification with dreams of freedom, material success, upward mobility, youth and beauty. In the 1950s, rock 'n' roll music helped germinate a new national community of teenagers, with profound effects on the culture of the entire country in the second half of the twentieth century. In the late 1970s, fear of nuclear accidents like the one at Three Mile Island brought concerned citizens together in communities around the country and encouraged a national movement opposing nuclear power.

The title for our book was suggested by the Latin phrase selected by John Adams, Benjamin Franklin, and Thomas Jefferson for the Great Seal of the United States: *E Pluribus Unum*—"Out of Many Comes Unity." These men understood that unity could not be imposed by a powerful central authority but had to develop out of mutual respect among Americans of different backgrounds. The revolutionary leadership expressed the hope that such respect could grow on the basis of a remarkable proposition: "We hold these truths to be self-evident, that all men are created equal; that they are endowed by their Creator with certain unalienable rights; that among these are life, liberty, and the pursuit of happiness." The national government of the United States would preserve local and state authority but would guarantee individual rights. The nation would be strengthened by guarantees of difference.

"Out of Many" comes strength. That is the promise of America and the premise of this book. The underlying dialectic of American history, we believe, is that as a people we must locate our national unity in the celebration of the differences that exist among us; these differences can be our strength, as long as we affirm the promise of the Declaration. Protecting the "right to be different," in other words, is absolutely fundamental to the continued existence of democracy, and that right is best protected by the existence of strong and vital communities. We are bound together as a nation by the ideal of local and cultural differences protected by our common commitment to the values of the American Revolution.

Today those values are endangered by those who use the tactics of mass terror. In the wake of the September 11, 2001 attack on the United States, and with the continuing threat of biological, chemical, or even nuclear assaults, Americans can not afford to lose faith in our historic vision. The thousands of victims buried in the smoking ruins of the World Trade Center included people from dozens of different ethnic and national groups. The United States is a multicultural and transnational society. We must rededicate ourselves to the protection and defense of the promise of diversity and unity.

Our history demonstrates that the promise has always been problematic. Centrifugal forces have been powerful in the American past, and at times the country seemed about to fracture into its component parts. Our transformation from a collection of groups and regions into a nation was marked by painful and often violent struggles. Our past is filled with conflicts between Indians and colonists, masters and slaves, Patriots and Loyalists, Northerners and Southerners, Easterners and Westerners, capitalists and workers, and sometimes the government and the people. War can bring out our best, but it can also bring out our worst. During World War II thousands of Japanese American citizens were deprived of their rights and locked up in isolated detention centers because of their ethnic background. Americans often appear to be

Thomas Satterwhite Noble, Last Sale of Slaves on the *Courthouse Steps*, 1860, oil on canvas, Missouri Historical Society.

little more than a contentious collection of peoples with conflicting interests, divided by region and background, race and class.

Our most influential leaders have also sometimes suffered a crisis of faith in the American project of "liberty and justice for all." Thomas Jefferson not only believed in the inferiority of African Americans but feared that immigrants from outside the Anglo-American tradition might "warp and bias" the development of the nation "and render it a heterogeneous, incoherent, distracted mass." We have not always lived up to the American promise and there is a dark side to our history. It took the bloodiest war in American history to secure the human rights of African Americans, and the struggle for full equality for all our citizens has yet to be won. During the great influx of immigrants in the early twentieth century, fears much like Jefferson's led to movements to Americanize the foreign born by forcing them, in the words of one leader, "to give up the languages, customs, and methods of life which they have brought with them across the ocean, and adopt instead the language, habits, and customs of this country, and the general standards and ways of American living." Similar thinking motivated Congress at various times to bar the immigration of Africans, Asians, and other people of color into the country, and to force assimilation on American Indians by denying them the freedom to practice their religion or even to speak their own language. Such calls for restrictive unity resound in our own day.

But other Americans have argued for a more fulsome version of Americanization. "What is the American, this new man?" asked the French immigrant Michel Crévecoeur in 1782. "A strange mixture of blood which you will find in no other country." In America, he wrote, "individuals of all nations are melted into a new race of men." A century later Crévecoeur was echoed by historian Frederick Jackson Turner, who believed that "in the crucible of the frontier, the immigrants were Americanized, liberated, and fused into a mixed race, English in neither nationality nor characteristics. The process has gone on from the early days to our own."

The process by which diverse communities have come to share a set of common American values is one of the most fundamental aspects of our history. It did not occur, however, because of compulsory Americanization programs, but because of free public education, popular participation in democratic politics, and the impact of popular culture. Contemporary America does have a common culture: we share a commitment to freedom of thought and expression, we join in the aspirations to own our own homes and send our children to college, we laugh at the same television programs or video clips on YouTube.

To a degree that too few Americans appreciate, this common culture resulted from a complicated process of mutual discovery that took place when different ethnic and regional groups encountered one another. Consider just one small and unique aspect of our culture: the barbecue. Americans have been barbecuing since before the beginning of written history. Early settlers adopted this technique of cooking from the Indians—the word itself comes from a native term for a framework of sticks over a fire on which meat was slowly cooked. Colonists typically barbecued pork, fed on Indian corn. African slaves lent their own touch by introducing the use of spicy sauces. The ritual that is a part of nearly every American family's Fourth of July silently celebrates the heritage of diversity that went into making our common culture.

The American educator John Dewey recognized this diversity early in the last century. "The genuine American, the typical American, is himself a hyphenated character," he declared, "international and interracial in his make-up." It was up to all Americans, Dewey argued, "to see to it that the hyphen connects instead of separates." We, the authors of *Out of Many*, endorse Dewey's perspective. "Creation comes from the impact of diversity," the American philosopher Horace Kallen wrote about the same time. We also endorse Kallen's vision of the American promise: "A democracy of nationalities, cooperating voluntarily and autonomously through common institutions, . . . a multiplicity in a unity, an orchestration of mankind." And now, let the music begin.

Out of Many

1

Chapter 1 at www.myhistorylab.com ((•—[Hear the Audio

A Continent of Villages
to 1500

CHAPTER OUTLINE

Painting of Cahokia Mounds, Collinsville, Illinois by Michael Hampshire. Cahokia Mounds State Historic Site.

Cahokia: Thirteenth-Century Life on the Mississippi

As the sun rose over the rich floodplain, the people of the riverbank city set about their daily tasks. Some went to shops where they manufactured tools, crafted pottery, worked metal, or fashioned ornamental jewelry—goods destined to be exchanged in the far corners of the continent. Others left their densely populated neighborhoods for the outlying countryside, where in the summer heat they worked the seemingly endless fields that fed the city. From almost any point people could see the great temple that rose from the city center—the place where priests in splendid costumes acted out public rituals.

The Indian residents of this thirteenth-century city lived and worked on the east banks of the Mississippi River, across from present-day St. Louis, a place known today as Cahokia. In the thirteenth century, Cahokia was an urban cluster of 20,000 or 30,000 people. Its farm fields were abundant with corn, beans, and squash. The temple, a huge earthwork pyramid, covered fifteen acres at its base and rose as high as a ten-story building. On top were the sacred quarters of priests and chiefs, who wore elaborate headdresses made from the plumage of exotic birds.

By the fourteenth century Cahokia had been abandoned, but its great central temple mound and dozens of smaller ones in the surrounding area, as well as hundreds of other large mounds throughout the Mississippi

AMERICAN Communities

Valley, remained to puzzle the colonists and settlers who came in the eighteenth and nineteenth centuries. Treasure seekers plundered those mounds, and many were eventually dynamited and plowed under for farmland. Only a few were preserved inside parks and estates. Cahokia's great central mound survived because it became the site of a monastery, now long gone.

The Europeans and Americans who explored and excavated those mounds were convinced they were the ruins of a vanished civilization, not the work of Indians. They were wrong. The ancestors of contemporary Native Americans constructed massive earthworks in the Mississippi Valley. The vast urban complex of Cahokia, which at its height stretched six miles along the Mississippi River, flourished from the tenth to the fourteenth century. Its residents were not nomadic hunters but farmers, participants in a complex agricultural culture that archaeologists term "Mississippian." Hundreds of acres of crops fed the people of Cahokia, the largest urban community north of the Aztec civilization of central Mexico. Mississippian farmers constructed ingenious raised plots of land on which they heaped compost in wide ridges for improved drainage and protection against unseasonable frosts. To their square houses of wood and mud they attached pens in which they kept flocks of domesticated turkeys and small herds of young deer, slaughtered for meat, feathers, and hide. Cahokia stood at the center of a long-distance trading system that linked it to other Indian communities over a vast area. Copper came from Lake Superior, mica from the southern Appalachians, and conch shells from the Atlantic coast. Cahokia's specialized artisans were renowned for the manufacture of

Cahokia

high-quality flint hoes, which were exported throughout the Mississippi Valley.

Evidence suggests that Cahokia was a city-state supported by tribute and taxation. Like the awe-inspiring public works of other early urban societies in other parts of the world, most notably the pyramids of ancient Egypt and the acropolis of Athens, the great temple mound of Cahokia was intended to showcase the city's wealth and power. The mounds and other colossal public works at Cahokia were the monuments of a society ruled by a class of elite leaders. From their residences atop the mound, priests and chiefs looked down on their subjects both literally and figuratively.

The 1848 Smithsonian report on Cahokia reflected the stereotypical American view that all Indian people were hunters. It is a view that persists. But the long history of North America before European colonization reveals that the native inhabitants developed a great variety of societies. Beginning as migrant hunting and gathering bands, they found ways to fine-tune their subsistence strategies to fit environmental possibilities and limitations. Communities in the highlands of Mexico invented systems of farming that spread to all the regions where cultivation was possible. Not only the Aztecs of Mexico and the Mayans of Central America but also communities in the Southwest and the Mississippi Valley constructed densely settled urban civilizations. North America before colonization was, as historian Howard R. Lamar phrases it, "a continent of villages," a land spread with thousands of communities. The wonders and mystery of the lost city of Cahokia are but one aspect of the little-understood history of the Indians of the Americas.

AMERICAN·· ·
Communities

The First American Settlers

"Why do you call us Indians?" a Massachusetts native complained to Puritan missionary John Eliot in 1646. Christopher Columbus, who mistook the Taino people of the Caribbean for the people of the East Indies, called them "Indios." Within a short time this Spanish word had passed into English as "Indians" and was commonly used to refer to all the native peoples of the Americas. Today anthropologists sometimes employ the term "Amerindians," and others use "Native Americans." But in the United States most of the

descendants of the original inhabitants refer to themselves as "Indian people."

Who Are the Indian People?

At the time of their first contacts with Europeans at the beginning of the sixteenth century, the inhabitants of the Western Hemisphere represented over 2,000 separate cultures, spoke several hundred different languages, and made their livings in scores of different environments. Just as the term "European" includes many nations, so the term

1. How were the Americas first settled?

2. In what ways did native communities adapt to the distinct regions of North America?

3. What were the consequences of the development of farming for native communities?

4. What was the nature of the Indian cultures in the three regions where Europeans first invaded and settled?

FOCUS Questions

to 1500

"Indian" covers an enormous diversity among the peoples of the Americas.

No single physical type characterized all the peoples of the Americas. Although most had straight, black hair and dark, almond-shaped eyes, their skin color ranged from mahogany to light brown. Few fit the "redskin" descriptions used by North American colonists of the eighteenth and nineteenth centuries. Indeed, it was only when Europeans had compared Indian peoples with natives of other continents, such as Africans, that they seemed similar enough to be classified as a group.

Once Europeans realized that the Americas were in fact a "New World," rather than part of the Asian continent, a debate began over how people might have moved there from Europe and Asia, where (according to the Bible) God had created the first man and woman. In 1590, the Spanish Jesuit missionary Joseph de Acosta reasoned that because Old World animals were present in the Americas, they must have crossed by a land bridge that could have been used by humans as well. "And they followed this way quite unthinkingly," he wrote, "changing places and lands little by little, with some of them settling in the lands already discovered and others seeking new ones."

Migration from Asia

Read the Document

José de Acosta, Speculations on the Origins of the Indians (1590) at **www.myhistorylab.com**

Acosta was the first to propose the Asian migration hypothesis that is widely accepted today. Siberian and American Indian populations suggest that migrants to North America began leaving Asia approximately 30,000 years ago (see Map 1.1).

The migration was possible because during the last Ice Age, from 70,000 to 10,000 years ago, huge glaciers locked up massive volumes of water, and sea levels were as much as 300 feet lower than they are today. Asia and North America, now separated by the Bering Strait, were joined by a huge

subcontinent of ice-free, treeless grassland, 750 miles wide from north to south, which geologists have named Beringia. Summers there were warm, and winters were cold but almost snow free, so there was no glaciation. It was

A forensic artist reconstructed this bust from the skull of "Kennewick Man," whose skeletal remains were discovered along the Columbia River in 1996. Scientific testing suggested that the remains were more than 9,000 years old.

MAP 1.1 Migration Routes from Asia to America During the Ice Age, Asia and North America were joined where the Bering Strait is today, forming a migration route for hunting peoples. Either by boat along the coast, or through a narrow corridor between the huge northern glaciers, these migrants began making their way to the heartland of the continent as much as 30,000 years ago.

a perfect environment for large mammals—mammoth and mastodon, bison, horse, reindeer, camel, and saiga (a goat-like antelope). Small bands of Siberian hunter-gatherers were surely attracted by these animal populations. Accompanied by a husky-like species of dog, hunting bands gradually moved as far east as the Yukon River basin of northern Canada, where field excavations have uncovered the fossilized jawbones of several dogs and bone tools estimated to be about 27,000 years old.

Access to lands to the south, however, was blocked by huge ice sheets covering much of what is today Canada. How did the migrants get through those 2,000 miles of deep ice? The standard hypothesis is that with the warming of the climate and the end of the Ice

Age, about 13,000 BCE (before the common era), glacial melting created an ice-free corridor—an original "Pan-American Highway"—along the eastern front range of the Rocky Mountains. Using this thoroughfare, the hunters of big game reached the Great Plains as early as 11,000 BCE.

Recently, however, new archaeological finds along the Pacific coast of North and South America have complicated this hypothesis. Radiocarbon analysis of remains discovered at several newly excavated human sites suggested dates of 12,000 BCE or earlier. The most spectacular find, at Monte Verde in southern Chile, produced striking evidence of tool making, house building, and rock painting conservatively dated at 12,500 BCE. A number of archaeologists believe that the people who founded these settlements moved south in boats along a coastal route—an ancient "Pacific Coast Highway." These people were probably fishers and gatherers rather than hunters of big game.

There were two later migrations into North America. About 5000 BCE the Athapascan people moved across Beringia and began to settle the forests in the northwestern area of the continent. Eventually groups of Athapascan speakers, the ancestors of the Navajos and Apaches, migrated across the Great Plains to the Southwest. A third and final migration began about 3000 BCE, long after Beringia had disappeared under rising seas, when a maritime hunting people crossed the Bering Strait in small boats. The Inuits (also known as the Eskimos) colonized the polar coasts of the Arctic, the Yupiks the coast of southwestern Alaska, and the Aleuts the Aleutian Islands (which are named for them).

While scientists debate the timing and mapping of these various migrations, many Indian people hold to oral traditions that say they have always lived in North America. Every culture has its origin stories, offering explanations of the customs and beliefs of the group. A number of scholars believe these origin stories may shed light on ancient history. The Haida people of the Northwest Pacific coast tell of a time long ago when the offshore islands were much larger, but then the oceans rose, they say, and "flood tide woman" forced them to move to higher ground. Could these stories preserve a memory of the changes at the end of the Ice Age?

•••○─ Read the Document
Pima Creation Story at
www.myhistorylab.com

These Clovis points are typical of thousands that archaeologists have found at sites all over the continent, dating from a period about 12,000 years ago. When inserted in a spear shaft, these three- to six-inch fluted points made effective weapons for hunting mammoth and other big game. The ancient craftsmen who made these points often took advantage of the unique qualities of the stone they were working to enhance their aesthetic beauty.

The Clovis Culture: The First Environmental Adaptation

The tools found at the earliest North American archaeological sites, crude stone or bone choppers and scrapers, are similar to artifacts from the same period found in Europe or Asia. About 11,000 years ago, however, ancient Americans developed a much more sophisticated style of making fluted blades and lance points, a tradition named "Clovis," after the location of the initial discovery near Clovis, New Mexico, in 1926. In the years since, archaeologists have unearthed Clovis stone tools at sites throughout the continent all dating within 1,000 or 2,000 years of one another, suggesting that the Clovis technology spread quickly throughout the continent.

The evidence suggests that Clovis bands were mobile communities of foragers numbering perhaps thirty to fifty individuals from several interrelated families. They returned to the same hunting camps year after year, migrating seasonally within territories of several hundred square miles. Near Delbert, Nova Scotia, archaeologists discovered the floors of ten tents arranged in a semicircle, their doors opening south to avoid the prevailing northerly winds. Both this camp and others found throughout the continent overlooked watering places that would attract game. Clovis blades have been found amid the remains of mammoth, camel, horse, giant armadillo, and sloth.

The global warming trend that ended the Ice Age dramatically altered the North American climate. About 15,000 years ago the giant continental glaciers began to melt and the northern latitudes were colonized by plants, animals, and humans. Meltwater created the lake and river systems of today and raised the level of the surrounding seas, not only flooding Beringia but also vast stretches of the Atlantic and Gulf coasts, creating fertile tidal pools and offshore fishing banks.

New Ways of Living on the Land

These huge transformations produced new patterns of wind, rainfall, and temperature, reshaping the ecology of the entire continent and gradually producing the distinct North American regions of today (see Map 1.2). The great integrating force of a single continental climate faded, and with its passing the continental Clovis culture fragmented into a number of different regional patterns.

The retreat of the glaciers led to new ways of finding food: hunting in the Arctic, foraging in the arid deserts, fishing along the coasts, hunting and gathering in the forests. These developments took place roughly 10,000 to

MAP 1.2 Native North American Culture Areas and Trade Networks, ca. 1400 CE All peoples must adjust their diet, shelter, and other material aspects of their lives to the physical conditions of the world around them. By considering the ways in which Indian peoples developed distinct cultures and adapted to their environments, anthropologists developed the concept of "culture areas." They divide the continent into nine fundamental regions that have greatly influenced the history of North America over the past 10,000 years. Just as regions shaped the lifeways and history of Indian peoples, after the coming of the Europeans they nurtured the development of regional American cultures. By determining the origin of artifacts found at ancient sites, historians have devised a conjectural map of Indian trade networks. Among large regional centers and smaller local ones, trade connected Indian peoples of many different communities and regions.

2,500 years ago, during what archaeologists call the Archaic period (corresponding to the Mesolithic period in the archaeological chronology of Eurasia).

Hunting Traditions   One of the most important effects of this massive climatic shift was the stress it placed on the big-game animals best suited to an Ice Age environment. The archaeological record documents the extinction of thirty-two classes of large New World mammals, including not only the mammoth and mastodon but also the horse and

camel, both of which evolved in America, then migrated to Asia across Beringia. Changing climatic conditions lowered the reproduction and survival rates of these large mammals, forcing hunting bands to intensify their hunting.

As the other large-mammal populations declined, hunters on the Great Plains concentrated on the herds of American bison (known more familiarly as buffalo). To

See the **Map**

The First Americans: Location of Major Indian Groups and Culture Areas in the 1600s at **www.myhistorylab.com**

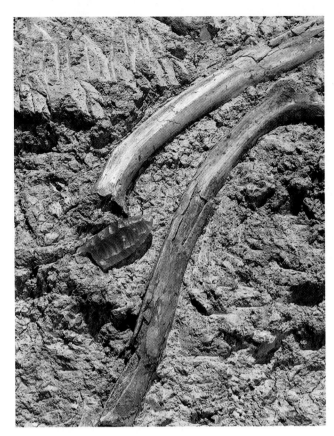

When, in 1927, archaeologists at Folsom, New Mexico, uncovered this dramatic example of a projectile point embedded in the ribs of a long-extinct species of bison, it was the first proof that Indians had been in North America for many thousands of years.

SOURCE: Courtesy of the Denver Museum of Nature and Science.

hunt these animals, people needed a weapon. In archaeological sites dating from about 10,000 years ago, a new style of tool is found mingled with animal remains. This technology, named "Folsom" (for the site of the first major find near Folsom, New Mexico) was a refinement of the Clovis culture that featured more delicate but deadlier spear points. Hunters probably hurled the lances to which these points were attached with wooden spear-throwers, attaining far greater momentum than possible using their arms alone.

These archaeological finds suggest the growing complexity of early Indian communities. Hunters frequently stampeded herds of bison into canyon traps or over cliffs. At one such kill site in southeastern Colorado, dated at about 6500 BCE, archaeologists uncovered the remains of nearly 200 bison that had been slaughtered and then systematically butchered on a single occasion. Such tasks required a sophisticated division of labor among dozens of men and women and the cooperation of a number of communities. Taking food in such great quantities also suggests a knowledge of basic preservation techniques.

Desert Culture   In the Great Basin, the warming trend created a desert where once there had been enormous inland seas. Here Indian people developed what anthropologists call "Desert culture," a way of life based on the pursuit of small game and the intensified foraging of plant foods. Small communities of desert foragers migrated seasonally within a small range. They collected seeds, fiber, and prickly pear from the yucca one season, then moved to highland mesas or plateaus to gather grass seed, acorns, juniper berries, and piñon nuts, and next to mountain streams to spear and net fish.

Archaeologists today find the artifacts of desert foragers in the caves and rock shelters in which they lived. In addition to stone tools, there are objects of wood, hide, and fiber, wonderfully preserved for thousands of years in the dry climate. Desert culture persisted into the nineteenth century among modern Shoshone and Ute communities.

The innovative practices of Desert culture gradually spread from the Great Basin to the Great Plains and the Southwest, where foraging for plant foods began to supplement hunting. About 6,000 years ago, these techniques were carried to California, where, in the natural abundance of the valleys and coasts, communities developed economies capable of supporting some of the densest populations and the first permanently settled villages in North America. Another dynamic center developed along the coast of the Pacific Northwest, where Indian communities developed a way of life based on the abundance of fish and sea mammals. Densely populated and permanently settled communities developed there as well.

Forest Efficiency   There were similar trends east of the Mississippi. In the centuries prior to colonization and settlement by Europeans, the whole of eastern North America was a vast forest. Communities of native people achieved a comfortable and secure life by developing a sophisticated knowledge of the rich and diverse available resources, a principle anthropologists term "forest efficiency." Forest peoples gathered wild plant foods and hunted small game. They developed a practice of burning the woodlands and prairies, creating meadows and edge environments that not only provided harvestable food but also attracted grazing animals, hunted for their meat and hides.

Archaeological sites in the East suggest that during the late Archaic period community populations grew and settlements became increasingly permanent, providing convincing evidence of the practicality of forest efficiency. The different roles of men and women were reflected in the artifacts these peoples buried with their dead: axes, fishhooks, and animal bones with males; nut-cracking stones, beads, and pestles with females.

The Origins of Foodways

One of the functions of myth is to offer explanations for the order of things, including foodways. Native foragers told tales that explained the origins of hunting. A myth common to many tribes on the Great Plains, here in a tale told to a nineteenth-century ethnographer by a Northern Arapaho of Wyoming, relates the story of male culture heroes, who as a result of their vision quests learn the essential skills of hunting, butchering, and cooking buffalo, the all-nourishing sacred food. Farming tribes, on the other hand, told stories in which hunting alone is not sufficient to feed the people. Thus, the spirit world provides them with the gift of corn. Such stories about the origins of corn are widespread wherever farming was important. The story printed here, told by the Penobscot of Maine in the early twentieth century, explains the willing self-sacrifice of First Mother on behalf of her children.

• **What do these two myths suggest about the roles of men and women?**

An Arapaho Legend

A man tried to think how the Arapahos might kill buffalo. He was a hard thinker. He would go off for several days and fast. He did this repeatedly. At last he dreamed that a voice spoke to him and told him what to do. He went back to the people and made an enclosure of trees set in the ground with willows wound between them. At one side of the enclosure, however, there was only a cliff with rocks at the bottom. Then four runners were sent out to the windward of a herd of buffalo, two of them on each side. They headed the buffalo and drove them toward the enclosure and into it. Then the buffalo were run about inside until a heavy cloud of dust rose and in this, unable to see, they ran over the precipice and were killed. . . .

The people had nothing to cut up meat with. A man took a buffalo shoulder blade and with flint cut out a narrow piece of it. He sharpened it, and thus had a knife. Then he also made a knife from flint by flaking it into shape. All the people learned how to make knives.

This man also made the first bow and arrows. He made the arrow point of the short rib of a buffalo. Having made a bow and four arrows, he went off alone and waited in the timber at a buffalo path. A buffalo came and he shot: the arrow disappeared into the body and the animal fell dead. Then he killed three more. He went back to camp and told the people: "Harness the dogs; there are four dead buffalo in the timber." So from this time the people were able to get meat without driving the buffalo into an enclosure.

The people used the fire drill. A man went off alone and fasted. He learned that certain stones, when struck, would give a spark and that this spark would light tinder. He gathered stones and filled a small horn with soft, dry wood. Then he went home. His wife said to him: "Please make a fire." He took out his horn and his flint stones, struck a spark, blew it,

> "A man tried to think how the Arapahos might kill buffalo. At last he dreamed that a voice . . . told him what to do."

The Development of Farming

At the end of the Stone Age, communities in different regions of the world independently created systems of farming, each based on a unique staple crop: rice in Southeast Asia, wheat in the Middle East, potatoes in the Andean highlands of South America, and maize (what Americans call "corn") in Mexico. The dynamic center of this development in North America was in the highlands of Mexico, from which the new technology spread north and east. Mexican farmers developed a great variety of other crops, most importantly beans and squash, but also tomatoes, chili peppers, avocados, cocoa (chocolate), and vanilla.

Origins in Mexico

Archaeological evidence suggests that plant cultivation in the highlands of central Mexico began about 5,000 years ago. Ancient Mexicans developed crops that responded well to human care and produced larger quantities of food in a limited space than did plants growing in the wild. Maize was particularly productive.

((•—[Hear the Audio
Ritual of the Maize at **www.myhistorylab.com**

put grass on it, and soon, to the astonishment of all who saw it, had a fire. This was much easier than using the fire drill, and the people soon all did it.

These . . . were the ones who brought the people to the condition in which they now live.

SOURCE: George Amos Dorsey and Alfred L. Kroeber, *Traditions of the Arapaho* (1903).

A Penobscot Legend

. . . Now the people increased and became numerous. They lived by hunting, and the more people there were, the less game they found. They were hunting it out, and as the animals decreased, starvation came upon the people. And First Mother pitied them.

The little children came to First Mother and said: "We are hungry. Feed us." But she had nothing to give them, and she wept. She told them: "Be patient. I will make some food. Then your little bellies will be full." But she kept weeping.

Her husband asked: "How can I make you smile? How can I make you happy?"

"There is only one thing that can stop my tears."

"What is it?" asked her husband.

"It is this: you must kill me," she said.

"I could never do that," he said. . . .

But First Mother said: "Tomorrow at high noon you must do it. After you have killed me, let two of our sons take hold of my hair and drag my body over that empty patch of earth. Let them drag me back and forth, back and forth, over every part of the patch, until all my flesh has been torn from my body. Afterwards, take my bones, gather them up, and bury them in the middle of this clearing. Then leave that place."

She smiled and said, "Wait seven moons and then come back, and you will find my flesh there, flesh given out of love, and it will nourish and strengthen you forever and ever."

So it was done. The husband slew his wife and her sons, praying, dragged her body to and fro as she had commanded, until her flesh covered all the earth. Then they took up her bones and buried them in the middle of it. Weeping loudly, they went away.

When the husband and his children and his children's children came back to that place after seven moons had passed, they found the earth covered with tall, green, tasseled plants. The plants' fruit, corn, was First Mother's flesh, given so that the people might live and flourish. And they partook of First Mother's flesh and found it sweet beyond words. Following her instructions, they did not eat all, but put many kernels back into the earth. In this way, her flesh and spirit renewed themselves every seven months, generation after generation.

"The . . . corn was First Mother's flesh, given so that the people might live. . . ."

And at the spot where they burned First Mother's bones, there grew another plant, broad leafed and fragrant. It was First Mother's breath, and they heard her spirit talking: "Burn this up and smoke it. It is sacred. It will clear your minds, help your prayers, and gladden your hearts."

And First Mother's husband called the first plant *skarmunal*, corn, and the second plant *utarmur-wayeh*, tobacco.

"Remember," he told the people, "and take good care of First Mother's flesh, because it is her goodness become substance. Take good care of her breath, because it is her breath turned into smoke. Remember her and think of her whenever you eat, whenever you smoke this sacred plant, because she has given her life so that you might live. Yet she is not dead, she lives: in undying love she renews herself again and again."

SOURCE: Richard Erdoes and Alfonso Ortiz, eds., *American Indian Myths and Legends* (New York: Pantheon, 1984), 11–13.

As farming became increasingly important, it radically reshaped social life. Where a foraging society might require 100 square miles to support 100 people, a farming society required only a single square mile. Farming provided not only the incentive for larger families (more workers for the fields) but also the means to feed them. People became less mobile, built more substantial residences near their crops, and developed more effective means of storage. Villages grew into towns and eventually into large, densely settled communities like Cahokia. Autumn harvests had to be stored during winter months,

and the storage and distribution of food had to be managed. The division of labor increased with the appearance of specialists like toolmakers, craft workers, administrators, priests, and rulers.

By 1000 BCE urban communities governed by permanent bureaucracies had begun to form in Mesoamerica, the region stretching from central Mexico to Central America. By the beginning of the first millennium CE (common era), highly productive farming was supporting complex urban civilizations in the Valley of Mexico (the location of present-day Mexico City), the Yucatan

Mesoamerican maize cultivation, as illustrated by an Aztec artist for the *Florentine Codex*, a book prepared several decades after the Spanish conquest. The peoples of Mesoamerica developed a greater variety of cultivated crops than those found in any other region in the world, and their agricultural productivity helped sustain one of the world's great civilizations.

SOURCE: Image #1739-3, courtesy the Library, American Museum of Natural History.

Peninsula, and other parts of Mesoamerica. Like many of the ancient civilizations of Asia and the Mediterranean, these Mesoamerican civilizations were characterized by the concentration of wealth and power in the hands of an elite class of priests and rulers, the construction of impressive temples and other public structures, and the development of systems of mathematics and astronomy and several forms of hieroglyphic writing. These civilizations also engaged in warfare between states and practiced ritual human sacrifice.

The great city of Teotihuacan in the Valley of Mexico, which emerged about 100 BCE, had a population of as many as 200,000 at the height of its power around 500 CE. Teotihuacan's elite class of religious and political leaders controlled an elaborate state-sponsored trading system that stretched from present-day Arizona to Central America and may have included coastal shipping connections with the civilizations of Peru. Teotihuacan began to decline in the sixth century, and by the eighth century it was mostly abandoned. A new empire, that of the Toltecs, dominated central Mexico from the tenth to the twelfth centuries. By the fourteenth century a people known as the Aztecs, migrants from the north, had settled in the

Valley of Mexico and begun a dramatic expansion into a formidable imperial power. The Aztecs settled a marshy lake district and built the great city of Tenochtitlán. By the early fifteenth century an estimated 200,000 people lived in the Aztec capital, making it one of the largest cities in the world, much larger than European cities of the time.

The Mayan peoples of the Yucatan Peninsula developed a group of competing city-states that flourished from about 300 BCE until 900 CE. Their achievements included advanced writing and calendar systems and a sophisticated knowledge of mathematics.

Increasing Social Complexity

In a few areas, farming truly did result in a revolutionary change in Indian communities, producing urban civilizations like those in Mesoamerica or on the banks of the Mississippi at Cahokia. It is likely that among the first social transformations was the development of significantly more elaborate systems of kinship. Greater population density prompted families to group themselves into clans, and separate clans gradually became responsible for different social, political, or ritual functions. Clans may have been an important mechanism for binding together the people of several communities into larger social units based on ethnic, linguistic, and territorial unity. These "tribes" were headed by leaders or chiefs from honored clans, often advised by councils of elders. Sometimes these councils arbitrated disputes between individuals or families, but it is likely that most crimes (theft, adultery, rape, murder) were avenged by aggrieved kinship groups. The city of Cahokia probably was governed by such a system.

Chiefs' primary functions were the supervision of the economy, the collection and storage of the harvest, and the distribution of food to the clans. Differences in wealth, though small by the standards of modern societies, might develop between the families of a farming tribe. These inequalities were kept in check by redistribution according to principles of sharing similar to those operating in foraging communities. Nowhere in North America did Indian cultures develop a concept of the private ownership of land or other resources, which were usually considered the common resource of the people and were worked collectively.

Indian communities practiced a rather strict division of labor according to gender. In foraging communities, hunting was generally men's work, while the gathering of food and the maintenance of home-base camps were the responsibility of women. The development of farming may have challenged that pattern. Where hunting remained an important activity, women took responsibility for the growing of crops. But in areas like Mexico, where communities were almost totally dependent on cultivated crops for their survival, both men and women worked the fields.

The creation of man and woman depicted on a pot (dated about 1000 CE) from the ancient villages of the Mimbres River of southwestern New Mexico, the area of Mogollon culture. Mimbres pottery is renowned for its spirited artistry. Such artifacts were usually intended as grave goods to honor the dead.

SOURCE: Mimbres black on white bowl, with painted representations of man and woman under a blanket. Grant County, New Mexico. Diam. 26.7 cm. Courtesy National Museum of the American Indian, Smithsonian Institution, 24/3198.

In most North American Indian farming communities, women and men belonged to separate social groupings, each with its own rituals and lore. Membership in these gender societies was one of the most important elements of a person's identity. Marriage ties, on the other hand, were relatively weak, and in most Indian communities divorce was a simple matter: the couple separated without a great deal of ceremony, and the children almost always remained with the mother.

Farming communities were far more complex than foraging communities, but they were also less stable. Growing populations demanded increasingly large surpluses of food, and this need often led to social conflict and warfare. Moreover, farming systems were especially vulnerable to changes in climate, such as drought, as well as to crises of their own making, such as soil depletion or erosion.

The Resisted Revolution

Some scholars describe the transition to farming as a revolution. Their argument is that farming offered such obvious advantages that communities rushed to adopt it. But there is very little evidence to support the notion that farming was a clearly superior way of life. Anthropologists have demonstrated that farmers work considerably longer and harder than do foragers. Moreover, farmers depend on a relatively narrow selection of plants and animals for food and are vulnerable to famine. Foragers experience periods of want, but they have a much higher probability of securing food under stressful conditions. Finally, compared to foragers, farmers experienced degenerative conditions of the spine (probably the result of hard labor), a threefold increase in iron-deficiency anemia, and twice the amount of tooth decay and loss.

Moreover, ignorance of cultivation was never the reason communities failed to take up farming. All foraging cultures understand a great deal about plant reproduction. When gathering wild rice, the Menominee Indians of the northern forests of Wisconsin purposely allowed some of it to fall back into the water to ensure a crop for the next season. Paiutes of the Great Basin systematically irrigated stands of their favorite wild food sources. Cultures in different regions assessed the relative advantages and disadvantages of adopting farming. In California and the Pacific Northwest, acorn gathering or salmon fishing made the cultivation of food crops seem a waste of time. In the Great Basin, there were attempts to farm but without much success. Before the invention of modern irrigation systems, which require sophisticated engineering, only the Archaic Desert culture could prevail in this harsh environment.

In the neighboring Southwest, however, farming resolved certain ecological dilemmas and transformed the way of life. Like the development of more sophisticated traditions of tool manufacture, farming represented another stage in *economic intensification* (like the advance in tool making represented by Clovis technology) that kept populations and available resources in balance. It seems that where the climate favored it, people tended to adopt farming as a way of increasing the production of food, thus continuing the Archaic tradition of squeezing as much productivity as they could from their environment.

Farming in Early North America

Maize farming spread north from Mexico into the area now part of the United States in the first millennium BCE. Over time maize was adapted to a range of climates and its cultivation spread to all the temperate regions.

Farmers of the Southwest

Farming communities began to emerge in the arid Southwest during the first millennium BCE. Among the first to develop a settled farming way of life was a culture known to archaeologists as Mogollon. These people farmed maize, beans, squash, and constructed ingenious food storage pits in permanent village sites along what is today the southern Arizona–New Mexico border. Those pits may have been the precursors of what southwestern peoples today call kivas, sites of community religious rituals.

During the same centuries, a culture known as Hohokam ("those who are gone," in the language of the modern tribes of the region) flourished in the region along the floodplain of the Salt and Gila Rivers in southern

Arizona. The Hohokam, who lived in farming villages, built and maintained the first irrigation system in America north of Mexico, channeling river water through 500 miles of canals to water desert fields of maize, beans, squash, tobacco, and cotton. Hohokam culture shared many traits with Mesoamerican civilization to the south, including platform mounds for religious ceremonies and large courts for ball playing.

The Anasazis

The best-known ancient farming culture of the Southwest is the Anasazi, which developed around the first century CE in the Four Corners area, where the states of Arizona, New Mexico, Utah, and Colorado meet on the great plateau of the Colorado River. Around 750 CE, possibly in response to population pressure and an increasingly dry climate, the residents of communities there began shifting from pit-house villages to densely populated, multistoried apartment complexes that the Spanish invaders called "pueblos." These farmers grew high-yield varieties of maize in terraced fields irrigated by canals flowing from mountain catchment basins. To supplement this vegetable diet, they hunted animals for their meat, using the bow and arrow that first appeared in the region in the sixth century.

Anasazi culture extended over a very large area. The sites of more than 25,000 Anasazi communities are known in New Mexico alone. Only a few have been excavated, so there is much that archaeologists do not yet understand. The most prominent center was Pueblo Bonito in Chaco Canyon. Completed in the twelfth century, this complex of 700 interconnected rooms is a monument to the Anasazi golden age.

The Anasazis faced a major challenge in the thirteenth and fourteenth centuries. The arid climate became even drier, and growing populations had to redouble their efforts to improve food production, building increasingly complex irrigation canals, dams, and terraced fields. A devastating drought from 1276 to 1293 (precisely dated by the aid of tree-ring analysis) resulted in repeated crop failures and eventual famine. The ecological crisis was heightened by the arrival in the fourteenth century of Athapascan migrants, ancestors of the Navajos and the Apaches. Athapascans raided Anasazi farming communities, taking food, goods, and possibly slaves. (Indeed, the name "Anasazi" means

Cliff Palace, at Mesa Verde National Park in southwest Colorado, was created 900 years ago when the Anasazis left the mesa tops and moved into more secure and inaccessible cliff dwellings. Facing southwest, the building gained heat from the rays of the low afternoon sun in winter, and overhanging rock protected the structure from rain, snow, and the hot midday summer sun. The numerous round kivas, each covered with a flat roof originally, suggest that Cliff Palace may have had a ceremonial importance.

"ancient enemies" in the Athapascan language.) Gradually Anasazi communities abandoned the Four Corners area altogether, most resettling along the Rio Grande, joining with local residents to form the Pueblo communities that were living there when the Spanish arrived.

Farmers of the Eastern Woodlands

Archaeologists date the beginning of the farming culture of eastern North America, known as Woodland culture, from the first appearances of pottery in the region about 3,000 years ago. Woodland culture was based on a sophisticated way of life that combined gathering and hunting with the cultivation of a few local crops. Sunflowers provided seeds and cooking oil. The presence of pipes in archaeological digs indicates that these farmers grew tobacco, which had spread north from the Caribbean, where it was first domesticated.

Woodland people began cultivating maize during the first millennium CE, but even before that they had begun to adopt an increasingly settled existence and a more complex social organization, evidenced by complex earthen constructions. Around 1000 BCE, at a place called Poverty Point in northeastern Louisiana, residents erected a remarkable series of concentric semicircular earthen mounds covering an area about a mile square.

Mound building was also a characteristic activity of the peoples living in the Ohio Valley during this period. The people of a culture known as Adena lived in semi permanent villages and constructed large burial mounds during the first millennium BCE. They were succeeded by a culture called Hopewell, which honored the dead with even larger and more elaborate burial mounds. Hopewell chiefs mobilized an elaborate trade network, acquiring obsidian from the Rocky Mountains, copper from the Great Lakes, mica from the Appalachians, and shells from the Gulf Coast. Hopewell artisans converted these materials into goods that played an important role in trade and were used to adorn the dead in their impressive graves.

Mississippian Society

The Hopewell culture collapsed in the fifth century CE, perhaps as a result of an ecological crisis brought on by shifting climate patterns. Over the next several centuries, however, a number of important technological innovations were introduced in the East. The bow and arrow, developed first on the Great Plains, appeared east of the Mississippi in about the seventh century, greatly increasing the efficiency of hunting. At about the same time maize farming spread widely through the East. Indian farmers developed a new variety (known today as Northern Flint) that matured in a short enough time to make it suitable for cultivation in temperate northern latitudes. A shift from digging sticks to flint hoes also took place about this time, further increasing the productive potential of maize farming.

On the basis of these innovations, a powerful new culture known as Mississippian arose in the seventh or eighth century CE. The peoples of Mississippian culture were master maize farmers living in permanent community sites along the floodplains of the Mississippi Valley. Cahokia was the largest and most spectacular, with its monumental temple mounds, its residential neighborhoods, and its surrounding farmlands. But there were dozens of other urban communities, each with thousands of residents. Archaeologists have excavated sites on the Arkansas River near Spiro, Oklahoma; on the Black Warrior River at Moundville, Alabama; at Hiawassee Island on the Tennessee River; and along the Etowah and Okmulgee Rivers in Georgia. The Great Serpent Mound, the largest effigy earthwork in the world, was constructed by Mississippian peoples in southern Ohio.

The Politics of Warfare and Violence

These centers, linked by the vast river transportation system of the Mississippi River and its many tributaries, became the earliest city-states north of Mexico, hierarchical chiefdoms that extended political control over the farmers of the surrounding countryside (see Map 1.2 for an illustration of trade networks). With continued population growth, these cities engaged in vigorous and probably violent competition for the limited space along the rivers. It may have been the need for more orderly ways of allocating territories that stimulated the evolution of political hierarchies. The tasks of preventing local conflict, storing large food surpluses, and redistributing foodstuffs from farmers to artisans and elites required a leadership class with the power to command. Mound building and the use of tribute labor in the construction of other public works testified to the power of chiefs, who lived in sumptuous quarters atop the mounds. The excavation of one mound at Cahokia uncovered the burial chamber of a chief who was accompanied in death by the bodies of dozens of young men and women, undoubtedly the victims of sacrifice.

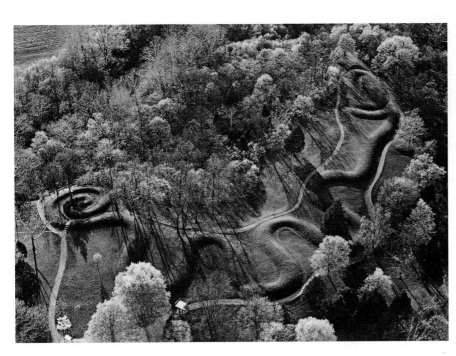

The Great Serpent Mound in southern Ohio, the shape of an uncoiling snake more than 1,300 feet long, is the largest effigy earthwork in the world. Monumental public works like these suggest the high degree of social organization of the Mississippian people.

Mississippian culture reached its height between the eleventh and thirteenth centuries CE, the same period in which the Anasazi culture constructed its desert cities. Both groups adapted to their own environment the technology that was spreading northward from Mexico. Both developed impressive artistic traditions, and their feats of engineering reflect the beginnings of science and technology. They were complex societies characterized by urbanism, social stratification, craft specialization, and regional trade—except for the absence of a writing system, all the traits of European civilization.

Warfare among Indian peoples certainly predated the colonial era. Organized violence was probably rare among hunting bands, which could seldom manage more than a small raid against an enemy. Certain hunting peoples, though, such as the southward-moving Athapascans, must have engaged in systematic raiding of settled farming communities. Warfare was also common among farming confederacies fighting to gain additional

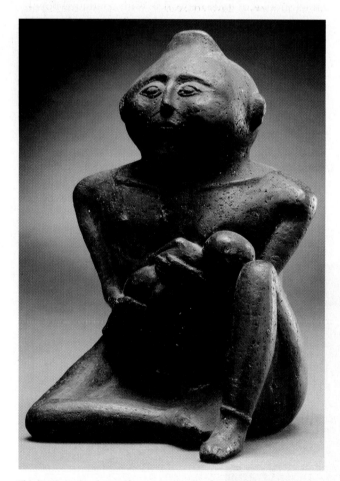

This bottle in the shape of a nursing mother (dated about 1300 BCE) was found at a Mississippian site. Historians can only speculate about the thoughts and feelings of the Mississippians, but such works of art are testimonials to the universal human emotion of maternal affection.

SOURCE: "Nursing Mother Effigy Bottle." From the Whelpley Collection at the St. Louis Science Center. Photograph © 1985 the Detroit Institute of Arts/The Bridgeman Art Library, NY.

lands for cultivation. The first Europeans to arrive in the southeastern part of the continent described highly organized combat among large tribal armies. The bow and arrow was a deadly weapon of war, and the practice of scalping seems to have originated among warring tribes who believed one could capture a warrior's spirit by taking his scalp lock.

The archaeological remains of Cahokia reveal that during the thirteenth and fourteenth centuries the residents enclosed the central sections of their city with a heavy log stockade. There must have been a great deal of violent warfare with other nearby communities. Also during this period, numerous towns were formed throughout the river valleys of the Mississippi, each based on the domination of farming countrysides by metropolitan centers. Eventually conditions in the upper Mississippi Valley deteriorated so badly that Cahokia and many other sites were abandoned altogether, and as the cities collapsed, people relocated in smaller, decentralized communities. Among the peoples of the South, however, Mississippian patterns continued into the period of colonization.

Cultural Regions of North America on the Eve of Colonization

An appreciation of the ways human cultures adapted to geography and climate is fundamental to an understanding of American history, for just as regions shaped the development of Indian cultures in the centuries before the arrival of Europeans, so they continued to influence the character of American life in the centuries thereafter.

In order to understand the impact of regions on Indian cultures, anthropologists divide North America into several distinct "culture areas" within which groups shared a significant number of cultural traits: Arctic, Subarctic, Great Basin, Great Plains, California, Northwest, Plateau, Southwest, South, and Northeast.

The Population of Indian America

In determining the precolonial population of the Americas, historical demographers consider a number of factors: the population densities that different technological and economic systems could support, the archaeological evidence, the very earliest European accounts, and the estimated impact of epidemic diseases. Determining the size of early human population is a tricky business, and estimates vary greatly, but there seems to be general agreement among historical demographers that the population of the North American continent (excluding Mesoamerica) numbered between 5 and 10 million at the time of the first European voyages of discovery. Millions more lived in the complex societies of Mexico and Central America (estimates run from 5 to 25 million). The population of the Western Hemisphere as a whole may have numbered 50 million or more, the same order of magnitude as Europe's population at the time.

Demographers may disagree about numbers but agree that population varied tremendously by cultural region (see Map 1.2). Although the cultural regions of the Arctic, Subarctic, Great Basin, and Great Plains made up more than half the physical space of the continent, they were inhabited by only a small fraction of the native population. Those regions were home to scattered bands who continued to practice the Archaic economy. Hunting and gathering continued in California as well, although the population there grew large and dense because of the region's natural abundance. In the Pacific Northwest, the strip of coast running 2,000 miles from northern California to southern Alaska, abundant salmon fisheries supported large populations concentrated in permanent villages. The people of the Plateau also made their living by fishing, although their communities were not as large or as concentrated.

The largest populations of the continent were concentrated in the farming regions of the Southwest, South, and Northeast. These were the areas in which European explorers, conquerors, and colonists concentrated their

first efforts, and they deserve more detailed examination (see Map 1.3).

The Southwest

The single overwhelming fact of life in the Southwest is aridity. Summer rains average only ten to twenty inches annually, and on much of the dry desert cultivation is impossible. A number of rivers, however, flow out of the pine-covered mountain plateaus. Flowing south to the Gulf of Mexico or the Gulf of California, these narrow bands of green winding through parched browns and reds have made possible irrigation farming along their courses.

On the eve of European colonization, Indian farmers in the Southwest had been cultivating their fields for nearly 3,000 years. In the floodplain of the Gila and Salt Rivers lived the Pimas and Tohono O'Odhams, descendants of the ancient Hohokam culture, and along the Colorado River, even on the floor of the Grand Canyon, the Yuman peoples worked small irrigated fields. In their oasis communities, desert farmers cultivated corn, beans, squash, sunflowers, and cotton, which they traded throughout the Southwest. Often described as individualists, desert farmers lived in dispersed settlements that the Spanish called rancherias,

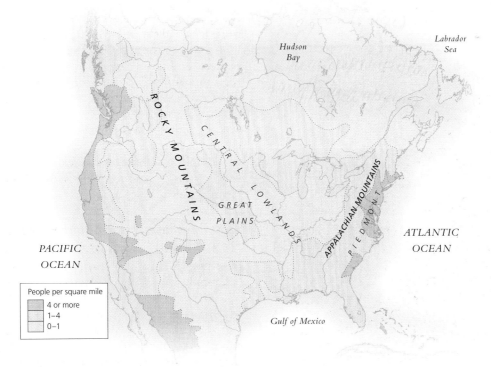

MAP 1.3 Population Density of Indian Societies in the Fifteenth Century Based on what is called the "carrying capacity" of different subsistence strategies—the population density they could support—historical demographers have mapped the hypothetical population density of Indian societies in the fifteenth century, before the era of European colonization. Populations were densest in farming societies or in coastal areas with marine resources and sparsest in extreme environments like the Great Basin.

From the very beginning of Europeans' contact with native American peoples, they depicted Indians as savages rather than as peoples with complex cultures. This woodcut by German artist Johann Froschauer was included in a 1505 German edition of Amerigo Vespucci's account of his voyage to the New World in 1499, and is among the very first images of Native Americans published. The image is a complete fantasy, lacking any ethnographic authenticity. Indians gather for a feast on the beach. The caption in the original publication read, in part: "The people are naked, handsome, brown, well-shaped in body. . . . No one has anything, but all things are in common. And the men have as wives those who please them, be they mothers, sisters, or friends; therein they make no distinction. They also fight with each other; and they eat each other, even those who are slain, and hang the flesh of them in the smoke." A cannibalized body is being devoured. A couple is kissing. Women display their breasts. The image sent a powerful message: that some of the strongest taboos of Europeans—nakedness, sexual promiscuity, and cannibalism—were practiced by the people of the New World. It is an unrelentingly negative picture. The arrival of European vessels in the background of the image suggests that all this was about to change. Images like these continued to dominate the depiction of Indians for the next 400 years, and were used as justifications for conquest.

● **How are European stereotypes of savage people conveyed visually in this image?**

OVERVIEW | Origins of Some Indian Tribal Names

Cherokee   A corruption of the Choctaw *chiluk-ki*, meaning "cave people," an allusion to the many caves in the Cherokee homeland in the highlands of present-day Georgia. The Cherokees called themselves *Ani-Yun-Wiya*, or the "real people."

Cheyenne   From the Sioux *Sha-hiyena*, "people of strange speech." The Cheyennes of the Northern Plains called themselves *Dzi-tsistas*, meaning "our people."

Hopi   A shortening of the name the Hopis of northern Arizona use for themselves, *Hópitu*, which means "peaceful ones."

Mohawk   From the Algonquian *Mohawaúuck*, meaning "man-eaters." The Mohawks of the upper Hudson Valley in New York called themselves *Kaniengehaga*, "people of the place of the flint."

Pawnee   From the Pawnee term *paríki*, which describes a distinctive style of dressing the hair with paint and fat to make it stand erect like a horn. The Pawnees, whose homeland was the Platte River valley in present-day Nebraska, called themselves *Chahiksichahiks*, "men of men."

---

their dwellings separated by as much as a mile. That way, say the Pimas, people avoid getting on each other's nerves. Rancherias were governed by councils of adult men whose decisions required unanimous consent, although a headman was chosen to manage the irrigation works.

East of the Grand Canyon lived the Pueblo peoples, named by the Spanish for their unique dwellings of stacked, interconnected apartments. Although speaking several languages, the Pueblos had a great deal in common, most notably their commitment to communal village life. A strict communal code of behavior that regulated personal conduct was enforced by a maze of matrilineal clans and secret religious societies; unique combinations of these clans and societies formed the governing systems of different Pueblo villages. Seasonal public ceremonies in the village squares included singing and chanting, dancing, colorful impersonations of the ancestral spirits called *kachinas*, and the comic antics of clowns who mocked in slapstick style those who did not conform to the communal ideal (pretending to drink urine or eat dirt, for example, in front of the home of a person who kept an unclean house).

The Pueblos inhabit the oldest continuously occupied towns in the United States. The village of Oraibi, Arizona, dates from the twelfth century, when the Hopis ("peaceful ones") founded it in the isolated central mesas of the Colorado Plateau. Using dry-farming methods and drought-resistant plants, the Hopis produced rich harvests of corn and squash amid shifting sand dunes. On a mesa top about fifty miles southwest of present-day Albuquerque, New Mexico, Anasazi immigrants from Mesa Verde built Acoma, the "sky city," in the late thirteenth century. The

Pueblo peoples established approximately seventy other villages over the next two centuries; fifty of these were still in existence in the seventeenth century when the Spanish founded Santa Fé, and two dozen survive today, including the large Indian towns of Laguna, Isleta, Santo Domingo, Jémez, San Felipe, and Taos.

The Athapascans, more recent immigrants to the Southwest, also lived in the arid deserts and mountains. They hunted and foraged, traded meat and medicinal herbs with farmers, and often raided and plundered these same villages and rancherias. One group of Athapascans, the Apaches, continued to maintain their nomadic ways. But another group, known as the Navajos, gradually adopted the farming and handicraft skills of their Pueblo neighbors.

The South

The South enjoys a mild, moist climate with short winters and long summers, ideal for farming. From the Atlantic and Gulf Coasts, a broad fertile plain extends inland to the Piedmont, a plateau separating the coastal plains from the Appalachian Mountains. The upper courses of the waterways originating in the Appalachian highlands offered ample rich bottom land for farming. The extensive forests, mostly of yellow pine, offered abundant animal resources. In the sixteenth century, large populations of Indian peoples farmed this rich land, fishing or hunting local fauna to supplement their diets. They lived in communities ranging from villages of twenty or so dwellings to large towns of a thousand or more inhabitants (see Map 1.4).

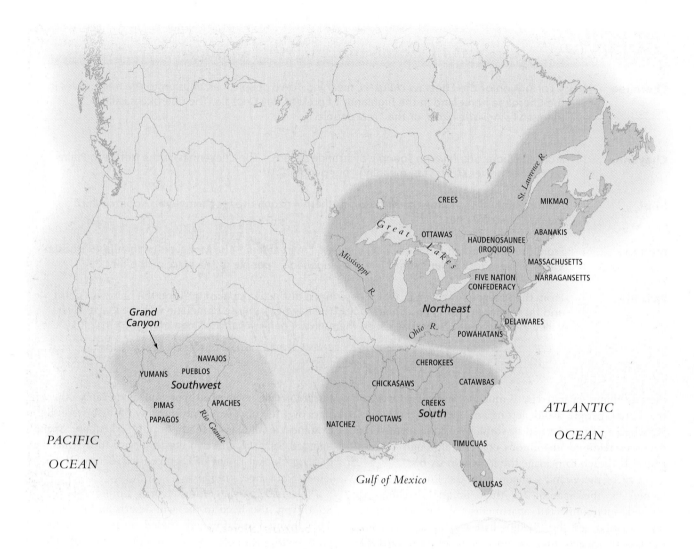

MAP 1.4 Indian Groups in the Areas of First Contact The Southwest was
populated by desert farmers like the Pimas, Tohono O'Odhams, Yumans, and Pueblos, as well as by
nomadic hunters and raiders like the Apaches and Navajos. On the eve of colonization, the Indian societies
of the South shared many traits of the complex Mississippian farming culture. The Indians of the Northeast
were mostly village peoples. In the fifteenth century, five Iroquois groups—the Mohawks, Oneidas,
Onondagas, Cayugas, and Senecas—joined together to form the Iroquois Five Nation Confederacy.

Mississippian cultural patterns continued among
many of the peoples of the South. Along the waterways,
many farming towns were organized into chiefdoms.
Because most of these groups were decimated by disease
in the first years of colonization, they are poorly documented. Archaeologists have excavated sites on the east
bank of the Mississippi, in what is now Arkansas, inhabited
by the Caddo people. The evidence suggests that in the fifteenth century they lived in complex ranked communities, built monumental temple mounds, and counted a
population of more than 200,000. There is historical evidence about the Natchez, who survived into the eighteenth century before being defeated and dispersed in a

war with the French. They too lived on the Mississippi, on
the opposite bank from the Caddos, where they farmed
the rich floodplains. The Natchez were also a ranked society, with a small group of nobility ruling over the majority.
Persistent territorial conflict with other confederacies ele-
vated warriors to an honored status. Public torture and
human sacrifice of enemies were common. The Natchez
give us our best glimpse of what life would have been like
in the community of Cahokia.

These chiefdoms were rather unstable. Under the
pressure of climate change, population growth, and warfare, many were weakened and others collapsed. As a
result, thousands of people left behind the grand mounds

"The New Queen Being Taken to the King," an engraving copied from a drawing by Jacques LeMoyne, an early French colonist of Florida, and published by the German Theodor de Bry in 1591. The communities of Florida were hierarchical, with classes and hereditary chiefs, some of whom were women. Here, LeMoyne depicted a "queen" being carried on an ornamental litter by men of rank.

SOURCE: Neg. No. 324281, Photographed by Rota, Engraving by DeBry. American Museum of Natural History Library.

and earthworks and migrated to the woodlands and hill country, where they took up hunting and foraging, returning to the tried and true methods of "forest efficiency." They formed communities and banded together in confederacies, which were less centralized and more egalitarian than the Mississippian chiefdoms and would prove considerably more resilient to conquest.

Among the most prominent of these new ethnic groups were a people in present-day Mississippi and Alabama who came to be known as the Choctaws. Another group in western Tennessee became known as the Chickasaws, and another people in Georgia later became known as the Creeks. On the mountain plateaus lived the Cherokees, the single largest confederacy, which included more than sixty towns. For these groups, farming was somewhat less important, hunting somewhat more so. There were no ruling classes or kings, and leaders included women as well as men. Women controlled household and village life and were influential in the matrilineal clans that linked communities together. Councils of elderly men governed the confederacies but were joined by clan matrons for annual meetings at the central council house.

The peoples of the South celebrated a common round of agricultural festivals that brought clans together from surrounding communities. At the harvest festival, for example, people cleaned their homes and villages. They fasted and purified themselves by consuming the "black drink," which induced visions. They extinguished the old fires and lit new ones, then celebrated the new crop of sweet corn with dancing and other festivities. During the days that followed, villages, clans, and groups of men and women competed in the ancient stick-and-ball game that the French named *lacrosse*; in the evenings men and women played *chunkey*, a gambling game.

This Hiawatha wampum belt of the Haudenosaunee or Iroquois Five Nation Confederacy is exquisitely constructed of nearly 7,000 purple and white drilled shell beads, woven together with buckskin thongs and hemp thread. It is a ceremonial artifact, a symbol of the unity of the five Iroquois nations. With the central tree or heart pointed up, the first two squares on the right represent the Mohawk and Oneida, the tree stands for the Onondaga, where the council met, and the third and fourth squares stand for the Cayuga and Seneca nations. The belt itself dates from the early eighteenth century, but the design is thought to have originated with the confederacy itself, perhaps in the twelfth century CE.

The Northeast

The Northeast, the colder sector of the eastern woodlands, has a varied geography of coastal plains and mountain highlands, great rivers, lakes, and valleys. In the first millennium CE, farming became the main support of the Indian economy in those places where the growing season was long enough to bring a crop of corn to maturity. In such areas of the Northeast, along the coasts and in the river valleys, Indian populations were large and dense (see Map 1.4).

The Iroquois of present-day Ontario and upstate New York have lived in the Northeast for at least 4,500 years and were among the first northeastern peoples to adopt cultivation. Iroquois women produced crops of corn, beans, squash, and sunflowers sufficient to support up to fifty longhouses, each occupied by a large matrilineal extended family. Some of those houses were truly long; archaeologists have excavated the foundations of some that extended 400 feet and would have housed dozens of families. Typically, these villages were surrounded by substantial wooden walls or palisades, clear evidence of conflict and warfare.

Population growth and the resulting intensification of farming in Iroquoia stimulated the development of chiefdoms there as it did elsewhere. By the eleventh century, several centers of population, each in a separate watershed, had coalesced from east to west across upstate New York. These were the five Iroquois chiefdoms or nations: the Mohawks, Oneidas, Onondagas, Cayugas, and Senecas. Oral histories collected from Iroquois speakers during the nineteenth century remember this as an era of persistent violence, possibly the consequence of conflicts over territory.

To control this violence, the five nations established a confederacy. According to Iroquois oral history, Chief Deganawida, speaking through the great orator Hiawatha, convinced the five nations to agree to prohibit warfare with each other, replacing revenge with payment and gift exchange. Iroquois legend refers to Deganawida "blocking out the sun" as a demonstration of his powers. From this bit of evidence, an astronomer and a historian have recently suggested that the founding might have taken place during the full solar eclipse that took place in the Northeast in 1142 CE. The Iroquois called their confederacy Haudenosaunee, meaning "people of the longhouse." Each nation, they said, occupied a separate hearth but acknowledged a common mother. As in the longhouse, women played important roles in the confederacy, choosing male leaders who would represent their lineages and chiefdom on the Iroquois council. The confederacy suppressed violence among its members but did not hesitate to encourage war against neighboring Iroquoian speakers, such as the Hurons or the Eries, who constructed defensive confederacies of their own at about the same time.

Read the Document

Dekanawida Myth & the Achievement of Iroquois Unity at **www.myhistorylab.com**

The other major language group of the Northeast was Algonquian, whose speakers divided among at least fifty distinct cultures. The Algonquian peoples north of the Great Lakes and in northern New England were hunters and foragers, organized into bands with loose ethnic affiliations. Several of these peoples, including the Mi'kmaq, Crees, Montagnais, and Ojibwas (also known as the Chippewas), were the first to become involved in the fur trade with European newcomers. Among the Algonquians of the Atlantic coast from present-day Massachusetts south to Virginia, as well as among those in the Ohio Valley, farming led to the development of settlements as densely populated as those of the Iroquois.

In contrast to the Iroquois, most Algonquian peoples were patrilineal. In general, they lived in less extensive dwellings and in smaller villages, often without palisade fortifications. Although Algonquian communities were relatively autonomous, they began to form confederacies during the fifteenth and sixteenth centuries. Among these groupings were those of the Massachusetts, Narragansetts, and Pequots of New England; the peoples of the Delaware Valley and Chesapeake Bay on the mid-Atlantic coast; and the Shawnees, Miamis, Kickapoos, and Potawatomis of the Ohio Valley.

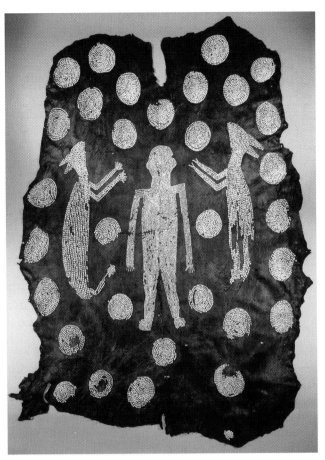

This deerskin cape, embroidered with shells by an Indian craftsman, is thought to be the chief's mantle that Powhatan, leader of a confederacy of Algonquian villages in the Chesapeake region, gave to an English captain as part of an exchange of presents in 1608. The animal effigies are suggestive of the complex of religious beliefs centering on the relationship of hunters to their prey.

SOURCE: Ashmolean Museum, Oxford, England, U.K.

Conclusion

Over the thousands of years that elapsed between the initial settlement of North America and the arrival of Europeans at the end of the fifteenth century, Indian peoples developed dozens of distinctive cultures, each fine-tuned to the geographic and climatic possibilities and limitations of their environments. In the northern forests they hunted game and perfected the art of processing furs and hides. Along the coasts and rivers they harvested the abundant runs of fish and learned to navigate the waters with sleek and graceful boats. In the arid Southwest they mastered irrigation farming and made the deserts bloom, while in the humid Southeast they mastered the large-scale production of crops that sustained large cities with sophisticated political systems. The ruins of the ancient city of Cahokia provide dramatic evidence that North America was not the "virgin" continent Europeans proclaimed it to be. Indians had transformed the natural world, making it into a human landscape.

"Columbus did not discover a new world," writes historian J. H. Perry, "he established contact between two

CHRONOLOGY

30,000 BCE	First humans populate Beringia	**200 BCE – 400 CE**	Hopewell culture flourishes
13,000 BCE	Global warming trend begins		
12,500 BCE	Monte Verde site in southern Chile flourishes	**650**	Bow and arrow, flint hoes, and Northern Flint corn in the Northeast
10,000 BCE	Clovis technology	**775–1150**	Hohokam culture flourishes
9000 BCE	Extinction of big-game animals	**1000**	Tobacco in use throughout North America
8000 BCE	Beginning of the Archaic period	**1142**	Founding of Haudenosaunee Confederacy
7000 BCE	First cultivation of plants in the Mexican highlands	**1150**	Founding of Hopi village of Oraibi, oldest continuously occupied town in the United States
5000 BCE	Athapascan migration to America begins		
4000 BCE	First settled communities along the Pacific coast	**1200**	High point of Mississippian and Anasazi cultures
3000 BCE	Inuit, Yupik, and Aleut migrations begin	**1276**	Severe drought begins in the Southwest
1500– 1000 BCE	Maize and other Mexican crops introduced into the Southwest	**1300**	Arrival of Athapascans in the Southwest
1000 BCE	First urban communities in Mexico		

worlds, both already old." North America had a rich history, one that European colonists did not understand and that later generations of Americans have too frequently ignored. The colonists and settlers who came to take the land encountered thousands of Indian communities with deep roots and vibrant traditions. In the confrontation that followed, Indian communities called on their own traditions and their own gods to help them defend their homelands.

Review Questions

1. List the evidence for the hypothesis that the Americas were settled by migrants from Asia.

2. Discuss the impact of environmental change and human hunting on the big-game populations of North America.

3. Review the principal regions of the North American continent and the human adaptations that made social life possible in each of them.

4. Define the concept of "forest efficiency." How does it help to illuminate the major development of the Archaic period?

5. Why did the development of farming lead to increasing social complexity? Discuss the reasons why organized political activity began in farming societies.

6. What were the hunting and agrarian traditions? In what ways did the religious beliefs of Indian peoples reflect their environmental adaptations?

7. What factors led to the organization of the Iroquois Five Nation Confederacy?

Recommended Reading

Colin G. Calloway, *One Vast Winter Count: The Native American West Before Lewis and Clark* (2003). A masterful synthesis that emphasizes the continuities between the precolonial and colonial history of North America.

Tom D. Dillehay, *The Settling of the Americas: A New Prehistory* (2000). A summary of the most recent archaeological findings, suggesting a much earlier migration to the Americas. For the newest discoveries, see recent issues and websites of *National Geographic* and *Scientific American*.

Patricia Galloway, *Choctaw Genesis, 1500–1700* (1995). A path-breaking work that uses both archaeological and written evidence to tie together the precolonial and colonial periods of a tribal people of the South.

Alvin M. Josephy Jr., ed., *America in 1492* (1992). Important essays by leading scholars of the North American Indian experience. Includes beautiful illustrations and maps as well as an excellent bibliography.

Alice Beck Kehoe, *America Before the European Invasions* (2002). A major new synthesis of the history of North America in the centuries before 1492.

Charles C. Mann, *1491: New Revelations of the Americas Before Columbus* (2005). A popular and engaging journalistic account of the increasing recognition among historians "that the Western Hemisphere played a role in the human story just as interesting and important as that of the Eastern Hemisphere."

Timothy R. Pauketat, *Cahokia: Ancient America's Great City on the Mississippi* (2009). An accessible account that summarizes current archaeological knowledge.

Stephen Plog, *Ancient Peoples of the American Southwest* (1998). Covers the shift to agriculture with a focus on both the costs and the benefits. An accessible text with wonderful photographs.

Sheri Marie Shuck-Hall, *Journey to the West: The Alabama and Coushatta Indians* (2008). An ethnohistory of these Southern native peoples that connects ancient and modern history.

Robert Silverberg, *Mound Builders of Ancient America: The Archaeology of a Myth* (1968). A history of opinion and theory about the mound builders.

David Hurst Thomas, *Skull Wars: Kennewick Man, Archaeology, and the Battle for Native American Identity* (2000). A page-turner that details the controversy over the discovery of "Kennewick Man" and changing ideas about ancient North American history.

Russell Thornton, *American Indian Holocaust and Survival: A Population History since 1492* (1987). The best introduction to the historical demography of North America. Provides a judicious review of all the evidence in a field of considerable controversy.

PEARSON myhistorylab Connections

Reinforce what you learned in this chapter by studying the many documents,
images, maps, review tools, and videos available at www.myhistorylab.com.

Read and Review

✓● Study and Review Chapter 1

●●● Read the Document

Pima Creation Story

*Dekanawida Myth & the Achievement of
    Iroquois Unity*

Iroquois Creation Story

Ottawa Origins Story (recorded ca. 1720)

*The Story of the Creation of the World, Told by a
    Zuñi Priest in 1885*

*Thomas Harriot, The Algonquian Peoples of the
    Atlantic Coast (1588)*

*José de Acosta, Speculations on the Origins of
    the Indians (1590)*

*History Bookshelf: Bartolome de las Casas, Brief
    Account of the Devastation of the Indies (1542)*

👁 See the Map

*The First Americans: Location of Major Indian
    Groups and Culture Areas in the 1600s*

Pre-Columbian Societies of the Americas

Research and Explore

●●● Read the Document

Exploring America: America and the Horse

Whose History Is It?: Images of Indians

Profiles
Trickster
Hiawatha (Deganawida)

((●● Hear the Audio *Ritual of the Maize*

((●● Hear the Audio

Hear the audio files for Chapter 1 at
www.myhistorylab.com.

Chapter 2 at www.myhistorylab.com

((•—Hear the Audio

When Worlds Collide

1492–1590

CHAPTER OUTLINE

The French, under the command of Jean Ribault, discover the River of May (St. Johns River) in Florida on 1 May 1562: colored engraving, 1591, by Theodor de Bry after a now lost drawing by Jacques Le Moyne de Morgues. The Granger Collection.

The English at Roanoke

AMERICAN · · Communities

It was late August 1590 when the English vessels sailed through Hatteras Inlet into Pamlico Sound, off the coast of present-day North Carolina, and made their way north through rough seas to Roanoke Island. Governor John White was returning to the first English community established in America. He had left three years before, sailing home to appeal for additional support. He was extremely anxious about the fate of the colonists, including his daughter, son-in-law, and granddaughter Virginia Dare, the first English child born in the New World. From the deck he saw no sign of life. Rowing ashore, he found the colonists' houses "taken down," their possessions "spoiled and scattered about." Looking around for some sign of hope, White noticed a word carved on a nearby tree trunk: "CROATOAN," the name of a friendly Indian village some fifty miles south. White had left instructions that in the event of trouble the colonists were to leave the sign of a cross, and not finding one he reassured himself that his people awaited him at Croatoan. He returned to his vessel, anxious to rescue them.

The Roanoke settlement had been sponsored by Sir Walter Raleigh, a wealthy English adventurer who sought profit and prestige by promoting colonies in the New World. In 1584 Raleigh sponsored a small group of adventurers who first landed on the island the Indians called Roanoke. The men found the coastal region densely populated by a "very handsome and goodly people" and were "entertained with all love and kindness" by a local chief named Wingina. To Wingina, the English were potential allies in his struggle to extend authority over more villages, and he granted the men permission to plan a large English settlement. He even sent two of his leading men back to England to help prepare the enterprise. Manteo and Wanchese, the Indian emissaries, worked with Thomas Harriot, an Oxford scholar, and John White, a surveyor and artist. When the Englishmen returned in 1585 to establish the colony of Virginia (christened in honor of England's virgin queen, Elizabeth I), the two Indians offered Wingina conflicting reports. Manteo, from the village of Croatoan, argued that English technology made these men powerful allies. But Wanchese told of the disturbing inequalities he had seen among the English and warned his chief of the potential brutality of these men. He rightly suspected their intentions, for Raleigh's plans were based on the expectation of exploiting the Indians. Raleigh hoped for profits from a lucrative trade in furs, a flourishing plantation agriculture, or the possibility of gold and silver mines. In each case the Indians were to supply the labor.

After building a rough fort on the island, the English requested supplies from Wingina. With the harvest in the storage pits, fish running in the streams, and fat game in the woods, the chief did the hospitable thing. But as fall turned to winter and the stores diminished, he grew weary of their persistent demands. He was also stunned by the new diseases the English brought. In the spring Wingina ran out of patience. Before the Indians could act, however, the Englishmen caught wind of the rising hostility and in a surprise attack in May 1586 they killed several leaders, including Wingina. Leaving his head on a stake, they fled back to England.

John White and Thomas Harriot, who had spent their time exploring the physical and human world of the coast and recording their findings in notes and sketches, were appalled by the turn of events. Back in England, Harriot insisted that the attack came "upon causes that on our part might easily enough have been borne" and argued for the possibility that the Indians, "through discreet dealing" might yet come to "honor, obey, fear and love us." White proposed a new plan for a colony of genuine settlers, families who would attempt to live in harmony with the natives.

In 1587, with Raleigh's financial support, John White returned to Virginia as governor of a new colony of 117 men, women, and children. They were supposed to land on Chesapeake Bay after checking on the situation at Roanoke. But the captain, eager to get on with the profitable activity of plundering Spanish shipping, insisted on dropping the colonists there. White found himself among Indians who had already been completely alienated, and within a month, one of the colonists had been shot full of arrows. White's counterattack only increased the Indians' resolve to expel the intruders. The colonists begged White to sail home in their only seaworthy vessel to ask Raleigh for additional support. He left reluctantly, arriving in England just as war began with Spain.

After three long and anxious years, Governor White now found the settlement destroyed, and the colonists gone. He returned to his vessel eager to leave for the village of Croatoan. But within minutes a great storm blew up, and the captain told White they had to sail for deeper waters. White would never glimpse the shores of America again. The English settlers of Roanoke became "The Lost Colony," their disappearance and ultimate fate one of the enduring mysteries of colonial history.

"The English," writes the historian and geographer Carl Sauer, were motivated by "naked imperial objectives." Blinded by their desire for immediate rewards, the colonists wasted the opportunity presented by the natives' initial welcome. But the Roanoke story also says something about the importance of community in the first attempts at colonization. Bits of evidence suggest that the so-called lost colonists lived out the rest of their lives as residents of Indian villages. In 1609, the English at Jamestown were told by the Indians there that the Roanoke colonists "were yet alive." Many decades later, natives of Croatoan Island told an Englishman that "several of their ancestors were white people," that the lost colonists had come to live with them, "and that in the process of time they conformed themselves to the manners of their Indian relations." Virginia Dare and other English children may have been adopted by Indian families, grown up and taken Indian spouses, in the process creating the first mixed

1. What was the European background to the colonization of North America?

2. What kind of an empire did the Spanish create in the New World, and why did it extend into North America?

3. In what ways did the exchange of peoples, crops, animals, and diseases shape the experience of European colonists and American natives?

4. What was the French role in the beginning of the North American fur trade?

5. Why did England enter the race for colonies?

FOCUS Questions

1492–1590

community of English and Indians in North America.

European colonists came to the Americas for a variety of reasons, but high on their list of priorities were plunder and profit. The invasion of America often included terrible violence, as well as frequent

Roanoke

possibilities for accommodation and cooperation between natives and newcomers. The invasion also introduced mortal epidemic diseases that devastated native communities. The encounter of communities at Roanoke was, in numerous ways, a template for New World colonization.

AMERICAN Communities

The Expansion of Europe

Roanoke and other European colonial settlements of the sixteenth century came in the wake of Christopher Columbus's voyage of 1492. But there may have been unrecorded contacts between the peoples of America and the Old World before Columbus. Archaeological excavations at L'Anse aux Meadows on the fogbound Newfoundland coast are evidence of the short-lived settlement of the Norse in the tenth or eleventh century. Implacably opposed by the native inhabitants, the Norse colony lasted only a few years and had no appreciable impact. The connection with America established by Columbus had earthshaking consequences. Within a generation, the exchanges of peoples, crops, animals, and germs had transformed the world. The key to understanding these remarkable events is the transformation of Europe during the several centuries preceding the voyage of Columbus.

Western Europe before Columbus

Western Europe was an agricultural society: most Europeans lived in family households clustered in farming villages. Farming and raising livestock had been practiced in Europe for thousands of years, but during the late Middle Ages there were great advances in technology. Water mills, iron plows, improved devices for harnessing ox and horse power, and systems of crop rotation greatly increased productivity. From the eleventh to the fourteenth centuries the quantity of land under cultivation in western Europe more than doubled. During the same period the population nearly tripled.

Europe was a world of social contrasts, characterized by a social system historians call "feudalism." The land was divided into hundreds of small territories, each ruled by a family of lords that held a monopoly of wealth and power. Feudal lords commanded labor service from peasants and tribute in the form of crops. They were the main beneficiaries of medieval economic expansion, accumulating great estates and building imposing castles. A relatively small class of freehold farmers prospered as well, but the majority of peasants experienced little improvement in their standard of living.

Western Europe was officially Christian, united under the authority of the Roman Catholic Church, whose complex organization spanned thousands of local communities with a hierarchy that extended from parish priests to the pope in Rome. At the core of Christian belief was a set of communal values: love of God the father, loving behavior toward other people, and the fellowship of all believers. Yet the Catholic Church itself was one of the most powerful feudal landowners in Europe. It insisted on its dogmas and actively persecuted heretics, nonbelievers, and devotees of older "pagan" religions. The Church provided legitimacy for the relationship of lord and peasant, counseling the poor and downtrodden to place their hopes in heavenly rewards.

For the great majority of Europeans, living conditions were harsh. Most rural people survived on bread and porridge, supplemented with seasonal vegetables and an occasional piece of meat or fish. Infectious diseases abounded; perhaps a third of all children died before their fifth birthday, and only half the population reached adulthood. Famines periodically ravaged the countryside. In the fourteenth century, for example, a series of crop failures resulted in widespread starvation and death. This episode prepared the way for the so-called Black Death, a widespread epidemic of bubonic plague that swept in from Asia and wiped out a third of Europe's population between 1347 and 1353.

Strengthened by the technological developments of the Middle Ages, Europe's agricultural economy quickly recovered. By 1500 the population had rebounded to its former high of 65 million.

The Merchant Class and the Renaissance

The economic growth of the late Middle Ages was accompanied by the expansion of commerce, especially the trade in basic goods such as minerals, salt, timber, fish, cereals, wool, and wine. Commercial expansion stimulated the growth of markets and towns.

The heart of this dynamic European commercialism lay in the city-states of Italy. During the late Middle Ages, the cities of Venice, Genoa, and Pisa launched armed commercial fleets that seized control of Mediterranean trade. The merchants of these cities became the principal outfitters of the Crusades, a series of great military expeditions promoted by the Catholic Church to recover Palestine from the Muslims. With the conquest of Jerusalem at the end of the eleventh century, the silk and spice trades of Asia were delivered into the hands of Italian merchants. Tropical spices—cloves, cinnamon, nutmeg, and pepper—were in great demand since they made the European diet far more palatable for the elites who could afford them. Asian civilization also supplied a number of technical innovations that further propelled European economic growth. From China alone came the compass, gunpowder, and use of movable type in printing. According to the seventeenth-century English philosopher Francis Bacon, these were "the three greatest inventions known to man."

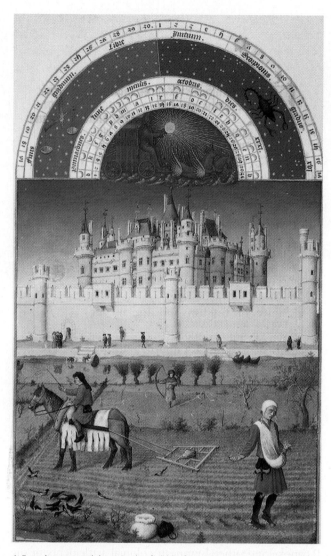

A French peasant labors in the field before a spectacular castle in a page taken from the illuminated manuscript *Tres Riches Heures*, made in the fifteenth century for the duc de Berry. In 1580 the essayist Montaigne talked with several American Indians at the French court who "noticed among us some men gorged to the full with things of every sort while their other halves were beggars at their doors, emaciated with hunger and poverty" and "found it strange that these poverty-stricken halves should suffer such injustice, and that they did not take the others by the throat or set fire to their houses."

Contact with Muslim civilization provided access to important ancient texts, long lost in Europe but preserved in the great libraries of Alexandria (Egypt) and Baghdad (Iraq). The revived interest in classical antiquity triggered a period of intellectual and artistic flowering from the fourteenth to sixteenth centuries that later generations called the Renaissance. The revolution in communication made possible by the printing press, the beginning of regular postal service, and the growth of universities helped spread Renaissance ideas throughout the elite circles of Europe.

The Renaissance celebrated human possibility. "You, constrained by no limits, in accordance with your own free will, shall ordain for yourself the limits of your nature," wrote the Italian intellectual Pico della Mirandola in 1486. This human-centered perspective was part of what became known as humanism, in which life on Earth took precedence over the afterlife of the soul. This outlook was a critical component of the inquisitive and acquisitive spirit that motivated the exploration of the Americas.

The New Monarchies

The Renaissance began amid the ruins of the plague. Famine and disease led to violence, as groups battled for their share of a shrinking economy. A series of peasant rebellions culminated in the great English Peasants' Revolt of 1381. "We are made men in the likeness of Christ," cried one rebel, "but you treat us like savage beasts!" Warfare among the nobility weakened and greatly reduced the power of the landed classes, and the Catholic Church was seriously destabilized by an internal struggle between French and Italian factions.

It was during this period of social and political chaos that the monarchs of western Europe began to replace the lords as the new centers of power. They built their legitimacy by promising internal order as they unified their realms (see Map 2.1). They built royal bureaucracies and standing armies and navies. In many cases, the new monarchs found support among the increasingly wealthy merchants, who in return sought lucrative royal contracts and trading monopolies. This alliance between commerce and political power was another important development that prepared the way for European expansion.

The Portuguese Voyages

Portugal, a narrow land along the western coast of the Iberian Peninsula with a long tradition of seafaring, became the first of the new Renaissance kingdoms to send out explorers on voyages to distant lands. Lisbon, the principal port on the sea route between the Mediterranean

MAP 2.1 Western Europe in the Fifteenth Century By the middle of the century, the monarchs of western Europe had unified their realms and begun to build royal bureaucracies and standing armies and navies. These states, all with extensive Atlantic coastlines, sponsored the voyages that inaugurated the era of European colonization.

The astrolabe, an instrument used for determining the precise position of heavenly bodies, was introduced into early modern Europe by the Arabs. This is one of the earliest examples, an intricately engraved brass astrolabe produced by a master craftsman in Syria in the thirteenth century.

SOURCE: © National Maritime Museum Picture Library, London, England. Neg. #E5555-3.

and northwestern Europe, was a bustling, cosmopolitan city with large enclaves of Italian merchants. By 1385 the local merchant community had grown powerful enough to place João I, their favorite, on the throne. João had ambitious plans to establish a Portuguese trading empire.

A central figure in this development was the king's son, Prince Henry, known to later generations as "the Navigator." Prince Henry established an academy of eminent geographers, instrument makers, shipbuilders, and seamen at his institute on the southwestern tip of Portugal at Sagres Point. By the mid-fifteenth century, as a result of their efforts, most educated Europeans knew the earth was round. Studying the seafaring traditions of Asia and the Muslim world, the learned men of Sagres Point incorporated them into the design of a new ship called the *caravel*, faster and better-handling than any ship

previously known in Europe. They promoted the use of Arab instruments for astronomical calculation. With such innovations, Europeans became the masters of the world's seas, a supremacy that would continue until the twentieth century.

The Portuguese explored the Atlantic coast of northwestern Africa for direct access to the lucrative gold and slave trades of that continent. By the time of Prince Henry's death in 1460, they had colonized the Atlantic islands of the Azores and the Madeiras and founded bases along the West African "Gold Coast." In 1488 Portuguese captain Bartholomeu Días rounded the southern tip of Africa, and ten years later Vasco da Gama, with the aid of Arab pilots, reached India. The Portuguese eventually built strategic trading forts along the coasts of Africa, India, Indonesia, and China, the first and longest-lasting outposts of European world colonization, and gained control of much of the Asian spice trade. Most important for the history of the Americas, the Portuguese established the Atlantic slave trade. (For a full discussion of slavery, see Chapter 4.)

Columbus Reaches the Americas

In 1476, Christopher Columbus, a young Genoan sailor, joined his brother in Lisbon, where he became a seafaring merchant for Italian traders. He developed the simple idea of opening a new route to the Indies by sailing west across the Atlantic Ocean, known at that time as the "Western Sea." Such a venture would require royal backing, but when he approached the various monarchs of Europe with his idea, their advisers laughed at his geographic ignorance, pointing out that his calculation of the distance to Asia was much too short. They were right: Columbus was wrong. But it turned out to be an error of monumental good fortune.

Columbus finally sold his plan to the monarchs of Castile and Aragon, Isabel and Ferdinand. These two had just completed the Reconquista, a centuries-long struggle between Catholics and Muslims that ended Muslim rule in Spain. The Catholic monarchs of Spain were eager for new lands to conquer, and observing the successful Portuguese push to the south along the west coast of Africa, they became interested in opening lucrative trade routes of their own to the Indies.

Columbus called his undertaking "the Enterprise of the Indies," which suggests his commercial hopes. But his mission was more than commercial. One of his prime goals was to "occupy" the islands he found, establishing title for Spain by the right of occupancy. Like the adventurers who later established the first English colony at Roanoke, Columbus's objectives were starkly imperial.

Columbus's three vessels reached the Bahamas in October 1492. But Columbus believed he was in the

Watch the **Video**
How Should We Think of Columbus? at **www.myhistorylab.com**

Columbus bids farewell to the monarchs Isabel and Ferdinand at the port of Palos in August 1492, illustrated in a copperplate engraving published in 1594 by Theodore de Bry of Frankfort. While armed men are ferried out to the vessels, three accountants in a room directly above the monarchs count out the gold to fund the journey.

Indies, somewhere near the Asian mainland. He explored the northern island coasts of Cuba and Hispaniola before heading home, fortuitously catching the westerly winds that blow from the American coast toward Europe north of the tropics. Perhaps Columbus's most important discovery was the clockwise circulation of the Atlantic winds and currents that would carry thousands of European ships back and forth to the Americas. This made possible entirely new global networks of trade and communication. The real discovery of 1492 was the Atlantic Ocean.

Leading Columbus's triumphal procession to the royal court were half a dozen Taíno Indians, taken by force from their homes, and dressed for the occasion in bright feathers with ornaments of gold. "Should your majesties command it," Columbus told the monarchs, "all the inhabitants could be made slaves." Moreover, he reported, "there are many spices and great mines of gold and of other metals." In fact, none of the Eastern spices familiar to Europeans grew in the Caribbean and there were only small quantities of alluvial gold in the riverbeds of the islands. But the sight of the gold ornaments worn by the Taínos infected Columbus with gold fever. He reported that he had left a small force behind in

Read the Document
From The Journal of Christopher Columbus (1492) at **www.myhistorylab.com**

a rough fort on the northern coast of Hispaniola to explore for gold—the first European foothold in the Americas.

The enthusiastic monarchs financed a return convoy of seventeen vessels and 1,500 men that sailed in late 1493 to begin the systematic colonization of the islands. Like the later English colonists at Roanoke, Columbus expected the Indians would provide the necessary labor. But returning to Hispaniola, Columbus found his fort in ruins and his men all killed by the Taínos who, like the Algonquians at Roanoke, lost patience with the continuing demands of the Europeans. Columbus directed his men to attack and destroy the nearby Taíno villages, enslaving the inhabitants and demanding tribute in gold.

Columbus's voyages were a disaster for the Taínos. The combined effects of warfare, famine, and demoralization resulted in the collapse of their society. Numbering perhaps 300,000 in 1492, they were reduced to fewer than 30,000 within fifteen years, and by the 1520s had been effectively eliminated as a people. As the native population fell, the colony plunged into depression. As early as 1500 the Spanish monarchs had grown so dissatisfied that they ordered Columbus arrested and sent back to Spain in irons.

Columbus made two additional voyages to the Caribbean, both characterized by the same obsessive searching for gold and violent raiding for slaves. He died in Spain in 1506, still convinced he had opened a new way to Asia. This belief persisted among many Europeans well into the sixteenth century. But others had already begun to see the discoveries from a different perspective. Amerigo Vespucci of Florence, who voyaged to the Caribbean in 1499, was the first to describe the discoveries as *Mundus Novus*, a "New World." When European geographers finally named the new lands early in the sixteenth century, they honored Vespucci's insight by calling them "America."

Watch the Video
What Is Columbus's Legacy? at **www.myhistorylab.com**

The Spanish in the Americas

Long before the English attempted to plant their first colony at Roanoke, the Spanish had created a huge and wealthy empire in the Americas. In theory, all law and policy for the empire came from Spain; in practice, the isolation of the settlements led to a good deal of local autonomy. The Spanish created a caste system, in which a small minority of settlers and their offspring controlled the lives and labor of millions of Indian and African workers. But it was also a society in which colonists, Indians, and Africans mixed to form a new people.

The Invasion of America

The first stages of the Spanish invasion of America included frightful violence. Armies marched across the Caribbean islands, plundering villages, slaughtering men, and capturing women. Columbus and his successors established an institution known as the *encomienda*, in which Indians were compelled to labor in the service of Spanish lords. The relationship was supposed to be reciprocal, with lords protecting Indians in exchange for service, but in practice it amounted to little more than slavery. Faced with labor shortages, slavers raided the Bahamas and soon depopulated them of native people. The depletion of gold on Hispaniola led to the invasion of the islands of Puerto Rico and Jamaica in 1508, then Cuba in 1511. Meanwhile, rumors of wealthy native societies to the west led to scores of probing expeditions (see Map 2.2). The Spanish invasion of Central America began in 1511, and

two years later Vasco Núñez de Balboa crossed the Isthmus of Panama to the Pacific Ocean. In 1517, Spaniards landed on the coast of Mexico, and within a year they made contact with the Aztec empire (see Chapter 1).

Hernán Cortés, a veteran of the conquest of Cuba, landed on the Mexican coast in 1519 with armed troops. Within two years he overthrew the Aztec empire, a spectacular military accomplishment that has few parallels in the annals of conquest. Cortés skillfully exploited the resentment of the many peoples who lived under Aztec domination, forging Spanish–Indian alliances that became a model for the subsequent European colonization of the Americas. He was also assisted by important "gobetweens." One of the most important was Malínche, an Indian slave girl who became Cortés's translator. Like many other indigenous people who decided it was in their best interest to ally with the invaders, she did not "betray" the native side, but simply made a rational choice based on what she knew. Here, as at Roanoke and dozens of other sites of European invasion, colonizers found Indians eager for allies to support them in their conflicts with other

This woodcut accompanied Columbus's account of his voyage, published originally in Latin and reissued in many other languages and editions that circulated throughout Europe. The Spanish King Ferdinand is shown directing the voyage to a tropical island, where the natives flee in terror. Columbus's impression of Native Americans as a people vulnerable to conquest shows clearly in this image.

MAP 2.2 The Invasion of America In the sixteenth century, the Spanish first invaded the Caribbean and used it to stage their successive wars of conquest in North and South America. In the seventeenth century, the French, English, and Dutch invaded the Atlantic coast. The Russians, sailing across the northern Pacific, mounted the last of the colonial invasions in the eighteenth century.

Indians. Even so, the Aztecs were militarily powerful. They succeeded in driving the Spaniards from Tenochtitlán, then put up a bitter and prolonged defense when Cortés returned with tens of thousands of Indian allies to besiege the capital. In the meantime, however, the Aztecs suffered a devastating epidemic of smallpox that killed thousands and undermined their ability to resist. In the aftermath of conquest, the Spanish plundered Aztec society, providing the Catholic monarchs with wealth beyond their wildest imagining.

The Destruction of the Indies

The Indian peoples of the Americas resisted Spanish conquest with determination, but most proved a poor match for mounted warriors with steel swords. The record of the conquest includes many brave Indian leaders and thousands of martyrs. The Carib people (for whom the Caribbean Sea is named) successfully defended the outermost islands until the end of the sixteenth century, and the nomadic tribes of arid northern Mexico, known collectively as the Chichimecs, proved equally difficult to subdue.

Some Europeans protested the horrors of the conquest. In 1511 the Catholic priest Antonio de Montesinos condemned the violence in a sermon delivered to colonists on Hispaniola. "On what authority have you waged a detestable war against these people, who dwelt quietly and peacefully on their own land?" he asked. "Are these Indians not men? Are you not obliged to love them as you love yourselves?" In the congregation was Bartolomé de las Casas, a man who had participated in the plunder of Cuba. Renouncing his own wealth, las Casas entered the priesthood and dedicated his life to the protection of the Indians. Long before the world recognized the concept of universal human rights, las Casas was proclaiming that "the entire human race is one," earning him a reputation as one of the towering moral figures in the early history of the Americas.

In his brilliant history of the conquest, *The Destruction of the Indies* (1552), las Casas blamed the Spanish for cruelties resulting in millions of Indian deaths—in effect he accused them of genocide. Translated into several languages and widely circulated throughout Europe, las Casas's book was cynically used by other European colonial powers to condemn Spain, thereby covering up their own dismal colonial practices and creating what has been called the "Black Legend" of Spanish colonization. Although later scholars disputed las Casas's estimates of huge population losses, recent demographic studies suggest he was more right than wrong. The destruction of the Taínos on Hispaniola was repeated elsewhere.

This map of Tenochtitlán, published in 1524 and attributed to the celebrated engraver Albrecht Dürer, shows the city before its destruction, with the principal Aztec temples in the main square, causeways connecting the city to the mainland, and an aqueduct supplying fresh water. The information on this map must have come from Aztec sources, as did much of the intelligence Cortés relied on for the Spanish conquest.

The Virgin Soil Epidemics

Las Casas was incorrect, however, in attributing most of these Indian deaths to warfare. Although lethal violence cost thousands of lives, and thousands more starved because their economies were destroyed, the primary cause of the drastic reduction in native populations was epidemic disease—influenza, plague, smallpox, measles, and typhus. Although preconquest America was by no means disease free—skeletal evidence suggests that natives suffered from arthritis, hepatitis, polio, and tuberculosis—there were no diseases of epidemic potential. Indian peoples lacked the antibodies necessary to protect them from European germs and viruses. Such devastating outbreaks of disease, striking for the first time against a completely unprotected population, are known as "virgin soil epidemics." Smallpox made its first appearance in America in 1518, exploding in an epidemic so virulent that, in the words of an early Spanish historian, "it left Hispaniola, Puerto Rico, Jamaica, and Cuba desolated of Indians." The epidemic hit Mexico in 1520, destroying the Aztecs and preparing the way for their conquest, then spreading along the Indian trade network. In 1524 it strategically weak-

ened the Inca civilization of the Andes eight years before their empire was conquered by Francisco Pizarro. Spanish chroniclers wrote that this single epidemic killed half the native Americans it touched. Disease was the secret weapon of the Spanish, and it helps explain their extraordinary success. After the conquest, Mexicans sang of an earlier time:

> *There was then no sickness.*
> *They had then no aching bones.*
> *They had then no high fever.*
> *They had then no smallpox.*
> *They had then no burning chest.*
> *They had then no abdominal pains.*
> *They had then no consumption.*
> *They had then no headache.*
> *At that time the course of humanity was orderly.*
> *The foreigners made it otherwise when they arrived here.*

Warfare, famine, lower birthrates, and epidemic disease knocked the native population of the Americas into a downward spiral that was not reversed until the twentieth century (see Figure 2.1). By that time native population had fallen by more than 90 percent. It was the greatest demographic disaster in world history. The most notable difference between the European colonial experience in the Americas compared to Africa or Asia was this radical reduction in the native population.

The Columbian Exchange

The passage of diseases between the Old and New Worlds was one part of the large-scale exchange of people, animals, plants, and goods—what the historian Alfred Crosby terms "the Columbian Exchange"—that marks the beginning of the modern era of world history (see Map 2.3). The most obvious exchange was the vast influx into Europe of the precious metals plundered from the Aztec and Incan empires of the New World. Most of this golden booty was melted down, destroying forever thousands of priceless native artifacts. Silver from mines the Spanish discovered and operated with Indian labor in Mexico and Peru tripled the amount of silver coin circulating in Europe between 1500 and 1550, then tripled it again before 1600. The result of so much new coin in circulation was runaway inflation, which stimulated commerce and raised profits but lowered the standard of living for most people.

Of even greater long-term importance were the New World crops brought to Europe. Maize (Indian corn), the staff of life for most native North Americans, became a staple crop in Mediterranean countries, the dominant feed for livestock elsewhere in Europe, and the primary provision for the slave ships of Africa. Potatoes provided the

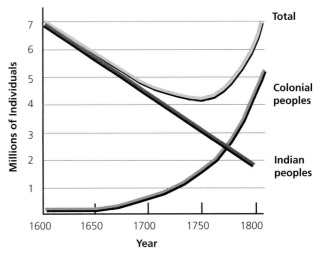

FIGURE 2.1 North America's Indian and Colonial Populations in the Seventeenth and Eighteenth Centuries The primary factor in the decimation of native peoples was epidemic disease, brought to the New World from the Old. In the eighteenth century, the colonial population overtook North America's Indian populations.

SOURCE: Historical Statistics of the United States (Washington, DC: Government Printing Office, 1976), 8, 1168; Russell Thornton, *American Indian Holocaust and Survival* (Norman: University of Oklahoma Press, 1987), 32.

margin between famine and subsistence for the peasant peoples of northern Europe and Ireland.

Although the Spanish failed to locate valuable spices such as black pepper or cloves in the New World, new tropical crops more than compensated. Tobacco, first introduced to Europe about 1550 as a cure for disease, was soon in wide use

This drawing of victims of the smallpox epidemic that struck the Aztec capital of Tenochtitlán in 1520 is taken from the *Florentine Codex*, a postconquest history written and illustrated by Aztec scribes. "There came amongst us a great sickness, a general plague," reads the account, "killing vast numbers of people. It covered many all over with sores: on the face, on the head, on the chest, everywhere. . . . The sores were so terrible that the victims could not lie face down, nor on their backs, nor move from one side to the other. And when they tried to move even a little, they cried out in agony."

as a stimulant. American vanilla and chocolate both became highly valued. American cotton proved far superior to Asian varieties for the production of cheap textiles. Each of these native plants—along with tropical transplants from the Old World to America, with sugar, rice, and coffee being the most important—supplied the basis for important new industries and markets that altered the course of world history.

Columbus introduced domesticated animals into Hispaniola and Cuba, and livestock were later transported to Mexico. The movement of Spanish settlement northward through Mexico was greatly aided by an advancing wave of livestock, for grazing animals did serious damage to native fields and forests. Horses, used by Spanish stockmen to tend their cattle, also spread northward. In the seventeenth century, horses reached the Great Plains of North America, where they eventually transformed the lives of the nomadic hunting Indians (see Chapter 5).

The Spanish in North America

Ponce de León, governor of Puerto Rico, was the first Spanish conquistador to attempt to extend the Spanish conquest to North America (see Map 2.4). In search of slaves, he made his first landing on the mainland coast, which he named Florida, in 1513. Warriors from the powerful Indian chiefdoms there beat back this and several other attempts at invasion, and in 1521 succeeded in killing de León. Seven years later, another Spanish attempt to colonize Florida, under the command of Pánfilo de Narváez, also ended in disaster. Most of Narváez's men were lost in a shipwreck, but a small group of them survived, living and wandering for several years among the native peoples of the Gulf Coast and the Southwest until they were finally rescued in 1536 by Spanish slave hunters in northern Mexico. One of these castaways, Alvar Núñez Cabeza de Vaca, published an account of his adventures in which he repeated rumors of a North American empire known as Cíbola, with golden cities "larger than the city of Mexico." These tales may have referred to Mississippian towns with platform mounds.

Cabeza de Vaca's report inspired two great Spanish expeditions into North America. The first was mounted in Cuba by Hernán de Soto, a veteran of the conquest of Peru. Landing in Florida in 1539 with over 700 men, de Soto pushed hundreds of miles through the heavily populated South, commandeering food and slaves from the Mississippian towns in his path. But de Soto failed

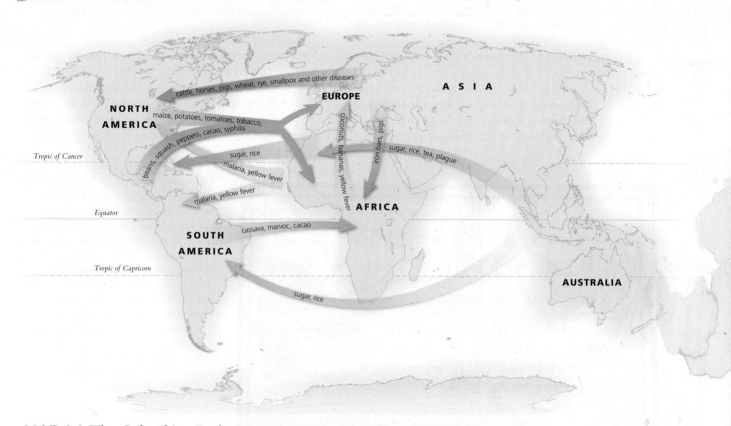

MAP 2.3 The Columbian Exchange Europeans voyaging between Europe, Africa, Asia, and the Americas in the fifteenth and sixteenth centuries began a vast intercontinental movement of plants, animals, and diseases that shaped the course of modern history. New World corn and potatoes became staple foods in Africa and Europe, while Eurasian and African diseases such as smallpox, malaria, and yellow fever devastated native communities in the Western Hemisphere.

Gulf of
Alaska

Hudson's
Bay

*Labrador
Sea*

Missouri R.

G r e a t   L a k e s

St. Lawrence R.

*Gulf of
St. Lawrence*

Mississippi R.

Ohio R.

**ATLANTIC
OCEAN**

Cibola
• Santa Fe

Rio Grande

Fort Caroline
• St. Augustine

*Gulf of
Mexico*

Mexico
City •
**AZTEC
EMPIRE**

*Yucatan
Peninsula*
**MAYAN
EMPIRE**

• Havana

• Santiago
de Cuba

• San Juan

*Caribbean
Sea*

**PACIFIC
OCEAN**

Isthmus of
Panama

**INCA
EMPIRE**

←— Spanish Voyages
←— English Voyages
←— French Voyages

MAP 2.4 European Exploration, 1492–1591 By the mid-sixteenth century, Europeans
had explored most of the Atlantic coast of North America and penetrated into the interior in the
disastrous expeditions of de Soto and Coronado.

The Debate over the Justice of the Conquest

In 1550 a historic debate took place at the Spanish court, in the city of Valladolid, over the justice of the conquest. Juan Gines Sepúlveda, official historian of the royal court, took the position that Indians were savages and deserved to be enslaved. He was opposed by the Dominican priest Bartolomé de las Casas, who believed the Indians to be fully capable of reason and that conversion to Christianity must be accomplished without force or coercion. Sepúlveda's position supported the interests of Spanish colonists, while the arguments of las Casas were taken up by church and crown, who sought to control the power of *encomenderos*. No transcript of the debate survives, but the arguments of the two men can be reconstructed from their other writings.

• **What principal argument does las Casas use to counter the logic of Sepúlveda?**

The Indians Are Natural Slaves

The Spanish have a perfect right to rule these barbarians of the New World and the adjacent islands, who in prudence, skill, virtues, and humanity are as inferior to the Spanish as children to adults, or women to men, for there exists between the two as great a difference as between savage and cruel races and the most merciful, between the most intemperate and the moderate and temperate and, I might even say, between apes and men.

. . . What temperance or mercy can you expect from men who are committed to all types of intemperance and base frivolity, and eat human flesh? And do not believe that before the arrival of the Christians they lived in that pacific age which the poets have invented; for, on the contrary, they waged continual and ferocious war upon one another with such fierceness that they did not consider a victory at all worthwhile unless they sated their monstrous hunger with the flesh of their enemies. . . . Although some of them show a certain ingenuity for various works of artisanship, this is no proof of human cleverness, for we can observe animals, birds, and spiders making certain structures which no human accomplishment can competently imitate. And as for the way of life of the inhabitants of New Spain and the province of Mexico . . . they have established their nation in such a way that no one possesses anything individually, neither a house nor a field, which he can leave to his heirs in his will, for everything belongs to their Masters whom, with improper nomenclature, they call kings, and by whose whims they live, more than by their own, ready to do the bidding and desire of these rulers and possessing no liberty. And the fulfillment of all this, not under the pressure of arms but in a voluntary and spontaneous way, is a definite sign of the service and base soul of these barbarians. . . . And if this type of servile and barbarous nation

> "[The Indians] have been born to slavery and not to civic and liberal life."

to locate another Aztec empire. Moving westward, his expedition was twice mauled by powerful native armies and reduced by half. When he reached the Mississippi, he was met by a great flotilla of 200 vessels said to have come down river from a great city to the west. There were hundreds of Indians "with their bows and arrows, painted with ocher and having great plumes of white and many colored feathers on either side." The Spaniards crossed the river and pushed westward through present-day Arkansas, but failing to find the great city, returned to the Mississippi. There de Soto fell sick and died. Some 300 dispirited survivors eventually made it back to Mexico on rafts. The native peoples of the South had successfully turned back Spanish invasion. But de Soto had introduced epidemic disease, which over the next several years drastically depopulated and undermined the Mississippian chiefdoms of the South.

In the same year of 1539, Spanish officials in Mexico launched a second attempt to conquer North America,

••• Read the Document

Alvar Núñez Cabeza de Vaca, "Indians of the Rio Grande" (1528–36) at **www.myhistorylab.com**

had not been to their liking and nature, it would have been easy for them, as it was not a hereditary monarchy, to take advantage of the death of a king in order to obtain a freer state and one more favorable to their interests; by not doing so, they have stated quite clearly that they have been born to slavery and not to civic and liberal life. Therefore, if you wish to reduce them, I do not say to our domination, but to a servitude a little less harsh, it will not be difficult for them to change their masters, and instead of the ones they had, who were barbarous and impious and inhuman, to accept the Christians, cultivators of human virtues and the true faith. . . .

SOURCE: Juan Ginés de Sepúlveda, "On the Just Causes for War Against the Indians" (1547).

The Indians Are Our Brothers

Now if we shall have shown that among our Indians of the western and southern shores (granting that we call them barbarians and that they are barbarians) there are important kingdoms, large numbers of people who live settled lives in a society, great cities, kings, judges and laws, persons who engage in commerce, buying, selling, lending, and the other contracts of the law of nations, will it not stand proved that the Reverend Doctor Sepúlveda has spoken wrongly and viciously against peoples like these, either out of malice or ignorance of Aristotle's teaching, and, therefore, has falsely and perhaps irreparably slandered them before the entire world? From the fact that the Indians are barbarians it does not necessarily follow that they are incapable of government and have to be ruled by others, except to be taught about the Catholic faith and to be admitted to the holy sacraments. They are not ignorant, inhuman, or bestial. Rather, long before they had heard the word Spaniard, they had properly organized states, wisely ordered by excellent laws, religion, and custom. They cultivated friendship and, bound together in common fellowship, lived in populous cities in which they wisely administered the affairs of both peace and war justly and equitably, truly governed by laws that at very many points surpass ours, and could have won the admiration of the sages of Athens. . . .

I call on the Spaniards who plunder that unhappy people. . . . For God's sake and man's faith in him, is this the way to impose the yoke of Christ on Christian men? Is this the way to remove wild barbarism from the minds of barbarians? Is it not, rather, to act like thieves, cut-throats, and cruel plunderers and to drive the gentlest of people headlong into despair? The Indian race is not that barbaric, nor are they dull witted or stupid, but they are easy to teach and very talented in learning all the liberal arts, and very ready to accept, honor, and observe the Christian religion and correct their sins (as experience has taught) once priests have introduced them to the sacred mysteries and taught them the word of God. . . .

"[L]ong before they had heard the word Spaniard, they had properly organized states . . . [and] excellent laws, . . ."

The Indians are our brothers, and Christ has given his life for them. Why, then, do we persecute them with such inhuman savagery when they do not deserve such treatment? The past, because it cannot be undone, must be attributed to our weakness, provided that what has been taken unjustly is restored.

SOURCE: Bartolomé de Las Casas, "In Defense of the Indians" (1552).

---

this one aimed at the Southwest. Francisco Vásquez de Coronado led 300 mounted men and infantry and 800 Indian porters north along well-marked Indian trading paths, passing through the settlements of Piman Indians near the present border of the United States and Mexico and finally reaching the Pueblo villages along the Rio Grande. The initial resistance of the Pueblo people was quickly quashed. But Coronado was deeply disappointed by their towns built "of stone and mud, rudely fashioned." He sent out expeditions in all directions in search of the legendary golden cities of Cíbola. He led his army as far north as the Great Plains, where they observed great herds of "shaggy cows" (buffalo) and made contact with nomadic hunting peoples, but returned without gold. For the next fifty years Spain would lose all interest in the Southwest.

The Spanish New World Empire

A century after Columbus, some 250,000 European immigrants, most of them Spaniards, had settled in the Americas. Another 125,000 Africans had been forcibly resettled as slaves on the Spanish plantations of the Caribbean, as well as

Spanish adventurers attack a native village on the Columbian coast of the Caribbean in an engraving published by Theodore de Bry in 1594. This attack of 1509 began at dawn, when the residents awoke to find their houses on fire. They attempted to flee, but were cut down by swords as they ran from their homes. Several hundred died, with few survivors. Images like this, widely circulated in Europe and England, helped create the "Black Legend" of the Spanish conquest.

on the Portuguese plantations of Brazil. (The Portuguese colonized Brazil under the terms of the Treaty of Tordesillas, a 1494 agreement dividing the Americas between Spain and Portugal. See Chapter 4.) Most of the Spanish settlers lived in the more than 200 urban communities founded during the conquest, including cities such as Santo Domingo in Hispaniola, Havana in Cuba, Mexico City, built atop the ruins of Tenochtitlán, and Quito and Lima in the conquered empire of the Incas.

Spanish women came to America as early as Columbus's second expedition, but over the course of the sixteenth century they made up only about 10 percent of the immigrants. Most male colonists married or cohabited with Indian or African women, and the result was what some historians call "a frontier of inclusion," a frontier society characterized by a great deal of mixing between male colonists and native or African women, with the corresponding growth of large mixed-ancestry groups that the Spanish labeled *mestizos* and *mulattoes*. Indians died by the thousands in the conquest, but Indian genes were passed on in mixed-ancestry people who quickly became the majority population in the mainland Spanish American empire.

Populated by Indians, Africans, Spanish colonists, and their hybrid descendants, the New World colonies of Spain made up one of the largest and most powerful empires in world history. In theory the empire operated as a highly centralized and bureaucratic system. But the Council of the Indies, the advisers of the Spanish king who made all the laws and regulations for the empire, was

located far away in Spain. What looked in the abstract like a centrally administered empire was in fact a fragmented collection of colonial regions that tolerated a great deal of local decision making.

Northern Explorations and Encounters

When the Spanish empire was at the height of its power in the sixteenth century, the merchants and monarchs of other European seafaring states began looking across the Atlantic for opportunities of their own (see Map 2.4). France was first to sponsor expeditions to the New World in the early sixteenth century. The French first attempted to plant settlements on the coasts of Brazil and Florida, but Spanish opposition forced them to concentrate on the North Atlantic. England did not develop its own plans to colonize North America until the second half of the sixteenth century.

Trade, Not Conquest: Fish and Furs

Long before France and England made attempts to found colonies, however, European fishermen were exploiting the coastal North American waters of the North Atlantic. Although there is no solid historical evidence, it is possible that European fishermen were working those waters before Columbus's voyages. Certainly by 1500, hundreds of ships and thousands of sailors were sailing annually to the Grand Banks, fishing for cod.

The first European voyages of exploration in the North Atlantic used the talents of these experienced European sailors and fishermen. With a crew from Bristol, England, Genovese explorer Giovanni Caboto (or John Cabot) reached Labrador in 1497, but the English did little to follow up on his voyage. In 1524, Tuscan captain Giovanni da Verrazano, sailing for the French, explored the North American coast from Cape Fear (North Carolina) to the Penobscot River (Maine). Encouraged by his report, the French crown commissioned experienced captain Jacques Cartier to locate a "Northwest Passage" to the Indies. In a series of voyages undertaken in 1534, 1535, and 1541, Cartier failed to locate such a passage but became the first European to explore the St. Lawrence River, which led to the Great Lakes, and provided easy access to the Ohio and Mississippi rivers. Although Cartier failed in his attempt to plant French settlements on the St. Lawrence, his exploration established France's imperial claim to the lands of Canada and provided the French with an incomparable geographic advantage over other colonial powers.

The French and other northern Europeans thus discovered the Indian people of the northern woodlands, and

Read the Document

Jacques Cartier on Meeting the Mi'kmaq Indians (1534) at **www.myhistorylab.com**

A Mi'kmaq Indian petroglyph or rock carving depicting a European vessel and crew, photographed in 1946 at Kejimkujik National Park, Nova Scotia, by Arthur and Olive Kelsall, who traced the lines of the image with white ink to enhance the contrast. The vessel appears to be a small pinnace with lanteen sails, similar to those used by French merchants and explorers in the early seventeenth century. Living along the southern shore of the Gulf of Saint Lawrence and on the Acadian peninsula, the Mi'kmaq were among the first natives in North America to establish contact with European traders, and understanding immediately the value of iron and textiles, they soon developed a system of coastal barter.

the Indians in turn discovered them. Contacts here were quite different than those of the tropics, and were based on commerce rather than conquest. The natives immediately appreciated the usefulness of textiles, glass, copper, and ironware. For his part, Cartier was interested in the fur coats of the Indians. Europeans, like Indians, used furs for winter clothing, but the growing population of the late Middle Ages had so depleted European wild game that the price of furs had risen beyond the reach of most people. Thus, the North American fur trade filled an important demand and produced high profits.

The fur trade would continue to play an important role in the Atlantic economy for the next three centuries. By no means were Indians simply the victims of European traders. They had a sharp eye for quality goods, and cutthroat competition among traders provided them with the opportunity to hold out for good prices. But the fur trade was essentially an unequal exchange, with furs selling in Europe for ten or twenty times what Indians received for them. The trade also had familiar negative consequences. European epidemic disease soon followed in the wake of the traders, and violent warfare broke out between tribes over access to hunting grounds. Moreover, as European-manufactured goods, such as metal knives, kettles, and firearms, became essential to their way of life, Indians grew dependent upon European suppliers. Ultimately, the fur trade was stacked in favor of Europeans.

By the end of the sixteenth century over a thousand European ships were trading for furs each year along the northern Atlantic coast. The village of Tadoussac on the St. Lawrence, where a wide bay offered Europeans safe anchorage, became the customary place for a late summer trading fair. Within a few years the French would attempt to monopolize the northern trade by planting colonies along the coast and on the St. Lawrence. The first French colonies in North America, however, were planted farther south by a group of French Protestant religious dissenters known as the Huguenots.

The Protestant Reformation and the First French Colonies

The Protestant Reformation—the religious revolt against the Roman Catholic Church—began in 1517 when German priest Martin Luther publicized his differences with Rome. Luther declared that eternal salvation was a gift from God and not related to works or service to the Catholic Church. His protests (thus, the term "Protestantism") fit into a climate of widespread dissatisfaction with the power and prosperity of the Catholic Church. Luther soon was attracting followers all over northwestern Europe, and just as soon, Catholic authorities were working to quash his nascent movement. One of Luther's most prominent converts was Jean Chauvin (known to English speakers as John Calvin), a young theology student in Paris.

In 1533, as the persecution of Protestants intensified, Calvin fled France, eventually taking up residence in Geneva, Switzerland, where civic leaders had renounced the Catholic Church and expelled the city's bishop. Working with those leaders, Calvin established a Protestant theocracy in Geneva. His systematic writings and teachings concerning theology, liturgy, ritual, and church government proved highly influential among Protestants. His followers in France, known as Huguenots, largely came from the urban middle class but also included a portion of the nobility, those opposed to the central

This watercolor depicts the friendly relations between the Timucuas of coastal Florida and the colonists of the short-lived French colony of Fort Caroline. The Timucuas hoped that the French would help defend them against the Spanish, who plundered the coast in pursuit of Indian slaves.

SOURCE: Jacques Le Moyne, *Rene de Loudonniere and Chief Athore*, 1564. Gouache and metallic pigments on vellum. Print Collection, The New York Public Library, New York. The New York Public Library/Art Resource, NY.

authority of the Catholic monarch. In 1560 the French crown successfully defeated a plot among powerful Huguenots to seize royal power, inaugurating nearly forty years of violent religious conflict in France.

The first French colonies developed as attempts to establish a religious refuge in the New World for Huguenots. In 1562 French naval officer Jean Ribault and a group of 150 Huguenots from Normandy landed on Parris Island, near present-day Beaufort, South Carolina, and began construction of a fort and crude mud huts. Ribault soon returned to France for supplies, where he was caught up in the religious wars. The colonists nearly starved and were forced to resort to cannibalism before being rescued by a passing English ship. In 1564, Ribault and his followers established a second Huguenot colony, Fort Caroline, on the St. Johns River of Florida, south of present-day Jacksonville.

The Spanish were alarmed by these moves. They had shown little interest themselves in colonizing Florida but worried about protecting their convoys, riding home to Spain on the offshore Gulf Stream, loaded with gold and silver. Not only was Fort Caroline manned by Frenchmen but also by Protestants—mortal enemies of the Catholic monarchs of Spain. "We are compelled to pass in front of their port," wrote one official, "and with the greatest ease they can sally out with their armadas to seek us." In 1565 King Philip II of Spain sent Don Pedro Menéndez de Avilés, captain general of the Indies, to crush the Huguenots. After founding a settlement south of Fort Caroline at a place called St. Augustine, he marched his men overland through the swamps, surprising the Huguenots from the rear. "I put Jean Ribault and all the rest of them to the knife," Menéndez wrote triumphantly to the king, "judging it to be necessary to the service of the Lord Our God and of Your Majesty." To prevent further French incursions the Spanish built massive Castillo San Marcos (still standing) and established a garrison at St. Augustine, which has the distinction of being the oldest continuously occupied European city in North America.

Social Change in Sixteenth-Century England

The English movement across the Atlantic, like the French, was tied to social change at home. Perhaps most important were changes in the economy. As prices for goods rose steeply—the result of New World inflation—English landlords, their rents fixed by custom, sought ways to increase their incomes. Seeking profits in the woolen trade, many converted the common pasturage used by tenants into grazing land for sheep, dislocating large numbers of farmers. Between 1500 and 1650 a third of all the common lands in England were "enclosed" in this way. Deprived of their livelihoods, thousands of families left their traditional rural homes and sought employment in English cities. The roads were crowded with homeless people.

Sixteenth-century England also became deeply involved in the Protestant Reformation. At first King Henry VIII of England (reigned 1509–47) supported the Catholic Church and opposed the Protestants. But there was great public resentment in England over the vast properties owned by the church and the loss of revenue to Rome. When the pope refused to grant Henry an annulment of his marriage to Catherine of Aragon, daughter of Ferdinand and Isabel of Spain, the king exploited this popular mood. Taking up the cause of reform in 1534, he declared himself head of a separate Church of England. He later took over the English estates of the Catholic Church—about a quarter of the country's land—and utilized their revenues in the construction of a powerful English state system, including a standing army and navy. Working through Parliament, Henry carefully enlisted the support of the merchants and landed gentry for his program, parceling out a measure of royal prosperity in the form of titles, offices, lands, and commercial favors. By 1547, when Henry died, he had forged a solid alliance between the English monarchy and the wealthy merchant class.

Henry was succeeded by his young and sickly son Edward VI (reigned 1547–53), who soon died. Next in succession was Edward's Catholic half-sister Mary (reigned 1553–1558), who persecuted and martyred hundreds of English Protestants (gaining her the nickname "Bloody Mary") and married Philip II of Spain, self-declared defender of the Catholic faith. With Mary's premature death, however, her Protestant half-sister Elizabeth I (reigned 1558–1603) reversed course, tolerating a variety of perspectives within the English church. Spain's monarch, Mary's widower, head of the most powerful empire in the world, vowed to overthrow Elizabeth.

Fearing Spanish subversion on the neighboring Catholic island of Ireland, Elizabeth urged enterprising

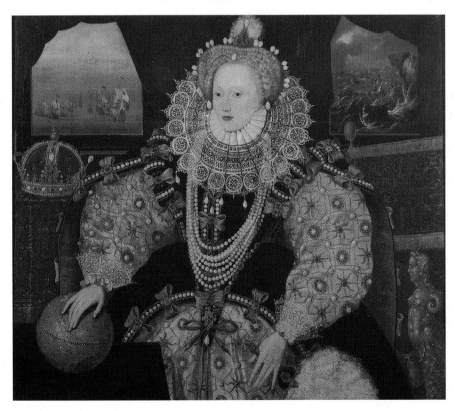

Elizabeth I, thought to be the work of court artist George Gower in 1588. The queen places her hand on the globe, covering North America, symbolizing England's ambitions there. Through the open windows, we see the battle against the Spanish Armada in 1588 and the destruction of the Spanish ships in a providential storm, which the Queen interpreted as an act of divine intervention.

SOURCE: *Elizabeth I*, Armada portrait, c. 1588 (oil on panel) by English School (C 16th) Private Collection/The Bridgeman Art Library, London/New York.

A Watercolor from the First Algonquian–English Encounter

Some of the first accurate images of the native inhabitants of North America were produced by the artist John White during his stay in 1585 at the first English colony in North America, at Roanoke Island on North Carolina's Outer Banks. Two years later White would become governor of the famous "Lost Colony." This image of an Indian mother and daughter illustrates the care White brought to the task of recording as fully as possible the Indians' way of life. The woman wears an apron-skirt of fringed deerskin, its borders edged with white beads, and a woven beadwork necklace. The body decorations on her face and upper arms are tattooed. One of her arms rests in a sling, an unusual posture, something quite unique to this culture. In the other hand she holds an empty gourd container for carrying water. The little girl holds an English wooden doll, a gift from White, and it seems to greatly please her. In the written account that accompanied White's images, Thomas Harriot wrote that all the Indian girls "are greatly delighted with puppetts and babes which were brought out of England" as gifts of exchange. Historic images bear close observation, for it is often small details like this one that are most revealing.

• **In what ways does this image document John White's powers of observation?**

supporters such as Walter Raleigh and his half-brother Humphrey Gilbert to subdue the Irish Catholics and settle homeless English families on their land. During the 1560s, Raleigh, Humphrey, and many other commanders invaded the island and viciously attacked the Irish, forcing them to retreat beyond a frontier line of English settlement along the coast. The English considered the Irish an inferior race, and the notion that civilized people could not mix with such "savages" was an assumption English colonists would carry with them to the Americas.

Early English Efforts in the Americas

England's first ventures in the New World were made against the backdrop of its conflict with Spain. In 1562, John Hawkins violated Spanish regulations by transporting a load of African slaves to the Caribbean, bringing back valuable tropical goods. (For a full discussion of the slave trade, see Chapter 4.) The Spanish attacked Hawkins on another of his voyages in 1567, an event English privateers such as Francis Drake used as an excuse for launching a series of devastating and lucrative raids against Spanish New World ports and fleets. The voyages of these English

CHRONOLOGY

1000	Norse settlement at L'Anse aux Meadows
1347–53	Black Death in Europe
1381	English Peasants' Revolt
1488	Bartolomeu Días sails around the African continent
1492	Christopher Columbus first arrives in the Caribbean
1494	Treaty of Tordesillas
1497	John Cabot explores Newfoundland
1500	High point of the Renaissance
1508	Spanish invade Puerto Rico
1513	Juan Ponce de León lands in Florida
1514	Bartolomé de las Casas begins preaching against the conquest
1516	Smallpox introduced to the New World
1517	Martin Luther breaks with the Roman Catholic Church
1519	Hernán Cortés lands in Mexico
1534	Jacques Cartier first explores the St. Lawrence River
1539–40	Hernán de Soto and Francisco Vásquez de Coronado expeditions
1550	Tobacco introduced to Europe
1552	Bartolomé de las Casas's *Destruction of the Indies* published
1558	Elizabeth I of England begins her reign
1562	Huguenot colony planted along the mid-Atlantic coast
1565	St. Augustine founded
1583	Humphrey Gilbert attempts to plant a colony in Newfoundland
1584–87	Walter Raleigh's colony on Roanoke Island
1588	English defeat the Spanish Armada
1590	John White returns to find Roanoke colony abandoned

"Sea Dogs" greatly enriched their investors, including Elizabeth herself. The English, thus, began their American adventures by slaving and plundering.

A consensus soon developed among Elizabeth's closest advisers that the time had come to enter the competition for American colonies. Elizabeth authorized several private attempts at exploration and colonization. In the late 1570s, Martin Frobisher conducted three voyages of exploration in the North Atlantic. Next Gilbert and Raleigh, fresh from the Irish wars, planned the first true colonizing ventures. In 1583 Gilbert sailed with a flotilla of ships from Plymouth and landed at St. John's Bay, Newfoundland. He encountered fishermen from several other nations but nevertheless claimed the territory for his queen. His ship was lost, however, on the return voyage.

Following his brother's death, Raleigh moved to establish a colony to the south, in the more hospitable climate of the mid-Atlantic coast. The Roanoke enterprise of 1584–1587 seemed far more promising than Gilbert's, but it too failed. In contrast to the French, who concentrated on commerce, the English attempted to dominate and conquer the natives, drawing on their Irish experience. The most positive legacy of the Roanoke experience was the work of Thomas Harriot and John White, who mapped the area, surveyed its commercial potential, and observed the Indian inhabitants. Harriot's *A Briefe and True Report of the Newfound Land of Virginia* (1588), illustrated with impressive engravings of White's original watercolors, provided the single most accurate description of North American Indians at the moment of their contact with Europeans.

Philip II was outraged at the English incursions into territory reserved by the pope for Catholics. He had authorized the destruction of the French colony in Florida, and now he committed himself to smashing England. In 1588, he sent a fleet of 130 ships carrying 30,000 men to invade the British Isles. Countered by captains such as Drake and Hawkins, who commanded smaller and more maneuverable ships, and frustrated by an ill-timed storm that the English chose to interpret as an act of divine intervention, the Spanish Armada foundered. The Spanish monopoly of the New World had been broken in the English Channel.

Conclusion

The era of European colonization in the Americas opened with Columbus's voyage in 1492. The subsequent Spanish invasion of America had catastrophic consequences for the Indian peoples of the Caribbean, Mesoamerica, and beyond. Wars of conquest and dispossession, and especially the introduction of epidemic disease, took an enormous toll in human life. Civilizations collapsed and whole cultures disappeared. Amidst this destruction, the Spanish succeeded in constructing the world's most powerful empire through the use of forced labor. Enormous wealth flowed across the Atlantic to Spain.

Inspired by the Spanish success, the French and the English sought to plant colonies on the coast of North America in the second half of the century, but neither succeeded in establishing lasting communities. Meanwhile, a very different kind of colonial encounter, one based on commerce rather than conquest, was taking place along the coasts of northeastern North America. Early in the next century the French would turn this development to their advantage.

The English would move in a different direction. The colony of Roanoke in the land the English called Virginia failed because of the imperial assumptions and the brutal behavior of the first colonists toward the native residents. The experience might have suggested the importance and necessity of "discreet dealing" with native peoples. But instead the English would put their Irish experience to use, pioneering an altogether new kind of American colonialism.

Review Questions

1. Discuss the roles played by the rising merchant class, the new monarchies, Renaissance humanism, and the Reformation in the development of European colonialism.

2. Define a "frontier of inclusion." In what ways does this description apply to the Spanish empire in the Americas?

3. Make a list of the major exchanges that took place between the Old World and the New World in the centuries following the European invasion of America. Discuss some of the effects these exchanges had on the course of modern history.

4. In what ways did colonial contact in the Northeast differ from contacts in the Caribbean and Mexico?

5. In what ways might the English experience in Ireland have shaped expectations about American colonization?

Recommended Reading

David Noble Cook, *Born to Die: Disease and New World Conquest, 1492–1650* (1998). A history of the impact of disease, including Indian and European views.

Alfred W. Crosby Jr., *The Columbian Exchange: Biological and Cultural Consequences of 1492* (1972). The path breaking account of the intersection of Old World and New World biospheres.

J. H. Elliott, *Empires of the Atlantic World: Britain and Spain in America, 1492–1830* (2006). A comparison of the two empires by a master historian. An incomparable introduction to the early Atlantic world.

Richard Flint, *Great Cruelties Have Been Reported: The 1544 Investigation of the Coronado Expedition* (2001). Testimony regarding the treatment of Indians and subsequent human rights debates in Spain.

Alison Games, *The Web of Empire: English Cosmopolitans in an Age of Expansion, 1560–1660* (2008). The story of the English struggle for world empire.

Lewis Hanke, *The Spanish Struggle for Justice in the Conquest of America* (1949). The classic account of las Casas's attempts to rectify the wrongs committed by the Spanish against the Indians.

Charles M. Hudson, *Knights of Spain, Warriors of the Sun: Hernando de Soto and the South's Ancient Chiefdoms* (1997). A very readable history of the de Soto expedition, told from the viewpoint of the Indians.

Henry Kamen, *Spain's Road to Empire: The Making of a World Power, 1492–1763* (2002). A fascinating account arguing that it was not Spain that made the empire but rather the empire that made Spain.

John T. McGrath, *The French in Early Florida: In the Eye of the Hurricane* (2000). A meticulously researched history of the French Huguenot colony in Florida.

Samuel Eliot Morison, *The European Discovery of America: The Northern Voyages, a.d. 500–1600* (1971) and *The Southern Voyages, a.d. 1492–1616* (1974). The most detailed treatment of all the important European explorations of the Americas.

Karen Vieira Powers, *Women in the Crucible of Conquest: The Gendered Genesis of Spanish American Society, 1500–1600* (2005). A new interpretation of the conquest that demonstrates how native women adapted to the new order.

Matthew Restall, *Seven Myths of the Spanish Conquest* (2003). A concise and refreshing new perspective on Spain's invasion of the New World.

David Beers Quinn, *Set Fair for Roanoke: Voyages and Colonies, 1584–1606* (1985). The story of Roanoke—the Indian village, the English settlement, and the Lost Colony.

Carl Ortwin Sauer, *Sixteenth Century North America: The Land and the People as Seen by the Europeans* (1971). A classic source for the explorations of the continent, providing abundant descriptions of American Indians at the point of contact.

Hugh Thomas, *Conquest: Montezuma, Cortés, and the Fall of Old Mexico* (1993). A fascinating account, written by a master of historical style, that incorporates the Aztec view as well as the words of the conquerors.

Gustavo Verdesio, *Forgotten Conquests: Rereading New World History from the Margins* (2001). An argument that the old historical narrative represented only one of many possible histories.

PEARSON myhistorylab Connections

Reinforce what you learned in this chapter by studying the many documents, images, maps, review tools, and videos available at www.myhistorylab.com.

Read and Review

✓ • Study and Review Chapter 2

•••• Read the Document

From The Journal of Christopher Columbus (1492)

Christopher Columbus, Letter to Luis de Sant' Angel (1493)

Alvar Núñez Cabeza de Vaca, "Indians of the Rio Grande" (1528–36)

Jacques Cartier on Meeting the Mi'kmaq Indians (1534)

Mi'kmaq Chief's Observations of the French (1691)

Bartolomè de Las Casas, "Of the Island of Hispaniola" (1542)

Research and Explore

•••• Read the Document

Exploring America: Exploitation of the Americas

Cultures Meet: Europeans View the New World

Profiles
  Virginia Dare
  Bartolomè de Las Casas

•••• Watch the Video

How Should We Think of Columbus?

What Is Columbus's Legacy?

((•••• Hear the Audio

Hear the audio files for Chapter 2 at
www.myhistorylab.com.

3

((•–[Hear the Audio
Chapter 3 at www.myhistorylab.com

Planting Colonies
in North America 1588–1701

Pueblo de Taos, New Mexico. The Beinecke Rare Book Library and Manuscript Library.

Communities and Diversity in Seventeenth-Century Santa Fé

It was a hot August day in 1680 when the frantic messengers rode into the small mission outpost of El Paso with the news that the Pueblo Indians to the north had risen in revolt. The corpses of more than 400 Spanish colonists lay bleeding in the dust. Two thousand survivors huddled inside the Palace of Governors in Santa Fé, surrounded by 3,000 angry warriors. The Pueblo leaders had sent two crosses into the palace—white for surrender, red for death. Which would the colonists choose?

Spanish colonists had been in New Mexico for a century. Franciscan priests from Mexico came first, in the 1580s, followed by a military expedition in search of precious metals. In 1609, high in the picturesque foothills of the Sangre de Cristo Mountains, colonial authorities founded La Villa Real de la Santa Fé de San Francisco—"the royal town of the holy faith of St. Francis"—soon known simply as Santa Fé. The Pueblos were to be converted to Christianity, subjected to the authority of the king of Spain, and forced to labor for the Hispanic colonists. The Pueblos at first resisted, but in the face of Spanish armed might, they were forced to give in.

AMERICAN Communities

51

Colonization took a tremendous toll on them. Epidemic disease, striking in successive waves, claimed thousands of lives. Taxes, tribute, and labor service left Pueblo storehouses empty, and starving times came much more frequently. Nomadic Apache neighbors, mounted on stolen Spanish horses, raided their villages with increasing frequency. From 1610 to 1680 the number of Pueblo communities fell by more than half, from 81 to 31, and their population plummeted by two-thirds to fewer than 20,000 people.

A devastating drought in the 1670s seemed a sign of final and complete collapse. Over the decades thousands of Pueblos had accepted Christianity, but in the face of disaster there was a revival of their traditional religious rituals. Outraged Franciscan missionaries invaded the underground *kivas*, destroyed sacred Indian artifacts, and publicly humiliated holy men. In 1675 the Spanish governor rounded up religious leaders from many villages, publicly executed three of them, and whipped the others. One of those men, Popé of San Juan Pueblo, vowed to overthrow the regime. During the next several years he and other rebel leaders organized a conspiracy among more than twenty Pueblo communities.

In Santa Fé, in response to the Pueblo demand of surrender, the besieged colonists were defiant, sending back the red cross. Three days later, with supplies running out, they counterattacked, winning just enough time to allow for the evacuation of the capital. Harassed by the Pueblos, they made their way south to El Paso, "the poor women and children on foot and unshod," in the words of one account, and "of such a hue that they looked like dead people." The Pueblos ransacked the missions, desecrating the holy furnishings and leaving the mutilated bodies of priests lying upon the altars. They transformed the governor's chapel into a traditional kiva, his palace into a communal dwelling. On the elegant inlaid stone floors where colonial governors had held court, Pueblo women now ground their corn.

Santa Fé became the capital of a Pueblo confederacy led by Popé. He forced Christian Indians "to plunge into the rivers" to wash away the taint of baptism and ordered the destruction of everything Spanish. Getting rid of Jesus was one thing, but the rest was harder. Horses and sheep, fruit trees and wheat, new tools and new crafts—these things the Pueblos found useful. They also found that they missed the support of the Spanish in their struggle against the Apaches. With chaos mounting, Popé was deposed in 1690.

In 1692, a Spanish force under Governor Diego de Vargas returned to New Mexico in an attempt to reestablish the colonial regime. Some communities welcomed him while others resisted. In 1696 there was another attempt at revolt, but Vargas crushed it with overwhelming force. The Spanish succeeded in their reconquest, but they seemed to have learned something in the process. They began to practice greater restraint, which enabled the Pueblos to accept their authority. As long as Pueblos dutifully observed Catholic rituals in the missionary chapels, missionaries looked the other way when the people also resorted to their kivas and their old faith. Royal officials promised the inviolability of Pueblo title to their lands, and Pueblos in turn swore loyalty to the Spanish monarch. Pueblos turned out for service on colonial lands, while colonists abandoned the system of forced labor. Spanish and Pueblo communities remained autonomous, but together they managed to hold off the Apache attacks. New Mexico remained a colony under the authority of the Spanish. But in the aftermath of the Pueblo Revolt, the governing principle was accommodation.

Thus did the Spanish in New Mexico and elsewhere seek to include native peoples as subjects of the king and communicants of the Church. Because the French developed a commercial empire, they too came to rely on a policy of native inclusion. In New England, Virginia, and Carolina, however, where English settlers developed agricultural colonies, the policy was one of exclusion. Indians were pushed to the periphery. These differences help explain the very different histories of the three principal colonial empires in North America.

Santa Fé

1. In what ways were the Spanish, French, and English colonies in North America similar? In what ways were they different?

2. What was the nature of the colonial encounter between English newcomers and Algonquian natives in the Chesapeake?

3. How did religious dissent shape the history of the New England colonies?

4. What role did the restored Stuart monarchy play in the creation of new proprietary colonies?

5. Why did warfare and internal conflict characterize the late seventeenth century?

FOCUS Questions

1588–1701

The Spanish, the French, and the Dutch in North America

At the beginning of the seventeenth century the Spanish controlled the only colonial outposts on the North American mainland, a series of forts along the Florida coast to protect the Gulf Stream sea-lanes used by the convoys carrying wealth from their New World colonies to Spain. During the first two decades of the new century, however, the Spanish, French, Dutch, and English were all drawn into planting far more substantial colonies in North America.

Instead of sending colonists, both Spain and France relied on a policy of converting Indians into subjects, and as a result there was a great deal of cultural mixing between colonists and natives. New Spain and New France became "frontiers of inclusion," where native peoples were incorporated into colonial society. The Dutch at first followed the French model when they established their colony on the Hudson River on the northeastern Atlantic coast. But soon they changed course, emulating the English, who from the beginning of their colonial experience took a different approach, sending colonists who dispossessed the Indians and pushed them to the periphery of their colonies. In Virginia and New England, colonists and Indians lived in separate communities. The English established "frontiers of exclusion" in dramatic contrast to New Spain and New France.

New Mexico

After the 1539 expedition of Francisco Vásquez de Coronado failed to turn up vast Indian empires to conquer in the northern Mexican deserts, Spanish interest in the Southwest faded. The densely settled farming communities of the Pueblos did offer a harvest of converts for Christianity, however, and by the 1580s Franciscan missionaries were at work there. Soon rumors drifted back to

Acoma Pueblo, the "sky city," was founded in the thirteenth century and is one of the oldest continuously inhabited sites in the United States. In 1598, Juan de Oñate attacked and laid waste to the pueblo, killing some 800 inhabitants and enslaving another 500.

Moving north into the upper Rio Grande Valley, Oñate encountered varying degrees of resistance. He laid siege at Acoma, set high atop a great outcropping of desert rock. Indian warriors killed dozens of Spaniards with their arrows, and women and children bombarded them with stones. But in the end, the attackers succeeded in climbing the rock walls and laying waste to the town, killing 800 men, women, and children. All surviving warriors had one of their feet severed, and more than 500 people were enslaved. In 1606 Spanish authorities in Mexico recalled Oñate for his failure to locate the fabled gold mines. The church, however, convinced the Spanish monarchy to subsidize New Mexico as a special missionary colony. In 1609, a new governor founded the capital of Santa Fé, and from this base the Franciscan missionaries penetrated all the surrounding Indian villages (see Map 3.1).

The colonial economy of New Mexico, based on small-scale agriculture and sheep raising, was never very prosperous. Spanish expectations, never very high, were even lower after the Pueblo Revolt and the reconquest. Very few newcomers came from Mexico. Population growth was almost entirely the result of marriages between colonial men and Indian women. By 1700 this northernmost outpost of the Spanish empire in America contained some 3,000 *mestizos* in a few towns along the Rio Grande, surrounded by an estimated 50,000 Pueblos in some fifty villages. New Mexico was a "frontier of inclusion."

Read the Document
Don Juan de Oñate, Letter from New Mexico to the Viceroy (1599) at **www.myhistorylab.com**

New France

In the early seventeenth century the French devised a strategy to monopolize the northern fur trade. In 1605 Samuel de Champlain, acting as the agent of a royal monopoly, helped establish the outpost of Port Royal on the Bay of Fundy in what became known as the colony of Acadia. It proved impossible, however, to control the coastal trade from that location. In 1608 he founded the settlement of Québec on the St. Lawrence River at a site where he could intercept the traffic in furs. He forged an alliance with the Huron Indians, who controlled access to the rich fur grounds of the Great Lakes, and in 1609 and 1610 joined them in making war on their traditional enemies, the Five Nation Iroquois Confederacy. Champlain sent agents and traders to live among native peoples, where they learned native languages and customs, and directed the flow of furs to Québec.

The St. Lawrence River is a great aquatic highway leading to the heart of the continent, and it provided the French with strategic geographic and political advantage. But because of its northern latitude the river froze solid during the winter, isolating colonists, and the growing season was short, limiting agricultural productivity. Thousands

MAP 3.1 New Mexico in the Seventeenth Century By the end of the seventeenth century, New Mexico numbered 3,000 colonial settlers in several towns, surrounded by an estimated 50,000 Pueblo Indians living in some fifty farming villages. The isolation and sense of danger among the Hispanic settlers are evident in their name for the road linking the colony with New Spain, *Jornada del Muerto*, "Road of Death."

Mexico City of rich mines along the Rio Grande, raising the hopes of finding another Aztec empire. In 1598, Juan de Oñate, the son of a wealthy mining family of New Spain, financed an expedition made up of Indians and *mestizos* (people of mixed Indian and European ancestry) with the purpose of mining both gold and souls.

This drawing, based on a sketch by Samuel de Champlain, depicts French and Hurons attacking an Iroquois village in what is now upstate New York. The Iroquois people lived in large, fortified enclosures that the English called "castles."

peoples, sought to build an empire through alliance and commerce with independent Indian nations. There were also important differences between Spanish and French missionary efforts. Unlike Franciscans in seventeenth-century Santa Fé, who insisted that natives must accept European cultural norms as part of their conversion, Jesuit missionaries in New France learned native languages and attempted to understand native customs, in an effort to introduce Christianity as a part of the existing Indian way of life.

New Netherland

The United Provinces of the Netherlands, commonly known as Holland, was only a fraction of the size of France, but in the sixteenth century it became the center of Europe's economic transformation. Amsterdam became the site of the world's first stock exchange and investment banks. Dutch investors built the largest commercial fleet in Europe and captured the lucrative Baltic and North Sea trade in fish, lumber, iron, and grain. It was said that the North Sea was Holland's "America."

Soon, however, the Dutch were establishing trading outposts in America itself. Early in the

of Frenchmen went to New France as *engagés* ("hired men") in the fur trade or the fishery, but nine out of ten returned to France when the term of their service ended. The French might have populated their American empire with thousands of willing Huguenot religious dissenters, but the state resolved that New France would be exclusively Catholic. As a result, the population grew very slowly, reaching a total of only 15,000 colonists by 1700. Rather than facing the Atlantic, the communities of Canada tended to look westward toward the continental interior. It was typical for the sons of habitants to take to the woods, working as independent traders or *coureurs de bois*, paid agents of the fur companies. Most eventually returned to their home communities, but others married Indian women and raised mixed-ancestry families in distant Indian villages. French traders were living on the Great Lakes as early as the 1620s, and both missionaries and traders were exploring the upper Mississippi River by the 1670s. In 1681–82, fur-trade commandant Robert Sieur de La Salle navigated the mighty river to its mouth on the Gulf of Mexico and claimed its entire watershed for France (see Map 3.2).

Thus, the French, like the Spanish, established a frontier of inclusion in North America. But in other ways the two colonial systems were quite different. The Spanish program was the conquest of native peoples and their exploitation as a labor force in mining, farming, or livestock raising. The French, on the other hand, lacking sufficient manpower to bully, dispossess, or enslave native

MAP 3.2 New France in the Seventeenth Century By the late seventeenth century, French settlements were spread from the town of Port Royal in Acadia to the post and mission at Sault Ste. Marie on the Great Lakes. But the heart of New France comprised the communities stretching along the St. Lawrence River between the towns of Québec and Montreal.

seventeenth century the United Netherlands organized two great monopolies, the Dutch East India Company and the Dutch West India Company, combining naval military might and commercial strength in campaigns to seize the maritime trade of Asia and the Atlantic. Backed by powerful armed vessels known as men-of-war, Dutch traders constructed a series of trading posts in China, Indonesia, India, Africa, Brazil, the Caribbean, and North America, making Holland into the world's greatest commercial power. The Dutch first established themselves in North America with the explorations of Henry Hudson in 1609, and within a few years had founded settlements on the Hudson River at the head of oceangoing navigation, a place they called Fort Orange (today's Albany), and at New Amsterdam on Manhattan Island, which guards the entrance to the river. In the 1640s the Dutch also succeeded in overwhelming a small colony of Swedes planted by a Swedish company on the lower Delaware River in 1637, incorporating that region as well into their sphere of influence (see Map 3.3).

MAP 3.3 European Colonies of the Atlantic Coast, 1607–39 Virginia, on Chesapeake Bay, was the first English colony in North America, but by the mid-seventeenth century, Virginia was joined by settlements of Scandinavians on the Delaware River and Dutch on the Hudson River, as well as English religious dissenters in New England. The territories indicated here reflect the vague boundaries of the early colonies.

Seeking to match French success in the fur trade, the Dutch West India Company negotiated a commercial alliance with the Five Nation Iroquois Confederacy. Access to Dutch products, including metal tools and firearms, greatly augmented the power of the Iroquois, and they soon launched a campaign to make themselves into the strategic middlemen of the fur trade. Beginning in the 1640s the Iroquois conducted a series of military expeditions against their northern, western, and southern neighbors, known as the Beaver Wars. They attacked and dispersed the Hurons, who had long controlled the flow of furs from the Great Lakes to their French allies.

The Chesapeake: Virginia and Maryland

England first attempted to plant colonies in North America during the 1580s in Newfoundland and at Roanoke Island in present-day North Carolina (see Chapter 2). Both attempts were dramatic failures. England's war with Spain (1588–1604) suspended further efforts, but thereafter the English once again turned to the Americas.

Jamestown and the Powhatan Confederacy

In 1607, a group of London investors known as the Virginia Company sent a small convoy of vessels to Chesapeake Bay, where a hundred men built a fort they named Jamestown in honor of King James I (reigned 1603–25). It was destined to become the first permanent English settlement in North America.

Read the Document
Exploring America: Jamestown at **www.myhistorylab.com**

The Chesapeake was already home to an estimated 14,000 Indian inhabitants. By what right did the English think they could seize lands occupied by another people? "These Savages have no particular propertie in any parcell of that country, but only a general residence there, as wild beasts have in the forest," an English minister preached to the departing Jamestown colonists. "They range and wander up and downe the country, without any law or government, being led only by their own lusts and sensualitie." Indians were savages with no rights that Christians were obliged to respect.

In fact the village communities of the Chesapeake were united in a politically sophisticated union known as the Powhatan Confederacy, led by a powerful chief named Wahunsonacook, whom the Jamestown colonists called "King Powhatan" (a little like calling James I "King England"). Powhatan's feelings about Europeans were mixed. He knew they could mean trouble. In 1571, Spanish missionaries had attempted to plant a colony on the Chesapeake shore, but

Read the Document
Remarks by Chief Powhatan to John Smith (ca. 1609) at **www.myhistorylab.com**

after they interfered with the practice of native religion they were violently expelled. Still, Powhatan was eager to forge an alliance with these people from across the sea to obtain access to supplies of metal tools and weapons. He allowed the English colonists to build their outpost at Jamestown. As was the case elsewhere in the Americas, Indians attempted to use Europeans to pursue ends of their own.

The Jamestown colonists had come to find gold and a passage to the Indies, and failing at both they spent their time gambling and drinking. They survived only because of Powhatan's help. But as more colonists arrived from England and demands for food multiplied, Powhatan had second thoughts. He now realized, he declared to Smith, that the English had come "not for trade, but to invade my people and possess my country." During the terrible winter of 1609–10 more than 400 colonists starved and a number resorted to cannibalism. Of the 500 colonists at Jamestown in the fall, only 60 remained alive by the spring.

Determined to prevail, the Virginia Company sent out a large additional force of men, women, and livestock,

•••|**Read** the **Document**

John Smith, "The Starving Time" (1624) at **www.myhistorylab.com**

committing itself to a protracted war against native men, women, and children. The grim fighting persisted until 1613, when the English captured one of Powhatan's favorite daughters, Matoaka, a girl of about fifteen whom the colonists knew by her nickname, Pocahontas. Eager for the return of his child, and worn down by violence and disease, the next year Powhatan accepted a treaty of peace. The peace was sealed by the marriage of Pocahontas, who converted to Christianity, to John Rolfe, one of the leading colonists.

For a brief moment it seemed the English too might move in the direction of a society of inclusion. In 1617 Rolfe traveled with his wife and son to England, where they were greeted as a new American noble line. But Pocahontas fell ill and died there. Crushed by the news, Powhatan abdicated in favor of his brother Opechancanough before dying of despair. Economic and social developments, however, were already pushing Virginia in the direction of a frontier of exclusion.

C. Smith taketh the King of Pamavnkee prisoner – 1608.

This illustration, from John Smith's memoirs (1624), was engraved by the artist Robert Vaughn. Seizing Chief Opechancanough, Powhatan's brother, by the scalplock, Smith attempts to obtain needed supplies from the Indians. Opechancanough later succeeded Powhatan and ruled the Chesapeake Algonquian Confederacy for a quarter century.

Tobacco, Expansion, and Warfare

The Virginia colonists struggled to find the "merchantable commodity" for which Thomas Hariot, the scientist who accompanied the Roanoke expedition, had searched (see Chapter 2). They finally found it in tobacco. Tobacco had been introduced to the English by Francis Drake in the 1580s, and by the 1610s a craze for smoking had created strong demand for the product. Pocahontas's husband John Rolfe developed a mild hybrid variety, and soon the first commercial shipments of cured Virginia leaf reached England. Tobacco provided the Virginia Company with the first returns on its investment.

Questions of land and labor would dominate the history of colonial Virginia. Tobacco cultivation required a great deal of hand labor, and it quickly exhausted the soil. The Virginia Company instituted a program of "headright

SEEING History

This illustration, taken from Samuel de Champlain's 1613 account of the founding of New France, depicts him joining a Huron attack on the Iroquois on July 30, 1609. The French sought to build a commercial empire by allying with the powerful Huron confederacy to control access to the great fur grounds of the West. The image depicts the moment when Champlain fired his arquebus (a muzzle-loading firearm), killing two of the Iroquois leaders. After this confrontation, the Iroquois formed an alliance of their own with the Dutch, who founded a trading colony on the Hudson River. The contrast between the heavily armored Frenchmen and the naked Indians was part of the convention of depicting "civilized" and "savage" nations. The palm trees in the background of this drawing suggest that it was not executed by an eyewitness, but rather by an illustrator more familiar with South American scenes.

• **What kind of relationship between Europeans and Indians is depicted in this image?**

This 1628 engraving depicts the surprise attack of Indians on Virginia colonists in 1622. While it includes numerous inaccuracies (the Indians did not possess such large knives and the colonists lived in far more primitive conditions) the image effectively conveys the surprise and horror of the English.

grants," awards of large plantations to wealthy colonists who agreed to transport workers from England at their own cost. Because thousands of English families were being thrown off the land (see Chapter 2), many were attracted to Virginia. Thus, English colonization took a different turn from the Spanish, who mostly sent male colonists. Moreover, the English concentration on plantation agriculture contrasted with the French emphasis on trade. With little need to incorporate Indians into the colony as workers or marriage partners, the English pushed natives out. Virginia became a "frontier of exclusion."

Pressed for additional lands on which to grow tobacco, Chief Opechancanough decided on an assault that would expel the English for good. He encouraged a cultural revival under the guidance of a native shaman named Nemattanew, who instructed his followers to reject the English and their ways, much as Popé would do among the Pueblos. This was the first of many Indian resistance movements led jointly by strong political and religious figures. Opechancanough's uprising, which began on Good Friday, March 22,

1622, completely surprised the English, claiming the lives of 347 colonists, nearly a third of Virginia's colonial population. Yet the colony managed to hang on. The attack stretched into a ten-year war of attrition with horrors committed by both sides.

The Powhatans finally sued for peace in 1632. In the meantime, however, the war had bankrupted the Virginia Company. In 1624 England converted Virginia into a royal colony with civil authorities appointed by the crown, although property-owning colonists continued to elect representatives to the colony's House of Burgesses, created in 1619 in an attempt to encourage immigration. Although disease, famine, and warfare took a heavy toll, continuous emigration from England produced a doubling of the colonial population every five years, and by 1640 it numbered approximately 10,000 (see Figure 3.1). Now the English outnumbered the Powhatans, who were decimated by violence and disease.

In 1644 Opechancanough organized a final desperate revolt in which more than 500 colonists were killed. But the next year the Virginians crushed the Powhatans, capturing and executing their leader. A formal treaty granted the Indians a number of small reserved territories. By 1670 the Indian population had fallen to just 2,000, overwhelmed by the 40,000 English colonists.

In this eighteenth-century engraving used to promote the sale of tobacco, slaves pack tobacco leaves into "hogsheads" for shipment to England, overseen by a Virginia planter and his clerk. Note the incorporation of the Indian motif.

FIGURE 3.1 Population Growth of the British Colonies in the Seventeenth Century
The British colonial population grew steadily through the century, then increased sharply in the closing decade as a result of the new settlements of the proprietary colonies.

Maryland

In 1632, King Charles I (reigned 1625–49) granted 10 million acres at the northern end of Chesapeake Bay to the Calvert family, the Lords Baltimore, important Catholic supporters of the English monarchy. The Calverts named their colony Maryland, in honor of the king's wife, and in 1634 sent the first party of colonists to found the settlement of St. Mary's near the mouth of the Potomac River. Two features distinguished Maryland from Virginia. First, it was a "proprietary" colony in which the Calvert family held the sole power to appoint civil officers and was sole owner of all the land, which they planned to carve into feudal manors providing them with rents. Second, the Calvert family encouraged settlement by Catholics, a persecuted minority in seventeenth-century England. In fact, Maryland became the only English colony in North America with a substantial Catholic minority. Wealthy Catholic landlords were appointed to the governing council, and they came to dominate Maryland's House of Delegates, founded in 1635.

Read the Document
The Charter of Maryland (1632) at **www.myhistorylab.com**

Yet Maryland quickly became much like neighboring Virginia. The tobacco plantation economy created pressures for labor and land that could not be met by the Calverts' original feudal plans. In 1640, the colony adopted the system of headright grants previously developed in Virginia, and settlements of independent planters quickly spread out on both sides of Chesapeake Bay. By the 1670s, Maryland's English population numbered more than 15,000.

Community Life in the Chesapeake

At least three-quarters of the English migrants to the Chesapeake came as indentured servants. In exchange for the cost of their transportation to the New World, men and women contracted to labor for a master for a fixed term. Most were young, unskilled males, who served for two to seven years, but some were skilled craftsmen, unmarried women, or even orphan children.

African slaves were first introduced to the Chesapeake in 1619, but slaves were more expensive than servants, and as late as 1680 they made up less than 7 percent of the population. In the hard-driving economy of the Chesapeake, however, masters treated servants as cruelly as they treated slaves. They poked muscles and peered into the open mouths of newly arrived laborers to assess their health. Because of the high mortality resulting from epidemics of typhus and malaria, approximately two of every five servants died during the term of their indenture. Indentured labor may not have been slavery, but this may have seemed like a distinction without a difference (see Chapter 4 for a full discussion of slavery).

Many indentured servants who survived their terms and were able to raise the price of passage quickly returned to England. Those who remained became eligible for "freedom dues"—clothing, tools, a gun, or a spinning wheel to help them get started on their own. They often headed west in the hope of cutting a farm from the forest.

Because most emigrants were men, whether free or indentured, free unmarried women often married as soon as they arrived. Moreover, in the disease-ridden environment of the early Chesapeake, English men seemed to suffer a higher rate of mortality than did women, and widows remarried quickly, sometimes within days. Their scarcity provided women with certain advantages. Shrewd widows bargained for a remarriage agreement that gave them a larger share of the estate than what was set by common law. So notable was the concentration of wealth in the hands of these widows that one historian has suggested early Virginia was a "matriarchy." But because of high mortality rates, family size was smaller and kinship bonds— one of the most important components of community— were weaker than in England.

English visitors often remarked on the crude conditions of community life. Prosperous planters, investing everything in tobacco production, lived in rough wooden dwellings. On the western edge of the settlements, freed servants lived with their families in shacks, huts, or even caves. Colonists spread across the countryside in search of new tobacco lands, creating dispersed settlements with hardly any towns. Before 1650 there were few community institutions such as schools and churches.

Nevertheless, the Chesapeake was a growing region. By the end of the seventeenth century the combined population of the Maryland and Virginia colonies was nearly 90,000. In contrast to the colonists of New France, who were developing a distinctive identity because of their connections with native peoples, the English residents of the Chesapeake maintained close emotional ties to the mother country.

The New England Colonies

Both in climate and in geography, the northern coast of North America was far different from the Chesapeake. "Merchantable commodities" such as tobacco could not be produced there, and thus it was far less favored for investment and settlement. Instead, the region became a haven for Protestant dissenters from England, who gave the colonies of the north a distinctive character of their own (see Map 3.3).

Puritanism

Most English men and women continued to practice a Christianity little different from traditional Catholicism. But the English followers of John Calvin, known as Puritans because they wished to purify and reform the English church from within, grew increasingly influential during the last years of Elizabeth's reign at the end of the sixteenth century. The Calvinist emphasis on enterprise meant that Puritanism appealed to merchants, entrepreneurs, and commercial farmers, those most responsible for the rapid economic and social transformation of England. Yet the Puritans were also the most vocal critics of the disruptive effects of that change, condemning the decline of the traditional rural community and the growing number of "idle and masterless men" produced by the enclosure of common lands. They argued for reviving communities by placing reformed Christian congregations at their core to monitor the behavior of individuals.

James I abandoned Queen Elizabeth's policy of religious tolerance. His persecution of the Puritans, however, merely stiffened their resolve and turned them toward open political opposition. James's son and successor, Charles I (reigned 1625–49), was heavily criticized by the increasingly vocal Puritan minority for marrying a French Roman Catholic princess and supporting "High Church" policies, emphasizing the authority of the clerical hierarchy and traditional forms of worship. In 1629, determined to rule without these troublesome opponents, Charles dismissed Parliament and launched a campaign of repression against the Puritans. This political turmoil provided the context for the migration of thousands of English Protestants to New England.

Plymouth Colony

The first English colony in New England was founded by a group of religious dissenters known to later generations as the Pilgrims. At the time they were called Separatists because they believed the English church was so corrupt they had to establish independent congregations. One

group moved to Holland in 1609, but fearful that tolerant and secular Dutch society was seducing their children, they decided on emigration to North America. Backed by the Virginia Company of London and led by tradesman William Bradford, 102 people sailed from England on the *Mayflower* in September 1620.

The little group, mostly families but including a substantial number of single men hired by the investors, arrived in Massachusetts Bay at the site of the former Indian village of Pawtuxet, which the English renamed Plymouth. Soon the hired men began to grumble about being excluded from decision making, and to reassure them Bradford drafted an agreement by which all the male members of the expedition did "covenant and combine together into a civil body politic." The Mayflower Compact was the first document of self-government in North America.

Read the Document
Agreement between the Settlers at New Plymouth (Mayflower Compact) (1620) at **www.myhistorylab.com**

Weakened by scurvy and malnutrition, nearly half the colonists perished over the first winter. Like the earlier settlers of Roanoke and Jamestown, however, they were rescued by Indians. Massasoit, the *sachem*, or chief, of the Pokanokets, offered the newcomers food and advice in return for an alliance against his enemies, the Narragansetts. It was the familiar pattern of Indians attempting to incorporate European colonists into their own world.

The Pilgrims supported themselves by farming, but like all colonies Plymouth needed a source of revenue, in their case in order to pay off their English investors. The foundation of their commercial economy was the cod fishery in the rich coastal banks of the Atlantic. With this revenue the Pilgrims were able to establish a self-sufficient community.

The Massachusetts Bay Colony

In England, the political climate of the late 1620s convinced growing numbers of influential Puritans that the only way to protect their congregations was by emigration. In 1629 a royal charter was granted to a group of wealthy Puritans who called their enterprise the Massachusetts Bay Company, and an advance force of 200 settlers left for the fishing settlement of Naumkeag on Massachusetts Bay, which they renamed Salem.

The colonists hoped to establish what John Winthrop, their leader and first governor, called "a city on a hill," a New England model of reform for old England. In this they differed from the Pilgrims, who never considered returning. Between 1629 and 1643 some 20,000 individuals relocated to Massachusetts, establishing the port town of Boston and ringing it with towns. By the 1640s their settlements had spread seventy-five miles west to the Connecticut River Valley, where they

Read the Document
John Winthrop, A Model of Christian Charity (1630) at **www.myhistorylab.com**

Governor John Winthrop, a portrait painted by an unknown artist, about 1640. Winthrop was first elected governor of Massachusetts Bay Colony in 1629 and reelected a total of twelve times.

mingled with settlers spreading north from the Puritan New Haven Colony on Long Island Sound.

Taking advantage of a loophole in their charter, in 1629 Puritan leaders transferred company operations from England to Massachusetts, and within a few years had transformed the company into a civil government. The original charter established a General Court composed of a governor and his deputy, a board of magistrates (or advisers), and the members of the corporation, known as freemen. In 1632, Governor Winthrop and his advisers declared that all the male heads of households in Massachusetts, who were also church members, were freemen. Two years later, the freemen secured their right to select delegates to represent the towns in drafting the laws of the colony. These delegates and the magistrates later became the colony's two legislative houses. Thus, the procedures of a joint-stock company provided the origins for democratic suffrage and the bicameral division of legislative authority in America.

Dissent and New Communities

The Puritans immigrated to North America in order to practice their variety of Christianity. But like the Pilgrims they had little tolerance for religious difference. Doctrinal disagreements among them often led to the establishment of new colonies. In 1636 Thomas Hooker, minister of the congregation at Cambridge, after objecting to the Massachusetts policy of restricting male suffrage to church members, led his followers west to the Connecticut River, where they founded the town of Hartford. The same year Roger Williams, the minister at Salem, was banished from Massachusetts for advocating religious tolerance. With a group of his followers, Williams immigrated to the country surrounding Narragansett Bay.

In 1637 religious controversy produced another schism. Anne Hutchinson, the brilliant and outspoken wife of a Puritan merchant, criticized a number of Boston ministers. Their concentration on good works, she argued, led people to believe they could earn their way to heaven. Hutchinson was called before the General Court, and in an extraordinary hearing was reprimanded, excommunicated, and banished. She and a group of followers relocated to the Williams colony on Narragansett Bay.

To protect the dissenters in his settlement from Puritan interference, Williams won royal charters in 1644 and 1663 establishing the independent colony of Rhode Island (named for the principal island in Narragansett Bay), with guarantees of self-government and complete religious liberty.

Indians and Puritans

The Indian communities of southern New England discovered soon after the arrival of the Pilgrims and the Puritans that these colonists were quite different from the French and Dutch traders who had preceded them. Although the fur trade was an important part of the economy of Plymouth and Massachusetts, the principal concern of the colonists was the acquisition of Indian land for their growing settlements.

Like the Jamestown colonists, most Puritans believed they had the right to take what they considered "unused" lands, that is, lands not used in the English way. "As for the natives in New England," wrote Puritan leader John Winthrop, "they inclose no land, neither have any settled habytation, nor any tame Cattle to improve the land by, and soe have noe other but a Naturall Right to those Countries, soe as if we leave them sufficient for their use, we may lawfully take the rest." Not everyone agreed on this. One of the reasons Roger Williams was banished was his insistence that colonists had no absolute right to Indian land but must bargain for it in good faith. More typical, however, was a Massachusetts town meeting that resolved the matter by a show of hands: "Voted that the earth is the Lord's and the fulness thereof; voted that the earth is given to the Saints; voted that we are the Saints."

Potential conflicts among settlers over title, however, made it necessary to obtain original deeds from Indians, and the English used a variety of tactics to pressure leaders into signing "quitclaims," relinquishing all claim to specified properties. Colonists allowed livestock to graze in native fields, destroying their subsistence. They fined Indians for violations of English law, such as working on the Sabbath, and demanded land as payment. They made deals with corrupt Indian leaders. Meanwhile epidemic disease continued to devastate Indian villages. Disorganized and demoralized, many coastal native communities not only gave up their lands but also placed themselves under the protection of the English.

By the late 1630s only a few tribes in southern New England retained the power to challenge Puritan expansion. The Pequots, who lived along the shores of Long Island Sound near the mouth of the Connecticut River, were one of the most powerful. Allies of the Dutch, the Pequots controlled the production of wampum, woven belts of seashells used as a medium of exchange in the Indian trade. In 1637, Puritan leaders pressured the Pequots' traditional enemies, the Narragansetts of present-day Rhode Island, to join them in waging war on the Pequots. Narragansett warriors and English troops attacked the main Pequot village, burning the houses and killing most of their slumbering residents. "It was a fearful sight to see them thus frying in the fire," wrote William Bradford, "and horrible was the stink and scent thereof." The indiscriminate slaughter shocked the Narragansetts, who condemned the English way of war. It was "too furious and slays too many," they declared.

The English commander dismissed their complaints. "The Scripture declareth that women and children must perish with their parents," he declared. "We had sufficient light from the Word of God for our proceedings."

The Economy: New England Merchants

In England, the dispute between King Charles I and the Puritans in Parliament escalated into armed conflict in 1642. Several years of revolutionary confrontation finally led to Charles's arrest, his execution in 1649, and the creation of an English Commonwealth, headed by the Puritan military leader Oliver Cromwell. Because the Puritans were on the victorious side in the English civil war, they no longer had the same incentive to migrate to New England. A number of colonists returned to England.

New England's economy had depended on the sale of supplies and land to arriving immigrants, but this market collapsed as the migration tailed off. Puritan merchants turned to the flourishing fishery, shipping cod (in addition to lumber and farm products) to the West Indies, where they bartered for sugar, molasses, and rum. By mid-century New England had constructed a commercial fleet of more than 300 vessels, and by the end of the century Boston had become the third largest English commercial center in the Atlantic (after London and Bristol). The development of a diversified economy provided New England with important long-term strength and offered a striking contrast with the specialized fur-trade economy of New France.

Community and Family in New England

Pilgrims and Puritans stressed the importance of well-ordered communities. The Massachusetts General Court, the governing body of the colony, granted townships to a group of proprietors, the leaders of a congregation wishing to settle new lands. These men then distributed fields, pasture, and woodlands in quantities proportional to the social status of the recipient, with wealthy families receiving more than others. The Puritans believed that social hierarchy was ordained by God and made for well-ordered communities. Settlers typically clustered their dwellings in a central village, near the meetinghouse that served as both church and civic center. Some towns, particularly those along the coast such as Boston, became centers

The first map printed in the English colonies, this view of New England was published in Boston in 1677. With north oriented to the right, it looks west from Massachusetts Bay, the two vertical black lines indicating the approximate boundaries of the Commonwealth of Massachusetts. The territory west of Rhode Island is noted as an Indian stronghold, the homelands of the Narragansett, Pequot, and Nipmuck peoples.

The Maypole at Merrymount

In 1625 a small group of English fur traders established a small coastal outpost some thirty miles to the north of the Pilgrims' colony of Plymouth. The fur trade was important to the Pilgrim economy, and they did not appreciate the appearance of competitors. They were even less fond of Thomas Morton, leader of the outpost, who was very successful at establishing good relations with local native groups, in part by supplying them with firearms for use in hunting. When in 1628 Morton organized a May Day celebration, which included Indian participants, Governor William Bradford of Plymouth ordered his arrest, his deportation to England, and the destruction of the settlement. The following accounts, written by Bradford and Morton, emphasize the differences between the two communities. Two centuries later, Nathaniel Hawthorne wrote a famous short story about the conflict at Merrymount (or Ma-Re Mount), the name Morton gave to his community.

• **How do Bradford's and Morton's accounts reveal the differences between their two communities?**

The Lord of Misrule

After this they fell to great licentiousness, and led a dissolute life, powering out themselves into all profaneness. And Morton became lord of misrule, and maintained (as it were) a school of Atheism. And after they had got some goods into their hands, and got much by trading with the Indians, they spent it as vainly, in quaffing and drinking both wine and strong waters in great excess, and, as some reported, £10 worth in a morning. They also set up a May-pole, drinking and dancing about it many days together, inviting the Indian women, for their consorts, dancing and frisking together, (like so many fairies, or furies rather,) and worse practices. . . . Morton likewise (to show his poetry) composed sundry rhymes and verses, some tending to lasciviousness, and others to the detraction and scandal of some persons, which he affixed to this idle or idol Maypole. They changed also the name of their place, . . .[calling it] Merrymount, as if this jollity would have lasted ever.

Now to maintain this riotous prodigality and profuse excess, Morton, thinking himself lawless, and hearing what gain the French and fisher-men made by trading of pieces, powder, and shot to the Indians, he, as the head of this consortship, began the practice of the same in these parts; and first he taught them how to use them, to charge, and discharge, and what proportion of powder to give the piece, according to the size or bigness of the same; and what shot to use for fowl, and what for deer. And having thus instructed them, he employed some of them to hunt and fowl for him, so as they became far more active in that employment than any of the English, by reason of their swiftness of foot, and nimbleness of body, being also quick sighted, and by continual exercise well knowing the haunts of all sorts of game.

. . . This Morton having thus taught them the use of pieces, he sold them all he could spare; and he and his consorts determined to send for many out of England, and had by some of the ships sent for above a score. The which being known, and his neighbors meeting the Indians in

> "They also set up a May-pole, drinking and dancing about it many days together, . . ."

of shipping. Clustered settlements and strong communities distinguished New England from the dispersed and weak communities of the Chesapeake.

The ideal Puritan family was also well ordered. Parents often participated in the choice of mates for their offspring, and children typically married in the order of their births, younger children waiting until arrangements had been made for their elder siblings. But well-disciplined children also

needed education. Another source of New England's strength was the impressive Puritan education system. In 1647 the Massachusetts General Court required that towns with 50 families or more support a public school; those with 100 families were to establish a grammar school instructing students in Latin, knowledge of which was required for admission to Harvard College, founded in 1636. The Puritan colony of Connecticut enacted similar requirements.

the woods armed with guns in this way, it was a terror unto them. . . . And other places (though more remote) saw this mischief would quickly spread over all, if not prevented. Besides, they saw they should keep no servants, for Morton would entertain any, how vile so ever, and all the scum of the country, or any discontents, would flock to him from all places, if this nest was not broken; and they should stand in more fear of their lives and goods (in short time) from this wicked and debased crew than from the salvages themselves.

. . . Upon which they saw there was no way but to take him by force; and having so far proceeded, now to give over would make him far more haughty and insolent. So they mutually resolved to proceed, and obtained of the Governor of Plymouth to send Captain Standish, and some other aide with him, to take Morton by force. The which accordingly was done. . . . After Morton was sent for England, . . . shortly after came over that worthy gentleman, Mr. John Endecott, who brought over a patent under the broad seal, for the government of the Massachusetts, who visiting those parts caused that Maypole to be cut down, and rebuked them for their profanities, and admonished them . . .; so they now, or others, changed the name of their place again, and called it Mount-Dagon.

SOURCE: William Bradford, *History of Plimoth Plantation* (1620–1647).

Lasses in Beaver Coats Come Away

The Inhabitants of Pasonagessit, having translated the name of their habitation from that ancient Salvage name to Ma-re Mount, and being resolved to have the new name confirmed for a memorial to after ages, did devise amongst themselves to have it performed in a solemn manner, with Revels and merriment after the old English custom. [They] prepared to set up a Maypole upon the festival day of Philip and Jacob, and therefore brewed a barrel of excellent beer and provided a case of bottles, to be spent, with other good cheer, for all comers of that day. And because they would have it in a complete form, they had prepared a song fitting to the time and present occasion. And upon Mayday they brought the Maypole to the place appointed, with drums, guns, pistols and other fitting instruments, for that purpose; and there erected it with the help of Salvages, that came thither of purpose to see the manner of our Revels. A goodly pine tree of 80 foot long was reared up, with a pair of buck's horns nailed one somewhat near unto the top of it: where it stood, as a faire sea mark for directions how to find out the way to mine Host of Ma-re Mount. . . . There was likewise a merry song made, which, (to make their Revels more fashionable,) was sung with a Chorus, every man bearing his part; which they performed in a dance, hand in hand about the Maypole. . . .

> Make green garlands, bring bottles out
> And fill sweet Nectar freely about.
> Uncover thy head and fear no harm,
> For here's good liquor to keep it warm.
> [Chorus] Drink and be merry, merry, merry boys;
> Let all your delight be in the Hymen's joys;
> Joy to Hymen, now the day is come,
> About the merry Maypole take a Room.
> Give to the Nymphs that's free from scorn
> No Irish stuff nor Scotch over worn.
> Lasses in beaver coats come away,
> Ye shall be welcome to us night and day.

"... The setting up of this Maypole was a lamentable spectacle to the precise separatists...."

. . . The setting up of this Maypole was a lamentable spectacle to the precise separatists, that lived at new Plymouth. They termed it an Idol; yea, they called it the [Golden] Calf, . . . and stood at defiance with the place, naming it Mount Dagon; threatening to make it a woeful mount and not a merry mount.

SOURCE: Thomas Morton, *New English Canaan* (1637).

In 1640 the first printing press in the English colonies had issued the first English book published in North America, *The Bay Psalm Book*. By the mid-seventeenth century, New England men boasted the highest rates of literacy in North America and much of Europe. Because girls were excluded from grammar schools, however, women's literacy remained relatively low.

The Puritans were not "puritanical" in the modern sense of the word. Although they treated adultery as a capital crime, they celebrated sexual expression within marriage. Courting couples were encouraged to engage in "petting," and married couples were expected to enjoy sexual relations. There were many loving Puritan households. Anne Bradstreet, a Massachusetts wife and mother,

The Mason children, by an unknown Boston artist, ca. 1670. These Puritan children—David, Joanna, and Abigail Mason—are dressed in finery, an indication of the wealth and prominence of their family. The cane in young David's hand indicates his position as the male heir, while the rose held by Abigail is a symbol of childhood innocence.

SOURCE: The Freake-Gibbs Painter (American, Active 1670), "David, Joanna, and Abigail Mason," 1670. Oil on canvas, 39 ½ × 42 ½ in.; Frame: 42 ¾ × 45 ½ × 1 ½ in. Fine Arts Museums of San Francisco, Gift of Mr. and Mrs. John D. Rockefeller 3rd to The Fine Arts Museums of San Francisco, 1979.7.3.

and the first published poet of New England, wrote about her husband and marriage:

> *If ever two are one, then surely we.*
> *If ever man were lov'd by wife, then thee;*
> *If ever wife was happy in a man,*
> *Compare with me ye women if you can.*

The Position of Women

Families were supposed to operate as "little commonwealths," with everyone working cooperatively. The domestic economy required the combined efforts of husband and wife. Men were generally responsible for field-work, women for the work of the household, garden, henhouse, and dairy. Women managed a rich array of tasks, and some independently traded garden products, milk, and eggs. "I meddle not with the geese nor turkeys," one husband wrote of his wife's domestic management, "for they are hers for she hath been and is a good wife to me."

Still, the cultural ideal was the subordination of women to men. "I am but a wife, and therefore it is sufficient for me to follow my husband," wrote Lucy Winthrop Downing, and her brother John Winthrop declared that "a true wife accounts her subjection her honor and freedom." Married women could not make contracts, own property, vote, or hold office. A typical woman, marrying in her early twenties

and surviving through her forties, could expect to bear eight children and devote herself to husband and family. Aside from abstinence, there was no form of birth control. Wives who failed to have children, or widows who were economically independent, aroused significant suspicion among their neighbors. One Boston resident wrote that to be an "old maid is thought such a curse as nothing can exceed it, and look'd on as a dismal Spectacle."

The Salem Witch Trials

The cultural mistrust of women came to the surface most notably in periodic witchcraft scares. During the seventeenth century, according to one historian, 342 New England women were accused by their neighbors of witchcraft. The majority of the accused were unmarried, childless, widowed, or had reputations in their communities for assertiveness and independence. In the vast majority of cases, the charges were dismissed by authorities as baseless. In the infamous 1692 case of Salem, Massachusetts, however, the whole community was thrown into a panic of accusations when a group of girls claimed that they had been bewitched by a number of old women. Before the colonial governor finally called a halt to the persecutions in 1693, twenty people had been tried, condemned, and executed.

Read the **Document**
The Examination and Confession of Ann Foster at Salem (1692) at **www.myhistorylab.com**

The Salem witchcraft scare may have reflected social tensions that found their outlet through an attack on people perceived as outsiders. Salem was a booming commercial port, but while some residents were prospering, others were not. Most of the victims came from the commercial eastern end of town, the majority of their accusers from the economically stagnant western side. Most of the accused also came from Anglican, Quaker, or Baptist families. Finally, a majority of the victims were old women, suspect because they lived alone, without the guidance of men. The Salem witchcraft crisis exposed the dark side of Puritan thinking about women.

By the time of the witchcraft crisis New England's population was rapidly approaching 100,000. Massachusetts (which absorbed Plymouth colony in 1691) was the residence of considerably more than half this number, most concentrated in communities surrounding the port of Boston, although others were planted as far west as the Connecticut River Valley and as far north as the coast of Maine (not separated from Massachusetts until 1820). Connecticut claimed 26,000 residents, Rhode Island about 6,000, and New Hampshire, set off as a royal colony in 1680, another 5,000.

The Proprietary Colonies

Oliver Cromwell died in 1658 and two years later Parliament, anxious for stability, restored the Stuart monarchy, placing on the throne Charles II (reigned

1660–85), eldest son of the deposed king. Charles took an active interest in North America, establishing several new proprietary colonies on the model of Maryland (see Map 3.4).

The Carolinas

Charles II issued the first of his charters in 1663, establishing a new colony called Carolina, which stretched along the Atlantic coast from Virginia south to the northern limits of Spanish Florida. Virginians had already begun moving into the vicinity of Albermarle Sound in the northern part of this territory, and in 1664 the Carolina proprietors appointed a governor and created a popularly elected assembly. By 1700 North Carolina, as it became known, included 11,000 small farmers and large tobacco planters.

Settlement farther south began in 1670 with the founding of coastal Charles Town (renamed Charleston in 1783). Most South Carolina settlers came from the sugar colony of Barbados, a Caribbean colony founded by the

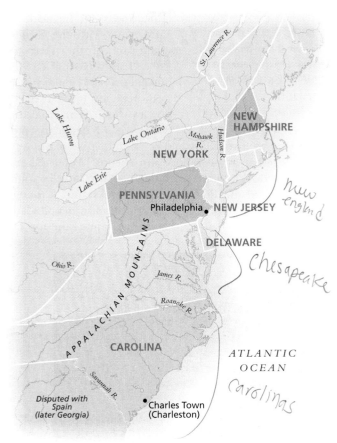

MAP 3.4 The Proprietary Colonies After the restoration of the Stuart monarchy in 1660, King Charles II of England created the new proprietary colonies of Carolina, New York, Pennsylvania, and New Jersey. New Hampshire was set off as a royal colony in 1680, and in 1704, the lower counties of Pennsylvania became the colony of Delaware.

English in 1627. Encouraged by liberal grants of land, hundreds of Barbadian planters relocated to South Carolina with their slaves during the last quarter of the seventeenth century. They lent a distinctly West Indian character to the colony. By 1700 South Carolina's population was more than 6,000, including some 3,000 enslaved Africans. (For a complete discussion of slavery see Chapter 4.)

New York and New Jersey

Charles also coveted the lucrative Dutch colony of New Netherland. In response to the growth of New England's population and its merchant economy, the Dutch West India Company changed course in the 1640s. Shifting from the French model to the English, it began sponsoring the immigration of European settlers to the Hudson River Valley, seeking to develop the colony as a diversified supply center for the West Indies. In 1651, Parliament passed a Trade and Navigation Act that barred Dutch vessels from English colonial possessions. This led to an inconclusive naval war between the two nations from 1652 to 1654. Ten years later the two powers clashed once again, this time along the West African coast, leading to a second Anglo-Dutch war. In September 1664 a small English fleet sailed into Manhattan harbor and forced the surrender of New Amsterdam without firing a shot. When the war ended with an inconclusive peace in 1667, the English were left in possession. Holland briefly regained control during a third and final conflict from 1672 to 1674, but the English won the war and won possession of the colony in the peace negotiations. This final war bankrupted the Dutch West India Company and marked the ascension of the English to dominance in the Atlantic, although Holland remained supreme in the Baltic and the East Indies.

Charles II issued a proprietary charter granting the former Dutch colony to his brother James, the Duke of York, renaming it New York in his honor. Otherwise the English did little to disturb the existing order, preferring simply to reap the benefits of this profitable colony. Ethnically and linguistically diversified, and accommodating a wide range of religious sects, New York society was the most heterogeneous in North America. In 1665, the communities of the Delaware Valley were split off as the proprietary colony of New Jersey, although it continued to be governed by New York until the 1680s. By the end of the century more than 33,000 residents lived in these two colonies.

The Founding of Pennsylvania

In 1676, the proprietary rights to the western portion of New Jersey were sold to a group of English religious dissenters, including William Penn. A member of the Society of Friends (known popularly as the Quakers), Penn

FORT NEW AMSTERDAM (NEW YORK), 1651.

The earliest known view of New Amsterdam, published in 1651. Indian traders are shown arriving with their goods in a dugout canoe of distinctive design known to have been produced by the native people of Long Island Sound. Twenty-five years after its founding, the Dutch settlement still occupied only the lower tip of Manhattan Island.

SOURCE: Fort New Amsterdam, New York, 1651. Engraving. Collection of The New-York Historical Society, 77354d.

the king. In 1681, to settle a large debt he owed Admiral Penn, King Charles issued to his son a proprietary grant to a huge territory west of the Delaware River. The next year, Penn sailed to America and supervised the laying out of the port of Philadelphia.

Penn wanted this colony to be a "holy experiment." In his first Frame of Government, drafted in 1682, he included guarantees of religious freedom, civil liberties, and elected representation. He also attempted to deal fairly with the native peoples, refusing to permit colonization to begin until settlement rights were negotiated and lands purchased. In 1682 and 1683, he made an agreement with the sachem Tammany of the Delaware tribe. "I am very sensible of the unkindness and injustice that hath been too much exercised toward you," Penn told the Delawares. "I desire to enjoy this land with your love and consent, that we may always live together as neighbors and friends." Penn did not know it, but his words might have applied as well to New Mexico and the Pueblos as to Pennsylvania. Although relations between Pennsylvania and Indian peoples later soured, during Penn's lifetime his reputation for fair

intended to make the colony a haven for religious toleration and pacifism. Penn himself had been imprisoned in England

●●●—Read the Document

William Penn, Description of Pennsylvania (1681) at
www.myhistorylab.com

several times for publicly expressing such views. But he was the son of a wealthy and influential English admiral who was a close adviser to

The Delawares presented William Penn with this wampum belt after the Shackamaxon Treaty of 1682. In friendship, a Quaker in distinctive hat clasps the hand of an Indian. The diagonal stripes on either side of the figures represent the "open paths" between the English and the Delawares. Wampum belts like this one, made from strings of white and purple shell beads, were used to commemorate treaties throughout the colonial period, and were the most widely accepted form of money in the northeastern colonies during the seventeenth century.

dealing led a number of native groups to resettle in the Quaker colony.

During the first two decades of Pennsylvania's settlement, nearly 20,000 settlers spread agricultural communities from the banks of the Delaware to the fertile interior valleys. In the eighteenth century Pennsylvania would be known as America's breadbasket, and Philadelphia would become North America's most important port. In 1704 Penn approved the creation of a separate colony called Delaware for the governance of the counties near the mouth of the river formerly controlled first by the Swedes and then the Dutch.

Conflict and War

Pennsylvania's ability to maintain peaceful relations with the Indians proved the great exception. The last quarter of the seventeenth century became a time of great violence throughout the colonial regions of the continent, mostly because of the expansion of European settlement (see Map 3.5). Much of this warfare was between colonists and Indians, but intertribal warfare and intercolonial rivalry greatly contributed to the violence. The pattern of violent conflict extended from Santa Fé, where the revolt of the Pueblos was the single most effective instance of Indian

MAP 3.5 Spread of Settlement: British Colonies, 1650–1700 The spread of settlement in the English colonies in the late seventeenth century created the conditions for a number of violent conflicts, including King Philip's War, Bacon's Rebellion, and King William's War.

resistance to colonization, to the shores of Hudson Bay, where French and English traders fought for access to the rich fur-producing region of the north, to the English colonies on the Atlantic coast.

King Philip's War

In New England, nearly forty years of peace followed the Pequot War of 1637. Natives and colonists lived in close, if tense, contact. Several Puritan ministers, including John Eliot and Thomas Mayhew, began to preach to the Indians, and some 2,000 native converts eventually relocated to Christian communities known as "praying towns." But there remained several independent tribes, including the Pokanokets, the Narragansetts, and the Abenakis of northern New England. The extraordinary expansion of the colonial population, and the increasing hunger for land, created inexorable pressures for expansion into their territories.

The Pokanokets, whose homeland lay between Rhode Island and Plymouth, were led by the sachem Metacom, whom the English called King Philip. The son of Massasoit, who forged the original alliance with the Pilgrims, Metacom had been raised among English colonists and educated in their schools. He operated on the assumption that his people had a future in the English colonial world but was gradually forced to conclude that the colonists had no room for the Pokanokets. In 1671 the colonial authorities of Plymouth pressured Metacom into granting them sovereign authority over his homeland. This humiliation convinced him that he had to break the half-century alliance with Plymouth and take up armed resistance. The Puritan colonies, meanwhile, prepared for a war of conquest.

War came in the spring of 1675, after Plymouth magistrates arrested and executed three Pokanoket men for the murder of a Christian Indian. Metacom appealed to the Narragansetts for a defensive alliance, which the New England colonies interpreted as an act of aggression. They sent armed forces into Pokanoket and Narragansett country, attacking and burning a number of villages. That opened the floodgates. Soon all New England was engulfed in what became known as King Philip's War.

At first things went well for the Indians. They forced the abandonment of English settlements on the Connecticut River and torched towns less than twenty miles from Boston. By the beginning of 1676, however, their campaign was collapsing. A combined colonial army defeated a large Indian force in a battle known as the Great Swamp Fight in Narragansett country. Metacom led his men and fled west to the border with New York where he appealed for support from the Iroquois. But instead of helping, the Iroquois attacked, forcing Metacom back to Pokanoket territory, where colonists annihilated his army in August 1676. Metacom was quartered, his severed head mounted on a pike at Plymouth.

Indians and New Englanders skirmish during King Philip's War in a detail from John Seller's "A Mapp of New England," published immediately after the war.

In attacking the Pequots, the Iroquois were motivated by interests of their own. Extending the role they had played in the Dutch trading system, they now cast themselves as powerful intermediaries between other tribes and the English. In a series of negotiations conducted at Albany in 1677, the Iroquois Confederacy and the colony of New York created an alliance known as the Covenant Chain. It envisioned Iroquois dominance over all other tribes, thus putting New York in an economically and politically dominant position among the other colonies.

An estimated 4,000 natives and 2,000 colonists died during the war, and dozens of native and colonial towns lay in ruins. Fearing attack from Indians close at hand, colonists also destroyed most of the Indian praying towns, killing many of the Christian residents. Calculated in the number of lives lost, King Philip's War was the most destructive Indian–colonist conflict in early American history, although the Pueblo Revolt claimed a greater proportion of the colonial population.

Bacon's Rebellion and Southern Conflicts

While King Philip's War raged in New England, another English–Indian confrontation took shape in the Chesapeake and mutated into civil war. The basic cause of the conflict was the old problem of land and labor. By the 1670s Indian communities residing on the frontier of the colony were under assault by colonists in search of new tobacco lands. The insatiable hunger came not only from established planters with lands reaching exhaustion but also from former servants who had served out their indentures. Governor William Berkeley, in office since the 1640s, ruled in alliance with the big planters, who feared landless freemen even more than they did Indians. In 1670 the Burgesses had enacted legislation restricting the suffrage to property owners; nevertheless, every man still had to pay taxes. Smoldering class antagonism thus added to the volatile mix. When in 1675 the governor declined to send the militia against the Indians, colonists under the leadership

of wealthy backcountry planter Nathaniel Bacon embarked on unauthorized raids resulting in the indiscriminate murder of many natives, including those allied with the colony. Bacon became a hero to former servants, and although Berkeley fumed, he ordered the first elections in many years in an attempt to appease the people. The new assembly—including Bacon, who was elected by his neighbors—restored the suffrage to freemen without property.

But Berkeley's move backfired when Bacon went further, demanding the death or removal of all Indians from the colony as well as an end to the rule of aristocratic "grandees" and "parasites." Berkeley fled across the Chesapeake, Bacon seized control, and his volunteer force burned Jamestown to the ground. Soon thereafter, however, the rebel leader came down with dysentery. He died and the rebellion collapsed. Berkeley returned, reestablished control, and ordered the execution of Bacon's lieutenants.

This brief but violent clash signaled a developing conflict between backcountry districts and more established coastal regions where the "Indian problem" had long since been settled. Backcountry men in the Albermarle region of North Carolina staged a similar revolt in 1677, an episode known as Culpeper's Rebellion. They overthrew the established government and held power for two years before the proprietors reestablished authority. These rebellions revealed the power of class antagonism, but they also suggested that the Indians could play the role of convenient scapegoats. As one historian writes, "resentment of an alien race might be more powerful than resentment of an upper class."

Colonial officials in South Carolina seemed to be paying attention. They encouraged Indians allied with the colony—Yamasees, Creeks, Cherokees, and Chickasaws—to wage war on tribes affiliated with rival colonial powers, including the mission Indians of Spanish Florida, the Choctaw allies of the French, and the Tuscaroras, trading partners of the Virginians. In addition to opening new lands for settlement, the brutal fighting resulted in the capture of many thousands of Indians who were sold into slavery. These wars continued into the first quarter of the eighteenth century.

The Glorious Revolution in America

Dynastic change in England was another factor in the violence in North America. After Charles II died in 1685, his brother and successor, James II (reigned 1685–88), began a concerted effort to strengthen royal control over the colonies. The king's ministers believed colonial assemblies had grown too powerful and independent and were determined to rein them in. The New York assembly, considered particularly troublesome, was abolished and all power placed in the hands of the colony's royal governor. In the other colonies governors challenged the authority of assemblies. The king annulled the charter governments of New England, New York, and New Jersey and combined them into a single supercolony known as the Dominion of New England. Edmund Andros, appointed royal governor, imposed Anglican forms of worship in Puritan areas and overthrew long-standing traditions of local autonomy.

James ruled England in the same imperious style. He was a practicing Catholic, and his appointment of Catholics to high positions of state added to rising discontent and protest. The last straw was the birth of a royal son in 1688. Fearing the establishment of a Catholic dynasty, Parliamentary leaders deposed James and replaced him with his Protestant daughter Mary, who was married to William of Orange, hereditary head of state of the Netherlands. When the army refused to prevent William and Mary from landing in England, James fled to France. The relatively nonviolent "Glorious Revolution," as it came to be known, included a Bill of Rights, issued by the new monarchs at the insistence of Parliament, in which they promised to respect traditional civil liberties, to summon and consult with Parliament annually, and to enforce and administer its legislation. These were significant concessions with profound implications for the future of English politics. In essence, England had become a "constitutional monarchy."

In North America, news of the Glorious Revolution sparked a series of colonial rebellions against the authorities set in place by King James. In the spring of 1689, Governor Andros was attacked by a Boston mob. He escaped their wrath but was arrested and deported. The Boston uprising inspired another in New York led by merchant Jacob Leisler that included many prominent Dutch residents. They seized control of the city and called for the formation of a new legislature. In Maryland, rumors of a Catholic plot led to the overthrow of the proprietary rule of the Calvert family by an insurgent group calling itself the Protestant Association.

The new regime in London carefully measured its response to these uprisings. When Jacob Leisler attempted to prevent the landing of the king's troops in New York, he was arrested, tried, and executed. But William and Mary also consented to the breakup of the Dominion of New England and the termination of proprietary rule in Maryland. All the affected colonies quickly revived their assemblies and returned to their tradition of self-government. The monarchs strengthened royal authority, however, by decreeing that henceforth Massachusetts, New York, and Maryland would be royal colonies.

King William's War

The year 1689 also marked the beginning of nearly seventy-five years of armed conflict between English and French forces for control of the North American interior. The Iroquois–English Covenant Chain alliance challenged New France's fur-trade empire, and in response the French pressed farther west in search of commercial opportunities. In the far north, the English countered with the establishment of Hudson's Bay Company, a royal fur-trade monopoly that sought to exploit the watershed of the great northern bay.

The competition in the colonies was part of a larger conflict between England and France over the European balance of power. Armed conflict in what is known as the War of the Grand Alliance began in Europe in 1688 and spread to the colonies, where it was known as King William's War (for the new king of England). In 1690, the French and their Indian allies attacked and burned frontier settlements in New York, New Hampshire, and Maine, and invaded the homeland of the Iroquois. The same year, a Massachusetts fleet captured and briefly held the strategic French port of Port Royal on the Bay of Fundy, but a combined English and colonial force failed to conquer the French settlements along the St. Lawrence. The inconclusive war ended in 1697 with an equally inconclusive peace. War between England and France would resume only five years later.

The persistent violence of the last quarter of the seventeenth century greatly concerned English authorities, who began to fear the loss of their North American possessions by outside attack or internal disorder. In 1701 the English Board of Trade converted the remaining charter and proprietary colonies into royal ones. Eventually William Penn succeeded in regaining private control of Pennsylvania, and Rhode Island and Connecticut won reinstatement of their charter governments. But the most lasting result of this quarter-century of turmoil was the tightening of English control over its North American colonies.

Conclusion

At the beginning of the seventeenth century, the European presence north of Mexico was extremely limited: Spanish bases in Florida, a few Franciscan missions among the Pueblos, and fishermen along the North Atlantic coast. By 1700 the human landscape of the Southwest, the South, and the Northeast had been transformed. More than a quarter million migrants from the Old World had come to North America, the great majority of them to the English colonies. Indian societies had been disrupted, depopulated, and in some cases destroyed. The violence that flared during the last quarter of the seventeenth century was a measure of the cost of empire. Indian people resisted colonial rule in New Mexico, New England, and the Chesapeake.

Like King Philip's War and Bacon's Rebellion, the Pueblo Revolt was an episode of great violence and destruction. Yet it resulted in a long period of accommodation between the Pueblos and the Spanish colonists. The English colonists, however, took a different lesson from the violent conflicts in their colonies. They renewed their commitment to establishing communities of exclusion with ominous implications for the future of relations between colonists and natives.

CHRONOLOGY

1598	Juan de Oñate leads Spanish into New Mexico
1607	English found Jamestown
1608	French found Québec
1609	Spanish found Santa Fé
1620	Pilgrim emigration
1622	Indian uprising in Virginia
1625	Jesuit missionaries arrive in New France
1629	Puritans begin settlement of Massachusetts Bay
1637	Pequot War
1649	Charles I executed
1660	Stuart monarchy restored, Charles II becomes king
1675	King Philip's War; Bacon's Rebellion
1680	Pueblo Revolt
1681–82	Robert Sieur de La Salle explores the Mississippi
1688	The Glorious Revolution
1689	King William's War
1696	Spanish reconquest of the Pueblos completed
1701	English impose royal governments on all colonies but Massachusetts, Connecticut, and Pennsylvania

Review Questions

1. Using examples drawn from this chapter, discuss the differences between colonizing "frontiers of inclusion" and "exclusion."

2. What factors turned England's Chesapeake colony of Virginia from stark failure to brilliant success?

3. Discuss the role of religious dissent in the founding of the first New England colonies and in stimulating the creation of others.

4. Compare and contrast William Penn's policy with respect to Indian tribes with the policies of other English settlers, in the Chesapeake and New England, and with the policies of the Spanish, the French, and the Dutch.

5. What were the principal causes of colonial violence and warfare of the late seventeenth century?

Recommended Reading

James Axtell, *The European and the Indian: Essays in the Ethnohistory of Colonial America* (1981). A readable introduction to the dynamics of mutual discovery between natives and colonizers.

Leslie Choquette, *Frenchmen into Peasants: Modernity and Tradition in the Peopling of French Canada* (1997). A history of French immigrants to North America, based on a comprehensive database of hundreds of individuals. The most detailed study of French colonization.

Jack P. Greene and Philip D. Morgan, Eds., *Atlantic History: A Critical Appraisal* (2009). A collection of original essays offering a comprehensive examination of how Atlantic history has been interpreted by historians.

Andrew L. Knaut, *The Pueblo Revolt of 1680* (1995). The most complete and sophisticated account of the revolt.

Edmund S. Morgan, *American Slavery, American Freedom* (1975). A classic interpretation of early Virginia, arguing that early American ideas of freedom for some were based on the reality of slavery for many.

Diana Newton, *Papists, Protestants, and Puritans, 1559–1714* (1998). The best survey of religious change during the Protestant Reformation with a focus on the turmoil in England.

Daniel K. Richter, *Facing East from Indian Country: A Native History of Early America* (2001). Colonial history from the point of view of the Indians. Includes remarkable biographical chapters on Pocahontas and Metacom.

Nicholas A. Robins, *Native Insurgencies and the Genocidal Impulse in the Americas* (2005). A comparative study of several native insurgencies on the Spanish frontier, prominently featuring the Pueblo Revolt.

Helen C. Rountree, *Pocahontas, Powhatan, Opechancanough: Three Indian Lives Changed by Jamestown* (2005). The leading authority on the Indians of eastern Virginia tells the story of colonization from the native perspective.

Susan Sleeper-Smith, *Indian Women and French Men: Rethinking Cultural Encounter in the Western Great Lakes* (2001). A study of Indian women who married French traders and became cultural intermediaries.

David J. Weber, *The Spanish Frontier in North America* (1992). A powerful overview that includes comprehensive histories of New Mexico and Florida.

PEARSON

myhistorylab™ Connections

Reinforce what you learned in this chapter by studying the many documents, images, maps, review tools, and videos available at www.myhistorylab.com.

Read and Review

✓●─[Study and **Review** Chapter 3

•••●─[Read the Document

Don Juan de Oñate, Letter from New Mexico to the Viceroy (1599)

Remarks by Chief Powhatan to John Smith (ca. 1609)

John Smith, "The Starving Time" (1624)

The Charter of Maryland (1632)

Agreement between the Settlers at New Plymouth (Mayflower Compact) (1620)

John Winthrop, A Model of Christian Charity (1630)

The Examination and Confession of Ann Foster at Salem (1692)

Ann Putnam's Deposition (1692)

William Penn, Description of Pennsylvania (1681)

👁●─[See the **Map**

The Colonies to 1740

French America, 1608–1763

Research and Explore

•••●─[Read the Document

Exploring America: Jamestown

Exploring America: Witches in the American Imagination

Profiles
Pocahontas
John Winthrop

History Bookshelf: William Bradford Of Plymouth Plantation *(1650)*

((●─[**Hear** the **Audio**

Hear the audio files for Chapter 3 at
www.myhistorylab.com.

4

Chapter 4 at www.myhistorylab.com

((•- Hear the Audio

Slavery and Empire
1441–1770

C H A P T E R   O U T L I N E

A model of the slave ship Brookes, showing plan view of slave positions, c.1790. Courtesy of Dorling Kindersley.

Rebellion in Stono, South Carolina

On Sunday morning, September 9, 1739, while most planter families were attending church, a group of twenty slaves gathered on the banks of the Stono River, twenty miles south of Charles Town, South Carolina. Led by an Angolan known in some accounts as Jemmy, in others as Cato, the slaves made their way to Hutchinson's general store in the hamlet of Stono Bridge. They killed the two storekeepers, ransacked the place, and arming themselves with firearms and ammunition, set off on the road headed southwest for Florida, where the Spanish governor had issued a proclamation promising freedom for all runaway British slaves. They made no attempt to hide themselves but marched boldly to the beat of drummers and shouts of "Liberty!" The commotion drew the attention of curious slaves from the numerous rice plantations scattered across the swampy countryside, and dozens joined the marchers, women and children as well as men. They plundered and burned the homes of planters and pursued and killed every white person they encountered along the way, with the exception of an innkeeper, who was spared when several rebels spoke up in his defense, saying he had been kind to his slaves. According to the official government report of the incident, a total of twenty-three whites lost their lives.

For the planters, this was the worst nightmare imaginable. Enslaved Africans greatly outnumbered white colonists in South Carolina. Word of the rebellion quickly spread throughout the planter community, and soon a heavily armed and mounted posse was hot on the rebels' trail. Late in the afternoon, near the crossing of the Edisto River, the posse overtook them. The rebel band, grown to nearly a hundred strong, had halted in a field where, in the words of the report, they "set to dancing, singing, and beating drums to draw more Negroes to them." Bottles of rum were passed and there was a good deal of drinking. Quietly the planters surrounded the field, then opened fire. Most of the slaves scattered, although according to the report the group of original conspirators "behaved boldly," forming themselves into a body and returning several volleys with the stolen firearms. But they were outmanned and outgunned, and at least two dozen slaves were killed. According to another account, the posse "cutt off their heads and set them up at every mile post" along the road leading back to Charles Town. Over the next few weeks the remaining fugitives were tracked down and killed by Indian allies of the South Carolina colony. A total of forty-five or fifty African Americans died. Thus ended the Stono Rebellion, the most violent slave uprising of the colonial period.

That slaves would rise up with the odds so stacked against them was a sign of their desperation. Most of these men and women were West Africans who had endured the shock of enslavement. Ripped from their homeland communities by slave raiders, they had been packed into the stinking holds of transport vessels and forced to endure a nightmarish passage across the Atlantic, a voyage that claimed the lives of many tens of thousands over several centuries. Unloaded on a strange continent, the survivors were sold at dockside auctions, shackled together, and marched to their destinations. On the rice plantations of low-country South Carolina, they suffered from overwork, poor diet, minimal clothing, and inadequate housing. Colonial laws permitted masters to discipline and punish harshly and indiscriminately. Slaves were whipped, confined in irons, mutilated, sold away, even murdered.

That slaves would rise up was also a sign of their community. The Stono Rebellion required the kind of careful organization possible only with the social trust and confidence built by community ties. Plantation slaves married, raised children, and constructed kinship networks. They passed on African names and traditions and created new ones. Many of the slaves of coastal South Carolina came from the central African rice coast, from Angola or the Kingdom of the Kongo, where men not only knew about the cultivation of rice but also shared a military tradition and knew how to handle firearms. We know almost nothing about the central group of conspirators in the Stono Rebellion, but very likely they were leaders of the emerging local African American community.

Community is also what enables a people to remember their history, to pass tales down the generations. In the 1930s, nearly 200 years after the uprising at Stono, George Cato, great-great-grandson of the leader of the Stono Rebellion, had family stories to tell. "My granddaddy and daddy tell me plenty 'bout it," Cato told an interviewer at his home, near the site of the uprising. "As it come down to me, I thinks de first Cato take a darin' chance on losin' his life, not so much for his own benefit as it was to help others." He and the other rebels died in their attempt to free themselves, and not only did slavery continue, but it grew harsher and more oppressive as planters sought to stamp out the merest possibility of revolt. Yet the slaves' cry of "Liberty!" had not been in vain. Although in the twentieth century most white Americans had never heard of the Stono Rebellion, stories of the rebels' bravery and daring continued to inspire the local African American community. "I sho' does come from dat old stock who had de misfortune to be slaves," said Cato, who had been born into slavery himself. But the rebels "decided to be men," he declared, "and I's right proud of it."

The history of slavery in early America includes some of the most troubling stories from our past, among them the horrid misery of the Atlantic slave trade, the shocking plunder of Africa, the use of forced labor for the production of sugar and other

1. How did the modern system of slavery develop?

2. What is the history of the slave trade and the Middle Passage?

3. How did Africans manage to create communities under the brutal slave system?

4. What were the connections between the institution of slavery and the imperial system of the eighteenth century?

5. How and why did racism develop in America?

FOCUS
Questions

1441–1770

tropical commodities, and the foundational profits of empire. The conflicts of European nations over the access to and control of this shameful commerce led directly to colonial

Stono, SC

wars of great devastation. Yet amid this history are also stories of the making of African American families, kin networks, and communities under the most difficult of all imaginable circumstances.

AMERICAN·
Communities

The Beginnings of African Slavery

Household slaves had been a part of the Mediterranean world since ancient times. In the fifteenth century, Venetian and Genoese merchants did a booming business in the sale of captive Slavs—the word "slave" derives from "Slav"—as well as Muslims and Africans. Many Europeans were disturbed, however, by the moral implications of enslaving other Europeans, and in the early fifteenth century the pope excommunicated a number of merchants engaged in selling Christians. The penalty did not apply to selling Africans and Muslims.

One of the goals of Portuguese expansion in the fifteenth century was to gain access to the lucrative West African trade in gold, ivory, textiles, and slaves previously dominated by the Moors of northern Africa. The first African slaves to arrive in Lisbon were kidnapped by a Portuguese captain in 1441. But European traders found it more efficient to leave the dirty work of taking captives to Africans who were willing to exchange slaves for European commodities. By the mid-fifteenth century, the Portuguese were shipping a thousand or more slaves each year from Africa. Most were sent to labor on the sugar

plantations on the Portuguese island colony of Madeira, which lies off the northern African coast.

Sugar and Slavery

Sugar and slaves had gone together since Italian merchants of the fourteenth century set up the first modern sugar plantations on islands in the Mediterranean. Columbus introduced sugar to Hispaniola on his second voyage, and plantations were soon in operation there. Because the Indian population had been devastated by warfare and disease, colonists imported African slaves as laborers. Meanwhile, the Portuguese, aided by Dutch financiers, created a center of sugar production in their Brazilian colony that became a model for the efficient and brutal exploitation of African labor. By 1600, at least 25,000 enslaved Africans were laboring on plantations in Hispaniola and Brazil.

Skilled at finance and commerce, the Dutch greatly expanded the European market for sugar, converting it from a luxury item for the rich to a staple for ordinary people. Along with other tropical commodities such as tobacco, coffee, and tea, sugar helped sustain Europeans

A portion of the *Catalan Atlas*, a magnificent map presented to the king of France in 1381 by his cousin, the king of Aragon, showing Iberia and north Africa, with the Straits of Gibralter connecting the Atlantic Ocean to the Mediterranean Sea. A depiction of Mansa Musa (1312–37), ruler of the Muslim kingdom of Mali, is bottom right. The accompanying inscription describes Musa as "the richest, the most noble lord in all this region on account of the abundance of gold that is gathered in his land." He holds what was thought to be the world's largest gold nugget. Under Musa's reign, Timbuktu became a capital of world renown.

through the increasingly long working day that accompanied the modernization process. Once the demand for sugar and its profitability had been demonstrated, England and France began seeking West Indian sugar colonies of their own. With the Spanish in control of the big islands of Cuba, Hispaniola, Jamaica, and Puerto Rico, they began by seizing islands of the Lesser Antilles, constructing plantations, and importing slaves. By the 1640s, English Barbados and French Martinique had become highly profitable sugar colonies. In 1655 the English seized the island of Jamaica from the Spanish, and by 1670 the French had established effective control over the western portion of Hispaniola, which they renamed Saint Domingue (present-day Haiti). By then, Caribbean sugar and slavery had become the centerpiece of the European colonial system.

West Africans

The men and women whose labor made these tropical colonies so profitable came from the long-established societies and local communities of West Africa. In the sixteenth century more than a hundred different peoples lived along the coast of West Africa, from Cape Verde south to Angola. In the north were the Wolofs, Mandingos, Hausas, Ashantis, and Yorubas; to the south the Ibos, Sekes, Bakongos, and Mbundus.

West African societies were based on sophisticated farming systems many thousands of years old. Farming sustained large populations and thriving networks of commerce, and in some areas kingdoms and states developed. Along the upper Niger River, where the grassland gradually turns to desert, towns such as Timbuktu developed into trading centers. There were a number of lesser states and kingdoms along the coast, and it was with these that the Portuguese first bargained for Africans who could be sold as slaves.

Varieties of household slavery were common in West African societies, although slaves there were often treated as subordinate members of the family. They were allowed to marry, and their children were born free. "With us they did no more work than other members of the community, even their master," remembered Olaudah Equiano, an Ibo captured and shipped to America as a slave in 1756, when he was a boy of eleven. "Their food, clothing, and lodging were nearly the same as [the others], except that they were not permitted to eat with those who were born free." When African merchants sold the first slaves to the Portuguese, they may have thought that European slavery

African slaves operate a sugar mill on the Spanish island colony of Hispaniola, illustated in a copperplate engraving published by Theodore de Bry in 1595. Columbus introduced sugar on his second voyage, and plantations were soon in operation. Because the native population was devastated by warfare and disease, colonists imported African slaves as laborers.

sugar production—nearly half to the Caribbean, and more than 40 percent to Portuguese Brazil (see Map 4.1). A much smaller proportion, about 1 in every 25 transported Africans, a total of more than 389,000 individuals, were transported to the British colonies of North America (see Figure 4.1).

Among the Africans transported to the Americas, men generally outnumbered women two to one. This ratio probably reflected the preferences of plantation masters, who wanted workers for the fields. The majority were young people, between the ages of fifteen and thirty. Nearly every ethnic group in West Africa was represented among them.

All the nations of Western Europe participated in the slave trade, but it was dominated by the Portuguese and the British. The Portuguese were the most important traders until the end of the sixteenth century, when the Dutch and English began to challenge their control. England became the largest

would be similar. But as Equiano declared: "How different was their condition from that of the slaves in the West Indies!" Yet the West African familiarity with "unfree" labor made it possible for African and European traders to begin the trade in human merchandise.

The African Slave Trade

The movement of Africans across the Atlantic to the Americas was the largest forced migration in world history (see Map 4.1). With the benefit of new compilations of

●●●[Read the Document
Alexander Falconbridge, The African Slave Trade (1788) at
www.myhistorylab.com

shipping records for the trans-Atlantic slave trade, historians now believe that more than 12.5 million people were crowed on vessels and transported. This makes Africans the single largest group of people to come to the Americas before the nineteenth century, outnumbering European migrants of the same period by a ratio of six to one. The Atlantic slave trade began with the Portuguese in the fifteenth century and did not end in the United States until 1807, and it continued elsewhere in the Americas until 1867. It is one of the most brutal chapters in the story of America.

A Global Enterprise

Approximately 10.5 million Africans arrived in the Americas during the four-century history of the slave trade. Ninety percent of them went directly to areas of

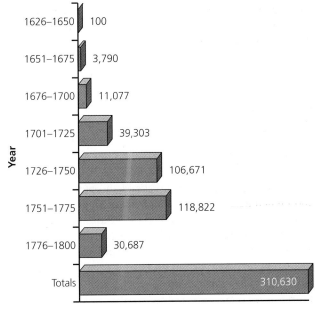

Numbers of Individuals

FIGURE 4.1 Africans Imported to Mainland British North America, 1626–1800 These statistics, generated by the computer database of all documented trans-Atlantic slave voyages, demonstrate the rising importance of the slave trade in the British mainland North American colonies.

SOURCE: *Voyages: The Trans-Atlantic Slave Trade Database.* http://www.slavevoyages.org (accessed 2010).

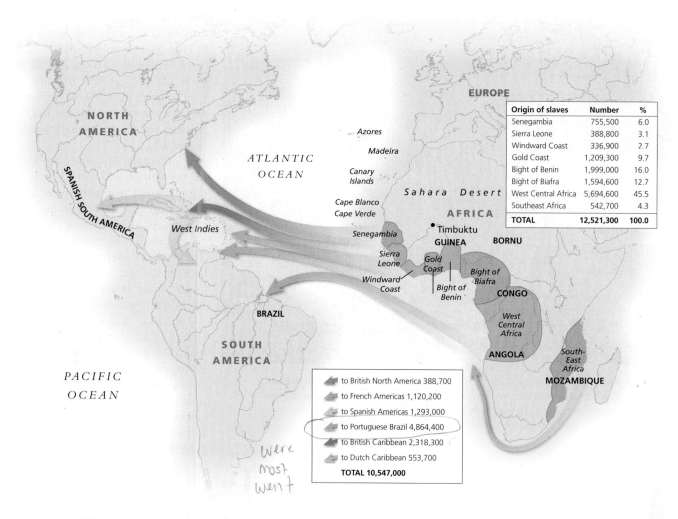

Origin of slaves	Number	%
Senegambia	755,500	6.0
Sierra Leone	388,800	3.1
Windward Coast	336,900	2.7
Gold Coast	1,209,300	9.7
Bight of Benin	1,999,000	16.0
Bight of Biafra	1,594,600	12.7
West Central Africa	5,694,600	45.5
Southeast Africa	542,700	4.3
TOTAL	**12,521,300**	**100.0**

to British North America 388,700
to French Americas 1,120,200
to Spanish Americas 1,293,000
to Portuguese Brazil 4,864,400
to British Caribbean 2,318,300
to Dutch Caribbean 553,700
TOTAL 10,547,000

MAP 4.1 The African Slave Trade The enslaved men, women, and children transported to the Americas came from West Africa, the majority from the lower Niger River (called the Slave Coast) and the region of the Congo and Angola.

slave-trading nation after 1640. The Royal African Company, chartered in London in 1672, held a monopoly of the trade until 1698 when Parliament opened it to independent merchants. Soon hundreds of ships from Bristol and Liverpool were competing with those from London, and the number of slaves shipped to North America skyrocketed. From 1650 to 1807 English and Anglo-American vessels carried half of all the slaves from Africa to the Americas. The Dutch, the French, and especially the Portuguese, however, continued to play important roles.

The European presence in Africa generally was confined to coastal outposts. By the early eighteenth century, more than two dozen trading forts crowded the 220 miles of the African Gold Coast. As the volume of slave trading expanded, the forts of trading companies gave way to the smaller coastal posts of independent traders who set up operations with the cooperation of local headmen or chiefs. This informal manner of trading offered

opportunities for small operators, such as slave traders from New England. Many early American fortunes were built from profits in the slave trade.

The slave trade was a collaboration between European or American and African traders. Dependent on the favor of local rulers, many colonial slave traders lived permanently in coastal forts and married African women, reinforcing their commercial ties with kinship relations. In many areas their mixed-ancestry children and grandchildren became prominent players in the slave trade. Continuing the practice of the Portuguese, the grim business of slave raiding was left to the Africans themselves. Slaves were not at all reticent about condemning the participation of their fellow Africans. "I must own, to the shame of my own countrymen," wrote Ottobah Cugoano of Ghana, who was sold into slavery in the 1750s, "that I was first kidnapped and betrayed by those of my own complexion."

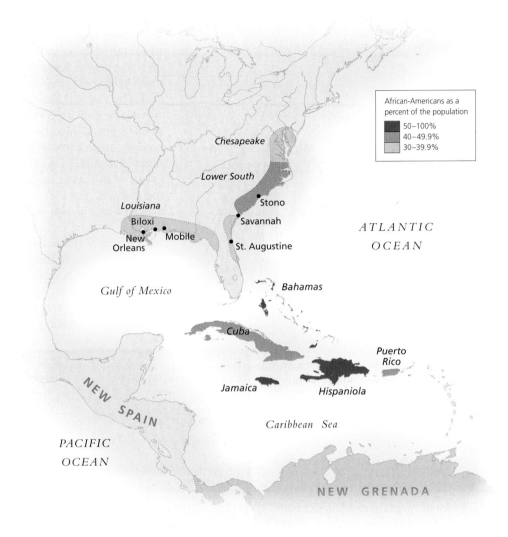

MAP 4.2 Slave Colonies of the Seventeenth and Eighteenth Centuries
By the eighteenth century, the system of slavery had created societies with large African populations throughout the Caribbean and along the southern coast of North America.

The Shock of Enslavement

Most Africans were enslaved through warfare. Sometimes large armies launched massive attacks, burning whole towns, killing many and enslaving others. More common were smaller raids in which a group of armed men attacked at nightfall, seized everyone within reach, then escaped with their captives. Wars and raids killed at least as many Africans as were captured, and this toll remains one of the great uncounted costs of the slave trade. Capture and enslavement was an unparalleled shock. Venture Smith, an African born in Guinea in 1729, was eight years old when he was captured. After many years in North American slavery, he still vividly recalled the attack on his village, the torture and murder of his father, and the long march of his people to the coast. "The shocking scene is to this day fresh in my mind," he wrote, "and I have often been overcome while thinking on it."

On the coast, European traders and African raiders assembled their captives. Prisoners waited in dark dungeons or in open pens called "barracoons." To lessen the possibility of collective resistance, traders split up families and ethnic groups. Captains carefully inspected each man and woman, and those selected for transport were branded on the back or buttocks with the mark of the buyer. Olaudah Equiano remembered that "those white men with horrible looks, red faces, and long hair, looked and acted in so savage a manner; I had never seen among any people such instances of brutal cruelty." Equiano's narrative, written after he secured his freedom in the 1780s, is one of a small number that provide an African account of enslavement. He and his fellow captives became convinced that they "had got into a world of bad spirits" and were about to be eaten by cannibals. A French trader wrote that

A group of slaves being led from the interior to the West African coast by two traders, from Rene Geoffroy de Villeneuve, *l' Afrique* (1814).

length of the bulwarks. After a breakfast of beans the crew commanded men and women to jump up and down, a bizarre session of exercise known as "dancing the slave." A day spent chained on deck was concluded by a second bland meal and then the stowing away. During the night, according to one seaman, there issued from below "a howling melancholy noise, expressive of extreme anguish." Down in the hold, the groans of the dying, the shrieks of women and children, and the suffocating heat and stench were, in the words of Olaudah Equiano, "a scene of horror almost inconceivable" (see Communities in Conflict, Two Views of the Middle Passage).

Among the horrors was the absence of any adequate sanitation. There were "necessary tubs" set below deck, but Africans, "endeavoring to get to them,

many prisoners were "positively prepossessed with the opinion that we transport them into our country in order to kill and eat them."

The Middle Passage

English sailors christened the voyage of slave vessels across the Atlantic from Africa to America as the "Middle Passage," that is, the middle part of the trading triangle linking Europe to Africa, Africa to America, and America back to Europe. From coastal forts and barracoons, crews rowed small groups of slaves to the waiting transports and packed them into shelves below deck only six feet long by two and a half feet high. "Rammed like herring in a barrel," wrote one observer, slaves were "chained to each other hand and foot, and stowed so close, that they were not allowed above a foot and a half for each in breadth." People were forced to sleep "spoon fashion," and the tossing of the ship knocked them about so violently that the skin over their elbows sometimes was worn to the bone from scraping on the planks. "It was more than a week after I left the ship before I could straighten my limbs," a former slave later remembered. One vessel designed to carry 450 slaves regularly crossed the Atlantic tightly packed with more than 600.

Their holds filled with human cargo, the transports headed up the African coast to Cape Verde where they caught the trade winds blowing toward America. A favorable voyage from Senegambia to Barbados might be accomplished in as little as three weeks, but a ship from Guinea or Angola, becalmed in the doldrums or driven back by storms, might take as much as three months.

Most voyages were marked by a daily routine. In the morning the crew opened the hatch and brought the captives on deck, attaching their leg irons to a great chain running the

Portrait of Olaudah Equiano, by an unknown English artist, ca. 1780. His autobiography, *The Interesting Narrative of the Life of Olaudah Equiano* (1789), was published in numerous editions, translated into several languages, and became the prototype for dozens of other slave narratives in the nineteenth century. In the book, Equiano described his capture in west Africa in 1756, when he was eleven years old, his "middle passage" voyage to America, and his eventual purchase by an English sea captain. After ten years as a slave, Equiano succeeded in purchasing his freedom and dedicated himself thereafter to the antislavery cause.

SOURCE: Royal Albert Memorial Museum, Exeter, Devon, UK/Bridgeman Art Library.

Slaves below deck on the Portugese vessel *Albaroz,* a sketch made by Lt. Francis Meynell of the British Navy shortly after his warship captured the slaver in 1845. Slaves were "stowed so close, that they were not allowed above a foot and a half for each in breadth," wrote one observer. This practice of "tight packing," which originated in the fifteenth century, continued to the end of the trade in the late 1860s.

tumble over their companions," as one eighteenth-century ship's surgeon wrote. "And as the necessities of nature are not to be resisted, they ease themselves as they lie." Crews were supposed to swab the holds daily, but so sickening was the task that it was rarely performed, and the captives were left to wallow in their own wastes. When first taken below deck, the boy Equiano remembered, "I received such a salutation in my nostrils as I had never experienced in my life," and "became so sick and low that I was not able to eat." According to Atlantic sailors, they could "smell a slaver five miles downwind." In these conditions many captives sickened and died.

Other captives contracted infectious diseases, and those exacted the greatest toll. Dysentery, known as the "flux," was common. Frequent shipboard epidemics of smallpox, measles, and yellow fever added to the misery. The sickening and dying often began as the ships were loaded and continued even after they anchored at their destinations. One comparative study of trans-oceanic voyages during the colonial period found that mortality on slave vessels was significantly higher than on the ships of migrating colonists, indentured servants, or even convict laborers. The consensus among historians is that approximately one of every seven transported Africans perished during the Middle Passage.

The unwilling voyagers offered plenty of resistance. As long as ships were still within sight of the African coast, hope remained alive and the danger of revolt was great. One historian found evidence of hundreds of slave revolts at sea, and estimates that insurrections occurred on one of every ten trans-Atlantic slaving voyages. Once on the open sea, however, the captives' resistance took more desperate form. The sight of the disappearing African coast "left me abandoned to despair," wrote Equiano. "I

now saw myself deprived of all chance of returning to my native country, or even the least glimpse of hope of gaining the shore." He witnessed several Africans jump overboard and drown, "and I believe many more would very soon have done the same if they had not been prevented by the ship's crew." Captains took the precaution of spreading netting along the sides of their ships. "Could I have got over the nettings," Equiano declared, "I would have jumped over the side."

As the vessels approached their destination, crews prepared the human cargo for market. All but the most rebellious were freed from their chains and allowed to wash themselves and move about the deck. To impress buyers, captains might parade Africans off the ship to the tune of an accordion or the beat of a drum. But the toll of the Middle Passage was difficult to disguise. One observer described a disembarking group as "walking skeletons covered over with a piece of tanned leather."

Some cargoes were destined for a single wealthy planter or consigned to a merchant who sold the captives in return for a commission. In other cases the captain himself was responsible. Buyers painstakingly examined the Africans, who once again suffered the indignity of probing eyes and poking fingers. This caused "much dread and trembling among us," wrote Equiano. In ports such as Charles Town in South Carolina, sales were generally made by auction or by a cruel method known as the scram-

Read the Document

Olaudah Equiano, The Middle Passage (1788) at **www.myhistorylab.com**

ble: with prices fixed in advance the Africans were driven into a corral, and on cue the buyers would rush in among them, grabbing their pick. The noise, clamor, and eagerness of the buyers, Equiano remembered, renewed all their apprehensions. "In this manner, without scruple, are

Two Views of the Middle Passage

Antislavery opinion developed very slowly over the course of the eighteenth century. Opponents focused first on the Atlantic slave trade, particularly the brutal voyage from Africa to the Americas known as the Middle Passage. In 1734, in response to early critics, Captain William Snelgrave of Bristol, England, published an account of his travels that included a defense of the slave trade and the treatment of slaves on his vessel. Snelgrave, who had been captain of a slave vessel for thirty years, believed he was transporting his captive cargo to a better, Christian life. More than fifty years passed before an African responded with a firsthand account of his own Middle Passage. Olaudah Equiano, from the region of Nigeria, was captured in 1756 and transported across the Atlantic in chains. In the passage taken from his autobiography, published in 1789, Equiano provides a vivid and contrasting description of conditions on board a slave ship.

• **In what ways do these two accounts differ? In what ways do they seem to agree?**

William Snelgrave Defends His Treatment of Slaves

Wherever I have commanded, it has been my principal Care, to have the Negroes on board my Ship kindly used; and I have always strictly charged my white People to treat them with Humanity and Tenderness; In which I have usually found my Account, both in keeping them from mutinying, and preserving them in health.

And whereas it may seem strange to those that are unacquainted with the method of managing them, how we can carry so many hundreds together in a small Ship, and keep them in order, I shall just mention what is generally practiced. When we purchase grown People, I acquaint them by the Interpreter, That, now they are become my Property, I think fit to let them know what they are bought for, that they may be easy in their Minds: (For these poor People are generally under terrible Apprehensions upon their being bought by white Men, many being afraid that we design to eat them; which, I have been told, is a story much credited by the inland Negroes;) So after informing them, That they are bought to till the Ground in our Country, with several other Matters; I then acquaint them, how they are to behave themselves on board towards the white Men; that if any one abuses them, they are to complain to the Linguist [translator], who is to inform me of it, and I will do them Justice; But if they make a Disturbance, or offer to strike a white Man, they must expect to be severely punished.

> "... [T]here has been no Attempt made by our Negroes to mutiny; which, I believe, was owing chiefly, to their being kindly used, ..."

When we purchase the Negroes, we couple the sturdy Men together with Irons; but we suffer the Women and Children to go freely about: And soon after we have sail'd from the Coast, we undo all the Mens Irons.

They are fed twice a day, and are allowed in fair Weather to come on Deck at seven a Clock in the Morning, and to remain there, if they think proper, till Sun setting. Every Monday Morning they are served with Pipes and Tobacco, which they are very fond of. The Men Negroes lodge separate from the Women and Children: and the places where they all lye are cleaned every day, some white Men being appointed to see them do it.

I have been several Voyages, when there has been no Attempt made by our Negroes to mutiny; which, I believe, was owing chiefly, to their

relations and friends separated, most of them never to see each other again." Bought by a Virginian, Equiano was taken to an isolated tobacco plantation where he found himself unable to communicate with any of his fellow slaves, who spoke other African languages.

Political and Economic Effects on Africa

Africa began the sixteenth century with genuine independence. But as surely as Europe and America grew stronger as a result of the transport of captive Africans, so Africa grew weaker by their loss. For every individual being kindly used, and to my Officers Care in keeping a good Watch. But sometimes we meet with stout stubborn People amongst them, who are never to be made easy. . . . [He recounts a near mutiny aboard his vessel off the African coast in 1721.] I called the Linguists, and ordered them to bid the Men-Negroes between Decks be quiet; (for there was a great noise amongst them). On their being silent, I asked, "What had induced them to mutiny?" They answered, "I was a great Rogue to buy them, in order to carry them away from their own Country, and that they were resolved to regain their Liberty if possible." I replied, "That they had forfeited their Freedom before I bought them, either by Crimes or by being taken in War, according to the Custom of their Country; and they being now my Property, I was resolved to let them feel my Resentment, if they abused my Kindness."

SOURCE: William Snelgrave, *A New Account of Some Parts of Guinea, and the Slave Trade* (1734).

Olaudah Equiano Describes His Own Middle Passage

At last, when the ship we were in had got in all her cargo, they made ready with many fearful noises, and we were all put under deck, so that we could not see how they managed the vessel. But this disappointment was the least of my sorrow. The stench of the hold while we were on the coast was so intolerably loathsome, that it was dangerous to remain there for any time, and some of us had been permitted to stay on the deck for the fresh air; but now that the whole ship's cargo were confined together, it became absolutely pestilential. The closeness of the place, and the heat of the climate, added to the number in the ship, which was so crowded that each had scarcely room to turn himself, almost suffocated us. This produced copious perspirations, so that the air soon became unfit for respiration, from a variety of loathsome smells, and brought on a sickness among the slaves, of which many died—thus falling victims to the improvident avarice, as I may call it, of their purchasers. This wretched situation was again aggravated by the gaffing of the chains, now became insupportable, and the filth of the necessary tubs, into which the children often fell, and were almost suffocated. The shrieks of the women, and the groans of the dying, rendered the whole a scene of horror almost inconceivable.

Happily perhaps, for myself, I was soon reduced so low here that it was thought necessary to keep me almost always on deck; and from my extreme youth I was not put in fetters. In this situation I expected every hour to share the fate of my companions, some of whom were almost daily brought upon deck at the point of death, which I began to hope would soon put an end to my miseries. Often did I think many of the inhabitants of the deep much more happy than myself. I envied them the freedom they enjoyed, and as often wished I could change my condition for theirs. Every circumstance I met with, served only to render my state more painful, and heightened my apprehensions, and my opinion of the cruelty of the whites.

One day, when we had a smooth sea and moderate wind, two of my wearied countrymen who were chained together (I was near them at the time), preferring death to such a life of misery, somehow made through the nettings and jumped into the sea; immediately, another quite dejected fellow, who, on account of his illness, was suffered to be out of irons, also followed their example; and I believe many more would very soon have done the same, if they had not been prevented by the ship's crew, who were instantly alarmed. Those of us that were the most active, were in a moment put down under the deck; and there was such a noise and confusion amongst the people of the ship as I never heard before, to stop her, and get

"The shrieks of the women, and the groans of the dying, rendered the whole a scene of horror almost inconceivable."

the boat out to go after the slaves. However, two of the wretches were drowned, but they got the other, and afterwards flogged him unmercifully, for thus attempting to prefer death to slavery. In this manner we continued to undergo more hardships than I can now relate, hardships which are inseparable from this accursed trade.

Many a time we were near suffocation from the want of fresh air, which we were often without for whole days together. This, and the stench of the necessary tubs, carried off many.

SOURCE: Olaudah Equiano, *The Interesting Narrative of the Life of Olaudah Equiano, or Gus-tavus Vassa, the African, Written by Himself* (1789).

---

taken captive, at least another died in the chronic slave raiding. Death and destruction spread deep into the African interior. Coastal slave-trading kingdoms drew slaves from central Africa. Many of the new states became little more than machines for supplying captives to European traders, and a "gun-slave cycle" pushed them into a destructive arms race with each other. Soldiers captured in these wars were themselves enslaved.

More serious still was the long-term stagnation of the West African economy. Labor was drawn away from

The Lower South

The Chesapeake did not become a slave society until almost a century after its founding. South Carolina, however, was a slave society from the beginning. The most valuable part of the early Carolina economy was the Indian slave trade. Practicing a strategy of divide and conquer, using Indian tribes to fight one another, Carolinians established a trade in Indian captives during the 1670s. By the early eighteenth century more than 12,000 mission Indians from Florida had been captured and sold into slavery and thousands more killed or dispersed. Most of the men were shipped from Charles Town to Caribbean or northern colonies; the women remained in South Carolina, where many eventually formed relationships and had children with male African slaves, forming a racial-ethnic group known as the "mustees."

In the early eighteenth century, however, planter preference turned toward African rather than Indian slaves. Rice production had become the most dynamic sector of the South Carolina economy, and their experience in agriculture made West Africans much preferred as rice workers. Another important crop was added to the mix in the 1740s when a young South Carolina woman named Elizabeth Lucas Pinckney successfully adapted West Indian indigo to the low-country climate. The indigo plant, native to India, produced a deep blue dye important in textile manufacture. Rice grew in the lowlands, but indigo could be cultivated on high ground, and with different seasonal growing patterns, planters were able to harmonize their production. Rice and indigo became two of the most valuable commodities exported from the mainland colonies of North America. The boom in these two crops depended on the growth of African slavery. Before the international slave trade to the United States was ended in 1808, at least 100,000 slaves landed in South Carolina. It is estimated that one of every five ancestors of today's African Americans entered North America through Charles Town (or Charleston, as it was renamed in 1781).

By the 1740s many of these arriving Africans were being taken to Georgia, a colony created by an act of the English Parliament in 1732. Its leader, James Edward Oglethorpe, hoped to establish a buffer against Spanish invasion from Florida and make the colony a haven for poor British farmers who could sell their products in the markets of South

Read the Document

James Oglethorpe, Establishing the Colony of Georgia (1733) at **www.myhistorylab.com**

Artist Thomas Coram painted this image of Mulberry Plantation, near Charleston, South Carolina, about 1800. The cabins of the slaves line the path to the mansion. Their steep roofs, an architectural feature introduced in America by enslaved African builders, kept living quarters cool by allowing the heat to rise and dissipate in the rafters.

SOURCE: Thomas Coram, *View of Mulberry Street, House and Street.* Oil on paper, 10 × 17.6 cm. Gibbes Museum of Art/Carolina Art Association. 68.18.01.

Carolina. Under Oglethorpe's influence, Parliament agreed to prohibit slavery in Georgia. But soon Georgia's coastal regions were being colonized by South Carolina rice planters and their slaves. By the time Oglethorpe and Georgia's trustees opened their colony to slavery in 1752, the Georgia coast had already become an extension of the Carolina low-country slave system.

By 1770 nearly 90,000 African Americans made up about 80 percent of the coastal population of South Carolina and Georgia. In the words of one eighteenth-century observer, "Carolina looks more like a negro country than like a country settled by white people." The African American communities of the Lower South had achieved self-sustained growth by the middle of the eighteenth century, a generation later than those in the Chesapeake.

Slavery in the Spanish Colonies

Slavery was basic to the Spanish colonial labor system, yet doubts about the enslavement of Africans were raised by both church and crown. The papacy denounced slavery as a violation of Christian principles. But the institution remained intact, and later in the eighteenth century, when sugar production expanded in Cuba, the slave system there turned as brutal as any in the history of the Americas.

The character of slavery in the Spanish colonies varied with local conditions. One of the most benign forms operated in Florida. In many Florida settlements, the conditions of servitude more resembled the household slavery common in African communities than the plantation slavery of South Carolina and Georgia. In 1699, in an attempt to undermine the English colonies of the Lower South, Spanish authorities declared Florida a refuge for escaped slaves, offering free land to any fugitive who would help defend the colony. Over the next half century, refugee Indians and fugitive Africans established many communities in the countryside surrounding St. Augustine. North of the city, Fort Mose was manned by African American troops commanded by their own officers. By 1763, 3,000 African Americans, a quarter of them free, made up 25 percent of St. Augustine's population.

In New Mexico, the Spanish depended on Indian slavery. In the sixteenth century the colonial governor sent Indian slaves to the mines of Mexico. The enslavement of Indians was one of the causes of the Pueblo Revolt (see Chapter 3). In the aftermath of the revolt the Spanish became much more cautious in their treatment of the Pueblos, who were officially considered Catholics. But they participated in a robust trade in captured and enslaved "infidel Indians," mostly nomadic people from the Great Plains, employing them as house servants and fieldworkers.

Slavery in French Louisiana

Slavery was also important in Louisiana, the colony founded by the French in the lower Mississippi Valley. In the early eighteenth century, French colonists established settlements and forts at Biloxi and Mobile on the Gulf of Mexico and in 1718 laid out the city of New Orleans on the lower Mississippi River. The French Company of the Indies imported some 6,000 African slaves, and planters invested in tobacco and indigo plantations along the river banks north of the city. This was the country of the Natchez Indians, who greatly resented the French intrusion. In 1729 the Natchez joined forces with rebellious slaves in an armed uprising. The Natchez Rebellion claimed the lives of more than 200 French settlers, 10 percent of the population. Planters elsewhere did everything they could to pit Indians and Africans against one another, employing Indians as slave-catchers, as they did after the Stono Rebellion. An alliance of slaves and Indians was the greatest of all planter fears. The French colonial militia put down the rebellion with brutal force, crushing and dispersing the Natchez people in the process.

Bitter memories of the Natchez Rebellion kept the Louisiana French from committing themselves totally to slavery. In 1750 African slaves amounted to less than a third of the colonial population of 10,000. It was not until the end of the century that the colony of Louisiana became an important North American slave society.

Slavery in the North

Slavery was a fundamental, acceptable, thoroughly American institution. None of the northern colonies could be characterized as slave societies, but slavery was an important form of labor in a number of localities. During the eighteenth century it grew increasingly significant in the commercial farming regions of southeast Pennsylvania, central New Jersey, and Long Island, areas where slaves made up about 10 percent of rural residents. In Rhode Island—a center of the slave trade—large gangs of slaves were used in cattle and dairy operations, and the proportion of slaves in the population reached nearly a third.

Slavery was common in all northern port cities, including Boston. There was "not a house that has not one or two," a visitor to that city wrote in the 1680s, and a visitor to Philadelphia about the same time noted that slaves were bought "by almost everyone who could afford [them]." Slave ownership was nearly universal among the wealthy and ordinary among craftsmen and professionals. By 1750 slaves, along with small populations of free blacks, made up 15 to 20 percent of the residents of Boston, New York City, and Philadelphia.

The Quakers of Pennsylvania and New Jersey, many of whom kept slaves, were the first colonists to voice antislavery sentiment. In 1715, John Hepburn of New Jersey published the first North American critique of slavery, but his was a lonely voice. By midcentury, however, there was a significant antislavery movement among Quakers. John Woolman's *Considerations on the Keeping of Negroes* (1754) was the first antislavery publication in American history. In 1758 the Philadelphia Friends Meeting voted to condemn slavery and urged masters to voluntarily free their slaves.

London Coffee House.

The London Coffee House, near the docks of Philadelphia, was the center of the city's business and political life in the mid-eighteenth century. Sea captains and merchants congregated here to do business, and as this contemporary print illustrates (in the detail on the far right), it was the site of many slave auctions. Slavery was a vital part of the economy of northern cities.

SOURCE: John F. Watson, *Annals of Philadelphia*, being a collection of memoirs, anecdotes, & incidents of Philadelphia. The London Coffee House. The Library Company of Philadelphia.

But it was not until the Revolution that antislavery attitudes became more widespread in the northern colonies.

African to African American

In 1774 a group of enslaved Massachusetts Africans spoke for tens of thousands of others when they petitioned the British authorities for their freedom. "We were unjustly dragged by the cruel hand of power from our dearest friends," they wrote, "and some of us stolen from the bosoms of our tender parents and from a populous, pleasant and plentiful country, and brought hither to be made slaves for life in a Christian land." Men and women from dozens of ethnic groups, representing many different languages, religions, and customs, were transported across the Atlantic without any of their cultural possessions. In America they were subjected to the control of masters intent on maximizing their work and minimizing their liberty. Nevertheless, African Americans carved out lives of their own with a degree of independence. Their African heritage was not erased; it provided them with a fundamental outlook, the basis for a common identity.

The majority of Africans transported to North America arrived during the eighteenth century. They joined a rapidly growing population of country-born slaves or "creoles" (from the Spanish *criollo* and Portuguese *creole*, meaning "born" or "raised"), a term first used by slaves in Brazil to distinguish their children, born in the New World, from newly arrived Africans. The perspective of creoles was shaped by their having grown up under slavery, and that perspective helped them to determine which elements of African culture they would incorporate into the emerging culture of the African American community. That community was

(((•—(Hear the Audio

On Being Brought from Africa to America at **www.myhistorylab.com**

formed out of the relationship between creoles and Africans, and between slaves and their European masters.

The Daily Life of Slaves

Slaves did the work that made plantation colonies so profitable. As an agricultural people, Africans, both women and men, were accustomed to the routines of field labor. Most slaves were field hands, and even domestic servants labored in the fields when necessary. Masters provided their workers with rude clothing, sufficient in the summer but nearly always inadequate in the winter.

On small plantations and farms, typical in the tobacco country of the Chesapeake, Africans might work side by side with their owners and, depending on the character of the master, might enjoy a standard of living not too different from that of other family members. The work was more demanding and living conditions far worse on the great rice and indigo plantations of the Lower South, where slaves usually lived separately from the master in their own quarters. But large plantations, with large numbers of slaves, created a concentration of population that made for more resilient African American communities. This was one of the profound ironies of American slavery: life was much harder on the great plantations, but slaves there had more opportunity for autonomy.

Families and Communities

The family was the most important institution for the development of community and culture, but slave codes did not provide for legal slave marriages—that would have contradicted the master's freedom to dispose of his property as he saw fit. "The endearing ties of husband and wife are strangers to us," declared the Massachusetts slaves who petitioned for their freedom in 1774, "for we are no longer man and wife than our masters or mistresses think proper."

Planters commonly separated families by sale or bequest, dividing husbands from wives and even separating mothers from children. Charles Ball was a mere boy in Virginia when his family was separated by sale. "Oh, master, do not take me from my child!" his mother cried. But her new owner gave her two or three heavy blows on the shoulders with a rawhide whip, "snatched me from her arms, and seizing her by one arm, dragged her back towards the place of sale." Ball never saw her again. Later, after he had grown and married, his master sold him to a rice planter in Georgia. "My heart died away within me," Ball remembered vividly. "I felt incapable of weeping or speaking, and in my despair I laughed loudly." On his journey south he dreamed his wife and children were "beseeching and imploring my master on their knees." He never saw them again.

Despite the odds against them, however, slaves in both the Chesapeake and the Lower South created the families that were essential for the development of African American culture. On large plantations throughout the southern colonies, travelers found Africans living in family households. In the Lower South, where there were greater concentrations of slaves on the rice plantations, husbands and wives often lived together in the slave quarters. On the smaller plantations of the Upper South, men frequently married women from neighboring farms, and with the permission of both owners visited their families in the evenings or on Sundays.

Emotional ties to particular places, connections between the generations, and relations of kinship and friendship linking neighboring plantations and farms were the foundation stones of African American community life. Kinship was especially important. African American parents encouraged their children to use family terms in addressing unrelated persons: "auntie" or "uncle" became a respectful way of addressing older men and women, "brother" and "sister" affectionate terms for age mates. This may have been one of the first devices enslaved Africans used to humanize the world of slavery.

African American Culture

The eighteenth century was the formative period in the development of the African American community, for it was then that the high birthrate and the growing numbers of country-born provided the necessary stability for the evolution of culture. During this period, men and women from dozens of African ethnic groups molded themselves into a new people. Distinctive patterns in music and dance, religion, and oral tradition illustrate the resilience of the human spirit under bondage as well as the successful struggle of African Americans to create a spiritually sustaining culture of their own.

((•• Hear the Audio

"Ghana: Ewe-Atsiagbekor" from Roots of Black Music in America at **www.myhistorylab.com**

Eighteenth-century masters were reluctant to allow their slaves to become Christians, fearing that baptism would open the way to claims of freedom or give Africans dangerous notions of universal brotherhood and equality with masters. One frustrated missionary was told by a planter that a slave was "ten times worse when a Christian than in his state of paganism." The majority of black southerners before the American Revolution practiced some form of African religion. Large numbers of African Americans were not converted to Christianity until the Great Awakening, which swept across the South just before the American Revolution (see Chapter 5).

One crucial area of religious practice concerned the rituals of death and burial. In their separate graveyards, African Americans often decorated graves with shells and pottery, an old African custom. African Americans generally believed that the spirits of their dead would return to Africa. The burial ceremony was often held at night to keep it secret from masters, who objected to the continuation of African traditions. The deceased was laid out, and around the body men and women would move counterclockwise in a slow dance step while singing ancestral songs. The pace gradually increased, finally reaching a frenzied but joyful conclusion. As slaves from different backgrounds joined together in the circle, they were beginning the process of cultural unification.

Music and dance may have formed the foundation of African American culture, coming even before a common language. Many eighteenth-century observers commented on the musical and rhythmic gifts of Africans. Olaudah Equiano remembered his people, the Ibos, as "a nation of dancers, musicians, and poets." Thomas Jefferson, raised on a Virginia plantation, wrote that blacks "are more generally gifted than the whites, with accurate ears for tune and time." Many Africans were accomplished players of stringed instruments and drums, and their style featured improvisation and rhythmic complexity, elements that would become prominent in African American music. In America, slaves re-created African instruments such as the banjo, and mastered the European violin and guitar. Fearing that slaves might communicate by code, authorities often outlawed drums. But using bones, spoons, sticks, or simply "patting juba" (slapping thighs), slaves produced elaborate multi-rhythmic patterns.

One of the most important developments of the eighteenth century was the invention of an African American language. An English traveler during the 1770s complained he could not understand Virginia slaves who spoke "a mixed dialect between the Guinea and English." But such a language made it possible for country-born and "saltwater" Africans to communicate. The two most important dialects were Gullah and Geechee, named after two of the African peoples most prominent in the Carolina and Georgia low country, the Golas and Gizzis of the African Windward Coast. These creole languages were a transitional phenomenon, gradually giving way to distinctive forms of black English, although in certain isolated areas,

A Musical Celebration in the Slave Quarters

This anonymous watercolor, discovered in South Carolina, dates from the last quarter of the eighteenth century. It offers a wonderfully detailed depiction of Africans or African Americans gathered together in the slave quarters, celebrating with music. This is clearly a community celebration, involving several families. Seated on the right, two men play instruments that suggest continuity with the African heritage. One plucks on something that looks like a banjo, and indeed, the banjo can be traced back to West Africa. "The instrument proper to them," Thomas Jefferson wrote of his slaves, "is the banjar, which they brought hither from Africa." The other man plays a drum that resembles the gudugudu, a small wooden kettledrum from Nigeria played with two long, thin rawhide sticks.

The dancing man with the carved stick may indicate that this is a wedding ceremony that involves jumping the broom, a custom that may have originated in Africa, although versions of it were practiced in medieval Europe as well. One planter's description of a slave dance seems to fit this scene: the men leading the women in "a slow shuffling gait, edging along by some unseen exertion of the feet, from one side to the other—sometimes courtesying down and remaining in that posture while the edging motion from one side to the other continued." The women, he wrote, "always carried a handkerchief held at arm's length, which was waved in a graceful motion to and fro as she moved." The painting is a tribute to the celebration of life amidst adversity.

• **Why do you think the plantation master is omitted from this painting?**

such as the sea islands of the Carolinas and Georgia, they persisted into the twentieth century.

The Africanization of the South

The African American community often looked to recently arrived Africans for religious leadership and medical magic. Throughout the South, many whites had as much faith in slave conjurers and herb doctors as the slaves did themselves, and slaves won fame for their healing powers. This was one of many ways in which white and black southerners came to share a common culture. Acculturation was by no means a one-way street; English men and women in the South were also being Africanized.

Slaves worked in the kitchens of their masters and thus introduced an African style of cooking into colonial diets already transformed by Indian crops. African American culinary arts are responsible for such southern culinary specialties as barbecue, fried chicken, black-eyed peas, and collard greens. And the liberal African use of red pepper, sesame seeds, and other sharp flavors established the southern preference for highly spiced foods. In Louisiana a combination of African, French, and Indian elements produced a distinguished American regional cuisine, exemplified by gumbos (soups) and jambalayas (stews).

Mutual acculturation was also evident in many aspects of material culture. Southern basket weaving used Indian techniques and African designs. Woodcarving often featured African motifs. African architectural designs featuring high, peaked roofs (to drain off the heat) and broad, shady porches gradually became part of a distinctive southern style. The West African iron-working tradition was evident throughout the South, especially in the ornamentation of the homes of Charles Town and New Orleans.

Even more important were less tangible aspects of culture. Slave mothers nursed white children as well as their own. As one English observer wrote, "each child has its [black] Momma, whose gestures and accent it will necessarily copy, for children, we all know, are imitative beings." In this way many Africanisms passed into the English language of the South: goober (peanut), yam (sweet potato), banjo, okay, tote, buddy. Some linguists have argued that the southern "drawl," evident among both black and white speakers, derived from the incorporation of African intonations of words and syllables.

Violence and Resistance

Slavery was made possible by the threat and reality of violence. The only way to make slaves work, Virginia planter Robert "King" Carter instructed his overseer, was "to make them stand in fear." Humane slave masters like George Washington did not wish to be harsh. He sought, as he wrote it, "tranquility with a certain income." But the tranquility of Mount Vernon rested on the threat of violence. Washington ordered his overseers to carefully monitor the work of the slaves and punish their offenses with regular whippings. Even the most cultured plantation owners thought nothing about floggings of fifty or seventy-five lashes. "Der prayer was answered," sang the Africans of South Carolina, "wid de song of a whip." Some masters were downright sadistic, raping, stabbing, burning, maiming, mutilating, and even castrating their slaves.

Yet African Americans demonstrated a resisting spirit. In their day-to-day existence they often refused to cooperate: they malingered, they mistreated animals and broke tools, they wantonly destroyed the master's property. "Let an hundred men shew him how to hoe, or drive a wheelbarrow," wrote one frustrated planter, "he'll still take the one by the bottom, and the other by the wheel." Flight was another option, and judging from the advertisements placed by masters in colonial newspapers, even the most trusted Africans ran away. "That this slave should run away and attempt getting his liberty, is very alarming," read the notice of one Maryland master in 1755. "He has always been too kindly used" and was "one in whom his master has put great confidence, and depended on him to overlook the rest of the slaves, and he had no kind of provocation to go off." An analysis of hundreds of eighteenth-century advertisements for runaways concludes that 80 percent were young men in their twenties, suggesting that flight was an option mostly exercised by unattached males.

Read the Document
Runaway Notices from the South Carolina Gazette 1732 and 1737 at **www.myhistorylab.com**

Runaways sometimes collected together in isolated and hidden communities called "maroons," from the Spanish word *cimarron*, meaning "wild and untamed." Slaves who escaped from South Carolina or Georgia into Spanish Florida created maroon communities among the Creek Indians there. These mixed African and Indian peoples came to call themselves "Seminoles," a name derived from their pronunciation of "cimarron." Maroons also lay hidden in the backcountry of the Lower South, and although they were less common in the Upper South, there were a number of them in the Great Dismal Swamp, the coastal region between Virginia and North Carolina.

The most direct form of resistance was revolt. The first notable slave uprising of the colonial era occurred in New York City in 1712. Taking an oath of secrecy, twenty-three Africans vowed revenge for what they called the "hard usage" of their masters. They armed themselves with guns, swords, daggers, and hatchets, killed nine colonists, and burned several buildings before being surrounded by the militia. Six of the conspirators committed suicide rather than surrender. Thirteen were hanged, another was starved to death in chains, another broken on the wheel, and three more burned at the stake. In 1741, New York authorities uncovered what they believed was another conspiracy. Thirteen black leaders were burned alive, eighteen more hanged, and eighty sold and shipped off to the West Indies. A family of colonists and a Catholic priest, accused of providing weapons, were also executed.

Fugitive slaves flee through the swamps in Thomas Moran's *Slave Hunt, Dismal Swamp, Virginia* (1862). Many slaves ran away from their masters, and colonial newspapers included notices urging readers to be on the lookout for them. Some fled in groups or collected together in isolated communities called "maroon" colonies, located in inaccessible swamps and woods.

SOURCE: Thomas Moran (American, 1837–1926), *Slave Hunt, Dismal Swamp, Virginia*, 1862. Gift of Laura A. Clubb, 1947.8.44. ©2008 The Philbrook Museum of Art, Inc.,Tulsa, Oklahoma.

A series of small rebellions and rumors of large ones in Virginia during the 1720s culminated in the Chesapeake Rebellion of 1730, the largest slave uprising of the colonial period. Several hundred slaves assembled in Norfolk and Princess Anne counties where they chose commanders for their "insurrection." More than 300 escaped en masse into the Dismal Swamp. Hunted down by Indians in the employ of the colony, their community was soon destroyed. Twenty-nine leaders were executed and the rest were returned to their masters.

In the Lower South, where slaves were a majority of the population, there were isolated but violent uprisings in 1704, 1720, and 1730. In 1738 a series of revolts broke out in South Carolina and Georgia. These prepared the way for the Stono Rebellion of 1739 (see the Introduction), the most violent slave rebellion of the colonial period. In the aftermath of Stono several similar uprisings were quickly crushed by planters. Attributing these revolts to the influence of newly

Read the Document

James Oglethorpe, The Stono Rebellion (1739) at **www.myhistorylab.com**

arrived Africans, colonial officials shut down the slave trade through Charles Town for the next ten years.

Wherever masters held slaves, fears of uprisings persisted. But compared with such slave colonies as Jamaica, Guiana, or Brazil, there were relatively few revolts in North America. The conditions favoring revolt (large African majorities, brutal exploitation with correspondingly low survival rates, little acculturation, and geographic isolation) prevailed only in some areas of the Lower South. Indeed, the very success of African Americans in British North America at establishing families, communities, and a culture of their own inevitably made them less likely to take the risks that rebellions required.

Slavery and the Economics of Empire

The British slave colonies—the sugar plantations of the West Indies, the tobacco plantations of the Chesapeake, and the rice and indigo plantations of the Lower South—accounted for 95 percent of exports from the Americas to Great Britain

Eighteenth-century ships being unloaded of their colonial cargoes on London's Old Custom House Quay. Most of the goods imported into England from the American colonies were produced by slave labor.

SOURCE: Samuel Scott, *Old Custom House Quay* Collection. V&A IMAGES, THE VICTORIA AND ALBERT MUSEUM, LONDON.

from 1714 to the eve of the American Revolution. Although approximately half of all British colonists lived in the northern colonies, that region contributed less than 5 percent of total exports. Moreover, there was the prime economic importance of the slave trade itself, which one eighteenth-century economist described as the "foundation" of the British economy, "the mainspring of the machine which sets every wheel in motion." The labor of African slaves was largely responsible for the economic success of the British Empire in the Americas. New World slavery contributed enormously to the growth and development of the Old World economy. During the eighteenth century slavery was the most dynamic force in the Atlantic economy, responsible for the capital formation that made possible the beginnings of the industrial economy.

Slavery: Foundation of the British Economy

Slavery contributed to the economic development of Great Britain in three principal ways. First, it generated enormous profits. Economic historians estimate that annual profit on invested capital during the eighteenth century averaged 15 percent in the slave trade and 10 percent in plantation agriculture. Some of the first of modern England's great fortunes were made from slavery's miseries.

Profits derived from the triangular trade in slaves, plantation products, and manufactured goods (see Map 4.3) furnished from 21 to 35 percent of Great Britain's fixed capital formation in the eighteenth century. This capital funded the first modern banks and insurance companies and, through loans and investments, found its way into a wide range of economic activities. Merchant capitalists were prominent investors in the expansion of the merchant marine, the improvement of harbors, and the construction of canals.

Second, slave colonies in the Caribbean supplied 69 percent of the raw cotton for British textile mills, the earliest sector of industrial development. The insatiable demand for cotton would eventually lead to the development of the cotton gin and the rise of cotton plantations in the United States (see Chapter 11).

MAP 4.3 Triangular Trade Across the Atlantic The pattern of commerce among Europe, Africa, and the Americas became known as the "triangular trade." Sailors called the voyage of slave ships from Africa to America the "Middle Passage" because it formed the crucial middle section of this trading triangle.

Third, slavery provided an enormous stimulus to the growth of manufacturing by creating a huge colonial market for exports. From 1700 to 1740, the growth in American and African demand for manufactured goods (principally textiles, metal products, and ship's wares) accounted for nearly 70 percent of the expansion of British exports.

The multiplier effects of these activities are best seen in the growth of English ports such as Liverpool and Bristol. There African and American commerce provided employment for ships' crews, dockmen, construction workers, traders, shopkeepers, lawyers, clerks, factory workers, and officials of all ranks down to the humblest employees of the custom house. It was said of Bristol that "there is not a brick in the city but what is cemented with the blood of a slave." In the countryside surrounding Liverpool and elsewhere, capital acquired through slavery was invested in the new industrial methods of producing cotton textiles, the beginning of the Industrial Revolution.

The Politics of Mercantilism

Imperial officials argued that colonies existed solely for the benefit of the mother country. What they principally had in mind was the great wealth produced by slavery. To ensure that this wealth benefited their own nation-state, imperialists created a system of regulations that became known as "mercantilism." The essence of mercantilist policy was the political control of the economy by the

New England artist John Greenwood painted this satirical image of New England sea captains drinking and carousing in the Caribbean. By the early eighteenth century, New England merchant traders had become important participants in the traffic in slaves and sugar to and from the West Indies. Northern ports thus became important pivots in the expanding commercial network linking slave plantations with Atlantic markets.

SOURCE: John Greenwood, *Sea Captains Carousing in Surinam*, 1758. Oil on bed ticking, 95.9 × 191.1 cm. Saint Louis Art Museum, Museum Purchase.

state. First advanced during the seventeenth-century reign of Louis XIV of France, mercantilist politics were most successfully applied in the eighteenth century by Great Britain. The monarchy and Parliament established a uniform national monetary system, regulated wages, subsidized agriculture and manufacturing, and protected themselves from foreign competition by erecting tariff barriers. Britain also sought to organize and control colonial trade to the maximum advantage of its own shippers, merchants, manufacturers, and bureaucrats.

The mercantilists viewed the economy as a "zero-sum game," in which total economic gains were equal to total losses. The essence of the competition between states, the mercantilists argued, was the struggle to acquire and hoard the fixed amount of wealth that existed in the world. The nation that accumulated the largest treasure of gold and silver would be the most powerful.

British Colonial Regulation

The Spanish monarchy created the Casa de Contratación, the first state trading monopoly, to manage the commerce of its empire in the sixteenth century. It was widely emulated by other powers. The Dutch East Indies Company, the French Company of the Indies, the English East India Company, the Hudson's Bay Company, and the Royal African Company were all state-sponsored trading monopolies.

English manufacturers complained that the nation's trading monopolies too frequently carried foreign (particularly Dutch) products to colonial markets, ignoring English domestic industry. Parliament reacted by passing a series of Navigation Acts between 1651 and 1696, creating the legal and institutional structure of Britain's eighteenth-century colonial system. The acts defined the colonies as both suppliers of raw materials and as markets for English manufactured goods. Merchants from other nations were forbidden from doing business in the English colonies, and colonial commodities were required to be transported in English vessels.

The regulations specified a list of "enumerated commodities" that could be shipped to England only. Those included the products of the southern slave colonies (sugar, molasses, rum, tobacco, rice, and indigo), those of the northern Indian trade (furs, pelts, and skins), and those essential for supplying the shipping industry (pine masts, tar, pitch, resin, and turpentine). The bulk of these products was not destined for English consumption but was exported elsewhere at great profit.

England also placed limitations on colonial enterprises that might compete with those at home. A series of enactments—including the Wool Act of 1699, the Hat Act of 1732, and the Iron Act of 1750—forbade the manufacture of those products in the colonies. Moreover, colonial assemblies were forbidden to impose tariffs on

English imports as a way to protect colonial industries. Banking was disallowed, local coinage prohibited, and the export of coin from England forbidden.

Robert Walpole, prime minister of the king's government from 1721 to 1742, argued that it made little sense to tamper with such a prosperous system. Walpole pursued a policy later characterized as "salutary neglect." Any colonial rules and regulations deemed contrary to good business practice were simply ignored and not enforced. Between 1700 and 1760 the quantity of goods exported from the colonies to the mother country rose 165 percent, while imports from Britain to North America increased by more than 400 percent. In part because of the lax enforcement, but mostly because the system operated to the profit of colonial merchants, colonists complained very little about the operation of the mercantilist system before the 1760s. It seemed that everyone was getting rich off the labor of slaves—except the slaves, of course.

Wars for Empire

During the 1720s and 1730s, Prime Minister Walpole steered Great Britain away from war with other mercantilist powers. Earlier in the century, a war pitting Great Britain against Spain and France (known as the War of the Spanish Succession in Europe, Queen Anne's War in America) had ended in a significant British victory, and in the Peace of Utrecht in 1713 it gained a good deal. France was forced to cede Acadia, Newfoundland, and Hudson Bay to Great Britain in exchange for guarantees of security for the French-speaking residents of those provinces. Spain was forced to open its American ports to British traders, who were also granted the exclusive right to supply slaves to the Spanish colonies.

Despite continuing tensions with Spain and France, Walpole saw considerable advantages in peace. The Spanish empire in America lay completely open to British traders, he argued. "Spain herself is no more than the canal through which all these [colonial] treasures are conveyed over the rest of Europe." For more than fifteen years Walpole prevailed over militant factions in the House of Commons that demanded complete elimination of Spanish competition in the Americas. But in 1739, at their urging, a one-eared sea captain by the name of Robert Jenkins testified about the indignities suffered by British merchant sailors at the hands of Spanish authorities in Caribbean ports. In a dramatic flourish, Jenkins produced a dried and withered ear, which he claimed the Spanish had cut from his head. The public outrage that followed forced Walpole to agree to a war of Caribbean conquest known as the War of Jenkins's Ear. "They now ring the bells," Walpole declared, "but they will soon wring their hands."

Walpole was right. While the Royal Navy conducted punitive raids against Spanish ports in the Caribbean, Governor Oglethorpe of Georgia raised a regiment of troops, invaded Florida, and besieged St. Augustine. The siege went on for six months, but Oglethorpe failed to break the town's defenses. Meanwhile, a regiment of 3,000 volunteers from the colonies joined forces with the British fleet in the Caribbean. Their attempt to seize Panama and Cuba ended in complete disaster. The British underestimated Spanish strength and the troops were ravaged by yellow fever and other diseases. The only success of the war for the British came when the Georgia militia blocked a Spanish invasion from Florida in 1742. The war ended with no territorial gains on either side.

The war with Spain merged into a war with France that began in 1744. Known as King George's War in America (the War of the Austrian Succession in Europe), it began with a French invasion of their former colony of Acadia, which the British had renamed Nova Scotia. Indian and Canadian raids again devastated the border towns of New England and New York, and hundreds of British subjects were killed or captured. In return, New England forces attacked and conquered the great French fortress at Louisbourg. But Great Britain fared less well in the European fighting, and the war ended in stalemate with the return of all territory.

The Colonial Economy

Despite the resumption of warfare, the colonial economy continued to operate to the great benefit of planters, merchants, and white colonists in general. Southern slave owners made healthy profits on the sale of their commodities. They enjoyed a protected market in which competing goods from outside the empire were heavily taxed. Planters found themselves with steadily increasing purchasing power. Pennsylvania, New York, and New England, and increasingly the Chesapeake as well, produced grain, flour, meat, and dairy products. None of these was included in the list of enumerated goods and could be sold freely abroad. Most of this trade was carried in New England ships.

The greatest benefits for the port cities of the North came from their commercial relationship to the slave colonies (see Figure 4.3). In addition to entering the slave trade itself, New England merchants began to make inroads into the export trade of the West Indian colonies. It was in the Caribbean that northern merchants most blatantly ignored mercantilist laws. In violation of Spanish, French, and Dutch regulations prohibiting foreign trade, New Englanders traded foodstuffs for sugar in foreign colonies. By 1750, more than sixty distilleries in Massachusetts were exporting more than 2 million gallons of rum, most of it produced from molasses obtained illegally. Because the restrictive rules and regulations enacted by Britain for its colonies were not enforced, the

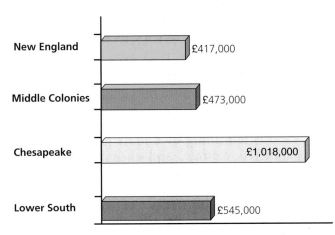

FIGURE 4.3 Value of Colonial Exports by Region, Annual Average, 1768–72 With tobacco, rice, grain, and indigo, the Chesapeake and Lower South accounted for nearly two-thirds of colonial exports in the years preceding the American Revolution.

SOURCE: *Shipping, Maritime Trade and the Economic Development of Colonial America*, James J. Shepherd, and Gary M. Walton, Eds. Copyright © 1972 Cambridge University Press. Reprinted with the permission of Cambridge University Press.

merchants and manufacturers of the port cities of the North prospered.

By the mid-eighteenth century, the Chesapeake and Lower South regions were major exporters of tobacco, rice, and indigo to Europe, and the middle colonies were major exporters of grain. The carrying trade in the products of slave labor made it possible for the northern and middle colonies to earn the income necessary to purchase British imports despite the lack of valuable products from their own regions. Gradually, the commercial economies of the Northeast and the South were becoming integrated. Like London, Liverpool, and Bristol—though on a smaller scale—the port cities of the North became pivots in the expanding trade network linking slave plantations with Atlantic markets. This trade provided northern merchants with the capital that financed commercial growth and development in their cities and the surrounding countryside. Slavery thus contributed to the growth of a score of northern port cities, forming an indirect but essential part of their economies.

Slavery, Prosperity, and Freedom

The prosperity of the eighteenth-century plantation economy thus improved the living conditions for the residents of northern cities as well as for a large segment of the white population of the South, providing them with the opportunity for a kind of freedom unknown in the previous century. The price of this prosperity and freedom, however, was the enslavement and exploitation of millions of Africans and African Americans. Freedom for white men based on the enslavement of black people is one of the most glaring contradictions in American history.

The Social Structure of the Slave Colonies

Slavery produced a highly stratified class society. At the summit of power stood an elite of wealthy planters who held more than half the cultivated land and over 60 percent of the wealth. Although there was no formal colonial aristocracy—no royal recognition of social rank—the landed elite of the slave colonies sought to present itself as one. Binding themselves together through strategic marriage alliances and carefully crafted business dealings; dressing themselves in silk, lace, and powdered wigs; and staging elaborate public rituals designed to awe common folk and slaves, they made up what one historian calls an "interlocking directorate."

The typical wealthy Virginia planter of the eighteenth century lived in a Tidewater county, owned several thousand acres of prime farmland and more than a hundred slaves, resided in a luxurious plantation mansion, and possessed an estate valued at more than £10,000. Elected to the House of Burgesses and forming the group from which the magistrates and counselors of the colony were chosen, these "first families of Virginia"—the Carters, Harrisons, Lees, Fitzhughs, Washingtons, Randolphs, and others—constituted a self-perpetuating governing class. A similar elite ruled the Lower South, although wealthy landowners spent little time on their plantations. They lived instead in fashionable Charles Town, where they made up a close-knit group who controlled the colonial government. "They live in as high a style here, I believe, as any part of the world," a visitor wrote.

A considerable distance separated this elite from typical southern landowners. About half the adult white males were small planters and farmers. But while the gap between rich and middling colonists grew larger during the eighteenth century, the prosperity of the plantation economy created generally favorable conditions for the landowning class as a whole. Slave ownership, for example, became widespread among this group during the eighteenth century. In Virginia at midcentury, 45 percent of heads of household held one to four slaves and even poorer farmers kept one or two.

Despite the prosperity that accompanied slavery, however, a substantial number of white colonists owned no land or slaves at all. Some rented land or worked as tenant farmers, some hired out as overseers or farm workers, and still others were indentured servants. Throughout the plantation region, landless men constituted about 40 percent of the population. A New England visitor found a "much greater disparity between the rich and poor in Virginia" than at home.

White Skin Privilege

But all the white colonists of eighteenth-century North America shared the privileged status of their color. In the early seventeenth century, there had been more diversity in views about race. For some, black skin was thought to be a sign of God's curse. "The blackness of the Negroes," one Englishman argued, "proceedeth of some natural infection." But not everyone shared those views. "I can't think there is any intrinsic value in one colour more than another," another Englishman remarked, "nor that white is better than black, only we think it so because we are so."

As slavery became increasingly important, however, Virginia officials took considerable care to create legal distinctions between the status of colonists and that of Africans. Beginning in 1670, free Africans were prohibited from owning Christian servants. Ten years later, another law declared that any African, free or slave, who struck a Christian would receive thirty lashes on his bare back. One of the most important measures was designed to suppress intimate interracial contacts between white servants and enslaved Africans. A 1691 act "for prevention of that abominable mixture and spurious issue which hereafter may encrease in this dominion" established severe penalties for interracial sexual relationships.

Such penalties were rarely applied to masters who had sexual relations with their slave women. Because by law the children of slave mothers were born into bondage, many plantations included light-skinned slaves who were the masters' kin. For many years it was rumored that Thomas Jefferson was the father of several children by his slave Sally Hemings. These claims were rejected by most historians. But in the late twentieth century a study of a descendant's DNA indicated the "high probability," in the words of an official report, that Jefferson indeed was the father. Hemings herself was the slave child of Jefferson's father-in-law and thus the half sister of Jefferson's deceased wife. Less well known is the fact that at George Washington's Mount Vernon, the household slave Ann Dandridge was the daughter of Martha Washington's father. Hemings and Dandridge may have been kin to wealthy planters and future presidents, but they spent their entire lives as slaves. Slavery, as one historian has written, "required certain evasions, denials, and psychological cruelties."

RUN away from the subscriber in *Albemarle*, a Mulatto slave called *Sandy*, about 35 years of age, his stature is rather low, inclining to corpulence, and his complexion light; he is a shoemaker by trade, in which he uses his left hand principally, can do coarse carpenters work, and is something of a horse jockey; he is greatly addicted to drink, and when drunk is insolent and disorderly, in his conversation he swears much, and in his behaviour is artful and knavish. He took with him a white horse, much scarred with traces, of which it is expected he will endeavour to dispose; he also carried his shoemakers tools, and will probably endeavour to get employment that way. Whoever conveys the said slave to me, in *Albemarle*, shall have 40 s. reward, if taken up within the county, 4 l. if elsewhere within the colony, and 10 l. if in any other colony, from
THOMAS JEFFERSON.

Thomas Jefferson placed this advertisement in the *Virginia Gazette* on September 14, 1769. Americans need to seriously consider the historical relationship between the prosperity and freedom of white people and the oppression and exploitation of Africans and African Americans.

Relationships between free whites and enslaved blacks produced a large mixed-ancestry group known as mulattoes. The majority of them were slaves. A minority, the children of European women and African men, were free. According to a Maryland census of 1755, more than 60 percent of the mulattoes of that colony were slaves. But mulattoes also made up three-quarters of the small free African American population. This group, numbering about 4,000 in the 1770s, was denied the right to vote, to hold office, or to testify in court—all on the basis of racial background. Denied the status of citizenship enjoyed by even the poorest white men, free blacks were an outcast group who raised the status of white colonials by contrast. Racial distinctions were a constant reminder of the freedom of white colonists and the debasement of all blacks, slave or free.

Racism set up a wall of contempt between colonists and African Americans. Jefferson was a believer in "the real distinctions which nature has made" between the races. "In memory they are equal to the whites," he wrote of his slaves, but "in reason much inferior." He gave no consideration to the argument of freed slave Olaudah Equiano that "slavery debases the mind." Jefferson was on firmer ground when he argued that the two peoples were divided by "deep rooted prejudices entertained by the whites" and

••• Read the Document

Exploring America: Racism in American History at **www.myhistorylab.com**

CHRONOLOGY

1441	African slaves first brought to Portugal
1619	First Africans brought to Virginia
1655	English seize Jamaica
1662	Virginia law makes slavery hereditary
1672	Royal African Company organized
1691	Virginia prohibits interracial sexual contact
1698	Britain opens the slave trade to all its merchants
1699	Spanish declare Florida a refuge for escaped slaves
1702	South Carolinians burn St. Augustine
1705	Virginia Slave Code established
1706	French and Spanish navies bombard Charles Town
1710	English capture Port Royal in Acadia
1712	Slave uprising in New York City
1713	Peace of Utrecht
1721–48	Robert Walpole leads British cabinet
1729	Natchez Rebellion in French Louisiana
1739	Stono Rebellion in South Carolina
1739–43	War of Jenkins's Ear
1741	Africans executed in New York for conspiracy
1744–48	King George's War
1752	Georgia officially opened to slavery
1770s	Peak period of the English colonies' slave trade
1808	Importation of slaves into the United States ends

"ten thousand recollections, by the blacks, of the injuries they have sustained." Perhaps he knew of these feelings from his long relationship with Sally Hemings. "I tremble for my country when I reflect that God is just," Jefferson concluded in a deservedly famous discussion of slavery and "that his justice cannot sleep forever."

Conclusion

During the eighteenth century, hundreds of thousands of Africans were kidnapped from their homes, marched to the African coast, and packed into ships for up to three months before arriving in British North America. They provided the labor that made colonialism profitable. Southern planters, northern merchants, and especially British traders and capitalists benefited greatly from the commerce in slave-produced crops. That prosperity trickled down to the ordinary white colonists of British North America. Mercantilism was a system designed to channel colonial wealth produced by slaves to the nation-state, but as long as profits remained high, the British tended to wink at colonists' violations of mercantilist regulations. In short, slavery was fundamental to the operation of the British empire in North America.

Review Questions

1. Trace the development of the system of slavery and discuss the way it became entrenched in the Americas.

2. Describe the effects of the slave trade both on enslaved Africans and on the economic and political life of Africa.

3. Describe the process of acculturation involved in becoming an African American. In what ways did slaves "Africanize" the South?

4. Explain the connection between the institution of slavery and the building of a commercial empire.

5. In what ways did colonial policy encourage the growth of racism?

Recommended Reading

Ira Berlin, *Many Thousands Gone: The First Two Centuries of Slavery in North America* (1998). A history of colonial slavery with attention to the differences between the regions of the Chesapeake, the Lower South,

Louisiana, and the North. Emphasizes the distinction between slave societies and societies with slaves.

Michael Craton, *Sinews of Empire: A Short History of British Slavery* (1974). An introduction to the British mercantilist system that emphasizes the importance of slavery. Includes a comparison of the mainland colonies with the Caribbean.

Annette Gordon-Reed, *The Hemingses of Monticello: An American Family* (2008). A prize-winning history of the intimate connections between a family of planters and a family of slaves.

Winthrop D. Jordan, *White over Black: American Attitudes Toward the Negro, 1550–1812* (1968). Remains the best and most comprehensive history of racial attitudes. A searching examination of British and American literature, folklore, and history.

Herbert S. Klein, *The Atlantic Slave Trade* (1999). A new and important synthesis of the most recent studies of the slave trade, covering the social and cultural effects of the trade, especially for Africans.

Philip D. Morgan, *Slave Counterpoint: Black Culture in the Eighteenth-Century Chesapeake and Lowcountry* (1998). A comprehensive and detailed examination of cultural forms and ways of life in the two regions that leaves hardly a stone unturned.

Anthony S. Parent Jr., *Foul Means: The Formation of a Slave Society in Virginia, 1660–1740* (2003). A vivid and disturbing portrayal of colonial Virginia's patriarchal and violent character. An analysis of the apparatus of oppression from the planters' seizure of land to the efforts to keep poor whites and slaves apart.

Marcus Rediker, *The Slave Ship: A Human History* (2007). A powerful history of the Atlantic slave trade, focusing on the relationships of crew and slaves during the terror-filled and deadly journey between the coasts of Africa and America.

Walter Rodney, *How Europe Underdeveloped Africa* (1974). This highly influential book traces the relationship between Europe and Africa from the fifteenth to the twentieth centuries, and demonstrates how Europe's industrialization became Africa's impoverishment.

Mechal Sobel, *The World They Made Together: Black and White Values in Eighteenth-Century Virginia* (1987). Demonstrates the ways in which both Africans and Europeans shaped the formation of American values, perceptions, and identities.

Ian K. Steele, *Warpaths: Invasions of North America* (1994). A new synthesis of the colonial wars from the sixteenth to the eighteenth centuries that places Indians as well as empires at the center of the action.

Henry Wiencek, *Imperfect God: George Washington, His Slaves, and the Creation of America* (2003). The story of Washington as planter and slave master, a man tormented by the contradictions.

myhistorylab Connections

PEARSON

Reinforce what you learned in this chapter by studying the many documents, images, maps, review tools, and videos available at www.myhistorylab.com.

Read and Review

✓• Study and Review Chapter 4

•••• Read the Document

Alexander Falconbridge, The African Slave Trade (1788)

Olaudah Equiano, The Middle Passage (1788)

Of the Servants and Slaves in Virginia (1705)

James Oglethorpe, Establishing the Colony of Georgia (1733)

Runaway Notices from the South Carolina Gazette, (1732 and 1737)

James Oglethorpe, The Stono Rebellion (1739)

👁• See the Map African Slave Trade, 1500–1870

Research and Explore

•••• Read the Document

Exploring America: Racism in American History

Profiles
Olaudah Equiano
John Woolman

Whose History Is It?: The Living Legacy of Slavery

History Bookshelf: Olaudah Equiano, The Interesting Narrative of the Life of Olaudah Equiano (1791)

Watson and the Shark: Reading the Representation of Race

((•• Hear the Audio

"Ghana: Ewe-Atsiagbekor" from Roots of Black Music in America

Phillis Wheatley, On Being Brought from Africa to America

((•• Hear the **Audio**

Hear the audio files for Chapter 4 at
www.myhistorylab.com.

5

Chapter 5
((•— Hear the Audio
Chapter 5 at www.myhistorylab.com

The Cultures
of Colonial North America

1700–1780

CHAPTER OUTLINE

The Old State House, historic Philadelphia, Pennsylvania in the late 1700s. Hand colored engraving. North Wind Pictures.

The Revival of Religion and Community in Northampton

Jonathan Edwards, minister of the Puritan church in Northampton, a rural town on the Connecticut River in western Massachusetts, rose before his congregation and began to preach. His words were frightening: "God will crush you under his feet without mercy, He will crush out your blood and make it fly, and it shall be sprinkled on His garments." Such torments would continue for "millions of millions of ages," and there could be no hope of relief from hell's fires. "It would be no wonder if some persons, that now sit here in some seats of this meeting house in health, quiet and secure, should be there before tomorrow morning." The people needed to "have their hearts touched," Edwards believed, and he was gratified by their response to his

sermon. "It was in the latter part of December 1734," he wrote, "that the Spirit of God began extraordinarily to set in, and wonderfully to work among us."

"Before the sermon was done," one Northampton parishioner later recalled, "there was a great moaning and crying through the whole house—What shall I do to be saved?—I am going to Hell!—Oh what shall I do for Christ?" Sarah Edwards, the minister's wife, lost "all ability to stand or speak," sometimes jerking involuntarily. In the height of her ecstasy, her husband wrote, her "soul dwelt on high, and was lost in God, and seemed almost to

AMERICAN Communities

leave the body." Religious fervor swept through the community, and church membership increased. A few years later an even greater revival known as the Great Awakening swept through all the colonies and plunged Northampton into turmoil once again. Important underlying issues prepared the ground for these religious revivals. They reflected the tensions that had arisen in the maturing communities of the colonies in which frontier opportunity was giving way to class inequity.

Founded in 1654 on the site of an Algonquian village, Northampton had grown from the original 50 households to more than 200 by the time of the 1734 revival. The last of the community's land had been parceled out to its residents. With the French and their Indian allies barring movement northward, and the colony of New York to the west, there was little opportunity for young men. Few could afford to buy land at the high market prices, so they had to rely on gifts or bequests from their fathers. Meanwhile, a small elite of well-to-do families, known as the "River Gods," controlled a disproportionately large share of local real estate. From their ranks came the majority of the officials of local and county government, as well as the ministers and elders of the Puritan congregations.

By the time Edwards became pastor in 1729, the authority and influence of the church had declined greatly from the heyday of Puritan power in the seventeenth century. In those early days, church and community had been one, but as Northampton's leaders devoted their energies to the pursuit of wealth, the fires of religious enthusiasm dimmed. The congregation adopted rules allowing church membership without evidence of a conversion experience. Some families simply fell away. The congregation built a new meetinghouse, scrapping the old seating plan in which people were sorted by age and sex in favor of a new one ranking families according to wealth. It was an important symbol of change. The Northampton community, Edwards believed, had been divided into "two parties," the rich and the envious.

Many of the town's young people faced a bleak future. The farm household was the most important economic unit, and the tight supply of real estate meant that most couples were forced to postpone marriage until they were in their late twenties. In the meantime they continued to live with their parents, and there were growing discipline problems in Northampton homes. Restless young people of both sexes began to meet together at nightly "frolics," and pastor Edwards

issued a warning about the "growth of uncleanness that has been in the land."

This group became Edwards's special constituency. The revival of religious enthusiasm began during special services he directed at them, but it was the same everywhere throughout the British colonies. Young people in their early twenties played the most important role in the movement to restore religious enthusiasm. Reversing a long-standing tendency for women to be more active in the church, young men predominated among the reborn. Edwards and other revival preachers called for a return to the Calvinist traditions of the Puritan faith, criticizing what they saw as the growing materialism, joining the rising generation in questioning the order of the world into which they had been born.

The revival of religion that shook communities throughout the British colonies in the mid-eighteenth century was one of the first unifying events in American history. Thousands of people experienced conversion, new sects and churches sprang up, and old ones split into opposing factions. The followers of one enthusiastic preacher burned their wigs, jewelry, and fine clothes in a bonfire, around which they marched, chanting curses at their opponents, whose religious writings they tossed into the flames. In the town of South Hadley, near Northampton, the congregation voted to dismiss their minister, who lacked the emotional fire they desired in a preacher. When he refused to vacate his pulpit they pulled him down, roughed him up, and threw him out the church door. Such episodes spoke clearly of the popular passions aroused during the Awakening. According to one minister: "Multitudes were seriously, soberly, and solemnly out of their wits."

The disaffection of young people with the social and economic conditions of the mid-eighteenth century created the conditions for the Great Awakening, but the revival remained a religious event. The social order in Northampton was challenged, but it remained intact. The "River Gods" had always been uncomfortable with the message Edwards preached, and when the fervor died down, as it inevitably did, they succeeded in voting him out. In the meantime Edwards had begun to produce a series of creative religious and theological writings in which he struggled to harmonize sixteenth-century Calvinism with the eighteenth-century philosophy of the Enlightenment. But this meant little to men and women seeking to reestablish tranquility in their community. Edwards spent several years ministering to a congregation

1. What were the similarities and differences among eighteenth-century Spanish, French, and British colonies?

2. What was the impact on British culture of increasing European immigration?

3. In what ways did Indian America change as a result of contact with European customs and lifeways?

4. What were the patterns of work and class in eighteenth-century North America?

5. How did tension between Enlightenment thought and traditional culture lead to the Great Awakening?

FOCUS Questions

1700–1780

of Christian "praying Indians" in the Berkshire hills on the Massachusetts frontier, then accepted a call to become president of the College of New Jersey (which later would become Princeton University). The turmoil in Northampton subsided, yet the tensions remained.

Rising tensions were typical in many of the colonial communities of British North America. Things went on much as they had in the French and Spanish colonies. But in British colonial communities a growing population meant narrowing opportunities for the ownership of local land, creating strong pressure for expansion into Indian homelands. Expanding economies led to increasing class inequality. Meanwhile, new secular and rationalist ways of thinking challenged traditional values. Simmering social conflict set the stage for religious and cultural turmoil.

Northampton, MA

AMERICAN Communities

North American Regions

American history too often is written as if only the British colonists really mattered. It is an error residents of the British colonies could not afford to make. Most critically, there was Indian America. In the mid-eighteenth century Indian peoples retained their majority in North America (see Table 5.1). From the fringes of colonial societies to the native heart of the continent, from the eastern foothills of the Appalachians where Reverend Edwards preached to the western flank of the Sierra Nevada in California, thousands of native communities, despite being deeply affected by the spread of colonial cultures, remained firmly in control of their homelands.

Neither could British colonists afford to ignore their colonial competitors. North and west of the English-speaking enclaves along the Atlantic coast, French-speaking communities were clustered along the St. Lawrence and scattered down the Mississippi to the Gulf of Mexico. South and west, isolated Spanish-speaking communities of the northern Spanish borderlands stretched from Florida to Texas and on to California. There were impressive similarities

TABLE 5.1

Population of North America in 1750

Region	Population
New France	70,000
New England	400,000
New York	100,000
Pennsylvania	230,000
Chesapeake	390,000
Lower South	100,000
Backcountry	100,000
Northern New Spain	20,000
Indian America	1,500,000
TOTAL	2,910,000

among these colonial communities, representing a continuation in the New World of Old World traditions and beliefs, customs, and institutions. But there was also a general pattern of European adaptation to American conditions (see Map 5.1).

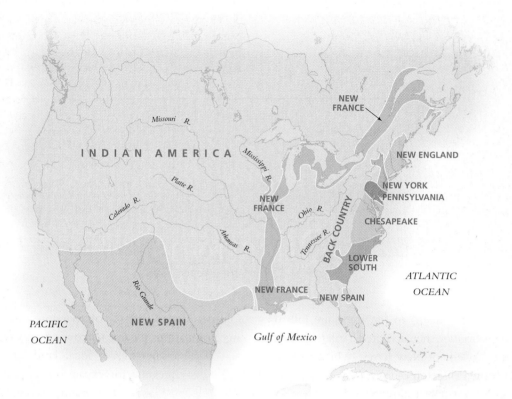

MAP 5.1 Regions in Eighteenth-Century North America By the middle of the eighteenth century, European colonists had established a number of distinctive colonial regions in North America. The northern periphery of New Spain, the oldest and most prosperous European colony, stretched from Baja California to eastern Texas, then jumped to the settlements on the northern end of the Florida peninsula; cattle ranching was the dominant way of life in this thinly populated region. New France was like a great crescent, extending from the plantation communities along the Mississippi near New Orleans to the French colonial communities along the St. Lawrence; in between were isolated settlements and forts connected only by the extensive French trading network.

Indian America

After two centuries of European colonization, Indian peoples had adapted and changed. They incorporated firearms and metal tools and learned to build their homes of logs. They participated enthusiastically in the fur trade. But in the process they became dependent on European commerce. "The clothes we wear, we cannot make ourselves, they are made for us," a Cherokee chief lamented. "We cannot make our guns. Every necessary thing in life we must have from the White People."

Yet Indian peoples continued to assert a proud independence and demonstrated considerable skill in playing colonial powers against each other. In 1701 the Iroquois, allies of the British, signed a treaty of neutrality with the French. Exploiting the vulnerabilities of these two powers, the Iroquois Confederacy became a major power broker during the first half of the eighteenth century. In the Lower South native peoples found similar room to maneuver between the competing interests of Britain, France, and Spain.

But native leaders confronted enormous difficulties. In the eastern portion of the continent the preeminent concern was the tremendous growth of the population in the British colonies and especially the movement of settlers westward. In the 1730s and 1740s Pennsylvania abandoned its tradition of fair dealing and perpetrated a series of fraudulent seizures of western lands from the Delawares. It was a disturbing sign of things to come.

Meanwhile, Indian communities continued to suffer from long-term population decline as the result of epidemic Old World diseases. Historical demographers estimate that from a high of 7 to 10 million north of Mexico in 1500, the native population had fallen to around a million by 1800. At some point in the mid-eighteenth century the colonial population became the majority. Population loss did not affect all Indian tribes equally, however. Native peoples with a century or more of colonial contact and interaction had lost 50 percent or more of their numbers, but most Indian societies in the interior had yet to be struck by the epidemics.

A portrait of the Delaware chief Tishcohan by Gustavus Hesselius, painted in 1735. In his purse of chipmunk hide is a clay pipe, a common item of the Indian trade. Tishcohan was one of the Delaware leaders forced by Pennsylvania authorities into signing a fraudulent land deal that reversed that colony's history of fair dealing with Indians over land. He moved west to the Ohio River as settlers poured into his former homeland.

SOURCE: Gustavus Hesselius, *Tishcohan*, Native American Portrait, 1735. Courtesy of the Historical Society of Pennsylvania Collection, Atwater Kent Museum of Philadelphia.

Other changes offered opportunity. By the early eighteenth century, Indians on the southern fringe of the Great Plains had acquired horses from Spanish colonists in New Mexico (see Map 5.2). Horses enabled Indian hunters to exploit the buffalo herds much more efficiently, and on the basis of this more productive economy peoples

●●●—[Read the Document
Exploring America:
America and the Horse at
www.myhistorylab.com

like the Comanches, Cheyennes, and Sioux built distinctive and elaborate nomadic cultures. Great numbers of Indian peoples moved onto the plains during the eighteenth century, pulled by this new way of life and pushed by colonial invasions and disruptions radiating southwest from Canada and north from the Spanish borderlands. The invention of nomadic Plains Indian culture was another of the dramatic cultural innovations of the eighteenth century. The mounted Plains Indian, so often used as a symbol of native America, was actually a product of the colonial era.

The Spanish Borderlands

In the mid-eighteenth century the region now known as the Sunbelt formed the periphery of the largest and most prosperous European colony on the North American continent,

the viceroyalty of New Spain, with a population of approximately 1 million Spanish-speaking inhabitants and 2 million Indians. Mexico City, the administrative capital of New Spain, was the most sophisticated city in the Western Hemisphere, the location of one of the world's great universities, with broad avenues and spectacular architecture. New Spain's northern provinces of Florida, Texas, New Mexico, and California, however, were far removed from this sophistication. Officials who oversaw these colonies thought of them as buffer zones, protecting New Spain from the expanding empires of Spain's rivals. Compared to the dynamic changes going on in the English colonies, society in the Spanish borderland was relatively static.

In Florida, the oldest of the European colonies in North America, fierce fighting with the British and their Indian allies had reduced the Spanish presence to little more than the forts of St. Augustine on the Atlantic and Pensacola on the Gulf of Mexico, each surrounded by small colonized territories populated with the families of Spanish troops. In their weakened condition, the Spanish had no choice but to establish cooperative relations with the Creek

MAP 5.2 Growing Use of the Horse by Plains Indians In the seventeenth and eighteenth centuries, Spanish settlers introduced horses into their New Mexican colony. Through trading and raiding, horses spread northward in streams both west and east of the Rocky Mountains. The horse, whose genetic ancestor had been native to the American continent in pre-Archaic times, offered the Indian peoples of the Great Plains the opportunity to create a distinctive hunting and warrior culture.

A mounted Soldado de Cuera (Leather-Coated Soldier), a watercolor by Ramón de Murillo, c. 1803. Thick leather coats offered protection from Indian arrows for the cavalry posted to the northern frontiers of eighteenth-century New Spain.

and Seminole Indians who dominated the region, as well as hundreds of African American runaways who fled to Florida. In 1750 Florida included a growing mestizo population and a considerable number of free African Americans and Hispanicized Indians from the old missions.

Nearly 2,000 miles to the west, New Mexico was similarly isolated from the mainstream of New Spain. In 1750 New Mexico included some 20,000 Pueblo Indians (their numbers greatly reduced by disease) and perhaps 10,000 mestizo colonists. The prosperity of these colonists, who supported themselves with subsistence agriculture, was severely limited by a restrictive colonial economic policy that required them to exchange their wool, pottery, and buffalo hides for imported goods at unfavorable rates. But unlike the population of Florida, that of colonial New Mexico was gradually expanding, as settlers left the original colonial outposts along the upper Rio Grande to follow the valleys and streams leading north and east.

Concerned about the expansion of other colonial empires, the Spanish founded several new northern outposts in the eighteenth century. French activity in the Mississippi Valley prompted authorities to establish a number of military posts or presidios on the fringes of Louisiana and in 1716 to begin the construction of a

string of Franciscan missions among the Indian peoples of Texas. By 1750 the settlement of San Antonio had become the center of a developing frontier province known as Tejas (Texas). New colonial outposts were also founded west of New Mexico in what is today southern Arizona. In the 1690s, Jesuit missionaries built missions among the desert Indians of the lower Colorado River and Gila River Valleys and introduced cattle herding, which remained the dominant economic activity for the next two centuries.

In 1769, acting on rumors of Russian expansion in the north Pacific (for a discussion of Russian America, see Chapter 9), officials in Mexico City ordered Gaspar de Portolá, governor of what is today Baja California, to establish a Spanish presence along the Pacific coast to the north. With Portolá were Franciscan missionaries led by Junípero Serra, president of the missions in Baja. At the harbor of San Diego their company, composed of some 200 men, founded the first mission and presidio in present-day California. Over the next fifty years the number of California settlements grew to include twenty-one missions and a half-dozen presidios and pueblos (towns), including Los Angeles, founded in 1781 by a group of mestizo pioneers. By the end of the century Los Angeles, with a population of only 300, was California's largest settlement.

The Spanish plan for California called for converting the natives to Catholicism, subjecting them to the rule of the crown, and putting them to work raising the subsistence necessary for a small civil and military establishment that would hold the province against colonial rivals. The first contacts between Franciscans and natives were not encouraging. "What is it you seek here," a chief and his entourage of warriors shouted at the missionaries. "Get out of our country!" But numerous native families were attracted by offerings of food and clothing, by new tools and crafts, and by fascination with the spiritual power of the newcomers. Gradually the Spanish built a flourishing local economy based on irrigated farming and livestock raising. Mission San Gabriel, near the pueblo of Los Angeles, was the most prosperous, with large vineyards and orchards that produced wine and brandy. Indian workers also constructed the adobe and stone churches, built on Spanish and Moorish patterns, whose ruins later came to symbolize California's colonial society.

Indians were not forced to join the missions, but once they did so they were not permitted to leave. The Franciscan missionaries resorted to cruel and sometimes violent means of controlling their Indian subjects, including shackles, solitary confinement, and whipping posts. Resistance developed early. In 1775, the natives at San Diego rose up and killed several priests, and over the years several other missions experienced similar revolts. But Spanish soldiers suppressed the uprisings. Another form of protest was flight. Soldiers hunted down the runaways and brought many back. Aggressive tribes in the hills and deserts, however, often proved even more threatening than the Spanish, so many Indians remained at the missions despite the harsh discipline. Overwork, inadequate nutrition, overcrowding, poor sanitation, and epidemic disease contributed to death rates that exceeded birthrates. During the period of the mission system, the native population of coastal California fell by 74 percent.

Throughout the Spanish borderlands the Catholic Church played a dominant role in community life. Religion was no private affair but a deadly serious business dividing nations into warring camps, and the Spanish considered themselves the special protectors of the traditions of Rome. The object of colonization, one colonial promoter wrote in 1584, was "enlarging the glorious gospel of Christ, and leading the infinite multitudes of these simple people that are in error into the right and perfect way of salvation." Although these were the words of the English imperialist Richard Hakluyt, they could as easily have come from a Jesuit missionary in New France or the Spanish padres Kino or Serra. There was no tradition of religious dissent. Certain of the truth of their "right and perfect way," the Spanish could see no reason for tolerating the errors of others.

The French Crescent

In France, as in Spain, church and state were closely interwoven. During the seventeenth century the chief ministers to the French monarchy, Cardinal Richelieu and his successor Cardinal Mazarin, laid out a fundamentally Catholic imperial policy, and under their guidance colonists constructed a second Catholic empire in North America. In 1674 church and state collaborated in establishing the bishopric of Québec, which founded local seminaries, oversaw the appointment and review of priests, and laid the foundation of the resolutely Catholic culture of New France. Jesuit missionaries, meanwhile, continued to carry Catholicism deep into the continent.

The Church of San Xavier del Bac, constructed in the late eighteenth century, is located a few miles south of the city of Tucson, where Jesuit Father Eusebio Kino founded a mission among the Pima Indians in 1700. Known as the White Dove of the Desert, it is acclaimed as the most striking example of Spanish colonial architecture in the United States.

The French sent few colonists to New France, but by natural increase the population rose from fewer than 15,000 in 1700 to more than 70,000 by 1750. The French used their trade and alliance network to establish colonies, military posts, and settlements that extended in a great crescent from the mouth of the St. Lawrence River southwest through the Great Lakes, then down the Mississippi River to the Gulf of Mexico (see Map 5.3). After the loss in 1713 of the maritime colony of Acadia to the British (see Chapter 4), French authorities constructed the great port and fortress of Louisbourg on Ile Royale (Cape Breton Island) to guard the northern approach to New France. The southern approach was protected by French troops at the port of New Orleans in Louisiana. Between these two points, the French laid a thin colonial veneer, the beginning of what they planned as a great commercial empire that would confine the Protestant British to the Atlantic coastline. By the middle of the century, the French were ascending the Missouri and Arkansas Rivers, placing missionaries and traders in Indian communities on the fringe of the Great Plains.

MAP 5.3 The French Crescent The French empire in North America was based on a series of alliances and trade relations with Indian nations linking a great crescent of colonies, settlements, and outposts that extended from the mouth of the St. Lawrence River, through the Great Lakes, and down the Mississippi River to the Gulf of Mexico. In 1713, Acadia was ceded to the British, but the French established the fortress of Louisbourg to anchor the eastern end of the crescent.

At the heart of the French empire in North America were the communities of farmers or habitants that stretched along the banks of the St. Lawrence between the provincial capital of Québec and the fur trade center of Montreal. There were also farming communities in the Illinois country, supplying wheat to sugar plantations in Louisiana. By the 1750s, those plantations, extending along the Mississippi from Natchez and Baton Rouge to New Orleans, had become the most profitable French enterprise in North America.

Among the most distinctive French stamps on the North American landscape were the "long lots" stretching back from the rivers, providing each settler a share of good bottomland to farm and frontage on the waterways, the "interstate highway system" of the French Crescent. Long lots were laid out along the Mississippi River in Louisiana and Illinois and at the strategic passages of the Great Lakes. Detroit, the most important of those, was a stockaded town with a military garrison, a small administrative center, several stores, a Catholic church, and 100 households of métis (French for mestizo) families. Farmers worked the land along the Detroit River, not far from communities inhabited by several thousand Indians from the Ottawa, Potawatomi, and Huron tribes.

The persistence of French colonial long lots in the pattern of modern landholding is clear in this enhanced satellite photograph of the Mississippi River near New Orleans. Long lots, the characteristic form of property holding in New France, were designed to offer as many settlers as possible a share of good bottomland as well as a frontage on the waterways, which served as the basic transportation network.

Communities of this sort, combining both European and native American elements, were in the tradition of the inclusive frontier. Detroit looked like "an old French village," said one observer, except that its houses were "mostly covered with bark," in Indian style. "It is not uncommon to see a Frenchman with Indian shoes and stockings, without breeches, wearing a strip of woolen cloth to cover what decency requires him to conceal," wrote another. "Yet at the same time he wears a fine ruffled shirt and a laced waistcoat, with a fine handkerchief on his head." Detroit had much of the character of a mixed community. Family and kinship were cast in the Indian pattern, yet the people focused their activities on commerce and overwhelmingly identified themselves as Catholics.

New England

Just as New Spain and New France had their official church, so too did the inhabitants of New England. Rather than the centralized authority of the Catholic hierarchy, however, communities in New England (except Rhode Island) were governed by Puritan congregations. Adult male church members constituted the freemen of the town, so there was very little distinction between religious and secular authority. At the town meeting the freemen chose their minister, voted on his salary, and elected local men to offices ranging from town clerk to animal warden.

The Puritan tradition was a curious mix of freedom and repression. Although local communities had considerable autonomy, they were tightly bound by the religious restrictions. The Puritans had not come to America to create a society where religion could be freely practiced but in order to establish their own version of the "right and perfect way." Puritan authorities banned and exiled Anglicans, Baptists, Quakers, and other dissidents. Quakers who returned to Massachusetts to preach their pacifist faith were branded with "H" for heretic, had their tongues bored with hot irons, or had their ears cut off. Between 1659 and 1661 four Quakers were executed for proselytizing.

Soon after the last of these executions King Charles II, newly placed on the throne, ordered a stop to religious persecution in Massachusetts. Several years later Roger Williams, whose Rhode Island colony had no established religion, made one of the first formal arguments for religious toleration. "Forced worship," Williams wrote in 1670, "stinks in God's nostrils." The new climate of opinion was best expressed by English political philosopher John Locke in "A Letter Concerning Tolerance," written in 1689. Churches were voluntary societies, Locke argued, and could gain genuine converts only through persuasion. The state, he asserted, had no legitimate concern with religious belief. That same year Parliament passed the Act of Toleration, granting religious freedom to Protestant dissenters (but not to Catholics). It was at first resisted by

The Turner House (immortalized by Nathaniel Hawthorne in his novel *The House of the Seven Gables*) in Salem, Massachusetts, was constructed in the seventeenth century. In this style of architecture, function prevailed over form as structures grew to accommodate their residents; rooms were added where and when they were needed. In England, wood for building was scarce, but the abundance of forests in North America created the conditions for a golden age of wood construction.

SOURCE: Photograph courtesy Peabody Essex Museum.

New England Puritans, but in 1700, under pressure from English authorities, Massachusetts and Connecticut reluctantly permitted other Protestant denominations to meet openly, although Puritan congregations continued to be supported officially through taxation. In the early eighteenth century Anglican, Baptist, and Presbyterian churches were organized in many New England towns.

By then New Englanders were less concerned with religious conformity than with the problem of land. As population grew, groups of residents left established towns, "hiving off" to form new congregations and towns elsewhere. By the 1730s, Puritan communities had taken up most of the available land of Massachusetts, Connecticut, and Rhode Island, leaving only a few isolated reservations for small communities of Pequots, Narragansetts, and Wampanoags. Northern Algonquians allied with the French in Québec maintained a defensive barrier that prevented expansion northward. New England had reached the limit of its land supply.

The Middle Colonies

In striking contrast to the ethnically homogeneous colonies of Connecticut and Massachusetts, populated almost entirely by English families, New York featured one of the most ethnically diverse populations on the continent. At midcentury, society along the lower Hudson River, including the counties in northern New Jersey, was a veritable mosaic of ethnic communities, including the Dutch of Flatbush, the Huguenots of New Rochelle, the Flemish of Bergen, and the Scots of Perth Amboy. African Americans, both slave and free, constituted more than 15 percent of the population of the lower Hudson.

Puritan, Baptist, Quaker, and Catholic congregations worshiped without legal hindrance, and in New York City, several hundred Jewish families built North America's first synagogue in 1730. There was intermingling, but these different communities would long retain their ethnic and religious distinctions, making colonial New York more of a cultural "salad bowl" than a "melting pot."

Although New York City grew by leaps and bounds in the eighteenth century, the colony as a whole was less attractive to immigrants than neighboring Pennsylvania. The New York elite who owned the rich lands and great manors along the upper Hudson chose to rent to tenants rather than to sell, but Pennsylvania's proprietors were willing to sell land to anyone who could pay the modest prices, making the Quaker colony, in the words of one German immigrant, "heaven for farmers." The region along the Delaware River—encompassing not only Pennsylvania but New Jersey, Delaware, and the northern portion of Maryland—grew more dramatically than any other in North America during the eighteenth century. Immigration played the dominant role in achieving the astonishing annual growth rate of nearly 4 percent. With access to some of the best farmland in North America, farmers and merchants were soon exporting abundant produce through the prosperous port at Philadelphia.

The Quakers quickly became a minority, but unlike the Puritans they were generally comfortable with religious and ethnic pluralism. Many of the founders of the Society of Friends had been imprisoned for their beliefs in pre-Restoration England, and they were determined to prevent a repetition of this injustice in their own province. This was a perspective well suited to the ethnically and

This view of the Philadelphia waterfront, painted about 1720, conveys the impression of a city firmly anchored to maritime commerce. The long, narrow canvas was probably intended for display over the mantel of a public room.

SOURCE: Peter Cooper, *The South East Prospect of the City of Philadelphia*, ca. 1720. The Library Company of Philadelphia.

religiously diverse population of the colony. Most German immigrants were Lutherans or Calvinists, most North Britons were Presbyterians, and there were plenty of Anglicans and Baptists as well.

The institutions of government were another pillar of community organization. Colonial officials appointed justices of the peace who provided judicial authority for the countryside. Property-owning farmers chose their own local officials. Country communities were bound together by kinship bonds as well as economic relations between neighbors. The substantial stone houses and great barns of the countryside testified to the social stability and prosperity of the Pennsylvania system. These communities were more loosely bound than those of New England. Rates of mobility were considerably higher, with about half the population moving on during any given decade. Because land was sold in individual lots rather than in communal parcels, farmers tended to disperse themselves over the open countryside. Villages gradually developed at crossroads and ferries but with little forethought or planning. The individual settlement pattern of Pennsylvania would provide the basic model for American expansion across the continent.

The Backcountry

By 1750 Pennsylvania's exploding population had pushed beyond the first range of the Appalachian highlands (see Map 5.4). Settlers moved southwest, through western Maryland and down the valley of the Shenandoah River into western Virginia. Although they hoped to become commercial farmers, these families began more modestly, planting Indian corn and raising hogs, hunting in the woods for meat and furs, and building log cabins (see Seeing History).

The movement into the Pennsylvania and Virginia backcountry that began during the 1720s was the first of the great pioneer treks that would take white pioneers into the continental interior. Many, perhaps most, of these pioneers held no legal title to the lands they occupied. They simply hacked out and defended squatters' claims from native proprietors and all other comers. To the Delawares and Shawnees, who had been pushed into the interior, or

the Cherokees, who occupied the Appalachian highlands to the south, these settlers presented a new and deadly threat. Rising fears and resentments over this expanding population triggered much eighteenth-century violence.

MAP 5.4 Spread of Settlement: Movement into the Backcountry, 1720–60 The spread of settlement from 1720 to 1760 shows the movement of population into the backcountry during the midcentury.

A Plan of an American New Cleared Farm

Patrick Campbell, a Scottish gentleman traveler, included this delightful plate in the account of his tour of the American backcountry, published in 1793. The illustration provides a composite view of the raw frontier farms he visited, entirely typical of the eighteenth century. Note the way the pioneers hacked out their farms from the forest, leaving stumps standing in the fields. See how they fenced their fields to keep out livestock, which were allowed to forage freely. The engraving illustrates four different types of fencing: plain log (marked 4), worm fence made of split poles (5), post-and-rail (6), and Virginia rail fence of crossed stakes (7). The use of wood from the abundant forest was an essential economic strategy. Campbell was notably free of the prejudice of many British visitors to the frontier, but he could not disguise his scorn of pioneer cabins, which he described as "miserable little hovels covered with bark." He included one of them in the engraving (14), one of the first illustrations of a log cabin to appear in print. Also notable here are the Indian canoes, one poled by a man, the other paddled by two women with what Campbell's note mistakenly labels a "Babose." Campbell made the entire trip with his own hunting dog, seen in the front of the canoe on the left. Note also the wonderful little "Indian dog" (15).

• **How does the presence of Indians in this image contradict the popular view of frontier life?**

The South

The Chesapeake and the Lower South were triracial societies, with intermingled communities of white colonists and black slaves, along with substantial Indian communities living on the fringes of colonial settlement. Much of the population growth of the region resulted from the forced migration of enslaved Africans, who by 1750 made up 40 percent of the population. Colonial settlement had filled not only the Tidewater area of the southern Atlantic coast but a good deal of the Piedmont as well. Specializing in rice, tobacco, and other commercial crops, these colonies were overwhelmingly rural. Farms and plantations were dispersed across the countryside, and villages or towns were few.

English authorities established the Church of England as the state religion in the Chesapeake colonies. Residents paid taxes to support the church and were required to attend services. No other churches were allowed into Virginia or Maryland (despite its founding by Catholics) and dissenters were excluded or exiled. Yet the Anglican establishment was internally weak. It maintained neither a colonial bishop nor local institutions for training clergy.

Along the rice coast, the dominant social institution was the large plantation. Transforming the tangle of woods and swamps along the region's rivers into an ordered pattern of dams, dikes, and flooded fields required heavy capital investment. Consequently, only men of means could undertake rice cultivation. By midcentury established rice plantations typically were dominated by a large main house, generally located on a spot of high ground overlooking the fields. Drayton Hall, a mansion of the period that still survives near Charleston, was built of pink brick in classically symmetrical style, with hand-carved interior moldings of imported Caribbean mahogany. Nearby, but a world apart, were the slave quarters, rough wooden cabins lining two sides of a muddy pathway near the outbuildings and barns.

Because tobacco, unlike rice, could be grown profitably in small plots, the Chesapeake included a greater variety of farmers and a correspondingly diverse landscape. Tobacco quickly drained the soil of its nutrients, and plantings had to be shifted to fresh ground every few years. Former tobacco land could be planted with corn for several years but then required twenty years or more of rest before reuse. Thus, the landscape was a patchwork of fields, many in various stages of ragged second growth. The poorest farmers lived in wooden cabins little better than the shacks of the slaves. More prosperous farm families lived with two or three slaves in houses that nevertheless were considerably smaller than the substantial homes of New England.

Compared to the Lower South, where there was almost no community life outside the plantation, the Chesapeake boasted well-developed neighborhoods constructed from kinship networks and economic connections. The most important community institution was the county court, which held both executive and judicial power. On court day white people of all ranks held a great gathering that included public business, horse racing, and perhaps a barbecue. The gentleman justices of the county, appointed by the governor, included the heads of the elite planter families. These men in turn selected the grand jury, composed of substantial freeholders. One of the most significant bonding forces in this free white population was a growing sense of racial solidarity in response to the increasing proportion of African slaves dispersed throughout the neighborhoods.

Social and Political Patterns

Despite important similarities among the colonial regions of North America, during the eighteenth century the trajectory of the British colonies began to diverge sharply from that of the French and Spanish. Immigration, economic growth, and provincial political struggles all pushed British colonists in a radically new direction.

The Persistence of Traditional Culture in the New World

In each of the regional North American societies, family and kinship, the church, and the local community were the most significant factors in everyday life. In this regard, Northampton was typical of settlement communities all over the continent. Everywhere colonists tended to live much as people had lived in European homeland communities at the time the colonies were settled. The residents of New Mexico, Québec, and New England continued to be attached to the religious passions of the seventeenth century long after their mother countries had put those religious controversies aside in favor of imperial geopolitics. Nostalgia for Europe helped to fix a conservative colonial attitude toward culture.

These were oral cultures, depending on the transmission of information by the spoken rather than the printed word, on the passage of traditions through oral story and song. North American colonial folk cultures, traditional and suspicious of change, preserved an essentially medieval worldview. The rhythms of life were regulated by the hours of sunlight and the seasons of the year. People rose with the sun and went to bed soon after sundown. The demands of the season determined their working routines. They farmed with simple tools, and drought, flood, or pestilence might quickly sweep away their efforts. Experience told them that the natural world imposed limitations within which men and women had to learn to live.

These were also communal cultures. In Québec, villagers worked side by side to repair the roads. In New Mexico they collectively maintained the irrigation ditches. In New England they gathered in town meetings to decide the dates when common fields were to be plowed, sowed, and harvested. Houses offered little privacy, with families often sleeping together in the same chamber, sitting together on benches rather than in chairs, and taking their supper from a common bowl or trencher. For most North American colonists of the mid-eighteenth century, the community was more important than the individual.

Most colonists continued the traditional European occupation of working the land. Commercial agriculture was practiced on slave plantations, of course. And it also developed in some areas of the northern colonies, such as fertile southeastern Pennsylvania—which became known as the breadbasket of North America—and in the rural districts surrounding colonial cities such as New York, Boston, and Quebéc. The majority of North American farmers, however, grew crops and raised livestock for their own needs or for local barter, and communities were largely self-sufficient. Most farmers attempted to produce small surpluses as well, which they sold to pay their taxes

and buy some manufactured goods. But rather than specializing in the production of one or two crops for sale, most farmers diversified production in order to remain as independent of the market as possible. The primary goal was ownership of land and the assurance that children and descendants would be able to settle on lands nearby.

Colonial cities, by contrast, were centers of commerce. Artisans and craftsmen worked at their trades full time, organizing themselves according to the European craft system. In Boston, New York, and Philadelphia carpenters, iron makers, blacksmiths, shipwrights, and scores of other tradesmen had their own self-governing associations. A young man who wished to pursue a trade served several years as an apprentice, working in exchange for learning the skills and secrets of the craft. After completing his apprenticeship, the young craftsman sought employment in a shop, often necessitating his migration to some

A spinner and potter from *The Book of Trades*, an eighteenth-century British survey of the crafts practiced in colonial America. In colonial cities, artisans organized themselves into the traditional European craft system with apprentices, journeymen, and masters. There were few opportunities for the employment of women outside the household, but women sometimes earned income by establishing sidelines as midwives or spinners.

other area, thus becoming a "journeyman." Most craftsmen remained at the journeyman level for the whole of

their careers. But by building a good
name and carefully saving, a journeyman hoped to become a master
craftsman, opening his own shop
and employing journeymen and
apprentices of his own. As in farming, the ultimate goal
was independence.

There were few opportunities for women outside the
household. By law, husbands held managerial rights over
family property, but widows received support in the form
of a one-third lifetime interest, known as "dower," in a
deceased husband's real estate (the rest of the estate being
divided among the heirs). In certain occupations, such as
printing (which had a tradition of employing women),
widows succeeded their husbands in business. As a result,
some colonial women played active roles in eighteenth-
century journalism. Ann Smith Franklin, Benjamin
Franklin's sister-in-law, took over the operation of her
husband's Rhode Island shop after his death. Widow
Cornelia Smith Bradford continued to publish her
deceased husband's Philadelphia paper and was an important force in publishing during the 1750s.

The Frontier Heritage

The colonial societies of eighteenth-century North
America also shared a set of assumptions originating in
their common frontier heritage. European colonists came
from Old World societies in which land was scarce and
monopolized by property-owning elites. They settled in a
continent where, for the most part, land was abundant and
cheap. The widespread and general expectation of property ownership was the most important cultural distinction between North America and Europe.

This expectation led to rising popular demands in all the
colonial regions of the continent that land be taken from the
Indian inhabitants and opened to colonial settlement. The
majority of colonists—whether British, Spanish, or French—
endorsed the violence directed against Indian peoples as an
essential aspect of colonial life. This attitude was as true of
inclusive as exclusive societies, with the difference that in the
former, native peoples were incorporated into colonial society, while in the latter, tribes were pushed from the frontier.

American historians once tied the existence of this
"free land" directly to the development of democracy. But
the frontier heritage encouraged the popular acceptance
of forced labor, a system that was anything but democratic.
When asked how to achieve a good living, a woman of
eighteenth-century South Carolina offered the following
advice: "get a few slaves and beat them well to make them
work hard." Labor was the key to prosperity, and it was in
short supply throughout the colonies. In a land where free
men and women could work for themselves on their own
plot of ground, there was little incentive to work for

wages. The use of forced labor was one of the few ways a
landowner could secure an agricultural workforce.

More than half the immigrants to eighteenth-century
British America arrived as indentured servants. Agents paid
for the Atlantic crossing of poor immigrants in exchange for
several years of service in America. But at the conclusion of
their indentures, eighteenth-century servants enjoyed considerably more opportunity than their seventeenth-century
counterparts. The chance of a former servant achieving a
position of moderate comfort rose from one in five in 1700
to better than fifty-fifty by 1750, probably because of the
rise in overall prosperity in the British colonies.

Population Growth and Immigration

All the colonial regions of North America experienced
unprecedented growth in the eighteenth century. "Our
people must at least be doubled every twenty years,"
Benjamin Franklin wrote in a remarkable 1751 essay on
population, and he was nearly right. In 1700, there were
290,000 colonists north of Mexico; fifty years later they
had grown to approximately 1.3 million, an average annual
growth rate of about 3 percent. Preindustrial societies typically grew at rates of less than 1 percent per year, approximately the pace of Europe's expansion in the eighteenth
century. But the colonial societies of North America
experienced what English economist Thomas Malthus,
writing at the end of the century, described as "a rapidity
of increase probably without parallel in history."

High fertility and low mortality played important
roles. Colonial women typically bore seven or more children during their childbearing years. And blessed with an
abundance of food, colonists enjoyed generally good
health and relatively low mortality. But the British
colonies grew far more rapidly than those of France or
Spain (see Figure 5.1). It was immigration that made the
difference. Fearful of depleting their population at home,
the Spanish severely limited the migration of their own
subjects and absolutely forbade the immigration of foreigners. Dedicated to keeping their colonies exclusively
Catholic, the French ignored the desire of Protestant
Huguenots to emigrate, instead sending thousands of
Catholic engagés to Canada, most of whom returned, discouraged by the climate and the lack of commercial
opportunity. But the English dispatched an estimated
400,000 of their own countrymen to populate their
North American colonies during the seventeenth and
eighteenth centuries.

Moreover, the British were the only colonial power to
encourage the immigration of foreign nationals. William
Penn was the first colonial official to promote the immigration of Europeans, in the 1680s sending agents to
recruit settlers in Holland, France, and the German princi-
palities along the Rhine River. Soon the leaders of other
British colonies were emulating his success. Shippers
developed a system that contemporaries called the "trade

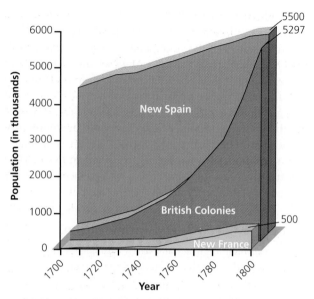

FIGURE 5.1 Estimated Total Population of New Spain, New France, and the British North American Colonies, 1700–1800 Although the populations of all three North American colonial empires grew in the eighteenth century, the explosive growth of the British colonies was unmatched.

SOURCE: *Historical Statistics of the United States* (Washington, DC: Government Printing Office, 1976), 1168.

The European crossing of the Atlantic was nowhere near as traumatic as the African Middle Passage, but it was harrowing. One immigrant described a voyage to Philadelphia with several hundred people packed like sardines in the vessel's hold. "The ship is filled with pitiful signs of distress," he wrote, "smells, fumes, horrors, vomiting, various kinds of sea sickness, fever, dysentery, headaches, heat, constipation, boils, scurvy, cancer, mouth-rot, and similar afflictions. In such misery all the people on board pray and cry pitifully together." In 1750 Pennsylvania was finally

in strangers." Vessels sent eastward across the Atlantic loaded with tobacco, rice, indigo, timber, and flour came back loaded with immigrants. The eighteenth-century trade in strangers was the prototype for the great waves of immigration to the United States in later centuries.

Early in the century, a number of British colonies enacted liberal naturalization laws that allowed immigrants who professed Protestantism and swore allegiance to the British crown to become free "denizens," with all the privileges of natural-born subjects. In 1740 Parliament extended these provisions to all the British colonies by enacting a general naturalization law.

Trans-Atlantic migration made for colonies characterized by extraordinary ethnic diversity (see Map 5.5 and Figure 5.2). First there were the Africans, the largest group to come to North America in the colonial period, larger even than the English. Forced relocation brought an estimated 600,000 to the colonies before the official end of the slave trade to the United States in 1807. Then there was the massive emigration from the northern British Isles. Squeezed by economic hardship, an estimated 150,000 Highland Scots and Protestant Irish from the Ulster region of northern Ireland (known as the "Scots-Irish") emigrated in the eighteenth century. German speakers were next in importance, at least 125,000 of them settling in the colonies. It is worth noting once again that a majority of these immigrants to British North America came as bonded servants or slaves.

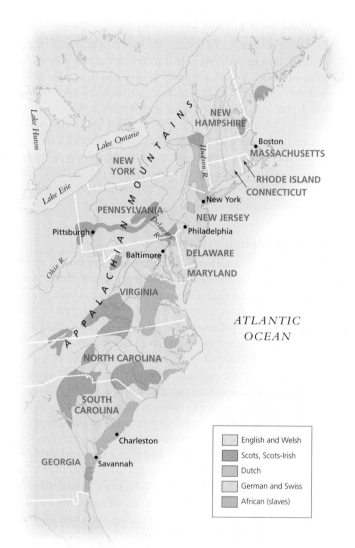

MAP 5.5 Ethnic Groups in Eighteenth-Century British North America The first federal census, taken in 1790, revealed remarkable ethnic diversity. New England was filled with people from the British Isles, but the rest of the colonies were a patchwork. Most states had at least three different ethnic groups within their borders, and although the English and Scots-Irish were heavily represented in all colonies, in some they had strong competition from Germans (eastern and southern Pennsylvania) and from African peoples (Virginia and South Carolina).

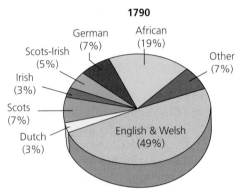

FIGURE 5.2 The Ancestry of the British Colonial Population The legacy of eighteenth-century immigration to the British colonies was a population of unprecedented ethnic diversity.

SOURCE: "The European Ancestry of the United States Population," by Thomas L. Purvis. *William and Mary Quarterly* 61 (1984): 85–101. Reprinted by permission of the *William and Mary Quarterly*.

compelled to pass a law to prevent the overcrowding of ships filled with indentured passengers.

Social Class

In New France, landowning seigneurs (lords) claimed privileges similar to those enjoyed by their aristocratic counterparts at home; the Spanish system of encomienda and the great manors created by the Dutch and continued by the English along the Hudson River also represented attempts to transplant European feudalism to North America. But because settlers in most areas had relatively free access to land, these monopolies proved difficult or impossible to maintain. North American society was not aristocratic in the European fashion, but neither was it without social hierarchy.

In New Spain the official criterion for status was racial purity. *Españoles* (Spaniards), also known as *gente de razon* (literally, "people of reason"), occupied the top rung of the social ladder, with mestizos, mulattoes, and others on descending levels, with Indians and African slaves at the bottom. In the isolated northern borderlands, however, such distinctions tended to blur, with castas (persons of mixed background)

enjoying considerably more opportunity. Mestizos who acquired land might suddenly be reclassified as españoles. Even so, Spanish and French colonial societies were cut in the style of the Old World, with its hereditary ranks and titles.

In the British colonies the upper class was made up of large landowners, merchants, and prosperous professionals. Despite the lack of titles, wealthy planters and merchants of the British colonies lived far more extravagantly than the seigneurs of New France or the dons of the Spanish borderlands. What separated the culture of class in the British colonies from that of New France or New Mexico was not so much the material conditions of life as the prevailing attitude toward social rank. In the Catholic cultures, the upper class attempted to obscure its origins, claiming descent from European nobility. But British North America celebrated social mobility. The class system was remarkably open, and the entrance of newly successful planters, commercial farmers, and merchants into the upper ranks was not only possible but also common, although by midcentury most upper-class families had inherited, not earned, their wealth.

There was also a large and impoverished lower class in the British colonies. Slaves, bound servants, and poor laboring families made up 40 percent or more of the population. For them the standard of living did not rise above bare subsistence. Most lived from hand to mouth, often suffering through seasons of severe privation. African American slaves stood apart from the gains in the standard of living enjoyed by immigrants from Europe. Their lives in America had been degraded beyond measure from the conditions that had prevailed in their native lands.

The feature of the class system most often commented on by eighteenth-century observers was not the character or composition of the lower ranks, but rather the size and strength of the middle class, a rank entirely absent in the colonies of France and Spain. More than half the population of the British colonies, and nearly 70 percent of all white settlers, might have been so classified. Most were landowning farmers of small to moderate means, but the group also included artisans, craftsmen, and small shopkeepers.

Households solidly in the center of this broad ranking owned land or other property worth approximately £500 and earned the equivalent of £100 per year. They enjoyed a standard of living higher than that of the great majority of people in England and Europe. As one economic historian has recently concluded, the British colonies "were much better places to live, with probably a much higher standard of living than the mother country."

Read the Document

A Boston Woman Writes about Her Trip to New York (1704) at **www.myhistorylab.com**

Economic Growth and Economic Inequality

One of the most important differences among North American colonial regions in the eighteenth century was the economic stagnation of New France and New Spain

Español con India.
Mestizo.

Mestizo con Española.
Castizo.

Castizo con Española.
Español.

Español con Mora.
Mulato.

5

6

Mulato con Española.
Morisco.

Morisco con Española.
Chino.

7

Chino con India.
Salta atras.

Salta atras con Mulata.
Lobo.

An eighteenth-century genre painting from New Spain showing various racial *castas*, the result of ethnic mixing.

compared with the impressive economic growth of the British colonies. Weighed down by royal bureaucracies and regulations, the communities of the French Crescent and New Spain never evidenced much prosperity. In eighteenth-century British North America, by contrast,

per capita production grew at an annual rate of 0.5 percent. Granted, this was considerably less than the average annual growth rate of 1.5 percent that prevailed during the era of American industrialization, from the early nineteenth through the mid-twentieth centuries. But as economic growth increased the size of the economic pie, most middle- and upper-class British Americans began to enjoy improved living conditions. Improving standards of living and open access to land encouraged British colonists to see theirs as a society where hard work and savings could translate into prosperity, thus producing an upward spiral of economic growth.

At the same time, economic growth produced increasing social inequality (see Table 5.2). In the commercial cities, for example, prosperity was accompanied by a concentration of assets in the hands of wealthy families. In Boston and Philadelphia at the beginning of the century, the wealthiest 10 percent of households owned about half of the taxable property; by midcentury their share had risen to more than 65 percent. In the commercial farming region of Chester County in southeastern Pennsylvania, the holdings of the wealthiest 10 percent of households increased more modestly, from 24 percent of taxable property in 1700 to 30 percent in 1750, but the share owned by the poorest third fell from 17 percent to 6 percent (see Figure 5.3). The general standard of living may have been rising, but the rich were getting richer and the poor poorer. The greatest concentrations of wealth occurred in the cities and in regions dominated by commercial farming, whether slave or free, while the greatest economic equality was found in areas of self-sufficient farming.

Another eighteenth-century trend, however, stymied upward economic mobility in the countryside. As population grew and as generations succeeded one another in older settlements, all the available land eventually was taken up. Under the pressure of increased demand, land prices rose beyond the reach of families of modest means. And as a family's land was divided among the heirs of the second and third generations, parcels became ever smaller and more intensively farmed. Eventually, the soil was exhausted. This is what happened in communities such as Northampton in New England, the region where this pattern was most pronounced. There were

TABLE 5.2

Wealth Held by Richest 10 Percent of Population in British Colonial America, 1770

Region	North	South
Frontier	33	40
Rural subsistence farming	35	45
Rural commercial farming	45	65
Cities	60	65
Overall	45	55

SOURCE: Jackson Turner Main, *The Social Structure of Revolutionary America* (Princeton, NJ: Princeton University Press, 1965), 276n.

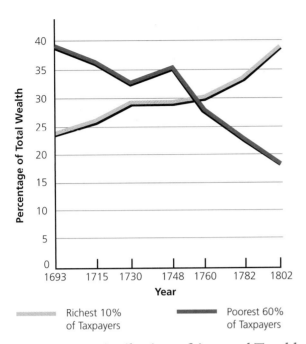

FIGURE 5.3 Distribution of Assessed Taxable Wealth in Eighteenth-Century Chester County This graph charts the concentration of assets in the hands of wealthy families. From 1693 to 1802, the percentage of total wealth held by the richest 10 percent of taxpayers rose from 24 to 38 percent, while the percentage held by the poorest 60 percent of taxpayers fell from 39 to 18 percent. This pattern was typical for regions dominated by commerce.

SOURCE: "The Distribution of Wealth in Eighteenth-Century America," by James Lemon and Gary Nash. *Journal of Social History* 2 (1968):1–24. Reprinted by permission of the George Mason University Press.

increases in the number of landless poor, as well as the disturbing appearance of what were called the "strolling poor," homeless people who traveled from town to town looking for work or simply a handout. Destitute families crowded into Boston, which by 1750 was spending more than £5,000 annually on relief for the poor, who were required to wear a large red "P" on their clothing. In other regions, land shortages in the older settlements almost inevitably prompted people to move to the frontier in search of cheap or free land.

Colonial Politics

The administration of the Spanish and French colonies was highly centralized. French Canada was ruled by a superior council including the royal governor (in charge of military affairs), the intendant (responsible for civil administration), and the bishop of Québec. New Spain was governed by the Council of the Indies, which sat in Spain, with the viceroy in Mexico City exercising direct executive authority over all political affairs. Although local communities had informal independence, these highly bureaucratized and centralized governments left little room for the development of vigorous traditions of self-government.

The situation in the British colonies was quite different. During the early eighteenth century the British government

of Prime Minister Robert Walpole assumed that a decentralized administration would best accomplish the nation's economic goals. Contented colonies, Walpole believed, would present far fewer problems. With the exception of Connecticut and Rhode Island, both of which retained their charters and continued to choose their own governors, the colonies were administered by royally appointed governors. But taxation and spending continued to be controlled by elected assemblies. The right to vote was restricted to men with property. Yet the proportion of adult white males who qualified approached 50 percent in the British colonies, considerably higher in New England, considerably lower in some southern jurisdictions. Proportionally, the electorate of the British colonies was the largest in the world.

That did not mean that the colonies were democratic. The basic principle of order in eighteenth-century British culture was the ideal of deference to natural hierarchy. The common metaphor for civil order was the well-ordered family, in which children were strictly governed by their parents, wives by their husbands. Members of subordinate groups, such as women, non-English immigrants, African American slaves, servants, and Indians, were not allowed to vote or hold public office. Moreover, for the most part, the men who did vote nearly always chose wealthy landowners, planters, or merchants to serve as their leaders. Consequently, provincial assemblies were controlled by colonial elites.

To educated British colonists the word "democracy" implied rule by the mob, the normal order of things turned upside-down. Yet over the century there was an important trend toward stronger institutions of representative government. By midcentury most colonial assemblies in British North America had achieved considerable power over provincial affairs, sharing authority with governors. They collected local revenues and allocated funds for government programs, asserted the right to audit the accounts of public officers, and in some cases even acquired the power to approve the appointment of provincial officials. Because the assemblies controlled the finances of government—the "purse strings"—most royal governors were unable to resist this trend.

The royal governors who were most successful at realizing their agendas were those who became adept at playing one provincial faction against another. All this had the important effect of schooling the colonial elite in the art of politics—not democratic politics, but the politics of patronage, coalition-building, and behind-the-scenes intrigue. This would have important implications for the development of American institutions.

The Cultural Transformation of British North America

The same ships that transported European immigrants and European goods across the Atlantic could also transport new ways of thinking that historians call "the Enlightenment."

Inspired by the sixteenth- and seventeenth-century revolution in scientific thought represented by giants such as Copernicus, Galileo, Descartes, and Newton, intellectuals in Europe and Great Britain became advocates for the power of human reason rather than spiritual revelation or mystical illumination as the sole way of discovering natural law. They sought to establish an authoritative canon of logic, ethics, and aesthetics, as well as political philosophy. In the 1690s, for example, Englishman John Locke proposed that individuals were endowed with inalienable rights to life, liberty, and property and that the state existed to protect those rights.

The Catholic Church banned the works of hundreds of rationalist thinkers whose opinions were considered threats to the authority of faith. In New Spain and New France colonial officials worked diligently to suppress such challenging ideas and writings. In Mexico, for example, officials of the Inquisition conducted house-to-house searches in pursuit of prohibited texts that they feared had been smuggled into the country. Cultural censorship in the French and Spanish colonies was effective because literacy was confined to a tiny minority of elite men. In the British colonies, by contrast, literacy was widespread. About half the white men and a quarter of the white women could read, rates comparable to those in England or Scandinavia. In New England, where public education was most developed, 85 percent of men and approximately 50 percent of women were literate, the highest rates in the Atlantic world. British colonial officials made little attempt at cultural censorship, and as a result these new ideas sparked a cultural transformation in eighteenth-century British North America.

The Enlightenment Challenge

The Enlightenment is a simple label for a complex movement encompassing many different thinkers with many different ideas. But Enlightenment writers shared some things in common. They were optimistic about the ability of the rational human mind to discover the natural laws that were thought to govern the physical world and human affairs. Coupled with their commitment to reason was their belief in progress, a conviction not only that the present was better than the past but also that the future would be better still. These themes were in stark contrast with the traditional emphasis of folk culture on the unfathomable mysteries of God and nature and the inevitability of human failure and disorder.

Such thinking was most attractive to the British colonial elite, families experiencing rising prosperity. This group had good reason to believe in progress. They sent their sons to colonial colleges, the focal point for the dissemination of Enlightenment ideas. Harvard, established in 1636, remained the only institution of higher education in British America until 1693, when Anglicans established the College of William and Mary at Williamsburg. Puritans in Connecticut, believing Harvard was too liberal,

founded Yale College in 1701. The curricula of these colleges, modeled on those of Oxford and Cambridge in England, were designed to train ministers, but gradually each institution changed to curricula influenced by Enlightenment thinking. By the 1730s students were studying Newton and reading Locke, as well as other British Enlightenment texts.

The tastes of ordinary readers ran to traditional rather than Enlightenment fare. Benjamin Harris, Boston publisher of the *New England Primer*, also issued religious works, broadsides, and in 1690 began printing the first newspaper in the colonies, *Public Occurrences both Foreign and Domestick*, which authorities suppressed after the first issue. In 1704, with a friendlier government in charge, the *Boston News-Letter* became the first continuously published newspaper in North America. By the mid-eighteenth century there were more than twenty newspapers in the British colonies. These papers did not employ reporters but instead depended on official government announcements, travelers' and correspondents' reports, and articles reprinted from other sources. Most literate people had access to them, and they were often read aloud in local taverns, making their information available to all within hearing.

The best-selling book of the colonial era, not surprisingly, was the Bible. But in second place was a unique American literary form, the captivity narrative. The genre originated with the appearance of *The Sovereignty and Goodness of God* (1682), Mary Rowlandson's tale of her captivity among Indians during King Philip's War. Appearing in fifteen editions over the next century, Rowlandson's account inspired the publication of at least 500 other similar narratives, most with a lot less religion and a lot more gore.

Another popular literary genre was the almanac, a combination calendar, astrological guide, sourcebook of medical advice, and farming tips that largely reflected the concerns of traditional folk culture. Best remembered is *Poor Richard's Almanac* (1732–57), published by Philadelphia printer and publisher Benjamin Franklin, but it was preceded and outlived by a great many others. What was so innovative about *Poor Richard's*, and what made it so important, was the manner in which Franklin used this traditional literary form to promote the new Enlightenment emphasis on useful and practical knowledge. Posing as the simple bumpkin Poor Richard, the highly sophisticated Franklin was one of the first Americans to bring Enlightenment thought to ordinary folk.

A mixture of traditional and Enlightenment views characterized the thinking of many colonial intellectuals. Boston minister Cotton Mather offers a good example. A conservative defender of the old order, Mather wrote of the existence of witches and supported the executions during the Salem witchcraft crisis (see Chapter 3). Yet he was also a member of the Royal

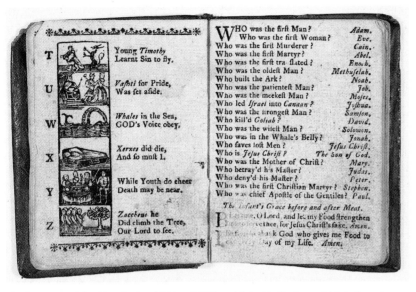

The first page of the *New England Primer* (1689), published in Boston, which in its various editions sold more than 5 million copies. In addition to the letters of the alphabet, illustrated by crude but charming woodcuts and couplets, the book contained simple moral texts based on biblical history and wisdom.

Society (Great Britain's national academy of science), a defender of the Copernican sun-centered model of the universe, and an early supporter of inoculation against smallpox (see Communities in Conflict: The Inoculation Controversy in Boston, 1721). Jonathan Edwards of Northampton was another who sought to reconcile old and new but in a considerably more sophisticated fashion. Edwards sought to defend traditional Calvinist doctrine, but he did so by employing the concepts of Enlightenment thought, in which he was very well read. Worrying, however, that the new thinking tended toward a philosophy of materialism, Edwards argued that natural law revealed the harmony of God's creation.

A Decline in Religious Devotion

As Enlightenment thinking gradually gained in popularity, religious commitment seemed to decline, much as Edwards feared. In the South, by the 1730s, only one adult in fifteen was affiliated with a church. The Anglican establishment in the Chesapeake and the Lower South was institutionally feeble, its ministers uninspiring, and many families "unchurched."

Puritan churches in New England also suffered declining membership and falling attendance, and ministers began to warn of Puritanism's "declension." By the second decade of the eighteenth century only one in five New Englanders belonged to an established congregation. And among the churched, an increasing number began to question the Calvinist theology of election, the belief that salvation was the result of God's sovereign decree, that only a small number of men and women would be the recipients of God's grace. Many turned instead to the view

that people had a natural ability to accept God's grace by developing their faith and doing good works.

The dispute between advocates of free will and determinism was ancient, but the idea that men and women were not helpless pawns but rational beings who could actively shape their own destinies was strengthened by Enlightenment thinking. It became a force at Harvard and Yale in the first quarter of the eighteenth century, and soon a generation of ministers with more liberal ideas were taking positions in New England churches. Their ideas appealed to the same men and women attracted to Enlightenment thinking, those experiencing rising prosperity and social improvement. Among ordinary people in the countryside, however, especially among those in communities with narrowing opportunities, there was a good deal of opposition to these unorthodox ideas.

The Great Awakening

The first stirrings of a movement challenging the rationalist approach to religion occurred during the 1730s, most notably in the revival sparked by Reverend Jonathan Edwards in the community of Northampton. Edwards was a committed Calvinist and used his charged preaching style to attack liberal theology. But there was more to this movement than the power of a single preacher. Similar revivals soon broke out in other New England communities, as well as among German Lutherans and Scots-Irish Presbyterians in Pennsylvania. Not all the revivalists were Calvinists. Some promoted a theology that emphasized human choice. But the common thread was a complaint of "spiritual coldness," of ministers whose sermons read like rational dissertations. People clamored for preaching that was more emotional.

Read the Document
Jonathan Edwards, Sinners in the Hands of an Angry God (1741) at **www.myhistorylab.com**

These local revivals became an intercolonial phenomenon thanks to the preaching of George Whitefield, an evangelical Anglican minister from England, who in 1738 made the first of several tours of the colonies. By all accounts, his preaching had a powerful effect. Even Benjamin Franklin, a religious skeptic, wrote of the "extraordinary influence of his oratory" after attending an outdoor service in Philadelphia where 30,000 people crowded the streets to hear him preach. Whitefield began as Edwards did, chastising his listeners as "half animals and half devils," but he parted company from Edwards by leaving them with the hope that God would be responsive to their desire for salvation. Whitefield avoided

Read the Document
Benjamin Franklin on George Whitefield (1771) at **www.myhistorylab.com**

The Inoculation Controversy in Boston, 1721

In the spring of 1721 a terrible smallpox epidemic swept through Boston. The Reverend Cotton Mather, who nearly lost three of his children in an earlier epidemic, had read in the journal of the British Royal Society about a preventive technique known as inoculation widely practiced in Asia and Africa. Mather's household slave, a man named Onesimus, who had been inoculated in Africa, explained the procedure. "Take the juice [pus] of the smallpox" [from a victim], and cut the skin [of the person to be inoculated] and put in a drop. . . . And nobody die of it; nobody have smallpox any more." Those who were inoculated generally contracted a mild case of the disease but developed immunity to further infection. At Mather's urging, the Boston doctor Zabdiel Boylston tried the procedure on his son and two of his slaves. All three survived and did not contract the disease. Boylston began inoculating others, a total of 248 Bostonians. Five of them died, about 2 percent of the total. But among those who contracted the disease naturally, the mortality rate was nearly 15 percent. Inoculation was soon widely practiced in Europe and America, until replaced by the more effective practice of vaccination in the 1790s.

Controversy erupted as soon as Boylston began his work. Ordinary people, as well as the town's physicians, interpreted the technique as "poisoning," and as soon as the first patient died they urged authorities to charge Boylston and Mather with murder. A bomb, which failed to go off, was thrown through the window of Mather's house. Attached was a note: "Mather, you dog, damn you," it read. "I will Enoculate you with this." The controversy played itself out in the pages of Boston's newspapers, as well as in a series of pamphlets. The varying opinions demonstrate the clash of traditional and progressive views in the early eighteenth century.

• **How does Cooper incorporate the perspectives of critics like Grainger in order to defend the practice of inoculation?**

There Are Destroying Angels

When the Almighty sends his Judgments among us to punish and humble us for our Sins, especially a wasting and Pestilential Distemper, what are the *Means* which may be lawfully us'd for our preservations FROM his desolating Judgments? . . . On all sides it is granted *lawful* to use Means for our *preservation* from a *Desolating Judgment* provided such Means be *Warranted by Gods Word*, to which we are more immediately directed, at the time *God* sends his Judgment, to seek what are the Ways to Escape the *Extremity* and *Destruction* at least, if not the TOUCH of it. This Mercy at all times *God* graciously affords us. Examine that carefully I entreat you Sir, and produce if you can, *any other appointed Means* for preventing or removing a *National Judgment* then that of a *National Repentance* and *Reformation*. And I hope you'll allow the best means of deliverance from National Calamities are those of *Gods appointment*, not our own. . . . And when we repent of the *Impulsive Cause* which brought it, God in his own good time will either Remove or mitigate the punishment, because he is *Faithful* in all his *Promises*, and *Just* in *performing* them. . . . There are Destroying Angels, as with Drawn Swords by a Commission from *God*, inflicting such a Sickness for the destruction, at least the vexation of the Inhabitants. The way to prevail, is to bring and plead a Sacrifice, for the *preventing* of such a *Dreadful Commission*. And what *Sacrifice* have we to plead in this Case? NONE truly but the ALL-SUFFICIENT Sacrifice of our Lord Jesus Christ; and by Faith in that great Sacrifice we may particularly procure our own Houses to be Sprinkled with that Blood, by which our Families may be *preserved in Jesus Christ*. . . . It is impossible that any *Humane Means*, or *preventive Physick* should defend us from, or Over-rule a *Judicial National Sickness;* for were it so, Wicked and Atheistical Men would have the same terms and conditions of *Security* in a *Physical Respect*, with the most Holy and Religious. And *National Judgments* would not have the Designed Ends for which they were sent, *National Amendment*. . . . As Gods

> "The way to prevail, is to bring and plead a Sacrifice, for the preventing of such a Dreadful Commission."

---

sectarian differences. "God help us to forget party names and become Christians in deed and truth," he declared.

This widespread colonial revival of religion, which later generations called the Great Awakening, was an American version of the second phase of the Protestant Reformation

(see Chapter 2). Religious leaders condemned the laxity, decadence, and bureaucracy of established Protestantism and sought to reinvigorate it with renewed piety and purity. People undergoing the economic and social stresses of the age, unsure about their ability to find land, marry, and

Designs in his Visitations is Repentance and Amendment, this practice [of inoculation] doubtless tends to take *off the fear of his Judgment,* and the *Spiritual Advantage* that *arises* from such *Fear.*

SOURCE: Samuel Grainger, *The Imposition of Inoculation as a Duty Religiously Considered* (1721).

New and Useful Discoveries

The new Method of receiving the Small-Pox by *Incision* (or *Inoculation* as 'tis commonly call'd) has been, you know, the Subject not only of plentiful Discourse, but of angry Debate and fierce Contention among us in this Town. . . . [Some say that] the *Small Pox is a Judgment of God, sent to punish and humble us for our Sins; and what shall we so evade it, and think to turn it away from us?* I fully agree to it, that it is a sore Judgment of God upon us for our Sins, which we have much deserv'd. And it is greatly to be lamented that it has no better Effect upon the hearts of Men. But is it Unlawful to use means for our Preservation from a desolating Judgment? *Especially,* if at the very time that God sends the Judgment, He shews us a way to escape the *Extremity* and Destruction at least, if not the Touch of it. If a gracious God Shews us so much *Mercy* as this under the judgment, does it become us to *put it away from our selves,* or rather should we not accept it with *Adoring Thankfulness?* If this Town was to suffer an *Innundation,* that would be a more terrible Judgment than this, and we should look upon it too as a righteous Punishment for our Sins; yet would any refuse to make use of a *Boat* or a *Plank that might providentially come in his Way,* thinking that to do it would be a criminal Evading the Judgment?

But some have said to me, *This Method tends to take off the fears of this Distemper from the Minds of people; and who knows of what Spiritual Advantage these fears might be to them?* In Answer to it I ask them, Whether GOD cannot make the *Mercy* of their Preservation and Recovery in this Way of Spiritual Advantage to them also, and by that *lead them to Repentance?* And, I truly hope, the Salvation of GOD bestow'd upon some in *this way,* as well as the other, will have a gracious sanctifying Effect upon them, under the powerful working of the Spirit of Grace. . . .

Some frame an Objection against this Practice from the *Decrees of GOD.* They say that *GOD has predetermin'd and fixed the Period of every ones life, beyond which nothing shall protract it; so that if this time be come Inoculation will not save the Persons life.* But this *Argument* may as well be urg'd against the Use of *all Physick,* nay even of *Food,* as against this Practice. I truly believe, aa my Bible teaches me, that GOD has fix'd the Period of every ones life; but I also believe that He has done it with a *Regard to second Causes,* or that Course of Nature which He has establish'd; *the End and Means are determined together.* He that has fix'd in His own Counsel how long we shall live, has also determin'd that by such and such means our

> "Every Age of the World produces some new and useful Discoveries. . ."

lives shall be continu'd to that Period of time. And how does any one know, but this is to be the *appointed Means,* of their Preservation in life? . . .

There is one thing more said against this Practice. . . . 'Tis this, *that it is originally from the Devil.* Sure this is the effect of *Transport,* etc. I will return a better answer to it than it deserves. If it be a *Method of Safety,* and a *Benefit to Mankind,* as hitherto it appears to be how came the Devil to be the Author of it? Was he ever a *Benefactor* to Mankind? No: But he is a *Murderer from the beginning.* Every Age of the World produces some *new* and useful Discoveries in one Profession, Art and Science or another: And if this Discovery very be reserv'd for our Day, why should it not be accepted *in all places with all Thankfulness?* In a word, I cannot but think, it's Original deriv'd elsewhere, because my *Bible* teaches me that *every good & perfect Gift comes down from the Father of Light.*

SOURCE: William Cooper, *A Letter to a Friend in the Country* (1721).

participate in the promise of a growing economy—like those in Northampton—found relief in religious enthusiasm.

Among Presbyterians, open conflict broke out between the revivalists and the old guard, and in some regions the church hierarchy divided into separate organizations. In New England, where these factions were known as the New Lights and the Old Lights, the two sides accused each other of heresy. New Lights railed against liberal theology as a "rationalist heresy" and called for a revival of Calvinism. Old Lights condemned emotional enthusiasm as a "lawless heresy," the

In this satirical British cartoon of 1760 evangelist George Whitefield preaches to a crowd of listeners while holding a bag of "cash." The crowd below adds critical comment, one man remarking that the "Rev. Mr. Humbug" is worth no more than a "halfpenny," and the woman next to him wishing that Whitefield's "spirit was in my flesh."

belief in a personal and direct relationship with God outside the order of the church. Itinerant preachers appeared in the countryside, stirring up trouble. Many congregations split into feuding factions, and ministers found themselves challenged by their newly awakened parishioners. Never had there been such turmoil in New England churches.

The revivals began somewhat later in the South, first developing in the mid-1740s, reaching full impact in the 1760s. They affected not only white southerners but also for the first time introduced many slaves to Christianity. Baptist churches of the South in the era of the American Revolution included members of both races and featured spontaneous preaching by slaves as well as masters. In the nineteenth century white and black Christians would go their separate ways, but the joint experience of the eighteenth-century Awakening shaped the religious cultures of both groups.

Many other "unchurched" colonists were brought back to Protestantism by revivalism. But a careful examination of

statistics suggests that the proportion of church members in the general population did not increase during the middle decades of the century. While the number of churches more than doubled from 1740 to 1780, the colonial population grew even faster, increasing threefold. The greatest impact was on families already associated with congregations. Before the Awakening, attendance at church had been mostly an adult affair, but throughout the colonies the revival of religion had its deepest effects on young people, who flocked to church in greater numbers than ever before. For years the number of people experiencing conversion had been steadily falling but now full membership surged. Church membership previously had been concentrated among women, leading Cotton Mather, for one, to speculate that perhaps women were indeed more godly. But men were particularly affected by the revival of religion, and their attendance and membership rose.

The Politics of Revivalism

Revivalism appealed most of all to groups that felt bypassed by the economic and cultural development of the British colonies during the first half of the eighteenth century. The New Lights tended to draw their greatest strength from small farmers and less prosperous craftsmen. Many members of the upper class and the comfortable "middling sort" viewed the excesses of revivalism as indications of anarchy, and they became even more committed to rational religion.

Revivalism sometimes had political implications. In Connecticut, for example, Old Lights politicized the religious dispute by passing a series of laws in the General Assembly designed to suppress revivalism. In one town, revivalists refused to pay taxes supporting the established church and were jailed. Judges sympathetic to New Light views were thrown off the bench, and others were denied their elected seats in the assembly. The arrogance of these actions was met with popular outrage: by the 1760s the Connecticut New Lights had organized themselves politically and, in what amounted to a political rebellion, succeeded in turning the Old Lights out of office. New Light politicians would provide the leadership for the American Revolution in Connecticut.

Such direct connections between religion and politics were rare. There can be little doubt, however, that for many people revivalism offered the first opportunity to participate actively in public debate and public action that affected the direction of their lives. Choices about religious styles, ministers, and doctrine were thrown open for public discourse, and ordinary people began to believe that their opinions actually counted for something. Underlying the debate over these issues were insecurities about warfare, economic growth, and the development of colonial society. Revivalism empowered ordinary people to question their leaders, an experience that would prove critical in the political struggles to come.

Baptism by Full Immersion in the Schuylkill River of Pennsylvania, an engraving by Henry Dawkins illustrating events in the history of American Baptists, was published in Philadelphia in 1770. With calls for renewed piety and purity, the Great Awakening reinvigorated American Protestantism. The Baptists preached an egalitarian message, and their congregations in the South often included both white and black Protestants.

SOURCE: Henry Dawkins, *Baptismal Ceremony Beside the Schuylkill*. Engraving, 1770. John Carter Brown Library at Brown University.

Conclusion

By the middle of the eighteenth century a number of distinct colonial regions had emerged in North America, all of them with rising populations demanding that more land be seized from the Indians. Some colonies attempted to ensure homogeneity, whereas others embraced diversity. Within the British colonies, New England in particular seemed bound to the past, whereas the middle colonies and the backcountry pointed the way toward pluralism and expansion. These developments placed them in direct competition with the expansionist plans of the French and at odds with Indian peoples committed to the defense of their homelands.

The economic development of the British colonies introduced new social and cultural tensions that led to the Great Awakening, a massive revival of religion that was the first transcolonial event in American history. Beginning in small communities like Northampton, Massachusetts, the revivals affected thousands of people, leading to a renewal of religious passions. Rather than resuscitating old traditions, however, the Awakening seemed to point people toward a more active role in their own political futures. Those transformations added to the differences between the British colonies, on the one hand, and New Spain and the French Crescent on the other.

Review Questions

1. What were the principal colonial regions of North America? Discuss their similarities and their differences. Contrast the development of their political systems.

2. Why did the Spanish and the French close their colonies to immigration? Why did the British open their colonies? How do you explain the ethnic homogeneity of New England and the ethnic pluralism of New York and Pennsylvania?

3. What were the principal trends in the history of Indian America in the eighteenth century?

4. Discuss the development of class differences in the Spanish, French, and British colonies in the eighteenth century.

5. Discuss the effects of the Great Awakening on the subsequent history of the British colonies.

Recommended Reading

Jon Butler, *Becoming America: The Revolution Before 1776* (2000). A history that emphasizes the diversity, economic prosperity, participatory politics, and religious pluralism of the eighteenth-century British colonies.

CHRONOLOGY

1636	Harvard College founded
1674	Bishopric of Québec established
1680s	William Penn begins recruiting settlers from the European continent
1682	Mary Rowlandson's *The Sovereignty and Goodness of God*
1689	Toleration Act passed by Parliament
1690s	Beginnings of Jesuit missions in Arizona
1693	College of William and Mary founded
1700s	Plains Indians begin adoption of the horse
1701	Yale College founded; Iroquois sign treaty of neutrality with France
1716	Spanish begin construction of Texas missions

1732	Franklin begins publishing *Poor Richard's Almanac*
1738	George Whitefield first tours the colonies
1740s	Great Awakening gets under way in the Northeast
1740	Parliament passes a naturalization law for the colonies
1746	College of New Jersey (Princeton University) founded
1760s	Great Awakening achieves full impact in the South
1769	Spanish colonization of California begins
1775	Indian revolt at San Diego
1781	Los Angeles founded

Edward Countryman, *Americans: A Collision of Histories* (1996). An important synthesis that includes the many peoples and cultures of North America.

W. J. Eccles, *The Canadian Frontier, 1534–1760* (1983). An introduction to the history of French America by a leading scholar of colonial Canada.

David Hackett Fischer, *Albion's Seed: Four British Folkways in America* (1990). An engaging history with fascinating details on the regions of New England, Pennsylvania, Virginia, and the backcountry.

Jack P. Greene, *Pursuits of Happiness: The Social Development of Early Modern British Colonies and the Formation of American Culture* (1986). A distillation of a tremendous amount of historical material on community life in British North America.

Pekka Hämäläinen, *The Comanche Empire* (2008). A prize-winning history of the most powerful people of the southern Great Plains during the eighteenth and early nineteenth.

Frank Lambert, *Inventing the "Great Awakening"* (1999). Argues that the revivialists themselves created the idea of the Great Awakening to further their evangelical work.

Jackson Turner Main, *The Social Structure of Revolutionary America* (1965). A classic study of colonial social structure, with statistics, tables, and enlightening interpretations.

George Marsden, *Jonathan Edwards: A Life* (2003). A new and comprehensive biography that emphasizes Edwards's work as both a pastor and an intellectual.

Lucy Eldersveld Murphy, *A Gathering of Rivers: Indians, Métis, and Mining in the Western Great Lakes, 1737–1832* (2000). Demonstrates the success of Indian communities in adapting to colonialism through the diversification of their economies, intermarriage, and constructing multiethnic communities.

James A. Sandos, *Converting California: Indians and Franciscans in the Missions* (2004). A balanced treatment of missionaries and natives in eighteenth- and nineteenth-century California.

David J. Weber, *The Spanish Frontier in North America* (1992). A magnificent treatment of the entire Spanish borderlands from Florida to California. Includes important chapters on colonial government and social life.

Marianne S. Wokeck, *Trade in Strangers: The Beginning of Mass Migration to North America* (1999). The first important study of immigration in the eighteenth century, arguing that these migrations served as models for European mass migration of the next century.

PEARSON myhistorylab Connections

Reinforce what you learned in this chapter by studying the many documents, images, maps, review tools, and videos available at www.myhistorylab.com.

Read and Review

✓• Study and Review Chapter 5

•••• Read the Document

An Older Businessman Advises a Young One (1748)

A Boston Woman Writes about Her Trip to New York (1704)

Jonathan Edwards, Sinners in the Hands of an Angry God (1741)

Benjamin Franklin on George Whitefield (1771)

👁 See the Map *Colonial Products*

Research and Explore

•••• Read the Document

Exploring America: America and the Horse

Profiles
Martha Ballard
Benjamin Franklin

History Bookshelf: The Autobiography of Benjamin Franklin *(1788)*

👁 Watch the Video *Chief Plenty Coups, Crow*

((•• Hear the Audio

Hear the audio files for Chapter 5 at
www.myhistorylab.com.

6

Chapter 6 at www.myhistorylab.com

((•—Hear the Audio

From Empire to Independence 1750–1776

CHAPTER OUTLINE

Continental Congress. Chaplain Jacob Duché leading the first prayer in the First Continental Congress at Carpenter's Hall, Philadelphia, September 1774; mezzotint, 1848. The Granger Collection.

The First Continental Congress Begins to Shape a National Political Community

The opening of the First Continental Congress, held in Philadelphia in September 1774, did not bode well. One of the delegates moved that the session open with prayer, but others objected. "We were so divided in religious sentiments," wrote John Adams, a representative from Massachusetts, "that we could not join in the same act of worship." Was the Congress to be stymied, here at the very beginning, by the things separating them? Adams's cousin and fellow Massachusetts delegate Samuel Adams leapt to his feet. He was no bigot, he proclaimed, and was willing to hear a prayer "from any gentleman of piety and virtue who was at the same time a friend to his country." Putting aside their religious differences, the delegates agreed to ask a local clergyman to give the invocation. He took as his text the Thirty-fifth Psalm: "Plead my cause, O Lord, with them that strive with me; fight against them that fight against me." He "prayed with such fervor, such Ardor, such Earnestness and Pathos, and in Language so elegant and sublime," wrote John Adams to his wife, that "it has had an excellent Effect upon every Body here."

The incident highlights the most important task confronting the First Continental Congress—strengthening their common cause without compromising their local identities. The delegates, noted

AMERICAN Communities

133

Adams, were like "ambassadors from a dozen belligerent powers of Europe." They represented distinct colonies with traditions and histories as different as those of separate countries. Moreover, these lawyers, merchants, and planters, leaders in their respective colonies, were strangers to one another. "Every man," Adams worried, "is a great man, an orator, a critic, a statesman, and therefore every man, upon every question, must show his oratory, his criticism, and his political abilities." As a result, "business is drawn and spun out to an immeasurable length. I believe that if it was moved and seconded that we should come to a resolution that three and two make five, we should be entertained with logic and rhetorick, law, history, politicks and mathematics concerning the subject for two whole days."

Britain's North American colonies enjoyed considerable prosperity during the first half of the eighteenth century. So in 1765 British authorities thought it only fair that colonists shoulder some of the expense of the late great war for empire—the Seven Years' War—during which Great Britain soundly defeated France and forced the cession of the French North American colonies. But the new taxes and trade restrictions inspired resistance among the colonists. By the opening session of the First Continental Congress, peaceful protest had escalated into violent riot, and in an attempt to force the colonists to acknowledge the power of Parliament to make laws binding them "in all cases whatsoever," the British had proclaimed a series of repressive measures, including the closure of ports in Massachusetts and the suspension of that colony's elected government. In this atmosphere of crisis, most of the colonial assemblies elected delegates for a "Continental Congress" to map out a coordinated response. If the fifty-six men assembled in Philadelphia failed to act collectively, declared delegate Arthur Lee of Virginia, they would be "attacked and destroyed by piece-meal." Abigail Adams, the politically astute wife of John Adams, agreed. "You have before you," she wrote her husband, "the greatest national concerns that ever came before any people."

Despite their differences, during seven weeks of deliberations the delegates succeeded in forging an agreement on the principles and policies they would follow in this, the most serious crisis in the history of the British North American colonies. At the outset they resolved that each colony would have one vote, thereby committing themselves to the preservation of provincial autonomy. Their most vexing problems they sent to committees, whose members could sound each other out without committing themselves on the public record. They added to their daily routine dinners, parties, and much late-night tavern-hopping. And in so doing they began to construct a community of interest and friendship among themselves. "It has taken us much time to get acquainted," John Adams wrote to Abigail, but by the time he departed Philadelphia he had begun to think of his fellow representatives as "a collection of the greatest men upon this continent."

These were the first tentative steps toward the creation of an American national political community. Communities are not simply local but can also be regional, national, and even international. In a town or village, feelings of association come from daily, face-to-face contacts, but for larger groups those connections must be deliberately constructed. In their final declaration the delegates pledged to "firmly agree and associate, under the sacred ties of virtue, honor and love of our country." They asked their countrymen to remember "the poorer sort" among them during the time of trouble they knew was coming. They demanded that patriotic Americans "break off all dealings" with those refusing to act, thus drawing a distinction between "insiders" and "outsiders," one of the essential first steps in the construction of community identity.

Patrick Henry, a Virginia delegate strongly committed to American independence, was exuberant by the time the Congress adjourned in late October. "The distinctions between Virginians, Pennsylvanians, New Yorkers, and New Englanders, are no more," he declared. "I am not a Virginian, but an American." He exaggerated the unity. It remained very much a work in progress. Local, provincial, and regional differences would continue to clash. But Henry voiced an important hope.

In its attempt to force the colonists to pay a share of the costs of empire through taxation, Great Britain had sparked a revolt of both elite and ordinary colonists. The road to a shared community of interest among British colonists, distinguishing them from the mother country, was marked by milestones with legendary names: the Stamp Act, the Boston Massacre, the Tea Party, the Intolerable Acts. The violent events that would follow

1. What were the conflicts that led to the Seven Years' War, and what were the outcomes for Great Britain, France, and the American Indians?

2. Why did American nationalism develop in the aftermath of the French and Indian War?

3. What was Great Britain's changing policy toward its North American colonies in the 1760s?

4. What were the assumptions of American republicanism?

5. How did the colonies attempt to achieve unity in their confrontation with Great Britain?

FOCUS Questions

1750–1776

the First Continental Congress—the first clash of arms at Lexington and Concord, the siege of Boston, and the Battle of Bunker Hill—would lead to a second session of the Congress. Reluctantly at first, then enthusiastically, the delegates would move toward independence. The difficult months and years of warfare would sorely test the imagined community of the united colonies, and the differences among them would frequently threaten to abort the nation being born. But the sessions of the First Continental Congress marked the moment when Americans first began the struggle to overcome local differences in pursuit of national goals.

Philadelphia

AMERICAN Communities

The Seven Years' War in America

Leaders of the British colonies made an early attempt at cooperation in 1754, when representatives from New England, New York, Pennsylvania, and Maryland met to consider a joint approach to military challenges from the French and their Indian allies. Even as the delegates met, fighting between French Canadians and Virginians began near the headwaters of the Ohio River in the Appalachian Mountains, the first shots in a great global war for empire pitting Great Britain (and Prussia) against the combined might of France, Spain, and Austria. In North America this would be the final and most destructive armed conflict between the British and the French empires. Ultimately the war would decide the future of the vast region between the Appalachian Mountains and the Mississippi River. It would also lay the groundwork for the conflict between the British and the colonists that led to the American Revolution.

The Albany Conference of 1754

The British Board of Trade convened the 1754 meeting in the New York town of Albany on the Hudson River. They wanted the colonies to consider a collective response to

This woodcut cartoon, created by Benjamin Franklin, was published in his newspaper, the *Pennsylvania Gazette*, on May 9, 1754. It accompanied Franklin's editorial about the "disunited state" of the colonies on the eve of the French and Indian War, and helped make his point about the need for unity. It plays on the superstition that a snake that had been cut into pieces would come back to life if the pieces were put back together before sunset. The cartoon was reprinted widely, and used again, more than twenty years later, during the Revolutionary War.

SOURCE: The Library Company of Philadelphia

the continuing conflict with New France and the Indians of the interior. High on the agenda was the negotiation of a settlement with the leaders of the Iroquois Confederacy, who had grown impatient with colonial land grabbing. But as the negotiations began, behind the scenes real estate developers were bribing minor Iroquois chiefs, affixing their signatures on a "deed" for an enormous tract of land in Pennsylvania, and turning the meeting into a vehicle for the very abuses the British sought to correct. Angered by these manipulations, the official Iroquois delegation walked out of the conference refusing all offers to join a British alliance.

Despite this failure, the Albany Conference succeeded in adopting the "Plan of Union" put forward by Benjamin Franklin, a delegate from Pennsylvania. Franklin, whom the British had appointed Postmaster General of the North American colonies, was especially sensitive to the need for cooperation. His proposal would have placed Indian affairs, western settlement, and other items of mutual interest under the authority of a grand council composed of representatives elected by the colonial assemblies and led by a British-appointed president. Franklin was struck by the unity of the Iroquois Confederacy. "It would be a very strange thing," he declared, if "ignorant Savages should be capable of forming a Scheme for such a Union, and yet a like Union should be impracticable for ten or a Dozen English Colonies." British authorities, however, were suspicious of the plan, fearing it would create a powerful entity they would have difficulty controlling. They had nothing to fear, for all the colonies rejected the Albany Plan of Union, fearful of losing their autonomy. The absence of cooperation would prove one of the greatest weaknesses during the subsequent war with the French, which was fought in far-flung locations requiring the coordination of command.

France vs. Britain in America

There were three violent flash points in the conflict between Great Britain and France for control of North America. First was the northern Atlantic coast, the ragged boundary between New France and New England. In 1713 France had ceded this region, known as Acadia, to the British, who called it Nova Scotia. To protect the ocean approach to their colonial heartland, the French constructed the port and fortress of Louisbourg on Cape Breton Island. In 1745, during King George's War, New Englanders captured Louisbourg, but the French reclaimed it upon the settlement of that conflict in 1748 (see Chapter 4). In 1749 the British established a large naval facility at Halifax in Nova Scotia, but worried about the loyalty of the 18,000 French-speaking Acadians of the province.

The second flash point was the border region between New France and New York, extending from Niagara Falls to Lake Champlain, where Canadians and New Yorkers were rivals for the lucrative Indian trade. The French, who found it difficult to compete against superior English goods, resorted instead to military might, garrisoning fortifications on Lake George and at Niagara. In this zone the strategic advantage was held by the Iroquois Confederacy.

The third area of conflict was the Ohio country, the trans-Appalachian region bisected by the Ohio River. The rich lands along the Ohio were a prime target of British land speculators and backcountry settlers, whom the French feared would overrun their isolated outposts and threaten their entire Mississippi trading empire. To reinforce their claim, in 1749 the French sent a heavily armed force down the Ohio River to ward off the British, and in 1752 they attempted to expel all British traders from the region. Then, in 1753, French Canadian troops began the construction of a line of forts running south from Lake Erie to the headwaters of the Ohio River. The French "have stripped us of more than nine parts in ten of North America," complained one British official, "and left us only a skirt of coast along the Atlantic shore." In a direct challenge to the French claims in the West, the British government issued a royal charter for more than 200,000 acres to the Ohio Company, organized by London and Virginia investors.

The Indian peoples of the Ohio country had interests of their own to defend. In addition to native inhabitants, the region had become a refuge for Indian peoples who had fled the British seaborne colonies. Most of the Indians of the Ohio country opposed further British expansion and wished to make the Appalachians into a defensive wall. Meanwhile the Iroquois Confederacy continued the game of playing the British against the French. In the South the Creeks (and to a lesser extent the Cherokees and Choctaws) attempted to carve out a similar balancing role for themselves among the British in the Lower South, the French in Louisiana, and the Spanish in Florida. These Indian confederacies saw it as in their interest to perpetuate the existing colonial stalemate. Their position would be greatly undermined by an overwhelming victory for either side.

Frontier Warfare

As the delegates to the Albany Conference conducted their business, they received news of the first clash with the French. Colonel George Washington, a young militia officer sent by the governor of Virginia to expel the French from the upper Ohio, had been forced to surrender his troops to a French Canadian force. The French now commanded the interior country from Fort Duquesne at the "Forks of the Ohio," the junction of the Allegheny and Monongahela Rivers.

Taking up the challenge, in 1755 the British launched an effort to strike the French in all three zones. An army of New England militiamen succeeded in capturing two important French forts on the northern border of Nova Scotia. The British then began the systematic removal of the Acadian inhabitants, dispersing them widely throughout the Atlantic world, replacing them with settlers from New England. A substantial number of the Acadians ended up in Louisiana, where they became known as "Cajuns." The Acadian expulsion, so similar to modern episodes of "ethnic cleansing," is an infamous chapter in the British imperial record in North America.

Elsewhere the British military campaigns failed miserably. In northern New York a large colonial force was repulsed by the French. And on July 9, 1755, Major General Edward Braddock's 1,500 British troops were ambushed and destroyed by a much smaller force of 600 confederated Indian fighters supported by a mere 30 French Canadians. A total of 456 British soldiers and officers died, including Braddock himself. It was the worst military defeat of a British army during the eighteenth century.

Full-scale warfare between Great Britain (supported by Prussia) and France (supported by Spain) began the next year, 1756. This was truly a global war, fought in Europe, Asia, and America, and known to history as the Seven Years' War (or the French and Indian War in America) (see Map 6.1). The first two years were a near catastrophe for Great Britain. Indians raided backcountry settlements, killed thousands of settlers, and penetrated deep into the coastal colonies, throwing

See the Map
The Seven Years' War at
www.myhistorylab.com

MAP 6.1 The War for Empire in North America, 1754–1763 The Seven Years' War in America (also known as the French and Indian War) was fought in three principal areas: Nova Scotia and what was then Acadia, the frontier between New France and New York, and the upper Ohio River—gateway to the Old Northwest.

British colonists into absolute panic. French Canadians captured British forts in northern New York. The lack of colonial cooperation greatly hampered the British attempt to mount a counterattack. When British commanders tried to exert direct control over provincial troops, they succeeded only in angering local authorities.

The Conquest of Canada

In 1757 William Pitt, an enthusiastic advocate of British expansion, became prime minister of Great Britain. Believing that the global war could be won in North America, he subsidized Prussian allies to fight the war in Europe, reserving his own forces for naval and colonial operations. Pitt committed himself to the conquest of Canada and the final elimination of French competition in North America. Promising that the war would be fought "at His Majesty's expense," Pitt secured colonial cooperation with a massive infusion of British currency and credit. He dispatched over 20,000 regular British

troops across the Atlantic. In combination with colonial militias, Pitt massed more than 50,000 troops against Canada. This was unlike anything ever seen before in North America.

The British were also effective at attracting Indian support. In 1758, at a conference with representatives of the Iroquois and the Ohio Indians held in the Pennsylvania town of Easton, British officials promised to establish "clear and fixed boundaries between our settlements and their hunting grounds, so that each party may know their own and be a mutual protection to each other of their respective possessions." This succeeded in neutralizing a good deal of the Indian support for the French.

Thus did Pitt succeed in reversing the course of the war. Regular and provincial forces captured the French fortress of Louisbourg in July 1758, setting the stage for the invasion of New France. A month later a force of New Englanders captured the strategic French fort of Oswego

The death of General James Wolfe at the conclusion of the battle in which the British captured Québec in 1759 became the subject of American artist Benjamin West's most famous painting, which was exhibited to tremendous acclaim in London in 1770.

SOURCE: Benjamin West (1738–1820), *The Death of General Wolfe* 1770. Oil on canvas, 152.6 × 214.5 cm. Transfer from the Canadian War Memorials, 1921 (Gift of the 2nd Duke of Westminster, Eaton Hall, Cheshire, 1918). National Gallery of Canada, Ottawa, Ontario.

on Lake Ontario, thereby preventing the Canadians from resupplying their western posts. Encouraged by British promises, increasing numbers of Indians deserted the French, forcing them to abandon Fort Duquesne, which the British occupied and renamed Fort Pitt (today's Pittsburgh) in honor of the prime minister. The last of the French forts in northern New York fell in 1759. In the South, British troops crushed the Cherokees and opened negotiations with the Creeks and Choctaws.

British forces now converged on French Canada. In 1759 colonial and British troops, acting on General James Wolfe's order to "burn and lay waste the country," plundered farms along the St. Lawrence and shelled Québec City. Finally, in an epic battle fought on the Plains of Abraham before the city walls, more than 2,000 British, French, American, and Canadian men lost their lives, including both Wolfe and the Marquis de Montcalm, the French commander. The British army prevailed and

Québec fell. The next year another British force moved up the Hudson and conquered Montreal. Its fall marked the end of the French empire in America.

In the final two years of the war the British swept French ships from the seas, conquered the Spanish colony of Cuba, captured the Spanish Philippines, and achieved dominance in India. In the 1763 Treaty of Paris, France lost all its possessions on the North American mainland, ceding to Great Britain all its claims east of the Mississippi, with the exception of New Orleans, which Britain agreed that France would pass to Spain, along with other French claims to the huge trans-Mississippi region, which the British had no interest in administering. In exchange for the return of its Caribbean and Pacific colonies, Spain ceded Florida to Britain. Three centuries of European imperial rivalry in eastern North America ended with complete victory for the British Empire (see Map 6.2).

MAP 6.2 European Claims in North America, 1750 and 1763 As a result of the British victory in the Seven Years' War, the map of colonial claims in North America was fundamentally transformed.

The Struggle for the West

The Ohio Indians were shocked when told of the French cession. "The French had no right to give away [our] country," they responded. They were "never conquered by any nation." A new set of British policies soon shocked them even more. The French and the British had long used gift-giving as a way of gaining favor with Indians. Spanish officials who replaced the French in Louisiana continued that old policy. But in one of his first official acts, General Jeffery Amherst, British military governor of the western region, banned presents to Indian chiefs and tribes, arguing that "it would be madness to the highest degree ever to bestow favors on a race who have so treacherously . . . attacked our Posts and butchered our Garrisons." Not only were Indians angered by Amherst's policy, but they were also frustrated by his refusal to supply them with the ammunition they needed for hunting. Many were left destitute.

In this climate, hundreds of Ohio Indians became disciples of an Indian visionary named Neolin ("The Enlightened One"), known to the English as the Delaware Prophet. The core of Neolin's teaching was that Indians had been corrupted by European ways and needed to purify themselves by returning to their traditions and preparing for a holy war. In the spring of 1763 a confederacy of tribes inspired by Neolin's ideas laid plans for a coordinated attack on British frontier posts. The principal leader of this resistance was an Ottawa chief named Pontiac, renowned as an orator and political leader. "We tell you now," Pontiac declared to British officials, "the French never conquered us, neither did they purchase a foot of our Country, nor have they a right to give it to you." In May 1763 Pontiac's alliance simultaneously attacked all the British posts in the West, destroying eight of them, but failing to take the key forts at Niagara, Detroit, and the forks of the Ohio River (Fort Pitt). Pontiac and his followers fought on for another year, but most Indians sued for peace.

They were encouraged by the announcement of the British Royal Proclamation of 1763, which in keeping with the promise made in the Treaty of Easton declared the trans-Appalachian region to be "Indian Country,"

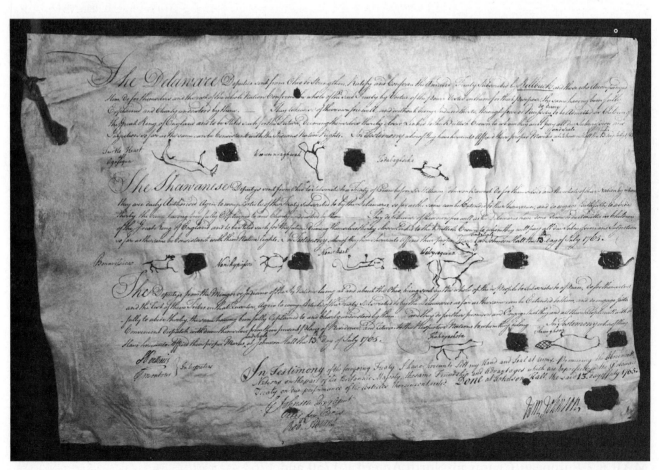

A treaty between the Delaware, Shawnee, and Mingo (western Iroquois) Indians and Great Britain, July 13, 1765, at the conclusion of the Indian uprising known as Pontiac's Rebellion. The Indian chiefs signed with pictographs symbolizing their clans, each notarized with an official wax seal.

reserved as a homeland for the Indian nations. It is "essential to our interest," the Proclamation stated, "that the several nations or tribes of Indians with whom we are connected, and who live under our protection, should not be molested or disturbed." British settlers had expected that the removal of the French threat would allow them to move into the West, but under the terms of the royal Proclamation specific authorization from the crown was now required for any movement onto protected Indian lands. Settlers were outraged that the British would award territory to mortal enemies who slaughtered more than 4,000 colonists during the war. In an act emblematic of the anger backcountry settlers felt about these restrictions, in December 1763 a mob of backcountry Pennsylvanians, calling themselves "the Paxton Boys," butchered twenty Christian Indians at the small village of Conestoga on the Susquehanna River. When colonial authorities attempted to arrest the murderers, 600 frontiersmen marched on Philadelphia in protest. Negotiations led by Benjamin Franklin helped prevent a bloody confrontation.

In fact, the British proved unable and ultimately unwilling to prevent the westward migration that was a dynamic part of the colonization of British North America. Within a few years of the war, New Englanders by the thousands were moving into the northern Green Mountain district, known as Vermont. In the middle colonies, New York settlers pushed ever closer to the homeland of the Iroquois, while others settled within the protective radius of Fort Pitt in western Pennsylvania. Hunters, stock herders, and farmers crossed over the first range of the Appalachians in Virginia and North Carolina, planting pioneer communities in what are now the states of West Virginia, Tennessee, and Kentucky. In response to demands by settlers and speculators, British authorities were soon pressing the Iroquois and Cherokees for cessions of land in Indian Country. No longer able to play off rival colonial powers, Indians were reduced to a choice between compliance and resistance. Weakened by the recent war, they chose to sign away lands. In the Treaty of Hard Labor in 1768, the Cherokees ceded a vast tract on the upper Tennessee River, where British settlers had already planted communities. In the Treaty of Fort Stanwix, signed the same year, the Iroquois gave up their claim to the Ohio Valley, hoping thereby to deflect English settlement away from their own homeland in New York.

The individual colonies were even more aggressive. Locked in a dispute with Pennsylvania about jurisdiction in the Ohio country, in 1773 Virginia governor John Murray, Earl of Dunmore, sent a force to occupy Fort Pitt. In 1774, in an attempt to gain legitimacy for his dispute with Pennsylvania, Dunmore provoked a frontier war with the Shawnees. After dealing them a humiliating defeat, Dunmore forced them to cede the upper Ohio River Valley to Virginia. The Ohio Indians angrily complained about the outcome of Dunmore's War. The king, they argued, had guaranteed that the boundary between colonial and Indian land "should forever after be looked upon as a barrier between us." But the Americans "entirely disregard and despise the settlement agreed upon by their Superiors and us," and despite the agreement, "are come in vast numbers to the Ohio, and gave our people to understand that they wou'd settle wherever they pleas'd. If this is the case we must look upon every engagement you made with us as void and of no effect." The continuing struggle for the West would be an important issue in the coming Revolutionary struggle.

The Emergence of American Nationalism

No colonial power of the mid-eighteenth century could match Britain in projecting imperial power over the face of the globe. During the years following its victory in the Seven Years' War, Britain turned confidently to the reorganization of its North American empire. The new colonial policy plunged British authorities into a new and ultimately more threatening conflict with the colonists, who had begun to develop a sense of a separate identity.

An American Identity

Despite the anger of frontier settlers over the Proclamation of 1763, the conclusion of the Seven Years' War left most colonists proud of their place in the British Empire. But many people had begun to note important contrasts between themselves and the mother country. The arrival of thousands of British troops raised the problem of where to house them. British commanders demanded they be quartered in private homes. British subjects at home were protected against such demands by an act of Parliament, but that protection had expressly not been extended to the colonies.

Americans who were thrown into contact with regular British troops were shocked by their profanity, lewdness, and violence. They were equally shocked by the swift and terrible punishment inflicted by aristocratic officers to keep those men in line. A Massachusetts militiaman wrote of witnessing the punishment of two soldiers sentenced to eight hundred lashes apiece. "The flesh appeared to be entirely whipped from their shoulders, and they hung as mute and motionless as though they had long since been deprived of life." A military doctor stood nearby with a vial of smelling salts, periodically reviving the men and taunting them: "damn you, you can bear it yet." It was, this observer concluded, "a specimen of British cruelty." Men who witnessed such scenes found it easy to believe the danger of British "slavery."

Colonial forces, by contrast, were composed of volunteer companies. Militia officers were moderate in the administration of punishment, knowing they had to maintain the enthusiasm of their troops. Discipline thus fell considerably below the standards to which British officers were accustomed. "Riff-raff," one British general labeled colonial troops, "the lowest dregs of the people, both officers and men." Americans believed British scorn blinded them to the important role played by the colonists in the Seven Years' War. Mutual suspicion was sometimes expressed in name-calling. Regular soldiers derisively called colonists "Yankees" (thought to be derived from the Dutch "Jan Kaas," or "John Cheese," pronounced "yan-kees"), while colonists heckled the red-coated British as "lobsters." It was during the Seven Years' War that many colonists began to view themselves as having an identity distinct from the British.

The Seven Years' War also strengthened a sense of intercolonial unity among the colonists. Farm boys who never before had ventured outside the communities of their birth fought in distant regions with men from other colonies. Such experiences reinforced a developing sense of national community. This sentiment built on previous developments, including the growth of intercolonial commerce, which involved the movement of people as well as goods. The first stagecoach lines linking seaboard cities began operation in the 1750s. And, encouraged by Postmaster Benjamin Franklin, the colonies constructed or improved post roads for transporting the mails.

The Press, Politics, and Republicanism

One of the most important means of intercolonial communication was the weekly newspaper. Early in the century the colonial press had functioned as a mouthpiece for British officialdom. But a bold stroke for freedom of the press was struck in 1735 when a New York City jury acquitted editor John Peter Zenger of seditious libel after he printed antigovernment articles. "Shall the press be silenced that evil governors may have their way?" Zenger's attorney asked. "The question before the court," he declared, was the cause "of every free man that lives under a British government on the main of America." Newspapers became a lively means of public discourse, and by 1760 more than twenty weekly papers were being published in the British colonies.

A protest against the Stamp Act from newspaper editor William Bradford, publisher of the *Pennsylvania Journal and Weekly Advertiser*. Bradford decorated his masthead with skull and crossbones, and in the bottom right corner included a satiric version of "the fatal Stamp," also with skull and crossbones.

The papers carried an increasing amount of colonial news. From the 1730s to the 1770s intercolonial coverage in the colonial press increased six fold. Editors began to look at events from what they called a "continental" perspective. This trend accelerated during the Seven Years' War, when communities demanded news of the distant places where their men were fighting. Thus did the war promote a new spirit of nationalism and a wider notion of community. Editors began using the

OVERVIEW | Eleven British Measures That Led to Revolution

Year	Legislation	
1764	**Sugar Act**	Placed prohibitive duty on imported sugar; provided for greater regulation of American shipping to suppress smuggling
1765	**Stamp Act**	Required the purchase of specially embossed paper for newspapers, legal documents, licenses, insurance policies, ships' papers, and playing cards; struck at printers, lawyers, tavern owners, and other influential colonists. Repealed in 1766
1766	**Declaratory Act**	Asserted the authority of Parliament to make laws binding the colonies "in all cases whatsoever"
1767	**Townshend Revenue Acts**	Placed import duties, collectible before goods entered colonial markets, on many commodities including lead, glass, paper, and tea. Repealed in 1770
1773	**Tea Act**	Gave the British East India Company a monopoly on all tea imports to America, hitting at American merchants
1774	**Coercive or Intolerable Acts**	
	Boston Port Bill	Closed Boston Harbor
	Massachusetts Government Act	Annulled the Massachusetts colonial charter
	Administration of Justice Act	Protected British officials from colonial courts by sending them home for trial if arrested
	Quartering Act	Legalized the housing of British troops in private homes
	Québec Act	Created a highly centralized government for Canada

term "American" to denote the common identity of British colonists. It was an early sign of the political community the delegates began to construct at the First Continental Congress.

Colonial editors frequently reprinted writings by British authors, including poems by Alexander Pope, satiric essays by Jonathan Swift, and political philosophy by John Locke. They also frequently reprinted political essays by British republicans, who warned of the growing threat to liberty posed by the unchecked exercise of state power. Some essayists suggested that a conspiracy existed among European monarchs, aristocrats, and Catholics to quash liberty and reinstitute tyranny. These ideas came to define a political consensus in the British colonies, a point of view that came to be called "republicanism."

Republicanism asserted that state power, by its very nature, was antithetical to liberty and, consequently, had to be limited; that the authority of rulers should be conditional rather than absolute; and that the people had an inherent right to withdraw their support from the government if it did not fulfill their expectations, and organize a new one. The best guarantee of good government, republicans argued, was a broad distribution of power to the people, who could not only select their own leaders but also vote them out of office. The theory of republican government relied on the virtue of the people, on their willingness to make the stability and justice of the political community their first priority. But that kind of virtue was possible only for an "independent" population in control of its own affairs. As Thomas Jefferson once wrote, "dependence begets subservience and venality, suffocates the germ of virtue, and prepares fit tools for the designs of ambition." The widespread individual ownership of property, Jefferson argued, especially the ownership of land, was the most secure foundation of an independent and virtuous people.

This was a political theory that fit well with the circumstances of American life, with its wide base of property ownership, its tradition of representative assemblies, and its history of struggle with royal authority. Contrast the assumptions of republicans with those of British monarchists, who argued that the good society was one in which a strong state, controlled by a hereditary elite, kept a vicious and unruly people in line.

The Sugar and Stamp Acts

The emerging sense of American political identity was soon tested by British measures designed to raise revenue in the colonies. To quell Indian uprisings and stifle discontent among the French and Spanish populations of Québec and Florida, at the conclusion of the Seven Years' War the British decided to keep 10,000 regular troops stationed in North America. The cost of maintaining this force added to the enormous debt run up during the fighting. In 1764 Prime Minister George Grenville decided to obtain the needed revenue from American colonists. Parliament passed a measure known as the Sugar Act, which placed a tariff on sugar imported into the colonies.

•••⌐Read the Document

Benjamin Franklin, Testimony against the Stamp Act (1766) at **www.myhistorylab.com**

Anticipating that American importers would attempt to avoid the duty by smuggling, Parliament also broadened the jurisdiction of the vice-admiralty court at Halifax, which had jurisdiction over customs cases. Courts of vice-admiralty were hated and feared because they neither provided for trial by jury nor acted on a presumption of innocence. Both merchants and artisans viewed the Sugar Act as a threat to their livelihoods, and there were public protests in many port towns. The residents of Boston were especially vocal. The town meeting proposed a boycott of certain English imports, and the tactic of nonimportation soon spread to other port towns.

James Otis, a brilliant Massachusetts lawyer, became one of the first Americans to give voice to these protests, striking a number of themes that were repeated many times over the next fifteen years. Every man, Otis declared, in rhetoric lifted directly from the Great Awakening, "was an independent sovereign, subject to no law but the law written on his heart and revealed to him by his Maker." No government, he argued, using the logic of British republicanism, could rightfully deprive a

•••⌐Read the Document

Otis, The Rights of the British Colonies Asserted and Proved (1763) at **www.myhistorylab.com**

man of the right "to his life, his liberty, and his property." Otis's most memorable phrase would echo throughout the subsequent decade: "Taxation without representation is tyranny."

The Stamp Act Crisis

But wasn't it only fair, Prime Minister Grenville responded, that the colonists help pay the costs of the empire? And what better way to do so than by taxation? Although colonial assemblies had raised taxes during the war, colonial tax rates remained significantly lower than those in the mother country. Ignoring American protests, in early 1765 Grenville pushed through a considerably more sweeping revenue measure known as the Stamp Act. This legislation required the purchase of specially embossed paper for all newspapers, legal documents, licenses, insurance policies, ships' papers, even dice and

Samuel Adams, a second cousin of John Adams, was a leader of the Boston radicals and an organizer of the Sons of Liberty. The artist of this portrait, John Singleton Copley, was known for setting his subjects in the midst of everyday objects; here he portrays Adams in a middle-class suit with the charter guaranteeing the liberties of Boston's freemen.

Source: John Singleton Copley (1738–1815), *Samuel Adams* ca. 1772. Oil on canvas, 49 ½ × 39 ½ in. (125.7 cm × 100.3 cm). Deposited by the City of Boston, 30.76c. Courtesy, Museum of Fine Arts, Boston. Reproduced with permission. ©2000 Museum of Fine Arts, Boston. All Rights Reserved.

playing cards. It affected nearly every colonial resident in one way or another.

The American reaction to the Stamp Act during the summer and autumn of 1765 created a crisis of unprecedented proportions. The stamped paper had to be purchased with hard money, and it came during a period of economic stagnation. Many colonists complained of being "miserably burdened and oppressed with taxes." But constitutional objections had more importance over the long term. Although colonial male property owners elected their own assemblies, they could not vote in British elections and had no representatives in Parliament. The British government argued that colonists were still subject to the acts of Parliament because of what they termed "virtual representation." As one British conservative put it, the colonists were "represented in Parliament in the same manner as those inhabitants of Britain are who have not voices in elections," such as women, children, and servants.

Americans did not take well to his analogy. They argued instead for "actual representation," emphasizing the direct relationship that should exist between the people and their political leaders. Just such constitutional issues were emphasized in the Virginia Stamp Act Resolutions, written by Patrick Henry, a passionate young backcountry lawyer and member of the House of Burgesses. Although Henry's colleagues rejected the most radical of his resolutions, all of them were reprinted in the colonial press. By the end of 1765 the assemblies of eight other colonies had approved similar measures denouncing the Stamp Act and proclaiming their support of "no taxation without representation."

The most violent protests took place in Boston. The city's elite had prospered over the previous decade, but conditions for workers and the poor had worsened. Unemployment, inflation, and high taxes greatly increased the level of poverty during the depression following the Seven Years' War. Ordinary Bostonians were resentful. Their discontent was channeled by Samuel Adams, the son of a brewer, who became a powerful local politician. Adams organized an anti-British alliance that spanned Boston's social classes. In the late summer of 1765 he and his associates organized a protest of Boston workingmen. On August 14 a large crowd assembled near Boston Common, and in an old elm, known as the "Liberty Tree," strung up effigies of several British officials, including Boston's stamp distributor, Andrew Oliver. The restless crowd then invaded and vandalized Oliver's office as well as his home. Soon thereafter, Oliver resigned his commission. Several days later another mob broke into the mansion of Thomas Hutchinson, lieutenant governor of the colony.

During the fall and winter, urban crowds protested in port towns from Halifax in the north to Savannah in the south (see Map 6.3). Growing alarmed at the rising potential for violence, merchants, lawyers, and respectable

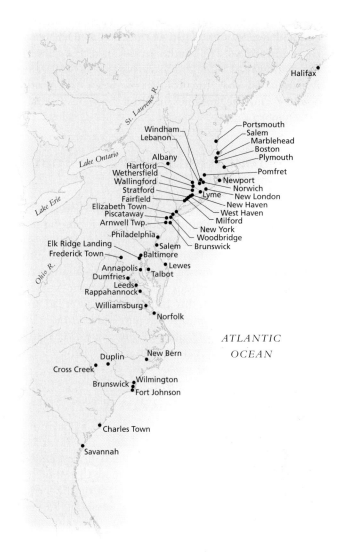

MAP 6.3 Demonstrations against the Stamp Act, 1765 From Halifax in the North to Savannah in the South, popular demonstrations against the Stamp Act forced the resignation of British tax officials. The propaganda of 1765 even reached the breakfast table, emblazoned on teapots.

craftsmen gained control of the resistance movement. Calling themselves the Sons of Liberty, these leaders encouraged more moderate forms of protest, such as circulating petitions and publishing pamphlets. There were few repetitions of mob attacks, but by the end of 1765 almost all the stamp distributors had resigned or fled, making it impossible for Britain to enforce the Stamp Act. Pressured by British merchants, who worried over the effects of the growing nonimportation movement among the colonists, in March 1766 Parliament repealed the Stamp Act and reduced the duties under the Sugar Act. This news was greeted with celebrations throughout the American colonies.

Overlooked, however, was the fact that Parliament coupled repeal with what was termed a "Declaratory Act," affirming its full authority to make laws binding the colonies "in all cases whatsoever." The Declaratory Act signaled that the conflict between the mother country and the colonies had not been resolved but merely postponed.

"Save Your Money and Save Your Country"

Colonial resistance to the Stamp Act was stronger in urban than in rural communities, stronger among merchants, craftsmen, and planters than among farmers and frontiersmen. When Parliament next moved to impose its will, as it had promised to do in the Declaratory Act, the American opposition again adopted the tactic of nonimportation. But this time resistance spread from the cities and towns into the countryside. As the editor of the *Boston Gazette* phrased the issue, "Save your money and you save your country." It became the slogan of the movement.

The Townshend Revenue Acts

The foremost problem facing the new British government in the mid-1760s was the national debt. Britain suffered massive unemployment, riots over high prices, and tax protests. Fearing opposition at home more than protest in the colonies, in June 1767, Chancellor of the Exchequer Charles Townshend proposed a new series of Revenue Acts placing tariffs on the importation of commodities such as lead, glass, paint, paper, and tea into the colonies. Import taxes, Townshend hoped, would redress colonists' opposition to internal taxes such as those imposed by the Stamp Act. For most colonists, it proved a distinction without a difference.

The most influential colonial response came in a series of articles by wealthy Philadelphia lawyer John Dickinson, which were reprinted in nearly every colonial newspaper. Posing as a humble farmer, Dickinson argued that Parliament had no constitutional authority to tax goods in order to raise revenue in America. Other Americans warned that the Revenue Acts were part of a British conspiracy to suppress American liberties. Their fears were reinforced by stringent enforcement.

●●●—Read the Document

John Dickinson, from Letters from a Farmer in Pennsylvania (1768) at **www.myhistorylab.com**

In response some colonists argued for violent resistance. But it was Dickinson's essays that had the greatest effect on the public debate, not only because of their convincing arguments but also because of their mild and reasonable tone. "Let us behave like dutiful children," Dickinson urged, "who have received unmerited blows from a beloved parent." Very little sentiment for independence yet existed in the British colonies.

An Early Political Boycott

In October 1767 the Boston town meeting revived the tactic of nonimportation, drawing up a long list of British products to boycott. Over the next few months other port cities, including Providence, Newport, and New York, set up nonimportation campaigns of their own. Artisans took to the streets in towns and cities throughout the colonies to pressure merchants to stop importing British goods. Uncooperative importers and retailers became the object of protesters. Coercion was very much a part of the movement, and there was occasional violence.

Protestors formed "nonimportation associations," pledging to curtail luxuries and stimulate local industry. These aims had great appeal in small towns and rural districts, which previously had been uninvolved in the anti-British struggle. In 1768 and 1769 colonial newspapers paid a great deal of attention to women's support for the boycott. Groups of women, some calling themselves Daughters of Liberty, organized spinning and weaving bees to produce homespun for local consumption. The actual work performed at these bees was less important than the symbolic message. "The industry and frugality of American ladies," wrote the editor of the *Boston Evening Post*, "are contributing to bring about the political salvation of a whole continent." Other women renounced silks and satins and pledged to stop serving tea to their husbands.

Nonimportation was greatly strengthened in May 1769 when the Virginia House of Burgesses enacted the first provincial legislation banning the importation of goods enumerated in the Townshend Acts. Over the next few months all the colonies but New Hampshire enacted similar legislation. Because of these efforts, the value of colonial imports from Britain declined by 41 percent over the next year.

The Massachusetts Circular Letter

Boston and Massachusetts were at the center of the agitation over the Townshend Revenue Acts. In February 1768 the Massachusetts House of Representatives approved a letter drawn up by Samuel Adams and addressed to the speakers of the other colonial assemblies. The letter denounced the Revenue Acts, attacked the British plan to make royal officials independent of colonial assemblies, and urged the colonies to find a way to "harmonize with each other." Massachusetts governor Francis Bernard condemned the document for stirring up rebellion and dissolved the legislature. In Britain, Lord Hillsborough, secretary of state for the colonies, ordered each royal governor in America to dissolve his colony's assembly if it

This British cartoon, "A Society of Patriotic Ladies," ridiculed the efforts of American women to support the Patriot cause by boycotting tea. The moderator of the meeting appears coarse and masculine, while an attractive scribe is swayed by the amorous attention of a gentleman. The activities under the table suggest that these women are neglecting their true duty.

should endorse the letter. Before this demand reached America, the assemblies of New Hampshire, New Jersey, and Connecticut had commended Massachusetts. Virginia, moreover, had issued a circular letter encouraging a "hearty union" among the colonies and urging common action against the British measures that "have an immediate tendency to enslave us."

Throughout this crisis there were rumors and threats of mob rule in Boston. "I am no friend to Riots, Tumult, and unlawful Assemblies," declared Samuel Adams, "but when the People are oppressed . . . they are not to be blamed." Because customs agents pressed on smugglers and honest traders alike, they enraged merchants, seamen, and dockworkers. John Hancock, reportedly the wealthiest merchant in the colonies, and a vocal opponent of the British measures, was a principal target of the customs officers. In June 1768 a crowd assaulted customs officials who had seized Hancock's sloop *Liberty* for nonpayment of duties. So terrorized were the officials that they fled the city. In September, the Boston town meeting called on

the people to arm themselves and issued an invitation for all the colony's towns to send delegates to a provincial convention. Although a number of delegates made threats of armed resistance, they received little support and the convention broke up in chaos. Fearful of insurrection, on October 1, 1768, the British occupied Boston with infantry and artillery regiments. This action added greatly to the growing tensions.

The Boston Massacre

The British troops stationed in the colonies were the object of scorn and hostility over the next two years. There were regular conflicts between soldiers and radicals in New York City, often focusing on protests organized by the Sons of Liberty. In Boston Sam Adams played up each and every rumor of soldiers harassing women, picking fights with residents, or simply taunting them with the derisive song "Yankee Doodle." There were a number of violent confrontations.

The BLOODY MASSACRE perpetrated in King Street BOSTON on March 5th 1770 by a party of the 29th REGT.

BUTCHER'S HALL

Engrav'd Printed & Sold by PAUL REVERE BOSTON

Unhappy Boston! see thy Sons deplore,
Thy hallow'd Walks besmear'd with guiltless Gore:
While faithless P—n and his savage Bands,
With murd'rous Rancour stretch their bloody Hands;
Like fierce Barbarians grinning o'er their Prey,
Approve the Carnage and enjoy the Day.

If scalding drops from Rage from Anguish Wrung,
If speechless Sorrows lab'ring for a Tongue,
Or if a weeping World can ought appease
The plaintive Ghosts of Victims such as these;
The Patriot's copious Tears for each are shed,
A glorious Tribute which embalms the Dead.

But know, Fate summons to that awful Goal,
Where Justice strips the Murd'rer of his Soul:
Should venal C—ts the scandal of the Land,
Snatch the relentless Villain from her Hand,
Keen Execrations on this Plate inscrib'd,
Shall reach a Judge who never can be brib'd.

The unhappy Sufferers were Mess.rs Sam.l Gray, Sam.l Maverick, Jam.s Caldwell, Crispus Attucks & Pat.k Carr
Killed. Six wounded; two of them (Christ.r Monk & John Clark) Mortally

In Paul Revere's version of the Boston Massacre, issued three weeks after the incident, the British fire an organized volley into a crowd of unresisting civilians. Revere's print—which he plagiarized from another Boston engraver—was historically inaccurate but enormously effective propaganda. It hung in so many Patriot homes that the judge hearing the murder trial of these British soldiers warned the jury not to be swayed by "the prints exhibited in our houses."

A persistent source of conflict was the competition between troops and townsmen over jobs. Soldiers were permitted to work on their days off-duty, thus competing with poor day laborers. In early March 1770 a British soldier walked into a Boston ropewalk in search of a job. "You can clean my shithouse," the scornful owner told him. The soldier later returned with some of his friends and a small riot resulted. Over the next few days sporadic fighting between soldiers and townsmen continued in the streets between the wharf and the Common, where the soldiers were encamped. Finally, on the evening of March 5, 1770, a crowd at the Customs House began taunting a guard, calling him a "damned rascally scoundrel lobster" and worse. A captain and a company of seven soldiers went to his rescue, only to be pelted with snowballs and stones. Suddenly someone shouted "Fire!" and the frightened soldiers shot indiscriminately into the crowd. Five men fell dead and six were wounded, two of them mortally. The soldiers escaped to their barracks, but a mob numbering in the hundreds rampaged through the streets demanding vengeance. What became known as "the Boston Massacre" was soon infamous throughout the colonies. For many colonists the incident was a disturbing reminder of the extent to which relations with the mother country had deteriorated. During the next two years many people found themselves pulling back from the brink.

The growth of American resistance was slowed as well by the news that Parliament had repealed most of the Revenue Acts. In the climate of apprehension and confusion, there were few celebrations of the repeal, and the nonimportation associations almost immediately collapsed. The parliamentary retreat on the question of duties, like the earlier repeal of the Stamp Act, was accompanied by a face-saving measure—retention of the tax on tea "as a mark of the supremacy of Parliament," in the words of the British prime minister, Frederick Lord North.

From Resistance to Rebellion

There was a lull in the American controversy during the early 1770s, but the situation turned violent once again in 1773, when Parliament infuriated the Americans by passing an ill-advised tax on tea. The tax pushed the colonists onto a fast track from resistance to outright rebellion.

Committees of Correspondence

In June 1772, Governor Hutchinson of Massachusetts inaugurated another controversy by announcing that henceforth his salary and those of other royally appointed officials would be paid by the crown. In effect, this made the executive and judiciary branches of the colony's government independent of control by elected representatives. In October, the Boston town meeting appointed a committee of correspondence to communicate with other communities regarding this challenge.

In March 1773 the Virginia House of Burgesses appointed a standing committee of correspondence "to obtain the most early and authentic intelligence" of British actions affecting America, "and to keep up and maintain a correspondence and communication with our sister colonies." The Virginia committee, including Patrick Henry, Richard Henry Lee, and young Thomas Jefferson, served as a model for the other colonies, and within a year all but Pennsylvania (where conservatives were in control of the legislature) had created committees of their own. The committees of correspondence became the principal channel for sharing information, shaping public opinion, and building cooperation among the colonies before the opening meeting of the First Continental Congress in 1774.

The information most damaging to British influence came from the radicals in Boston. In June 1773 the Boston committee circulated a set of confidential letters from Governor Hutchinson to the ministry in Britain. The letters revealed the governor's call for "an abridgement of what are called English liberties" in the colonies. "I wish to see some further restraint of liberty," he wrote, "rather than the connection with the parent state should be broken." His statement appeared to be the "smoking gun" of the conspiracy theory, and it created a torrent of anger against the British and their officials in the colonies.

The Boston Tea Party

It was in this context that the colonists received the news that Parliament had passed the Tea Act. Colonists were major consumers of tea, typically drinking from five to ten cups a day. But because of the Townshend duties the market for tea had collapsed. The British East India Company, the sole agent of British power in India, was on the brink of bankruptcy. Parliament considered it too big to fail, and devised a scheme to offer tea to Americans at prices that would tempt even the most patriotic drinker. The radicals argued that this was merely a device to make palatable the payment of unconstitutional taxes and further evidence of the British effort to seduce and corrupt the colonists.

In October 1773 a mass meeting in Philadelphia denounced anyone importing the tea as "an enemy of his country." A group calling itself "the Committee for Tarring and Feathering" published a broadside, plastered all over the city, asking if the captains of ships carrying the tea might like "ten gallons of liquid tar decanted on your pate—with the feathers of a dozen wild geese laid over that to enliven your appearance." The Philadelphia consignees resigned in terror. Similar protests in New York City forced resignations there as well. The town meeting in Boston soon passed resolutions patterned on those of Philadelphia.

The first of three tea ships arrived in Boston Harbor late in November. Mass meetings in Old South Church, including many country people drawn to the scene of the crisis, resolved to keep the tea from being unloaded. On the evening of December 16, 1773, 5,000 people crowded into the church to hear the captain of one of the vessels report

to Sam Adams that Governor Hutchinson had issued orders that the ship was to remain docked at the wharf. "This meeting can do nothing more to save the country," Adams declared. This was the signal for a disciplined

The Bostonians Paying the Excise-Man, or Tarring and Feathering

Political cartoons played an important role in the public controversy leading to the American Revolution. This print, published in London in 1774 and sold on the streets for a few pennies, depicts the violent attack of a Boston mob on customs commissioner John Malcolm several weeks after the "Tea Party." Malcolm, an ardent Loyalist, had been the frequent target of protests. In January 1774 he struck a prominent Patriot activist on the head with his cane, seriously injuring him. That night a mob dragged Malcolm from his house and covered him with tar and feathers, a ritual of public humiliation. Hot tar produced painful blistering of the skin, and the effort to remove it made the condition worse. The feathers made the victim into an object of ridicule. Hauled to the Liberty Tree in Boston Common, Malcolm was threatened with hanging if he did not apologize and renounce his commission. When he did he was allowed to return home. The pro-Loyalist print includes a number of telling details. Malcolm is attacked by a group that includes a leather-aproned artisan. A broadside announcing the Stamp Act is posted upside down on the Liberty Tree. A hangman's noose dangles from a branch. The Boston Tea Party takes place in the background. In the foreground is a tar bucket and a pole topped by a "liberty cap," a symbol of freedom adopted by American protesters (and later an icon of the French Revolution). These details were intended to mock the Americans.

But when the print found its way to North America it was embraced by Patriots and became an enduring American favorite. In the nineteenth century it was reprinted as a celebration of the righteous violence of the Revolution.

The BOSTONIAN'S Paying the EXCISE-MAN, or TARRING & FEATHERING

• **How could this image, intended to ridicule and shame the American patriots, have been embraced and celebrated by them?**

group of fifty or sixty men, including farmers, artisans, merchants, professionals, and apprentices, to march to the wharf. Dressed as Indians and cheered on by Boston's citizens, they boarded the ships and dumped into the harbor some forty-five tons of tea, valued at £18,000.

Boston's was the first tea party, and other incidents of property destruction soon followed. But it was the initial action in Boston that infuriated the British. The government became convinced that something had to be done about the rebellious colony of Massachusetts. Strong measures were required, King George III (reigned 1760–1820) wrote to Lord North, for "we are now to dispute whether we have, or have not, any authority in that country."

The Intolerable Acts

During the spring of 1774 an angry Parliament passed a series of acts—officially called the Coercive Acts but known by Americans as the Intolerable Acts—calculated to punish the colony of Massachusetts and strengthen the British hand. The Boston Port Bill prohibited the loading or unloading of ships in any part of Boston Harbor until the town fully compensated the East India Company and the customs service for the destroyed tea. The Massachusetts Government Act annulled the colonial charter: delegates to the upper house would no longer be elected by the assembly but henceforth were to be appointed by the king. Civil officers throughout the province were placed under the authority of the royal governor, and the selection of juries was given over to governor-appointed sheriffs. Town meetings, an important institution of the resistance movement, were prohibited from convening more than once a year except with the approval of the governor, who was placed in control of their agendas. With these acts, the British terminated the long history of self-rule by communities in the colony of Massachusetts.

Additional measures affected the other colonies and encouraged them to see themselves in league with suffering Massachusetts. The Administration of Justice Act protected British officials from colonial courts, thereby encouraging them to pursue the work of suppression. Those accused of committing capital crimes while putting down riots or collecting revenue—as in the Boston Massacre—were now to be sent to England for trial. The Quartering Act legalized the housing of troops at public expense not only in taverns and abandoned buildings but also in occupied dwellings and private homes.

Finally, in the Québec Act, the British authorized a permanent government for the territory taken from France during the Seven Years' War: a strictly anti-republican government with an appointed council. It

MAP 6.4 The Québec Act of 1774 With the Québec Act, Britain created a centralized colonial government for Canada and extended that colony's administrative control south west to the Ohio River, invalidating the sea-to-sea boundaries of many colonial charters.

confirmed the feudal system of land tenure along the St. Lawrence (see Map 6.4). The act also granted religious toleration to the Roman Catholic Church and upheld the Church's traditional right to collect tithes, in effect endorsing Catholicism as the state religion of Québec. To the American colonists it seemed a frightening preview of what imperial authorities had in store for them, and it confirmed the contention of the committees of correspondence that there was a British plot to destroy American liberty. In May General Thomas Gage arrived in Boston to replace Hutchinson as governor.

The First Continental Congress

It was amid this crisis that town meetings and colonial assemblies alike chose representatives for the First Continental Congress. The delegates who arrived in Philadelphia in September 1774 included the most important leaders of the American cause. Cousins Samuel and John Adams from Massachusetts were joined by Patrick Henry and George Washington of Virginia and Christopher Gadsden of South Carolina. Many of the delegates were conservatives, including John Dickinson and Joseph Galloway of Philadelphia, and John Jay and James Duane from New York. With the exception of Gadsden, a hothead who proposed an attack on British forces in Boston, the delegates wished to avoid war and favored a policy of economic coercion.

After one of their first debates, the delegates passed a "Declaration and Resolves," asserting that all the colonists sprang from a common tradition and enjoyed rights guaranteed "by the immutable laws of nature, the principles of the English constitution, and the several charters or compacts" of their provinces. Thirteen acts of Parliament, passed since 1763, were declared in violation of these rights. Until these acts were repealed, the delegates declared, they were imposing a set of sanctions against the British. These included not only the nonimportation and nonconsumption of British goods but a prohibition on the export of colonial commodities to Britain or its other colonies.

To enforce these sanctions, the Continental Congress urged that "a committee be chosen in every county, city, and town, by those who are qualified to vote for representatives in the legislature, whose business it shall be attentively to observe the conduct of all persons." This call for democratically elected local committees in each community had important political ramifications. Known as "Committees of Observation and Safety," these groups took over the functions of local government throughout the colonies. They organized militia companies, called extra legal courts, and combined to form colony-wide congresses or conventions. By dissolving the colonial legislatures, royal governors had unwittingly aided the work of these Committees. In addition to providing government, the committees also scrutinized the activities of fellow citizens, suppressed the expression of Loyalist opinion from pulpit or press, and practiced other forms of coercion. Throughout the colonies the Committees formed a bridge between the old colonial administrations and the revolutionary governments organized over the next few years. Committees began to link localities together in the cause of a wider American community. It was at this moment that people began for the first time to refer to the British colonies as the American "states."

Lexington and Concord

On September 1, 1774, General Gage sent troops to seize stores of gunpowder and arms from several storehouses on the outskirts of Boston. In response, the Massachusetts

Ignoring the Olive Branch Petition from the Continental Congress, on August 23, 1775, King George III issued this Proclamation, declaring that the colonies stood in open rebellion to his authority and were subject to severe penalty, as was any British subject who failed to report the knowledge of rebellion or conspiracy. This document literally transformed loyal subjects into traitorous rebels.

House of Representatives, calling itself the Provincial Congress, created a Committee of Safety, empowered to call up the militia. On October 15 the Committee authorized the creation of special units, to be known as "Minutemen," who stood ready to be called at a moment's notice. The armed militia of the towns and communities surrounding Boston now opposed the British army, quartered in the city. Gage wrote to London for instructions. These were no rabble he was up against, he told his superiors, but rather "the freeholders and farmers" of New England who believed they were defending their communities. Worrying that his forces were insufficient to suppress the rebellion, Gage requested reinforcements. The stalemate continued throughout the fall and winter as he awaited instructions.

British monarch George III believed the time for war had come. "The New England Governments are in a State of Rebellion," he wrote, and "blows must decide whether they are to be subject to this Country or independent." In Virginia, at almost the same moment, Patrick Henry was predicting that hostilities soon would begin. "Gentlemen may cry peace, peace!" he thundered in prose later memorized by several generations of American schoolchildren, "but there is no peace. Is life so dear, or peace so sweet, as to be purchased at the price of chains and slavery? Forbid it, Almighty God! I know not what course others may take, but as for me give me liberty or give me death!" Three weeks later, on April 14, 1775, General Gage received instructions to immediately strike against the Massachusetts militia.

Read the Document

Patrick Henry, "Give Me Liberty or Give Me Death" (1775) at **www.myhistorylab.com**

On the evening of April 18, Gage ordered 700 troops to Concord, some miles outside Boston, to take possession of the armory there. Learning of the operation, the Boston Committee dispatched two men, Paul Revere and William Dawes, to alert the militia of the countryside. By the time the British forces had reached Lexington, midway to their destination, some seventy armed minutemen were assembled on the green in the center of town. They were disorganized and confused. "Lay down your arms, you damned rebels, and disperse!" one of the British officers cried. In the face of what appeared overwhelming force, the American militiamen began to withdraw, taking their firearms. "Damn you, why don't you lay down your arms!" someone shouted from the British lines. "Damn them! We will have them!" No order to fire was given, but suddenly shots rang out spontaneously. Eight Americans were killed, ten wounded.

The British marched on to Concord where they burned a small quantity of supplies and cut down a liberty pole. Meanwhile, news of the deaths at Lexington had spread throughout the surrounding countryside, and the militia companies from communities from miles around converged on the town. Seeing smoke, they mistakenly concluded the British were burning homes. "Will you let them burn the town?" one man cried. At a Concord bridge they encountered the enemy and opened fire. Three regular soldiers were killed, the first British casualties. Seeing that their men were greatly outnumbered by Massachusetts militia, British officers immediately ordered a return to Boston, but at many points along the way they were subjected to withering fire. By the time the British force finally reached the city, 73 soldiers had been killed and 202 wounded (see Map 6.5). American losses were much lower. The engagement forecast what would be a central problem for the British: they would be forced to fight an armed population defending their own communities against outsiders.

Read the Document

Joseph Warren, "Account of the Battle of Lexington" (1775) at **www.myhistorylab.com**

MAP 6.5 The First Engagements of the Revolution The first military engagements of the American Revolution took place in the spring of 1775 in the countryside surrounding Boston.

Deciding for Independence

"We send you momentous intelligence," read the letter reporting the violence received by the committee of correspondence in Charleston, South Carolina, on May 8, 1775. Throughout the colonies community militia companies mobilized for war. At Boston, thousands of militiamen besieged the city, leaving the British no escape but by sea. The siege would last for nearly a year. Meanwhile, delegates from twelve colonies converged again on Philadelphia.

The Second Continental Congress

The Second Continental Congress, which opened on May 10, 1775, included representatives from twelve of the British colonies on the mainland of North America. Few conservatives or Loyalists were among them. Georgia, unrepresented at the First Continental Congress, remained absent at the opening of the Second. It depended heavily on British subsidies, and its leaders were cautious, fearing both slave and Indian uprisings. But the political balance soon shifted in favor of the radicals in Georgia, and by the end of the summer the colony had sent delegates to Philadelphia.

Among the men at the Congress were many familiar faces and a few new ones, including Thomas Jefferson, Virginia plantation master and lawyer, gifted with one of the most imaginative and analytical minds of his era. All the delegates carried news of the enthusiasm for war that raged in their home provinces. "A frenzy of revenge seems to have seized all ranks of people," Jefferson observed. George Washington attended all the sessions in uniform.

British soldiers fire upon Massachusetts militia at Lexington, the first of four hand-colored engravings included in Amos Doolittle's *View of the Battle of Lexington and Concord* (1775). It is the only contemporary pictorial record of the events of April 19, 1775, from an American point of view. Doolittle, a Connecticut silversmith, traveled to the site of the conflict in the weeks afterward, and his engravings are based on first-hand observation. Important buildings, individuals, or groups of people are keyed to a legend that explains what is happening. Doolittle intended his prints to be informative in the same sense as a photograph in a modern newspaper.

The delegates agreed that military defense was the most important issue on their agenda.

On May 15 the representatives resolved to put the colonies in a state of defense but were divided on how best to do it. They lacked the power and the funds to raise and supply an army. John Adams made the winning proposal that they simply designate as a Continental Army the militia forces besieging Boston. In order to emphasize their national aspirations, they decided to select a man from the South to command those New England forces. All eyes turned naturally to Washington. Although he had suffered defeat at the beginning of the Seven Years' War, he had subsequently compiled a distinguished record. On June 15 Jefferson and Adams nominated him to be commander-in-chief, and he was elected by acclaim. On June 22, in a highly significant move, the Congress voted to finance the army with an issue of $2 million in bills of credit, backed by the good faith of the "Confederated Colonies." Thus began the long and complicated process of financing the Revolution.

During the early summer of 1775 the Congress began to move cautiously toward independence. Few would admit, even to themselves, that this was their goal. On July 5, 1775, the delegates passed the so-called "Olive Branch Petition," written by John Dickinson of Pennsylvania, in which they professed their attachment to

King George and begged him to prevent further hostilities so that there might be an accommodation. The next day they approved a "Declaration of the Causes and Necessities of Taking Up Arms," written by Jefferson and Dickinson. In this the delegates adopted a harsher tone, resolving "to die freemen rather than to live slaves." Before the Second Continental Congress adjourned at the beginning of August, the delegates appointed commissioners to negotiate with the Indian nations in an attempt to keep them out of the conflict. They also reinstated Benjamin Franklin as postmaster general in order to keep the mails moving and protect communication among the colonies.

Canada and the Spanish Borderlands

How did the rest of North America react to the coming conflict? The Continental Congress made contact with leaders of all the British colonies. In one of their first acts, delegates called on "the oppressed inhabitants of Canada" to join in the struggle for "common liberty." French Canadians felt little sympathy for the British, but the Americans were traditional enemies, much feared because of their aggressive expansionism. Indeed, when the Canadians failed to respond positively and immediately, the Congress reversed itself and voted to authorize a military expedition against Québec to eliminate any possibility of a British invasion from that quarter, thus killing any chance of the Canadians joining the anti-British cause. This set a course toward the development of the separate nations of the United States and Canada.

In the British island colonies, there was at first considerable sympathy for the American struggle. The legislative assemblies of Jamaica, Grenada, and Barbados declared themselves in accord with the Continental Congress. But the British navy prevented them from sending representatives. A delegation from Bermuda succeeded in getting to Philadelphia, but the Americans were so preoccupied with more pressing matters they were unable to provide any assistance, and the spark of resistance on the island sputtered out. The island colonies would remain aloof from the imperial crisis, largely because the colonists there were dependent on a British military presence to guard against slave revolts.

Things at first seemed more promising in Nova Scotia (not then a part of Canada), where many New Englanders had relocated after the expulsion of the Acadians. There had been Stamp Act demonstrations in Halifax, and when the British attempted to recruit among the Nova Scotians for soldiers to serve in Boston, one community responded that since "almost all of us [were] born in New England, [we are] divided betwixt natural affection to our nearest relations and good faith and friendship to our king and country." The British naval stronghold at Halifax, however, secured the province for the empire. Large contingents of British troops also kept Florida (which Britain had divided into two colonies, East and West Florida) solidly in the empire.

In Cuba, some 3,000 exiled Spanish Floridians, who had fled there in 1763 rather than live under British rule, now clamored for Spain to take advantage of the situation and retake their homeland. Many of them were active supporters of American independence. Spanish colonial authorities, who also administered the newly acquired colony of Louisiana, were conflicted. They certainly felt no solidarity with the cause of the American rebels, whom they thought threatened the idea of monarchy and empire. But with painful memories of the British invasion of Havana in 1763, they looked forward to the prospect of taking revenge on their traditional enemy, as well as regaining control of the Floridas and eliminating the British threat to their Mexican and Caribbean colonies.

In 1775 Spain publicly declared itself neutral but secretly searched for an opportunity to support the Americans. One presented itself in the late spring of 1776 when a contingent of Americans arrived in Spanish New Orleans via the Mississippi River bearing a proposal from patriot forces in Virginia. British naval supremacy was making it impossible to obtain supplies from overseas. Would the Spanish be willing to quietly sell guns, ammunition, and other provisions to the Americans in New Orleans and allow them to be shipped by way of the Mississippi and Ohio Rivers? If the Spanish could be cooperative, the Americans might agree to a Spanish "protectorate" of the Floridas. The Spanish government eventually approved the plan, turning Havana and New Orleans into important supply centers for the Americans.

Fighting in the North and South

Violent conflict took place between British forces and American rebels in both the northern and southern colonies in 1775 and early 1776. On the evening of May 10, 1775, a small force of armed New Englanders jointly commanded by Ethan Allen of Vermont and Benedict Arnold of Connecticut, surprised the British garrison at Fort Ticonderoga on Lake Champlain. One account had Allen hailing the British commander, still in his nightshirt: "Come out of there, you damned old bastard." By whose authority? the commander shouted back. "In the name of Great Jehovah and the Continental Congress," Allen thundered. In fact, Allen was a notorious atheist, and the Congress knew nothing of this campaign. With great effort, the Americans hauled the fort's cannon overland to be used in the siege of Boston.

The Debate over Independence

The American colonists moved gradually toward declaring independence. It was a question that caused enormous controversy. As late as 1775 a majority of the delegates to the Continental Congress favored reconciliation, and during the Revolution a large minority remained Loyalists. Among the more prominent Loyalists was the Episcopal minister Jonathan Boucher, who migrated to Virginia from England in 1759 at the age of twenty-one. A firm supporter of established authority, Boucher was the subject of verbal attack and threats by local Patriots. He preached the sermon from which the following selection is taken in 1775, with two loaded pistols on the pulpit. His arguments were representative of the conservative Loyalist position. Shortly afterward, in fear of his life, Boucher returned to England, where he later published his American sermons.

The most effective argument for independence was made by Thomas Paine, a radical Englishman who immigrated to Philadelphia in 1774 and quickly took up the Patriot cause. The selection from Paine's pamphlet *Common Sense*, published in January 1776, provides a good summary of the Patriot response to Loyalists such as Boucher.

• **Boucher and Paine pursue contrasting forms of argument. Can you identify them?**

Will You Rebel for a Cause So Trivial?

Be it (for the sake of argument) admitted that the government under which till now you have lived happily is, most unaccountably, all at once become oppressive and severe; did you, of yourselves, make the discovery? No. I affirm, without any apprehension of being contradicted, that you are acquainted with these oppressions only from the report of others. For what, then (admitting you have a right to resist in any case), are you now urged to resist and rise against those whom you have hitherto always regarded (and certainly not without reason) as your nursing fathers and nursing mothers? . . . It is on account of an insignificant duty on tea, imposed by the British Parliament, and which, for aught we know, may or may not be constitutionally imposed, but which, we well know, two-thirds of the people of America can never be called on to pay. Is it the part of an understanding people, of loyal subjects, or of good Christians, instantly to resist and rebel for a cause so trivial? O my brethren, consult your own hearts and follow your own judgments! And learn not your "measures of obedience" from men who weakly or wickedly imagine there can be liberty unconnected with law—

"Is it the part of an understanding people, of loyal subjects, or of good Christians, instantly to resist and rebel for a cause so trivial?"

and whose aim it is to drive you on, step by step, to a resistance which will terminate, if it does not begin, in rebellion! On all such trying occasions, learn the line of conduct which it is your duty and interest to observe, from our constitution itself, which, in this particular, is a fair transcript or exemplification of the ordinance of God. Both the one and the other warn you against resistance; but you are not forbidden either to remonstrate or to petition. . . .

Let it be supposed, however, that even the worst may happen, which can happen: that our remonstrances are disregarded, our petitions rejected, and our grievances unredressed: what, you will naturally ask— what, in such a case, would I advise you to do? . . . Act the part of reasonable men and of Christians. . . . If you think the duty of three pence a pound upon tea laid on by the British Parliament a grievance, it is your duty to instruct your members to take all the constitutional means in their power to obtain redress; if those means fail of success, you cannot but be sorry and grieved, but you will better bear your disappointment by being able to reflect that it was not owing to any misconduct of your own. And what is the whole history of human life, public or private, but a series of disappointments? It might be hoped that Christians would not think it grievous to be doomed to submit to disappointments and calamities, as their Master submitted, even if they were as innocent. His disciples and first followers shrunk from no trials nor dangers. Treading in the steps of him who, when he was reviled, blessed, and when he was persecuted, suffered it, they willingly laid down their lives rather than resist some of the worst tyrants that ever disgraced the annals of history. Those persons are as little acquainted with general history, as they are with the particular doctrines of Christianity, who represent such submission as abject and servile. I affirm, with great authority, that there can be no better way of asserting the people's lawful rights, than disowning unlawful commands, by thus patiently suffering. When this doctrine was more generally embraced, our holy religion gained as much by submission as it is now in a fair way of losing for want of it. . . .

SOURCE: Jonathan Boucher, *A View of the Causes and Consequences of the American Revolution, with an Historical Preface* (1797).

The Sun Never Shone on a Cause of Greater Worth

In the following pages I offer nothing more than simple facts, plain arguments, and common sense: and have no other preliminaries to settle with the reader, than that he will divest himself of prejudice and prepossession, and suffer his reason and his feelings to determine for themselves: that he will put on, or rather that he will not put off, the true character of a man, and generously enlarge his views beyond the present day.

Volumes have been written on the subject of the struggle between England and America. Men of all ranks have embarked in the controversy, from different motives, and with various designs; but all have been ineffectual, and the period of debate is closed. Arms as the last resource decide the contest; the appeal was the choice of the king, and the continent has accepted the challenge.

The sun never shone on a cause of greater worth. 'Tis not the affair of a city, a county, a province, or a kingdom; but of a continent—of at least one eighth part of the habitable globe. 'Tis not the concern of a day, a year, or an age; posterity are virtually involved in the contest, and will be more or less affected even to the end of time, by the proceedings now. Now is the seed-time of continental union, faith and honor. The least fracture now will be like a name engraved with the point of a pin on the tender rind of a young oak; the wound would enlarge with the tree, and posterity read it in full grown characters.

By referring the matter from argument to arms, a new era for politics is struck, a new method of thinking has arisen. All plans, proposals, etc. prior to the nineteenth of April—to the commencement of hostilities—are like the almanacks of the last year; which though proper then, are superceded and useless now. . . .

Ye that tell us of harmony and reconciliation, can ye restore to us the time that is past? Can ye give to prostitution its former innocence? neither can ye reconcile Britain and America. The last cord now is broken, the people of England are presenting addresses against us. There are injuries which nature cannot forgive; she would cease to be nature if she did. As well can the lover forgive the ravisher of his mistress, as the continent forgive the murders of Britain. The Almighty hath implanted in us these unextinguishable feelings for good and wise purposes. They are the guardians of his image in our hearts. They distinguish us from the herd of common animals. The social compact would dissolve, and justice be extirpated from the earth, or have only a casual existence were we callous to the touches of affection. The robber and the murderer would often escape unpunished, did not the injuries which our tempers sustain, provoke us into justice. O! ye that love mankind! Ye that dare oppose not

> "The sun never shone on a cause of greater worth."

only the tyranny but the tyrant, stand forth! Every spot of the old world is overrun with oppression. Freedom hath been hunted round the globe. Asia and Africa have long expelled her. Europe regards her like a stranger, and England hath given her warning to depart. O! receive the fugitive, and prepare in time an asylum for mankind.

SOURCE: Thomas Paine, *Common Sense* (1776).

At Boston, the British reinforced Gage's forces, and by the middle of June had approximately 6,500 soldiers in the city. They were besieged by more than 10,000 New England militia. Fearing a move by Gage to occupy the heights south of town, the Americans made a counter-move, occupying the Charlestown peninsula on the north. Gage decided on a frontal assault to dislodge them. In bloody fighting at Breed's and Bunker Hill, the British overran the Americans, killing 140 men, but not before suffering over a thousand casualties of their own, including 226 dead. The fierce patriotic reaction in England to this enormous loss ended any possibility of a last-minute reconciliation. In August 1775 King George refused to hear the Olive Branch Petition and issued a royal proclamation declaring the colonists in "open and avowed rebellion." The rebellion was caused by "divers wicked and desperate persons," the king argued, and he called on his loyal subjects in America to "bring the traitors to justice."

Read the Document
Royal Proclamation of Rebellion (1775) at
www.myhistorylab.com

In June Congress assembled an expeditionary force against Canada. One thousand Americans moved north up the Hudson River corridor, and in November General Richard Montgomery forced the capitulation of Montreal. In the meantime Colonel Benedict Arnold set out from Massachusetts with another American army and, after a torturous march through the forests and mountains of Maine, joined Montgomery outside the walls of Québec. But the American assault failed to take the city. Montgomery and 100 Americans were killed and another 300 taken prisoner. Although Arnold held his position, the American siege was broken the following spring by British reinforcements. By the summer of 1776 the Americans had been forced back from Canada.

There were successes elsewhere. In the South local militias rose against the Loyalist forces of Virginia's Governor Dunmore, who alienated the planter class by promising freedom to any slave who would fight with the British. After Dunmore was decisively defeated, he

The Connecticut artist John Trumbull painted *The Battle of Bunker Hill* in 1785, the first of a series that earned him the informal title of "the Painter of the Revolution." Trumbull was careful to research the details of his paintings but composed them in the grand style of historical romance. In the early nineteenth century, he repainted this work and three other Revolutionary scenes for the rotunda of the Capitol in Washington, DC.

retreated to British naval vessels and shelled the city of Norfolk, nearly obliterating it. The next month the North Carolina rebel militia crushed a Loyalist force at the Battle of Moore's Creek Bridge near Wilmington, ending British plans for an invasion there. The British elected to attack Charles Town, but an American force turned back the assault. It would be more than two years before the British would try to invade the South again. At Boston, Washington installed the British artillery captured at Fort Ticonderoga on the heights south of town, placing the city and harbor within cannon range. The British had little choice but to evacuate. In March 1776 they sailed out of Boston Harbor heading northeast to Halifax, accompanied by at least a thousand American Loyalists.

No Turning Back

Any hope of reconciliation died with the mounting casualties. The Second Continental Congress, rapidly assuming the role of a general government for all the colonies, now called the states, reconvened in Philadelphia in September 1775, where the delegates received the royal proclamation that they were in open rebellion. Although the Congress continued to disclaim any intention of denying the sovereignty of the king, it now moved to organize an American navy, and declared British vessels open to capture. The Congress took further steps toward independence when it authorized contacts with foreign powers through its agents in Europe. In the spring of 1776 France joined Spain in approving the shipping of supplies to the rebellious provinces. The Continental Congress then declared colonial ports open to the trade of all nations but Britain.

But the emotional ties to Great Britain proved difficult to break. Help arrived in January 1776 in the form of a pamphlet written by Thomas Paine, a radical Englishman recently arrived in Philadelphia. In *Common Sense*, Paine proposed to offer "simple fact, plain argument, and common sense" on the crisis. For years Americans had defended their actions by wrapping themselves in the mantle of British tradition. But Paine argued that the British system rested on "the base remains of two ancient tyrannies," aristocracy and monarchy, neither of which was appropriate for America. Paine placed the blame for the oppression of the colonists on the shoulders of George III. *Common Sense* was the single most important piece of writing during the Revolutionary era, selling more than 100,000 copies within a few months of its publication. It reshaped popular thinking and put independence squarely on the agenda.

In April, the North Carolina convention, operating as the revolutionary substitute for the old colonial

The Manner in Which the American Colonies Declared Themselves INDEPENDENT of the King of ENGLAND, a 1783 English print. Understanding that the coming struggle would require the steady support of ordinary people, in the Declaration of Independence, the upper-class men of the Continental Congress asserted the right of popular revolution and the great principle of human equality.

assembly, became the first to empower its delegates to the Continental Congress to vote for independence. News that the British were recruiting a force of German mercenaries to use against the Americans provided an additional push toward what now began to seem inevitable. In May the Congress voted to recommend that the individual states move as quickly as possible toward the adoption of state constitutions. In the preamble to this statement John Adams wrote that "the exercise of every kind of authority under the said crown should be totally suppressed." This sent a strong signal that the delegates were on the verge of approving a momentous declaration.

●●●—Read the Document

Thomas Jefferson, "Original Rough Draught" of the Declaration of Independence (1776) at **www.myhistorylab.com**

The Declaration of Independence

On June 7, 1776, Richard Henry Lee of Virginia offered the first motion for independence: "That these united colonies are, and of right ought to be, free and independent states, that they are absolved from all allegiance to the British crown, and that all political connection between them and the state of Great Britain is, and ought to be, totally dissolved." After some debate, a vote was postponed until July, but a committee composed of John Adams, Thomas Jefferson, Benjamin Franklin, Roger Sherman of Connecticut, and Robert Livingston of New York was asked to prepare a draft declaration of American independence. The committee assigned the writing of a first draft to Jefferson.

The intervening time allowed the delegates to debate and receive instructions from their state conventions. By the end of the month all the states but New York had authorized a vote for independence, and when the question came up for debate again on July 1, there was a large majority in support. The final vote, taken on July 2, was twelve in favor of independence, none against, with New York abstaining. The delegates then turned to the Declaration itself and made a number of changes in Jefferson's draft, striking out, for example, a long passage condemning slavery. In this and a number of other ways the final version was more cautious than the draft. But it was still a stirring document.

> The first section of the Declaration expressed the highest ideals of the delegates: We hold these truths to be self-evident, that all men are created equal, that they are endowed by their creator with certain unalienable rights, that among these are life, liberty, and the pursuit of happiness. That to secure these rights, governments are instituted among men, deriving their just powers from the consent of the governed. That whenever any form of government becomes destructive of these ends, it is the right of the people to alter or to abolish it, and to institute a new government, laying its foundation on such principles, and organizing its powers in such form, as to them shall seem most likely to effect their safety and happiness.

There was very little debate over this extraordinary statement. John Adams later noted that Jefferson had put into elegant language what nearly every delegate already believed. The unanimity was the result of the widespread influence of Enlightenment and republican thought. Notably, there was no recourse to biblical authority. The delegates, mostly men of wealth and position, realized that the coming struggle for independence would require the steady support of ordinary people, and thus they asserted this great principle of equality and the right of revolution. There was little debate about the implications or the potential consequences. The statement of principles would resonate throughout subsequent American history. The ideal of equality would inspire the poor as well as the wealthy, women as well as men, blacks as well as whites.

It was the final section of the Declaration, however, that may have contained the most meaning for the delegates themselves: "And for the support of this declaration, with a firm reliance on the Protection of Divine Providence, we mutually pledge to each other our Lives, our Fortunes, and our sacred Honor." By voting for independence, these men were not only proclaiming a belief in their newly conceived national community, they were also committing treason against their king and empire. They would be condemned as traitors, hunted as criminals, and might stand on the scaffold in payment for their actions. "It is too late to pull different ways; the members of the Continental Congress must hang together," presiding officer John Hancock said to his colleagues shortly before signing the document. "Yes, we must, indeed, all hang together," replied Benjamin Franklin, "or, most assuredly, we shall all hang separately." On July 4, 1776, the Declaration of Independence was adopted without dissent.

Conclusion

Great Britain emerged from the Seven Years' War as the dominant power in North America. Yet despite its attempts at strict regulation and determination of the course of events in its colonies, it faced consistent resistance. Perhaps British leaders felt as John Adams had when he attended the first session of the Continental Congress in 1774: How could a motley collection of "ambassadors from a dozen belligerent powers" effectively organize as a single, independent, and defiant body? The British underestimated the political consensus that existed among the colonists about the importance of republican government. They also underestimated the ability of the colonists to inform one another, to work together, and to build the bonds of national community cutting across boundaries of ethnicity, region, and economic condition. Through newspapers, pamphlets, committees of correspondence, community organizations, and group protest, the colonists discovered the concerns they shared, and in so doing fostered a new American identity. Without that identity it would have been difficult for them to consent to the treasonous act of declaring independence, especially when the independence they sought was from an international power that dominated much of the globe.

CHRONOLOGY

1713	France cedes Acadia to Britain
1745	New Englanders capture Louisbourg
1749	French send an expeditionary force down the Ohio River
1753	French begin building forts from Lake Erie to the Ohio
1754	Albany Conference
1755	British General Edward Braddock defeated by a combined force of French and Indians
	Britain expels Acadians from Nova Scotia
1756	Seven Years' War begins in Europe
1757	William Pitt becomes prime minister
1758	Louisbourg captured by the British for the second time
1759	British capture Québec
1763	Treaty of Paris
	Pontiac's uprising
	Proclamation of 1763 creates "Indian Country"
	Paxton Boys massacre
1764	Sugar Act
1765	Stamp Act and Stamp Act Congress
1766	Declaratory Act
1767	Townshend Revenue Acts
1768	Treaties of Hard Labor and Fort Stanwix
1770	Boston Massacre
1772	First Committee of Correspondence organized in Boston
1773	Tea Act
	Boston Tea Party
1774	Intolerable Acts
	First Continental Congress
	Dunmore's War
1775	Fighting begins at Lexington and Concord
	Second Continental Congress
1776	Americans invade Canada
	Thomas Paine's *Common Sense*
	Declaration of Independence

Review Questions

1. How did overwhelming British success in the Seven Years' War lead to an imperial crisis in British North America?

2. Outline the changes in British policy toward the colonies from 1750 to 1776.

3. Trace the developing sense of an American national community over this same period.

4. What were the principal events leading to the beginning of armed conflict at Lexington and Concord?

5. How were the ideals of American republicanism expressed in the Declaration of Independence?

Recommended Reading

Benedict Anderson, *Imagined Communities: Reflections on the Origin and Spread of Nationalism*, rev. ed. (1991). An argument that the essential first act of national consciousness is the effort to create a community that encompasses more than just local individuals and groups.

Fred Anderson, *The Crucible of War: The Seven Years' War and the Fate of Empire in British North America, 1754–1766* (2000). A new and powerful history of the war, arguing that it created a "hollow British empire."

Bernard Bailyn, *The Ideological Origins of the American Revolution* (1967). This classic argument emphasizes the role of ideas in the advent of the Revolution. Includes an analysis of American views of the imperial crisis.

Gregory Evans Dowd, *War Under Heaven: Pontiac, the Indian Nations, and the British Empire* (2002). Artfully crafted and gracefully written, this book restores Pontiac as a preeminent figure in the uprisings that bore his name.

Eric Foner, *Tom Paine and Revolutionary America* (1976; revised ed. 2004). Combines a biography of Paine with a community study of the Revolution in Philadelphia and Pennsylvania.

Pauline Maier, *American Scripture: Making the Declaration of Independence* (1997). The deep background of this foundation of American democracy.

Richard L. Merritt, *Symbols of American Community, 1735–1775* (1966). A study of colonial newspapers that provides evidence for a rising sense of national community. The French and Indian War emerges as the key period for the growth of nationalist sentiment.

Gary B. Nash, *The Unknown American Revolution: The Unruly Birth of Democracy and the Struggle to Create America* (2005). A noted social historian focuses on the revolution's lesser-known freedom fighters.

Ray Raphael, *First American Revolution: Before Lexington and Concord* (2002). A vivid account of the turbulent days in Massachusetts from the time the province received word of the Massachusetts Government Act in August 1774 until the fighting broke out at Lexington and Concord the following April.

Peter Silver, *Our Savage Neighbors: How Indian War Transformed Early America* (2008). A prize-winning, elegantly written history, arguing that the hatred of Indians formed one of the essential components of early American identity.

PEARSON myhistorylab Connections

Reinforce what you learned in this chapter by studying the many documents, images, maps, review tools, and videos available at www.myhistorylab.com.

Read and Review

✓•—[Study and Review Chapter 6

•••—[Read the Document

Benjamin Franklin, *Testimony against the Stamp Act (1766)*

Otis, *The Rights of the British Colonies Asserted and Proved (1763)*

The Stamp Act Crisis

John Dickinson, *from Letters from a Farmer in Pennsylvania (1768)*

Boston Gazette Description of the Boston Massacre (1770)

John Andrew to William Barrell, *Boston Tea Party (1773)*

Patrick Henry, *"Give Me Liberty or Give Me Death" (1775)*

Joseph Warren, *"Account of the Battle of Lexington" (1775)*

Royal Proclamation of Rebellion (1775)

Thomas Jefferson, *"Original Rough Draught" of the Declaration of Independence (1776)*

👁—[See the Map *The Seven Years' War*

Research and Explore

•••—[Read the Document

Exploring America: The Stamp Act

Profiles
Samuel Adams
Thomas Hutchinson

History Bookshelf: Thomas Paine, Common Sense *(1776)*

((•—[Hear the Audio *The Connecticut Peddler*

((💿—[Watch the Video *The Revolution*

((•—[Hear the **Audio**

Hear the audio files for Chapter 6 at
www.myhistorylab.com.

Chapter 7 at www.myhistorylab.com

((•—[Hear the Audio

7

The American Revolution 1776–1786

CHAPTER OUTLINE

General Washington and Lafayette at Valley Forge, 1777: lithograph, 19th century. The Granger Collection.

A National Community Evolves at Valley Forge

A drum roll announced the dawn of a cold January morning in 1778. Along a two-mile line of rude log cabins, doors slowly opened and the ragged men of the Continental Army stepped out onto the frozen ground of Valley Forge. "There comes a soldier," wrote surgeon Albigense Waldo. "His bare feet are seen through his worn-out shoes, his legs nearly naked from the tattered remains of an only pair of stockings, his breeches not sufficient to cover his nakedness, his shirt hanging in strings, his hair disheveled, his face meagre." The reek of unwashed bodies and foul straw filled the air. "No bread, no soldier!" The chant began as a barely audible murmur, then was picked up by men all along the line. "No bread, no soldier! No bread, no soldier!" At last the chanting grew so loud it could be heard at General Washington's headquarters, a mile away. The 11,000 men of the American army were surviving on little more than "firecake," a mixture of flour and water baked hard before the fire that, according to Waldo, turned "guts to pasteboard." Two thousand men were without shoes; others were without blankets and had to sit up all night about the fires to keep from freezing. Washington fired off an appeal to the Continental Congress for supplies. "Three or four days of bad weather," he wrote, "would prove our destruction."

A year before the army had suffered through a terrible winter at their encampment in Morristown, New Jersey. It was the hard winter at Valley Forge, however, that rose in legend to become a national symbol of endurance. After suffering a series of shattering defeats at the hands of a British force nearly twice their number, the soldiers of the Continental Army straggled into winter headquarters in this valley, some twenty miles northwest of Philadelphia, only to find themselves at the mercy of indifferent local suppliers. Congress refused to pay the exorbitant rates demanded by contractors for food and clothing. Local farmers preferred to deal with the British, who paid in pounds sterling rather than depreciated Continental currency.

The 11,000 men of the Continental Army were divided into sixteen brigades composed of regiments from the individual states. Many were drawn from the ranks of the poor and disadvantaged. They included landless tenant farmers, indentured servants, and nearly a thousand African Americans, both slave and free. A majority of the men came from rural districts or small towns, places where precautions regarding sanitation were unnecessary. Every thaw that winter revealed ground covered with "much filth and nastiness," and officers ordered sentinels to fire on any man "easing himself elsewhere than at the vaults." Such conditions bred infectious epidemic diseases like typhoid that spread quickly among men already weakened by malnutrition, dysentery, and exposure. Some 2,500 men died that winter. The women encamped at Valley Forge—an estimated 700 laundresses, cooks, wives, lovers, and prostitutes—were kept busy nursing the sick and burying the dead. "What then is to become of this army?" Washington worried in December.

Yet the army that marched out of Valley Forge five months later was considerably stronger for its experience there. As twentieth-century psychologists learned from studying the experiences of soldiers in World War II, it is the spirit of community among fighting men that contributes most to their success in battle. The men of the Continental Army spent the late winter and spring drilling under the strict discipline of Friedrich Wilhelm Augustus von Steuben, a Prussian officer who came to America to volunteer for the American cause.

They were already resilient and tough; now they learned how to fight as a unit.

But most important were the bonds forged among the men. In their small cabins they "shared with each other their hardships, dangers, and sufferings," wrote Private Joseph Plumb Martin, "sympathized with each other in trouble and sickness, assisted in bearing each other's burdens, [and] endeavored to conceal each other's faults." In short, he concluded, the men fashioned "a band of brotherhood" among themselves. Thrown together under the most trying of circumstances, men from different localities and ethnic backgrounds found a common identity in their struggle. On May Day they celebrated the end of winter and the coming of spring by raising maypoles before the cabins of each state regiment. Led by a sergeant decked out as King Tammany, the great Delaware chief of American folklore, and accompanied by thirteen honor guards representing each of the states, the men paraded through the rough streets of camp, pausing at each maypole to dance together. It was a ritual of their new sense of national community.

To some American Patriots—as the supporters of the Revolution called themselves—the European-style Continental Army betrayed the revolutionary ideals of the citizen-soldier and the autonomy of local communities. Washington argued strongly, however, that the Revolution could not be won without a national army insulated from politics and able to withstand shifts in the popular mood. Moreover, during the critical period of the nation's founding, the Continental Army acted as a popular democratic force, counterbalancing the conservatism of the new republic's elite leadership. The national spirit built at places like Valley Forge sustained the fighting men through years of war and provided momentum for the long process of forging a national political system out of the persistent localism of American politics. The soldiers of the Continental Army were among the first of their countrymen to think of themselves as Americans.

The Revolutionary years were characterized by warfare not only between armed American and British forces but also between Patriots and Loyalists, settlers and Indians, masters and slaves. Jealous of their autonomy, the individual colonies shaped a weak central government that just barely managed to keep them unified. Battered and bruised by British armies,

1. What were the major alignments and divisions among Americans during the American Revolution?

2. What were the major campaigns of the Revolution?

3. What role did the Articles of Confederation and the Confederation Congress play in the Revolution?

4. In what ways were the states the sites for significant political change?

FOCUS Questions

1776–1786

the Continental Army pulled off an unexpected and remarkable victory against a large British force in upper New York State that led to financial support from Holland and a military alliance with France that in the end proved to be a

Valley Forge

decisive element in winning American independence. The glue that held Americans together during this long struggle was the sense of national community that emerged in places like Valley Forge during the winter of 1777.

AMERICAN Communities

The War for Independence

At the beginning of the Revolution, the British had the world's best-equipped and most disciplined army, as well as a navy that was unopposed in American waters. But this overwhelming force encouraged them to greatly underestimate the American capacity to fight. With a native officer corps and considerable experience in the colonial wars of the eighteenth century, Patriot forces proved formidable. The British also misperceived the sources of the conflict. Seeing the rebellion as the work of a small group of disgruntled conspirators, they defined their objective as defeating this Patriot opposition. They believed that in the wake of a military victory they could easily reassert political control. But the geography of eastern North America offered no single vital center whose conquest would end the war. The Patriots had the advantage of fighting on their own ground and among a population thinly spread over a territory stretching along 1,500 miles of coastline and extending 100 miles or more into the interior. When the British succeeded in defeating the Patriots in one area, resistance would spring up in another. The key factor in the outcome of the war for independence was popular support for the American cause.

Watch the Video
The American Revolution as Different Americans Saw It
at **www.myhistorylab.com**

The Patriot Forces

Most American men of fighting age had to face the call to arms. From a population of approximately 350,000 eligible men, more than 200,000 saw action, though no more than 25,000 were engaged at any time. About half served in the Continental Army under Washington's command, the other half in militia companies.

These militias—armed bodies of men drawn from local communities—proved important in the defense of their own areas, for they had homes as well as local reputations to protect. But the Revolution was not won by citizen-soldiers who traded plows for guns, or backcountry riflemen who picked off Redcoats from behind trees. In the exuberant days of 1776, many Patriots hoped that militias alone could win the war against the British. But serving short terms of enlistment, often with officers of their own choosing, militiamen resisted discipline. Indeed, in the face of battle, militia companies during the Revolution demonstrated appalling rates of desertion.

The final victory resulted primarily from the steady struggle of the Continental Army. The American Revolution had little in common with modern national liberation movements in which armed populations conduct guerrilla warfare. Washington and his officers wanted a force that could directly engage the British, and from the beginning of the war, he argued that victory could be won only with a full commitment to a truly national army. His views conflicted with popular fears of a standing army. Would they not be defeating their own purpose, many wondered, by adopting the corrupt institutions of their British enemies? Led by such views, Congress initially refused to invoke a draft or mandate army enlistments exceeding one year.

But the failings of the militias in the early battles of the war sobered Congress, and it responded with greatly enlarged state quotas for the Continental Army and terms of service that lasted for the duration of the conflict. To spur enlistment, Congress offered bounties, regular wages, and promises of free land after victory. By the spring of 1777, Washington's army had grown to nearly 9,000 men.

A wide chasm separated the officer corps from the rank and file in the Continental Army, a reflection of the class gradations of colonial society. Officers came from propertied and socially prominent families and considered themselves gentlemen, while enlisted men came mainly from the economically deprived and socially marginal elements of the population. Officers enjoyed significant advantages in pay and accommodations and scrupulously avoided fraternization with their enlisted inferiors. For soldiers, honorable behavior demanded unquestioning obedience to higher authority and acceptance of the hardships of army life.

The New England militia companies that made up the original core of the Continental Army included a small number of African Americans. But in late 1775, under pressure from southern delegates, the Continental Congress barred them from enlistment. What changed this policy was the British promise of liberty for all slaves who fought for the crown, first offered by Virginia's royal governor John Murray, Earl of Dunmore. Thousands of slaves fled their masters and enlisted, forcing the states of the Upper South—Maryland, Virginia, and North Carolina—to admit free persons of color and even slaves into the ranks. By

war's end, at least 5,000 African Americans had served in Patriot militias or the Continental Army, and in the Upper South some slaves won their freedom through military service. In the Lower South, however, where the numerical superiority of slaves inspired fears of rebellion among whites, there was no similar movement.

◆◆◆ Read the Document
Proclamation of Lord Dunmore (1775) at **www.myhistorylab.com**

The Continental Army played an important political role during the war. At a time when Americans identified most strongly with their local communities or their states, the Continental Army, through experiences like the Valley Forge winter, evolved into a powerful force for nationalist sentiment. Over 100,000 men from every state served in the Continental Army, contributing mightily to the unity of purpose—the formation of a national political community—that was essential to the process of nation making.

The Toll of War

Discipline was essential in a conflict in which men fired at close range, charged with bayonets drawn, and engaged in hand-to-hand combat. One Connecticut soldier wrote of the effects of cannon on his regiment: "The ball first cut off the head of Smith, a stout heavy man, and dashed it open, then took Taylor across the bowels; it then struck Sergeant Garret of our company on the hip, took off the point of the hip bone." The carnage was horrible. "Oh! What a sight that was, to see within a distance of six rods those men with their legs and arms and guns and packs all in a heap." A sergeant witnessed British troops slaughtering wounded Americans during the battles in New Jersey: "They dashed out their brains with their muskets and run them through with their bayonets, made them like sieves. This was barbarity to the utmost."

The best estimate is that 25,324 American men died in the fighting, approximately 6,800 from wounds suffered in battle, most of the rest from the effects of disease. But since

Jean Baptiste Antoine de Verger, a French officer serving with the Continental Army, made these watercolors of American soldiers during the Revolution. Some 200,000 men saw action, including at least 5,000 African Americans; more than half of these troops served with the Continental Army.

these numbers include only the major battles, the total death toll must have been considerably higher. The Continental Army experienced the heaviest casualty rates, losses in some regiments approaching 40 percent. Indeed, the casualty rate overall was higher than in any other American conflict except the Civil War. In New England and the Mid-Atlantic states the war claimed few civilian lives, for it was confined largely to direct engagements between armies. In the South and backcountry, however, where Patriot and Loyalist militias waged violent and often vicious campaigns, there were many noncombatant casualties. There are no overall statistics for Loyalist casualties, but British forces suffered at least 10,000 killed or wounded in the major battles of the war.

● ●●―[Read the Document
Letter from a Revolutionary War Soldier (1776) at **www.myhistorylab.com**

The Loyalists

Not all Americans were Patriots. Many were confused by the conflict and waited for a clear turn in the tide of the struggle before declaring their allegiance. Between a fifth and a third of the population, somewhere between a half a million and a million people, remained loyal to the British crown. They called themselves Loyalists but were known to Patriots as Tories, the popular name for the conservative party in England, traditionally supporters of the king's authority over that of Parliament.

A large proportion of the Loyalists were relatively recent migrants to the colonies, born in England, Scotland, or Ireland. Others, such as royal officeholders or Anglican clergymen, were dependent on the British government for their salaries. Many Loyalists were men of conservative temperament, fearful of political or social upheaval. The Loyalists included ethnic minorities who had been persecuted by the dominant majority, such as the Highland Scots of the Carolinas and western New York, or southern tenant farmers who had Patriot landlords. Loyalists were particularly strong in some colonies. They were nearly a majority in New York and were so numerous in Pennsylvania that an officer of the Continental Army described that colony as "the enemy's country." In Georgia, Loyalists made up such a large majority that the colony would probably have abandoned the revolutionary movement had the British not surrendered at Yorktown in 1781.

Patriots passed state treason acts that prohibited speaking or writing against the Revolution. They also punished Loyalists by issuing bills of attainder, a legal process (later made illegal by the United States Constitution) by means of which Loyalists were deprived of civil rights and property. In some areas, notably New York, South Carolina, Massachusetts, and Pennsylvania, Loyalists faced mob violence.

The British strategy for suppressing the Revolution depended on mobilizing the Loyalists, as many as 50,000 of whom took up arms for Great Britain. Many joined Loyalist militias or engaged in irregular warfare, especially in the Lower South. In 1780, when Washington's army numbered about 9,000, some 8,000 American Loyalists were serving in the British army in America.

As many as 80,000 Loyalists fled the country during and after the Revolution. Many went to England or the British West Indies, but the largest number settled in the northern British colonies that would later become the nation of Canada. Some 4,000 former slaves who fought for the British settled near Halifax in Nova Scotia, where they formed the largest independent black community outside Africa. Although the British government compensated many Loyalists for their losses when their property was confiscated by the states and sold at auction, most were unhappy exiles. "I earnestly wish to spend the remainder of my days in America," William Pepperell, formerly of Maine, wrote from London in 1778. "I love the country. I love the people." Former governor Thomas Hutchinson of Massachusetts wrote that he "had rather die in a little country farm-house

The TORY'S Day of JUDGMENT.

A Patriot mob torments Loyalists in this print published during the Revolution. One favorite punishment was the "grand Tory ride," in which a crowd hauled the victim through the streets astride a fence rail. In another, men were stripped to "buff and breeches" and their naked flesh coated liberally with heated tar and feathers.

in New England than in the best nobleman's seat in old England." Despite their disagreement with the Patriots on essential political questions, they remained Americans, and they mourned the loss of their country.

Among those exiles was the most infamous American supporter of the British cause, Benedict Arnold. Arnold was a hero of the early battles of the Revolution on the Patriot side (see Chapter 6), but in 1779, resentful of what he perceived to be humiliating assignments and rank below his station, he became a paid informer of the British. In 1780 Patriots uncovered Arnold's plot to betray the strategic post of West Point, which he commanded. He fled to the British, who paid him a handsome stipend and pension. During the last two years of the war he commanded British troops and led raids against his home state of Connecticut. He moved to London after the war, where he died in 1801, impoverished and unknown. But Arnold's name remained well known in the United States, where it is still synonymous with treason.

Women and the War

As men marched off to war, thousands of women assumed the management of farms and businesses. Abigail Adams ran the Adams family's farm at Quincy for years, reporting on operations in frequent letters to her husband John, letters that included commentary on the American struggle for independence and the political structure of the new republic. Some women participated even more directly in Patriot politics. Mercy Otis Warren, sister of the Massachusetts leader James Otis, turned her home into a center of Patriot political activity and published a series of satires supporting the American cause and scorning the Loyalists. Thousands of women volunteered to support the war effort by working as seamstresses, nurses, even spies.

Thousands of women also traveled with the armies of both sides. Some camp followers were prostitutes, but most were wives, nurses, cooks, and laundresses. In sharp contrast to the wives of officers who rode in coaches or wagons and were put up in the best available housing, working women were consigned to the back of the line with the baggage. For their services they got little respect and were often condemned as "wild beasts" or "furies."

These women not only shared the hardships of the soldiers but also were on the battlefields bringing water, food, and supplies to the front lines under withering cannon and musket fire and nursing the wounded and dying. Tales were told of "Molly Pitcher," a woman who carried water to thirsty fighters on the front lines and took her husband's place at the cannon when he was killed by shrapnel. Molly was a composite figure of folklore, inspired by the actions of real women. The Continental Congress and state legislatures awarded pensions to numerous women wounded in battle: to Margaret Corbin, struck while filling in for her mortally wounded husband; to Mary Hays McCauley, known to soldiers as "Sgt. McCauley"; and to Anna Maria Lane, wife of a Connecticut enlisted man, who "in the garb and with the courage of a soldier performed extraordinary

John Singleton Copley's portrait of Mercy Otis Warren captured her at the age of thirty-six, in 1765. During the Revolution, her home in Boston was a center of Patriot political activity.

SOURCE: John Singleton Copley (American, 1738–1815), *Mrs. James Warren (Mercy Otis)*, ca.1763. Oil on canvas. 49 ⅝ × 39 ½ in. (126 × 100.3 cm). Bequest of Winslow Warren. Courtesy, Museum of Fine Arts, Boston (31.212). Reproduced with permission. © 2000 Museum of Fine Arts, Boston. All Rights Reserved.

military services and received a severe wound at the Battle of Germantown." According to one estimate, several hundred women dressed themselves as men and enlisted. One of them, Deborah Sampson of Massachusetts, was the subject of a sensational biography after the war and became the first American woman to embark on a lecture tour.

The Campaign for New York and New Jersey

During the winter of 1775–76, the British developed a strategic plan for the war. From his base at Halifax, Sir William Howe would take his army to New York City, which the British navy would protect. From there Howe was to drive north along the Hudson, while another British army marched south from Canada. The two armies would converge at Albany, cutting New England off from the rest of the colonies, then turn eastward. Washington, in command of Patriot forces at Boston, shifted his forces southward toward New York in the spring of 1776.

In early July, as Congress adopted the Declaration of Independence, the British began their operation by landing 32,000 troops on Staten Island. The Patriots set up fortified positions across the harbor in Brooklyn. In late

August the British attacked, inflicting heavy casualties. The militia forces under Washington's command proved unreliable under fire. The Battle of Long Island ended in disaster for the Patriots, and they were forced to withdraw across the East River to Manhattan.

The British then offered Congress an opportunity to negotiate, and on September 6, Benjamin Franklin, John Adams, and Edward Rutledge sat down on Staten Island with General Howe and his brother, Admiral Richard Howe. But the meeting broke up when the Howes demanded repeal of the Declaration of Independence, setting the stage for another round of fighting. Six days later, the British invaded Manhattan, and only a desperate American stand at Harlem Heights prevented the destruction of a large portion of the Patriot army. Enjoying naval control of the harbor, the British quickly outflanked the American positions. In a series of battles over the next few months, they forced Washington back at White Plains and overran the American posts of Fort Washington and Fort Lee, on either side of the Hudson River. By November, the Americans were fleeing south across New Jersey in a frantic attempt to avoid the British under General Charles Cornwallis (see Map 7.1).

With morale desperately low, whole militia companies deserted. American resistance seemed to be collapsing, and Washington was pessimistic. "Our Troops will not do their duty," he wrote painfully to Congress as he crossed the Delaware River into Pennsylvania. But rather than fall back farther, which would surely have meant the dissolution of his entire force, he decided to risk a counterattack. On Christmas night 1776, Washington led 2,400 troops back across the Delaware, and the next morning defeated the Hessian forces in a surprise attack on their headquarters at Trenton, New Jersey. The Americans inflicted further heavy losses on the British at Princeton, then drove them all the way back to the environs of New York City.

These victories had little strategic importance, but they salvaged American morale. As Washington settled into winter headquarters at Morristown, he realized he had to pursue a defensive strategy, avoiding direct confrontations with the British while checking their advances and hurting them wherever possible. The most important thing would be the survival of the Continental Army.

⊙ See the Map
The American Revolution
at **www.myhistorylab.com**

The Northern Campaigns of 1777

The fighting with American forces prevented Howe from moving north up the Hudson River, and the British advance southward from Canada was stalled by American resistance at Lake Champlain. In 1777, however, the British decided to replay their strategy. From Canada they dispatched General John Burgoyne with nearly 8,000 British and allied German troops. Howe was to move his force from New York, first taking the city of Philadelphia, the seat of the Continental Congress, and then moving north to meet Burgoyne (see Map 7.2).

Fort Ticonderoga fell to Burgoyne on July 6, but by August the general found himself bogged down and harassed by Patriot militias in the rough country south of Lake George. After several defeats in September at the hands of an American army commanded by General Horatio Gates, Burgoyne retreated to Saratoga. There he was surrounded by a considerably larger force of Americans, and on October 18 he surrendered his army. It would be the biggest British defeat until Yorktown, decisive because it forced the nations of Europe to recognize that the Americans had a fighting chance to win their Revolution.

The Americans were less successful against Howe. A force of 15,000 British troops left New York in July and landed a month later at the northern end of Chesapeake Bay. In September, at Brandywine Creek outside Philadelphia, the British outflanked the Americans, inflicting heavy casualties and forcing a retreat. Ten days later they routed the Americans a second time at Paoli, clearing the way for the British occupation of Philadelphia on September 26. Congress fled to the Pennsylvania country town of York. Washington attempted a valiant counterattack at Germantown on October 4, but initial success was followed by a lack of coordination that eventually doomed the operation.

After this campaign, the Continentals headed into winter quarters at Valley Forge, the bitterness of their defeats muted somewhat by news of Burgoyne's surrender at Saratoga. The British had possession of Philadelphia, the most important city in North America, but it would prove of little strategic value to them. The Continental Congress continued to function, so the unified effort suffered little disruption. At the end of two years of fighting, despite numerous military victories, the British strategy for suppressing the Revolution had been a failure.

MAP 7.1 Campaign for New York and New Jersey, 1775–77

MAP 7.2 Northern Campaigns, 1777–78

A Global Conflict

During these two years of fighting, the Americans were sustained by loans from France and Spain, traditional enemies of Great Britain. Both saw an opportunity to win back North American territories lost as a result of the Seven Years' War. Seeking more support, the Continental Congress sent a diplomatic delegation to Paris headed by Benjamin Franklin. The urbane and cosmopolitan Franklin, who captured French hearts by dressing in homespun and wearing a "frontiersman" fur cap, established excellent relations with Comte de Vergennes, the French foreign minister. Franklin negotiated for recognition of American independence and a Franco-American alliance against the British, in addition to loans from the French to finance the Revolution. Vergennes longed to weaken the British Empire any way he could and was inclined to support the Americans. But he was reluctant to encourage a republican revolution against monarchy and colonialism.

The American victory at Saratoga, and the fear that Great Britain might enter into negotiations with the revolutionaries, persuaded Vergennes to recognize American independence in December 1777. In the treaty signed by the two nations the French pledged to "maintain effectually the liberty, sovereignty, and independence" of the United States, while the United States promised to recognize French acquisitions of British island colonies in the West Indies. Neither country was to conclude peace with the British "without the formal consent of the other." The treaty was to take effect "should war break out" between France and Great Britain. The alliance was sealed when fighting between the two traditional enemies began in June.

Americans also found much support in the Netherlands. Although officially allied with Great Britain, the Dutch maintained a position of neutrality and opened secret negotiations with the Americans for a treaty of trade and friendship. Clandestine trade through the Dutch island of St. Eustatius in the Caribbean helped sustain the Patriot cause. In 1779 the British shelled the Dutch colony and the next year declared war on the Netherlands. The Dutch became the second European nation to recognize the United States and its financiers became the most important source of loans for the new nation.

Spain had entered the war in 1779. As early as 1775, Spanish officials in New Orleans were providing substantial ammunition and provisions for American forts in the West, including supplies of beef from herds of cattle driven to New Orleans by vaqueros (cowboys) from Texas. The viceroy of New Spain levied a special tax to pay for these supplies, and borderland colonists in Sonora, Texas, New Mexico, and California contributed their share. But unlike France and the Netherlands, the Spanish refused to establish a formal alliance with the United States. They viewed the Revolution as an opportunity to regain Florida from the British and extend their control of the Mississippi Valley, but they feared the threat the Americans would pose to New Spain. "Its people are active, industrious, and aggressive," one official in Mexico wrote of the new nation, and "it would be culpable negligence on our part not to thwart their schemes for conquest."

Thus, the Spanish pursued an independent strategy against the British, seizing the weakly defended Mississippi River towns of Natchez and Baton Rouge in 1779, and winning the important Gulf ports of Mobile in 1780 and Pensacola in 1781. The victory at Pensacola was achieved with the help of several companies of Florida exiles, many of them African Americans. Alarmed by the quick spread of American settlements west of the Appalachians, the Spanish attempted to establish a claim of their own to the British territory north of the Ohio; they sent an expedition into the Northwest that in 1781 succeeded in taking the minor British post of St. Joseph, in present-day Michigan.

With France and Spain now in the war, the British rethought their military strategy. Considering their West Indies sugar colonies at risk, they shipped 5,000 troops from New York to the Caribbean, where they succeeded in beating back a French attack. Fearing the arrival of the French fleet along the North American coast, the new British commander in America, General Henry Clinton, evacuated Philadelphia in June 1778. Washington's Continentals, fresh out of Valley Forge, went in hot pursuit. In the Battle of Monmouth, fought in stifling New Jersey heat on June 28, the British blunted the American drive and succeeded in making an orderly retreat to New York City. After a failed American-French joint campaign against the British at Newport, Rhode Island, Washington decided on a defensive strategy. Although the Americans enjoyed several small successes in the Northeast over the next two years, the war there went into a stalemate.

The war at sea was mostly fought between the British and French, but Continental, state, and private vessels engaged in privateering raids against British merchant ships and isolated naval patrols. The foremost naval hero of the war was John Paul Jones, who raided the British coast of Scotland in 1777; in 1778, in command of a French ship he named *Bonhomme Richard* in honor of Franklin, he engaged in a celebrated sea battle with the British warship *Serapis*. When the two ships locked together, the British captain hailed Jones to see if he was ready to surrender. Jones's reply—"I have not yet begun to fight"—became one of the most quoted lines of the Revolution. The incident actually had little military value, and after the war Congress decommissioned the small number of American ships and dismissed its naval officers, including Jones, who went on to serve in the Russian navy.

Indian Peoples and the Revolution in the West

At the beginning of the conflict, both sides looked for Indian support. Most important was the stance of the Iroquois Confederacy, long one of the most potent political forces in colonial North America. A delegation from Congress told the Iroquois that the conflict was a "family quarrel" and urged them to keep out of it. British agents, on the other hand, pressed the Iroquois to unite against the Americans. Many Indian leaders were reluctant to get involved: "We are unwilling to join on either side of such a contest," declared one Oneida chief. "Let us Indians be all of one mind, and live with one another, and you white people settle your own disputes between yourselves."

Ultimately, however, the British proved persuasive. It became clear to Indians that a Patriot victory would mean the extension of American settlements into their homelands. Native peoples fought in the Revolution for some of the same reasons Patriots did—for political independence, cultural integrity, and the protection of their land and property—but Indian fears of American expansion led

Joseph Brant, the brilliant chief of the Mohawks who sided with Great Britain during the Revolution, in a 1786 painting by the American artist Gilbert Stuart. After the Treaty of Paris, Brant led a large faction of Iroquois people north into British Canada, where they established a separate Iroquois Confederacy.

them to oppose the Patriot rhetoric of natural rights and the equality of all men. Almost all the tribes that engaged in the fighting did so on the side of the British.

British officials marshaled the support of Cherokees, Creeks, Choctaws, and Chickasaws in the South, supplying them with arms from the British arsenal at Pensacola until it was seized by the Spanish in 1781. The consequence was a ferocious Indian war in the southern backcountry. In the summer of 1776 a large number of Cherokees, led by the warrior chief Dragging Canoe (Tsiyu-Gunsini), attacked dozens of American settlements. It required hard fighting before Patriot militia companies managed to drive the Cherokees into the mountains. Although the Cherokees eventually made an official peace, sporadic violence between Patriots and Indians continued along the southern frontier.

Among the Iroquois of New York, the Mohawk leader Joseph Brant (Thayendanegea) succeeded in bringing most Iroquois warriors into the British camp, although he was opposed by the chiefs of the Oneidas and Tuscaroras, who supported the Patriots. In 1777 and 1778, Iroquois and Loyalist forces raided the northern frontiers of New York and Pennsylvania. In retaliation an American army invaded the Iroquois homelands in 1779. Supported by Oneida and Tuscarora warriors, the Americans destroyed dozens of western villages and thousands of acres of crops. For the first time since the birth of their confederacy centuries before, the Iroquois were fighting each other (see Map 7.3).

Across the mountains, the Ohio Indians formed an effective alliance under the British at Detroit, and in 1777 and 1778 they sent warriors south against pioneer communities in western Virginia and Kentucky that had been founded in defiance of the Proclamation of 1763. Boonesborough, Kentucky, was nearly destroyed by repeated attacks, and the Americans barely held out. Virginian George Rogers Clark countered by organizing an expedition of Kentucky militia against the old French settlements in the Illinois country, which were controlled by the British. They succeeded in taking the British post at Kaskaskia in the summer of 1778, and in early 1779, in a daring winter raid on Vincennes, they captured Colonel Henry Hamilton, British commander in the West, infamously known as "the Scalp Buyer" because of the bounty he had placed on Patriots' lives.

But Clark lacked the strength to attack the strategic British garrison at Detroit. Coordinating his Iroquois forces with those in Ohio, Brant mounted a new set of offensives that cast a shadow over Clark's successes. Raids back and forth across the Ohio River by Indians and

MAP 7.3 Fighting in the West, 1778–79

Americans claimed hundreds of lives over the next three years. The war in the West would not end with the conclusion of hostilities in the East. With barely a pause, the fighting in the trans-Appalachian West between Americans and Indians would continue for another two decades.

The War in the South

The most important fighting of the Revolution took place in the South (see Map 7.4). General Clinton regained the initiative for Britain in December 1778 by sending a force from New York against Georgia, the weakest of the colonies. The British crushed the Patriot militia at Savannah and began to organize the Loyalists in an effort to reclaim the colony. Encouraged by their success in Georgia, the British decided to apply the lessons learned there throughout the South. This involved a fundamental change from a strategy of military conquest to one of pacification. Territory would be retaken step by step, then handed over to Loyalists who would reassert the crown's authority.

In October 1779 Clinton evacuated Rhode Island, the last British stronghold in New England, and proceeded with 8,000 troops for a campaign against Charleston.

Outflanking the American defenders, he forced the surrender of more than 5,000 troops in May. It was the most significant American defeat of the war. Patriot resistance collapsed in the Lower South, and American fortunes were suddenly at their lowest ebb since the beginning of the war.

The southern campaign was marked by vicious fighting between partisan militias of Patriots and Loyalists. The violence peaked in September 1780 with Cornwallis's invasion of North Carolina, where the Patriots were stronger and better organized. There the British found their southern strategy untenable: plundering towns and farms in order to feed the army in the interior had the effect of producing angry support for the Patriots. In October at Kings Mountain, in the backcountry near the boundary separating the Carolinas, Patriot sharpshooters outflanked and destroyed a Loyalist force, and in January 1781, Loyalists were again defeated at the Battle of the Cowpens, not far from Kings Mountain.

Into 1781 the Continentals and Patriot militias waged what General Greene called a fugitive war of hit and run against the British. "I am quite tired of marching about the country in quest of adventures," Cornwallis wrote. Finally

MAP 7.4 Fighting in the South, 1778–81

In 1845 Artist William Ranney depicted a famous moment during the Battle of Cowpens that took place in January 1781. Lieutenant Colonel William Washington, leader of the Patriot cavalry and a relative of George Washington, was attacked by a squadron of British dragoons. As Washington was about to be cut down, he was saved by his servant William Ball, who fired a pistol that wounded the attacker. Nothing more is known about Ball, but he was one of a number of African Americans who fought on the Patriot side in the battle.

SOURCE: William Ranney, *The Battle of Cowpens*. Oil on canvas. Photo by Sam Holland. Courtesy South Carolina State House.

in the summer of 1781, deciding he would not be able to hold the Carolinas as long as Virginia remained a base of support and supply for the Americans, Cornwallis led his army north. After marauding through the Virginia countryside, he reached the Chesapeake where he expected reinforcements from New York. The British withdrawal from North Carolina allowed Greene to reestablish Patriot control of the Lower South.

The Yorktown Surrender

While the British raged through the South, the stalemate continued in the Northeast. In the summer of 1780, taking advantage of the British evacuation of Rhode Island, the French landed 5,000 troops at Newport under the command of General Jean Baptiste Donatien de Vimeur, comte de Rochambeau. But it was not until the spring of 1781 that Rochambeau risked joining his force to Washington's Continentals north of New York City. In August Washington learned that the French Caribbean fleet was

headed for the Chesapeake. If he and Rochambeau could move their troops south, they might lock up Cornwallis in his camp at Yorktown. Leaving a small force behind as a decoy, they marched their 16,000 men overland to the Virginia shore in little more than a month.

The maneuver was a complete success. The French and Americans surrounded and besieged the British encampment. French and American heavy artillery hammered the British unmercifully until the middle of October. After the failure of a planned retreat across the York River, Cornwallis opened negotiations for the surrender of his army. Two days later, on October 19, 1781, between lines of victorious American and French soldiers, the British troops came out from their trenches to surrender. Pleading illness, Cornwallis sent his second-in-command, General Charles O'Hara, to surrender (see Seeing History). O'Hara first approached General Rochambeau, but the Frenchman waved him toward Washington. Washington, following the military protocol

SEEING History

The Surrender of Lord Cornwallis

American artist John Trumbull displayed a preliminary version of *Surrender of Lord Cornwallis* in 1797 along with three other history paintings of the Revolution, including his depiction of the signing of the Declaration of Independence, the surrender of General Burgoyne at Saratoga, and the resignation of General Washington from his military commission at the war's conclusion. Young Trumbull had been an officer in the Continental Army and served for a time as Washington's aide-de-camp, but he had not been at Yorktown. By that time he was in London studying with the American expatriate artist Benjamin West. This painting was done in the heroic style of nationalist art popular at the time in Great Britain and Europe. Trumbull was at pains to get the details right. He visited Yorktown to sketch the landscape and traveled across the United States and France to capture the likenesses of the senior American and French officers, including Washington and Rochambeau, shown lining the two sides, colors flying, as the British troops file by. But Trumbull was criticized by the public for getting one detail appallingly wrong. He depicted Cornwallis on horseback in the center, when in fact the British commander was not present at the ceremony but was sulking in his tent. Trumbull corrected his error by changing the color of the central figure's uniform from red to blue, thereby turning Cornwallis into General Benjamin Lincoln, who is seen reaching for the sword in the possession of the British second-in-command, General Charles O'Hara. In 1817 the Senate commissioned Trumbull to repaint his Revolutionary scenes for placement in the Rotunda of the Capitol.

• **In what ways does Trumbull create a heroic painting by the arrangement of his subjects?**

that directed him to accept the sword of surrender from no one other than the commander in chief, directed O'Hara to his second, General Benjamin Lincoln, who received it. Everyone was aware that it was an event of incalculable importance, but few guessed it was the end of the war. The British still controlled New York.

In London a month later Lord North received the news "as he would have taken a ball in the breast," the colonial secretary reported. "Oh God!" North moaned, "it is all over!" The American Revolution had turned into war with France and Spain, and British fortunes were at low ebb in India, the West Indies, Florida, and the Mediterranean. The cost of the war was enormous, and there was little support for it among either the British public or the members of Parliament. George III wished to press on, but North submitted his resignation, and in March 1782 the king was forced to offer the office of prime minister to Charles Watson-Wentworth, Lord Rockingham, who long had favored granting the Americans their independence.

The United States in Congress Assembled

The motion for independence, offered to the Continental Congress by Richard Henry Lee on June 7, 1776, called for a confederation of the states. The Articles of Confederation, the first written constitution of the United States, created a national government of sharply limited powers. This arrangement reflected the concerns of people fighting to free themselves from a coercive central government. But the weak Confederation government had a difficult time forging the unity and assembling the resources necessary to fight the war and win the peace.

The Articles of Confederation

The debate over confederation that took place in the Continental Congress during 1776 made it clear that delegates favoring a loose union of autonomous states outnumbered those who wanted a strong central government. A consensus finally emerged in 1777, and the "Articles of Confederation" were formally adopted by the Continental Congress in November and sent to the states for ratification. The Articles created a national assembly, called the Congress, in which each state had a single vote. Delegates, selected annually in a manner determined by the individual state legislatures, could serve no more than three years out of six. A presiding president, elected annually by Congress, was eligible to hold office no more than one year out of three. Votes would be decided by a simple majority of the states, except for major questions, which would require the agreement of nine states.

Congress was granted national authority in the conduct of foreign affairs, matters of war and peace, and

►○┤**Read** the **Document**

The Articles of Confederation (1777) at **www.myhistorylab.com**

maintenance of the armed forces. It could raise loans, issue bills of credit, establish a coinage, and regulate trade with Indian peoples, and it was to be the final authority in jurisdictional disputes between states. It was charged with establishing a national postal system as well as a common standard of weights and measures. Lacking the power to tax citizens directly, however, the national government was to apportion its financial burdens among the states according to the extent of their surveyed land. The Articles explicitly guaranteed the sovereignty of the individual states, reserving to them all powers not expressly delegated to Congress. Ratification or amendment required the agreement of all thirteen states. The Articles of Confederation thus created a national government of specific yet sharply circumscribed powers.

The legislatures of twelve states soon voted in favor of the Articles, but final ratification was held up for more than three years by the state of Maryland. Representing the interests of states without claims to lands west of the Appalachians, Maryland demanded that states cede to Congress their western claims, the new nation's most valuable resource, for "the good of the whole" (see Map 7.5). During the subsequent stalemate, Congress agreed to conduct business under the terms of the unratified document. It was 1781 before Virginia, the state with the largest western claims, broke the logjam by agreeing to the cession. Maryland then ratified the Articles of Confederation, and in March they took effect.

◉┤See the **Map**

Western Land Claims Ceded by the States at **www.myhistorylab.com**

►●►┤**Read** the **Document**

Congress Decides What to Do with the Western Lands (1785) at **www.myhistorylab.com**

Financing the War

Lacking the authority to levy direct taxes, Congress financed the Revolution through grants and loans from friendly foreign powers and by issuing paper currency. The total foreign subsidy by the end of the war approached $9 million, but this was not enough to back the circulating Continental currency that Congress authorized, the face value of which amounted to $200 million. In an attempt to retire this currency, Congress called on the states to raise taxes, payable in Continental dollars. But most of the states were unwilling to do this. In fact, most had resorted to printing currency of their own, estimated at a face value of another $200 million by war's end. The result of this expansion in the money supply was the rapid depreciation of Continental currency. People who received fixed incomes for services—Continental soldiers, for example, as well as landlords and other creditors—were devastated by runaway inflation. By the time Robert Morris, one of the wealthiest merchants in the country, became secretary of finance in May 1781, Continental currency had ceased to circulate. In the jargon of the day, things of no

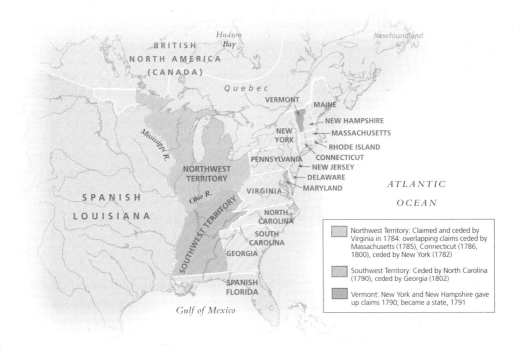

MAP 7.5 State Claims to Western Lands The ratification of the Articles of Confederation in 1781 awaited settlement of the western claims of eight states. Vermont, claimed by New Hampshire and New York, was not made a state until 1791, after disputes were settled the previous year. The territory north of the Ohio River was claimed in whole or in part by Virginia, New York, Connecticut, and Massachusetts. All of them had ceded their claims by 1786, except for Connecticut, which had claimed an area just south of Lake Erie, known as the Western Reserve; Connecticut ceded this land in 1800. The territory south of the Ohio was claimed by Virginia, North Carolina, South Carolina, and Georgia; in 1802, the latter became the last state to cede its claims.

value were "not worth a Continental." Yet the paper currency had funded a revolution.

Morris was able to turn things around. He persuaded Congress to charter a "Bank of North America" located in Philadelphia, the first private commercial bank in the United States. Into its vaults he deposited large quantities of gold and silver coin and bills of exchange obtained through loans from Holland and France. He then issued new paper currency backed by this treasure. Once he established confidence in the bank, Morris was able to supply the Continental Army through private contracts. He also began making interest payments on the debt, which in 1783 was estimated at $30 million.

Negotiating Independence

Peace talks between the United States and Great Britain opened in July 1782 when Benjamin Franklin sat down with the British emissary in Paris. Congress had issued its first set of war aims in 1779. The fundamental demand was recognition of American independence and withdrawal of British forces. American negotiators were instructed to press for the largest territorial limits possible, as well as

guarantees of American rights to fish North Atlantic waters. As for its French ally, Congress instructed the commissioners to be guided by friendly advice, but also by "knowledge of our interests, and by your own discretion, in which we repose the fullest confidence." The French were not happy with this, and partly as a result of French pressure, in June 1781 Congress issued a new set of instructions. The commissioners were to settle merely for a grant of independence and withdrawal of troops and to be subject to the guidance and control of the French in the negotiations.

Ben Franklin, John Jay, and John Adams, the peace commissioners in Paris, were well aware of French attempts to manipulate the outcome of negotiations and place limits on American power. In violation of both Congressional instructions and treaty obligations to France, they signed a preliminary treaty with Britain in November 1782 without consulting the French. In the treaty, Britain acknowledged the United States as "free, sovereign & independent" and agreed to withdraw its troops from all forts within American territory "with all convenient speed." The American commissioners pressed the British for Canada but settled for western territorial boundaries extending to

Eighteen Pence.

To counterfeit is *Death.*

Burlington in NEW-JERSEY,
Printed by Ifaac Collins, 1776.

The Continental Congress printed currency to finance the Revolution. Because of widespread counterfeiting, engravers attempted to incorporate complex designs, like the unique vein structure in the leaf on this eighteen-pence note. In case that wasn't enough, the engraver of this note also included the warning: "To counterfeit is Death."

the Mississippi (see Map 7.6) with unencumbered navigation of the river. The British guaranteed Americans "the right to take fish" in the waters of the North Atlantic. Britain received American promises that Congress would erect "no lawful impediments" to the recovery of debts, end the confiscation of Loyalist property, and attempt to persuade the states to fairly compensate Loyalist exiles. All in all, it was an astounding coup for the Americans. The peace terms, the commissioners wrote to Congress, "appear to leave us little to complain of and not much to desire."

See the Map
Territorial Claims in Eastern America after Treaty of Paris at
www.myhistorylab.com

The preliminary treaty confronted France with an accomplished fact. When French diplomats criticized the American commissioners, they responded by hinting that resistance to the treaty provisions could result in a British–American alliance. Thereupon France quickly made an agreement of its own with the British.

Spain did not participate in the negotiations with the Americans. But having waged a successful campaign against the British on the Mississippi and the Gulf Coast, its government issued a claim of sovereignty over much of the trans-Appalachian territory granted to the United States by Great Britain. Spain arranged a separate peace with Great Britain, in which it won the return of Florida. The final Treaty of Paris—actually a series of separate agreements among the United States, Great Britain, France, and Spain—was signed at Versailles on September 3, 1783.

The Crisis of Demobilization

In 1778 Continental officers had won from Congress a promise of life pensions at half pay in exchange for enlistment for the duration of the war. By 1783, however, Congress had still not made any specific provisions for officers' pensions. With peace at hand, the officers began to fear that the army would be disbanded before the problem was resolved, and they would lose whatever power they had to pressure Congress. In January 1783, a group of prominent senior officers petitioned Congress, demanding that pensions be converted to a bonus equal to five years of full pay. "Any further experiments on their patience," they warned, "may have fatal effects." Despite the barely veiled threat of military intervention, Congress rejected their petition.

With the backing of congressional nationalists, a group of army officers associated with General Horatio Gates circulated a letter arguing for direct military intervention and calling an extraordinary meeting of the officer corps at Newburgh. But General Washington, on whom the officers counted for support, criticized the meeting as "disorderly" and called an official meeting of his own (see Communities in Conflict). There was enormous tension as the officers assembled on March 15, 1783. Washington strode into the room and mounted the platform. Turning his back in disdain on Gates, he delivered an address from memory condemning the circular letter. Fearing he had not been convincing enough, he told the assembly he wished to conclude by reading a letter from a member of Congress and then pulled a pair of glasses from his pocket. None of his officers had seen their commander wearing glasses before. "Gentlemen, you must pardon me," said Washington, noting their surprise. "I have grown gray in your service and now find myself growing blind." It was this offhand remark that had the greatest impact. Who had sacrificed more than Washington? After he left, the officers adopted resolutions rejecting intervention, and a week later, on Washington's urging, Congress converted the promised pensions to bonuses.

MAP 7.6 North America After the Treaty of Paris, 1783 The map of European
and American claims to North America was radically altered by the results of the American Revolution.

Washington's role in this crisis was one of his greatest
contributions to the nation. At stake was nothing less than
the possibility of a military coup at the very moment of
victory. The American Revolution was the first of many
successful colonial revolutions, and in hindsight it is clear
that post independence military rule was a common outcome in many of them. In December 1783 Washington
resigned his commission as general of the army despite
calls for him to remain. There is little doubt he could have
assumed the role of an American dictator. Instead, by his
actions and example, the principle of military subordination to civil authority was firmly established.

As for the common soldiers, they wanted simply to be
discharged. In May 1783, Congress voted the soldiers three
months' pay as a bonus and instructed Washington to begin
dismissing them. By the beginning of 1784, the Continental
Army had shrunk to no more than a few hundred men.

The Problem of the West
Even during the Revolution thousands of Americans
migrated westward, and after the war settlers poured over
the mountains and down the Ohio River. Thousands of
Americans pressed against the Indian country north of the
Ohio River, and destructive violence continued along the

American artist Benjamin West never completed his painting of the *American Commissioners of the Preliminary Peace Negotiations with Great Britain, 1783–1785,* but left this study. It features portraits of (left to right) John Jay, John Adams, Henry Laurens, Benjamin Franklin, and William Temple Franklin, who served as secretary for his grandfather. West intended to include the British commissioners, but the death of one and the uncooperative attitude of the other aborted the project.

frontier. British troops continued to occupy posts in the Great Lakes region and encouraged Indian attacks on vulnerable settlements. Spain refused to accept the territorial settlement of the Treaty of Paris and closed the port of New Orleans to Americans, effectively blockading the Mississippi River. Westerners who saw that route as their primary access to markets were outraged.

John Jay, appointed secretary for foreign affairs by the Confederation Congress in 1784, attempted to negotiate with the British for their complete withdrawal but was told that was not possible until all outstanding debts from before the war were settled. Jay also negotiated with the Spanish for guarantees of territorial sovereignty and commercial relations, but they insisted that the Americans relinquish free navigation of the Mississippi. Congress would approve no treaty under those conditions, and some frustrated Westerners considered leaving the Confederation. In the West, local community interest continued to override the fragile development of national community sentiment.

In 1784, Congress took up the problem of extending national authority over the West. Legislation was drafted, principally by Thomas Jefferson, providing "Government for the Western Territory." The legislation proposed a remarkably republican colonial policy. The western public domain would be divided into states, fully the equals of the original thirteen, with Congressional guarantees of self-government and republican institutions. Once the

population of a territory numbered 20,000, the residents could call a convention and establish a constitution and government of their own choosing. And once the population grew to equal that of the smallest of the original thirteen states, the territory could petition for statehood, provided it agreed to remain forever a member of the Confederation. Congress accepted these proposals but rejected by a vote of seven to six Jefferson's clause forever prohibiting slavery in the West.

Passed the following year, the Land Ordinance of 1785 provided for the survey and sale of western lands. The settlement of Kentucky had been characterized by a chaos of overlapping surveys and land claims, a problem the Land Ordinance was designed to solve by creating an ordered system of survey, dividing the land into townships composed of thirty-six sections of one square mile (640 acres) each. This measure would have enormous impact on the North American landscape, as can be seen by anyone who has flown over the United States and looked down at the patchwork pattern below. Jefferson argued that land ought to be given away to actual settlers. But, eager to establish a revenue base for the government, Congress provided for the auction of public lands for not less than one dollar per acre.

In the treaties of Fort Stanwix in 1784 and Fort McIntosh in 1785, congressional commissioners forced the Iroquois and a number of Ohio tribes, respectively, to cede portions of their territory in what is now eastern Ohio. These treaties were not the result of negotiation but intimidation. The commissioners dictated the terms by seizing hostages and forcing compliance. Surveyors were immediately sent west to divide up the land. The first surveyed lands did not come onto the market until the fall of 1788, and in the meantime Congress, desperate for revenue, sold a tract of more than 1.5 million acres to the Ohio Company, a new consortium of land speculators, for a million dollars. Thousands of Westerners chose not to wait for the official opening of the public lands north of the Ohio River but simply settled illegally by making squatters' claims. In 1785 Congress raised troops and evicted many of them, but once the troops departed the squatters returned. The persistence of this problem convinced many congressmen to revise Jefferson's democratic territorial plan.

In the Northwest Ordinance of 1787, Congress established a system of government for the territory north of the Ohio (see Map 7.7). Three to five states were to be carved from the giant Northwest Territory. Slavery was prohibited. But the initial guarantee of self-government in Jefferson's plan was replaced by a congressionally appointed governor and court of judges. Once the free white male population of the territory had grown to 5,000, these citizens would be permitted to choose an assembly, but the governor had the power of absolute veto on all territorial legislation. National interest would be imposed on the local western communities.

The creation of the land system of the United States was the major achievement of the Confederation government. But there were other important accomplishments. Under the Articles of Confederation, Congress led the country through the Revolution and its commissioners negotiated the terms of a comprehensive peace treaty. And by organizing the departments of war, foreign affairs, finance, and the post office, the Confederation government created the beginnings of a national bureaucracy.

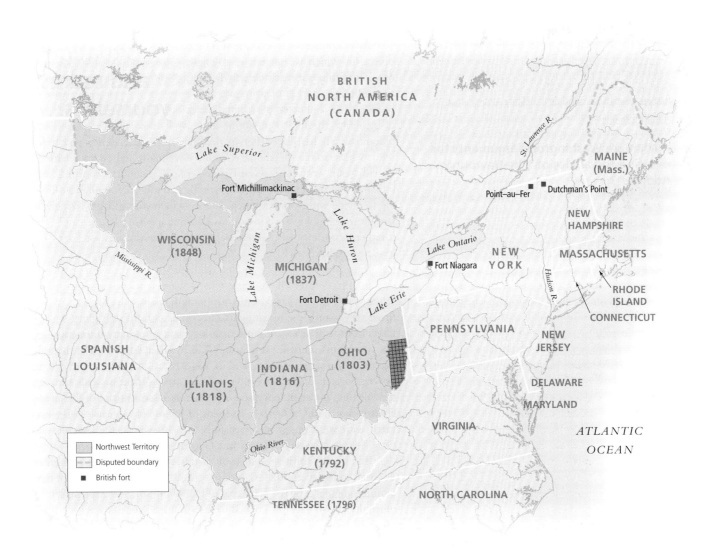

MAP 7.7 The Northwest Territory and the Land Survey System of the United States The Land Ordinance of 1785 created an ordered system of survey (revised by the Northwest Ordinance of 1787), dividing the land into townships and sections.

Washington and the Newburgh Conspiracy

In March 1783, as peace talks continued in Paris and the British remained in control of New York City, a crisis developed over civilian control of the Continental Army. Fearful of British intentions, Congress was unwilling to discharge the 10,000 troops encamped north of the city on the Hudson. But restricted in the power to levy taxes, Congress was unable to pay enlisted men or guarantee the pensions of their officers. A group of senior officers, led by General Horatio Gates, began to consider more direct action. Their position was announced in an anonymous circular letter known as "The Newburgh Address," which strongly hinted at the possibility of a military coup. The author of the letter was later revealed to be an aide to Gates, Major John Armstrong. Washington intervened, called a meeting of his senior officers, and responded to the letter in an address that established the principle of military subordination to civilian authority.

• **What are Washington's arguments for rejecting the advice of "the Newburgh Address"?**

The Army Has Its Alternative

To the Officers of the Army. GENTLEMEN,—A fellow soldier, whose interest and affections bind him strongly to you, whose past sufferings have been as great, and whose future fortune may be as desperate as yours—would beg leave to address you. . . . He has long shared in your toils and mingled in your dangers. He has felt the cold hand of poverty without a murmur, and has seen the insolence of wealth without a sigh. But, too much under the direction of his wishes, and sometimes weak enough to mistake desire for opinion, he has till lately—very lately—believed in the justice of his country. . . . But faith has its limits as well as temper, and there are points beyond which neither can be stretched, without sinking into cowardice or plunging into credulity. This, my friends, I conceive to be your situation. . . .

After a pursuit of seven long years, the object for which we set out is at length brought within our reach. Yes, my friends, that suffering courage of yours was active once—it has conducted the United States of America through a doubtful and a bloody war. It has placed her in the chair of independency, and peace returns again to bless—whom? A country willing to redress your wrongs, cherish your worth and reward your services, a country courting your return to private life, with tears of gratitude and smiles of admiration, longing to divide with you that independency which your gallantry has given, and those riches which your wounds have preserved? Is this the case? Or is it rather a country that tramples upon your rights, disdains your cries and insults your distresses? . . .

> "[A]wake; attend to your situation and redress yourselves. . . ."

If this, then, be your treatment, while the swords you wear are necessary for the defence of America, what have you to expect from peace, when your voice shall sink, and your strength dissipate by division? When those very swords, the instruments and companions of your glory, shall be taken from your sides, and no remaining mark of military distinction left but your wants, infirmities and scars? Can you then consent to be the only sufferers by this revolution, and retiring from the field, grow old in poverty, wretchedness and contempt? Can you consent to wade through the vile mire of dependency, and owe the miserable remnant of that life to charity; which has hitherto been spent in honor? If you can—GO—and carry with you the jest of tories and scorn of whigs—the ridicule, and what is worse, the pity of the world. Go, starve, and be forgotten!

But, if your spirit should revolt at this; if you have sense enough to discover, and spirit enough to oppose tyranny under whatever garb it may assume; whether it be the plain coat of republicanism, or the splendid robe of royalty; if you have yet learned to discriminate between a people and a cause, between men and principles—awake; attend to your situation and redress yourselves. If the present moment be lost, every future effort is in vain; and your threats then, will be as empty as your entreaties now.

I would advise you, therefore, to come to some final opinion upon what you can bear, and what you will suffer. If your determination be in any proportion to your wrongs, carry your appeal from the justice to the fears of government. . . . Tell them that, though you were the first, and would wish to be the last to encounter danger: though despair itself can never drive you into dishonor, it may drive you from the field: that the wound often irritated, and never healed, may at length become incurable; and that the slightest mark of indignity from Congress now, must operate like the grave, and part you forever: that in any political event, the army has its alternative. If peace, that nothing shall separate them from your arms but death: if war, that courting the auspices, and inviting the direction of your illustrious leader, you will retire to some unsettled country, smile in your turn, and "mock when their fear cometh on." But let it represent also, that should they comply with the request of your late memorial, it would make you more happy and them more respectable. That while war should continue, you would follow their standard into the field, and when it came to an end, you would withdraw into the shade of private life, and give the world another subject of wonder and applause; an army victorious over its enemies—victorious over itself.

SOURCE: David Ramsey, *The Life of George Washington* (1807).

In the Name of Our Common Country

By an anonymous summons, an attempt has been made to convene you together? how inconsistent with the rules of propriety! How unmilitary! And how subversive of all order and discipline. . . . If my conduct heretofore, has not evinced to you, that I have been a faithful friend to the army, my declaration of it at this time would be equally unavailing and improper. But as I was among the first who embarked in the cause of our common country—as I have never left your side one moment, but when called from you, on public duty—as I have been the constant companion and witness of your distresses, and not among the last to feel, and acknowledge your merits—as I have ever considered my own military reputation as inseparably connected with that of the army—as my Heart has ever expanded with joy, when I have heard its praises—and my indignation has arisen, when the mouth of detraction has been opened against it—it can scarcely be supposed, at this late stage of the war, that I am indifferent to its interests.

But—how are they to be promoted? The way is plain, says the anonymous addresser. If war continues, remove into the unsettled country—there establish yourselves, and leave an ungrateful country to defend itself. . . . If peace takes place, never sheath your sword says he until you have obtained full and ample justice. This dreadful alternative, of either deserting our country in the extremist hour of her distress, or turning our arms against it, (which is the apparent object, unless Congress can be compelled into instant compliance) has something so shocking in it, that humanity revolts at the idea.

My God! What can this writer have in view, by recommending such measures? Can he be a friend to the army? Can he be a friend to this country? Rather is he not an insidious foe? Some emissary, perhaps, from New York City [still occupied by the British], plotting the ruin of both, by sowing the seeds of discord and separation between the civil and military powers of the continent? . . .

I cannot, in justice to my own belief, and what I have great reason to conceive is the intention of Congress, conclude this address, without giving it as my decided opinion; that that honorable body entertain exalted sentiments of the services of the army; and, from a full conviction of its merits and sufferings, will do it complete justice. That their endeavors, to discover and establish funds for this purpose, have been unwearied, and will not cease, till they have succeeded, I have not a doubt. But, like all other large bodies, where there is a variety of different interests to reconcile, their deliberations are slow. Why then should we distrust them?—and, in consequence of that distrust, adopt measures, which may cast a shade over that glory which, has been so justly acquired; and tarnish the reputation of an army which is celebrated thro' all Europe, for its fortitude and patriotism? And for what is this done? To bring the object we seek for nearer? No! Most certainly, in my opinion, it will cast it at a greater distance.

. . . Let me entreat you, gentlemen, on your part, not to take any measures, which, viewed in the calm light of reason, will lessen the dignity, and sully the glory you have hitherto maintained—let me request you to rely on the plighted faith of your country, and place a full confidence in the purity of the intentions of Congress; that, previous to your dissolution as an Army they will cause all your accounts to be fairly liquidated,

> "[R]ely on the plighted faith of your country, and place a full confidence in . . . the intentions of Congress. . . ."

as directed in their resolutions, which were published to you two days ago—and that they will adopt the most effectual measures in their power, to render ample justice to you, for your faithful and meritorious Services. And let me conjure you, in the name of our common country—as you value your own sacred honor—as you respect the rights of humanity; as you regard the military and national character of America, to express your utmost horror and detestation of the man who wishes, under any specious pretences, to overturn the liberties of our country, and who wickedly attempts to open the flood gates of civil discord, and deluge our rising empire in blood.

SOURCE: David Ramsay, *The Life of George Washington* (1807).

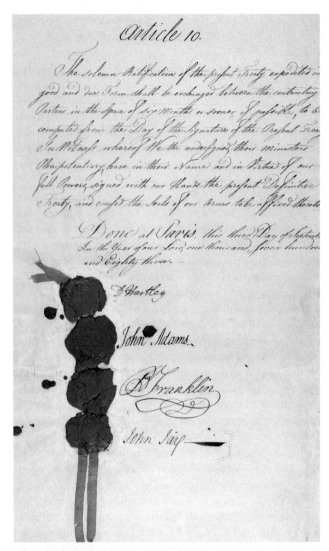

The last page of the Treaty of Paris, signed in Paris on September 3, 1783, by David Hartley for Great Britain, and for the United States by John Adams, Benjamin Franklin, and John Jay.

Revolutionary Politics in the States

Despite the accomplishments of the Confederation, most Americans were focused on the governments of their own states. The national government was distant and had relatively little effect on people's lives. Social and political identity was located in local communities and states rather than the American nation. People spoke of "these United States," emphasizing the plural. The national community feeling that developed during the Revolution at places like Valley Forge was not as powerful as persistent localism. The states were the setting for the most important political struggles of the Confederation period.

A New Democratic Ideology

The political mobilization that took place in 1774 and 1775 greatly broadened political participation. Mass meetings in which ordinary people expressed their opinions, voted, and gained political experience were common not only in the cities but in small towns and rural communities as well. During these years a greater proportion of the population began to participate in elections. Compared with the colonial assemblies, the new state legislatures included more men from rural and western districts—farmers and artisans as well as lawyers, merchants, and large landowners.

This transformation was accompanied by a dramatic shift in the content of political debate. During the colonial period, when only the upper classes were truly engaged in the political process, the principal argument followed the lines of the traditional Tory and Whig divide in Great Britain. The Tory position, taken by colonial officials, was that colonial governments were simply convenient instruments of royal prerogative, serving at the king's pleasure. The Whig position, adopted by colonial elites who sought to preserve and increase their own power, emphasized the need for a government balancing the power of a governor with an upper house and an assembly. As a result of the Revolution, the Tory position lost all legitimacy and the Whig position was challenged by farmers, artisans, and ordinary people armed with a new and radical democratic ideology. The spectrum of politics shifted to the left.

The First State Constitutions

One of the first post-Revolution debates focused on an appropriate governmental structure for the new states. The thinking of democrats was indicated by the title of a New England pamphlet of 1776: *The People the Best Governors.* Power, this anonymous author argued, should be vested in a single, popularly elected assembly. The people, in the words of this pamphlet, "best know their wants and necessities, and therefore are best able to govern themselves." The ideal form of government, according to Democrats, was the community or town meeting, in which the people set their own tax rates, created a militia, controlled their own schools and churches, and regulated the local economy. State government was necessary only for coordination among communities.

Conservative Americans took up the Whig argument of the need for balanced government. The "unthinking many," wrote a conservative pamphleteer, should be checked by a strong executive and an upper house. Both of these would be insulated from popular control by property qualifications and long terms in office. The greatest danger, according to conservatives, was the possibility of majority tyranny, which might lead to the violation of property rights and dictatorship. "We must take mankind as they are," one conservative wrote, "and not as we could wish them to be."

Fourteen states—the original thirteen plus Vermont, an independent republic from 1777 until 1791—adopted constitutions between 1776 and 1780. Each of those political charters was shaped by the debate between radicals and conservatives, Democrats and Whigs, and reflected a particular political alignment. Pennsylvania was the first state to adopt a radically democratic constitution, with a unicameral assembly elected annually by all free male taxpayers. North Carolina, Georgia, and Vermont followed the Pennsylvania model. Indeed, Vermont went even further and became the first state to adopt universal manhood suffrage. At the other extreme, South Carolina and Maryland created a conservative set of institutions designed to keep citizens and rulers as far apart as possible. The other states adopted constitutional systems somewhere in the middle.

Declarations of Rights

One of the most important innovations of the state constitutions were the guarantees of rights patterned on the Virginia "Declaration of Rights" of June 1776. Written by George Mason—a wealthy planter, Democrat, and brilliant political philosopher—the Virginia declaration set a distinct tone in its very first article: "That all men are by nature equally free and independent, and have certain inherent rights, namely, the enjoyment of life and liberty, with the means of acquiring and possessing property and pursuing and obtaining happiness and safety." The fifteen articles of the Virginia Declaration declared, among other things, that sovereignty resided in the people, that government was the servant of the people, and that the people had the "right to reform, alter, or abolish" that government. There were guarantees of due process and trial by jury in criminal prosecutions, as well as prohibitions against excessive bail and "cruel and unusual punishment." Freedom of the press was guaranteed as "one of the great bulwarks of liberty," and the people were assured of "the free exercise of religion, according to the dictates of conscience."

Eight state constitutions included a general declaration of rights similar to the first article of the Virginia declaration; others incorporated specific guarantees. A number of states proclaimed the right of the people to engage in free speech and free assembly, to instruct their representatives, and to petition for the redress of grievances—rights either inadvertently or deliberately omitted from Virginia's declaration. These declarations were important precedents for the Bill of Rights, the first ten amendments to the federal Constitution of 1789. Indeed, George Mason of Virginia would be the leader of the Democrats who insisted that the Constitution stipulate such rights.

The Spirit of Reform

The political upheaval of the Revolution raised the possibility of other reforms in American society. The New Jersey constitution of 1776 granted the vote to "all inhabitants of this colony, of full age, who are worth fifty pounds . . . and have resided within the county . . . for twelve months," thus enfranchising women as well as men. Because married women could own no property in their own names, only single women voted in New Jersey, but large numbers of them participated in elections and spoke out on political issues. There were male protests of this "irregular" situation,

and in 1807 the legislature passed a law explicitly limiting the right to vote to "free white male citizens."

The New Jersey controversy was something of an anomaly, yet women's participation in the Revolution wrought subtle but important changes. In 1776 Abigail Adams wrote to her husband John Adams at the Continental Congress. "In the new code of laws which I suppose it will be necessary for you to make I desire you would remember the ladies," she advised, "and be more generous and favourable to them than your ancestors." In the aftermath of the Revolution, there was evidence of increasing sympathy in the courts for women's property rights and fairer treatment of women's petitions for divorce. And the postwar years witnessed an increase in opportunities for women seeking an education.

From a strictly legal and political point of view, the Revolution may have done little to change women's role in society, but it did seem to help change expectations. Abigail Adams's request to her husband was directed less toward the shape of the new republic than toward the structure of family life. "Do not put such unlimited powers into the hands of husbands," she wrote, "for all men would be tyrants if they could." She had in mind a companionate ideal of marriage that contrasted with older notions of patriarchy. Husbands and wives ought to be more like partners, less like master and servant. That new ideal first took root in America during the era of the Revolution.

The most steadfast reformer of the day was Thomas Jefferson, who after completing work on the Declaration of Independence returned to Virginia to take a seat in its House of Delegates. In 1776 he introduced a bill in the Virginia legislature abolishing entail (restriction of inheritance to particular heirs in order that landed property remain undivided) and primogeniture (the inheritance of all the family property by the firstborn son), legal customs long in effect in aristocratic England that Jefferson believed had no place in a Republican society. Jefferson's reform of inheritance law passed and had a dramatic effect. By 1798, every state had followed Virginia's lead.

Jefferson's other notable success was his Bill for Establishing Religious Freedom. He considered it one of his greatest accomplishments. At the beginning of the Revolution, there were established churches—denominations officially supported and funded by the government—in nine of the thirteen colonies. Many Anglican clergymen harbored Loyalist sympathies, and as part of an anti-Loyalist backlash, New York, Maryland, the Carolinas, and Georgia had little difficulty passing acts that disestablished the Anglican Church. In Virginia, however, many planters viewed Anglicanism as a bulwark against Baptist and Methodist democratic thinkers, resulting in bitter and protracted opposition to Jefferson's bill. It did not pass until 1786.

New England Congregationalists proved even more resistant to change. Although Massachusetts, New Hampshire, and Connecticut allowed dissenting churches

By giving the vote to "all free inhabitants," the 1776 constitution of New Jersey enfranchised women as well as men who met the property requirements. The number of women voters eventually led to male protests. Wrote one: "What tho' we read, in days of yore, / The woman's occupation / Was to direct the wheel and loom, / Not to direct the nation." In 1807, a new state law explicitly limited the right of franchise to "free white male citizens."

to receive tax support, they maintained the official relationship between church and state well into the nineteenth century. Other states, despite disestablishment, retained certain religious tests in their legal codes. Georgia, the Carolinas, and New Jersey limited office holding to Protestants; New York required legislators to renounce allegiance to the pope; and even Pennsylvania, where religious toleration had a long history, required officials to swear to a belief in the divine inspiration of the Old and New Testaments.

Jefferson proposed several more reforms of Virginia law, all of which failed to pass. He would have created a system of public education, revised the penal code to restrict capital punishment to the crimes of murder and treason, and established the gradual emancipation of slaves by law. On the whole, Jefferson and the Revolutionary generation were more successful at raising questions than at accomplishing reforms. The problems of penal reform, public education, and slavery remained for later generations of Americans to resolve.

African Americans and the Revolution

For most African Americans there was little to celebrate, for the American victory guaranteed the continuation of slavery as an institution. Few people were surprised when thousands of black fighters and their families departed with the Loyalists and the British at the end of the war, settling in the West Indies, Canada, and Africa. Most of these refugees were fugitive slaves rather than committed Loyalists. In Virginia alone, some 30,000 slaves fled during the Revolution, including seventeen from George Washington's Mount Vernon plantation. Several of Washington's slaves were recaptured, but most left the country with the British.

There was an obvious contradiction in waging a war for liberty while continuing to support the institution of slavery. "How is it," English critic and essayist Samuel Johnson asked pointedly in 1775, "that we hear the loudest yelps for liberty among the drivers of Negroes?" The contradiction was not lost on Washington, who during the Revolution began to agonize over the morality of slavery. He was not alone. Revolutionary idealism, in combination with a shift away from tobacco farming, weakened the commitment of many Chesapeake planters to the slave system. After the Revolution, a sizable number of Virginians granted freedom to their slaves, and there was a small but important movement to encourage gradual emancipation by convincing masters to free their slaves in their wills.

George Washington was one of them, making a will that not only freed several hundred slaves upon his death but also included an elaborate plan for apprenticeship and tenancy for the able-bodied, and lodging and pensions for the aged. Planters in the Lower South, however, heavily dependent as they were on slave labor, resisted the growing calls for an end to slavery. Between 1776 and 1786 all the states but South Carolina and Georgia prohibited or heavily taxed the international slave trade, and this issue became an important point of conflict at the Constitutional Convention in 1787 (see Chapter 8).

Perhaps the most important result of this development was the growth of the free African American population. From a few thousand in 1750, their number grew to more than 200,000 by the end of the century. The increase was most notable in the Upper South. The free black population of Virginia, for example, grew from fewer than 2,000 in 1780 to more than 20,000 in 1800. Largely excluded from the institutions of white Americans, the African American community now had enough strength to establish schools, churches, and other institutions of its own. At first, this development was opposed by whites. In Williamsburg,

Virginia, for instance, the leader of a black congregation was seized and whipped when he attempted to gain recognition from the Baptist Association. But by the 1790s the Williamsburg African Church had grown to over 500 members, and the Baptist Association reluctantly recognized it. In Philadelphia, Reverend Absalom Jones established St. Thomas's African Episcopal Church. The incorporation of the word "African" in the names of churches, schools, and mutual benefit societies reflected the pride African Americans took in their heritage.

In the North, slavery was first abolished in the state constitution of Vermont in 1777, in Massachusetts in 1780, and New Hampshire in 1784. Pennsylvania, Connecticut, and Rhode Island adopted systems of gradual emancipation during these years, freeing the children of slaves at birth. By 1804, every northern state had provided for abolition or gradual emancipation, although as late as 1810, 30,000 African Americans remained enslaved in the North.

During the era of the Revolution, a small group of African American writers rose to prominence. Benjamin Banneker, born free in Maryland, where he received an education, became one of the most accomplished mathematicians and astronomers of late eighteenth-century

America. In the 1790s, he published a popular almanac that both white and black Americans consulted. Jupiter Hammon, a New York slave, took up contemporary issues in his poems and essays, one of the most important of which was his "Address to the Negroes of the State of New York," published in 1787. But the most famous African American writer was Phyllis Wheatley, who came to public attention when her *Poems on Various Subjects, Religious and Moral* appeared in London in 1773, while she was still serving as a domestic slave in Boston. Kidnapped in Africa as a young girl and converted to Christianity during the Great Awakening, Wheatley wrote poems combining piety with a concern for her people. Writing to the Mohegan Indian minister Samuel Occom in 1774, Wheatley penned a line that not only applied to African Americans but also to all Americans struggling to be free. "In every human breast God has implanted a principle, which we call love of freedom; it is impatient of oppression, and pants for deliverance. The same principle lives in us."

((•─ Hear the Audio
Phyllis Wheatly, On Being Brought from Africa to America at **www.myhistorylab.com**

Conclusion

The Revolution was a tumultuous era, marked by violent conflict between Patriots and Loyalists, masters and slaves, settlers and Indian peoples. The advocates of independence emerged successfully, largely because of their ability to pull together and consolidate their identification with the national community, an identity that emerged from national institutions like the Continental Army during periods of trial like the Valley Forge winter. Fearful of the power of central authority, however, Americans created a relatively weak national government. People identified strongly with their local and state communities, and these governments became the site for most of the struggles over political direction that characterized the Revolution and its immediate aftermath. But not all problems, it turned out, could be solved locally. Within a very few years, the nation would sink into a serious economic depression that sorely tested the resources of local communities. By the mid-1780s, many American nationalists were asking a question similar to the one Washington asked at Valley Forge in 1777: "What then is to become of this nation?"

Review Questions

1. Assess the relative strengths of the Patriots and the Loyalists in the American Revolution.

2. What roles did Indian peoples and African Americans play in the Revolution?

3. Describe the structure of the Articles of Confederation. What were its strengths and weaknesses?

This portrait of the African American poet Phyllis Wheatley was included in the collection of her work published in London in 1773 when she was only twenty years old. Kidnapped in Africa when a girl, then purchased off the Boston docks, she was more like a daughter than a slave to the Wheatley family. She later married and lived as a free woman of color before her untimely death in 1784.

CHRONOLOGY

1775	Lord Dunmore, royal governor of Virginia, appeals to slaves to support Britain
1776	July: Declaration of Independence
	August: Battle of Long Island initiates retreat of Continental Army
	September: British land on Manhattan Island
	December: George Washington counterattacks at Trenton
1777	Slavery abolished in Vermont
	September: British General William Howe captures Philadelphia
	October: British General John Burgoyne surrenders at Saratoga
	November: Continentals settle into winter quarters at Valley Forge
	December: France recognizes American independence
1778	June: France enters the war
	June: Battle of Monmouth hastens British retreat to New York
	July: George Rogers Clark captures Kaskaskia
	December: British capture Savannah

1779	Spain enters the war
1780	February: British land at Charleston
	July: French land at Newport
	September: British General Charles Cornwallis invades North Carolina
1781	March: Articles of Confederation ratified
	May: Robert Morris appointed secretary of finance
	October: Cornwallis surrenders at Yorktown
1782	Peace talks begin
1783	March: Washington mediates issue of officer pensions
	September: Treaty of Paris signed
	November: British evacuate New York
1784	Treaty of Fort Stanwix
	Postwar depression begins
1785	Land Ordinance of 1785
	Treaty of Fort McIntosh
1786	Jefferson's Bill for Establishing Religious Freedom

4. How did the Revolution affect politics within the states?

5. What was the effect of the Revolution on African Americans?

Recommended Reading

Carol Berkin, *Revolutionary Mothers: Women in the Struggle for America's Independence* (2005). Uses a topical and biographical approach to introduce to general readers women's experiences during the Revolution.

Wayne Bodle, *Valley Forge Winter: Civilians and Soldiers in War* (2002). The authoritative history, written by a historian who spent years on the staff at Valley Forge National Historical Park.

Caroline Cox, *A Proper Sense of Honor: Service and Sacrifice in George Washington's Army* (2004). A close investigation of officers and enlisted men in the Continental Army that reveals the persistence of class rank and standing throughout the armed struggle.

Thomas Fleming, *Liberty! The American Revolution* (1997). This well-written account, derived from a public television series, includes wonderful contemporary images.

Merrill Jensen, *The New Nation: A History of the United States during the Confederation, 1781–1789* (1950). Remains the standard work on the 1780s.

Max M. Mintz, *Seeds of Empire: The American Revolutionary Conquest of the Iroquois* (1999). The Revolution as a war for the control of Iroquois lands in upstate New York.

Ray Raphael, *A People's History of the American Revolution: How Common People Shaped the Fight for Independence* (2001). Demonstrates that the Revolution was much more fractious when viewed at the level of those who did the fighting and dying.

Charles Royster, *A Revolutionary People at War* (1979). A pathbreaking study of the Continental Army and popular attitudes toward it. Emphasizes the important role played by the officer corps and the enlisted men in the formation of the first nationalist constituency.

Simon Schama, *Rough Crossings: Britain, the Slaves, and the American Revolution* (2006). A detailed and engaging history of the African Americans who fought for the British.

Henry Wiencek, *Imperfect God: George Washington, His Slaves, and the Creation of America* (2003). An award-winning study of Washington's changing attitude toward slavery.

Alfred F. Young, *Masquerade: The Life and Times of Deborah Sampson, Continental Soldier* (2004). A meticulously researched account of the woman who passed for a man and served in the Continental Army.

myhistorylab Connections

Reinforce what you learned in this chapter by studying the many documents, images, maps, review tools, and videos available at www.myhistorylab.com.

Read and Review

✓• Study and Review Chapter 7

••• Read the Document

Proclamation of Lord Dunmore (1775)

Letter from a Revolutionary War Soldier (1776)

The Articles of Confederation (1777)

Congress Decides What to Do with the Western Lands (1785)

👁• See the Map

Revolutionary War: Northern Theater, 1775-1780

The American Revolution

Western Land Claims Ceded by the States

Territorial Claims in Eastern America after Treaty of Paris

Research and Explore

••• Read the Document

Exploring America: Exploring the Geography of the American Revolution

Profiles
Joseph Brant (Thayendanegea)
Mercy Otis Warren

History Bookshelf
Phillis Wheatley, Religious and Moral Poems (1773)
Thomas Paine, Crisis Papers (1776)

((•• Hear the Audio *Phillis Wheatley, On Being Brought from Africa to America*

📹• Watch the Video

The War for Independence

The American Revolution as Different Americans Saw It

((•• Hear the Audio

Hear the audio files for Chapter 7 at
www.myhistorylab.com.

Chapter 8 at www.myhistorylab.com

((•—[Hear the Audio

8

The New Nation

1786–1800

George Washington, Benjamin Franklin, and others signing the U.S. Constitution in Philadelphia, Pennsylvania. Painting by Henry Hintermeister, circa 1925. Courtesy of the Library of Congress.

A Rural Massachusetts Community Rises in Defense of Liberty

AMERICAN Communities

Several hundred farmers from the town of Pelham and scores of other rural communities in western Massachusetts converged on the courthouse in Northampton, the county seat, before sunrise on Tuesday, August 29, 1786. They arrived in military formation, fifes playing and drums beating, armed with muskets, broadswords, and cudgels, the men's tricorner hats festooned with sprigs of evergreen, symbols of freedom frequently worn by Yankee soldiers during the War for Independence, which had concluded only four years before. At least a third of the men and virtually all their officers were veterans. The country was in the midst of an economic depression that had hit farm communities particularly hard. Two-thirds of the men who marched on Northampton had been sued for debt, and many had spent time in debtor's prison. Dozens of rural towns petitioned the state government for relief, but not only did the merchant-dominated legislature reject their pleas, but it raised the property tax in order to pay off the enormous debt the state had accumulated during the Revolution. The new tax was considerably more oppressive than any levied by the British and was considered even more odious,

193

since the revenue would go to a small group of wealthy eastern Massachusetts creditors to whom the debt was owed.

The farmers decided to take matters into their own hands. When outsiders threatened a man's property, they argued, the community had the right, indeed the duty, to rise up in defense. During the Revolution, armed men had marched on the courts, shutting down the operation of government, and now they were doing it again. The judges of the Northampton court had no choice but to shut down, and that success led to similar actions in many other Massachusetts counties. "We have lately emerged from a bloody war in which liberty was the glorious prize," one man declared, "and in this glorious cause I am determined to stand with firmness and resolution."

This uprising quickly became known as Shays' Rebellion, named for Daniel Shays, a decorated Revolutionary officer and one of the leaders from the town of Pelham. Although rebellion was most widespread in the state of Massachusetts, similar disorders occurred in the country districts of New Hampshire, Vermont, Pennsylvania, Maryland, and Virginia. Conservatives around the country were thrown into panic. The rebels, wrote Secretary of War Henry Knox to George Washington, planned to seize the property of the wealthy and redistribute it to the poor. In the opinion of Washington's former aide Colonel David Humphreys of Connecticut, the rebels were "levelers" determined to "annihilate all debts public and private." Washington agreed and worried that rebellion threatened to break out everywhere. "There are combustibles in every State which a spark might set fire to."

Washington and other conservative leaders saw Shays' Rebellion as a class conflict pitting poor against rich, debtor against creditor. Yet the residents of Pelham and other rural towns acted in common, without regard to rank or property. Big farmers and small farmers alike marched on the county court. They came from tight-knit communities, bound together by family and kinship. Among the group of a hundred Pelham residents who marched on Northampton, for example, were twelve men from the Grey family, eight Johnsons, and six McMillans. More than two-thirds of the rebels were accompanied by kinsmen. Whether well-to-do or poor, they considered

themselves "husbandmen," and they directed their protest against "outsiders," the urban residents of Boston and other coastal towns. "I am a man that gets his living by hard labor," one rebel announced, "and I think that husbandry is as honest a calling as any in the world." The country would be a lot better off, he concluded, "if there were less white shirts and more black frocks."

The crisis in Massachusetts ended when a militia force raised by the "white shirts" in the eastern part of the state, and financed by the great merchants, marched west and crushed the Shaysites in January 1787. Daniel Shays fled the state and never returned. Fifteen of the leaders were tried and sentenced to death. Two were hanged before the remainder were pardoned, and some four thousand other farmers temporarily lost their right to vote, to sit on juries, or to hold office. Yet many of them considered their rebellion a success. The next year Massachusetts voters rejected the old governor and elected a new legislature, which passed a moratorium on debts and cut taxes to only 10 percent of what they had been.

Shays' Rebellion was the most prominent of hundreds of protests, uprisings, and revolts across the United States focusing on the hard times caused by the eco-

A mocking pamphlet of 1787 pictured Daniel Shays and Job Shattuck, two leaders of Shays' Rebellion. The artist gives them uniforms, a flag, and artillery, but the rebels were actually an unorganized group of farmers armed only with clubs and simple muskets. When the rebellion was crushed, Shattuck was wounded and jailed, and Shays, along with many others, left Massachusetts. He first settled in a remote region of Vermont, then later in New York.

SOURCE: Anonymous, 18th century, "Daniel Shay (c.1747–1825) and Job Shattuck (1725–1825?)", 1787, relief cut, 9 × 12.9 cm (3-9/16 × 5-1/16"). Published in Bickerstaff's Boston Almanack for 1787, third edition, Boston. National Portrait Gallery, Smithsonian Institution/Art Resource, NY ,

1. What were the tensions and conflicts between local and national authorities in the decades after the American Revolution?

2. How did Americans differ in their views of the new Constitution, and how were those differences reflected in the struggle to achieve ratification?

3. What were the essential structures of national government under the Constitution?

4. How did American political parties first begin?

5. What were the first stirrings of an authentic American national culture?

FOCUS Questions

1786–1800

nomic depression. But the most important consequence of this unrest was not relief for the poor and distressed. Rather it was the effect they had on conservative nationalists unhappy with the distribution of power between the states and national governments under the Articles of Confederation. "Without some alteration in our political creed," Washington wrote to James Madison, "the superstructure we have been seven years in raising, at the expence of so much blood and treasure, must fall. We are fast verging to anarchy and confusion!" Shays' Rebellion "wrought prodigious changes in the minds of men respecting the powers of government," noted Henry Knox. "Everybody says they must be strengthened and that unless this shall be effected, there is no security for liberty and property." Popular participation had been a necessity during the Revolution. But now the time had come, he declared, "to clip the wings of a mad democracy."

The economic and political crisis of the 1780s would lead to the Constitutional Convention and a new charter for a national state. It would be enthusiastically supported by many, passionately opposed by many others. Its ratification would bring a new and stronger government to power, headed by the leaders of the Revolution. Before the end of the century, that government would lay the groundwork for the longest-lived democratic republic in the world.

Pelham

AMERICAN Communities

The Crisis of the 1780s

The depression of the mid-1780s and the political protests it generated were instrumental in the development of strong nationalist sentiment among elite circles. In the aftermath of Shays' Rebellion, these sentiments coalesced into a powerful political movement dedicated to strengthening the national government.

The Economic Crisis

The economic crisis that produced Shays' Rebellion had its origins in the Revolution. The shortage of goods resulting from the British blockade, the demand for supplies by the army and the militias, and the flood of paper currency issued by the Confederation Congress and the states combined to create the worst inflation in American history. U.S. dollars traded against Spanish dollars at the rate of 3 to 1 in 1777, 40 to 1 in 1779, and 146 to 1 in 1781, by which time Congress had issued more than $190 million in currency (see Figure 8.1). Most of this paper money ended up in the hands of merchants who had paid only a fraction of its face value.

After the war ended, inflation gave way to depression. Political revolution could not alter economic realities: the independent United States continued to be a supplier of raw materials and an importer of manufactured products,

FIGURE 8.1 Postwar Inflation, 1777–80: The Depreciation of Continental Currency The flood of Continental currency issued by Congress, and the shortage of goods resulting from the British blockade, combined to create the worst inflation Americans have ever experienced. Things of no value were said to be "not worth a Continental."

SOURCE: From "How Much Is That in Real Money?" *Proceedings of the American Antiquarian Society*, N.S. 102 (1992): 297–359. Copyright © 1992 American Antiquarian Society. Courtesy of American Antiquarian Society. Used by permission.

and Great Britain remained the country's most important trading partner. In 1784, British merchants began dumping goods in the American market, offering easy terms of credit. But the production of exportable goods had been drastically reduced by the fighting, and thus the trade deficit with Britain for the period 1784–86 rose to approximately £5 million (see Figure 8.2). The deficit acted like a magnet, drawing hard currency from American accounts, leaving the country with little silver or gold coin in circulation. Commercial banks insisted on the repayment of old loans and refused to issue new ones. By the end of 1784, the country had fallen into the grip of economic depression, and within two years, prices had fallen by 25 percent.

The depression struck while the nation was attempting to dig out from the huge mountain of debt incurred during the Revolution. Creditors were owed more than $75 million by national and state governments. Not allowed to raise taxes on its own, the Confederation Congress requisitioned the states for the funds necessary for debt repayment. The states in turn taxed their residents. At a time when there was almost no money in circulation, ordinary Americans feared being crushed by the burden of private debt and public taxes. The economic problem became a political problem.

State Remedies

In the states, radicals called for regulation of the economy. The most controversial remedies were those designed to relieve the burden on debtors and ordinary taxpayers. Farmers and debtors pressed their state governments for legal tender laws, which required creditors to accept a state's paper currency at face value (rather than depreciated market value) for all debts public and private. Despite the opposition of creditors, seven states enacted such laws. For the most part, these were modest programs that worked rather well, caused little depreciation, and did not result in the problems creditors feared.

It was the plan of the state of Rhode Island, however, that received most of the attention. A rural political party campaigning under the slogan "To Relieve the Distressed" captured the legislature in 1786 and enacted a radical currency law. The supply of paper money issued in relation to the population was much greater under this program than in any other state. The law declared the currency legal tender for all debts. If creditors refused to accept it, debtors were allowed to satisfy their obligations by depositing the currency with a county judge, who would then advertise the debt as paid. "In the state of Rogue Island," one shocked merchant wrote, "fraud and injustice" had been permitted "by solemn law." Conservatives pointed to Rhode Island as an example of the evils that could accompany "unchecked democracy."

Some states erected high tariff barriers to curb imports and protect domestic industries. But foreign shippers found it easy to avoid these duties simply by unloading their cargo in states without tariffs and distributing the goods by overland transport. To be effective, commercial regulations had to be national. Local sentiment had to give way to the unity of a national community. The "means of preserving ourselves," wrote John Adams, will "never be secured entirely, until Congress shall be made supreme in foreign commerce, and shall have digested a plan for all the states."

Toward a New National Government

In 1786 the legislature of Virginia invited all the states to appoint delegates to a convention where they might consider political remedies for the economic crisis. The meeting, held in Annapolis, Maryland, in September, was sparsely attended (only twelve delegates from five states), but the men shared their alarm over the rebellion that was simultaneously taking place in Massachusetts, and the possibility of others like it. "What stronger evidence can be given of the want of energy in our governments than these disorders?" Washington wrote fellow Virginian James Madison, one of the delegates. "If there exists not a power to check them, what security has a man for life, liberty, or property?"

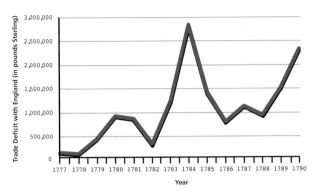

FIGURE 8.2 The Trade Deficit with Great Britain The American trade deficit with Great Britain rose dramatically with the conclusion of the Revolution.

SOURCE: *Historical Statistics of the United States* (Washington, DC: Government Printing Office, 1976), 1176.

Convinced of the absolute necessity of strengthening the national government, the Annapolis convention passed a resolution requesting that the Confederation Congress call on all the states to send delegates to a national convention that they might "render the constitution of the federal government adequate to the exigencies of the union." A few weeks later, with some reluctance, the Congress voted to endorse a convention to be held in Philadelphia in May 1787, "for the sole and express purpose of revising the Articles of Confederation."

Conservatives had in mind more than simply a revision of the Articles, however. They looked forward to a considerably strengthened national government. Louis Otto, French chargé d'affaires in the United States, believed these men were acting in the interests of their class. "Although there are no nobles in America," he informed his superiors at Versailles, "there is a class of men denominated 'gentlemen,' who by reason of their wealth, their talents, their education, their families, or the offices they hold, aspire to a preeminence which the people refuse to grant them." Believing that the consolidation of power in a strong central government would better serve their interests as merchants, bankers, and planters, the conservatives hid their motives behind the call for revision of the Articles.

The New Constitution

In late May 1787, a few weeks after the suppression of Shays' Rebellion, fifty-five men from twelve states (the radical government of Rhode Island refusing to send a delegation) assembled at the Pennsylvania State House in Philadelphia. A number of prominent men were missing. Thomas Jefferson and John Adams were serving as ambassadors in Europe, and Patrick Henry of backcountry Virginia declared that he "smelt a rat." But most of America's best-known leaders were present: George Washington, Benjamin Franklin, Alexander

Hamilton, James Madison, George Mason, and Robert Morris. Twenty-nine of the delegates were college educated, thirty-four were lawyers, twenty-four had served in Congress, and twenty-one were veterans of the officer corps of the Continental Army. At least nineteen owned slaves, and there were also land speculators and merchants. There were no ordinary farmers or artisans and, of course, no women, African Americans, or Indians. The Constitution was framed by white men who represented America's social and economic elite.

Read the Document
The United States Constitution (1789) at **www.myhistorylab.com**

These men were patriots, however, and committed to republicanism: that government must rest on the consent of the governed, and that the authority of rulers must be conditional on popular support. (For a discussion of republicanism see Chapter 6.) But they were not Democrats. They believed that the country already suffered from too much democracy. They feared that ordinary people, if given ready access to power, would enact policies against the interests of the privileged classes and, thus, the nation as a whole. The specter of Shays' Rebellion hung over the proceedings.

The Constitutional Convention

On their first day of work, the delegates agreed to vote by states, as was the procedure of Congress. They chose Washington to chair the meeting. Although the sessions were closed to the public, James Madison, a young, conservative Virginian with a profound knowledge of history and political philosophy, took voluminous daily minutes that provide the best record of the proceedings. Madison and his fellow Virginians had drafted what became known as the Virginia Plan. Presented to the convention shortly after it convened, their plan set the agenda for the convention.

The Virginia Plan proposed scrapping the Articles of Confederation in favor of a "consolidated government" with the power to tax and to enforce its laws directly rather than through the states. "A spirit of locality," Madison declared, was destroying "the aggregate interests of the community," by which he meant the great community of the nation. The Virginia Plan would have reduced the states to little more than administrative institutions, something like counties. There would be a bicameral national legislature with all seats apportioned by population; members of the House of Representatives would be elected by popular vote, but members of the Senate chosen indirectly by state legislators, insulating them from democratic pressure. The Senate would lead, controlling foreign affairs and the appointment of officials. An appointed chief executive and a national judiciary would together form a Council of Revision having the power to veto both national and state legislation.

Read the Document
James Madison, The Virginia (or Randolph) Plan (1787) at **www.myhistorylab.com**

The main opposition to the Virginia Plan came from the delegates of the small states who feared being swallowed up by the large ones. After two weeks of debate, William Paterson of New Jersey introduced an alternative, a set of "purely federal" principles that became known as the New Jersey Plan. This plan also proposed increasing the powers of the central government but retained the single-house Congress of the Confederation government in which the states were equally represented. After much debate and a series of votes that split the convention down the middle, the delegates finally agreed to what has been called the Great Compromise. Representation would be proportional to population in the House, with equal representation to each of the states in the Senate. The compromise allowed for the creation of a strong national government while still providing an important role for the states.

Part of this Great Compromise was a second fundamental agreement between North and South. In the opinion of James Madison, "The real difference of interests lay, not between the large and small but between the Northern and Southern states. The institution of slavery and its consequences formed the line of discrimination." Southern delegates wanted protections for slavery. They wanted provision for the mandatory return of fugitive southern slaves from the free northern states. To boost their power in Congress, they wanted slaves counted for the purpose of determining a state's proportional representation but excluded from the apportioning of taxes. Northern delegates, who wanted a central government with the power to regulate commerce, agreed to count five slaves as the equivalent of three free men—the so-called "three-fifths rule"—in exchange for southern support for a "commerce clause," providing the federal government with the power to regulate commerce with foreign nations, among the several states, and with Indian tribes. Furthermore, representatives from South Carolina and Georgia demanded protection for the slave trade, and after bitter debate the delegates also agreed to include a provision preventing any federal restriction on the importation of slaves for twenty years.

The word "slave" appeared nowhere in the text. It would, James Madison argued, be "wrong to admit in the Constitution the idea that there could be property in men." Instead the drafters employed phrases such as "persons held to labor." But these provisions amounted to national guarantees for southern slavery. Although a minority of delegates were opposed to slavery and regretted having to give in on this issue, they agreed with Madison, who wrote that "great as the evil is, a dismemberment of the union would be worse."

Watch the Video
Slavery and the Constitution
at **www.myhistorylab.com**

There was still much to decide regarding the other branches of government. Madison's Council of Revision was scratched in favor of a strong federal judiciary with the implicit power to declare unconstitutional acts of Congress. There were demands for a powerful chief executive, and Alexander Hamilton made the antirepublican proposal that the executive should be appointed for life, raising fears that the office might prove to be, in the words of Edmund Randolph of Virginia, "the fetus of monarchy." But there was considerable support for a president with veto power to check the legislature. To keep the president independent, the delegates decided he should be elected rather than appointed by the Congress, as was the procedure under the Articles of Confederation. But fearing that ordinary voters would never "be sufficiently informed" to select wisely, they insulated the process from popular choice by creating the electoral college. Voters in the states would not actually vote for president. Rather, each state would select a slate of "electors" equal in number to the state's total representation in the House and Senate. Following the general election, the electors in each state would meet to cast their ballots and elect the president.

The delegates voted their approval on September 17, 1787, and transmitted the document to the Confederation Congress, agreeing that it would become operative after ratification by nine states. A number of congressmen were outraged that the convention had exceeded its charge of simply modifying the Articles, but Congress agreed to issue a call for a special ratifying convention in each of the states.

George Washington presides over a session of the Constitutional Convention meeting in Philadelphia's State House (now known as Independence Hall) in an engraving of 1799.

Ratifying the New Constitution

The supporters of the new Constitution immediately adopted the name Federalists to describe themselves. In this, as in much of the subsequent process of ratification, the Federalists (or nationalists) grabbed the initiative, and their opponents had to content themselves with the negative label Anti-Federalists (see Map 8.1). The critics of the Constitution were by no means a unified group. But most believed it granted far too much power to the central government, weakening the autonomy of local communities and states (see Communities in Conflict).

The argument between Federalists and Anti-Federalists played out in dozens of essays published in the popular press in 1787 and early 1788. It is doubtful, however, whether any of them made much of a difference in the voting to select delegates for the state ratification conventions. The alignment of forces generally followed the lines laid down during the fights over economic issues in the years since the Revolution. An agrarian-localist versus commercial-cosmopolitan alignment characterized most of the states. The most critical convention took place in Massachusetts in early 1788. Five states—Delaware, Pennsylvania, New Jersey, Georgia, and Connecticut—had already voted to ratify, but the states with the strongest

MAP 8.1 The Ratification of the Constitution, 1787–90 The distribution of the vote for the ratification of the Constitution demonstrated its wide support in sections of the country linked to the commercial economy and its disapproval in more remote and backcountry sections. (Note that Maine remained a part of Massachusetts until admitted as a separate state in 1820.)

Anti-Federalist movements had yet to convene. If the Constitution lost in Massachusetts, its fate would be in great danger.

At the Massachusetts convention, the opponents of ratification—which included supporters of Shays' Rebellion—enjoyed a small majority. But several important Anti-Federalist leaders, including Governor John Hancock and Revolutionary leader Samuel Adams, were swayed by the enthusiastic support for the Constitution among Boston's townspeople, whose livelihoods were tied to the commercial economy. On February 16, the convention voted narrowly in favor of ratification. To no one's surprise, Rhode Island rejected the Constitution in March, but Maryland and South Carolina approved it in April and May. On June 21, 1788, New Hampshire became the ninth state to ratify. The Constitution was now the law of the land.

New York, Virginia, and North Carolina were left with the decision of whether to join the new Union. Anti-Federalist support was strong in these states. North Carolina voted to reject. (It would reconsider and join the next year, followed by a still reluctant Rhode Island in 1790.) In New York the delegates were moved to vote their support by a threat from New York City to secede from the state and join the Union separately if the state convention failed to ratify. The Virginia convention was almost evenly divided, but promises to amend the Constitution to protect the people from the potential abuses of the federal government persuaded enough delegates to produce a victory for the Constitution. The promise of such a "Bill of Rights" was important in the ratification vote of five of the states.

◆◆◆ Read the Document
The Debates in the Federal Convention of 1787 at
www.myhistorylab.com

The Bill of Rights

The Constitutional Convention had considered a bill of rights patterned on the declarations of rights included in several state constitutions but then rejected it as superfluous. Anti-Federalist delegates in numerous state ratification conventions, however, had proposed a grab bag of over 200 potential amendments protecting the rights of the people against the power of the central government. In June 1789, James Madison, elected to the first Congress as a representative from Virginia, set about transforming these proposed amendments into a coherent series of proposals. Congress approved twelve and sent them to the states, and ten survived the ratification process to become the Bill of Rights in 1791.

The First Amendment prohibited Congress from establishing an official religion and provided for the freedom of assembly. It also ensured freedom of speech, a free press, and the right of petition. The other amendments guaranteed the right to bear arms, to limit the government's power to quarter troops in private homes, and to restrain the government from unreasonable searches or seizures; they guaranteed the traditional legal rights under

The Controversy over Ratification

The drafting of the Constitution was followed by the process of ratification, first by the Confederation Congress and then by the states. According to George Washington, president of the convention, the new charter of government had been written in a "spirit of amity." But amity did not characterize the debate over ratification. In Massachusetts, where one of the most important struggles took place, rural activists who had been involved in Shays' Rebellion responded with a bitter attack on Washington as one of the "aristocratick gentlemen" whose interests would be served by the Constitution. Their point of view conveys the ferocious controversy of the times.

• **In what ways do the two arguments differ in regard to the question of "liberties"?**

George Washington Transmits the New Constitution to the Confederation Congress, September 17, 1787

To Arthur St. Clair, president of Congress.

Sir, We have now the honor to submit to the consideration of the United States in Congress assembled, that Constitution which has appeared to us the most advisable.

The friends of our country have long seen and desired, that the power of making war, peace, and treaties, that of levying money and regulating commerce, and the correspondent executive and judicial authorities should be fully and effectually vested in the general government of the Union: But the impropriety of delegating such extensive trust to one body of men is evident. Hence results the necessity of a different organization.

It is obviously impracticable in the federal government of these states, to secure all rights of independent sovereignty to each, and yet provide for the interest and safety of all—Individuals entering into society, must give up a share of liberty to preserve the rest. The magnitude of the sacrifice must depend as well on situation and circumstance, as on the object to be obtained. It is at all times difficult to draw with precision the line between those rights which must be surrendered, and those which may be reserved; and on the present occasion this difficulty was increased by a difference among the several states as to their situation, extent, habits, and particular interests. In all our deliberations on this subject we kept steadily in our view, that which appears to us the greatest interest of every true American, the consolidation of our Union, in which is involved our prosperity, felicity, safety, perhaps our national existence. This important consideration, seriously and deeply impressed on our minds, led each state in the Convention to be less rigid on points of inferior magnitude, than might have been otherwise expected; and thus the Constitution, which we now present, is the result of a spirit of amity, and of that mutual deference and concession which the peculiarity of our political situation rendered indispensible.

That it will meet the full and entire approbation of every state is not perhaps to be expected; but each will doubtless consider, that had her interest been alone consulted, the consequences might have been particularly disagreeable or injurious to others; that it is liable to as few exceptions as could reasonably have been expected, we hope and believe; that it may promote the lasting welfare of that country so dear to us all, and secure her freedom and happiness, is our most ardent wish.

> "[T]hat which appears to us the greatest interest of every true American, [is] the consolidation of our Union. . . ."

With great respect, We have the honor to be, Sir, Your Excellency's most obedient and humble servants,
George Washington, President.
By unanimous Order of the Convention.

SOURCE: Max Farrand, ed., *The Records of the Federal Convention of 1787* (1911), volume 2.

Anti-Federalists in Massachusetts Respond, January 25, 1788

To the Publick. Many are the arts made use of by our aristocratick gentlemen, to accomodate the federal constitution to the taste of the yeomanry of the country. But it is very unlucky for them, that they should be so far misled, as to attempt to trump up one thing which appears by no means to be founded in truth, viz that none but placemen [bureaucrats] and pensioners are opposed to it. This is so far from quadrating with truth, that we conceive it to be an absolute falsehood. We would ask the disinterested part of the community just to look over the characters w[h]ich are so fond of swallowing this creature, which exhibits all the portraits of an overbearing aristocracy, and see if they are not chiefly composed of salary men and pensioners, and those who at least think themselves fair candidates for places of honour and emolument, whenever the aristocratick wheels of the federal chariot shall be set in motion.

When we see the adherents to this constitution chiefly made up of civil and ecclesiastical gown men, and their dependents, the expedient they have hit upon is not likely to have the intended effect. There are many men destitute of eloquence, yet they can see and hear—They can think and judge, and are therefore not likely to be wheedled out of their senses by the sophistical reasonings of all the advocates for this new constitution in the country combined. We know this is not true; and as we well know the design of such representations, we would have those gentlemen know, that it will not take. They must pull upon some other string, or they must fail. Another thing they tell us, that the constitution must be good, from the characters which composed the Convention that framed it. It is graced with the names of a Washington and a Franklin. Illustrious names, we allow— worthy characters in civil society. Yet we cannot suppose them, to be infallible guides, neither yet that a man must necessarily incur guilt to himself merely by dissenting from them in opinion.

We cannot think the noble general, has the same ideas with ourselves, with regard to the rules of right and wrong. We cannot think, he acts a very consistent part, or did through the whole of the contest with Great Britain: who, notwithstanding he wielded the sword in defence of American liberty, yet at the same time was, and is to this day, living upon the labours of several hundreds of miserable Africans, as free born as himself; and some of them very likely descended from parents who, in point of property and dignity in their own country, might cope with any man in America. We do not conceive we are to be overborne by the weight of any names, however revered. "ALL MEN ARE BORN FREE AND EQUAL;" if so, every man hath a natural and unalienable right to his own opinion, and, for asserting this

> "We do not conceive we are to be overborne by the weight of any names, however revered."

right, ought not to be stigmatized with the epithets of tenacious and dogmatical. . . .

We are willing to have a federal constitution. We are willing another trial should be made; this may be done without derogating from the gentlemen, who composed the late convention. In framing a constitution for this commonwealth [of Massachusetts], two trials were made before one would stick. We are willing to relinquish so much, as to have a firm, energetick government, and this we are sensible may be done, without becoming slaves, to the capricious fancies of any sett of men whatever. It is argued, that there is no danger that the proposed rulers will be disposed to exercise any powers that this constitution puts into their hands, which may enable them to deprive the people of their liberties. But in case, say they, they should make such attempts, the people may, and will rise to arms and prevent it; in answer to which, we have only to say, we have had enough of fighting in the late war, and think it more eligible, to keep our liberties in our own hands, whilst it is in our power thus to do, than to place them in the hands of fallible men, like ourselves, who may if they please, entirely deprive us of them, and so we be at last reduced to the sad alternative of losing them forever, or recovering them back by the point of the sword. The aristocratic party are sensible, that these are the sentiments of the majority of the community, and their conduct plainly evinces the truth of a well known ancient adage—"Nothing cuts like the truth."

[signed] The Yeomanry of Massachusetts.

SOURCE: the *Massachusetts Gazette*, January 25, 1788.

A cartoon published in July 1788, when New York became the eleventh state to ratify the Constitution. After initially voting to reject, North Carolina soon reconsidered, but radical and still reluctant Rhode Island did not join the Union until 1790.

SOURCE: The Federal Edifice "On the Erection of the Eleventh Pillar," caricature from the *Massachusetts Centinal*, August 2, 1788. Neg. #33959. Collection of The New-York Historical Society.

the common law, including the prohibition of double jeopardy, the right not to be compelled to testify against oneself, and due process of law before life, liberty, or property could be taken away. Finally, the unenumerated rights of the people were protected, and the powers not delegated to the federal government were reserved to the states.

The first ten amendments to the Constitution have been a restraining influence on the growth of government power over American citizens.

▶ Read the Document

The Bill of Rights (1789) at **www.myhistorylab.com**

Their provisions have become an admired aspect of the American political tradition throughout the world. The Constitution was authored by the Federalists, but the Bill of Rights is the most important legal legacy of the Anti-Federalists.

The First Federal Administration

Ratification of the Constitution was followed in the fall of 1788 by the first federal elections for Congress and the presidency, and in the spring of 1789 the new federal government assumed power in the temporary capital of New York City. The inauguration of George Washington as the first president of the United States took place on April 30 on the balcony of Federal Hall, at the corner of Wall and Broad Streets. Reelected without opposition in 1792, Washington served until 1797. The first years under the new federal Constitution were especially important for the future because they shaped the structure of the American nation-state in ways that would be enormously significant for later generations.

The Washington Presidency

Although he dressed in plain American broadcloth at his inauguration and claimed to be content with a plain republican title, Washington was anything but a man of the people. By nature reserved and solemn, he chose to ride about

town in a grand carriage drawn by six horses and attended by uniformed liverymen. In the tradition of British royalty, he delivered his addresses personally to Congress and received from both houses an official reply. These customs were continued by Washington's successor, John Adams, but ended by Thomas Jefferson, who denounced them as "rags of royalty." On the other hand, Washington worked hard to adhere to the letter of the Constitution, refusing, for example, to use the veto power except where he thought Congress had acted unconstitutionally and personally seeking the "advice and consent" of the Senate.

Congress quickly moved to establish departments to run the affairs of state, and Washington soon appointed Thomas Jefferson as secretary of state, Alexander Hamilton as secretary of the treasury, Henry Knox as secretary of war (continuing in the position he held under the Confederation government), and Edmund Randolph as attorney general. The president consulted each of these men regularly and during his first term met with them as a group to discuss matters of policy. By the end of Washington's presidency the secretaries had coalesced in what came to be known as the cabinet, an institution that has survived to the present despite the absence of constitutional authority. Washington understood the importance of national unity, and in his style of leadership, his consultations, and his appointments he sought to achieve a balance of conflicting political perspectives and sectional interests. His intentions would be sorely tested during the eight years of his administration.

The Federal Judiciary

The most important piece of legislation to emerge from the first session of Congress was the Judiciary Act of 1789, implementing the judicial clause of the Constitution, which empowered Congress to set the number of justices on the Supreme Court and create a system of federal courts. The act established a High Court of six justices

Two coins from the first decade of the federal republic illustrate political controversies of the period. The Washington cent was proposed by Treasury Secretary Alexander Hamilton in 1792, in the hope of enhancing popular respect for the new government by having the president's bust impressed on coins in the manner of European kings. But after long debate, Congress defeated the plan, the opponents claiming it smacked of monarchy. The Liberty coin, issued by the Mint of the United States in 1795, when under the authority of Secretary of State Thomas Jefferson, features Liberty wearing a liberty cap and bearing a marked resemblance to the French Revolutionary icon Marianne.

(increased to nine in 1869) and established circuit and district federal courts. Strong nationalists argued for a powerful federal legal system that would provide a uniform code of civil and criminal justice throughout the country. But the localists in Congress, intent on preserving local community autonomy, successfully fought to retain the various bodies of law that had developed in the states. The act gave federal courts limited original jurisdiction, restricting them mostly to appeals from state courts. But it established the principle of federal judicial review of state legislation, despite the silence of the Constitution on this point.

Washington appointed and the Senate confirmed the six Supreme Court justices, including John Jay, who became Chief Justice. During the Court's first decade it heard relatively few cases yet managed to raise considerable political controversy. In *Chisholm* v. *Georgia* (1793) the Court ruled in favor of two South Carolina residents suing the State of Georgia for the recovery of confiscated property, thus supporting the Constitution's grant of federal jurisdiction over disputes "between a state and citizens of another state." Many localists believed the ruling threatened the integrity of the states, and in response, they proposed an Eleventh Amendment to the Constitution, protecting states against suits by citizens of another state. It was ratified in 1798. The Supreme Court nevertheless established itself as the final authority on questions of law when it invalidated a Virginia statute in *Ware* v. *Hylton* (1796) and upheld the constitutionality of an act of Congress in *Hylton* v. *United States* (1796).

Hamilton's Fiscal Program

Fiscal and economic affairs were important in the new government. It was, after all, the economic crisis and the resulting unrest in episodes like Shays' Rebellion that had provided the momentum for the new Constitution. Lacking revenue and facing the massive national debt run up during the Revolution, the government took power in a condition of virtual bankruptcy.

Treasury Secretary Hamilton took on the task of reorganizing the nation's finances. In 1790 he submitted a "Report on the Public Credit," recommending the federal "redemption" at full value of the national debt owed to foreign and domestic creditors, as well as the "assumption" of the obligations accumulated by the states during the previous fifteen years. Congress readily agreed to settle the $11 million owed to foreign creditors (through a combination of tax revenue and loans) but balked at the redemption of the domestic debt of $42 million and the assumption of the state debts of another $25 million. Hamilton proposed issuing new interest-bearing government bonds that would be exchanged for the full face value of all the notes, warrants, and securities the government had distributed during the Revolution.

Thousands of veterans had been rewarded for their service with warrants for land or money, but as they waited for Congress to mark out the territory or provide the funding, many had been forced by necessity to sell to speculators at deep discounts. Hamilton's proposal, his colleague James Madison objected, would result in windfall profits for speculators and create a permanent federal debt. Hamilton did not dispute these claims but instead argued that they were good things. The creation of a federal debt by the issue of securities would give the government the ability to finance national projects or provide for national defense in the event of war, and the possession of those securities in the hands of a wealthy class of citizens would offer a guarantee for the government's stability. There was even greater congressional opposition to Hamilton's proposal for the assumption of state debts. Some states (mostly in the South) had already arranged to pay off their debts, whereas others (mostly in the North) had not, so the plan seemed to reward the insolvent and punish the thrifty. Congress remained deadlocked on these issues for six months, until congressmen from Pennsylvania and Virginia arranged a compromise.

Final agreement, however, was stalled by a sectional dispute over the location of the new national capital. Southerners supported Washington's desire to plant it on the Potomac River, but Northerners argued for Philadelphia. In return for Madison's pledge to obtain enough southern votes to pass Hamilton's debt assumption plan, northern congressmen agreed to a location for the new federal district on the boundary of Virginia and Maryland. In July 1790, Congress passed legislation moving the temporary capital from New York to Philadelphia until the expected completion of the federal city in the District of Columbia in 1800. Two weeks later it adopted Hamilton's credit program. It was the first of many sectional compromises.

Hamilton now proposed a second component of his fiscal program, the establishment of a Bank of the United States. The bank, a public corporation funded by private capital, would serve as the depository of government funds and the fiscal agent of the Treasury. Congress narrowly approved it, but Madison's opposition raised doubts in the president's mind about the constitutionality of the measure, and Washington solicited the opinion of his cabinet.

Read the Document

Alexander Hamilton, An Opinion on the Constitutionality of an Act to Establish a Bank (1791) at **www.myhistorylab.com**

Here, for the first time, the classic interpretations of constitutional authority were articulated. Jefferson took a "strict constructionist" position, arguing that the powers of the federal government must be limited to those specifically enumerated in the Constitution. This position came closest to the basic agreement of the men who had drafted the document. Hamilton, on the other hand, reasoned that the Constitution "implied" the power to use whatever means were "necessary and proper" to carry out its enumerated powers, the "loose constructionist" position. Persuaded by Hamilton's opinion, Washington signed the bill, and the bank went into operation in 1791.

The final component of Hamilton's fiscal program, outlined in his famous "Report on Manufactures," was an ambitious plan, involving the use of government securities as investment capital for "infant industries" and high protective tariffs to encourage the development of an industrial economy. Congressmen from farming areas, whose previous objections to Hamilton's preference for the "monied interests" had not prevailed, were finally able to frustrate him on this last proposal. Hamilton's views, they argued, would limit them to roles exactly like those they had played within the British empire and would amount to exchanging British for Boston and New York masters. Of equal importance, the plan failed to inspire the enthusiasm of American capitalists, who continued to be more interested in investments in shipping or in land speculation than in industrial production. Many of Hamilton's specific proposals for increased tariff protection, however, became part of the revision of duties that took place in 1792. Moreover, his fiscal program as a whole dramatically restored the financial health of the United States.

The Federalist political coalition, forged during the ratification of the Constitution, was sorely strained by these debates over fiscal policy. By the middle of 1792, Jefferson—representing southern agrarians—and Hamilton—speaking for northern capitalists—were locked in a full-scale feud within the administration. Hamilton conducted himself

Alexander Hamilton (ca. 1804) by John Trumbull. Although Hamilton's fiscal program was controversial, it restored the financial health of the United States.

more like a prime minister than a cabinet secretary, greatly offending Jefferson, who considered himself the president's heir apparent. But the dispute went deeper than a mere conflict of personalities. Hamilton stated the difference clearly when he wrote that "one side appears to believe that there is a serious plot to overturn the State governments, and substitute a monarchy to the present republican system," while "the other side firmly believes that there is a serious plot to overturn the general government and elevate the separate powers of the States upon its ruins."

Distressed by these political disputes, Washington considered retiring at the end of his first term, but both factions encouraged him to remain in office to bridge their differences. The factions did contest the vice presidency. In December 1792 Washington was reelected by unanimous vote in the electoral college, but incumbent Vice President John Adams was only narrowly returned to office. It was an indication of things to come.

American Foreign Policy

The conflict between Hamilton and Jefferson grew even bitterer over the issue of American foreign policy. The commanding event of the Atlantic world during the 1790s was the French Revolution, which broke out in 1789. Most Americans enthusiastically welcomed the fall of the French monarchy. But with the inauguration of the Reign of Terror in 1793, which claimed the lives of hundreds of aristocrats and politicians upon the guillotine, American conservatives began to voice their opposition. The execution of King Louis XVI in January 1793 and the outbreak of war between revolutionary France and monarchical Great Britain a few weeks later firmly divided American opinion.

Most at issue was whether the Franco-American alliance of 1778 required the United States to support France in its war with Britain. All of Washington's cabinet agreed on the importance of American neutrality. With France and Britain prowling for each other's vessels on the high seas, the vast colonial trade of Europe was delivered up to neutral powers, the United States prominent among them. In other words, neutrality meant windfall profits. Jefferson believed it highly unlikely that the French would call upon the Americans to honor the 1778 treaty and that the administration should simply wait and see. But Hamilton argued that so great was the danger of American involvement in the war that Washington should immediately declare the treaty "temporarily and provisionally suspended."

These disagreements revealed two contrasting perspectives on the course the United States should chart in international waters. Hamilton and the nationalists believed in the necessity of an accommodation with Great Britain, the most important trading partner of the United States and the world's greatest naval power. Jefferson, Madison, and their supporters, on the other hand, looked for more international independence, less connection with the British, and thus closer relations with Britain's traditional rival, France. They pinned their hopes for the future on American western expansion.

The debate in the United States grew hotter with the arrival in early 1793 of French ambassador Edmond Genêt. Large crowds of supporters greeted him throughout the nation, and Genêt solicited contributions and distributed commissions authorizing American privateering raids against the British. A majority of Americans still nursed a hatred of imperial Britain and expressed a great deal of sympathy for republican France. Conservatives such as Hamilton, however, favored a continuation of traditional commercial relations with Britain and feared the anti-aristocratic violence of the French. Washington sympathized with Hamilton's position, but most of all he wished to preserve American independence and neutrality. Knowing he must act before "Citizen" Genêt (as the ambassador was popularly known) compromised American sovereignty and involved the United States in a war with Britain, the president issued a proclamation of neutrality on April 22, 1793. In it he assured the world that the United States intended to pursue "a conduct friendly and impartial towards the belligerent powers," while continuing to do business with all sides.

Hamilton's supporters applauded the president, but Jefferson's friends were outraged. Throughout the country, activists sympathetic to France organized Democratic Societies, political clubs modeled after the Sons of Liberty. Society members corresponded with each other, campaigned on behalf of candidates, and lobbied with congressmen. In a speech to Congress, President Washington denounced what he called these "self-created societies," declaring them "the most diabolical attempt to destroy the best fabric of human government and happiness."

Citizen Genêt miscalculated, however, alienating even his supporters, when he demanded that Washington call Congress into special session to debate neutrality. Jefferson, previously a confidant of the ambassador, now denounced Genêt as "hot-headed" and "indecent towards the President." But his words came too late to save his reputation with Washington, and at the end of 1793 Jefferson left the administration. The continuing upheaval in France soon swept Genêt's party from power and he was recalled, but fearing the guillotine, he claimed sanctuary and remained in the United States. During his time in the limelight, however, Genêt had furthered the division of the Federalist coalition into two factions, one identifying with Washington, Hamilton, and conservative principles, the other supporting Jefferson, Madison, democracy, and the French Revolution.

The United States and the Indian Peoples

One of the most pressing problems of the Washington presidency concerned the West. The American attempt to treat western Indian tribes as conquered peoples after the Revolution had resulted only in further violence and warfare. In the Northwest Ordinance of 1787 (see Chapter 7), the Confederation Congress abandoned that course for a new approach. "The utmost good faith shall always be observed towards the Indians," the ordinance read. "Their lands and property shall never be taken from them without their consent." Yet the ordinance was premised on the survey and sale to American settlers of Indian land north of the Ohio River and the creation of new state governments. The ordinance pointed in wildly contradictory directions.

The new federal government continued to pursue this inconsistent policy. In 1790 Congress passed the Intercourse Act, the basic law by which the United States would "regulate trade and intercourse with the Indian tribes." In an attempt to clarify the vexing problem of Indian sovereignty, the act declared public treaties between the United States and the Indian nations the only legal means of obtaining Indian land. Treaty making, thus, became the procedure for establishing and maintaining relations with Indian nations. In the twentieth century, a number of Indian communities have successfully appealed for the return of lands obtained by states or individuals in violation of this provision of the Intercourse Act. To eliminate the abuses of unscrupulous traders, the act also created a federal licensing system, and subsequent legislation authorized the creation of subsidized trading houses, or "factories," where Indians could obtain manufactured goods at reasonable prices. These provisions indicated the best intentions of the Washington administration.

On the other hand, one of the federal government's highest priorities was the acquisition of western Indian land to support a growing population of farmers (see Map 8.2). The federal government, in fact, was unable to control the flood of settlers coming down the Ohio River. An American expeditionary force was sent to evict squatters from Indian land, but inevitably the troops ended up protecting settlers and fighting Indians. In defense of their homelands, villages of Shawnees, Delawares, and other Indian peoples confederated with the Miamis under their war chief Little Turtle. In the fall of 1790 Little Turtle lured federal forces led by General Josiah Harmar into the confederacy's stronghold in Ohio and badly mauled them. In November 1791 the confederation inflicted an even more disastrous defeat on a large American force under General Arthur St. Clair, governor of the Northwest Territory and the former president of Congress. More than 900 Americans were killed or wounded, making this the worst defeat of an army by Indians in North American history (see Seeing History).

In the aftermath of this defeat the House of Representatives launched the first formal investigation of the executive branch undertaken by Congress. They found St. Clair's leadership "incompetent," and he soon resigned. Yet few Americans were willing to admit to the contradiction at the heart of American policy. "We

Little Turtle, a war chief of the Miami tribe of the Ohio Valley, led a large pan-Indian army to victory over the Americans in 1790 and 1791. After his forces were defeated at the Battle of Fallen Timbers in 1794, he became a friend of the United States. This lithograph is a copy of an oil portrait, which no longer survives, by the artist Gilbert Stuart.

SOURCE: Little Turtle, or Mich-i-kin-i-qua, Miami War Chief, Conqueror of Harmar and St. Clair. Lithograph made from a portrait painted in 1797 by Gilbert Stuart. Indiana Historical Society Library (negative no. C2584).

MAP 8.2 Spread of Settlement: The Backcountry Expands, 1770–90 From 1770 to 1790, American settlement moved across the Appalachians for the first time. The Ohio Valley became the focus of bitter warfare between Indians and settlers.

acknowledge the Indians as brothers," yet we "seize their lands," Senator Benjamin Hawkins of North Carolina wrote to President Washington. "This doctrine it might be expected would be disliked by the independent Tribes. It is the source of their hostility."

Spanish Florida and British Canada

The position of the United States in the West was made even more precarious by the hostility of Spain and Great Britain, which controlled the adjoining territories. Under the dynamic leadership of King Carlos III and his able ministers, Spain introduced liberal reforms to revitalize the rule-bound bureaucracy of its American empire. As a result the economy of New Spain grew rapidly in the 1780s. Moreover, Spain had reasserted itself in North America, acquiring the French claims to Louisiana before the end of the Seven Years' War, expanding into California, seizing the Gulf Coast during the American Revolution, and regaining Florida from Britain in the Treaty of Paris in 1783. The Spanish were deeply suspicious of the United States. American settlers, the Spanish governor of Florida declared, "were nomadic like Arabs, distinguished from savages only in their color, language, and the superiority of their depraved cunning and untrustworthiness." Spain claimed for itself much of the territory that today makes up the states of Tennessee, Alabama, and Mississippi and pursued a policy designed to block the continued expansion of the young republic (see Map 8.3).

Spain's anti-American policy in the West had several facets. Controlling both sides of the lower Mississippi, the Spanish closed the river to American shipping, making it impossible for western American farmers to market their crops through the port of New Orleans. They also sought to create a barrier to American settlement by promoting immigration to Louisiana and Florida. They succeeded in attracting several thousand Acadians, whom the British had deported from Nova Scotia during the Seven Years' War. Reassembling their distinctive communities in the bayou country of Louisiana, these tough emigrants became known as the Cajuns. But otherwise, the Spanish had little success with immigration and relied mostly on creating a barrier of pro-Spanish Indian nations in the lower Mississippi Valley. In the early 1790s the Spanish attempted to extend their control of the Mississippi River by constructing two new forts at sites that would later become the river cities of Vicksburg and Memphis.

North of the Ohio River, the situation was much the same. Thousands of Loyalists had fled the United States in the aftermath of the Revolution and settled north of lakes Ontario and Erie. They were understandably hostile to the new republic. In 1791 the British Parliament passed the Canada Act, creating the province of Upper Canada (later renamed Ontario) and granting the Loyalists limited self-government. To protect this province, British troops remained at a number of posts

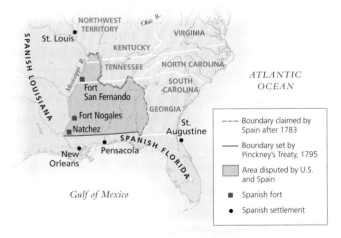

MAP 8.3 Spanish Claims to American Territory, 1783–95 Before 1795, the Spanish claimed the American territory of the Old Southwest and barred Americans from access to the port of New Orleans, effectively closing the Mississippi River. This dispute was settled by Pinckney's Treaty in 1795.

within American territory, such as Detroit, where they supplied arms to the Indian nations, in hopes of creating a buffer to American expansion.

The Crises of 1794

These conditions laid the groundwork for the gravest crisis of Washington's presidency in 1794. In the West, the inability of the federal government to subdue the Indians, eliminate the British from the northern fur trade, or arrange with the Spanish for unencumbered use of the Mississippi River stirred frontiersmen to loud protest. Secret agents for Great Britain and Spain sought to entice American settlers to quit the Union and join themselves to Canada or Florida. In the Atlantic, Great Britain declared a blockade of France and its colonies in the West Indies, and by early 1794 the Royal Navy had confiscated the cargoes of more than 250 American ships, threatening hundreds of merchants with ruin. The United States was being "kicked, cuffed, and plundered all over the ocean," declared James Madison, and in Congress, he introduced legislation imposing retaliatory duties on British ships and merchandise.

To make matters worse a rebellion broke out among farmers in western Pennsylvania in the summer of 1794. To produce needed revenue, Congress had placed an excise tax on the distillation of whiskey, which many farm families produced from their surpluses of corn. Throughout rural America, farmers protested that the new tax ran counter to the principles of the Revolution. "Internal taxes upon consumption," declared the citizens of Mingo Creek, in western Pennsylvania, are "most dangerous to the civil rights of freemen, and must in the end destroy the liberties of every country in which they are introduced." Hugh Henry Brackenridge, editor of the *Pittsburgh Gazette*, argued for a tax on the "unsettled lands which all around us have been purchased by speculating men, who keep them up in large bodies and obstruct the population of the country." In other words, Congress should tax land speculators like President Washington rather than backcountry settlers. Protest turned to riot when the Mingo Creek militia attempted to seize the tax collector, and several of their number were killed in the confrontation.

The "Whiskey Rebellion" came at a time when Washington considered the nation to be under siege. The combination of Indian attack, international intrigue, and domestic insurrection, he believed, posed the greatest threat to the nation since the Revolution. He called up a federal army of 13,000 men, approximately the same size as the one he had commanded during the Revolution, and ordered the occupation of western Pennsylvania. Federal troops dragged protesting farmers from their beds and confined them to open pens, where they remained for days in the freezing rain. Authorities arrested twenty people, and a judge convicted two of treason.

Read the **Document**
George Washington, Proclamation Regarding the Whiskey Rebellion (1794) at **www.myhistorylab.com**

The Columbian Tragedy

Broadsides—large sheets printed on one side, suitable for posting—were an important medium of popular communication in the late eighteenth and early nineteenth centuries. This one, lamenting the disastrous defeat of an American expeditionary force at the hands of the Ohio Indian confederacy in 1791 in which more than 900 Americans were killed or wounded, was published in Boston and sold throughout New England for the price of six cents. The struggle against the Ohio Indian confederacy was one of the most critical issues during Washington's presidency. Across the top are the names of the officers killed in battle, each accompanied by the icon of a black coffin. On the left is a woodcut of Major-General Richard Butler, the highest-ranking officer to die, and beneath it an Indian warrior alongside a skull and crossbones. On the right is a crude representation of the battleground. As one contemporary critic put it, all the images are "of the commonest description," yet the broadside survives in a number of copies, indicating that it probably sold quite well. The broadside did double duty—as both memorial for the dead and protest against the incompetence of the army's leaders. Most of the broadside is devoted to a mournful ballad that nevertheless concludes that the nation will ultimately prevail because "the *Lord* is on our side."

• **Why would Americans purchase this broadside and display it in their homes?**

In this 1794 painting, President George Washington reviews some 13,000 troops at Fort Cumberland on the Potomac before dispatching them to suppress the Whiskey Rebellion. Washington's mobilization of federal military power dramatically demonstrated the federal commitment to the preservation of the Union and the protection of the western boundary.

SOURCE: Francis Kemmelmeyer, *General George Washington Reviewing the Western Army at Fort Cumberland the 18th of October 1794*, after 1794. Oil on paper backed with linen, 18 ⅛ × 23 ⅛. Courtesy of Winterthur Museum.

The protests gradually died down and Washington pardoned the felons, sparing their lives. The president overreacted, for there was no organized insurrection in western Pennsylvania. Nevertheless, his mobilization of federal military power was a dramatic demonstration of his commitment to the preservation of the Union, the protection of the western boundary, and the supremacy of the national over the local community.

Washington's action was reinforced by an impressive American victory against the western Indian confederacy. Following the disastrous defeat of St. Clair by Little Turtle, the president directed General Anthony Wayne to lead a greatly strengthened American force to secure the Northwest. At the Battle of Fallen Timbers, fought in northern Ohio on August 20, 1794, Wayne crushed the Indians. British troops inside nearby Fort Miami barred the gates to the retreating warriors, unwilling to engage the powerful American force. This American victory set the stage for the Treaty of Greenville in 1795, in which the representatives of twelve Indian nations ceded a huge territory encompassing most of present-day Ohio, much of Indiana, and other enclaves in the Northwest, including the town of Detroit and the tiny village of Chicago.

Settling Disputes with Britain and Spain

The strengthened American position in the West encouraged the British finally to settle their dispute with the United States so that they might concentrate on defeating republican France. Washington dispatched Chief Justice John Jay to London to arrange a settlement with the British, and in November 1794 Jay and his British counterpart signed an agreement providing for British withdrawal from American soil by 1796, for limited American trade with British colonies, and for "most-favored-nation" status (meaning that each nation would enjoy terms of trade equal to the best terms accorded any other nation). The treaty represented a solid gain for the young republic. With only a small army and no navy to speak of, the United States was in no position to wage war.

Jay's Treaty enshrined Hamilton's conception of American neutrality. Hamilton's opponents, on the other hand, were enraged at what they considered an accommodation with the British at the expense of the French. Moreover, Southerners were alienated by Jay's failure to negotiate compensation for masters whose slaves had fled to the British during the Revolution. Throughout the country opponents of the treaty organized protests and demonstrations. Chief Justice Jay joked he found his way across country by the light of his burning effigies. Nevertheless, the Senate, dominated by supporters of Hamilton, ratified the agreement in June 1795. In the House, a coalition of southerners, westerners, and friends of France attempted to stall the treaty by threatening to withhold the necessary appropriations. They demanded they be allowed to examine the diplomatic correspondence regarding the whole affair, but the president refused, establishing the precedent of "executive privilege" in matters of state.

The deadlock continued until late in the year, when word arrived that the Spanish had abandoned their claims to the territory south of the Ohio River. Spain had declared war on revolutionary France but quickly suffered a humiliating defeat. Fearing the loss of its American empire, the Spanish found it expedient to come to an agreement with the Americans. In 1795 American envoy Thomas Pinckney negotiated a treaty setting the international boundary at the 31st parallel (the southern boundary of Mississippi and Alabama) and opening the Mississippi to American shipping. This treaty was compatible with the Jeffersonian conception of empire, and congressmen from the South and West were delighted with its terms. Administration supporters, however, demanded that the House agree in the matter of Jay's Treaty before the Senate would approve Pinckney's.

With the ratification of these important treaties, the United States established its sovereignty over the land west of the Appalachians and opened to American commerce a vast market extending from Atlantic ports to the Mississippi Valley. From a political standpoint, however, the events of 1794 and 1795 brought Washington down from his pedestal. Vilified by the opposition press, sick of politics, and longing to return to private life, Washington rejected the idea of a third term.

Washington's Farewell Address

During the last months of his term, Washington published a "Farewell Address" to the nation. He extolled the benefits of the federal government as "a main pillar in the edifice of your real independence" and praised the financial stability that had resulted from Hamilton's policy, surely one of the major accomplishments of his administration. In the best-remembered portion of the address, he urged that the United States seek commercial connections with all nations but "have with them as little political connection as possible." Why, he asked, "entangle our peace and prosperity in the toils of European ambition, rivalship, interest, humor, or caprice?" Looking forward, he expressed great concern about the growing acrimony between political factions, which, he argued, "agitates the community with ill-founded jealousies and false alarms, . . . and opens the door to foreign influence and corruption."

Federalists and Democratic-Republicans

The framers of the Constitution envisioned a one-party state in which partisan distinctions would be muted by patriotism and public virtue. "Among the numerous advantages promised by a well constructed Union," Madison had written, is "its tendency to break and control the violence of faction." Not only did he fail to anticipate the rise of political parties or factions, but also he saw them as potentially harmful to the new nation. Yet it was Madison who took the first steps toward organizing the opposition to the policies of the Washington administration, and it was Hamilton, Madison's coauthor of *The Federalist Papers*, who organized administration supporters into a disciplined political faction. Despite the intentions of the framers, in the twelve years between the ratification of the Constitution and the federal election of 1800, political parties became a fundamental part of the American system of government.

The Rise of Political Parties

Evident in the debates and votes of Congress from 1789 to 1795 was a series of shifting coalitions. These coalitions first began to polarize into opposing political factions during the debate over Jay's Treaty in 1795, when agrarians, westerners, southerners, and supporters of France came together in opposition. By the time of the election of 1796, the factions had taken names for themselves. Hamilton's supporters continued to claim the mantle of Federalism. But Jefferson's supporters christened themselves Republicans, suggesting by implication that the Federalists were really monarchists at heart. (Historians use the term "Democratic-Republicans" to distinguish them from the modern Republican Party, founded in 1854.) The two political factions played a fitful role in the presidential election of 1796, which pitted Vice President John Adams against Thomas Jefferson. Partisan organization was strongest in the Middle States, where there was a real contest of political forces, and weakest in New England and the South, where sectional loyalty prevailed and organized opposition was weaker. The absence of party discipline was demonstrated when the ballots of the presidential electors, cast in their respective state capitals, were counted in the Senate. Adams was victorious, but in accordance with the Constitution the vice presidency went to the candidate with the second-highest total, and that was Jefferson. The new administration was born divided.

The Adams Presidency

Adams was put in the difficult situation of facing a political opposition led by his own vice president. He nevertheless attempted to conduct his presidency along the lines laid down by Washington and retained most of the former president's appointees. This arrangement presented Adams with another problem. Although Hamilton had retired the year before, the members of the cabinet continued to seek his opinion and follow it, undercutting the president's authority.

On the other hand, Adams benefited from rising tensions between the United States and France. Angered by Jay's Treaty, the French suspended diplomatic relations with the United States at the end of 1796 and inaugurated a tough new policy toward American shipping. During the next two years they seized more than 300 American vessels and confiscated cargoes valued at an estimated $20 million. Hoping to resolve the crisis, Adams sent an American delegation to France. But in dispatches sent back to the United States, the envoys reported that three agents of the French foreign ministry had demanded a bribe before any negotiations could begin. Skeptical Republicans demanded the release of the dispatches, which Adams agreed to in 1798, substituting the letters X, Y, Z for the names of the French agents. The documents upheld Adams's case and proved a major liability for the Republicans, sparking powerful anti-French sentiment throughout the country. "Millions for

OVERVIEW | The First American Party System

Federalist Party	Organized by figures in the Washington administration who were in favor of a strong federal government, friendship with the British, and opposition to the French Revolution; its power base was among merchants, property owners, and urban workers tied to the commercial economy. A minority party after 1800, it was regionally strong only in New England.
Democratic-Republican Party	Arose as the opposition to the Federalists; its adherents were in favor of limiting federal power; they were sympathetic to the French Revolution and hostile to Great Britain; the party drew strength from southern planters and northern farmers and was the majority party after 1800.

defense, but not one cent for tribute!" was the slogan of the day. The XYZ Affair, as it became known, sent Adams's popularity soaring.

The Alien and Sedition Acts

During the spring of 1798 Adams and the Federalists prepared the country for war with France. Congress authorized tripling the size of the army, and Washington came out of retirement to command the force. Fears of a French invasion declined after word arrived of a British naval victory over the French at Aboukir Bay in Egypt in August 1798, but what became known as the "Quasi-War" between France and the United States continued.

The Democratic-Republicans contested the Federalist war measures and began for the first time to act as a genuine opposition party, complete with caucuses, floor leaders, and partisan discipline. They contested the election of Speaker of the House of Representatives, which henceforth became a partisan office. The more effective the Republicans became as an opposition, the more treasonous they appeared in the eyes of the Federalists. With the Revolution still fresh in memory, Americans had a weak understanding of the concept of a loyal opposition. Disagreement with the administration was misconstrued by the Federalists as opposition to the state itself.

In the summer of 1798 the Federalist majority in Congress, with the acquiescence of President Adams, passed four acts severely limiting both freedom of speech and the freedom of the press and threatening the liberty of foreigners in the United States. The Naturalization Act extended the period of residence required for citizenship from five to fourteen years. The Alien Act and the Alien Enemies Act authorized the president to order the imprisonment or deportation of suspected aliens during wartime. Finally, the Sedition Act provided heavy fines and imprisonment for anyone convicted of writing, publishing, or speaking anything of "a false, scandalous and malicious" nature against the government or any of its officers.

The Federalists intended these repressive laws as weapons to defeat the Democratic-Republicans. They prosecuted dissent by indicting leading opposition newspaper editors and writers, fining and imprisoning at least twenty-five of them. The most vilified was Congressman Matthew Lyon of Vermont, scorned by Federalists as "Ragged Matt the Democrat." In July 1798 Lyon was convicted of publishing libelous statements about President Adams and thrown into prison. Later that year, he conducted a campaign from his jail cell and was reelected to Congress.

The Sedition Act, Madison wrote, "ought to produce universal alarm, because it is levelled against the right of freely examining public characters and measures, and of free communication among the people thereon, which has ever been deemed the only effectual guardian of every other right." He and Jefferson anonymously authored resolutions, passed by the Virginia and Kentucky legislatures, declaring the Constitution a compact among sovereign states and advocating the power of the states to "nullify" unconstitutional laws. When threatened with overbearing central authority, they argued, the states had the right to go their own way. The Virginia and Kentucky Resolves, as they were known, would later be used to justify the secession of the Southern states at the beginning of the Civil War.

•**•**[Read the Document
*The Alien and Sedition
Acts (1798)* at
www.myhistorylab.com

The Revolution of 1800

In 1799 the French convinced President Adams that they were willing to settle their dispute with the United States when they released seized American ships and requested negotiations. Adams sensed a public mood running toward peace. But the Hamiltonian wing of the party, always scornful of public sentiment, continued to beat the drums of war. When Federalists in Congress attempted to block the negotiations, Adams threatened to resign and turn the government over to Vice President Jefferson. "The end of war is peace," Adams declared, "and peace was offered me."

In this contemporary cartoon, *Congressional Pugilists, Congress Hall in Philadelphia, February 15, 1798*, Roger Griswold, a Connecticut Federalist, uses his cane to attack Matthew Lyon, a Vermont Democratic-Republican, who retaliates with fire tongs.

SOURCE: Collection of The New-York Historical Society, Neg. #33995.

Adams considered the settlement of this conflict with France to be one of the greatest accomplishments of his career, but it earned him the scorn of conservative Federalists, including Hamilton.

The presidential campaign of 1800 was the first to be contested by two disciplined political parties. Caucuses of congressmen nominated respective slates: Adams and Charles Cotesworth Pinckney of South Carolina for the Federalists, Jefferson and Aaron Burr of New York for the Republicans. Both tickets thus represented attempts at sectional balance. The Democratic-Republicans presented themselves as the party of traditional agrarian purity, of liberty and states' rights, of "government rigorously frugal and simple," in the words of Jefferson. They were optimistic, convinced they were riding the wave of the future. The Federalists, divided and embittered, waged a defensive struggle for strong central government and public order and often resorted to negative campaigning. They denounced Jefferson as an atheist, a Jacobin, and the father of mulatto children (a charge now substantiated by the results of DNA testing, as noted in Chapter 4).

Adams won in New England but elsewhere was overwhelmed (see Map 8.4). Jefferson called it "the Revolution of 1800." Party discipline was so effective, in fact, that it created a constitutional crisis. By casting all their ballots for Jefferson and Burr, Republican electors thoughtlessly produced a tie vote, thus forcing the election into the lame duck House of Representatives controlled by the Federalists. Given a last chance to decide the election, Federalist representatives attempted to cut a deal with Burr. Although Burr refused, he also declined to withdraw his name from consideration. Finally, on the thirty-fifth ballot the Federalists arranged with their opponents to elect Jefferson without any of them having to vote in his favor. Congressman Matthew Lyon cast the symbolic final ballot in a gesture of sweet revenge. Afterward, Congress passed and the states ratified the Twelfth Amendment, creating separate ballots for president and vice president in time for the next presidential election.

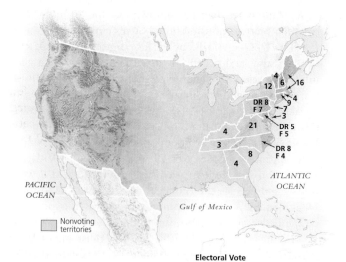

	Electoral Vote (%)
THOMAS JEFFERSON (Jeffersonian Republican)	73 (53)
JOHN ADAMS (Federalist)	65 (47)

MAP 8.4 The Election of 1800 In the presidential election of 1800, Democratic-Republican victories in New York and the divided vote in Pennsylvania threw the election to Jefferson. The combination of the South and these crucial Middle States would keep the Democratic-Republicans in control of the federal government for the next generation.

The presidential election of 1800 was the first to feature campaign advertising. "T. Jefferson, President of the United States of America; John Adams—no more," reads the streamer on this election banner, illustrated with an American eagle and a portrait of Jefferson. This was mild rhetoric in a campaign characterized by wild charges. The Republicans labeled Adams a warmonger and a monarchist, while the Federalists denounced Jefferson as an atheist, Jacobin, and sexual libertine.

Popular pressure resulted in the introduction of universal white manhood suffrage in four states by 1800 and the reduction of property requirements in others. Thus was inaugurated a movement that would sweep the nation over the next quarter century. As a consequence, voter turnout increased in all the states. The growth of popular interest in politics was a transformation as important as the peaceful transition from Federalists to Democratic-Republicans in national government.

"The Rising Glory of America"

In 1771, Philip Freneau and Hugh Henry Brackenridge addressed their graduating class at Princeton on "The Rising Glory of America." Thus far American contributions to learning and the arts had been slim, they admitted, but they were boundlessly optimistic about the potential of their country. Indeed, judged against the creative work of the colonial period, the Revolutionary generation accomplished a great deal in their effort to build a national culture.

The Liberty of the Press

At the beginning of the Revolution in 1775, there were thirty-seven weekly or semiweekly newspapers in the thirteen colonies, only seven of which were Loyalist in sentiment. By 1789, the number of papers in the United States had grown to ninety-two, including eight dailies; three papers were being published west of the Appalachians. Relative to population, there were more newspapers in the United States than in any other country in the world—a reflection of the remarkably high literacy rate of the American people. In New England, almost 90 percent of the population could read, and even on the frontier about two-thirds of the males were literate. During the political controversy of the 1790s, the press became the principal medium of Federalist and Democratic-Republican opinion, and papers came to be identified by their politics. In 1789, John Fenno, aided by Alexander Hamilton, began publication of the Federalist *Gazette of the United States*, and in 1791, Jefferson encouraged Philip Freneau to establish the competing *National Gazette*. The columns of these papers broadcast the feud between the two cabinet secretaries.

The prosecutions under the Sedition Act, however, threatened to curb the further development of the media,

Democratic Political Culture

Accompanying the rise of partisan politics was a transformation in popular political participation. Consider the custom of celebrating Independence Day. At the beginning of the 1790s, in many communities, the day featured demonstrations of military prowess by veteran officers, followed by banquets for leaders. Relatively few Americans played a direct role. But during the political controversies of the decade, a tradition of popular celebration developed. People took to the streets, set off fireworks, erected liberty poles, and listened to readings of the preamble of the Declaration of Independence, which more than any other document encapsulated and symbolized republican ideology.

There was a corresponding increase in the suffrage. In 1789 state regulations limited the franchise to a small percentage of the adult population. Women, African Americans, and Indians could not vote, but neither could a third to a half of all free adult males, who were excluded by tax-paying or property-owning requirements. Moreover, even among the eligible, the turnout was generally low. The traditional manner of voting was *viva voce*, by voice. At the polling place in each community individuals announced their selections aloud to the clerk of elections who wrote them down. Not surprisingly, this system allowed wealthy men, landlords, and employers to pressure poorer voters.

The situation changed with the increasing competition between Democratic-Republicans and Federalists.

and in their opposition to these measures Democratic-Republicans played an important role in establishing the principle of a free press. In *An Essay on Liberty of the Press* (1799), the Virginia lawyer George Hay, later appointed to the federal bench by President Jefferson, wrote that "a man may say everything which his passions suggest." Were this not true, he argued, the First Amendment would have been "the grossest absurdity that was ever conceived by the human mind." In his first inaugural address, Jefferson echoed this early champion of the freedom of expression. "Error of opinion may be tolerated," he declared, "where reason is left free to combat it." During Jefferson's presidency the Alien and Sedition Acts, which had justified the suppression of political opinion, were repealed or allowed to expire.

Books, Books, Books

During the post-Revolutionary years there was an enormous outpouring of American publications. In the cities the number of bookstores grew in response to the demand for reading matter. Perhaps even more significant was the appearance in the countryside of numerous book peddlers who supplied farm households with Bibles, gazettes, almanacs, sermons, and political pamphlets. One of them wrote that he found his customers "uninformed, their minds bitter, and their manners savage," but they cried out for "books, books, books!"

Some of the most interesting American books of the postwar years examined the developing American character. The French emigrant Michel-Guillaume Jean de Crevecoeur, in *Letters from an American Farmer* (1782), proposed that the American, a product of many cultures, was a "new man" with ideas new to the world. John Filson, the author of *The Discovery, Settlement, and Present State of Kentucke* (1784), presented the narrative of one such new man, the Kentucky pioneer Daniel Boone. In doing so, he took an important step toward the creation of that most American of literary genres, the western.

But for Americans, the most important "new man" was George Washington. In 1800, an itinerant bookseller, Mason Locke Weems, published a short biography of the first president that became the new nation's first bestseller. Weems's *Life of Washington* introduced a series of popular and completely fabricated anecdotes, including the story of young Washington and the cherry tree. The book was a pioneering effort in mass culture, and Weems, as one historian puts it, was "the father of the Father of his Country." The biography was beloved by ordinary Americans of all political persuasions. Decades later, Abraham Lincoln recalled that he had read Weems "away back in my childhood, the earliest days of my being able to read," and had been profoundly impressed by "the struggles for the liberties of the country." Although Washington had in fact become a partisan leader of the Federalists during his second term, Weems presented him as a unifying

figure for the political culture of the new nation, and that was the way he would be remembered.

Women on the Intellectual Scene

One of the most interesting literary trends of the 1790s was the growing demand for books appealing to women readers. Susanna Haswell Rowson's *Charlotte Temple* (1791) and Hannah Webster Foster's *The Coquette* (1797), tales of seduction and abandonment, ran up tremendous sales and remained in print for much of the next century. The young republic thus marked the first dramatic appearance of women writers and women readers. Although women's literacy rates continued lower than men's, they rose steadily as girls joined boys in common schools. This increase was one of the most important social legacies of the democratic struggles of the Revolutionary era.

Some writers argued that the new republican order ought to provide new roles for women as well as for

Judith Sargent Murray, a portrait by John Singleton Copley, completed in 1771. Born into an elite merchant family in Gloucester, Massachusetts, she became a wife and mother but also a poet, essayist, playwright, novelist, and historian. In 1779 she published an essay on the equality of the sexes that distinguished her as the first avowed feminist in American history.

SOURCE: John Singleton Copley (1738–1815), *Portrait of Mrs. John Stevens (Judith Sargent, later Mrs. John Murray)*, 1770–72. Commissioned on the occasion of her first marriage, at age eighteen. Oil on canvas, 50 × 40 in. Daniel J. Terra Art Acquisition Endowment Fund, 2000.6. © Terra Foundation for American Art, Chicago / Art Resource, New York.

CHRONOLOGY

1786	Shays' Rebellion
	Annapolis Convention
1787	Constitutional Convention
1787–88	*The Federalist Papers* published
1788	Constitution ratified
	First federal elections
1789	President George Washington inaugurated in New York City
	Judiciary Act
	French Revolution begins
1790	Agreement on site on the Potomac River for the nation's capital
	Indian Intercourse Act
	Judith Sargent Murray publishes "On the Equality of the Sexes"
1791	Bill of Rights ratified
	Bank of the United States chartered
	Alexander Hamilton's "Report on Manufactures"
	Ohio Indians defeat General Arthur St. Clair's army
1792	Washington reelected
1793	England and France at war; America reaps trade windfall
	Citizen Genêt affair
	President Washington proclaims American neutrality in Europe
	Supreme Court asserts itself as final authority in *Chisholm* v. *Georgia*
1794	Whiskey Rebellion
	Battle of Fallen Timbers
	Jay's Treaty with the British concluded
1795	Pinckney's Treaty negotiated with the Spanish
	Treaty of Greenville
1796	President Washington's Farewell Address
	John Adams elected president
1797–98	French seize American ships
1798	XYZ Affair
	"Quasi-War" with France
	Alien and Sedition Acts
	Kentucky and Virginia Resolves
1800	Convention of 1800
	Thomas Jefferson elected president
	Mason Locke Weems publishes *Life of Washington*

men. The first avowed feminist in American history was Judith Sargent Murray, who publicly stated her belief that women "should be taught to depend on their own efforts, for the procurement of an establishment in life." She was greatly influenced by the English feminist Mary Wollstonecraft but developed her line of thinking independently. Her essay "On the Equality of the Sexes," written in 1779 and published in 1790, threw down a bold challenge to men. "Yes, ye lordly, ye haughty sex," she wrote, "our souls are by nature equal to yours," and predicted that American women would commence "a new era in female history." Federalists listened to such opinions with horror. "Women of masculine minds," one Boston minister sneered, "have generally masculine manners."

There seemed to be general agreement among all parties, however, that the time had come for women to be better educated. Republican institutions of self-government were widely thought to depend on the wisdom and self-discipline of the American people. Civic virtue, so indispensable for the republic, needed to be taught at home. By placing her learning at the service of her family, the "republican mother" was spared the criticism leveled at independent-minded women such as Murray. "A woman will have more commendation in being the mother of heroes," wrote one Federalist, "than in setting up, Amazon-like, for a heroine herself." Thus were women provided the opportunity to be not simply "helpmates" but also people "learned and wise." But they were also expected to be content with a narrow role, not to wish for fuller participation in the American experiment.

Conclusion

During the last years of the eighteenth century, the United States adopted a new constitution and established a new national government. It repaid the debt run up during the Revolution and made peace with adversaries abroad and Indian peoples at home. Americans began to learn how to channel their disagreements into political struggle. The new government, born in the economic and political crisis that surrounded Shays' Rebellion, had withstood a first decade of stress, but tensions would continue to divide the people. At the beginning of the new century, it remained uncertain whether the new nation would find a way to control and channel the energies of an expanding people.

Review Questions

1. Discuss the conflicting ideals of local and national authority in the debate over the Constitution.

2. What were the major crises faced by the Washington and Adams administrations?

3. Describe the roles of Madison and Hamilton in the formation of the first American political parties.

4. What did Jefferson mean when he talked of "the Revolution of 1800"?

5. Discuss the contributions of the Revolutionary generation to the construction of a national culture.

Recommended Reading

Akhil Reed Amar, *The Bill of Rights: Creation and Reconstruction* (1998). A legal analysis arguing that the first ten amendments were meant to protect the majority from the potential tyranny of the federal government.

Robert A. Dahl, *How Democratic Is the American Constitution?* (2003). An eminent political scientist examines the antidemocratic character of the nation's defining political document.

Stanley Elkins and Eric McKitrick, *The Age of Federalism* (1993). A massive and informative account of the politics of the 1790s, from the ratification of the Constitution to the election of Jefferson.

Paul Finkelman, *Slavery and the Founders: Race and Liberty in the Age of Jefferson* (2001). A persuasive historical argument that the Constitution legitimated a "slave-holders' republic."

Joanne B. Freeman, *Affairs of Honor: National Politics in the New Republic* (2001). A major reassessment of political culture in the new republic, stressing the importance of the culture of honor.

Woody Holton, *Unruly Americans and the Origins of the Constitution* (2007). A colorful introduction to the "unruly" Americans who opposed the adoption of the Constitution and supported the passage of the Bill of Rights.

Reginald Horsman, *The Frontier in the Formative Years, 1783–1815* (1970). A sensitive survey of developments in the West, emphasizing that the "western question" was one of the most important facing the young republic.

Calvin H. Johnson, *Righteous Anger at the Wicked States: The Meaning of the Founders' Constitution* (2005). An argument that the authors of the Constitution were responding to the turmoil of the "wicked states," particularly their economic and fiscal policies.

Simon P. Newman, *Parades and the Politics of the Street: Festive Culture in the Early American Republic* (1997). The participation of ordinary Americans in the political culture of the new republic.

Leonard L. Richards, *Shays' Rebellion: The American Revolution's Final Battle* (2002). A new interpretation that significantly broadens the meaning of the uprising of farmers in western Massachusetts.

James M. Smith, *Freedom's Fetters: The Alien and Sedition Laws and American Civil Liberties* (1966). Remains the best overview of the Federalist threat to liberty, as well as the Democratic-Republican counterattack.

Bernard A. Weisberger, *America Afire: Jefferson, Adams, and the Revolutionary Election of 1800* (2000). Shows that the election and the transfer of power were victories for popular self-government and that they set a major precedent for all other elections.

Gordon Wood, *The Creation of the American Republic, 1776–1787* (1969). This general survey provides the best overview of the Constitutional Convention.

Rosemarie Zagarri, *Revolutionary Backlash: Women and Politics in the Early American Republic* (2007). A path breaking account of the women who participated in the political process during the revolutionary era.

PEARSON myhistorylab Connections

Reinforce what you learned in this chapter by studying the many documents, images, maps, review tools, and videos available at www.myhistorylab.com.

Read and Review

✓ Study and Review **Chapter 8**

Read the Document

The United States Constitution (1789)

James Madison, The Virginia (or Randolph) Plan (1787)

The Debates in the Federal Convention of 1787

The Bill of Rights (1789)

Alexander Hamilton, An Opinion on the Constitutionality of an Act to Establish a Bank (1791)

George Washington, Proclamation Regarding the Whiskey Rebellion (1794)

The Alien and Sedition Acts (1798)

James Madison Defends the Constitution (1788)

Patrick Henry against Ratification of the Constitution (1788)

A Free African American Petitions the Government for Emancipation of All Slaves (1777)

See the Map *The Ratification of the Constitution, 1787–90*

Research and Explore

Read the Document

Are you an Anti-Federalist?

Exploring America: The Partisan Press

Exploring America: Ratification of the Constitution

Profiles
Matthew Lyon
Charles Wilson
Peale

History Bookshelf: Alexander Hamilton, John Jay, and James Madison, The Federalist Papers *(1787–1788)*

Watch the Video *Slavery and the Constitution*

((•— Hear the Audio

Hear the audio files for Chapter 8 at
www.myhistorylab.com.

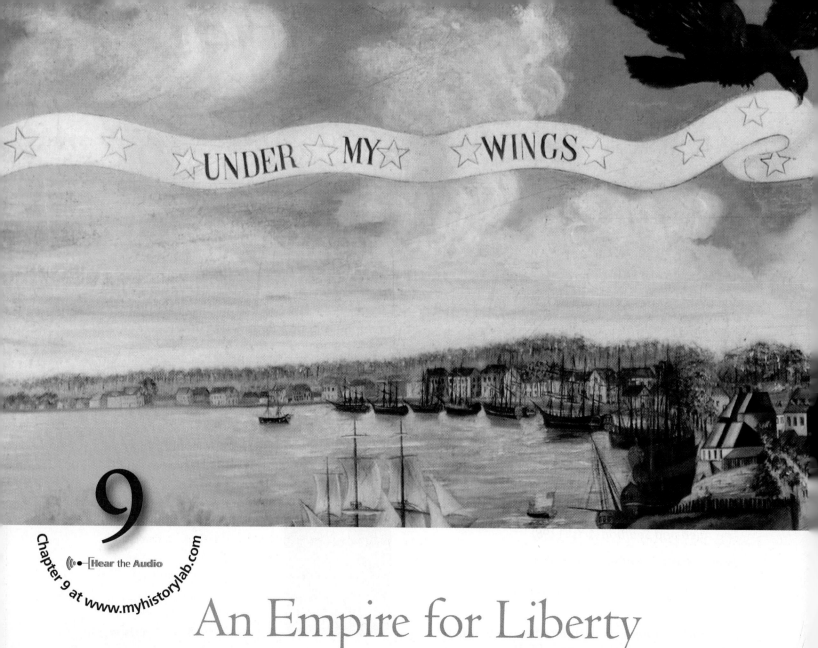

UNDER ☆ MY ☆ WINGS

Chapter 9 at www.myhistorylab.com

((•—Hear the Audio

An Empire for Liberty
1790–1824

CHAPTER OUTLINE

EVERY ☆ ☆THING☆ ☆ ☆ ☆ PROSPERS☆ ☆

A View of New Orleans, November 1803 by Boqueto de Woiserie. An eagle carrying a banner flies over the booming coastal town of New Orleans, Louisiana. Oil on canvas. Chicago Historical Museum.

Expansion Touches Mandan Villages on the Upper Missouri

In mid-October 1804, news arrived at the Mandan villages, prominently situated on bluffs overlooking the upper Missouri River, that an American military party led by Meriwether Lewis and William Clark was coming up the river. The principal chiefs, hoping for expanded trade and support against their enemies the Sioux, welcomed these first American visitors. As the expedition's three boats and forty-three men approached the village, Clark wrote, "great numbers on both sides flocked down to the bank to view us." That evening, the Mandans welcomed the Americans with an enthusiastic dance and gifts of food.

Since the fourteenth century, when they had migrated from the East, the Mandans had lived along the Missouri, on the edge of the Great Plains in what is now North Dakota. They believed their homeland was "the very center of the world," and indeed it is in the heart of the North American continent. Mandan men hunted buffalo and Mandan women kept storage pits full with abundant crops of corn, beans, squash, sunflowers, and tobacco grown on the fertile soil of the river bottomlands. The Mandan villages were also the central marketplace of the northern Plains; at trading time in late summer they filled with Crows, Assiniboins, Cheyennes, Kiowas, and Arapahoes. Well

AMERICAN Communities

219

before any of these people, or those of other tribes, had met a European, they were trading in kettles, knives, and guns acquired from the French and English to the east, and leatherwork, glassware, and horses acquired from the Spanish in the Southwest.

The eighteenth century had been a golden age for the Mandan, who with their closely related Hidatsa neighbors numbered about 3,000 in 1804. In each of their five villages, earth lodges surrounded a central plaza. One large ceremonial lodge was used for community gatherings, and each of the other earth lodges was home to a senior woman, her husband, her sisters (perhaps married to the same man as she, for the Mandans practiced polygamy), their daughters and their unmarried sons, along with numerous grandchildren. Matrilineal clans, the principal institution of the community, distributed food to the sick, adopted orphans, cared for the dependent elderly, and punished wrongdoers. A village council of male clan leaders selected chiefs who led by consensus and lost power when people no longer accepted their opinions.

Lewis and Clark had been sent by President Thomas Jefferson to survey the Louisiana Purchase and to find an overland route to the Pacific Ocean. They were also instructed to inform the Indians that they

Watch the Video
Lewis and Clark: What Were They Trying to Accomplish? at **www.myhistorylab.com**

now owed loyalty—and trade—to the American government, thereby challenging British economic control over the lucrative North American fur trade. Meeting with the village chiefs, the Americans offered the Mandans a military and economic alliance. His people would like nothing better, responded Chief Black Cat, for the Mandans had fallen on hard times over the past decade. [Some twenty years earlier], "the smallpox destroyed the greater part of the nation," the chief said. "All the nations before this malady [were] afraid of them, [but] after they were reduced, the Sioux and other Indians waged war, and killed a great many." Black Cat was skeptical that the Americans would deter the Sioux, but Clark reassured him. "We were ready to protect them," Clark reported in his journal, "and kill those who would not listen to our good talk."

The Americans spent the winter with the Mandans, joining in their communal life and establishing firm and friendly relations with them. There were dances and joint hunting parties, frequent visits to the earth lodges, long talks around the fire, and, for many of the men,

pleasant nights in the company of Mandan women. Lewis and Clark spent many hours acquiring important geographic information from the Mandans, who drew charts and maps showing the course of the Missouri, the ranges of the Rocky Mountains, and places where one could cross the Continental Divide. The information provided by the Mandans and other Indian peoples to the west was vital to the success of the expedition. Lewis and Clark's "voyage of discovery" depended largely on the willingness of Indian peoples to share their knowledge of the land with the Americans.

In need of interpreters who could help them communicate with other Indian communities on their way, the Americans hired several multilingual Frenchmen who lived with the Mandans. They also acquired the services of Sacajawea, the fifteen-year-old Lemhi Shoshone wife of one of the Frenchmen, who became the only woman to join the westward journey. The presence of Sacajawea and her baby son was a signal, as Clark noted, to "all the Indians as to our friendly intentions"; everyone knew that women and children did not go on war parties.

Read the Document
Thomas Jefferson to Meriweather Lewis (1803) at **www.myhistorylab.com**

When the party left the Mandan villages in March, Clark wrote, his men were "generally healthy, except venereal complaints which is very common amongst the natives and the men catch it from them." After an arduous journey across the Rockies, the party reached the Pacific Ocean at the mouth of the Columbia River, where they spent the winter. Overdue and feared lost, they returned in triumph to St. Louis in September 1806. Before long the Americans had established Fort Clark at the Mandan villages, giving American traders a base for challenging British dominance of the western fur trade. The permanent American presence brought increased contact, and with it much more disease. In 1837, a terrible smallpox epidemic carried away the vast majority of the Mandans, reducing the population to fewer than 150. Four Bears, a Mandan chief who had been a child at the time of the Lewis and Clark visit, spoke these last words to the remnants of his people:

"I have loved the whites," he declared. "I have lived with them ever since I was a boy." But in return for the kindness of the Mandans, the Americans had brought this plague. "I do not fear death, my friends," he said, "but to die with my face rotten, that even the wolves will shrink with horror at seeing me, and say to themselves, that is Four Bears, the friend of the whites. They

1. Where did the new nation find economic opportunities in the world market?

2. How did President Jefferson calm the political hostilities of the 1790s?

3. What values were embodied in republican agrarianism?

4. What unresolved issues between the United States and Britain led to the War of 1812?

5. What were the causes of Indian resistance and how did the War of 1812 resolve them?

6. How did the Missouri Compromise reveal the dangers of expansion?

FOCUS Questions

1790–1824

have deceived me," he pronounced with his last breath. "Those that I always considered as brothers turned out to be my worst enemies."

In sending Lewis and Clark on their "voyage of discovery" to claim the land and the loyalty of the Mandans and other western Indian communities, President Jefferson was motivated by his vision of an expanding American republic of self-sufficient farmers. During his and succeeding presidencies, expansion became a key element of national policy and pride. Yet, as the experience of the Mandans showed, what Jefferson viewed as enlargement of "the empire for liberty" had a dark side—the destruction, from

Mandan Villages

disease and coerced displacement, of the communities created by America's first peoples.

In the first quarter of the nineteenth century, the young American nation was preoccupied with defining its place on the North American continent and in the larger world of independent nations. At the same time that America found opportunities in world trade and in territorial expansion, it encountered international opposition from Britain and resistance at home from hard-pressed Indian nations. This chapter describes the ways in which, through war and diplomacy, the United States defined and controlled the nation's expanded boundaries, a vital step in building a sense of national identity and community.

AMERICAN Communities

North American Communities From Coast to Coast

In spite of the political turmoil of the 1790s, the young United States entered the new century full of national pride and energy. But the larger issue, America's place in the world, was still uncertain, beginning with its situation on the North American continent (see Map 9.1).

The New Nation

The United States of America in 1800 seemed much like it had been before the American Revolution: a loosely-connected group of scattered states clinging to the Atlantic seaboard. Two-thirds of the young nation's people still lived within fifty miles of the Atlantic coast. From New

Hampshire to Georgia, most people lived on farms or in small towns. Because they rarely traveled far from home, peoples' horizons were limited and local. The exception was the Atlantic seaports which looked outward to the world. Although only 3 percent of the nation's population lived in cities, the Atlantic ports continued to dominate the nation economically and politically. In 1800, the nation's most important urban centers were all Atlantic seaports: Charleston (population 20,000), Baltimore (26,000), Philadelphia (70,000), New York (60,000), and Boston (25,000).

Nevertheless, the new nation was already transforming itself: between 1790 and 1800, according to the first and second federal censuses, the American population grew from 3.9 million to 5.3 million. Growth by migration was greatest in the trans-Appalachian West, a region

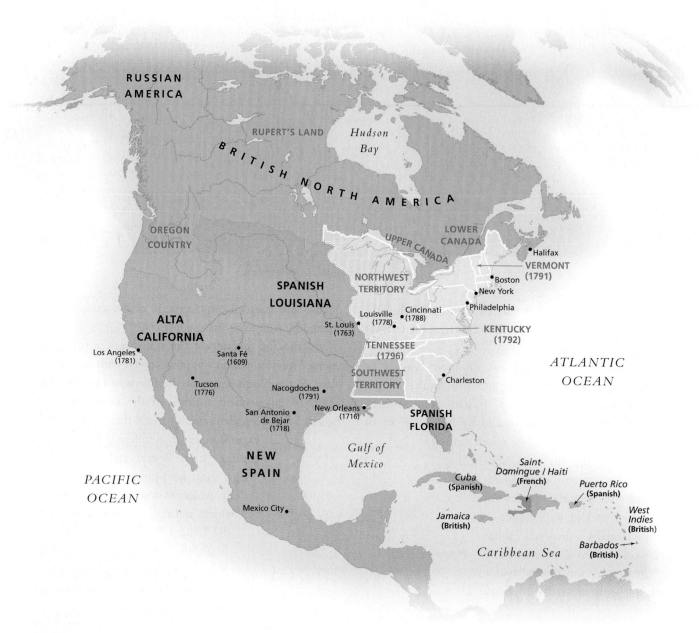

MAP 9.1 North America in 1800 In 1800, the new United States of America shared the North American continent with territories held by the European powers: British Canada, French Louisiana (secretly ceded that year to France by Spain), Spanish Florida, Spanish Mexico, and Russian Alaska, expanding southward along the Pacific Coast. Few people could have imagined that by 1850, the United States would span the continent. But the American settlers who had crossed the Appalachians to the Ohio River Valley were already convinced that opportunity lay in the West.

that was already home to approximately 100,000 Indians. Soon, expansion was to transform the nation, but in 1800 the United States of America was a new and weak country sharing a continent with the potentially hostile colonies of most of the world's great powers. To the immediate north was the continuing presence of the British in what is now Canada and the growing Russian presence in Alaska. To the west and south loomed the

Spanish empire, while closer still was the nearby racial powder keg in the Caribbean.

To the North: British North America and Russian America

Although Britain had lost its war to keep the American colonies, it kept a firm grasp on British North America, which had once been French Canada (see Chapter 6). In

1800, its heart remained the former French colony of Quebec (at that time called Lower Canada). Most of the rest of the settlers elsewhere were American, many of them Loyalists driven out at the time of the Revolution. They were clustered in the Maritime Provinces, dominated by Nova Scotia's great port, Halifax, with a scattering in Upper Canada, the first inland colony north of the Great Lakes, established in 1791. Farther west (and closed to settlement) lay Rupert's Land, administered by the Hudson's Bay Company.

British North America dominated the continental fur trade and the great succession of waterways—the St. Lawrence River, the Great Lakes, and the rivers beyond—that made it possible. Britain was on friendly terms with many of the native peoples north and south of the border who were part of the fur trade. This economic grip was a challenge and frustration to many westward-moving Americans. At the same time, the dispersed nature of the Canadian colonies made them, at least in the eyes of some Americans, ripe for conquest.

Russian settlement of what is now Alaska posed another potential threat to the United States. Alaska was an extension of the Russian conquest of Siberia, which was driven by the fur trade as well. In 1741, the Danish-born naval officer Vitus Bering, sailing for Russia, ventured east from Kamchatka across the sea that now bears his name and made landfall on the southern coast of Alaska. By the 1750s, Russian and Siberian fur trappers, known as *promyshleniki*, were shipping a steady supply of furs from Russian America.

The Russians sometimes took furs by force, holding whole villages hostage and brutalizing the native Inuit and Aleut peoples. After the Aleut Revolt of 1766, the Russian authorities promised to end the abuse, but by 1800, the precontact population of 25,000 Aleuts had been greatly reduced. At the same time, sexual relations and intermarriage between fur trappers and Aleut women created a large group of Russian creoles who assumed an increasingly prominent position in the Alaskan fur trade as navigators, explorers, clerks, and traders.

The Russian-American Company, chartered by the tsar in 1799, set up American headquarters in Sitka, in what is now the southeastern panhandle of Alaska, only to have their first fortress destroyed in the Tlingit Revolt of 1802. The Russians reestablished Sitka by force in 1804, and over the next generation, they reached south along the Pacific Coast, cooperating with the Spanish in California at Fort Ross and also with Hudson's Bay officials at Fort Vancouver in Oregon Country.

To the West and South: The Spanish Empire, Haiti, and the Caribbean

Spain posed the greatest threat to the United States because it possessed most of North and South America. Mexico City, with a population of 200,000, was by far the largest and most elegant city on the continent. But Spanish control crumbled rapidly in the 1790s. Tensions mounted between the Spanish-born *peninsulares* high officials and bureaucrats, and the native-born *criollos* of Spanish descent, who chafed at their subordination, especially after the success of the American Revolution. In the 1790s, there were two abortive criollo conspiracies on behalf of independence in Mexico City alone. Furthermore, none of New Spain's northern provinces, created to protect Mexico's fabulously wealthy silver mines, thrived. In all of the older settlements—San Antonio, Santa Fé, and Tucson—only a handful of persons of Spanish descent lived among a preponderantly native population. This was true even in the most recently founded northern province, Alta (Upper) California.

In 1769, in their last effort to protect their rich colony of Mexico, the Spanish established a chain of twenty-one missions in Alta California that stretched north from San Diego (1769) to Sonoma (1823). Despite Spain's desire to seal its territory from commerce with other nations, a brisk but illegal trade in otter skins, hides, and tallow developed between the United States and California after the first American ship, the *Lelia Bird*, arrived in 1803.

This view shows Sitka, the center of Russian activities in Alaska, in 1827. Russian architectural styles and building techniques are apparent in the Church of St. Michael the Archangel in the right background, contrasting with the Asian and Indian origins of most of Sitka's inhabitants.

American traders were making inroads on Spanish-held territory along the Mississippi River as well. New Orleans, acquired by Spain from France at the end of the Seven Years' War in 1763, was becoming a thriving international port. In 1801, it shipped more than $3 million worth of tobacco, sugar, rice, cotton, fruits, and vegetables to Europe. Every year, a greater proportion of products for the New Orleans trade was supplied by Americans living some distance up the Mississippi River. Pinckney's 1795 treaty with Spain guaranteed Americans free navigation of the Mississippi River and the right to deposit goods at the port of New Orleans. Nevertheless, Americans were uncomfortably aware that the city's crucial location at the mouth of the Mississippi meant that whatever foreign nation possessed New Orleans had the power to choke off the flourishing trade in the vast Mississippi Valley river system.

More than 600 miles north was the small trading town of St. Louis, founded by the New Orleans trader Pierre Laclède in 1763. By 1800, the town had fewer than a thousand residents, three-quarters of whom were involved in the Indian trade of the Missouri River. Spanish officials tried to supervise that trade from their offices in the town, but real control rested in the hands of the Laclèdes and other French traders. Americans visiting this

shabby little place laughed at Pierre Laclède's prediction that St. Louis would become "one of the finest cities in America," but he was right.

The Caribbean posed a racial challenge to the United States. The rich sugar-producing islands, variously colonies of Spain (Cuba, Puerto Rico, and Santo Domingo), France (Martinique, Guadaloupe, and Saint-Domingue), and Britain (Barbados, Jamaica, and a number of smaller islands), provided 80 to 90 percent of the European supply of sugar. All the sugar plantations used enslaved Africans as the labor force. Thus, they shared with the slaveholding American South a distinctive Afro–North American society that cut across national boundaries. This world was jolted in 1791 by the revolt of black slaves in Saint-Domingue, France's richest colony. Under the leadership of Toussaint L'Ouverture, the former colony, renamed Haiti, became North America's first independent black nation. Its existence struck fear into the hearts of white slave owners at the same time that it served as a beacon of hope to the enslaved.

Trans-Appalachia

Within the United States itself, the region of greatest growth was territory west of the Appalachian Mountains, and it was this area that was most affected by fears of

The launching of a ship from Becket's Shipyard in Essex, Massachusetts, in 1802. Shipbuilding was a major New England industry and, as this picture shows, a launching was a community event.

continuing British influence on Indian peoples. By 1800, about 500,000 people (the vast majority from Virginia and North Carolina) had found rich and fertile land along the Ohio River system. Soon there was enough population for statehood. Kentucky (1792) and Tennessee (1796) were the first trans-Appalachian states admitted to the Union.

Cincinnati, strategically situated 450 miles downstream from Pittsburgh, was a particularly dramatic example of the rapid community growth and development that characterized the trans-Appalachian region. Founded in 1788, Cincinnati began life as a military fort, defending settlers in the fertile Miami River Valley of Ohio from resistance by Shawnee and Miami Indians. Conflict between these Indian peoples and the new settlers was so fierce that the district was grimly referred to as "the slaughterhouse." After the battle of Fallen Timbers broke Indian resistance in 1794, Cincinnati became the point of departure for immigrants arriving by the Ohio River on their way to settle the interior of the Old Northwest: Ohio, Indiana, and Illinois. In 1800, Cincinnati had a population of about 750 people. By 1810, it had tripled in size, confirming its boast to be "the Queen City of the West."

Cincinnati merchants were soon shipping farm goods from the fertile Miami Valley down the Ohio–Mississippi River system to New Orleans, 1,500 miles away. River hazards like snags and sandbars made the downriver trip by barge or keelboat hazardous, and the return trip upriver was slow, more than three months from New Orleans to Cincinnati. Frequently, river men simply abandoned their flatboats in New Orleans and traveled home overland, on foot or horseback, by the long and dangerous Natchez Trace, an old Indian trail that linked Natchez on the Mississippi with Nashville, Tennessee. Nevertheless, river traffic increased yearly, and control of New Orleans became a key concern of western farmers and merchants. If New Orleans refused to accept American goods, Cincinnati merchants and many thousands of trans-Appalachian farmers would be ruined.

A National Economy

Concern about New Orleans illustrates the new nation's weak position in international trade. In 1800, the United States was a producer of raw materials. It faced the same challenge that developing nations confront today. At the mercy of fluctuating world commodity prices they cannot control, such countries have great difficulty protecting themselves from economic dominance by stronger, more established nations.

Cotton and the Economy of the Young Republic

In 1800, the United States was predominantly rural and agricultural. According to the census, 94 of 100 Americans lived in communities of fewer than 2,500 people, and four of five families farmed the land. Farming families followed centuries-old traditions of working with hand tools and draft animals, producing most of their own food and fiber. Crops were grown for subsistence (home use) rather than for sale. Commodities such as whiskey and hogs (both easy to transport) provided small and irregular cash incomes or items for barter. As late as 1820, only 20 percent of the produce of American farms was consumed outside the local community.

The situation was different in the South, where plantation agriculture based on enslaved African workers was both commercial and international. The demand for cotton was growing rapidly in response to the boom in the industrial production of textiles in England and Europe, but extracting the seeds from the fibers of the variety of cotton that grew best in the southern interior required an enormous investment of labor. The cotton gin, which mechanized this process, was invented in 1793; soon cotton, and the slave labor system that produced it, assumed a commanding place in southern life and in the foreign trade of the United States. The essential contribution of cotton to the nation's economy was the most important social and political reality of the early nineteenth century.

In 1790, however, increasing foreign demand for American goods and services hardly seemed likely. Britain, still the biggest customer for American raw materials, no longer gave its former colony preferential tariffs, with the result that trade between the two countries diminished. Britain and France both excluded Americans from their lucrative West Indian trade and taxed American ships with discriminatory duties. It was difficult to be independent in a world dominated by great powers.

Neutral Shipping in a World at War

Despite these restrictions on American commerce, the strong shipping trade begun during the colonial era and centered in the Atlantic ports became a major asset in the 1790s, when events in Europe provided America with extraordinary opportunities. The French Revolution, which began in 1789, initiated nearly twenty-five years of warfare between Britain and France. All along the Atlantic seaboard, urban centers thrived as American ships carried European goods that could no longer be transported on British ships without danger of French attack (and vice versa). Because America was neutral, its merchants had the legal right to import European goods and promptly reexport them to other European countries. In spite of British and French efforts to prevent the practice (see Chapter 8), reexports amounted to half of the profits in the booming shipping trade (see Figure 9.1).

The vigorous international shipping trade had dramatic effects within the United States. The active American participation in international trade fostered a strong and diversified shipbuilding industry. All the

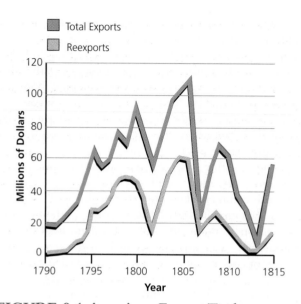

FIGURE 9.1 American Export Trade, 1790–1815 This graph shows how completely the American shipping boom was tied to European events. Exports, half of which were reexports, surged when Britain and France were at war and America could take advantage of its neutral status. Exports slumped in the brief period of European peace from 1803 to 1805 and plunged following the Embargo Act of 1807 and the outbreak of the War of 1812.

major Atlantic ports boasted expanding shipbuilding enterprises. The coastal cities all grew substantially from 1790 to 1820. This rapid urbanization was a sign of real economic growth (rather than a sign that poverty was pushing rural workers off the farms, as occurs in some developing countries today), for it reflected expanding opportunities in the cities. In fact, the rapid growth of cities stimulated farmers to produce the food to feed the new urban dwellers.

The long series of European wars also allowed enterprising Americans to seize such lucrative international opportunities as the China trade. In 1784, the *Empress of China* set sail from New York for Canton with forty tons of ginseng. When it returned in 1785 with a cargo of teas, silks, and chinaware, the sponsors of the voyage made a 30 percent profit. Other merchants were quick to follow. In 1787, Robert Gray left Boston in the *Columbia*, sailing south around Cape Horn, then north to the Pacific Northwest, where he bought sea otter skins (the same that the Russians sought in Alaska) cheaply from the coastal Indians. Then Gray sailed west across the Pacific to China, where he sold the furs at fabulous profits before rounding the Cape of Good Hope and returning to Boston laden with tea. In his second voyage in 1792, Gray discovered the mouth of a major Northwest river, which he named for his ship. (When Lewis and Clark ventured west in 1804, part of their task was to

chart the exact path of Gray's "Columbia's River.") Soon New England so dominated the seaborne trade in furs to China that the Pacific Northwest Indians called all Americans "Bostons."

The Jefferson Presidency

At noon on March 4, 1801, Thomas Jefferson walked from his modest boardinghouse through the swampy streets of the new federal city of Washington to the unfinished Capitol. George Washington and John Adams had ridden in decorated carriages to their inaugurals. Jefferson, although accepting a military honor guard, demonstrated by his actions that he rejected the elaborate, quasi-monarchical style of the two Federalist presidents and (to his mind) their autocratic style of government as well.

For all its lack of pretension, Jefferson's inauguration as the third president of the United States was a momentous occasion in American history, for it marked the peaceful transition from one political party, the Federalists, to their hated rivals, the Jeffersonian Republicans. Beginning in an atmosphere of exceptional political bitterness, Jefferson's presidency was to demonstrate that a strongly led party system could shape national policy without leading either to dictatorship or to revolt. Jefferson's own hope for moderation may have been the crucial factor. Trying to overcome the bitter political disagreements of the 1790s, Jefferson set a tone of conciliation in his inaugural address, announcing, "We are all republicans; we are all federalists" and during his eight years in office he paid close attention to ways to attract moderate Federalists to the Jeffersonian Republican party.

Read the Document
Margaret Bayard Smith, Reflections upon Meeting Jefferson (1809) at **www.myhistorylab.com**

Republican Agrarianism

Jefferson brought to the presidency a clearly defined political philosophy. Behind all the events of his administration (1801–09) and those of his successors, in what became known as the Virginia Dynasty (James Madison, 1809–17; James Monroe, 1817–25), was a clear set of beliefs that embodied Jefferson's interpretation of the meaning of republicanism for Americans.

Jefferson's years as ambassador to France in the 1780s were particularly important in shaping his political thinking. Recoiling from the extremes of wealth and poverty he saw there, he came to believe that it was impossible for Europe to achieve a just society that could guarantee to most of its members the "life, liberty and . . . pursuit of happiness" of which he had written in the Declaration of Independence. Only America, he believed, provided fertile earth for the true citizenship necessary to a republican form of government. What America had, and Europe lacked, was room to grow.

Jefferson's thinking about growth was directly influenced by Englishman Thomas Malthus's deeply pessimistic

Tall, ungainly, and diffident in manner, Thomas Jefferson was nonetheless a man of genius: an architect, naturalist, philosopher, and politician. His political philosophy, republican agrarianism, exemplified Jefferson's hopes for America in the efforts of the ordinary farmer. As he said, "those who labor in the earth are the chosen people of God."

and widely influential *Essay on the Principle of Population*, published in 1798. Warning of an impending population explosion, Malthus predicted that unless population growth was checked, misery and poverty would soon be widespread throughout Europe and even, Malthus warned, in America. His prediction alarmed many Americans, who had taken pride in having one of the fastest rates of population growth in the world, close to 40 percent per decade. Thomas Jefferson was not worried. He used Malthus to underline the opportunity created by America's vast land resources. The Malthusian prediction need not trouble the United States, Jefferson said, as long as the country kept expanding.

Jefferson envisaged a nation of small family farms clustered together in rural communities—an agrarian republic. He believed that only a nation of roughly equal yeoman farmers, each secure in his own possessions and not dependent on someone else for his livelihood, would exhibit the concern for the community good that was essential in a republic. Indeed, Jefferson said that "those who labor in the earth are the chosen people of God," and so he viewed himself, though his "farm" was the large slave-owning plantation of Monticello.

Jefferson's vision of an expanding agrarian republic remains to this day one of our most compelling ideas about America's uniqueness and special destiny. But expansionism contained some negative aspects. The lure of the western lands fostered constant mobility and dissatisfaction rather than the stable, settled communities Jefferson envisaged. Expansionism caused environmental damage, in particular soil exhaustion—a consequence of abandoning old lands, rather than conserving them, and moving on to new ones. Expansionism encouraged the spread of plantations based on slave labor in the South (see Chapter 10). Finally, it bred a ruthlessness toward Indian peoples, who were pushed out of the way for white settlement or who, like the Mandans, were devastated by the diseases that accompanied European trade and contact. Jefferson's agrarianism thus bred some of the best and some of the worst traits of the developing nation.

Jefferson's Government

Thomas Jefferson came to office determined to reverse the Federalist policies of the 1790s and to ensure an agrarian "republic of virtue." Accordingly, he proposed a program of "simplicity and frugality," promising to cut all internal taxes, to reduce the size of the army (from 4,000 to 2,500 men), the navy (from twenty-five ships to seven), and the government staff, and to eliminate the entire national debt inherited from the Federalists. He kept all of these promises, even the last, although the Louisiana Purchase of 1803 cost the Treasury $15 million. This diminishment of government was a key matter of republican principle to Jefferson. If his ideal yeoman farmer was to be a truly self-governing citizen, the federal government must not, Jefferson believed, be either large or powerful. His cost-cutting measures simply carried out the pledge he had made in his inaugural address for "a wise and frugal government, which shall restrain men from injuring one another, [and] shall leave them otherwise free to regulate their own pursuits."

Perhaps one reason for Jefferson's success was that the federal government he headed was small and unimportant by today's standards. For instance, Jefferson found only 130 federal officials in Washington (a grand total of nine in the State Department, including the secretary of state). The national government's main service to ordinary people was mail delivery, and already in 1800 there were persistent complaints about the slowness, unreliability, and expense of the Postal Service! Everything else—law and order, education, welfare, road maintenance, economic control—rested with state or local governments. Power and political loyalty were still local, not national.

This small national government also explains why for years the nation's capital was so unimpressive. The French designer Pierre L'Enfant had laid out a magnificent plan of broad streets and sweeping vistas reminiscent of Paris.

This 1800 watercolor by William Russell Birch shows the original Capitol building. This simple rectangular structure is a far cry from the imposing domed structure we recognize today, yet it was typical of the modest beginnings of the nation's capital city.

Congress had planned to pay for the grand buildings with money from land sales in the new city, but few people besides politicians and boardinghouse keepers (a largely female occupation) chose to live in Washington. Construction lagged: the President's House lacked a staircase to the second floor until 1808, and although the House and Senate chambers were soon completed, the central portion of the Capitol was missing. Instead of the imposing dome we know so well today, the early Capitol consisted of first one white box and later two white marble boxes connected by a boardwalk. It is a telling indicator of the true location of national power that a people who had no trouble building new local communities across the continent should have had such difficulty establishing their federal city.

An Independent Judiciary

Although determined to reverse Federalist fiscal policies, Jefferson was much more moderate concerning Federalist officeholders. He resisted demands by other Jeffersonian

Republicans that "the board should be swept" and all Federalist officeholders replaced with party loyalists. During his term of office, Jefferson allowed 132 Federalists to remain at their posts, while placing Jeffersonian Republicans in 158 other posts. Jefferson's restraint, however, did not extend to the most notorious Federalist appointees, the so-called midnight judges.

In the last days of the Adams administration, the Federalist-dominated Congress passed several acts that created new judgeships and other positions within the federal judiciary. Jeffersonian Republicans feared that the losing Federalist Party was trying to politicize the judiciary by appointing Federalists who would use their positions to strengthen the powers of the federal government, a policy the Jeffersonians opposed. In one of his last acts in office, President Adams appointed Federalists—quickly dubbed the "midnight judges"—to these new positions. William Marbury, whom President Adams had appointed justice of the peace for Washington, DC, and three other appointees sued James Madison, Jefferson's secretary of state, to receive their commissions for their offices. Before the case came to trial, however, Congress, controlled by Jeffersonian Republicans, repealed the acts. This case, *Marbury* v. *Madison*, provoked a landmark decision from the U.S. Supreme Court.

At issue was a fundamental constitutional point: Was the judiciary independent of politics? In his celebrated 1803 decision in *Marbury* v. *Madison*, Chief Justice John Marshall, himself a strong Federalist and an Adams appointee, managed to find a way to please both parties. Marshall ruled that Marbury was entitled to his commis-

●●●┌Read the **Document**

Supreme Court Retains Right to Overrule Legislation (1803) at **www.myhistorylab.com**

sion but that the Supreme Court did not have the power to force the executive branch to give it to him. At first glance, Jefferson's government appeared to have won the

battle. But in the long run, Marshall established the principle that only the federal judiciary could "say what the law is," thus unequivocally defending the independence of the judiciary and the principle of judicial review. This was a vital step in realizing the three-way balance of power among the branches of the federal government—executive (president), legislative (Congress), and judiciary (courts)—envisaged in the Constitution. Equally important, during his long tenure in office (1801–35), Chief Justice Marshall consistently led the Supreme Court in a series of decisions that favored the federal government over state governments (see Chapter 12). Under Marshall's direction, the Supreme Court became a powerful nationalizing force, often to the dismay of defenders of states' rights, Jefferson's Republicans among them.

Opportunity: The Louisiana Purchase

In 1800, the United States was a new and fragile democracy in a world dominated by two contending great powers: Britain and France, who were almost continuously at war from 1789 (the French Revolution) until 1815, when Napoleon Bonaparte was defeated at the battle of Waterloo. Jefferson, who had once ardently supported the goals of the French Revolution, viewed Napoleon's ambitions with increasing apprehension. He feared a resumption of the political animosity of the 1790s, when Federalists and Jeffersonian Republicans had so bitterly disagreed on policy toward France (see Chapter 8).

In his planning for battles with the British, Napoleon looked at the Caribbean, where he planned to reconquer Haiti, the world's first independent black nation, reenslave its people, and use the rich profits from sugar to finance his European wars. As a first step, in 1800, France secretly reacquired the Louisiana Territory, the vast western drainage of the Mississippi and Missouri Rivers, from Spain, which held the region since 1763. Napoleon planned to use Louisiana to grow food for sugar-producing Haiti, to counterbalance the British in Canada, and to check any American expansion that might threaten Spain's North

American colonies. In 1802, he launched the plan by sending an army of 30,000 to reconquer Haiti.

In 1801, when President Jefferson first learned of the French–Spanish secret agreement about Louisiana, he was concerned about the threat to American commerce on the Mississippi River. In fact, in 1802, the Spanish commander at New Orleans (the French had not yet taken formal control) closed the port to American shippers, thus disrupting commerce as far away as Cincinnati. As Jefferson feared, Federalists in Congress clamored for military action to reopen the port. Jefferson was willing to fight for American commerce.as he showed in 1801, when to protect American shipping in the Mediterranean, he refused to continue to pay tribute to the Barbary pirates and authorized a naval blockade and raids on Tripoli in North Africa. The so-called First Barbary War continued until 1805, when Tripoli sued for peace. In the case of New Orleans, however, Jefferson first tried diplomacy, with spectacular results.

In the summer of 1802, Jefferson instructed Robert Livingston, the American ambassador to France, to try to buy New Orleans and the surrounding area for $2 million (or up to $10 million, if necessary). The initial bargaining went badly, but suddenly, in early 1803, Napoleon was ready to sell. His army of 30,000 men had been forced to withdraw from Haiti, defeated by yellow fever and by an army of former slaves led by Toussaint L'Ouverture. In need of money for European military campaigns, Napoleon suddenly offered the entire Louisiana Territory, including the crucial port of New Orleans, to the Americans for $15 million. In an age when it took at least two months for messages to cross the Atlantic, special American envoy James Monroe and Ambassador Livingston could not wait to consult Jefferson. They seized the opportunity: they bought the entire Louisiana Territory from Napoleon in Paris in April 1803. President Jefferson first learned the news two months later, on July 3, the eve of Independence Day. Overnight, the size of the United States more than doubled. It was the largest peaceful acquisition of territory in U.S. history.

At home, Jefferson suffered brief qualms. The Constitution did not authorize the president to purchase territory, and Jefferson had always rigidly insisted on a limited interpretation of executive rights. Spain was certain to be upset, and no one quite knew where the boundaries of Louisiana were. But Jefferson had long held a sense of destiny about the West and had planned the Lewis and Clark expedition before the Louisiana Purchase was a reality. In any case, the prize was too rich to pass up. Jefferson now argued that Louisiana was vital to the nation's republican future. "By enlarging the empire of liberty," Jefferson wrote, "we . . . provide new sources of renovation, should its principles, at any time, degenerate, in those portions of our country which gave them birth." In other words, expansion was essential to liberty. But for African American slaves and Native Americans, the Louisiana Purchase simply increased the

◉ See the Map
Louisiana Purchase at
www.myhistorylab.com

scope of their enslavement and destruction. By 1850, four of the six states in the Louisiana Purchase had entered the Union as slave states (see Chapter 10), and Indian Territory, envisaged by Jefferson as a distant refuge for beleaguered eastern Indian peoples, was surrounded by new settlements (see Chapter 15). No matter how noble Jefferson's rhetoric, neither African Americans nor American Indians shared in his "empire of liberty" (see Map 9.2).

Incorporating Louisiana

The immediate issue following the Louisiana Purchase was how to treat the French and Spanish inhabitants of the Louisiana Territory. Many politicians thought the only way

to deal with a population so "foreign" was to wipe out its customs and laws and to impose American ones as quickly as possible. But this could not happen, because the treaty with France that sealed the purchase specifically stated:

> The inhabitants of Louisiana shall be incorporated in the union of the United States…[with] the enjoyment of all the rights, advantages and immunities of citizens of the United States; and in the mean time they shall be maintained and protected in the free enjoyment of their liberty, property, and the religion which they profess.

In 1803, when the region that is now the state of Louisiana became American property, it had a racially

MAP 9.2 Louisiana Purchase The Louisiana Purchase of 1803, the largest peaceful acquisition of territory in U.S. history, more than doubled the size of the nation. The Lewis and Clark expedition (1804–06) was the first to survey and document the natural and human richness of the area. The American sense of expansiveness and continental destiny owes much to the extraordinary opportunity provided by the Louisiana Purchase.

and ethnically diverse population of 43,000 people, of whom only 6,000 were American. French and French-speaking people were numerically and culturally dominant, especially in the city of New Orleans. The city itself was, in the words of one American, "a veritable tower of Babel." In a population of about 8,000, in addition to the French, there were Germans, Spanish, Irish, Americans and native born Creoles (persons of French descent). Two-thirds of the non-white half of the population were slaves, while the remainder were "free persons of color," who under French law enjoyed legal rights equal to those of white people, and there was a sizable number of Indians as well. The incorporation of Louisiana into the American federal system thus posed a novel challenge to the many different communities involved, with differing results.

The U.S. representative in New Orleans and governor of Lower Louisiana Territory, William Claiborne, slowly learned how to negotiate with the French and Creole elite. With Claiborne's full support, Louisiana adopted a legal code in 1808 that was based on French civil law rather than English common law. This was not a small concession. French law differed from English law in many fundamental respects, such as in family property (communal versus male ownership), in inheritance (forced heirship versus free disposal), and even in contracts, which were much more strictly regulated in the French system. Remnants of the French legal system remain part of Louisiana state law to this day. The losers in the process were the free people of color whose legal rights were curtailed, and the Caddo Indians, in particular, who struggled to maintain the region known as the Neutral Ground on the Texas–Louisiana border.

Texas and the Struggle for Mexican Independence

Spain objected in vain to Napoleon's 1803 sale of Louisiana to America. For years, Spain had attempted to seal off its rich colony of Mexico from commerce with other nations. Now, American Louisiana shared a vague and disputed boundary (including the Neutral Ground) with Mexico's northern province of Texas, which was already coveted by some Americans.

Soon Napoleon brought turmoil to all of Mexico. In 1808, having invaded Spain, he installed his brother Joseph Bonaparte as king, forcing Spain's king, Charles IV, to renounce his throne. For the next six years, as warfare convulsed Spain, the country's long-prized New World empire slipped away. Mexico, divided between royalists loyal to Spain and populists seeking social and economic justice for mestizos and Indians, edged toward independence. Two populist revolts—one in 1810 led by Father Miguel Hidalgo and the other in 1813 led by Father José María Morelos—were suppressed by the royalists, who executed both revolutionary leaders.

In 1812, a small force, led by Mexican republican Bernardo Gutiérrez but composed mostly of American adventurers, invaded Texas, captured San Antonio, assassinated the provincial governor Manuel Salcedo, and declared Texas independent. A year later, however, the Mexican republicans were defeated by a royalist army, which then killed suspected collaborators and pillaged the province so thoroughly that the local economy was devastated. The Mexican population declined to fewer than 2,000. Under these circumstances, Mexico's difficult path toward independence seemed, at least to some Americans, to offer yet another opportunity for expansion. For years Louisiana seethed with rumors of American plots to invade Texas and set up a separate nation. Among the plotters may have been former Vice President Aaron Burr, who was tried but acquitted in 1807 of treason for his purported plans.

Renewed Imperial Rivalry in North America

Fresh from the triumph of the Louisiana Purchase, Jefferson scored a major victory over the Federalist Charles Cotesworth Pinckney in the presidential election of 1804, garnering 162 electoral votes to Pinckney's 14. Jefferson's shrewd wooing of moderate Federalists had been so successful that the remaining Federalists dwindled to a highly principled but sectional group, unable to attract voters outside of its home base in New England. Vice President Aaron Burr, who was indicted but acquitted of murder for killing Alexander Hamilton in a duel in 1804, was replaced by George Clinton. Jefferson's second term was fraught with fruitless efforts to remain neutral in the ongoing struggle between Britain and France.

Problems with Neutral Rights

In his first inaugural address in 1801, Jefferson had announced a foreign policy of "peace, commerce, and honest friendship with all nations, entangling alliances with none." This was a difficult policy to pursue after 1803, when the Napoleonic Wars resumed. By 1805, Napoleon had conquered most of Europe, but Britain, the victor at the great naval battle of Trafalgar, controlled the seas. The United States, trying to profit from trade with both countries, was caught in the middle. Beginning in 1805, the British targeted the American reexport trade between the Caribbean and France by seizing American ships that were bringing French West Indian goods to Europe. Angry Americans viewed these seizures as violations of their rights as shippers of a neutral nation.

An even more contentious issue arose from the substantial desertion rate of British sailors. Many deserters promptly signed up on American ships, where they drew

Christianizing the Indian

Thomas Jefferson encouraged efforts by Protestant missionary groups to convert American Indians, but many native people resisted. The two opinions expressed here, one by a missionary and one by an Indian leader, illustrate how religion itself became a cause of conflict. Responding to questions from Congress in 1822 about the effectiveness of its efforts, the United Foreign Missionary Society defended its work. On the other hand, Sagoyewatha, or Red Jacket, was an important leader and orator of the Seneca people of northern New York State who defended native religion against the 1805 request of a Boston missionary society to proselytize among his people.

• **It is often said that religion expresses a culture's deepest values. Does that mean, then, that religion must always be a point of conflict when, as in this case, one group insists that another group adopt its ways?**

A Missionary Society Defends Its Activities

The objects of the United Foreign Missionary Society, are to civilize and christianize the American Indians; and the Managers are convinced, from their own experience, as well as that of kindred Institutions, that each of these objects can be more easily and successfully attained, when combined, than when separately attempted. The history of eighteen centuries testifies, that no pagan nation ever became civilized to any important degree, until it had renounced its idols, and abandoned the whole train of superstitious rites connected with its idolatrous worship; and that no one ever became evangelized without acquiring, in some measure, the arts and habits of civilized life. Whether the object, therefore, be to civilize or christianize, both must be carried on with an equal and united effort. . . . At all Missionary Stations under the care of this Board, it shall be the object to promote, not only the knowledge of Christianity, but also the arts of civilized life. Besides the branches of learning taught in common

> **"[No] pagan nation ever became civilized to any important degree, until it had renounced its idols, . . ."**

---

better pay and sometimes obtained false naturalization papers as well. The numbers involved were large: as many as a quarter of the 100,000 seamen on American ships were British. Soon the British were stopping American merchant vessels and removing any man they believed to be British, regardless of his papers. The British refusal to recognize genuine naturalization papers (on the principle "once a British subject, always a British subject") was particularly insulting to the new American sense of nationhood. At least 6,000 innocent American citizens suffered forced impressment into the British navy from 1803 to 1812. In 1807, impressment turned bloody when the British ship *Leopard* stopped the American ship *Chesapeake* in American territorial waters and demanded to search for deserters. When the American captain refused, the *Leopard* opened fire, killing three men, wounding eighteen, and removing four deserters (three with American naturalization papers) from the damaged ship. An indignant public protested British interference and the death of innocent sailors.

The Embargo Act

Jefferson insisted on America's right as a neutral nation to ship goods to Europe. He first tried diplomatic protests, then negotiations, and finally threats, all to no avail. In 1806, Congress passed the Non-Importation Act, hoping that a boycott of British goods, which had worked so well during the Revolutionary War, would be effective once again. It was not. Finally, in desperation, Jefferson imposed the Embargo Act in December 1807. This act forbade American ships from sailing to any foreign port, thereby cutting off all exports as well as imports. The intent of the act was to force both Britain and France to recognize neutral rights by depriving them of American-shipped raw materials.

But the results were a disaster for American trade. The commerce of the new nation, which Jefferson himself had done so much to promote, came to a standstill. Exports fell from $108 million in 1807 to $22 million in 1808, and the schools, the boys shall be instructed in agriculture and the mechanic arts; and the girls in spinning, weaving, sewing, knitting, and household business.

SOURCE: Letter to a member of Congress in relation to Indian civilization by the domestic secretary of the United Foreign Missionary Society (New York: D. Fanshaw, 1822), 3–4.

Red Jacket Defends Native Religion

Brother, our seats were once large, and yours were very small; you have now become a great people, and we have scarcely a place left to spread our blankets; you have got our country, but are not satisfied; you want to force your religion upon us.

Brother, continue to listen. You say you are sent to instruct us how to worship the Great Spirit agreeably to his mind, and if we do not take hold of the religion which you white people teach, we shall be unhappy hereafter. You say that you are right, and we are lost; how do we know this to be true? We understand that your religion is written in a book; if it was intended for us as well as you, why has not the Great Spirit given it to us, and not only to us, but why did he not give to our forefathers the knowledge of that book, with the means of understanding it rightly? We only know what you tell us about it. How shall we know when to believe, being so often deceived by the white people?

Brother, you say there is but one way to worship and serve the Great Spirit; if there is but one religion, why do you white people differ so much about it? Why not all agree, as you can all read the book?

Brother, the Great Spirit has made us all; but he has made a great difference between his white and red children; he has given us a different complexion, and different customs; to you he has given the arts; to these he has not opened our eyes; we know these things to be true. Since he has made so great a difference between us in other things, why may we not conclude that he has given us a different religion according to

> "How shall we know when to believe, being so often deceived by the white people?"

our understanding. The Great Spirit does right; he knows what is best for his children; we are satisfied.

Brother, we do not wish to destroy your religion, or take it from you; we only want to enjoy our own.

SOURCE: Daniel Drake, *Lives of Celebrated American Indians* (Boston: Bradbury, Soden & Co., 1843), 283–87.

---

nation was driven into a deep depression. There was widespread evasion of the embargo. A remarkable number of ships in the coastal trade found themselves "blown off course" to the West Indies or Canada. Other ships simply left port illegally. Smuggling flourished. Pointing out that the American navy's weakness was due largely to the deep cuts Jefferson had inflicted on it, the Federalists sprang to life with a campaign of outspoken opposition, and they found a ready audience in New England, the area hardest hit by the embargo.

Madison and the Failure of "Peaceable Coercion"

In this troubled atmosphere, Thomas Jefferson despondently ended his second term, acknowledging the failure of what he called "peaceable coercion." He was followed in office by his friend and colleague James Madison of Virginia. Although Madison defeated the Federalist candidate—again Charles Cotesworth Pinckney—by 122 electoral votes to 47, Pinckney's share of the votes was three times what it had been in 1804.

Ironically, the Embargo Act had almost no effect on its intended victims. The French used the embargo as a pretext for seizing American ships, claiming they must be British ships in disguise. The British, in the absence of American competition, developed new markets for their goods in South America. And at home, as John Randolph sarcastically remarked, the embargo was attempting "to cure corns by cutting off the toes." In March 1809, Congress admitted failure, and the Embargo Act was repealed. But the struggle to remain neutral in the confrontation between the European giants continued. The next two years saw passage of several acts—among them the Non-Intercourse Act of 1809 and Macon's Bill Number 2 in 1810—that unsuccessfully attempted to prohibit trade with Britain and France unless they ceased their hostile treatment of U.S. shipping. Frustration with the ineffectiveness of government policy mounted.

A Contradictory Indian Policy

The United States faced other conflicts besides those with Britain and France over neutral shipping rights. In the West, the powerful Indian nations of the Ohio Valley were determined to resist the wave of expansion that had carried thousands of white settlers onto their lands. North of the Ohio River lived the Northwest Confederation of the Shawnees, Delawares, Miamis, Potawatomis, and several smaller tribes. To the south of the Ohio were the Five Southern Tribes, the Cherokees, Chickasaws, Choctaws, Creeks, and (in Florida) the Seminoles.

According to the Indian Intercourse Act of 1790, the United States could not simply seize Indian land; it could only acquire it when the Indians ceded it by treaty. But this policy conflicted with the harsh reality of westward expansion. Commonly, settlers pushed ahead of treaty boundaries. When Indian peoples resisted the invasion of their lands, the pioneers fought back and called for military protection. Defeat of an Indian people led to further land cessions. The result for the Indians was a relentless cycle of invasion, resistance, and defeat.

Thomas Jefferson was deeply concerned with the fate of the western Indian peoples. Convinced that Indians had to give up hunting in favor of the yeoman-farmer lifestyle he so favored for all Americans, Jefferson directed the governors of the Northwest Territories to "promote energetically" his vision for civilizing the Indians, which included Christianizing them and teaching them to read. Many Indian peoples actively resisted these efforts at conversion (see Communities in Conflict). In addition, Jefferson's Indian civilization plan was never fully supported by territorial governors and settlers.

After the Louisiana Purchase, Jefferson offered traditionalist Indian groups new lands west of the Mississippi River, where they could live undisturbed by white settlers. But he failed to consider the pace of westward expansion. Less than twenty years later, Missouri, the first trans-Mississippi state, was admitted to the Union. Western Indians like the Mandans, who had seemed so remote, were now threatened by further westward expansion. In fact, Jefferson's Indian policy, because it did nothing to slow down the ever-accelerating westward expansion, offered little hope to Indian peoples. The alternatives they faced were stark: acculturation, removal, or extinction. Deprived of hunting lands, decimated by disease, increasingly dependent on the white economy for trade goods and annuity payments in exchange for land cessions, many Indian peoples despaired. Like the Mandans after Lewis and Clark's visit, they came to dread the effects of white contact. Nearly every tribe found itself bitterly split between accommodationists and traditionalists.

Indian Alternatives

There was no escape from white encroachment. Between 1801 and 1809, William Henry Harrison, governor of Indiana Territory, concluded fifteen treaties with the Delawares, Potawatomis, Miamis, and other tribes. These treaties opened eastern Michigan, southern Indiana, and most of Illinois to white settlement and forced the Indians onto ever-smaller reservations. Many of these treaties were obtained by coercion, bribery, and outright trickery, and most Indians did not accept them.

The Shawnees, a seminomadic hunting and farming tribe (the men hunted, the women farmed) of the Ohio Valley, had resisted white settlement in Kentucky and Ohio since the 1750s. Anthony Wayne's decisive defeat of the Indian confederacy led by Little Turtle at Fallen Timbers (1794) and the continuing pressure of American settlement, however, had left the Shawnees divided. One group, about one quarter of the total, led by Black Hoof, tried to retain tribal homelands by accepting acculturation directed by government officials and missionaries. The rest of the tribe tried to maintain traditional ways. The vast majority broke into small bands and moved west of the Mississippi to an area of mixed Indian settlement in Missouri, along the Mississippi River south of St. Louis, where they remained until removed to eastern Kansas (part of the original Indian Territory) in 1825. One small group of militant Shawnees, however, led by the warrior Tecumseh, refused to move west and embarked on a pan-Indian resistance movement that rapidly became famous.

In 1805, Tecumseh's brother, Tenskwatawa, known as The Prophet, began preaching a message of Indian revitalization: a rejection of all contact with the Americans, including the use of American alcohol, clothing, and trade goods, and a return to traditional practices of hunting and farming. If the Northwest Indians returned to traditional ways, Tenskwatawa promised, "the land will be overturned so that all the white people will be covered and you alone shall inhabit the land." This was a powerful message, but it was not new. Just six years earlier, Handsome Lake had led the Seneca people of upstate New York in a similar revitalization movement. Tecumseh, however, succeeded in molding his brother's religious following into a powerful pan-Indian military resistance movement. With each new treaty that Harrison concluded, Tecumseh gained new followers among the Northwest Confederation tribes. Significantly, he also had the support of the British, who, after 1807, began sending food and guns to him from Canada, and who promised an alliance with the Indians if war broke out between Britain and America.

Tecumseh's pan-Indian strategy was at first primarily defensive, aimed at preventing further westward expansion. But after the Treaty of Fort Wayne in 1809, in which the United States gained 3 million acres of Delaware and

(left) Tecumseh, a Shawnee military leader, and (right) his brother Tenskwatawa, a religious leader called
The Prophet, led a pan-Indian revitalization and resistance movement that posed a serious threat to
American westward expansion. Tecumseh traveled widely, attempting to build a military alliance on his
brother's spiritual message. He achieved considerable success in the Old Northwest but less in the Old
Southwest, where many Indian peoples put their faith in accommodation. Tecumseh's death at the Battle
of the Thames (1813) and British abandonment of their Shawnee allies at the end of the War of 1812
brought an end to organized Indian resistance in the Old Northwest.

SOURCE: (right) 1830. Oil on canvas. 29 × 24 in. (73.7 × 60.9 cm) Location: Smithsonian American Art Museum,
Washington, DC, U.S.A.

Potawatomi land in Indiana, Tecumseh moved from passive to active resistance. Confronting Harrison directly,
Tecumseh argued that the land belonged to the larger
community of all the Indian peoples; no one tribe could
give away the common property of all. He then warned
that any surveyors or settlers who ventured into the 3 million acres would risk their lives.

Tecumseh took his message of common land ownership and military resistance to all the Indian peoples of the
Northwest Confederacy. He was not uniformly successful,
even among the Shawnees. Black· Hoof, for example,
refused to join. Tecumseh also recruited, with mixed success, among the tribes south of the Ohio River. In councils with Choctaws, Chickasaws, Creeks, and Cherokees
(see Map 9.3), he preached a stark message:

> The white race is a wicked race. Since the days
> when the white race first came in contact with the
> red men, there has been a continual series of aggres-
> sions. The hunting grounds are fast disappearing, and
> they are driving the red man farther and farther to
> the west. Such has been the fate of the Shawnees,
> and surely will be the fate of all tribes if the power of
> the whites is not forever crushed.

In November 1811, while Tecumseh was still recruiting among the southern tribes, Harrison marched to the
pan-Indian village of Tippecanoe with 1,000 soldiers. The
600 to 700 Indian warriors at the town, urged on by
Tenskwatawa, attacked Harrison's forces before dawn on
November 7, hoping to surprise
them. The attack failed, and in the
battle that followed, the Americans
inflicted about 150 Indian casualties, while sustaining
about as many themselves. Although Harrison claimed
victory, the truth was far different. Dispersed from
Tippecanoe, Tecumseh's angry followers fell on American
settlements in Indiana and southern Michigan, killing
many pioneers and forcing the rest to flee to fortified
towns. Tecumseh himself entered into a formal alliance
with the British. For western settlers, the Indian threat was
greater than ever.

See the **Map**
Native American Removal
at **www.myhistorylab.com**

MAP 9.3 Indian Removals and Resistance, 1790–1814 American westward expansion put relentless pressure on the Indian nations in the trans-Appalachian South and West. The trans-Appalachian region was marked by constant displacement and warfare from the time of the earliest settlements in Kentucky in the 1780s to the War of 1812. Tecumseh's Alliance in the Old Northwest (1809–11) and the Creek Rebellion in the Old Southwest (1813–14) were the culminating struggles in Indian resistance to the American invasion of the trans-Appalachian region. Indian resistance was a major reason for the War of 1812.

The War of 1812

Many Westerners blamed the British for Tecumseh's attacks on pioneer settlements in the Northwest. British support of western Indians and the long-standing difficulties over neutral shipping rights were the two grievances cited by President Madison when he asked Congress for a declaration of war against Britain on June 1, 1812. Congress obliged him on June 18. But the war had other, more general causes as well.

The War Hawks

A rising young generation of political leaders, first elected to Congress in 1810, strongly resented the continuing influence of Britain on American affairs. These War Hawks, who included such future leaders as Henry Clay of Kentucky and John C. Calhoun of South Carolina, were young Jeffersonian Republicans from the West and South. They found all aspects of British interference, such as impressment of sailors and support for

Artist Charles Munger graphically recorded the devastation in Washington after the British burned it in August, 1814. The fire damaged both the Senate and House wings of the Capitol and destroyed the wooden causeway between the buildings.

western Indians, intolerable. Eager to assert independence from England once and for all, these young men saw themselves finishing the job begun by the aging revolutionary generation. They also wanted to occupy Florida to prevent runaway slaves from seeking refuge with the Seminole Indians. Westerners wanted to invade Canada, hoping thereby to end threats from British-backed Indians in the Northwest, such as Tecumseh and his followers. As resentments against England and frustrations over border issues merged, the pressure for war—always a strong force for national unity—mounted.

●●●–[Read the Document
A War Hawk Speaks About the British (1811) at www.myhistorylab.com

Unaware that the British, seriously hurt by the American trade embargo, were about to adopt a more conciliatory policy, President James Madison yielded to the War Hawks' clamor for action in June 1812, and his declaration of war passed the U.S. Senate by the close vote of 19 to 13, the House by 79 to 49. All the Federalists voted against the war. (The division along party lines continued in the 1812 presidential election, in which Madison garnered 128 electoral votes to 89 for his Federalist opponent, DeWitt Clinton.) The vote was sectional, with New England and the Middle States in opposition and the West and South strongly prowar. Thus, the United States entered the War of 1812 more deeply divided along sectional lines than during any other foreign war in American history.

As a result of Jefferson's economizing, the American army and navy were small and weak. In contrast, the British, fresh from almost ten years of Napoleonic Wars, were in fighting trim. At sea, the British navy quickly established a strong blockade, harassing coastal shipping along the Atlantic seaboard and attacking coastal settlements at will. In the most humiliating attack, the British burned Washington in the summer of 1814, forcing the president and Congress to flee. Dolley Madison, the president's wife, achieved a permanent footnote in history by saving a portrait of George Washington from the White House as she fled. There were a few American naval successes. The American frigate *Constitution*, known as "Old Ironsides," destroyed two British men-of-war, the *Guerrière* and the *Java*, in classic naval battles, but these failed to lift the British blockade (see Map 9.4).

The Campaigns against the Northern and Southern Indians

The American goal of expansion fared badly as well. Americans envisaged a quick victory over sparsely populated British Canada that would destroy British support for Tecumseh and his Northwest Indian allies, but instead the British–Indian alliance defeated them (see Seeing History). In July 1812, an American foray into western Canada was repulsed. A joint British and Indian force went on, in August, to capture Detroit and

●●●–[Read the Document
Indian Hostilities (1812) at www.myhistorylab.com

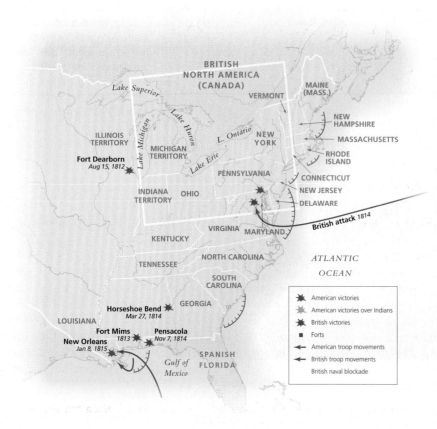

MAP 9.4 The War of 1812 On land, the War of 1812 was fought to define the nation's boundaries. In the North, where military action was most intense, American armies attacked British forts in the Great Lakes region with little success, and several invasions of Canada failed. In the South, the Battle of New Orleans made a national hero of Andrew Jackson, but it occurred after the peace treaty had been signed. On the sea, with the exception of Oliver Perry's victory in the Great Lakes, Britain's dominance was so complete and its blockade so effective that British troops were able to invade the Chesapeake and burn the capital of the United States.

Fort Dearborn (site of Chicago). In September 1813, at the battle of Put-in-Bay, Captain Oliver H. Perry established American control over Lake Erie, leading to the recapture of Detroit by William Henry Harrison. Assisted by naval forces commanded by Perry, Harrison defeated British and Indian defenders in the battle of the Thames in October 1813. Among those slain in the battle was Tecumseh, fighting on the British side. Later attempts by the United States to invade Canada in the Niagara area failed, but so too did British attempts to invade the United States in the same area.

One reason for the failure of the invasion of Canada, aside from failure to appreciate the strength of the British–Indian forces, was that the New England states actively opposed the war. Massachusetts, Rhode Island, and Connecticut refused to provide militia or supplies, and other New England governors turned a blind eye to the flourishing illegal trade across the U.S.–Canadian border. Another reason was the reaction of Canadians themselves, the majority of whom were former Americans. Ironically, the most decisive effect of the American attacks was the formation of a Canadian sense of national identity and a determination never to be invaded or absorbed by the United States.

In the South, warfare similar to that waged against Tecumseh's pan-Indian resistance movement in the Northwest dramatically affected the southern Indian peoples. The first of the Indian peoples to battle the Americans were the Creeks, a trading nation with a long history of contacts with the Spanish and French. When white settlers began to occupy Indian lands in northwestern Georgia and central Alabama early in the nineteenth century, the Creeks, like the Shawnees in the Northwest, were divided in their response. Although many Creek bands argued for accommodation, a group known as the Red Sticks was determined to fight. During the War of 1812, the Red Sticks, allied with the British and Spanish, fought not only the Americans but also other Indian groups.

In August 1813, the Red Sticks attacked Fort Mims on the Alabama River, killing more than 500 Americans and mixed-race Creeks who had gathered there for safety. Led by Andrew Jackson, troops from the Tennessee and

SEEING History

"A Scene on the Frontiers as Practiced by the 'Humane' British and their 'Worthy' Allies"

This American cartoon, published during the War of 1812, shows a British officer paying for a scalp from an Indian, while another man is shown in the act of scalping a dead American soldier. The cartoon may have been prompted by an actual event: the offer of bounties for scalps made by British Colonel Proctor at Fort Dearborn (Chicago) in August 1815. In any case, the cartoon mocking the "humane" British and their "worthy allies" was intended to spur "Columbia's Sons" to avenge "Your Country's wrongs."

The figures in the cartoon are familiar types dating back to before the American Revolution: the fat British officer, the dead American victims, and the Indians with their scalping knives. What made the cartoon effective in the War of 1812? Was it the familiar scenario? The sarcastic jibe at the "humane" British? The long-held fear of "savage" Indians? How did the cartoon mobilize these familiar feelings to support the war?

• **This cartoon relied on popular fears of Indians and resentment of the British that existed long before the War of 1812. In what way did these familiar images contribute to the American war effort?**

A SCENE ON THE FRONTIERS AS PRACTICED BY THE HUMANE BRITISH AND THEIR WORTHY ALLIES!

Bring me the Scalps and the King our Master will reward you!

Reward for 16 — Scalps.

Arise Columbia's Sons and forward press,
Your Country's wrongs call loudly for redress,
The savage Indian with his scalping knife
Or tomahawk, may seek to take your life.

By bravery aw'd, they'll in a dreadfull fright
Shrink back for refuge to the woods in flight,
Their British leaders then will quickly shake,
And for those wrongs shall restitution make.

Kentucky militias combined with the Creeks' traditional foes—the Cherokees, Choctaws, and Chickasaws—to exact revenge. Jackson's troops matched the Creeks in ferocity, shooting the Red Sticks "like dogs," one soldier reported. At the battle of Horseshoe Bend in March 1814, the Creeks were trapped between American cannon fire and their Indian enemies: more than 800 were killed, more than in any other battle in the history of Indian–white warfare.

At the end of the Creek War in 1814, Jackson demanded huge land concessions from the Creeks (including concessions from some Creek bands that had fought on his side): 23 million acres, or more than half the Creek domain. The Treaty of Fort Jackson (1814) confirming these land concessions earned Jackson his Indian name, Sharp Knife. In early 1815 (after the peace treaty had been signed but before news of it arrived in America), Andrew Jackson achieved his best-known victory, an improbable win over veteran British troops in the Battle of New Orleans.

Ending the War: The Hartford Convention and the Treaty of Ghent

America's occasional successes failed to diminish the angry opposition of New England Federalists to the War of 1812. That opposition culminated in the Hartford Convention of 1814, where Federalist representatives from the five New England states met to discuss their grievances. At first the air was full of talk of secession from the Union, but soon cooler heads prevailed. The convention did insist, however, that a state had the right "to interpose its authority" to protect its citizens against unconstitutional federal laws. This nullification doctrine was not new; Madison and Jefferson had proposed it in the Virginia and Kentucky Resolves opposing the Alien and Sedition Acts in 1798 (see Chapter 8). In any event, the nullification threat from Hartford was ignored, for peace with Britain was announced as delegates from the convention made their way to Washington to deliver their message to Congress. There the convention's grievances were treated not as serious business but as an anticlimactic joke.

By 1814, the long Napoleonic Wars in Europe were slowly drawing to a close, and the British decided to end their war with the Americans. The peace treaty, after months of hard negotiation, was signed at Ghent, Belgium, on Christmas Eve in 1814. Like the war itself, the treaty was inconclusive. The major issues of impressment and neutral rights were not mentioned, but the British did agree to evacuate their western posts, and late in the negotiations they abandoned their insistence on a buffer state for neutral Indian peoples in the Northwest.

For all its international inconsequence, the war did have an important effect on national morale. Andrew Jackson's victory at New Orleans allowed Americans to believe that they had defeated the British. It would be more accurate to say that by not losing the war the Americans had ended their own feelings of colonial dependency. Equally important, they convinced the British government to stop thinking of America as its colony.

The War of 1812 was one of America's most divisive wars, arousing more intense sectional opposition than any other American conflict except the Civil War. Today, most historians regard the war as both unnecessary and a dangerous risk to new and fragile ideas of national unity. Fortunately for its future, the United States as a whole came out unscathed, and the Battle of New Orleans provided last-minute balm for its hurt pride.

The only clear losers of the war were the northwestern Indian nations and their southern allies. With the death of Tecumseh at the Battle of the Thames in 1813 and the defeat of the southern Creeks in 1814, the last hope of a united Indian resistance to white expansion perished forever. Britain's abandonment of its Indian allies in the Treaty of Ghent sealed their fate. By 1815, American settlers were on their way west again.

Defining the Boundaries

With the War of 1812 behind them, Americans turned, more seriously than ever before, to the tasks of expansion and national development. The so-called Era of Good Feelings (1817–23) found politicians largely in agreement on a national agenda, and a string of diplomatic achievements forged by John Quincy Adams gave the nation sharper definition. But the limits to expansion also became clear: the Panic of 1819 showed the dangers in economic growth, and the Missouri Crisis laid bare the sectional split that attended westward expansion.

Another Westward Surge

The end of the War of 1812 was followed by a westward surge to the Mississippi River that populated the Old Northwest (Ohio, Indiana, Illinois, Michigan, and Wisconsin) and the Old Southwest (western Georgia, Alabama, Mississippi, and Louisiana). The extent of the population redistribution was dramatic: in 1790, about 95 percent of the nation's population had lived in states bordering the Atlantic Ocean; by 1820 fully 25 percent of the population lived west of the Appalachians (see Map 9.5).

What accounted for this extraordinary westward surge? There were both push and pull factors. Between 1800 and 1820, the nation's population almost doubled, increasing from 5.3 million to 9.6 million. Overpopulated farmland in all of the seaboard states pushed farmers off the land, while new land pulled them westward. The defeat and removal of Indians in the War of 1812 was another important pull factor.

The most important pull factor, however, was the attractive price of western land. The Land Ordinance of 1785 priced western lands too high for all but speculators and the wealthy (see Chapter 7), but subsequent realities

MAP 9.5 Spread of Settlement: Westward Surge, 1800–1820 Within a period of twenty years, a quarter of the nation's population had moved west of the Appalachian Mountains. The westward surge was a dynamic source of American optimism.

had slowly forced Congress to enact land laws more favorable to the small farmer. The most sustained challenge came from "squatters," who repeatedly took up land before it was officially open for sale and then claimed a "preemption" right of purchase at a lower price that reflected the value of improvements they had made to the land. Congress sought to suppress this illegal settlement and ordered the expulsion of squatters on several occasions but to no avail. When federal lands were officially opened for sale in Illinois in 1814, for example, there were already 13,000 settlers, forcing Congress to reverse itself and grant them all preemption rights.

Finally, in the Land Act of 1820, Congress set the price of land at $1.25 an acre, the minimum purchase at eighty acres (in contrast to the 640-acre minimum in 1785), and a down payment of $100 in cash. This was the most liberal land law yet passed in American history, but the cash requirement still favored speculators, who had more cash than most small farmers (see Figure 9.2).

Read the Document
"The Western Country"
Letter in Niles Weekly
Register at
www.myhistorylab.com

The major migration routes west favored cultural transplantation. Because of lateral westward movement, Northerners tended to migrate to the Old Northwest, Southerners to the Old Southwest. Except in southern Ohio and parts of Kentucky and Tennessee, there was very little contact among regional cultures. New Englanders carried their values and lifestyles directly west and settled largely with their own communities; Southerners did the same (see Map 9.5).

One section of northern Ohio along Lake Erie, for example, had been Connecticut's western land claim since the days of its colonial charter. Rather than give up the land when the Northwest Territory was established in 1787, Connecticut held onto the Western Reserve (as it was known) and encouraged its citizens to move there. Group settlement was common. General Moses Cleaveland of the Revolutionary War led one of the first groups of Yankees, fifty-two in all. In 1795, they settled the community that bears his name (though not his spelling of it). Many other groups followed, naming towns such as Norwalk after those they had left in Connecticut. These New Englanders brought

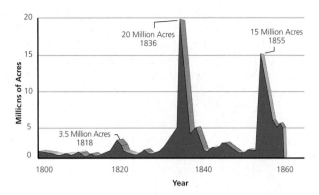

FIGURE 9.2 Western Land Sales Surges in western land sales reflect surges in westward expansion. Western land sales following the War of 1812 reached an unprecedented 3.5 million acres, but that was small in comparison with what was to come in the 1830s and 1850s. Not all land sales reflected actual settlement, however, and speculation in western lands was rampant. Collapse of the postwar speculative boom contributed to the Panic of 1819, and the abrupt end to the boom of the 1830s led to the Panic of 1837.
SOURCE: From Riegel, R., AMERICA MOVES WEST 5th Edition. © 1971 Wadsworth, a part of Cengage Learning, Inc. Reproduced by permission. www.cengage.com/permissions.

to the Western Reserve their religion (Congregational), their love of learning (tiny Norwalk soon boasted a three-story academy), and their adamant opposition to slavery.

Western migration in the South was very different. On this frontier, the people clearing the land were African American slaves creating plantations not for themelves but for their owners. After the War of 1812, as cotton growing expanded, hopeful slave owners from older parts of the South (Virginia, North and South Carolina, Georgia) flooded into the region, bringing their slaves with them or, increasingly, purchasing new ones supplied by the internal slave trade. The migration was like a gold rush, characterized by high hopes, land speculation, and riches—for a few. Most of the white settlers in the Old Southwest were small farm families who did not own slaves, but they hoped to, for ownership of slaves was the means to wealth. More than half of the migrants to the Old Southwest after 1812 were enslaved African Americans. This involuntary migration of slaves tore African American families apart at the same time that white families viewed migration as a chance to replicate the lifestyle and values of older southern states on this new frontier (see Chapter 10).

The western transplantation of distinctive regional cultures explains why, although by 1820 western states accounted for more than a third of all states (eight out of twenty-three), the West did not form a third, unified political region. Although there were common western issues—in particular, the demand for better roads and other transportation routes—communities in the Old Northwest, in general, shared New England political attitudes, whereas those in the Old Southwest shared southern attitudes. Then too, while slavery was banned in the

The hopes of every westward migrant are exemplified in this series of four illustrations imagining inevitable progress from pioneer cabin to prosperous farm. The illustrations, "The Pioneer Settler and His Progress," appeared in a booster history advertising land in western New York.

Old Northwest, it was not in the Old Southwest, thus sowing the seeds of the sectionalism to come.

The Election of 1816 and the Era of Good Feelings

In 1816, James Monroe, the last of the Virginia Dynasty, was easily elected president over his Federalist opponent Rufus King (183 to 34 electoral votes). This was the last election in which Federalists ran a candidate. Monroe had no opponent in 1820 and was reelected nearly unanimously (231 to 1). The triumph of the Jeffersonian Republicans over the Federalists seemed complete.

Tall, dignified, dressed in the old-fashioned style of knee breeches and white-topped boots that Washington had worn, Monroe looked like a traditional figure. But his politics reflected changing times. When he visited Boston, as recently as 1815 the heart of a secession-minded Federalist region, he received an enthusiastic welcome, prompting the Federalist *Columbian Centinel* to proclaim an "Era of Good Feelings." The phrase has been applied to Monroe's presidency (1817–25) ever since.

Monroe sought a government of national unity, and he chose men from North and South, Jeffersonian Republicans and Federalists, for his cabinet. He selected John Quincy Adams, a former Federalist, as his secretary of state, virtually assuring that Adams, like his father, would become president. To balance Adams, Monroe picked John C. Calhoun of South Carolina, a prominent War Hawk, as secretary of war. And Monroe supported the American System, a program of national economic development that became identified with westerner Henry Clay, Speaker of the House of Representatives.

In supporting the American System, Monroe broke with Jefferson's agrarianism to embrace much of the Federalist program for economic development, including the chartering of a national bank, a tax on imported goods to protect American manufacturers, and a national system of roads and canals. All three of these had first been proposed by Alexander Hamilton in the 1790s (see Chapter 8). At the time, these proposals had met with bitter Jeffersonian Republican opposition. The support that Monroe gave to Hamilton's ideas following the War of 1812 was a crucial sign of the dynamism of the American commercial economy. Many Republicans now acknowledged that the federal government had a role to play in fostering the economic and commercial conditions in which both yeoman farmer and merchant could succeed.

In 1816, Congress chartered the Second Bank of the United States for twenty years. The bank was a private institution supported by some of the nation's wealthiest men with whom the government cooperated. Located in Philadelphia, the bank had capital of $35 million, of which the government contributed $7 million. The bank was expected to provide the large-scale financing that the smaller state banks could not handle and to create a strong national currency. Because they feared the economic

power of rich men, Jeffersonian Republicans had allowed the charter of the original Bank of the United States, founded in 1791, to expire in 1811. The Republican about-face in 1816 was a sign that the strength of commercial interests had grown to rival that of farmers, whose distrust for central banks persisted.

The Tariff of 1816 was the first substantial protective tariff in American history. In 1815, British manufacturers, who had been excluded for eight years (from the Embargo Act of 1807 to the end of the War of 1812), flooded the U.S. market with their products. American manufacturers complained that the British were dumping goods below cost in order to prevent the growth of American industries. Congress responded with a tariff on imported woolens and cottons, on iron, leather, hats, paper, and sugar. The measure had southern as well as northern support, although in later years, differences over the passage of higher tariffs would become one of the most persistent sources of sectional conflict.

The third item in the American System, funding for roads and canals—internal improvements, as they came to be known—was more controversial. Monroe supported genuinely national (that is, interstate) projects such as the National Road from Cumberland, Maryland, to Vandalia, Illinois. Congressmen, however, aware of the urgent need to improve transportation in general, and sensing the political advantages from directing funds to their districts, proposed spending federal money on local projects. Monroe vetoed such local proposals, believing them to be unconstitutional. Thus it happened that some of the most famous projects of the day, such as the Erie Canal, which lay wholly within New York State, and the early railroads, were financed by state or private money (see Chapter 12).

Monroe's support for measures initially identified with his political opposition was an indicator of his realism. The three aspects of the American System—bank, tariff, roads—were all parts of the basic infrastructure that the American economy needed in order to develop. Briefly, during the Era of Good Feelings, politicians agreed about the need for all three. Later, each would be a source of heated partisan argument.

The Diplomacy of John Quincy Adams

The diplomatic achievements of the Era of Good Feelings were due almost entirely to the efforts of one man, John Quincy Adams, Monroe's secretary of state. Adams set himself the task of tidying up the borders of the United States. Two accords with Britain—the Rush-Bagot Treaty of 1817 and the Convention of 1818—fixed the border between the United States and Canada at the 49th parallel and resolved conflicting U.S. and British claims to Oregon with an agreement to occupy it jointly for ten (eventually twenty) years. The American claim to Oregon (present-day British Columbia, Washington, Oregon, northern Idaho, and parts of Montana) was based on China trader

Robert Gray's discovery of the Columbia River in 1792 and on the Lewis and Clark expedition of 1804–06.

Adams's major diplomatic accomplishment was the Adams-Onís or Transcontinental Treaty of 1819, in which he skillfully wrested concessions from the faltering Spanish empire. Adams convinced Spain not only to cede Florida but also to drop all previous claims it had to the Louisiana Territory and Oregon. In return, the United States relinquished claims on Texas and assumed responsibility for the $5 million in claims that U.S. citizens had against Spain.

Finally, Adams picked his way through the remarkable changes occurring in Latin America, developing the policy that bears his president's name, the Monroe Doctrine. The United States was the first country outside

Latin America to recognize the independence of Spain's former colonies. When the European powers (France, Austria, Russia, and Prussia) began to talk of a plan to help Spain recover the lost colonies, what was the United States to do? The British, suspicious of the European powers, proposed a British-American declaration against European intervention in the hemisphere. Others might have been flattered by an approach from the British empire, but Adams would have none of it. Showing the national pride that was so characteristic of the era, Adams insisted on an independent American policy. He therefore drafted for the president the hemispheric policy that the United States has followed ever since.

On December 2, 1823, the president presented the Monroe Doctrine to Congress and the world. He called for the end of colonization of the Western Hemisphere by European nations (this was aimed as much at Russia and its Pacific Coast settlements as at other European powers). Intervention by European powers in the affairs of the independent New World nations would be considered by the United States a danger to its own peace and safety. Finally, Monroe pledged that the United States would not interfere in the affairs of European countries or in the affairs of their remaining New World colonies.

All of this was a very loud bark from a very small dog. In 1823, the United States lacked the military and economic force to back up its grand statement. In fact, what kept the European powers out of Latin America was British opposition to European intervention, enforced by the Royal Navy. The Monroe Doctrine was, however, useful in Adams's last diplomatic achievement, the Convention of 1824, in which Russia gave up its claim to the Oregon Territory and accepted 54°40' north latitude as the southern border of Russian America. Thus, Adams had contained another possible threat to American continental expansion (see Map 9.6).

In the short space of twenty years, the position of the United States on the North American continent had been transformed. Not only was America a much larger nation,

but also the Spanish presence was much diminished, Russian expansion on the West Coast contained, and peace prevailed with Britain. This string of diplomatic achievements—the treaties with Russia, Britain, and Spain and the Monroe Doctrine—represented a great personal triumph for the stubborn, principled John Quincy Adams. A committed nationalist and expansionist, he showed that reason and diplomacy were in some circumstances more effective than force. Adams's diplomatic achievements were a fitting end to the period dominated by the Virginia Dynasty, the trio of enlightened revolutionaries who did so much to shape the new nation.

The Panic of 1819

Across this impressive record of political and economic nation building fell the shadow of the Panic of 1819. A delayed reaction to the end of the War of 1812 and the Napoleonic Wars, the panic forced Americans to come to terms with their economic place in a peaceful world. As British merchant ships resumed trade on routes they had abandoned during the wars, the American shipping boom ended. And as European farm production recovered from the wars, the international demand for American foodstuffs declined and American farmers and shippers suffered.

Domestic economic conditions made matters worse. The western land boom that began in 1815 turned into a speculative frenzy. Land sales, which had totaled 1 million acres in 1815, mushroomed to 3.5 million in 1818. Some lands in Mississippi and Alabama, made valuable by the international demand for cotton, were selling for $100 an acre. Many settlers bought on credit, aided by small "wildcat" state banks that made loans far beyond their resources. This was not the first—or the last—speculative boom in western lands. But it ended like all the rest—with a sharp contraction of credit, begun on this occasion by the Second Bank of the United States, which in 1819 forced state banks to foreclose on many bad loans. Many small farmers were ruined, and they blamed the faraway Bank of the United States for their troubles. In the 1830s, Andrew Jackson would build a political movement on their resentment.

Urban workers lost their jobs as international trade declined and as manufacturers failed because of competition from British imports. As they lobbied for local relief, many workers became deeply involved in urban politics, where they could express their resentment against the merchants and owners who had laid them off. Thus developed another component of Andrew Jackson's new political coalition.

Another confrontation arose over the tariff. Southern planters, hurt by a decline in the price of cotton, began to actively protest the protective tariff, which kept the price of imported goods high even when cotton prices were low. Manufacturers, hurt by British competition, lobbied for even higher rates, which they achieved in 1824 over southern protests. Southerners then began to express

---

◆►▶ Read the Document

The President Addresses the Union (1823) at
www.myhistorylab.com

MAP 9.6 John Quincy Adams's Border Treaties John Quincy Adams, secretary of state in the Monroe administration (1817–25), solidified the nation's boundaries in several treaties with Britain and Spain. The Rush-Bagot Treaty of 1817 and the Conventions of 1818 and 1824 settled the northern boundary with Canada and the terms of a joint occupancy of Oregon. The Adams-Onís Treaty of 1819 added Florida to the United States and settled the disputed border between the American Louisiana Territory and Spanish possessions in the West.

doubts about the fairness of a political system in which they were always outvoted.

The Panic of 1819 was a symbol of this transitional time. It showed how far the country had moved since 1800, from Jefferson's republic of yeoman farmers toward a nation dominated by commerce. And the anger and resentment expressed by the groups harmed by the depression—farmers, urban workers, and southern planters—were portents of the politics of the upcoming Jackson era.

The Missouri Compromise

In the Missouri Crisis of 1819–21, the nation confronted the momentous issue that had been buried in the general enthusiasm for expansion: as America moved west, would the largely southern system of slavery expand as well? Until 1819, this question was decided regionally. The Northwest Ordinance of 1787 explicitly banned slavery in the northern section of trans-Appalachia but made no mention of it elsewhere. Because so much of the expansion into the Old Northwest and Southwest was lateral (Northerners stayed in the North, Southerners in the South), there was little conflict over sectional differences. In 1819, however, the sections collided in Missouri, which applied for admission to the Union as a slave state (see Map 9.7).

The northern states, all of which had abolished slavery by 1819, were opposed to the extension of slavery. In addition to the moral issue, the Missouri question raised the political issue of sectional balance. Northern politicians did not want to admit another slave state. To do so would tip the balance of power in the Senate, where the 1819

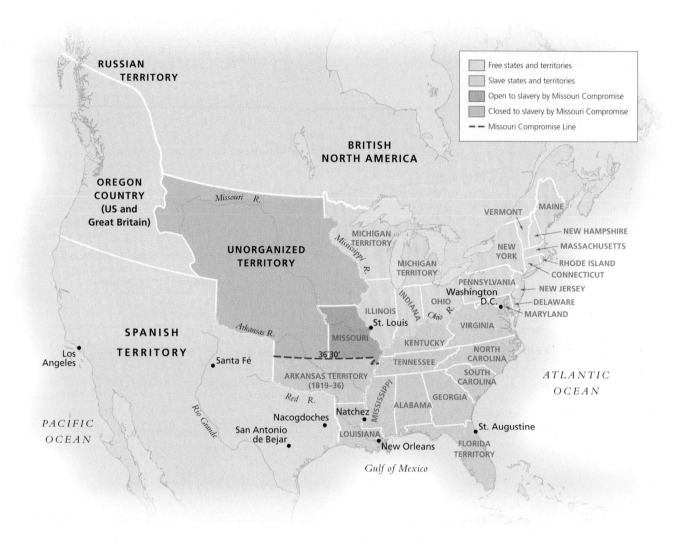

MAP 9.7 The Missouri Compromise Before the Missouri Compromise of 1820, the Ohio River was the dividing line between the free states of the Old Northwest and the slaveholding states of the Old Southwest. The compromise stipulated that Missouri would enter the Union as a slave state (balanced by Maine, a free state), but slavery would be prohibited in the Louisiana Territory north of 36°30' (Missouri's southern boundary). This awkward compromise lasted until 1846, when the Mexican-American War reopened the issue of the expansion of slavery.

count of slave and free states was eleven apiece. For their part, Southerners believed they needed an advantage in the Senate; because of faster population growth in the North, they were already outnumbered (105 to 81) in the House of Representatives.

But above all, Southerners did not believe Congress had the power to limit the expansion of slavery. They were deeply alarmed that Northerners wanted to pass national legislation on the matter. Slavery, in southern eyes, was a question of property and, therefore, a matter for state rather than federal legislation. Thus, from the very beginning, the expansion of slavery exposed vital constitutional issues. Indeed, the aging politician of Monticello, Thomas

Jefferson, immediately grasped the seriousness of the question of the expansion of slavery. As he prophetically wrote to a friend, "This momentous question like a fire bell in the night, awakened and filled me with terror. I considered it at once the [death] knell of the Union."

In 1819, Representative James Tallmadge Jr. of New York began more than a year of congressional controversy when he demanded that Missouri agree to the gradual end of slavery as the price of entering the Union. At first, the general public paid little attention, but religious reformers (Quakers prominent among them) organized a number of antislavery rallies in northern cities that made politicians take notice. Former Federalists in the North who had seen

CHRONOLOGY

1800	Thomas Jefferson elected president
1802	Russian-American Company headquarters established at Sitka, Alaska
	First Barbary War begins
1803	Louisiana Purchase
	Marbury v. *Madison*
	Ohio admitted to the Union
1804	Lewis and Clark expedition leaves St. Louis
	Vice President Aaron Burr kills Alexander Hamilton in a duel
	Thomas Jefferson reelected president
1807	*Chesapeake–Leopard* incident
	Embargo Act
	Former Vice President Aaron Burr tried for treason but acquitted
1808	James Madison elected president
1809	Tecumseh forms military alliance among Northwest Confederacy peoples
1811	Battle of Tippecanoe
1812	War of 1812 begins

	James Madison reelected president
	Louisiana admitted to the Union
1814	Treaty of Ghent
1815	Battle of New Orleans
1816	James Monroe elected president
	Congress charters Second Bank of the United States
	Indiana admitted to the Union
1817	Mississippi admitted to the Union
1818	Illinois admitted to the Union
1819	Panic of 1819
	Adams-Onís Treaty
	Alabama admitted to the Union
1819–20	Missouri Crisis and Compromise
1820	James Monroe reelected president
	Maine admitted to the Union
1821	Missouri admitted to the Union as a slave state
1823	Monroe Doctrine

their party destroyed by the achievements of Jefferson and his successors in the Virginia Dynasty eagerly seized on the Missouri issue. This was the first time that the growing northern reform impulse had intersected with sectional politics. It was also the first time that southern threats of secession were made openly in Congress.

The Senate debate over the admission of Missouri, held in the early months of 1820, was the nation's first extended debate over slavery. Observers noted the high proportion of free African Americans among the listeners in the Senate gallery. But the full realization that the question of slavery was central to the future of the nation would not become apparent to the general public until the 1850s, in part because the irreconcilable nature of the argument convinced most politicians that it was a topic best treated by silence.

In 1820, Congress achieved compromise over the sectional differences. Henry Clay forged the first of the many agreements that were to earn him the title of "the Great Pacificator" (peacemaker). The Missouri Compromise maintained the balance between free and slave states:

Maine (which had been part of Massachusetts) was admitted as a free state in 1820 and Missouri as a slave state in the following year. A policy was also enacted with respect to slavery in the rest of the Louisiana Purchase: slavery was prohibited north of 36°30′ north latitude—the southern boundary of Missouri—and permitted south of that line. This meant that the vast majority of the Louisiana Territory would be free. In reality, then, the Missouri Compromise could be only a temporary solution, because it left open the question of how the balance between slave and free states would be maintained. But the Compromise did have one immediate effect: Southerners now realized that slavery was under attack and quickly built new arguments to defend it (see Chapter 10).

Conclusion

In complex ways a developing economy, geographical expansion, and even a minor war helped shape American unity. Local, small, settled, face-to-face communities in both the North and the South began to send their more mobile, expectant members to new occupations in urban centers or west to form new settlements.

The westward movement was the novel element in the American national drama. Europeans believed that large size and a population in motion bred instability and political disintegration. Thomas Jefferson thought otherwise, and the Louisiana Purchase was the gamble that confirmed his thinking. The westward population movement dramatically changed the political landscape and Americans' view of themselves. But expansion did not create the "empire for liberty" that Jefferson had hoped for. While expansion did indeed create economic opportunity, it also displaced and destroyed Indian communities such as the Mandans, the Shawnee, and many others. And it also created an even greater denial of liberty, as we shall see in the next chapter, in a greatly expanded community tied to cotton and to the slave labor that produced it.

Review Questions

1. What economic and political problems did the United States face as a new nation in a world dominated by war between Britain and France? How successful were the efforts by the Jefferson, Madison, and Monroe administrations to solve these problems?

2. The anti-European cast of Jefferson's republican agrarianism made it appealing to many Americans who wished to believe in their nation's uniqueness, but how realistic was it?

3. Some Federalists opposed the Louisiana Purchase, warning of the dangers of westward expansion. What are arguments for and against expansion?

4. What contradictions in American Indian policy did the confrontations between Tecumseh's alliance and soldiers and settlers in the Old Northwest reveal? Can you suggest solutions to these contradictions?

5. What did the War of 1812 accomplish?

6. What were the issues that made it impossible for the Era of Good Feelings to last?

Recommended Reading

Walter Borneman, *1812: The War That Forged a Nation* (2004). A very readable account.

Robert Pierce Forbes, *The Missouri Compromise and Its Aftermath: Slavery and the Meaning of America* (2007). A compelling discussion of contemporary debates over slavery and the impact of the compromise.

Carolyn Gilman, *Lewis and Clark Across the Divide* (2003). Illustrated, informative account published to mark the bicentennial of the expedition and its contacts with western Indians.

Jay Gitlin, *The Bourgeois Frontier: French Towns, French Trader, and American Expansion* (2009). Traces the transition of French towns such as St. Louis to American rule.

Nancy Isenberg, *Fallen Founder: The Life of Aaron Burr* (2007). A persuasive effort to rehabilitate a scandal-ridden founding father.

Peter J. Kastor, *The Nation's Crucible: The Louisiana Purchase and the Creation of America* (2004). A complicated story of the incorporation of all the groups—white, black, Indian, mixed race—in Louisiana.

Peter S. Onuf, *Jefferson's Empire* (2000). A thoughtful study of Jefferson's ideas about republicanism, empire, and nationalism.

Robert Owens, *Mr. Jefferson's Hammer: William Henry Harrison and the Origins of American Indian Policy* (2007). Harrison's Indian policy considered in the military, political and social world of the early Ohio Valley.

Stephen Warren, *The Shawnees and Their Neighbors 1795–1870* (2005). Examines Tecumseh in the wider context of choices by of other Shawnees, especially those who moved west.

PEARSON myhistorylab Connections

Reinforce what you learned in this chapter by studying the many documents, images, maps, review tools, and videos available at www.myhistorylab.com.

Read and Review

✓ Study and Review Chapter 9

Read the Document

Thomas Jefferson to Meriweather Lewis (1803)

Supreme Court Retains Right to Overrule Legislation (1803)

Constitutionality of the Louisiana Purchase (1803)

Lewis and Clark Meet the Shoshone (1805)

Margaret Bayard Smith, Reflections upon Meeting Jefferson (1809)

A War Hawk Speaks About the British (1811)

Indian Hostilities (1812)

"The Western Country" Letter in Niles Weekly Register

The President Addresses the Union (1823)

See the Map

Louisiana Purchase

Native American Removal

The War of 1812

Research and Explore

Read the Document

Exploring America: Continentalism

Whose History Is It: In the Footsteps of Lewis and Clark

Profiles
Dolley Madison
Tenskwatawa

Hear the Audio

Jefferson and Liberty

The Star Spangled Banner

Watch the Video *Lewis and Clark: What Were They Trying to Accomplish?*

((•─ Hear the Audio

Hear the audio files for Chapter 9 at
www.myhistorylab.com.

10

((•—[Hear the Audio

Chapter 10 at www.myhistorylab.com

The South and Slavery

1790s–1850s

CHAPTER OUTLINE

Slavery and the Old South, 1800–1860. A Slave auction in Virginia. 1861. English engraving. The Granger Collection.

Cotton Communities in the Old Southwest

In 1834, Samuel Townes of South Carolina caught "Alabama Fever." Restive under what seemed to him excessive demands from his large and well-connected family, Samuel rebelled by marrying a woman of whom his family disapproved and moving with her and his slaves to Perry County, Alabama, a newly opened part of the Old Southwest suitable for growing cotton. There, beyond the reach of most family obligations, he practiced law in the village of Marion, bought a plantation on the banks of the Cahaba River, and acquired ten to fifteen more slaves. Almost all of Samuel's new workers were bought on credit, which was plentiful at this "flush time" of high cotton prices and rich new land just coming into cultivation. Samuel's desire for wealth caused him to drive his slaves very hard, demanding that his overseer "whip them like the devil" to pick more cotton. Samuel was fortunate that his wife Joanna shared his pride in being counted among the "rising prosperous people" in Perry County. Although Joanna Townes apparently relished their independence, many plantation women in the Old Southwest felt their isolation from kinfolk deeply. One such woman was Samuel's sister Eliza, who with her husband William Blassingame also settled in Perry County. William rarely allowed Eliza to leave the plantation, which was ruled by his unchecked alcoholism,

AMERICAN·
Communities

domestic violence, and molestation of female slaves. Without support from nearby kin (Samuel apparently only intervened once), Eliza had no choice but to endure until William's death in 1841.

The Panic of 1837 devastated Samuel's ambitions. As the price of cotton fell to seven cents a pound, banks demanded repayment of their generous loans. Samuel sold some slaves, rented out the labor of others, but he was forced to ask for loans from the family he had been so eager to escape. In 1844 his plantation was sold at auction. Three years later, his health failed, and he and Joanna returned to South Carolina and the charity of kinfolk.

The rapid westward expansion of cotton cultivation exposed the undeveloped state of community formation among the southern elite. The plantation form of agriculture, which had been the rule in the South since its earliest days, meant that cities were few and community institutions like churches and schools were rare. Slave-owning families depended almost entirely on kinship networks for assistance (and the obligations that Samuel Townes wished to avoid) and for sociability. Families who moved west frequently found themselves lost without their customary family connections. Judging from the experiences of the Townes and Blassingame families, it seems that the expansion of slavery encouraged independent and irresponsible behavior among slave-owning men while tearing slave-owning women from the security of the family networks on which they depended. Probably other families had happier experiences, but it is clear that wider community connections and support lagged behind the pursuit of profits to be made from cotton.

What of the slaves that Samuel brought with him? Once part of a larger Townes family group in South Carolina, the slaves that Samuel owned were separated from their kinfolk permanently and had to adjust to living with a number of newly purchased slaves in Alabama. Most of the new slaves were bought as individuals and were usually still in their teens or even younger. Young male slaves were favored for the backbreaking work of cutting trees and clearing land for cultivation. Sometimes owners worked side by side with their workers at this initial stage. But generally, uniformity and strict discipline were the rule on cotton plantations. Owners eager to clear land rapidly and make quick profits often drove the clearing crews at an unmerciful pace. And, as Samuel Townes had, they attempted to impose strict discipline and a rapid pace on the work gangs that planted, hoed, and harvested cotton. Slaves from other parts of the South, used to more individual and less intense work, hated the cotton regime and most of all hated the overseers who enforced it.

Only long-practiced African American community-building strategies saved these young transported slaves from complete isolation. Beginning in the earliest days of slavery, Africans from many different tribes built their own communities by using the language of kinship (for example, "brother," "sister," "uncle," "aunt," and "child") to encompass everyone in new imagined families. On one hand, the cultivation of cotton required many workers, thus creating the conditions necessary for large slave communities in the Old Southwest. On the other hand, because the price of cotton was unstable, probably many shared the experience of the Townes slaves, who were sold again when the plantation failed.

Thus, the new land in the Old Southwest that appeared to offer so much opportunity for owners bred tensions caused by forcible sale and migration, by the organization and pace of cotton cultivation, and by the owners' often violent efforts to control their slaves in a new region where community bonds were undeveloped. For planters and slaves alike, migration broke long-standing family ties that were the most common form of community throughout the South. The irony is that African Americans, who were the most cruelly affected, knew better how to build new communities than did their privileged owners.

In the first half of the nineteenth century, world demand for cotton transformed the South, promoting rapid expansion and unprecedented prosperity. But it also tied the South to a slave system that was inherently unstable and violent. Although southern slave owners frequently talked about their plantations as communities and their slaves as family, the slave system was not one community but two with the strengths of the slave community largely invisible to the owners.

Marion, AL

1. How did attitudes in the South toward slavery change after the invention of the cotton gin?

2. What is a "slave society"?

3. What was life like for slaves in the American South?

4. What role did religion play in African American slave communities?

5. What were the values of yeoman farmers?

6. Who were the planter elite?

7. Why was the white South increasingly defensive after 1830?

FOCUS Questions

1790s–1850s

King Cotton and Southern Expansion

Slavery had long dominated southern life. African American slaves grew the great export crops of the colonial period—tobacco, rice, and indigo—on which slave owners' fortunes were made, and their presence shaped southern society and culture (see Chapter 4). Briefly, in the early days of American independence, the slave system waned, only to be revived by the immense profitability of cotton in a newly industrializing world. Cotton became the dominant crop in a rapidly expanding South that more than doubled in size (see Map 10.1), and as it expanded, attitudes toward slavery hardened. As the years passed, Southern spokesmen, who once spoke of slavery as a regrettable necessity came to describe slavery as a benevolent system, a "positive good." The overwhelming economic success of cotton and of the slave system on which it depended created a distinctive regional culture quite different from that developing in the North.

See the Map
United States Territorial Expansion in the 1850s at **www.myhistorylab.com**

Cotton and Expansion into the Old Southwest

Short-staple cotton had long been recognized as a crop ideally suited to southern soils and growing conditions. But it had one major drawback: the seeds were so difficult to remove from the lint that it took an entire day to hand-clean a single pound of cotton. The invention in 1793 that made cotton growing profitable was the result of collaboration between a young Northerner named Eli Whitney who had been hired to tutor the children of Catherine Greene, a South Carolina plantation owner and widow of Revolutionary War General Nathanael Greene. Whitney built a prototype cotton engine, dubbed "gin" for short, a simple device consisting of a hand-cranked cylinder with

teeth that tore the lint away from the seeds. At Greene's suggestion, the teeth were made of wire. With the cotton gin, it was possible to clean more than fifty pounds of cotton a day. Soon large and small planters in the inland regions of Georgia and South Carolina had begun to grow cotton. By 1811, this area was producing 60 million pounds of cotton a year and exporting most of it to England.

Other areas of the South quickly followed South Carolina and Georgia into cotton production. New land was needed because cotton growing rapidly depleted the soil. The profits to be made from cotton growing drew a rush of southern farmers into the so-called black belt—an area stretching through western Georgia, Alabama, and Mississippi that was blessed with exceptionally fertile soil.

This model of Eli Whitney's cotton gin, invented in 1793, was a simple device with huge consequences. It transformed the South, condemned millions of African Americans to slavery, and was the largest source of American economic growth before 1860.

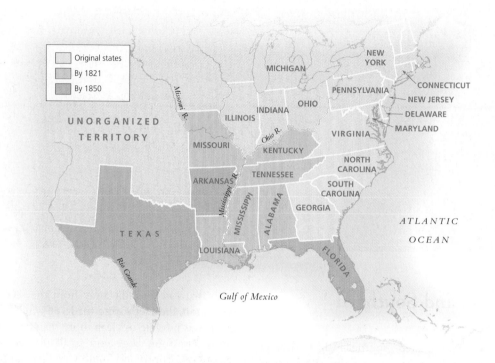

MAP 10.1 The South Expands, 1790–1850 This map shows the dramatic effect cotton production had on southern expansion. From the original six states of 1790, westward expansion, fueled by the search for new cotton lands, added another six states by 1821 and three more by 1850.

Following the War of 1812, Southerners were seized by "Alabama Fever." In one of the swiftest migrations in American history, white Southerners and their slaves flooded into western Georgia and the areas that would become Alabama and Mississippi (the Old Southwest). On this frontier, African American pioneers (albeit involuntary ones) cleared the forests, drained the swamps, broke the ground, built houses and barns, and planted the first crops. This migration caused the population of Mississippi to double (from 31,306 to 74,448) and that of Alabama to grow sixteen fold (from 9,046 to 144,317) between 1810 and 1820.

Like the simultaneous expansion into the Old Northwest, settlement of the Old Southwest took place at the expense of the region's Indian population (see Chapter 9). Beginning with the defeat of the Creeks at Horseshoe Bend in 1814 and ending with the Cherokee forced migration along the "Trail of Tears" in 1838, the Five Civilized Tribes—the Cherokees, Chickasaws, Choctaws, Creeks, and Seminoles—were forced to give up their lands and move to Indian Territory (see Chapter 11).

Following the "Alabama Fever" of 1816–20, several later surges of southern expansion (1832–38, and again in the mid-1850s) carried cotton planting over the Mississippi River into Louisiana and deep into Texas. Each surge ignited feverish speculative frenzies, remembered in terms like the "Flush Times" for the heated rush of the 1830s. In the minds of the mobile, enterprising Southerners who sought their fortunes in the West, cotton profits and expansion went hand in hand. But the expansion of cotton meant the expansion of slavery.

Slavery the Mainspring—Again

The export of cotton from the South was the dynamic force in the developing American economy in the 1790–1840 period. Just as the international slave trade had been the dynamic force in the Atlantic economy of the eighteenth century (see Chapter 4), southern slavery financed northern industrial development in the nineteenth century.

The rapid growth of cotton production was an international phenomenon, prompted by events occurring far from the American South. The insatiable demand for cotton was a result of the technological and social changes that we know today as the Industrial Revolution. Beginning early in the eighteenth century, a series of inventions resulted in the mechanized spinning and weaving of cloth in the world's first factories in the north of England. The ability of these factories to produce unprecedented amounts of cotton cloth revolutionized the world economy. The invention of the cotton gin came at just the right time. British textile manufacturers were eager to buy all the cotton that the South could produce. The figures for cotton production soared: from 720,000 bales in 1830, to 2.85 million bales in 1850, to nearly 5 million in 1860. By the time of the Civil War, cotton accounted for almost 60 percent of American exports, representing a total value of nearly $200 million a year (see Figure 10.1).

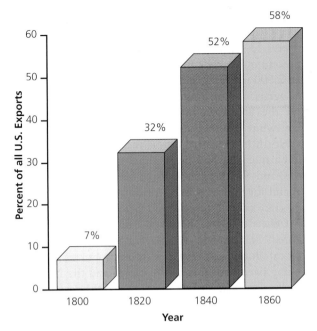

FIGURE 10.1 Cotton Exports as a Percentage of All U.S. Exports, 1800–1860 One consequence of the growth of cotton production was its importance in international trade. The growing share of the export market and the great value (nearly $200 million in 1860) led southern slave owners to assert that "Cotton is King." They believed that the importance of cotton to the national economy entitled the South to a commanding voice in national policy.

SOURCE: From *Atlas of Antebellum Southern Agriculture*, by Sam B. Hilliard. (Baton Rouge: Louisiana State University Press, 1984), pp. 67–71. Copyright © 1984 Louisiana State University Press. Reprinted by permission.

Cotton's central place in the national economy and its international importance led Senator James Henry Hammond of South Carolina to make a famous boast in 1858:

Without firing a gun, without drawing a sword, should they make war on us, we could bring the whole world to our feet. . . . What would happen if no cotton was furnished for three years? . . . England would topple headlong and carry the whole civilized world with her save the South. No, you dare not to make war on cotton. No power on the earth dares to make war upon it. Cotton is King.

The connection between southern slavery and northern industry was very direct. Most mercantile services associated with the cotton trade (insurance, for example) were in northern hands and, significantly, so was shipping. This economic structure was not new. In colonial times,

New England ships dominated the African slave trade. Some New England families—like the Browns of Providence who made fortunes in the slave trade—invested some of their profits in the new technology of textile manufacturing in the 1790s. Other merchants—such as the Boston Associates who financed the cotton textile mills at Lowell—made their money from cotton shipping and brokerage. Thus, as cotton boomed, it provided capital for the new factories of the North (see Chapter 12).

A Slave Society in a Changing World

In the flush of freedom following the American Revolution, all the northern states abolished slavery or passed laws for gradual emancipation, and a number of slave owners in the Upper South freed their slaves (see Chapter 7). Thomas Jefferson, ever the optimist, claimed that "a total emancipation with the consent of the masters" could not be too far in the future. Tellingly, however, Jefferson himself could not envisage an equal biracial society, and therefore advocated gradual emancipation coupled with removal of former slaves to Haiti or Africa. Throughout the South, legislatures were unwilling to write steps toward emancipation into law, preferring to depend on the charity of individual slave owners.

Attitudes toward slavery rapidly changed following the invention of the cotton gin in 1793 and the realization of the riches to be made from cotton. While slave owners in the Upper South still spoke of gradual emancipation, the opportunity for expansion offered by the Louisiana Purchase of 1803 convinced many residents of

Read the **Document**

Thomas Jefferson, Notes on Virginia (1787) at **www.myhistorylab.com**

The immense size of the internal slave trade made sights like this commonplace on southern roads. Groups of slaves, chained together in gangs called coffles, were marched from their homes in the Upper South to cities in the Lower South, where they were auctioned to new owners.

the Lower South that slavery was essential. White Southerners firmly believed that only African slaves could be forced to work day after day, year after year, at the rapid and brutal pace required in the cotton fields in the steamy southern summer. As the production of cotton climbed higher every year in response to a seemingly inexhaustible international demand, so too did the demand for slaves and the conviction of Southerners that slavery was an economic necessity. Figures from the international slave trade in the decade before it was banned demonstrate this conclusively: nearly 75,000 new slaves were imported from Africa in 1800–1808, more than any other decade's total in the entire history of American slavery. Yet at the same time Southerners continued to argue that slavery was a problem that they themselves would someday resolve. Opinions and interference from the North were unwelcome.

As had been true since colonial times, the centrality of slavery to the economy and the need to keep slaves under firm control required the South to become a slave society, rather than merely a society with slaves, as had been the case in the North. What this meant was that one particular form of social relationship, that of master and slave (one dominant, the other subordinate), became the model for all relationships, including personal interactions between white husbands and wives as well as interactions in politics and at work. The profitability of cotton reconfirmed this model and extended it far beyond its original boundaries, thus creating a different kind of society in the South than the one emerging in the North.

●◦●—Read the Document

State Laws Govern Slavery (1824) at **www.myhistorylab.com**

At a time when the North was experiencing the greatest spurt of urban growth in the nation's history (see Chapter 13), most of the South remained rural: less than 3 percent of Mississippi's population lived in cities of more than 2,500 residents, and only 10 percent of Virginia's did. The agrarian ideal, bolstered by the cotton boom, encouraged the antiurban and anticommercial sentiments of many white Southerners. The South also lagged behind the North in industrialization and in canals and railroads (see Chapter 12). Southern capital was tied up in land and slaves, and Southerners, buoyed by the world's insatiable demand for cotton, saw no reason to invest in economically risky railroads, canals, and factories.

Other changes, however, could not be so easily ignored. Nationwide, the slave states were losing their political dominance because their population was not keeping pace with that of the North and the Northwest. Equally alarming, outside the South, antislavery sentiment was growing rapidly. Southerners felt directly threatened by growing abolitionist sentiment in the North and by the 1834 action of the British government eliminating slavery on the sugar plantations of the West Indies. The South felt increasingly hemmed in by northern opposition to the expansion of slavery.

The Second Middle Passage: the Internal Slave Trade

The cotton boom caused a huge increase in the domestic slave trade. Plantation owners in the Upper South (Delaware, Kentucky, Maryland, Virginia, and Tennessee) sold their slaves to meet the demand for labor in the new and expanding cotton-growing regions of the Old

This engraving from *Harper's Weekly* shows slaves, dressed in new clothing, lined up outside a New Orleans slave pen for inspection by potential buyers before the actual auction began. They were often threatened with punishment if they did not present a good appearance and manner that would fetch a high price.

Southwest. In every decade after 1820, at least 150,000 slaves were uprooted either by slave trading or planter migration to new areas, and in the expansions of the 1830s and the 1850s, the number reached a quarter of a million. Cumulatively, between 1820 and 1860, nearly 50 percent of the slave population of the Upper South took part against their will in southern expansion (see Map 10.2).

More slaves—an estimated 1 million—were uprooted by this internal slave trade and enforced migration in the early nineteenth century than were brought to North America during the entire time the international slave trade was legal (see Chapter 4).

Purchased by slave traders from owners in the Upper South, slaves were gathered together in notorious "slave pens" in places like Richmond and Charleston and then moved south by train or boat. In the interior, they were carried as cargo on steamboats on the Mississippi River, hence the dreaded phrase "sold down the river." Often slaves moved on foot, chained together in groups of fifty or more known as "coffles." Chained slaves in coffles were a common sight on southern roads and one difficult to reconcile with the notion of slavery as a benevolent institution. Arriving at a central market in the Lower South like Natchez, New Orleans, or Mobile, the slaves, after being carefully inspected by potential buyers, were sold at auction to the highest bidder (see Map 10.3).

In New Orleans, in the streets outside large slave pens near the French Quarter, thousands of slaves were displayed and sold each year. Dressed in new clothes provided by the traders and exhorted by the traders to walk, run, and otherwise show their stamina, slaves were presented to buyers. For their part, suspicious buyers, unsure that traders and slaves themselves were truthful, poked, prodded, and frequently stripped male and female slaves to be sure they were as healthy as the traders claimed. Aside from obvious signs of illness, buyers often looked for scars on a slave's back: too many scars were a sign of the frequent whippings that a rebellious or "uppity" slave had provoked. Most slaves were sold as individuals: buyers rarely responded to pleas to buy an "extra" slave to keep a family together.

*••┤*Read the Document
A Slave Tells of His Sale at Auction (1848) at
www.myhistorylab.com

Although popular stereotype portrayed slave traders as unscrupulous outsiders who persuaded kind and reluctant masters to sell their slaves, the historical truth is much harsher. Traders, far from being shunned by slave-owning society, were often respected community members. One Charleston trader, Alexander McDonald, served as both an alderman and a bank president and was described as "a man of large means and responsible for all his engagements." Similarly, the sheer scale of the slave trade makes it impossible to believe that slave

owners only reluctantly parted with their slaves at times of economic distress. Instead, it is clear that many owners sold slaves and separated slave families not out of necessity but to increase their profits. The sheer size and profitability of the internal slave trade made a mockery of southern claims for the benevolence of the slave system.

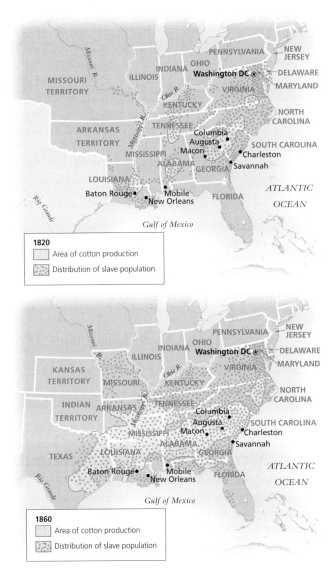

MAP 10.2 Cotton Production and the Slave Population, 1820–60 In the forty years from 1820–60, cotton production grew dramatically in both quantity and extent. Rapid westward expansion meant that by 1860 cotton production was concentrated in the black belt (so called for its rich soils) in the Lower South. As cotton production moved west and south, so did the enslaved African American population that produced it, causing a dramatic rise in the internal slave trade.

SOURCE: From *Atlas of Antebellum Southern Agriculture*, by Sam B. Hilliard. (Baton Rouge: Louisiana State University Press, 1984), pp. 67–71. Copyright © 1984 Louisiana State University Press. Reprinted by permission.

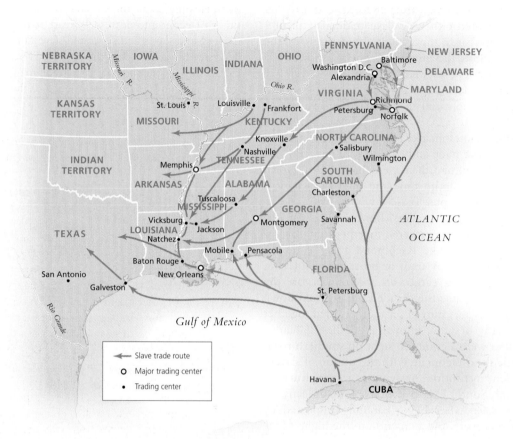

MAP 10.3 Internal Slave Trade, 1820–60 Between 1820 and 1860, nearly 50 percent of the slave population of the Upper South was sold to labor on the cotton plantations of the Lower South. This map shows the various routes by which they were "sold down the river," shipped by boat or marched south.

SOURCE: From *Historical Atlas of the United States* (Washington, DC: National Geographic Society, 1988). Copyright © 1988 National Geographic Society. Reprinted by permission.

The African American Community

Surely no group in American history has faced a harder job of community building than the black people of the antebellum South. Living in intimate, daily contact with their oppressors, African Americans nevertheless created an enduring culture of their own, a culture that had far-reaching and lasting influence on all of southern life and American society as a whole (see Chapter 4). Within their own communities, African American values and attitudes, and especially their own forms of Christianity, played a vital part in shaping a culture of endurance and resistance.

The Mature American Slave System

On January 1, 1808, the United States ended its participation in the international slave trade. Although a small number of slaves continued to be smuggled in from Africa, the growth of the slave labor force depended primarily on natural increase—that is, through births within the slave population. The slave population, estimated at 700,000 in 1790, grew to more than 4 million in 1860. A distinctive African American slave community, which had first emerged in the eighteenth century (see Chapter 4), expanded dramatically in the early years of the nineteenth century. This community was as much shaped by King Cotton as was the white South.

The size of cotton plantations fostered the growth of slave communities: now 75 percent of all slaves lived in groups of ten or more, in contrast to the more dispersed distribution on smaller farms in earlier generations. Over half of all slaves lived on plantations with twenty or more other slaves, and others, on smaller farms, had links with slaves on nearby properties. Urban slaves were able to make and sustain so many secret contacts with other African Americans in cities or towns that slave owners wondered whether slave discipline could be maintained in cities. There can be no question that the bonds that African Americans created with each other were what sustained them during the years of slavery.

In law, slaves were property, to be bought, sold, rented, worked, and otherwise used (but not abused or killed) as the owner saw fit. But slaves were also human beings, with feelings, needs, and hopes. Even though most white Southerners believed black people to be members of an inferior, childish race, all but the most brutal masters acknowledged the humanity of their slaves. White masters learned to live with the two key institutions of African American community life: the family and the African American church, and in their turn slaves learned, however painfully, to survive slavery.

The Growth of the Slave Community

Of all the New World slave societies, the one that existed in the American South was the only one that grew by natural increase rather than through the constant importation of captured Africans. This fact alone made the African American community of the South different from the slave societies of Cuba, the Caribbean islands, and Brazil. In order to understand, we must examine the circumstances of survival and growth.

The growth of the African American slave population was not due to better treatment than in other New World slave societies, but to the higher fertility of African American women, who in 1808 (the year the international slave trade ended) had a crude birthrate of thirty-five to forty, causing a 2.2 percent yearly population growth. This was still below the fertility rate of white women, who had a crude birthrate of fifty-five and a 2.9 percent annual population growth. The ending of African importations may have affected black population growth, for while African women usually breastfed for two years, a form of natural birth control that produced fewer births per mother, African American slave women adopted the white practice of breastfeeding for only one year, and on average gave birth to six or eight children at year-and-a-half intervals. But they also suffered from the contradictory demands of slave owners, who wanted them to work hard while still having children, for every slave baby increased the wealth of the owners.

Health remained a lifelong issue for slaves. Malaria and infectious diseases such as yellow fever and cholera were endemic in the South. White people as well as black died, as the life expectancy figures for 1850 show: forty to forty-three years for white people and thirty to thirty-three years for African Americans. Slaves were more at risk because of the circumstances of slave life: poor housing, poor diet, and constant, usually heavy, work. Sickness was chronic: 20 percent or more of the slave labor force on most plantations were sick at any one time. Many owners believed sick slaves were only "malingering." Because of the poor medical knowledge of the time, they failed to realize that adequate diet, warm housing, and basic sanitation might have prevented the pneumonia and dysentery that killed or weakened many slaves and that exacted an especially high toll on children under five, who died at twice the rate of their white counterparts.

From Cradle to Grave

Slavery was a lifelong labor system, and the constant and inescapable issue between master and slave was how much work the slave would—or could be forced to—do. Southern white slave owners claimed that by housing, feeding, and clothing their slaves from infancy to death they were acting more humanely than northern industrialists who employed people only during their working years. But in spite of occasional instances of manumission—the freeing of a slave—the child born of a slave was destined to remain a slave.

Children lived with their parents (or with their mother if the father was a slave on another farm or plantation) in housing provided by the owner. Husband and wife cooperated in loving and sheltering their children and teaching them survival skills. From birth to about age seven, slave children played with one another and with white children, observing and learning how to survive. They saw the penalties: black adults, perhaps their own parents, whipped for disobedience; black women, perhaps their own sisters, violated by white men. And they might see one or both parents sold away as punishment or for financial gain. They would also see signs of white benevolence: special treats for children at holidays, appeals to loyalty from the master or mistress, perhaps friendship with a white child. One former slave recalled:

> Yessum, when they used to have company in the big house, Miss Ross would bring them to the door to show them us children. And, my blessed, the yard would be black with us children, all string up there next the doorstep looking up in they eyes. Old Missus would say, "Ain't I got a pretty crop of little niggers coming on?"

Of course, black children had no schooling of any kind; in most of the southern states, it was against the law to teach a slave to read, although indulgent owners often rewarded their "pet" slaves by teaching them in spite of the law. Instead of learning to read, most children learned slave ways of getting along: apparent acquiescence to white demands, pilfering, malingering, incomprehension, sabotage, and other methods of slowing the relentless work pace. Many white Southerners genuinely believed that their slaves were both less intelligent and more loyal than they really were. Frederick Douglass, whose fearless leadership of the abolitionist movement made him the most famous African American of his time, wryly noted, "As the master studies to keep the slave ignorant, the slave is cunning enough to make the master think he succeeds."

Whatever their particular childhood circumstances, at age twelve, slaves were considered full grown and put to work in the fields or in their designated occupation.

Field Work and the Gang System

In 1850, 55 percent of all slaves were engaged in cotton growing. Another 20 percent labored to produce other crops: tobacco (10 percent), rice, sugar, and hemp. About 15 percent of all slaves were domestic servants, and the remaining 10 percent worked in mining, lumbering, industry, and construction (see Figure 10.2).

The field workers, 75 percent of all slaves, both male and female, were most directly affected by the gang labor system employed on cotton plantations (as well as in tobacco and sugar). Cotton was a crop that demanded nearly year-round labor: from planting in April, to constant hoeing and cultivation through June, to a picking season that began in August and lasted until December. Owners divided their slaves into gangs of twenty to twenty-five, a communal labor pattern reminiscent of parts of Africa, but with a crucial difference—these workers were supervised by overseers with whips. On most plantations, the bell sounded an hour before sunup, and slaves were expected to be on their way to the fields as soon as it was light. Work continued till noon, and after an hour or so for lunch and rest, the slaves worked until nearly dark. In the evening, the women prepared dinner at the cabins and everyone snatched a few hours of unsupervised socializing before bedtime. Work days were shorter in the winter, perhaps only ten hours.

Work was tedious in the hot and humid southern fields, and the overseer's whip was never far away. Cotton growing was hard and demanding work demanding real skill: plowing and planting, chopping weeds with a heavy hoe, and picking the ripe cotton from the stiff and scratchy bolls, at the rate of 150 pounds a day. A strong, hardworking slave—a "prime field hand"—was valuable property, worth at least $1,000 to the master. Slaves justifiably took pride in their strength, as observed by a white Northerner traveling in Mississippi in 1854, who came across a work gang happy to be going home early because of rain:

> First came forty of the largest and strongest women I ever saw together . . . they carried themselves loftily, each having a hoe over the shoulder, and walking with a free, powerful stride. Behind them came the . . . [plowhands and their mules], thirty strong, mostly men, but a few of them women. . . . A lean and vigilant white overseer, on a brisk pony, brought up the rear.

That, of course, is only one side of the story. Compare former slave Solomon Northup's memory of cotton picking:

> It was rarely that a day passed by without one or more whippings. The delinquent [who had not picked enough cotton] was taken out, stripped, made to lie upon the ground, face downwards, when he received a punishment proportioned to his offence. It is the literal, unvarnished truth, that the crack of the lash, and the shrieking of the slaves, can be heard from dark till bed time, on [this] plantation, any day almost during the entire period of the cotton-picking season.

Slaves aged fast in this regime. Poor diet and heavy labor undermined health. When they were too old to work, they took on other tasks within the black community, such as caring for young children. Honored by the slave community, the elderly were tolerated by white owners, who continued to feed and clothe them until their deaths. Few actions show the hypocrisy of southern paternalism more clearly than the speed with which white owners evicted their elderly slaves in the 1860s when the end of the slave system was in sight.

Read the Document
Frances Ann Kemble, Journal of a Residence on a Georgia Plantation (1838) at **www.myhistorylab.com**

House Servants and Skilled Workers

In the eighteenth century, as profits from slavery grew, slave owners diverted an increasing proportion of slave labor from the fields to the house service necessary to sustain their rich lifestyles. By one calculation, fully one-third of the female slaves in Virginia worked as house servants by 1800, but the figures were much lower in the newly opened cotton lands in the West.

At first glance, working in the big house might seem to have been preferable to working in the fields. Physically,

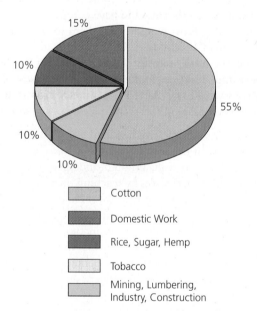

15%
10%
10%
10%
55%

- Cotton
- Domestic Work
- Rice, Sugar, Hemp
- Tobacco
- Mining, Lumbering, Industry, Construction

FIGURE 10.2 Distribution of Slave Labor, 1850 In 1850, 55 percent of all slaves worked in cotton, 10 percent in tobacco, and another 10 percent in rice, sugar, and hemp. Ten percent worked in mining, lumbering, industry, and construction, and 15 percent worked as domestic servants. Slave labor was not generally used to grow corn, the staple crop of the yeoman farmer.

it was much less demanding, and house slaves were often better fed and clothed. They also had much more access to information, for white people, accustomed to servants and generally confident of their loyalty, often forgot their presence and spoke among themselves about matters of interest to the slaves: local gossip, changes in laws or attitudes, policies toward disobedient or rebellious slaves.

For many white people, one of the worst surprises of the Civil War was the eagerness of their house slaves to flee. Considered by their masters the best treated and the most loyal, these slaves were commonly the first to leave or to organize mass desertions. Even the Confederacy's first family, President Jefferson Davis and his wife Varina, was chagrined by the desertion of their house servants in 1864.

From the point of view of the slave, the most unpleasant thing about being a house servant (or the single slave of a small owner) was the constant presence of white people. There was no escape from white supervision. Many slaves who were personal maids and children's nurses were required to live in the big house and rarely saw their own families. Cooks and other house servants were exposed to the tempers and whims of all members of the white family, including the children, who prepared themselves for lives of mastery by practicing giving orders to slaves many times their own age. And house servants, more than any others, were forced to act grateful and ingratiating. An escaped slave, Jermain Loguen, recalled with distaste the charade of "servile bows and counterfeit smiles . . . and other false expressions of gladness" with which he placated his master and mistress. At the same time, genuine intimacy was sometimes possible, especially between black nurses and white children. But these were bonds that the white children were ultimately forced to reject as the price of joining the master class.

A small number of slaves were skilled workers: weavers, seamstresses, carpenters, blacksmiths, and mechanics. More slave men than women achieved skilled status (partly because many jobs considered appropriate for women, like cooking, were not thought of as skilled). Black people worked as lumberjacks (of the 16,000 lumber workers in the South, almost all were slaves), as miners, as deckhands and stokers on Mississippi riverboats, as stevedores loading cotton on the docks of Charleston, Savannah, and New Orleans, and sometimes as workers in the handful of southern factories. Because slaves were their masters' property, the wages of the slave belonged to the owner, not the slave.

The extent to which slaves made up the laboring class was most apparent in cities. A British visitor to Natchez in 1835 noted slave "mechanics, draymen, hostelers, labourers, hucksters and washwomen and the heterogeneous

Thomas Jefferson used this revolving bookstand with five adjustable bookrests at Monticello. It was built of walnut in 1810 by slaves from the plantation whom Jefferson had directed to be trained as skilled carpenters.

multitude of every other occupation." In the North, all these jobs were performed by white workers. In part because the South failed to attract as much immigrant labor as the North, southern cities offered both enslaved and free black people opportunities in skilled occupations such as blacksmithing and carpentering that free African Americans in the North were denied.

Slave Families

As had been true in the eighteenth century, families remained essential to African American culture (see Chapter 4). No southern state recognized slave marriages in law. Most owners, though, not only recognized but also encouraged them, sometimes even performing a kind of wedding ceremony for the couple. Masters encouraged marriage among their slaves, believing it made the men less rebellious, and because they were eager for the slave women to have children. Whatever marriages meant to the masters, to slaves they were a haven of love and intimacy in a cruel world and the basis of the African American community. Husbands and wives had a chance, in their own cabins, to live their own lives among loved ones. The relationship between slave husband and wife was different from that of the white husband and wife. The master–slave system dictated that the white marriage be unequal, for the man had to be dominant and the woman dependent and submissive. Slave marriages were ironically more equal, for husband and wife were both powerless within the slave system. Both knew that neither could protect the other from abuse at the hands of white people.

Slave quarters built by slave owners, like these pictured on a South Carolina plantation, provided more than basic shelter. Slave quarters were the center of the African American community life that developed during slavery.

SOURCE: Collection of The New-York Historical Society. Photograph by G.N. Barnard, Bagoe Collection, ca. 1865, negative number 48169.

age "aunt" or "uncle," and to call children of their own age "brother" or "sister" (see Chapter 4). Thus, in the absence of their own family, separated children could quickly find a place and a source of comfort in the slave community to which they had been sold.

This emphasis on family and on kinship networks had an even more fundamental purpose. The kinship of the entire community, where old people were respected and young ones cared for, represented a conscious rejection of white paternalism. The slaves' ability, in the most difficult of situations, to structure a community that expressed their values, not those of their masters, was extraordinary. Equally remarkable was the way in which African Americans reshaped Christianity to serve their needs.

Freedom and Resistance

Whatever their dreams, most slaves knew they would never escape. Freedom was too far away. Almost all successful escapes in the nineteenth century (approximately a thousand a year) were from the Upper South (Delaware, Maryland, Virginia, Kentucky, and Missouri). A slave in the Lower South or the Southwest simply had too far to go to reach freedom. That meant that ways to endure and to resist became all the more important.

African American Religion

Black Christianity was an enabling religion: it helped slaves to survive, not as passive victims of white tyranny but as active opponents of an oppressive system that they daily protested in small but meaningful ways. In their faith, African Americans expressed a spiritual freedom that white people could not destroy.

African religions managed to survive from the earliest days of slavery in forms that white people considered as "superstition" or "folk belief," such as the medicinal use of roots by conjurers. Religious ceremonies survived, too, in late-night gatherings deep in the woods where the sound of drumming, singing, and dancing could not reach white ears (see Chapter 4). In the nineteenth century, these African traditions allowed African Americans to reshape white Christianity into their own distinctive faith that expressed their deep resistance to slavery.

The Great Awakening, which swept the South after the 1760s, introduced many slaves to Christianity, often in mixed congregations with white people (see Chapter 5). The transformation was completed by the Second Great Awakening, which took root among black and white

Marriage was more than a haven from cruelty: it was the foundation of community. Family meant continuity. Parents made great efforts to teach their children the family history and to surround them with a supportive and protective kinship network. The strength of these ties is shown by the many husbands, wives, children, and parents who searched for each other after the Civil War when slavery came to an end. Observing African Americans' postwar migrations, a Freedmen's Bureau agent commented that "every mother's son among them seemed to be in search of his mother; every mother in search of her children." As the ads in black newspapers indicate, some family searches went on into the 1870s and 1880s, and many ended in failure.

Given the vast size of the internal slave trade, fear of separation was constant—and real. One in every five slave marriages was broken, and one in every three children sold away from their families. These figures clearly show that slave owners' support for slave marriages was secondary to their desire for profits. The scale of the trade was a strong indication of the economic reality that underlay their protestations of paternalism.

In the face of constant separation, slave communities attempted to act like larger families. Following practices developed early in slavery, children were taught to respect and learn from all the elders, to call all adults of a certain

Southerners in the 1790s. The number of African American converts, preachers, and lay teachers grew rapidly, and a distinctive form of Christianity took shape. Free African Americans founded their own independent churches and denominations. The first African American Baptist and Methodist churches were founded in Philadelphia in 1794 by the Reverend Absalom Jones and the Reverend Richard Allen. In 1816, the Reverend Allen joined with African American ministers from other cities to form the African Methodist Episcopal (AME) denomination. By the 1830s, free African American ministers like Andrew Marshall of Savannah and many more enslaved black preachers and lay ministers preached, sometimes secretly, to slaves. Their message was one of faith and love, of deliverance, of the coming of the promised land.

African Americans found in Christianity a powerful vehicle to express their longings for freedom and justice. But why did their white masters allow it? Some white people, themselves converted by the revivals, doubtless believed that they should not deny their slaves the same religious experience. But many southern slave owners expected Christianity to make their slaves obedient and peaceful. Forbidding their slaves to

●●●─ Read the Document
Slave Culture Documented in Song (1867) at
www.myhistorylab.com

hold their own religious gatherings, owners insisted that their slaves attend white church services. Slaves were quick to realize the owners' purpose. As a former Texas slave recalled: "We went to church on the place and you ought to heard that preachin'. Obey your massa and missy, don't steal chickens and eggs and meat, but nary a word havin' a soul to save." On many plantations, slaves attended religious services with their masters every Sunday, sitting quietly in the back of the church or in the balcony, as the minister preached messages justifying slavery and urging obedience. But at night, away from white eyes, they held their own prayer meetings.

In churches and in spontaneous religious expressions, the black community made Christianity its own. Fusing Christian texts with African elements of group activity, such as the circle dance, the call-and-response pattern, and, above all, group singing, black people created a unique community religion full of emotion, enthusiasm, and protest. Nowhere is this spirit more compelling than in the famous spirituals: "Go Down Moses," with its mournful refrain "Let my people go"; the rousing "Didn't My Lord Deliver Daniel . . . and why not every man"; the haunting "Steal Away." Some of these spirituals became as well known to white people as to black people, but only African Americans seem to have appreciated the full meaning of their subversive messages.

African cultural patterns persisted in the preference for night funerals and for solemn pageantry and song, as depicted in British artist John Antrobus's *Plantation Burial*, ca. 1860. Like other African American customs, the community care of the dead contained an implied rebuke to the masters' care of the living slaves.

SOURCE: John Antrobus, *Plantation Burial*. Oil painting. The Historic New Orleans Collection. #1960.46.

Other Kinds of Resistance

The rapid geographical spread of cotton introduced a new source of tension and resistance into the slave–master relationship. White Southerners did everything they could to prevent escapes and rebellions. Slave patrols were a common sight on southern roads: any black person without a pass from his or her master was captured (usually roughly) and returned home to certain punishment. But despite almost certain recapture, slaves continued to flee and to help others do the same. Escaped slave Harriet Tubman of Maryland, who made twelve rescue missions freeing sixty to seventy slaves in all (later inflated to three hundred as Tubman's rescues became legendary), had extraordinary determination and skill. As a female runaway, she was unusual, too: most escapees were young men, for women often had small children they were unable to take and unwilling to leave behind.

Much more common was the practice of "running away nearby." Slaves who knew they could not reach freedom still frequently demonstrated their desire for liberty or their discontent over mistreatment by taking unauthorized

◦•◦ Read the Document

Runaway Slave Advertisements (1838–1839) at **www.myhistorylab.com**

leave from their plantation. Hidden in nearby forests or swamps, provided with food smuggled by other slaves from the plantation, the runaway might return home after a week or so, often to rather mild punishment. Although in reality, most slaves could have little hope of gaining freedom, even failed attempts at rebellion shook the foundations of the slave system, and thus temporary flight by any slave was a warning sign of discontent that a wise master did not ignore.

Slave Revolts

The ultimate resistance, however, was the slave revolt. Southern history was dotted with stories of former slave conspiracies and rumors of current plots (see Chapter 4). Every white Southerner knew about the last-minute failure of Gabriel Prosser's insurrection in Richmond in 1800 and the chance discovery of Denmark Vesey's plot in Charleston in 1822. But when in 1831, Nat Turner actually started a rebellion in which a number of white people were killed, southern fears were greatly magnified.

A literate man, Nat Turner was a lay preacher, but he was also a slave. It was Turner's intelligence and strong religious commitment that made him a leader in the slave community. Turner began plotting his revolt after a religious vision in which he saw "white spirits and black spirits engaged in battle"; "the sun was darkened—the thunder rolled in the Heavens, and blood flowed in streams." Turner and five other slaves struck on the night of August 20, 1831, first killing Travis, who, Turner said, "was to me a kind master, and placed the greatest confidence in me; in fact, I had no cause to complain of his treatment of me."

Moving from plantation to plantation and killing a total of fifty-five white people, the rebels numbered sixty by the

Harriet Tubman was 40 years old when this photograph (later hand-tinted) was taken. Already famous for her daring rescues, she gained further fame by serving as a scout, spy, and nurse during the Civil War.

next morning, when they fled from a group of armed white men. More than forty blacks were executed after the revolt, including Turner, who was captured accidentally after he had hidden for two months in the woods. Thomas R. Gray, a white lawyer to whom Turner dictated a lengthy confession before his death, was impressed by Turner's composure. "I looked on him," Gray said, "and my blood curdled in my veins." If intelligent, well-treated slaves such as Turner could plot revolts, how could white Southerners ever feel safe?

◦•◦ Read the Document

The Confession of Nat Turner (1831) at **www.myhistorylab.com**

Gabriel's Rebellion, the Denmark Vesey plot, and Nat Turner's revolt were the most prominent examples of organized slave resistance, but they were far from the only ones. Conspiracies and actual or rumored slave resistance began in colonial times (see Chapter 4) and never ceased. These plots exposed the truth white Southerners preferred to ignore: only force kept Africans and African Americans enslaved, and because no system of control could ever be total, white Southerners could never be completely safe from the possibility of revolt. Nat Turner brought white Southerners' fears to the surface. After 1831, the possibility of slave insurrection was never far from their minds.

Free African Americans

Another source of white disquiet was the growing number of free African Americans. By 1860, nearly 250,000 free black people lived in the South. For most, freedom dated from before 1800, when antislavery feeling among slave owners in the Upper South was widespread and cotton cultivation had yet to boom.

Most free black people lived in the countryside of the Upper South, where they worked as tenant farmers or farm laborers. Urban African Americans were much more visible. Life was especially difficult for female-headed families, because only the most menial work—street peddling and laundry work, for example—was available to free black women. The situation for African American males was somewhat better. Although they were discriminated against in employment and in social life, there were opportunities for skilled black craftsmen in trades such as blacksmithing and carpentry. Cities such as Charleston, Savannah, and Natchez were home to flourishing free African American communities that formed their own churches and fraternal orders.

After 1830, manumission was virtually impossible throughout the South. In the 1830s, state legislatures tightened black codes—laws concerning free black people. Free African Americans could not carry firearms, could not purchase slaves (unless they were members of their own family),

One of the ways Charleston attempted to control its African American population was to require all slaves to wear badges showing their occupation. After 1848, free black people also had to wear badges, which were decorated, ironically, with a liberty cap.

and were liable to the criminal penalties meted out to slaves (that is, whippings and summary judgments without a jury trial). They could not testify against whites, hold office, vote, or serve in the militia. In other words, except for the right to own property, free blacks had no civil rights. White people increasingly feared the influence free black people might have on slaves, for free African Americans were a living challenge to the slave system. Their very existence disproved the basic southern equations of white equals free, and black equals slave. No one believed more fervently in those equations than the South's largest population group, white people who did not own slaves.

The White Majority

The pervasive influence of the slave system in the South is reflected in the startling contrast of two facts: two-thirds of all Southerners did not own slaves, yet slave owners dominated the social and political life of the region. Although slave owners occupied the most productive land, the poor white people and small farmers—southern "plain folk"— occupied the rest of the rural land, and a small middle class lived in the cities of the South.

Poor White People

From 30 to 50 percent of all southern white people were landless, a proportion similar to that in the North. But the existence of slavery limited the opportunities for poor white people. Slaves made up the permanent, stable workforce in agriculture and in many skilled trades. Many poor white people led highly transient lives in search of work, such as farm labor at harvest time, which was only temporary. Others were tenant farmers working under share-tenancy arrangements that kept them in debt to the landowner. Although they farmed poorer land with less equipment than landowning farmers, most tenant farmers grew enough food to sustain their families. Like their landowning neighbors, tenant farmers aspired to independence.

This drawing shows the moment, almost two months after the failure of his famous and bloody slave revolt, when Nat Turner was accidentally discovered in the woods near his home plantation. Turner's cool murder of his owner and methodical organization of his revolt deeply frightened many white Southerners.

Relationships between poor whites and black slaves were complex. White men and women often worked side by side with black slaves in the fields and were socially and sexually intimate with enslaved and free African Americans. White people engaged in clandestine trade to supply slaves with items like liquor that slave owners prohibited, helped slaves to escape, and even (in an 1835 Mississippi case) were executed for their participation in planning a slave revolt. At the same time, the majority of poor white people insisted, sometimes violently, on their racial superiority over blacks. For their part, many African American slaves, better dressed, better nourished, and healthier, dismissed them as "poor white trash." But the fact was that the difficult lives of poor whites, whom one contemporary described as "a third class of white people," served to blur the crucial racial distinction between independent whites and supposedly inferior, dependent black people on which the system of slavery rested.

Southern "Plain Folk"

The word "yeoman," originally a British term for a farmer who works his own land, is often applied to independent farmers of the South, most of whom lived on family-sized farms. Southerners themselves referred to them as "plain folk," as opposed to the gentry who owned slaves. Although yeoman farmers sometimes owned a few slaves, in general they and their families worked their land by themselves. Typical of the yeoman-farmer community was northwestern Georgia, once home to the Creeks and Cherokees, but now populated by communities of small farmers who grew enough vegetables to feed their families, including corn, which they either ate themselves or fed to hogs. In addition, these farmers raised enough cotton every year (usually no more than one or two bales) to

bring in a little cash. At least 60 percent owned their own farms.

Just as elsewhere in the South, family was the mainstay of community. Farm men and women depended on their relatives and neighbors for assistance in large farm tasks such as planing, harvesting, and construction. Projects requiring lots of hands, like logrollings, corn shuckings, and quilting bees, were community events. Farmers repaid this help and obtained needed goods through complex systems of barter with other members of the community. In their organization, southern farm communities were no different from northern ones, with one major exception—slavery. In the South, one of the key items in the community barter system was the labor of slaves, who were frequently loaned out to neighbors by small slave owners to fulfill an obligation to another farmer.

Where yeomen and large slave owners lived side by side, as in the Georgia black belt where cotton was the major crop, slavery again provided a link between the rich and the "plain folk." Large plantation owners often bought food for their slaves from small local farmers, ground the latter's corn in the plantation mill, ginned their cotton, and transported and marketed it as well. But although planters and much smaller yeomen were part of a larger community network, in the black belt the large slave owners were clearly dominant. Only in their own up-country communities did yeomen feel truly independent.

Many southern yeomen lived apart from large slaveholders in the up-country regions where plantation agriculture was unsuitable. The very high value southern yeomen placed on freedom grew directly from their own experience as self-sufficient property-owning farmers in small, family-based communities, and from the absolute, patriarchal control they exercised over their own wives

Yeoman farmer Robert Smith, who owned 11 slaves and 800 acres, was much wealthier than most other yeoman, but like them he conducted a mixed farming and grazing operation. Today, the Tullie Smith house and its many outbuildings is preserved as a living history farm at the Atlanta History Center as a reminder to visitors that yeoman farms were much more common in Georgia than large single-crop plantations.

and children. This was a way of life that southern "plain folk" were determined to preserve. It made them resistant to the economic opportunities and challenges that capitalism and industrialization posed for northern farmers, which southern yeomen perceived as encroachments on their freedom.

The irony was that the freedom yeomen so prized rested on slavery. White people could count on slaves to perform the hardest and worst labor, and the degradation of slave life was a daily reminder of the freedom they enjoyed in comparison. Slavery meant that all white people, rich and poor, were equal in the sense that they were all free. This belief in white skin privilege had begun in the eighteenth century as slavery became the answer to the South's labor problem (see Chapter 4). The democratization of politics in the early nineteenth century and the enactment of nearly universal white manhood suffrage perpetuated the belief in white skin privilege, even though the gap between rich and poor white people was widening.

The Middling Ranks

In the predominantly rural South, cities provided a home for a small commercial middle class of merchants, bankers, factors (agents), and lawyers on whom the agricultural economy depended to sell its produce to a world market. Adding to them small businessmen such as shopkeepers, teachers, doctors and ministers, the professional class as a whole made up about ten percent of the population. Urban growth lagged far behind the North, but increased rapidly in the 1840s and the 1850s. The cities that grew first were major shipping centers for agricultural goods: the river cities of Louisville, St. Louis, Memphis, and New Orleans, and the cotton ports of Mobile and Savannah. The urban middle class in the South founded educational institutions, libraries, and cultural activities, as in the North, and increasingly they espoused the same middle class beliefs in progress, technology, industrialization and the importance of the family. Although many scorned the "backwardness" of the plantation elite and yeoman farmers, these middle class Southerners were not abolitionists. Indeed, most believed that the slave system was essential to maintaining social peace as industrialization went forward. As in the North, small industrial cities, often including textile mills and heavier industry, clustered along the fall line where the rivers dropped down from the highlands to the coastal plains. Columbus, Georgia, located at the falls of the Chattahoochee River, was an example of such an industrial small city.

The effort of William Gregg of South Carolina to establish the cotton textile industry illustrates some of the problems facing southern entrepreneurs. Gregg, a successful jeweler from Columbia, South Carolina, became convinced that textile factories were a good way to diversify the southern economy and to provide a living for poor whites who could not find work in the slave-dominated employment system. He enthusiastically

publicized the findings of his tour of northern textile mills but found a cool reception. His request to the planter-dominated South Carolina legislature for a charter of incorporation for a textile mill passed by only one vote. In 1846, he built a model mill and a company town in Graniteville, South Carolina, that attracted poor white families as employees. Gregg adapted southern paternalism to industry, providing a school and churches and prohibiting alcohol and dancing, yet paying his workers 20 percent less than northern wages. His experience in the competitive textile industry led him to favor the protective tariff, thus putting him at odds with the general attitude in South Carolina that had solidified at the time of the Nullification Crisis (see Chapter 11).

Another noteworthy exception was the Tredegar Iron Works, near Richmond, which by 1837 was the third largest foundry in the nation. Joseph Anderson, who became its manager (and later owner) in 1841 broke southern precedent by using slave labor in the mills, thus proving that enslaved workers were capable of factory work (a fact that many Southerners disputed).

Many southern planters scorned members of the commercial middle class like Joseph Anderson because they had to please their suppliers and customers and thus lacked, in planter's eyes, true independence. This was an attitude strikingly different from that in the North, where the commercial acumen of the middle class was increasingly valued (see Chapter 12).

Planters

Remarkably few slave owners fit the popular stereotype of the rich and leisured plantation owner with hundreds of acres of land and hundreds of slaves. Only 36 percent of southern white people owned slaves in 1830, and only 2.5 percent owned fifty slaves or more. Just as yeomen and poor whites were diverse, so, too, were southern slave owners (see Figure 10.3).

Small Slave Owners

The largest group of slave owners was small yeomen taking the step from subsistence agriculture to commercial production. To do this in the South's agricultural economy, they had to own slaves. But upward mobility was difficult. Owning one or two slaves increased farm production only slightly, and it was hard to accumulate the capital to buy more. Getting a secure footing on the bottom rung of the slave-owner ladder was very difficult. In good economic times, the owner might buy a new slave or two, but a poor crop or a downturn in cotton prices could wipe out his gains and force him to sell all of his slaves. The roller-coaster economy of the early nineteenth century did not help matters, and the Panic of 1837 was a serious setback to many small farmers.

For a smaller group of slave owners, the economic struggle was not so hard. Middle-class professional men—lawyers, doctors, and merchants—frequently managed to

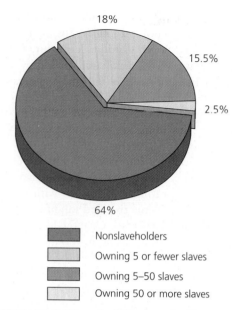

FIGURE 10.3 Slaveholding and Class Structure in the South, 1830 The great majority of the southern white population was yeoman farmers. In 1830, slave owners made up only 36 percent of the southern white population; owners of more than fifty slaves constituted a tiny 2.5 percent. Yet they and the others who were middling planters dominated politics, retaining the support of yeomen who prized their freedom as white men above class-based politics.

SOURCE: U.S. Bureau of the Census.

become large slave owners because they already had capital (the pay from their professions) to invest in land and slaves. Sometimes they received payment for their services, not in money, but in slaves. These owners were the most likely to own skilled slaves—carpenters, blacksmiths, and other artisans—and to rent them out for profit. By steady accumulation, the most successful members of this middle class were able to buy their way into the slave-owning elite and to confirm that position by marrying their sons or daughters into the aristocracy.

The Planter Elite

The slave-owning elite, those 2.5 percent who owned fifty slaves or more, enjoyed the prestige, the political leadership, and the lifestyle to which many white Southerners aspired. Almost all great slave owners inherited their wealth. They were rarely self-made men, although most tried to add to the land and slaves they had inherited. Men of wealth and property had led southern politics since colonial times. Increasingly after 1820, as universal manhood suffrage spread, planters had to learn how to appeal to the popular vote, but most never acquired "the common touch." The smaller slave owners, not the great planters, formed a clear majority in every southern state legislature.

The eastern seaboard had first given rise to a class of rich planters in the colonial period, as attested by the plantations of William Byrd and Robert "King" Carter of

Virginia and the cultured life of the planter elite, centered in Charleston, which had established itself in the South Carolina low country and Sea Islands. In the nineteenth century, these planters ranged from land rich but labor poor Thomas Chaplin of Tombee Plantation, who grew sea-island cotton, to rice planter Nathaniel Heyward, who through wealthy marriages and land purchases amassed 45,000 acres of land and over 2,000 slaves.

As Southerners and slave owning spread westward, membership in the elite broadened to include the new wealth of Alabama, Mississippi, Louisiana, and Texas. Natchez, on the Mississippi River, became so wealthy that its rich planters were popularly called "nabobs" (from a Hindi word for Europeans who had amassed fabulous wealth in India). One great Natchez family, the Surgets, of French origin, traced its wealth back to a Spanish land grant of 2,500 acres. In the 1850s, Frank and James Surget controlled some 93,000 acres in Mississippi, Arkansas, and Louisiana (half of it plantation land and half bought on speculation for resale). Each brother sold 4,000 bales of cotton a year, and between them they owned upwards of 1,000 slaves. Each also owned palatial mansions in Natchez which, thanks to cotton, in 1850 was the richest county in the nation.

Creating a Plantation Ideology

The urban life of the Natchez planters was unusual. Many wealthy planters, especially those on new lands in the Old Southwest, lived in isolation on their plantations with their families and slaves. Through family networks, common boarding school experience, political activity, and frequent visiting, the small new planter elite consciously worked to create and maintain a distinctive lifestyle that was modeled on that of the English aristocracy, as Southerners understood it. This entailed a large estate, a spacious, elegant mansion, and lavish hospitality. For men, the gentlemanly lifestyle meant immersion in masculine activities such as hunting, soldiering, or politics, and a touchy concern with "honor" that could lead to duels and other acts of bravado. Women of the slave-owning elite, in contrast, were expected to be gentle, charming, and always welcoming of relatives, friends, and other guests.

The economic reality of plantation life was that large numbers of black slaves had to be forced to work to produce the wealth that supported the planters' gracious lifestyle. Each plantation, like the yeoman farm but on a larger scale, aimed to be self-sufficient, producing not only the cash crop but also most of the food and clothing for both slaves and family. There were stables full of horses for plowing, transportation, and show. There were livestock and vegetable gardens to be tended, and carpentry, blacksmithing, weaving, and sewing to be done. A large plantation was an enterprise that required many hands, many skills, and a lot of management. Large plantation owners

Read the Document

Overseer's Report from Chicora Wood Plantation (1858) at **www.myhistorylab.com**

might have overseers or black drivers to supervise field work, but frequently they themselves had direct financial control of daily operations. Even if they were absentee landlords (such as Thomas Chaplin in South Carolina and the richest of the Natchez elite), planters usually required careful accounts from their overseers and often exercised the right to overrule their decisions.

Plantation mistresses spent most of their lives tending "family" members—including slaves—in illness and in childbirth, and supervising their slaves' performance of such daily tasks as cooking, housecleaning, weaving, and sewing. In addition, the plantation mistress often had to spend hours, even days, of behind-the-scenes preparation for the crowds of guests she was expected to welcome in her role as elegant and gracious hostess.

Many southern women also suffered deeply from their isolation from friends and kin. Sometimes the isolation of life on rural plantations could be overcome by long visits, but women with many small children and extensive responsibilities found it difficult to leave. Plantation masters, on the other hand, often traveled widely for political and business reasons. John C. Calhoun, for example, spent much less time than his wife on the family plantation, Fort Hill. He spent years in Washington as a politician, while Floride Calhoun, who had accompanied him in his early career, remained at Fort Hill after the first five of their ten children were born.

The planter elite developed a paternalistic ideology to justify their rigorous insistence on the master–slave relationship. According to this ideology, each plantation was a family composed of both black and white. The master, as head of the plantation, was head of the family, and the mistress was his "helpmate." The master was obligated to provide for all of his family, both black and white, and to treat them with humanity. In return, slaves were to work properly and do as they were told, as children would. Most elite slave owners spoke of their position of privilege as a duty and a burden. (Their wives were even more outspoken about the burdensome aspects of supervising slave labor, which they bore more directly than their husbands.) John C. Calhoun spoke for many slave owners when he described the plantation as "a little community" in which the master directed all operations so that the abilities and needs of every member, black and white, were "perfectly harmonized." Convinced of their own benevolence, slave owners expected not only obedience but also gratitude from all members of their great "families."

Coercion and Violence

There were generous and benevolent masters, but most large slave owners believed that constant discipline and coercion were necessary to make slaves work hard (see Seeing History). Some slave owners used their slaves with great brutality. Owners who killed slaves were occasionally brought to trial (and usually acquitted), but no legal action was taken in the much more frequent cases of excessive punishment, general abuse, and rape. All southern slave owners, not just those who experienced the special tensions of new and isolated plantations in the Old Southwest, were engaged in a constant battle of wills with their slaves that owners frequently resolved by violence.

One of the most common violations of the paternalistic code of behavior (and of southern law) was the sexual abuse of female slaves by their masters. Usually, masters forcibly raped their women slaves at will, and slave women had little hope of defending themselves from these attacks. Occasionally long-term intimate relationships between masters and slaves developed, such as the one that apparently existed between Thomas Jefferson and Sally Hemmings.

It was rare for slave owners to publicly acknowledge fathering slave children or to free these children, and black women and their families were helpless to protest their treatment. Equally silenced was the master's wife, who for reasons of modesty as well as her subordinate position was not supposed to notice either her husband's infidelity or his flagrant crossing of the color lines. As Mary Boykin Chesnut, wife of a South Carolina slave owner, vehemently confided to her diary: "God forgive us, but ours is a monstrous system. . . . Like the patriarchs of old, our men live all

SCENE ON A COTTON PLANTATION.   GATHERING COTTON.

The gang system used in cotton cultivation necessitated overseers to keep the gang at work. Hence scenes like this where slaves work hard to pick and bale cotton while white overseers with whips stand lazily.

in one house with their wives and their concubines, and the mulattoes one sees in every family partly resemble the white children. Any lady is ready to tell you who is the father of all the mulatto children in everybody's household but her own. Those, she seems to think, drop from the clouds."

Perhaps as common but veiled by the gentle female stereotype was the daily violence practiced by plantation mistresses. Although a number of southern white women railed against "the curse of slavery," few meant the inhumanity of the system; most were actually complaining

about the extra work entailed by housekeeping with slaves. As one plantation mistress explained, "Slaves are a continual source of more trouble to housekeepers than all other things, vexing them, and causing much sin. We are compelled to keep them in ignorance and much responsibility rests on us." House servants bore the brunt of the brunt of petty and persistent punishment by their mistresses, and personal servants often suffered mental cruelty. Although on every plantation black women served as nursemaids to white children and as lifelong maids to white women, there

SEEING HISTORY

"Gordon under Medical Inspection"

This horrifying image of the badly scarred back of a former slave named Gordon appeared in *Harper's Weekly* in July 1863. He was an escaped slave who entered Union lines in Baton Rouge in March 1863, arriving in the bedraggled condition shown on the left. Under medical examination, he revealed the scars from a whipping three months earlier. As the third picture shows, he promptly joined the Union Army.

Although abolitionist literature frequently described brutal whippings endured by slaves, few people in the North can have seen such graphic examples before the

publication of this article in 1863. A photographic image of "The Scourged Back" is one of the earliest examples of the impact of photography as propaganda. Since that time, the picture of Gordon's back has frequently been used to illustrate the violence of the slave system. There is no question that whipping was a frequent punishment in the slaveholding South and that masters, mistresses, and overseers, in fits of temper, whipped harshly. Although we do not know if Gordon's scars were representative, the image makes it impossible to deny the reality of brutality in the slave system.

• **After viewing this image, how seriously would you consider claims that southern slavery was a benign, paternalistic system?**

are few historical examples of genuine sympathy between women across racial lines. Few white women seemed to realize the sadness, frustration and despair often experienced by their lifelong maids, who were forced to leave their own husbands and children to serve their mistresses as they married and moved to new homes. Years later many former slaves remembered their mistresses as being kinder than their masters, but fully a third of such accounts mention cruel whippings and other punishments by women.

An owner could do what he chose on his plantation, and his sons and daughters grew up expecting to do likewise. Unchecked power is always dangerous, and it is not surprising that it was frequently misused, often in the name of "discipline." Perhaps the most surprising thing about the southern slave system is how much humanity survived despite the intolerable conditions. For that, most of the credit goes not to white paternalism, but to African Americans and the communities they created under slavery.

The Defense of Slavery

"Slavery informs all our modes of life, all our habits of thought, lies at the basis of our social existence, and of our political faith," announced South Carolina planter William Henry Trescot in 1850, explaining why the South would secede from the Union before giving up slavery. Slavery bound white and black Southerners together in tortuous ways that eventually led, as Trescot had warned, to the Civil War. Population figures tell much of the story of the complex relationship between whites and blacks: of the 12 million people who lived in the South in 1860, 4 million were slaves. Indeed, in the richest agricultural regions, such as the Sea Islands of South Carolina and Georgia and parts of the black belt, black people outnumbered whites. These sheer numbers of African Americans reinforced white people's perpetual fears of black retaliation for the violence exercised by the slave master. Every rumor of slave revolts, real or imagined, kept those fears alive. The basic question was this: What might slaves do if they were not controlled? Thomas Jefferson summed up this dilemma: "We have the wolf by the ears; and we can neither hold him nor safely let him go. Justice is in one scale, and self-preservation in the other."

Developing Proslavery Arguments

Once the cotton boom began in the 1790s, Southerners increasingly sought to justify slavery. They found justifications for slavery in the Bible and in the histories of Greece and Rome, both slave-owning societies. The strongest defense was a legal one: the Constitution allowed slavery. Though never specifically mentioned in the final document, slavery had been a major issue between North and South at the Constitutional Convention in 1787. In the end, the delegates agreed that seats in the House of

Representatives would be apportioned by counting all of the white population and three-fifths of the black people (Article I, Section 2, Paragraph 3); they included a clause requiring the return of runaway slaves who had crossed state lines (Article IV, Section 2, Paragraph 3); and they agreed that Congress could not abolish the international slave trade for twenty years (Article I, Section 9, Paragraph 1). There was absolutely no question: the Constitution did recognize slavery. Just as important, but unwritten, was the implicit understanding in 1787 that slavery was a sectional problem that Southern politicians, not the federal government, would work to eliminate. That unvoiced agreement, of course, occurred before cotton became the South's economic mainspring.

The Missouri Crisis of 1819–20 deeply alarmed most Southerners, who were shocked by the evidence of widespread antislavery feeling in the North, and northern willingness to intervene in southern politics. South Carolinians viewed Denmark Vesey's conspiracy, occurring only two years after the Missouri debate, as an example of the harm that irresponsible northern antislavery talk could cause. In the wake of the Vesey conspiracy, Charlestonians turned their fear and anger outward by attempting to seal off the city from dangerous outside influences. In December 1822, the South Carolina legislature passed a bill requiring that all black seamen be seized and jailed while their ships were in Charleston harbor. Initially most alarmed about free black people from Haiti, Charlestonians soon came to believe that northern free black seamen were spreading antislavery ideas among their slaves.

After Nat Turner's revolt in 1831, Governor John Floyd of Virginia blamed the uprising on "Yankee peddlers and traders" who supposedly told slaves that "all men were born free and equal." Thus, northern antislavery opinion and the fear of slave uprisings were firmly linked in southern minds. This extreme reaction, which Northerners viewed as paranoid, stemmed from the basic nature of a slave society: *anything* that challenged the master–slave relationship was viewed as a basic threat to the entire system.

After Nat Turner

In 1831, the South began to close ranks in defense of slavery. Several factors contributed to this regional solidarity. Nat Turner's revolt was important, linked as it was in the minds of many Southerners with antislavery agitation from the North. Militant abolitionist William Lloyd Garrison began publishing the *Liberator*, the newspaper that was to become the leading antislavery organ, in 1831 The British gave notice that they would soon abolish slavery on the sugar plantations of the West Indies, an action that seemed to many Southerners much too close to home. Emancipation for West Indian slaves came in 1834. Finally, 1831 was the year before the Nullification Crisis (see Chapter 11) was resolved.

COMMUNITIES *in* CONFLICT

Who Benefits from Slavery?

Although we often use the term "community" to describe the entire southern slave system, no community is ever monolithic in its views. In these two excerpts, we see first a famous defense of slavery offered by South Carolina Senator James Henry Hammond (slave owner) in a speech to the U.S. Senate on March 4, 1858, and second, the much less well-known view of a nonslaveholder as expressed by Hinton Helper in 1857. Hinton Helper was the rare Southerner who published his opposition to slavery. His book, *The Impending Crisis of the South: How to Meet It*, was an economic comparison of North and South aimed at the southern majority that did not own slaves.

• **Why did the majority of Southerners, who did not own slaves themselves, support the slave system?**

Senator James Henry Hammond Defends Slavery

IN ALL SOCIAL SYSTEMS THERE MUST BE A CLASS to do the menial duties, to perform the drudgery of life. That is, a class requiring but a low order of intellect and but little skill. Its requisites are vigor, docility, fidelity. Such a class you must have, or you would not have that other class which leads progress, civilization, and refinement. It constitutes the very mud-sill of society and of political government; and you might as well attempt to build a house in the air, as to build either the one or the other, except on this mud-sill. Fortunately for the South, she found a race adapted to that purpose to her hand. A race inferior to her own, but eminently qualified in temper, in vigor, in docility, in capacity to stand the climate, to answer all her purposes. We use them for our purpose, and call them slaves. . . .

The Senator from New York said yesterday that the whole world had abolished slavery. Aye, the name, but not the thing; all the powers of the earth cannot abolish that. God only can do it when he repeals the fiat, "the poor ye always have with you"; for the man who

> "[O]ur slaves are hired for life and well compensated; there is no starvation, no begging, no want of employment, . . ."

Although the other southern states did not support the hotheaded South Carolinians who called for secession, they did sympathize with the argument that the federal government had no right to interfere with a state's special interest (namely, slavery). Following the crisis, other southern states joined with South Carolina in the belief that the only effective way to prevent other federal encroachment was through the militant and vehement defense of slavery.

In the 1830s, southern states began to barricade themselves against "outside" antislavery propaganda. In 1835, a crowd broke into a Charleston post office, made off with bundles of antislavery literature, and set an enormous bonfire to fervent state and regional acclaim. By 1835, every southern legislature had tightened its laws concerning control of slaves. For example, they tried to blunt the effect of abolitionist literature by passing laws forbidding slaves to learn how to read. In only three border states—Kentucky, Tennessee, and Maryland—did slave literacy remain legal. By 1860, it is estimated, only 5 percent of all slaves could read. Slaves were forbidden to gather for dances, religious services, or any kind of organized social activity without a white person present. They were forbidden to have whiskey because it might encourage them toward revolt. The penalty for plotting insurrection was death. Other laws made manumission illegal and placed even more restrictions on the lives of free black people. In many areas, slave patrols were augmented and became more vigilant in restricting African American movement and communication between plantations.

In 1836, Southerners introduced a "gag rule" in Washington to prevent congressional consideration of abolitionist petitions. Attempts were made to stifle all open debate about slavery within the South; dissenters were pressured to remain silent or to leave. A few, such as James G. Birney and Sarah and Angelina Grimké of South Carolina, left for the North to act on their antislavery convictions, but most chose silence. Among those under the greatest pressure to conform were Christian ministers, many of whom professed to believe that preaching obedience to slaves was a vital part of making slavery a humane system.

lives by daily labor, and scarcely lives at that, and who has to put out his labor in the market, and take the best he can get for it; in short, your whole hireling class of manual laborers and "operatives," as you call them, are essentially slaves. The difference between us is, that our slaves are hired for life and well compensated; there is no starvation, no begging, no want of employment among our people, and not too much employment either. Yours are hired by the day, not cared for, and scantily compensated, which may be proved in the most painful manner, at any hour in any street in any of your large towns. Why, you meet more beggars in one day, in any single street of the city of New York, than you would meet in a lifetime in the whole South.

SOURCE: Selection from the *Letters and Speeches of the Hon. James H. Hammond of South Carolina* (New York: John F. Trow and Co., 1866).

Hinton Helper Exhorts White Southerners

Non-slaveholders of the South! Farmers, mechanics, and workingmen, we take this occasion to assure you that the slaveholders, the arrogant demagogues whom you have elected to offices of honor and profit, have hoodwinked you, trifled with you, and used you as mere tools for the consummation of their wicked designs. They have purposely kept you in ignorance, and have, by moulding your passions and prejudices to suit themselves, induced you to act in direct opposition to your dearest rights and interests. By a system of the grossest subterfuge and misrepresentation, and in order to avert, for a season, the vengeance that will most assuredly overtake them ere long, they have taught you to hate the abolitionists, who are your best and only true friends. Now, as one of your own number, we appeal to you to join us in our patriotic endeavors to rescue the generous soil of the South from the usurped and desolating control of these political vampires. Once and forever, at least so far as this country is concerned, the infernal question of slavery must be disposed of; a speedy and perfect abolishment of the whole institution is the true policy of the South—and this is the policy which we propose to pursue. Will you aid us, will you assist us, will you be freemen, or will you be slaves?

SOURCE: Hinton Rowan Helper, *The Impending Crisis of the South: How to Meet It* (New York: Burdick Brothers, 1857).

"[T]he infernal question of slavery must be disposed of; a speedy . . . abolishment of the whole institution is the true policy of the South. . . ."

In addition to fueling fears of slave rebellions, the growing abolitionist sentiment of the 1830s raised the worry that southern opportunities for expansion would be cut off. Southern politicians painted melodramatic pictures of a beleaguered white South hemmed in on all sides by "fanatic" antislavery states. At home, Southerners were forced to contemplate what might happen when they had "to let loose among them, freed from the wholesome restraints of patriarchal authority . . . an idle, worthless, profligate set of free negroes" whom they feared would "prowl the . . . streets at night and [haunt] the woods during the day armed with whatever weapons they could lay their hands on."

Finally, southern apologists moved beyond defensiveness to develop proslavery arguments. One of the first to do this was James Henry Hammond, elected a South Carolina congressman in 1834. In 1836, Hammond delivered a major address to Congress in which he denied that slavery was evil. Rather, he claimed, it had produced "the highest toned, the purest, best organization of society that has ever existed on the face of the earth" (see Communities in Conflict). In 1838, Senator John C. Calhoun of South Carolina took the argument a step further by claiming that slavery was "the most safe and stable basis for free institutions in the world" because it subordinated an "inferior" race to benevolent white paternalists devoted to their well-being and moral improvement. Calhoun spoke not only of the plantation as a family, as we have seen, but of the entire South as a collection of paternalistic communities. In 1858, another southern spokesman, George Fitzhugh, asserted that "the negro slaves of the South are the happiest, and, in some sense, the freest people in the world" because all the responsibility for their care was borne by concerned white masters. Fitzhugh contrasted southern paternalism with the heartless individualism that ruled the lives of northern "wage slaves." Northern employers did not take care of their workers, Fitzhugh claimed, because "selfishness is almost the only motive of human conduct in free society, where every man is taught that it is his first duty to change and better his pecuniary situation." In contrast, Fitzhugh argued, southern

Read the **Document**
George Fitzhugh, Slavery Justified (1854) at **www.myhistorylab.com**

masters and their slaves were bound together by a "community of interests."

Changes in the South

In spite of these defensive and repressive proslavery measures, which made the South seem monolithic in northern eyes, there were some surprising indicators of dissent. One protest occurred in the Virginia state legislature in 1832, when nonslaveholding delegates, alarmed by the Nat Turner rebellion, forced a two-week debate on the merits of gradual abolition. In the final vote, abolition was defeated seventy-three to fifty-eight. Although the subject was never raised again, this debate was a startling indicator of frequently unvoiced doubts about slavery that existed in the South.

But slavery was not a static system. From the 1830s on, financial changes increasingly underlined class differences among southern whites. It was much harder to become a slaveholder: from 1830 to 1860, slave owners declined from 36 to 25 percent of the population. In 1860, the average slaveholder was ten times as wealthy as the average nonslaveholder. A major reason for the shrinking number of slave owners and their increased wealth was the rapidly increasing price of slaves: a "prime field hand" was worth more than $1,500 in 1855. Such prices caused the internal slave trade to flourish: during the 1850s, slave owners from the Upper South sold some 250,000 slaves to the Lower South for handsome profits. By 1850, in the Chesapeake (Virginia, Maryland, and Delaware), where American slavery had its origin, the percentage of slave owners had fallen to 28 percent, while the comparable figures for Louisiana and Mississippi were 45 percent. Agriculture was diversifying in the Upper South, while the plantation system flourished in the Lower South, as indicated by the fact that 85 percent of the great planters with more than a hundred slaves lived there. Such differences in the extent of slaveholding between the Upper and Lower South threatened regional political unity (see Map 10.4).

Another alarming trend was the disintegration of the slave system in southern cities. The number of urban slaves greatly decreased because plantation owners deeply distrusted the effect of cities on the institution of slavery.

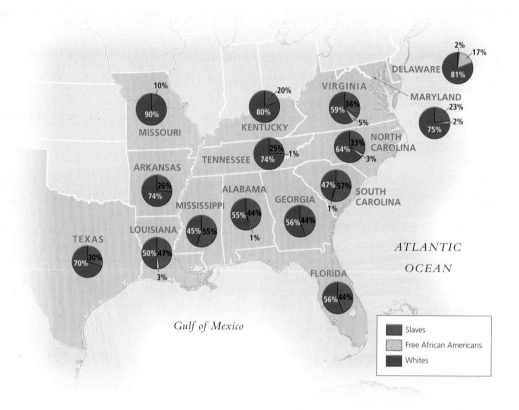

MAP 10.4 Population Patterns in the South, 1850 In South Carolina and Mississippi, the enslaved African American population outnumbered the white population; in four other Lower South states, the percentage was above 40 percent. These ratios frightened many white Southerners. White people also feared the free black population, though only three states in the Upper South and Louisiana had free black populations of over 3 percent. Six states had free black populations that were so small (less than 1 percent) as to be statistically insignificant.

CHRONOLOGY

1790s	Second Great Awakening
	Black Baptist and African Methodist Episcopal churches founded
1793	Cotton gin invented
1800	Gabriel Prosser's revolt discovered in Virginia
1806	Virginia tightens law on manumission of slaves
1808	Congress prohibits U.S. participation in the international slave trade
1816–20	"Alabama Fever": migration to the Old Southwest
1819–20	Missouri Crisis
1822	Denmark Vesey's conspiracy in Charleston
1831	Nat Turner's revolt in Virginia
	William Lloyd Garrison begins publishing an antislavery newspaper, the *Liberator*
1832	Nullification Crisis
1832–38	"Flush Times": second wave of westward expansion
1832	Virginia legislature debates and defeats a measure for gradual emancipation
1834	Britain frees slaves throughout the empire, including in its Caribbean colonies
1835	Charleston crowd burns abolitionist literature
	Tightening of black codes completed by southern legislatures
1836	Congress passes "gag rule" to prevent discussion of antislavery petitions
	James Henry Hammond announces to Congress that slavery is not evil
1846	William Gregg opens model textile mill at Graniteville, South Carolina
1854	George Fitzhugh publishes *Sociology for the South*, a defense of slavery
1857	Hinton Helper publishes *The Impending Crisis*, an attack on slavery
1858	James Henry Hammond's "King Cotton" speech

Urban slaves led much more informed lives than rural ones and were often in daily contact with free blacks and urban poor whites. Many slaves were hired out and a number even hired out their own time, making them nearly indistinguishable from northern "free labor." Other urban slaves worked in commercial and industrial enterprises in jobs that were nearly indistinguishable from those of whites. Planters viewed all of these changes with suspicion, yet they also had to acknowledge that southern cities were successful and bustling centers of commerce.

Economic changes adversely affected poor whites and yeomen as well. Increased commercialization of agriculture (other than cotton) led to higher land prices that made it harder for poor whites to buy or rent land. Extensive railroad building in up-country regions during the boom of the 1850s ended the isolation of many yeomen, exposing them for the first time to the temptations and dangers of the market economy. While slave owners grew increasingly worried about threats from the abolitionist and capitalist North, yeomen worried about local threats to their independence from banks, railroads, and activist state governments. In North Carolina, disputes between slave owners and nonslaveholders erupted in

print in 1857, when Hinton Helper published an attack on slavery in a book titled *The Impending Crisis*. His protest was an indicator of the growing tensions between the haves and the have-nots in the South (see Communities in Conflict). Equally significant, though, Helper's book was published in New York, where he was forced to move once his views became known.

In spite of these signs of tension and dissent, the main lines of the southern argument were drawn in the 1830s and remained fixed thereafter. The defense of slavery stifled debate within the South, prevented a search for alternative labor systems, and narrowed the possibility of cooperation in national politics. In time, it made compromise impossible.

Conclusion

The amazing growth of cotton production after 1793 transformed the South and the nation. Physically, the South expanded explosively westward: in all, seven southern states were admitted to the Union between 1800 and 1845. Cotton production fastened the slave system of labor upon the region. Although the international slave trade was abolished in 1808, the internal slave trade flourished, with devastating effects on African American families. Nationally, the profitable cotton trade fueled economic development and provided much of the original capital for the infant factory system of the North. Cotton production was based on the labor of African American slaves, who built strong communities under extremely difficult circumstances. The cohesion of African American families and the powerful faith of African American Christianity were the key community elements that bred a spirit of endurance and resistance. White Southerners, two-thirds of whom did not own slaves, denied their real dependence on slave labor by claiming equality in white skin privilege, while slave owners boasted of their own paternalism. But the extreme fear generated by a handful of slave revolts and the growing number of free African Americans in many areas gave the lie to white claims of benevolence. In the 1830s, the South defensively closed ranks against real and perceived threats to the slave system. In this sense, the white South was nearly as trapped as the African American slaves they claimed to control. And in its growing concern for the defense of the slave system, the South's role in national politics became more rigid, as we shall see in the next chapter.

Review Questions

1. How did cotton production after 1793 transform the social and political history of the South? How did the rest of the nation benefit? In what way was it an "international phenomenon"?

2. What were the two key institutions of the African American slave community? How did they function, and what beliefs did they express?

3. The circumstances of two groups—poor whites and free African Americans—put them outside the dominant southern equations of white equals free and black equals slave. Analyze the difficulty each group encountered in the slave-owning South.

4. Who were the yeoman farmers? What was their interest in slavery?

5. Southern slaveholders claimed that their paternalism justified their ownership of slaves, but paternalism implied obligations as well as privileges. How well

do you think slaveholders lived up to their paternalistic obligations?

6. How did slave owners justify slavery? How did their defense change over time?

Recommended Reading

Edward E. Baptist, *Creating an Old South: Middle Florida's Plantation Frontier before the Civil War* (2002). Traces the development of a rough plantation frontier to a consciously constructed genteel plantation lifestyle.

Ira Berlin, *Generations of Captivity* (2003). A compelling survey of the changing nature of American slavery.

Daina Ramey Berry, *"Swing the Sickle for the Harvest Is Ripe": Gender and Slavery in Antebellum Georgia* (2007). Focuses on female labor in two different labor systems in Georgia.

Joan E. Cashin, *A Family Venture: Men and Women on the Southern Frontier* (1991). Explores the effects on slave owners of separation from family networks.

Steven Deyle, *Carry Me Back: The Domestic Slave Trade in American Life* (2005). The effects of the trade on American life.

Lacy Ford, *Deliver Us from Evil* (2009). Introduces dynamism into the history of American slavery by suggesting a periodization of Southern defenses of the system.

Jeff Forret, *Race Relations at the Margins: Slaves and Poor Whites in the Antebellum Southern Countryside* (2007). Studies the mostly-hidden social contacts between slaves and poor whites in Virginia, North and South Carolina.

Thavolia Glymph, *Out of the House of Bondage: The Transformation of the Plantation Household* (2008). Explores the persistent violence of white plantation women toward their black female slaves.

Annette Gordon-Reed, *The Hemingses of Monticello: An American Family* (2008) An award-winning account of three generations of Jefferson's favorite slave family.

Anthony E. Kaye, *Joining Places: Slave Neighborhoods in the Old South* (2007). An innovative study about the ways the informal and unnoticed ways of slaves linked plantations into African American neighborhoods.

Edward Bartlett Rugemer, *The Problem of Emancipation: The Caribbean Roots of the American Civil War* (2009). Explores the little-studied impact on the South of British emancipation in 1834.

PEARSON myhistorylab Connections

Reinforce what you learned in this chapter by studying the many documents, images, maps, review tools, and videos available at www.myhistorylab.com.

Read and Review

✓• Study and Review Chapter 10

•••• Read the Document

Thomas Jefferson, Notes on Virginia (1787)

State Laws Govern Slavery (1824)

A Slave Tells of His Sale at Auction (1848)

Frances E.W. Harper, The Slave Auction (1854)

Frances Ann Kemble, Journal of a Residence on a Georgia Plantation (1838)

A Catechism for Slaves (1854)

Slave Culture Documented in Song (1867)

Runaway Slave Advertisements (1838–1839)

The Confession of Nat Turner (1831)

Overseer's Report from Chicora Wood Plantation (1858)

George Fitzhugh, Slavery Justified (1854)

👁• See the Map *United States Territorial Expansion in the 1850s*

Research and Explore

•••• Read the Document

Exploring America: Alexis de Tocqueville

Profiles
  Hinton Rowan Helper
  Harriet Jacobs

⊙• Watch the Video *The Plantation System*

((•• Hear the Audio

Hear the audio files for Chapter 10 at
www.myhistorylab.com.

11

The Growth of Democracy 1824–1840

CHAPTER OUTLINE

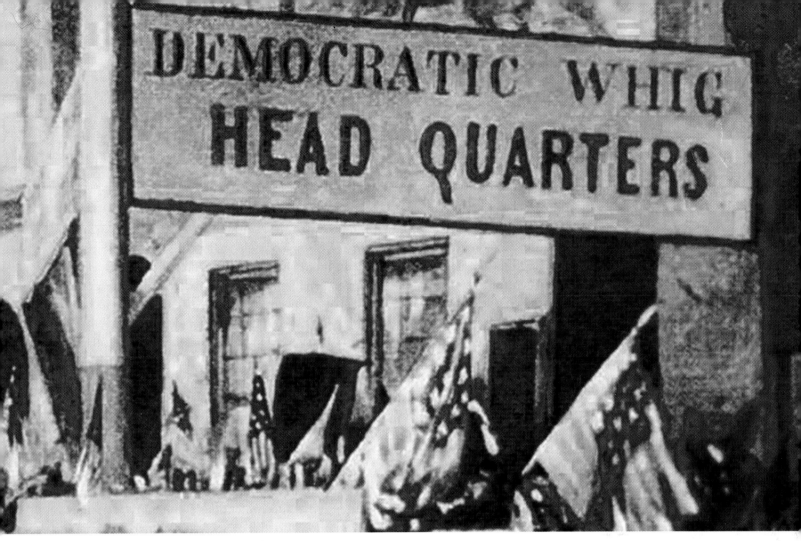

Whig Parade, 1840s. Courtesy of the Library of Congress.

A Political Community Abandons Deference for Democracy

Philadelphia had long been a stronghold of craft associations for skilled workers. Their organizations, and their parades and celebrations, were recognized parts of the urban community. Groups of master craftsmen marching in community parades with signs such as "By Hammer and Hand All Arts Do Stand" not only demonstrated pride in their craft but also asserted their importance to the community as a whole. Pennsylvania enfranchised all men who were taxpayers in 1776, enabling many of Philadelphia's skilled workers to vote, but they were willing to follow the leadership of the city's political elite. This was the accepted rule of republican government as understood by leaders such as Thomas Jefferson: an independent and virtuous people willingly deferred to wealthy and enlightened leaders who would govern in the public interest. In reality, most states limited the vote to property owners, and so many ordinary men had little choice but to accept the decisions of the wealthy.

By the 1820s, the lives of workers in Philadelphia had changed. As the Market Revolution transformed the economy, many skilled workers lost their independence and became wage earners in factories owned by others. Members of urban workers' associations realized that their own economic interests were different from those of the owners. In other states, where many men

AMERICAN Communities

279

gained the vote for the first time in the 1820s, a similar process of identifying common interests at odds with the traditional political elite was also underway. The spread of universal manhood suffrage marked the transition from traditional deferential politics to democracy.

In 1827, the British-born shoemaker William Heighton urged his fellow workers in Philadelphia to band together under "the banner of equal rights" and form their own political party to press for issues of direct concern to workingmen, including the ten-hour day, free public education for their children, the end of imprisonment for debt, and curbing the powers of banks. Until producers (by which he meant both urban workers and rural farmers) united and formed their own political party, Heighton warned, politicians would continue to ignore their concerns. "Surely we, the working class, who constitute a vast majority of the nation . . . have a right to expect [that] an improvement in our *individual condition* will be the natural result of legislative proceedings."

Heighton saw in the rising tide of universal manhood suffrage the possibility of reaching his overarching aim of "economic democracy." In response to his new vision of majority rule, the Philadelphia Working Men's Party was formed in 1828 and elected a slate of local officials as well as voting for Andrew Jackson for president. Andrew Jackson, who was so untraditional that at first national politicians did not take him seriously as a candidate, perfectly personified the new democratic mood and its animosity toward what was often termed "the monied aristocracy."

Thus, when a committee of the Philadelphia Working Men's Party attacked the banking system in 1829, Andrew Jackson paid attention. Their report decried the control by wealthy men of banks and of the paper money each bank issued (there was no national government-controlled currency until 1862), concluding: "If the present system of banking and paper money be perpetuated, the great body of the working people must give over all hopes of ever acquiring any property." This fear of the threat to democracy from a moneyed aristocracy was common among voters in rural areas of the South and West as well as in urban areas. Jackson not only understood this public resentment, but he also shared it. In 1832 he had Philadelphia's workers and others in mind when, speaking for "the humble members of society—the farmers, mechanics and laborers," he refused to renew the charter of the Bank of the United States and thereby instigated the events that we call the Bank War.

The Philadelphia Working Men's Party did not last very long. Too small and too narrowly focused to have wide appeal, it was quickly absorbed into Jackson's Democratic Party, with most of its specific demands unmet. Nevertheless, its brief history is significant for marking the end of traditional ideas about a unitary local political community and the transition to the more diverse and contentious community of competing interests that has characterized American democracy ever since. But it also set some limits. Politicians were quick to note that most Americans were uncomfortable with President Jackson's use of the language of class warfare in his veto message. Henceforth, whatever the competing interests might be, appeal to resentment alone was rarely successful. Rather, politicians sought to create national coalitions of voters with similar interests, creating new and more democratic political communities than had existed before.

Philadelphia

The New Democratic Politics in North America

The early years of the nineteenth century were a time of extraordinary growth and change, not only for the United States but for all the countries of North America as well. Seen in continental perspective, the American embrace of popular democracy was unusual. Elsewhere, crises over popular rights dominated.

Struggles over Popular Rights: Mexico, the Caribbean, Canada

In 1821, after eleven years of revolts (see Chapter 9), Mexico achieved its independence from Spain. Briefly united under the leadership of Colonel Agustin de Iturbide, Mexico declared itself a constitutional monarchy that promised equality for everyone—peninsulares, criollos, mestizos, and Indians alike. But because Spanish

1. How did suffrage expand between 1800 and 1840?

2. In what ways did Andrew Jackson's presidency affirm the new democratic politics?

3. How did the major political struggles of the Jackson years strengthen the executive branch of government?

4. How did the basic two-party pattern of American political democracy take shape?

5. How was a distinctive American cultural identity shaped by writers and artists?

FOCUS
Questions

1824–1840

colonial rule had left a legacy of deep social divisions, the initial unity was short-lived. Iturbide reigned as Emperor of Mexico for little more than a year before he was overthrown by a military junta and later executed as a traitor. A series of weak presidents repeatedly invoked emergency powers and relied on the army, as they attempted to revive a faltering economy and reconcile the differences between the centralists—the vested interests of clergy, large land owners, and the military—and the federalists, largely criollos and mestizos, who hoped to create a liberal republic modeled on the American one. The unresolved issue of elite versus popular rule continued to undermine the hope for unity, popular rights, and stable government in an independent Mexico.

The independence of Haiti in 1804 (see Chapter 9) set the pattern for events in many other Caribbean islands in subsequent years. Independence destroyed the sugar industry, for freed slaves asserted their popular rights by refusing to perform the killing labor demanded of them on sugar plantations. The British Caribbean islands were racked with revolts, the largest occurring on Barbados in 1816 and on Jamaica in 1831. In response the British Parliament abolished slavery in all British colonies in 1834. As in Haiti, sugar production then plunged. The only island where sugar production increased was Spanish Cuba, where slavery remained legal until 1880. Elsewhere, economic collapse following emancipation destroyed the political authority of local white elites, forcing the British government to impose direct rule. This sequence of events—revolt, emancipation, economic collapse, loss of local political autonomy—was closely observed by slave owners in the American South and made them fear for their own futures.

Still a third crisis of popular rights occurred in British North America. In 1837, both Upper and Lower Canada rebelled against the limited representative government that

the British government had imposed in the Constitutional Act of 1791. By far the most serious revolt was in predominantly French Lower Canada, where armed uprisings were brutally suppressed by British troops. In 1840, Britain abolished the local government of Lower Canada and joined it to Upper Canada in a union that most French Canadians opposed and in which they were a minority. In his report to the British government, Lord Durham announced that the purpose of union was to end the ethnic enmity between British and French by forcing the latter to assimilate and "abandon their vain hopes of nationality." Lord Durham suggested increased colonial self-government, but the British government, fearing further trouble, refused to grant it.

In comparison to these experiences, the rapid spread of suffrage in the United States and the growth of a vibrant but stable democratic political culture seemed all the more extraordinary. But after a brilliant start, in the 1850s the United States, like its neighbors, foundered on a basic sectional difference—slavery—that not even political democracy could reconcile (see Chapter 15).

The Expansion and Limits of Suffrage

Before 1800, most of the original thirteen states had limited the vote to property owners or taxpayers, thereby excluding about half of the white male population. Westward expansion changed the nature of American politics by undermining the traditional authority structures in the older states. "Old America seems to be breaking up and moving westward" and thereby breaking the old networks of personal authority, an observer commented in 1817—fostering a more democratic structure in the newer states (see Map 11.1).

Most of the new states extended the right to vote to all white males over the age of twenty-one. Vermont led

MAP 11.1 Population Trends: Westward Expansion, 1830 Westward population movement, only a trickle in 1800, had become a flood by 1830. Between 1800 and 1830, the U.S. white and African American population more than doubled (from 5.3 million to 12.9 million), but the trans-Appalachian population grew tenfold (from 370,000 to 3.7 million). By 1830, more than a third of the nation's inhabitants lived west of the original thirteen states.

the way in 1791, followed by Kentucky in 1792. Tennessee (1796) and Ohio (1803) entered with low taxpayer qualifications that approached universal suffrage. By 1820, most of the older states had followed suit. The War of 1812 was an important impetus to change in many states, for the propertyless men called up for militia service in that war questioned why they were eligible to fight but not to vote. There were laggards—Rhode Island, Virginia, and Louisiana did not liberalize their voting qualifications until later—but by 1840, more than 90 percent of adult white males in the nation could vote. And they could vote for

more officials: governors and (most important) presidential electors were now elected by direct vote, rather than chosen by small groups of state legislators.

Universal white manhood suffrage, of course, was far from true universal suffrage: the right to vote remained barred to most of the nation's free African American males and to women of any race. Only in five New England states (Maine, New Hampshire, Vermont, Massachusetts, and Rhode Island) could free African American men vote before 1865. In the rest of the northern states, the right of free African American men to vote was restricted to only the most affluent property owners. Free African American men were denied the vote in the all of the new western states as well. The Ohio constitution of 1802 denied them the right to vote, to hold public office, and to testify against white men in court cases. The constitutions of other western states—Illinois, Indiana, Michigan, Iowa, Wisconsin, and (later) Oregon—attempted to solve the "problem" of free African Americans by simply denying them entry into the state at all. Of course, all free black men were prohibited from voting in the slave states of the South (see Figure 11.1).

What accounted for this nearly universal denial of voting rights to free black men? Racism—the assumption that African Americans were a different and less capable people—accounted for much of it, an attitude that was strengthened by the backlash against the extremely controversial abolitionist movement of the 1830s and 1840s (see Chapter 13). In addition, as party lines hardened, northern Democrats, the party most closely aligned with the slave South, opposed enfranchising African American men who were almost certain to vote for their opponents. Above all, it was a sign of the growing influence that the southern slave system cast over all of American politics.

In contrast, the reason for the denial of suffrage to white women was boringly traditional, stemming from the patriarchal belief that men headed households and represented the interests of all household members. Even wealthy single women who lived alone were considered subordinate to male relatives and denied the right to vote. (New Jersey had been an exception to this rule until it amended its constitution in 1807 to withdraw the franchise from propertied women.) Although unable to vote, women of the upper classes had long played important informal roles in national politics, especially in Washington, DC, where presidents' wives like Abigail Adams and Dolley Madison wielded behind-the-scenes power. At the local level as well, women—often the wives of leading citizens—were accustomed to engaging informally in politics through their benevolent groups. These groups, often church related, had since colonial times not only provided charity to the poor but also raised money to support basic community institutions such as schools, churches, and libraries, in effect setting community priorities in the process.

Although the extension of suffrage to all classes of white men seemed to indicate that women had no role in public affairs, in fact women's informal involvement in politics grew along with the increasing pace of political activity. At the same time, however, as "manhood" rather than property became the qualification for voting, men began to ignore women's customary political activity and to regard their participation as inappropriate, an attitude that politically active women increasingly resented.

Thus, in a period famous for democratization and "the rise of the common man," the exclusion of important groups—African American men and women of all races—marked the limits of liberalization. It is also true that nowhere else in the world was the right to vote as widespread as it was in the United States. This unprecedented confidence in popular opinion made American politics and politicians unique in the changing world of the early nineteenth century. The extension of suffrage to propertyless farm workers and members of the laboring poor in the nation's cities left European observers wondering: Could "mob rule" possibly succeed?

●●─[Read the Document

A Legal Scholar Opposes Spreading the Vote (1821) at **www.myhistorylab.com**

The Election of 1824

The 1824 election marked a dramatic end to the political truce that James Monroe had established in 1817 and to the idea of leadership by a small nonpartisan political elite. Five candidates, all of them members of the Republican Party, ran for president in the elections of 1824: William H. Crawford of Georgia, Secretary of State John Quincy Adams of Massachusetts, Henry Clay of Kentucky, Andrew Jackson of Tennessee, and John C. Calhoun of South Carolina, who withdrew before the election to run for vice president. Jackson, a latecomer to the race, was at first not taken seriously because his record as a legislator was lackluster and his political views

FIGURE 11.1 Race Exclusions for Suffrage, 1790–1855
This graph shows that as the number of states increased so did the percentage that excluded African American men from voting. None of the states that entered the Union after 1819 allowed African American suffrage.

SOURCE: From *The Right to Vote*, by Alexander Keyssar. Copyright © 2009 Alexander Keyssar. Reprinted by permission of Basic Books, a member of the Perseus Books Group.

unknown. He was not a member of the elite political group that had made up the governing class since 1790. However, owing to his national reputation as a military leader, Jackson won 43 percent of the popular vote and ninety-nine electoral votes—more than any other candidate. The runner-up, John Quincy Adams, won 31 percent of the popular vote and eighty-four electoral votes. But neither had an electoral majority, leaving it up to the House of Representatives, as in the election of 1800, to pick the winner.

After some political dealing, Henry Clay threw his support to Adams, and the House elected Adams president. This was customary and proper: the Constitution gave the House the power to decide, and Clay had every right to advise his followers how to vote.

Read the Document

John Quincy Adams, Inaugural Address (1825) at **www.myhistorylab.com**

But when Adams named Clay his secretary of state, the traditional stepping-stone to the highest office, Jackson's supporters promptly accused them of a "corrupt bargain." Popular opinion, the new element in politics, supported Jackson. John Quincy Adams served four miserable years as president, knowing that Jackson would challenge him, and win, in 1828 (see Map 11.2).

The legislative accomplishments of Adams's presidency were scanty. Adams tried to enact the coordinated plan for economic development embodied in Henry Clay's American System (see Chapter 9) but was rebuffed by a hostile Congress, although he did succeed in obtaining funding for an extension of the National Road west from Wheeling—an issue on which he could count on western votes. Southerners blocked Adams's desire to play an important role in hemispheric affairs by refusing his request to send American delegates to a conference in Panama called by the Latin American liberator Simón Bolívar, in part because they feared it might lead to recognition of the revolutionary black republic of Haiti. Adams's desire to lead the nation from a position above politics was frustrated by a political opposition that was an early sign of the emerging two-party system.

The New Popular Democratic Culture

In 1834, the French visitor Michel Chevalier witnessed a mile-long nighttime parade in support of Andrew Jackson. Stunned by the orderly stream of banners lit by torchlight, the portraits of George Washington, Thomas Jefferson, and Jackson, and the enthusiastic cheering of the crowd, Chevalier wrote, "These scenes belong to history. They are

Read the Document

Michel Chevalier, Society, Manner and Politics in the U.S. (1834) at **www.myhistorylab.com**

the episodes of a wondrous epic which will bequeath a lasting memory to posterity, that of the coming of democracy." Mass campaigns—huge political rallies, parades, and candidates with wide "name recognition," such as military heroes—were the hallmarks of the new popular democratic culture. So were less savory customs, such as the distribution of lavish food and (especially) drink at polling places, which frequently turned elections into rowdy, brawling occasions. As Chevalier noted, the spirit that motivated the new mass

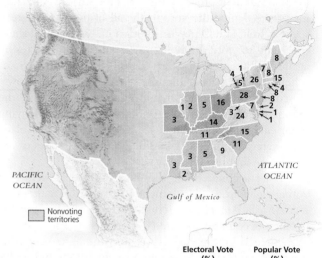

	Electoral Vote (%)	Popular Vote (%)
Andrew Jackson	99 (38)	153,544 (43)
JOHN QUINCY ADAMS	84 (32)	108,740 (31)
William H. Crawford	41 (16)	46,618 (13)
Henry Clay	37 (14)	47,136 (13)

MAP 11.2 The Election of 1824 The presidential vote of 1824 was clearly sectional. John Quincy Adams carried his native New England and little else, Henry Clay carried only his own state of Kentucky and two adjoining states, and Crawford's appeal was limited to Virginia and Georgia. Only Andrew Jackson moved beyond the regional support of the Old Southwest to wider appeal and the greatest number of electoral votes. Because no candidate had a majority, however, the election was thrown into the House of Representatives, which chose Adams.

politics was democratic pride in participation. And as the election of 1824 showed, along with the spread of universal male suffrage went a change in popular attitudes that spelled the end of the customary dominance of small political elites. However, the new mass of voters was quickly absorbed into a new political structure. New national parties that superseded sectional interests emerged: to succeed, they had to appeal to the interests of a diverse range of voters.

In New York State, master political tactician Martin Van Buren forged a tightly organized, broad-based political group nicknamed the Albany Regency that wrested political control away from the former elite. In doing so, he became a major architect of the new democratic politics of mass participation, based, he claimed, on his "faith in the capacity of the masses of the people of our Country to govern themselves, and in their general integrity in the exercise of that function." In other states, a Virginia group known as the Richmond Junto, the Nashville Junto in Tennessee, and New Hampshire's Concord Regency all aspired to the same discipline and control. Coordinated by Van Buren, they

This well-known painting by George Caleb Bingham, *Stump Speaking*, shows a group of men (and boys and dogs) of all social classes brought together by their common interest in politics.

SOURCE: George Caleb Bingham (American, 1811–1879), *Stump Speaking*, 1853–54. Oil on canvas, 42 ½ × 58 in. Saint Louis Art Museum, Gift of Bank of America.

formed the coalition that nearly elected Andrew Jackson president in 1824. One of the keys to their success was their use of newspapers to reach a broad audience.

A print revolution helped to democratize politics by spreading word far beyond the nation's cities about the parades, protests, and celebrations that became a basic part of popular democracy. The print revolution had begun in 1826, when a reform organization, the American Tract Society, installed the country's first steam-powered press and rapidly turned out 300,000 Bibles and 6 million religious tracts. The greatest growth, however, was in newspapers that reached a mass audience. The number of newspapers soared from 376 in 1810 to 1,200 in 1835. This rise paralleled the growth of interest in politics, for most news papers, like Heighton's *Mechanics Free Press* in Philadelphia, were published by political parties and were openly partisan. Packed with articles that today would be considered libelous and scandalous, newspapers were entertaining and popular reading, and they rapidly became a key part of democratic popular culture (see Figure 11.2).

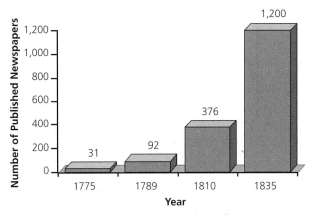

FIGURE 11.2 The Burgeoning of Newspapers
Newspapers have a long history in the United States. Even before the American Revolution, the colonies boasted thirty-seven newspapers, and within little more than a decade, that number had nearly tripled. Toward the end of the century, however, the number of newspapers expanded rapidly, by 1835 numbering more than thirty times that of 1775.

The new politics appealed to new voters by placing great emphasis on participation and party loyalty. One way for ordinary citizens to show their loyalty was to turn out for parades, which derived from processions like those of Philadelphia artisans' associations in earlier times. Political processions were huge affairs, marked by the often spontaneous participation of men carrying badges and party regalia, banners and placards, and portraits of the candidates, accompanied by bands, fireworks, and the shouting and singing of party slogans and songs. The political party provided some of the same satisfactions that popular sports offer today: excitement, entertainment, and a sense of belonging. In effect, political parties functioned as giant national men's clubs. They made politics an immediate and engrossing topic of conversation and argument for men of all walks of life. In this sense, the political party was the political manifestation of a wider social impulse toward community (see Figure 11.3).

The Election of 1828

The election of 1828 was the first to demonstrate the power and effectiveness of the new popular democratic culture and party system. With the help of Martin Van Buren, his campaign manager, Andrew Jackson rode the wave of the new democratic politics to the presidency. Voter turnout in 1828 was more than twice that of 1824. Jackson's party, the Democratic-Republicans (they soon dropped "Republicans" and became simply the

Politics, abetted by the publication of inexpensive party newspapers, was a great topic of conversation among men in early nineteenth-century America, as Richard Caton Woodville's 1845 painting *Politics in an Oyster House* suggests.

SOURCE: Richard Caton Woodville, *Politics in an Oyster House*, 1848. Oil on canvas. The Walters Art Museum, Baltimore.

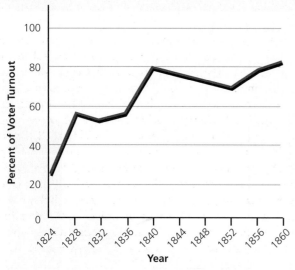

FIGURE 11.3 Pre–Civil War Voter Turnout

The turnout of voters in presidential elections more than doubled from 1824 to 1828, the year Andrew Jackson was first elected. Turnout surged to 80 percent in 1840, the year the Whigs triumphed. The extension of suffrage to all white men, and heated competition between two political parties with nationwide membership, turned presidential election campaigns into events with great popular appeal.

Democrats), spoke the language of democracy, and they opposed the special privilege personified for them by President John Quincy Adams and his National Republican (as distinguished from the earlier Jeffersonian Republican) Party. Neither Jackson nor Adams campaigned on his own—that was considered undignified. But the supporters of both candidates campaigned vigorously, freely, and negatively. Jackson's supporters, playing on popular resentment of a wealthy political elite, portrayed the campaign as a contest between "the democracy of the country, on the one hand, and a lordly purse-proud aristocracy on the other." In their turn, Adams's supporters depicted Jackson as an illiterate backwoodsman, a murderer (he had ordered the execution of deserters in the Tennessee militia), and an adulterer (apparently unwittingly, he had married Rachel Robards before her divorce was final). Jackson's running mate for vice president was John C. Calhoun of South Carolina. Although this choice assured Jackson of valuable southern support, it also illustrated the transitional nature of politics, for

••• Read the Document

Ballad of General Jackson and the Six Militia Men (1827) at **www.myhistorylab.com**

Calhoun was at the time of the election serving as vice president to John Quincy Adams, Jackson's opponent. That Calhoun was easily able to lend his support to a rival faction was a holdover from the old elite and personal politics that would soon be impossible in the new democratic political system.

Jackson won 56 percent of the popular vote (well over 80 percent in much of the South and West) and a decisive electoral majority of 178 votes to Adams's 83. The vote was interpreted as a victory for the common man. But the most important thing about Jackson's victory was the coalition that achieved it. The new democratically based political organizations—the Richmond and Nashville juntos, the Albany and Concord regencies, with help from Calhoun's organization in South Carolina—worked together to elect him. Popular appeal, which Jackson the military hero certainly possessed, was not enough to ensure victory. To be truly national, a party had to create and maintain a coalition of North, South, and West. The Democrats were the first to do this (see Map 11.3).

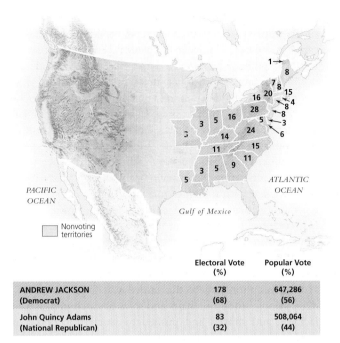

	Electoral Vote (%)	Popular Vote (%)
ANDREW JACKSON (Democrat)	178 (68)	647,286 (56)
John Quincy Adams (National Republican)	83 (32)	508,064 (44)

MAP 11.3 The Election of 1828 Andrew Jackson's victory in 1828 was the first success of the new national party system. The coalition of state parties that elected him was national, not regional. Although his support was strongest in the South and West, his ability to carry Pennsylvania and parts of New York demonstrated his national appeal.

This anti-Jackson "coffin bill" from the election of 1828 accuses Jackson of murder because he ordered three men executed for desertion during the War of 1812.

The Jackson Presidency

Andrew Jackson's election ushered in a new era in American politics, an era that historians have called the "Age of the Common Man." Jackson himself, however, was no common man: he was a military hero, a rich slave owner, and an imperious and decidedly undemocratic personality. "Old Hickory," as Jackson was affectionately called, was tough and unbending, just like hickory itself, one of the hardest of woods. Yet he had a mass appeal to ordinary people, unmatched—and indeed unsought—by earlier presidents. The secret to Jackson's extraordinary appeal lies in the changing nature of American society. Jackson was the first to respond to the ways in which westward expansion and the extension of the suffrage were changing politics at the national as well as the local and state levels.

A Popular President

Jackson was born in 1767 and raised in North Carolina. During the American Revolution, he was captured and beaten by the British, an insult he never forgot. As a young man without wealth or family support, he moved west to the frontier station (fort) at Nashville, Tennessee, in 1788. There he made his career as a lawyer and his considerable wealth as a slave-owning planter. He first became a national hero with his underdog win against the British in the Battle of New Orleans in 1815. In the popular mind, his fierce belligerence came to symbolize pioneer independence. The fact that he had little political experience, which would have made his nomination impossible under the traditional system of politics, was not a hindrance in the new age of popular politics.

On March 4, 1829, Andrew Jackson was inaugurated as president of the United States. Jackson himself was still in mourning for his beloved wife Rachel, whose recent death he attributed to the slanders of the campaign. But everyone else was celebrating. The small community of Washington was crowded with strangers, many of them Westerners and common people who had come especially for Jackson's inauguration. Jackson's brief inaugural address was almost drowned out by the cheering of the crowd, and after the ceremony the new president was mobbed by well-wishers. The same unrestrained enthusiasm was evident at a White House reception, where the crowd was large and disorderly. People stood on chairs and sofas to catch glimpses of Jackson, and shoved and pushed to reach the food and drink, which was finally carried out to the lawn. In the rush to follow, some people exited through windows rather than the doors (see Seeing History). This was the exuberance of democracy in action. It marked something new in American politics. Indeed, Jackson's administration was different from all those before it.

A Strong Executive

The mob scene that accompanied Jackson's inauguration was more than a reflection of the popular enthusiasm for Old Hickory. It also signaled a higher level of controversy in national politics. Jackson's personal style quickly stripped national politics of the polite and gentlemanly aura of cooperation it had acquired during the Era of Good Feelings and that Adams had vainly tried to maintain. Jackson had played rough all his life, and he relished controversy. His administration (1829–37) had plenty of it. Andrew Jackson dominated his administration. Except for Martin Van Buren, whom he appointed secretary of state, he mostly ignored the heads of government departments who made up his official cabinet. Instead he consulted with an informal group, dubbed the "Kitchen Cabinet," made up of Van Buren and old western friends. The Kitchen Cabinet did not include John C. Calhoun, the vice president, or either of the other two great sectional representatives, Henry Clay and Daniel Webster. Jackson never forgave Clay for his role in the "corrupt bargain" of 1825, and he saw Daniel Webster as a representative of his favorite political target, the privileged elite.

Jackson used social distance to separate himself from other politicians. When Jackson's secretary of war, John Henry Eaton, married a beautiful woman of flamboyant reputation, he transgressed the social code of the time. It was rumored that Peggy Eaton had been Eaton's mistress and that there were other men in her past. She was, in nineteenth-century thinking, a fallen woman and unfit for polite society. The respectable ladies of Washington shunned her. But Jackson, aroused by memories of the slanders against his own wife, defended Peggy Eaton and urged his cabinet members to force their wives to call on her. When, to a woman, they refused, Jackson called the husbands henpecked.

This episode chilled the social life of cabinet members and their families and drove a wedge between Jackson and Calhoun, whose wife Floride was a leader in the anti-Eaton group. Although Jackson claimed to be motivated only by chivalry, he wanted to change Washington politics, and this episode helped him do it. The important although quiet role that women had played since 1800 in Washington politics came to an abrupt end. Ironically, the Eaton episode might never have occurred had Jackson not been a widower. Her own damaged reputation as a bigamist would surely have forced Rachel Jackson to side with Mrs. Calhoun in upholding the moral code of the time.

Jackson freely used the tools of his office to strengthen the executive branch of government at the expense of the legislature and judiciary. By using the veto more frequently than all previous presidents combined (twelve vetoes compared with nine by the first six presidents), Jackson forced Congress to constantly consider his opinions. Even more important, Jackson's "negative activism" restricted federal activity (see Chapter 9). Only his strong and popular leadership made this sharp change of direction possible.

The Nation's Leader versus Sectional Spokesmen

Despite his western origins, Jackson was a genuinely national figure. He believed that the president, who symbolized the popular will of the people, ought to dominate the government. As he put it in his first annual message, "the first principle of our system [is that] the majority is to govern." This was new. Voters were much more accustomed to thinking of politics in sectional terms. Jackson faced a Congress full of strong and immensely popular sectional figures. Three stood out: Southerner John C. Calhoun, Northerner Daniel Webster, and Westerner Henry Clay.

Intense, dogmatic, and uncompromising, John C. Calhoun of South Carolina had begun his political career as an ardent nationalist and expansionist in his early days as a War Hawk before the War of 1812. Since the debate over the Missouri Compromise in 1820, however, Calhoun had wholeheartedly identified with southern interests, first and foremost among which was the preservation and expansion of slavery. As the South's minority position in Congress became clear over the years, Calhoun's defense of southern economic interests and slavery became more and more rigid. Not for nothing did he earn his nickname the "Cast-Iron Man."

SEEING History

President's Levee, or all Creation Going to the White House

Until 1829, presidential inaugurations had been small, polite, and ceremonial occasions. Andrew Jackson's popularity, however, brought a horde of well-wishers to Washington for his inaugural. "Thousands and thousands of people, without distinction of rank," reported Washington resident Margaret Bayard Smith, "collected in an immense mass round the Capitol, silent, orderly and tranquil," to watch Jackson's swearing-in. But afterwards, when the crowd followed Jackson to an open house at the White House, says Smith, "what a scene did we witness! . . . a rabble, a mob of boys, negros, women, children, scrambling, fighting, romping. What a pity what a pity." Her consternation was echoed by many respectable people who feared that "the reign of King Mob" had begun.

This famous illustration of the raucous crowd at the White House reception is by the British caricature artist Robert Cruikshank. It was probably first shown, along with other pictures, in a London printmaker's window display in 1829, with copies sold for two shillings. For the British, amusement came from the fact that American democracy so quickly turned into a rowdy mob, just as the British had always predicted.

Cruikshank was not in Washington at the time of Jackson's inaugural. At best, the details of the illustration are based on accounts provided to him by others or perhaps simply invented. Nevertheless, the illustration captures the mood of the celebrating crowd.

• **Does it matter that the details are not correct?**

Three Great Sectional Leaders. The years of Jackson's presidency were also notable for the prominence of regional spokesmen, among them John C. Calhoun (top left), who spoke for the South and slavery, Henry Clay (top right) who spoke for the West, and Daniel Webster (bottom left), who represented northern business. Clay's great personal charm is captured in this 1824 portrait (right), contrasting with Calhoun's dour expression and Webster's stern image.

SOURCE: (top right) Matthew H. Joulett (1788–1827), *Henry Clay*, c. 1824. Oil on panel. (attr. to Jouett) © Chicago Historical Society, Chicago, USA.

Senator Daniel Webster of Massachusetts was the outstanding orator of the age. Large, dark, and stern, Webster delivered his speeches in a deep, booming voice that, listeners said, "shook the world." Webster became the main spokesman for the new northern commercial interests, supporting a high protective tariff, a national bank, and a strong federal government. Webster's fondness for comfortable living made him less effective as he grew older, but then, as a contemporary of his remarked, "No man could be as great as Daniel Webster looked."

In contrast with the other two, Henry Clay of Kentucky, spokesman of the West, was charming, witty, and always eager to forge political compromises. Clay held the powerful position of Speaker of the House of Representatives from 1811 to 1825 and later served several terms in the Senate. Well known for his ability to make a deal—he was known as "the Great Pacificator" (compromiser)—Clay worked to incorporate western desires for cheap and good transportation into national politics. It was he who promoted the national plan for economic development known as the American System: a national bank, a protective tariff, and the use of substantial federal funds for internal improvements such as roads, canals, and railroads (see Chapter 9). Clay might well have forged a political alliance between the North and the West if not for the policies of President Jackson, his fellow Westerner and greatest rival. Jackson's preeminence thwarted Clay's own ambition to be president.

The prominence and popularity of these three politicians show that sectional interests remained strong even under a president as determined as Jackson to override them and disrupt "politics as usual" by imposing his own personal style. Nothing showed the power of sectional interests more clearly than the unprecedented confrontation provoked by South Carolina in Jackson's first term, the Nullification Crisis.

The Nullification Crisis

The crisis raised the fundamental question concerning national unity in a federal system: What was the correct balance between local interests—the rights of the states—and the powers of the central government? The men who wrote the federal Constitution in Philadelphia in 1787 had not been able to reach agreement on this question. Because the Constitution deliberately left the federal structure ambiguous, all sectional disagreements automatically became constitutional issues that carried a threat to national unity.

The political issue that came to symbolize the divergent economic interests of North and South was the protective tariff that placed a duty (or surcharge) on imported goods. The first substantial tariff was enacted in 1816 after northern manufacturing interests clamored for protection from the ruthless British competition that followed the War of 1812 (see Chapter 9). As a group, wealthy southern planters were opposed to tariffs, both because duties raised the cost of the luxury goods they imported from Europe and because they feared that American tariffs would cause other countries to retaliate with tariffs against southern cotton. Most southern congressmen, assured that the 1816 tariff was a temporary postwar recovery measure, voted for it. But it was not temporary.

As the North industrialized and new industries demanded protection, tariff bills in 1824 and 1828 raised rates still higher and protected more items. Southerners protested, but they were outvoted in Congress by northern and western representatives. The 1828 tariff, nicknamed the "Tariff of Abominations," was a special target of southern anger because Jackson's supporters in Congress had passed it, over southern objections, in order to increase northern support for him in the presidential campaign of that year. It imposed especially high tariffs on imported textiles and iron; the tariffs ranged from a third to a half of the total value of those products.

Southern opponents of the tariff insisted that it was not a truly national measure but rather a sectional one that helped only some groups while harming others. Thus, they claimed, it was unconstitutional because it violated the rights of some of the states.

South Carolina, Calhoun's home state, reacted the most forcefully to the Tariff of 1828. Of the older southern states, South Carolina had been the hardest hit by the opening of the new cotton lands in the Old Southwest, which had drained both population and commerce from the state. To these economic woes were added the first real fears about national attitudes toward slavery.

South Carolinians, who had always had close personal ties with slave owners in the Caribbean islands, were shaken by the news that the British Parliament, bowing to popular pressure at home, was planning to emancipate all the slaves in the British West Indies. If Congress had the power to impose tariffs that were harmful to some states, South Carolinians asked, what would prevent it from enacting legislation like Britain's, depriving Southerners of their slaves and, thus, of their livelihood? In this sense, although the Nullification Crisis was about the tariff, it was also about the greatest of all sectional issues, slavery.

Read the Document
Proclamation Concerning Nullification (1832) at **www.myhistorylab.com**

The result of these fears was a renewed interest in the doctrine of nullification, a topic that became the subject of widespread discussion in South Carolina. The doctrine upheld the right of a state to declare a federal law null and void and to refuse to enforce it within the state. South Carolinian John C. Calhoun wrote a widely circulated defense of the doctrine, the *Exposition and Protest*, in 1828. Because Calhoun was soon to serve as Andrew Jackson's vice president, he wrote the *Exposition* anonymously. He hoped to use his influence with Jackson, a fellow slave owner, to gain support for nullification, but he was disappointed.

Where Calhoun saw nullification as a safeguard of the rights of the minority, Jackson saw it as a threat to national unity. The president and the vice president were thus in open disagreement on a matter of crucial national importance. The outcome was inevitable: Calhoun lost all influence with Jackson, and two years later, he took the unusual step of resigning the vice presidency. Martin Van Buren was elected to the office for Jackson's second term. Calhoun, his presidential aspirations in ruins, became a senator from South Carolina, and in that capacity, participated in the last act of the nullification drama.

In 1832, the nullification controversy became a full-blown crisis. In passing the Tariff of 1832, Congress (in spite of Jackson's disapproval) retained high taxes on woolens, iron, and hemp, although it reduced duties on other items. South Carolina responded with a special convention and an Ordinance of Nullification, in which it rejected the tariff and refused to collect the taxes it required. The state further issued a call for a volunteer militia and threatened to secede from the Union if Jackson used force against it. Jackson responded vehemently, denouncing the nullifiers—"Disunion by armed force is treason"—and obtaining from Congress a Force Bill authorizing the federal government to collect the tariff in South Carolina at gunpoint if necessary. Intimidated, the other southern states refused to follow South Carolina's lead. More quietly, Jackson also asked Congress to revise the tariff. Henry Clay, the Great Pacificator, swung into action and soon, with Calhoun's support, had crafted the Tariff Act of 1833. The South Carolina legislature, unwilling to act without the support of other southern states, quickly accepted this face-saving compromise and repealed its nullification of the Tariff of 1832. In a final burst of bravado, the legislature nullified the Force Bill, but Jackson defused the crisis by ignoring its action.

The Nullification Crisis was the most serious threat to national unity that the United States had ever experienced. South Carolinians, by threatening to secede, had forced concessions on a matter they believed of vital economic importance. They—and a number of other Southerners—believed that the resolution of the crisis illustrated the success of their uncompromising tactics. Most of the rest of the nation simply breathed a sigh of relief, echoing Daniel Webster's sentiment, spoken in the heat of the debate over nullification, "Liberty and Union, now and forever, one and inseparable!"

Read the Document
An American Senator Opposes Nullification, (1830) at **www.myhistorylab.com**

Changing the Course of Government

As Martin Van Buren later recalled, Jackson came to the presidency with a clear agenda: "First, the removal of the Indians from the vicinity of the white population and their settlement beyond the Mississippi. Second, to put a stop to the abuses of the Federal government in regard to internal improvements [and] Third, to oppose as well the existing re-incorporation of the existing National Bank." As Jackson enacted his agenda, which he believed expressed the popular will, he changed the course of the federal government as decisively as Jefferson had during his presidency (see Chapter 9). But the opposition that Jackson evoked also revealed the limits of presidential authority in an age of democratic politics.

Indian Removal

The official policy of the U.S. government from the time of Jefferson's administration was to promote the assimilation of Indian peoples by encouraging them to adopt white ways. To Indian groups that resisted "civilization" or that needed more time to adapt, Jefferson offered the alternative of removal from settled areas in the East to the new Indian Territory west of the Mississippi River. Following this logic, at the end of the War of 1812, the federal government signed removal treaties with a number of Indian nations of the Old Northwest, thereby opening up large tracts of land for white settlement (see Chapter 9). In the Southwest, however, the Five Southern Tribes—the Cherokees, Chickasaws, Choctaws, Creeks, and Seminoles—remained.

By the 1830s, under constant pressure from settlers, each of the five southern tribes had ceded most of its lands, but sizable self-governing groups lived in Georgia, Alabama, Mississippi, and Florida. All of these (except the Seminoles) had moved far in the direction of coexistence with whites, and they resisted suggestions that they should voluntarily remove themselves.

The Cherokees took the most extensive steps to adopt white ways. Their tribal lands in northwestern Georgia boasted prosperous farms, businesses, grain and lumber mills, and even plantations with black slaves. Intermarriage with whites and African Americans had produced an influential group of mixed-bloods within the Cherokee nation, some of whom were eager to accept white ways. Schooled by Congregationalist, Presbyterian, and Moravian missionaries, the Cherokees were almost totally literate in English.

Despite the evidence of the Cherokees' successful adaptation to the dominant white culture, in the 1820s, the legislatures of Georgia, Alabama, and Mississippi, responding to pressures from land-hungry whites, voted to invalidate federal treaties granting special self-governing status to Indian lands. Because the federal government, not the states, bore responsibility for Indian policy, these state actions constituted a sectional challenge to federal authority. In this instance, however, unlike the Nullification Crisis, the resisting states had presidential support. Living up to his reputation as a ruthless Indian fighter, Jackson determined on a federal policy of wholesale removal of the southern Indian tribes.

Read the Document
Memorial of the Cherokee Nation (1830) at **www.myhistorylab.com**

In 1830, at President Jackson's urging, the U.S. Congress passed the hotly debated Indian Removal Act, which appropriated funds for relocation, by force if necessary. When Jackson increased the pressure by sending federal officials to negotiate removal treaties with the southern tribes, most reluctantly signed and prepared to move. The Cherokees, however, fought their removal by using the white man's weapon—the law. At first they seemed to have won: in *Cherokee Nation* v. *Georgia* (1831) and *Worcester* v. *Georgia* (1832), Chief Justice John Marshall ruled that the Cherokees, though not a state or a foreign nation, were a "domestic dependent nation" that could not be forced by the state of Georgia to give up its land against its will. Ignoring the decision, Jackson continued his support for removal.

Although some Seminole bands mounted a successful resistance war in the Florida Everglades, the majority of Seminoles and members of

other tribes were much less fortunate: most of the Choctaws moved west in 1830; the last of the Creeks were forcibly moved by the military in 1836, and the Chickasaws a year later. And in 1838, in the last and most infamous removal, resisting Cherokees were driven west to Oklahoma along what came to be known as the "Trail of Tears." A 7,000-man army escorting them watched thousands (perhaps a quarter of the 16,000 Cherokees) die along the way (see Map 11.4).

Another futile effort to resist removal, the Black Hawk "war," occurred in the Old Northwest. In 1832, Sauk and Fox Indians, led by Black Hawk, attempted to move back to their old tribal grounds in Illinois following

removal, but settlers saw the move as an invasion and demanded military protection. Federal troops chased the Black Hawk band to Wisconsin, where more than 300 Indians died in a final battle, and Black Hawk himself was taken prisoner. As in the South, the last of the remaining Indians east of the Mississippi were removed by the end of the 1830s.

Indian removal was a deeply divisive national issue. President Jackson's sweeping policy undoubtedly expressed the opinion of most Southerners and Westerners. But northern opinion, led by Protestant missionaries and reform groups, was strongly opposed. Among the groups mobilized in protest were members of female benevolent societies who had a direct interest in the issue, for they had long raised money to support missionary activities aimed at assimilating, not removing, American Indians. Now, they joined together to organize the first national female petition drive. A surprised Congress was deluged by women's petitions against removal, many with hundreds

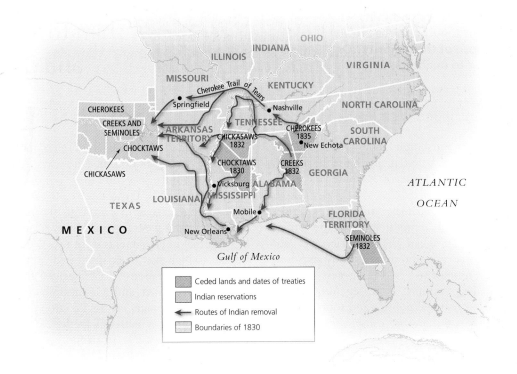

MAP 11.4 Southern Indian Cessions and Removals, 1830s Pressure on the five major southern Indian peoples—the Cherokees, Chickasaws, Choctaws, Creeks, and Seminoles—that began during the War of 1812 culminated with their removal in the 1830s. Some groups from every tribe ceded their southern homelands peacefully and moved to the newly established Indian Territory west of Arkansas and Missouri. Some, like the Seminoles, resisted by force. Others, like the Cherokees, resisted in the courts, but finally lost when President Andrew Jackson refused to enforce a Supreme Court decision in their favor. The Cherokees, the last to move, were forcibly removed by the U.S. Army along the "Trail of Tears" in 1838.

Indian Removal, Pro and Con

When Andrew Jackson became president in 1829, he placed the removal of the Five Southern Tribes to Indian Territory at the top of his political agenda, but he faced vehement opposition, especially in the North. Beyond the issue of land ownership (Alabamans and Georgians wanted the lands the Indians occupied) the debate revealed deeper questions of how to deal with cultural differences that are still relevant today. In these two excerpts, Jackson strongly advocates removal in his First Annual Message to Congress in December 1829 by arguing that "civilization" and "savagery" are incompatible. In response Senator Theodore Frelinghuysen of New Jersey, speaking during the Congressional debate on the Indian Removal Act in April 1830, argues for cultural integrity and autonomy.

• **Should the state recognize the cultural autonomy of communities within its population, even if their practices are different from those of the majority? Or should adaptation to majority standards be required?**

Andrew Jackson's Message on Indian Removal

A portion . . . of the Southern tribes, having mingled much with the whites and made some progress in the arts of civilized life, have lately attempted to erect an independent government within the limits of Georgia and Alabama . . . I informed the[m] their attempt to establish an independent government would not be countenanced . . . and advised them to emigrate beyond the Mississippi or submit to the laws of those states.

Our conduct toward these people is deeply interesting to our national character. Their present condition, contrasted with what they once were, makes a most powerful appeal to our

> [Indians are] surrounded by the whites with their arts of civilization, which . . . destroy the resources of the savage [and] doom him to weakness and decay.

---

of signatures (670 from Pittsburgh alone). In the end, the protest failed, but by the barest of margins: the Indian Removal Act passed the House of Representatives by only three votes (out of 200).

In contrast to the lesson of the Nullification Crisis, Jackson's policy on Indian removal showed how unfair majority rule could be when the minority was not strong enough to force a compromise. But just as South Carolinians were emboldened by the success of their resistance, benevolent women were encouraged by their intervention in national politics and soon focused their petitioning skills on another cause, abolition (see Chapter 13).

Internal Improvements

Because Jackson was a Westerner, his supporters expected him to recognize the nation's urgent need for better transportation and to provide federal funding for internal improvements, especially in the West. Jackson's veto of the Maysville Road Bill of 1830 was, therefore, one of his most unexpected actions. Jackson refused to allow federal funding of a southern spur of the National Road in Kentucky, claiming it should be paid for by the state.

Jackson argued that federal funding for extensive and expensive transportation measures was unconstitutional because it infringed on the "reserved powers" the Constitution left to the states. He also had the satisfaction of defeating a measure central to the American System proposed by his western rival, Henry Clay.

Internal improvements were a part of Clay's American System (which had been supported by the Monroe and Adams administrations) that envisaged the national government as planner and administrator of a coordinated policy to encourage economic growth and foster the development of a national market. But since 1816, it had proved impossible to propose a nationally funded transportation plan that satisfied everyone. Repeatedly, disappointed claimants for federal funds accused each administration of favoritism and corruption. Jackson ended most of the debate over internal improvements by refusing federal funds for all but the most obviously interstate projects (such as the National Road).

But the country still needed a basic infrastructure of roads, canals, and railroads to tie the national economy together. Without federal funding and planning, the initiative passed to private developers, who turned to individual states. The states actually spent more than the sympathies. Our ancestors found them the uncontrolled possessors of these vast regions. By persuasion and force they have been made to retire from river to river and mountain to mountain, until some of the tribes have become extinct and others have left but remnants to preserve for a while their once terrible names. Surrounded by the whites with their arts of civilization, which by destroying the resources of the savage doom him to weakness and decay, the fate of the Mohegan, the Narragansett, and the Delaware is fast overtaking the Choctaw, the Cherokee, and the Creek. That this fate surely awaits them if they remain within the limits of the States does not admit of a doubt.

Senator Theodore Frelinghuysen Responds

I believe, sir, it is not now seriously denied that the Indians are men, endowed with kindred faculties and powers with ourselves; that they have a place in human sympathy, and are justly entitled to a share in the common bounties of a benignant Providence. And, with this conceded, I ask in what code of the law of nations, or by what process of abstract deduction, their rights have been extinguished?

What is the decree or ordinance that has stripped these early and first lords of the soil? Sir, no record of such measure can be found. . . . However mere human policy, or the law of power, or the tyrant's pleas of expediency, may have found it convenient at any or in all times to recede from the unchangeable principles of eternal justice, no argument can shake the political maxim, that, where the Indian always has been, he enjoys an absolute right still to be, in the free exercise of his own modes of thought, government and conduct.

SOURCE: Francis Paul Prucha, ed., *Documents of United States Indian Policy, Second Edition, Expanded* (Lincoln, NE: University of Nebraska Press, 1990), pp. 47–52.

> Where the Indian always has been, he enjoys an absolute right still to be, in the free exercise of his own modes of thought, government and conduct.

federal government on internal improvements, with a fivefold increase from 1820 to 1840 (from $26 million to $108 million). States and towns, especially in newly populated areas of the West, competed in giving land, subsidies, and other forms of encouragement to road, canal, and railroad companies to provide transportation to their particular localities. Some of these commitments were overly generous and led to financial difficulty: by 1842, nine states (Arkansas, Florida, Illinois, Indiana, Louisiana, Maryland, Michigan, Mississippi, and Pennsylvania) had defaulted on some of their transportation loans, and Ohio and New York were forced to suspend dividends to investors. This was a financially chaotic and expensive situation.

Federal and State Support for Private Enterprise

At the same time that funding for internal improvements passed to the states, a series of decisions by federal courts asserted broad federal powers over interstate commerce. The effect of these decisions, contradictorily, was to vastly encourage commercial enterprise by limiting the regulatory power of the states at the same time that they were putting up most of the money for the new transportation network. By preventing states from interfering with interstate commerce, the courts encouraged development by assuring entrepreneurs the freedom and security to operate in the risky new national market.

Two key decisions were handed down by Chief Justice John Marshall (who had been on the bench since 1801). In *Dartmouth College v. Woodward* (1819), the Supreme Court prevented states from interfering in contracts, and in *Gibbons v. Ogden* (1824), it enjoined the State of New York from giving a monopoly over a steamboat line to Robert Fulton, inventor of the vessel. Although Fulton's invention was protected by a federal patent, its commercial application was not. Patenting thus encouraged technology, but not at the expense of competition. A decision handed down by Marshall's successor, Roger Taney, *Charles River Bridge v. Warren Bridge* (1837), again supported economic opportunity by denying a monopoly. All three cases involved federal reversal of decisions made at the state level, illustrating how the Supreme Court, under Marshall's leadership, weakened the powers of state governments in ways that aided the growth of private enterprise.

At the state level, another crucial commercial protection was the passage of laws concerning incorporation of businesses that had grown too large for individual proprietorship, family ownership, or limited partnership. Businesses that needed to raise large amounts of capital by attracting many investors found the contractual protections provided by incorporation to be essential. The protection investors wanted most was limited liability—the assurance that they would lose no more than what they had invested in a corporation if it were sued or went bankrupt. The net effect of state incorporation laws was to encourage large-scale economic activity and to hasten the commercialization of rural areas, both crucial aspects of the Market Revolution (see Chapter 12).

The Bank War

In the case of internal improvements, Jackson rejected, on behalf of popular democracy, the notion of coordinated economic planning by the government. His rejection set up the conditions for a speculative frenzy. Precisely the same result occurred in his epic battle with the Second Bank of the United States.

In 1816, Congress had granted a twenty-year charter to the Second Bank of the United States. The Bank was owned by private investors, with the U.S. government holding only one-fifth of the shares. With thirty branches, it was the nation's largest and performed a variety of functions, the most important of which was the control it exercised over state banks. Because state banks tended to issue more paper money than they could back with hard currency, the Bank always demanded repayment of its loans to them in hard currency. This policy forced state banks to maintain adequate reserves and restricted speculative activities. In times of recession, the Bank eased the pressure on state banks, demanding only partial payment in coin. Thus, the Bank acted as a currency stabilizer by helping to control the money supply. It brought a semblance of order to what we today would consider a chaotic money system—coins of various weights and a multitude of state banknotes, many of which were discounted (not accepted at full face value) in other states.

The concept of a strong national bank controlled by wealthy investors, not the federal government, was supported by the majority of the nation's merchants and businessmen. Nevertheless, the Bank had many opponents. Both western farmers and urban workers had bitter memories of the Panic of 1819, which the Bank had caused (at least in part) by sharply cutting back on available credit. Many ordinary people believed that a system based on paper currency would be manipulated by bankers—the "monied aristocracy"—in selfish and dangerous ways. Among those who held that opinion was Andrew Jackson, who had hated and feared banks ever since the 1790s, when he had lost a great deal of money in a speculative venture.

Early in his administration, Jackson hastened to tell Nicholas Biddle, the director of the Bank: "I do not dislike your Bank any more than all banks." By 1832, Jackson's opinion had changed, and he and Biddle were locked in a personal conflict that harmed not only the national economy but also the reputations of both men. Biddle, urged on by Henry Clay and Daniel Webster, precipitated the conflict by making early application for rechartering the Bank. Congress approved the application in July 1832. Jackson immediately decided on a stinging veto, announcing to Van Buren, "The bank . . . is trying to kill me, but I will kill it!"

And kill it he did that same July, with one of the strongest veto messages in American history. Asserting that the Bank's "exclusive privileges" were benefiting only the rich, Jackson claimed to speak for the "humble members of society—the farmers, mechanics and laborers" and to oppose injustice and inequality. Nevertheless, Jackson's veto message was a

••—Read the Document
Andrew Jackson, Veto of the Bank Bill (1832) at **www.myhistorylab.com**

"King Andrew." This Whig cartoon, published at the height of the Bank War, depicted Jackson as an absolute monarch trampling on the Constitution. The caption asked "Shall he reign over us, or shall the PEOPLE RULE?"

great popular success, and it set the terms for the presidential election of 1832. Henry Clay, the nominee of the anti-Jackson forces, lost the battle for popular opinion. Democrats successfully painted Clay as the defender of the Bank and of privilege. These were accusations with great popular appeal. Clay's defeat was decisive: he drew only forty-nine electoral votes to Jackson's 219.

Although the election was a triumph for Jackson, the Bank War continued because Jackson decided to kill the Bank by transferring its $10 million in government deposits to favored state banks ("pet banks," critics called them). Cabinet members objected, as did the Senate, but Jackson responded that the election had given him a popular mandate to act against the Bank. Short of impeachment, there was nothing Congress could do to prevent Jackson from acting on his expansive—and novel—interpretation of presidential powers.

Jackson's refusal to renew the charter of the Second Bank of the United States had lasting economic and political consequences. Economically, it inaugurated the economic policy known as *laissez-faire*, where decision-making power rests with commercial interests, not with government. Politically, it so infuriated Jackson's opponents that they formed a permanent opposition party. It was from the heat of the Bank War that the now characteristic American two-party system emerged.

Whigs, Van Buren, and the Panic of 1837

In 1833, as the government withdrew its deposits, Nicholas Biddle, the Bank's director, counterattacked by calling in the Bank's commercial loans, thereby causing a sharp panic and recession in the winter of 1833–34. Merchants, businessmen, and southern planters were all furious—at Jackson. His opponents, only a loose coalition up to this time, coalesced into a formal opposition party that called itself the Whigs. Evoking the memory of the Patriots who had resisted King George III in the American Revolution, the new party called on everyone to resist tyrannical "King Andrew." Just as Jackson's own calls for popular democracy had appealed to voters in all regions, so his opponents overcame their sectional differences to unite in opposition to his economic policies and arbitrary methods.

Vice President Martin Van Buren, Jackson's designated successor, won the presidential election of 1836 because the Whigs ran four sectional candidates, hoping their combined votes would deny Van Buren a majority and force the election into the House of Representatives. The strategy failed, but not by much: a shift of only 2,000 votes in Pennsylvania would have thrown the election into the House of Representatives, vindicating the Whig strategy. Their near success showed them that the basis for a united national opposition did exist. In 1840, the Whigs would prove that they had learned this lesson.

Meanwhile, the consequences of the Bank War continued. The recession of 1833–34 was followed by a wild speculative boom, caused as much by foreign investors as by the expiration of the Bank. Many new state banks were chartered that were eager to give loans, the price of cotton rose rapidly, and speculation in western lands was feverish (in Alabama and Mississippi, the mid-1830s were known as the "Flush Times"). A government surplus of $37 million distributed to the states in 1836 made the inflationary pressures worse. Jackson became alarmed at the widespread use of paper money (which he blamed for the inflation), and in July 1836, he issued the Specie Circular, announcing that the government would accept payment for public lands only in hard currency. At the same time, foreign investors, especially British banks, affected by a world recession, called in their American loans. The sharp contraction of credit led to the Panic of 1837 and a six-year recession, the worst the American economy had yet known.

In 1837, some 800 banks suspended business, refusing to pay out any of their $150 million in deposits. The collapse of the banking system led to business closures and outright failures. Nationwide, the unemployment rate reached more than 10 percent. In the winter of 1837–38 in New York City alone, one-third of all manual laborers were unemployed and an estimated 10,000 were living in abject poverty. The Panic of 1837 lasted six long years, causing widespread misery. Not until 1843 did the economy show signs of recovery.

In 1837 the federal government did nothing to aid victims of economic recession. No banks were bailed out, no bank depositors were saved by federal insurance, no laid-off workers got unemployment payments. Nor did the government undertake any public works projects or pump money into the economy. All of these steps, today seen as essential to prevent economic collapse and to alleviate human suffering, were unheard of then. Soup kitchens and charities were mobilized in major cities, but only by private, volunteer groups, not by local or state governments.

Panics and depressions were believed to be natural stages in the business cycle, and government intervention was considered unwarranted—although it was perfectly acceptable for government to intervene to promote growth. As a result, workers, farmers, and members of the new business middle class suddenly realized that participation in America's booming economy was very dangerous. The rewards could be great, but so could the penalties.

Martin Van Buren (quickly nicknamed "Van Ruin") spent a dismal four years in the White House presiding over bank failures, bankruptcies, and massive unemployment. Van Buren, who lacked Jackson's compelling personality, could find no remedies to the depression. His misfortune gave the opposition party, the newly formed Whigs, its opportunity.

This contemporary cartoon bitterly depicts the terrible effects of the Panic of 1837 on ordinary people—bank failures, unemployment, drunkenness, and destitution—which the artist links to the insistence of the rich on payment in specie (as Jackson had required in the Species Circular of 1836). Over the scene waves the American flag, accompanied by the ironic message, "61st Anniversary of Our Independence."

The Second American Party System

The First American Party System, the confrontation between the Federalists and the Jeffersonian Republicans that began in the 1790s, had been widely viewed at the time as an unfortunate factional squabble that threatened the common good of the republic (see Chapter 8). By the 1830s, with the expansion of suffrage, attitudes had changed. The political struggles of the Jackson era, coupled with the dramatic social changes caused by expansion and economic growth, created the basic pattern of American politics: two major parties, each with at least some appeal among voters of all social classes and in all sections of the country. That pattern, which we call the "Second American Party System," continues to this day.

Whigs and Democrats

There were genuine differences between the Whigs and the Democrats, but they were not sectional differences. Instead, the two parties reflected just-emerging class and cultural differences. The Democrats, as they themselves were quick to point out, had inherited Thomas Jefferson's belief in the democratic rights of the small, independent yeoman farmer. They had nationwide appeal, especially in the South and West, the most rural regions. As a result of Jackson's presidency, Democrats came to be identified with independence and a distaste for interference, whether from the government or from economic monopolies such as the Bank of the United States. They favored expansion, Indian removal, and the freedom to do as they chose on the frontier. Most Democratic voters were opposed to the rapid social and economic changes of the 1830s and 1840s.

The Whigs were themselves often the initiators and beneficiaries of economic change and were more receptive to it. Heirs of the Federalist belief in the importance of a strong federal role in the national economy (see Chapter 8), they supported Henry Clay's American System: a strong central government, the Bank of the United States, a protective tariff, and internal improvements. In fact, when it came to improvements, the

Whigs wanted to improve people as well as roads. Religion was an important element in political affiliation, and many Whigs were members of evangelical reforming denominations. Whigs favored government intervention in both economic and social affairs, calling for education and social reforms, such as temperance, that aimed to improve the ordinary citizen. Many rich men were Whigs, but so were many poorer men who had a democratic faith in the perfectibility of all Americans. The Whigs' greatest strength was in New England and the northern part of the West (the Old Northwest), the areas most affected by commercial agriculture and factory work (see Chapter 13).

Yet neither party was monolithic. As has continued to be true of American political parties, both the Democrats and the Whigs were a coalition of interests affected by local and regional factors. The job of the party leader, as the Democrats' Martin Van Buren had been among the first to realize, was to forge the divergent local party interests into a winning national majority. Although Jackson's appeal was strongest in the rural South and West, the Democrats also appealed to some workers in Philadelphia and other northern cities because they shared with Democrats from other regions a dislike of big business. On the other hand, a number of southern planters with close ties to merchant and banking interests were attracted to the Whig policy of a strong federal role in economic development, though they were less active than many northern Whigs in advocating sweeping social reform.

The Campaign of 1840

In 1840, the Whigs set out to beat the Democrats at their own game. Passing over the ever-hopeful Henry Clay, the Whigs nominated a man as much like Andrew Jackson as possible, the aging Indian fighter William Henry Harrison, former governor of the Indiana Territory from 1801 to 1812. In an effort to duplicate Jackson's winning appeal to the South as well as the West, the Whigs balanced the ticket by nominating a Southerner, John Tyler, for vice president. The campaign slogan was "Tippecanoe and Tyler too" (Tippecanoe was the site of Harrison's famous victory over Tecumseh's Indian confederation in 1811). The Whigs reached out to ordinary people with torchlight parades, barbecues, songs, coonskin caps, bottomless jugs of hard cider, and claims that Martin Van Buren, Harrison's hapless opponent, was a man of privilege and aristocratic tastes. Nothing could be further from the truth: Van Buren was the son of a tavern keeper. But Van Buren, a short man who lacked a commanding presence, had always dressed meticulously, and now even his taste in coats and ties was used against him.

The Whig campaign tactics, added to the popular anger at Van Buren because of the continuing depression, gave Harrison a sweeping electoral victory, 234 votes to 60. Even more remarkable, the campaign achieved the greatest voter turnout up to that time (and rarely equaled since): 80 percent (see Map 11.5).

The Whig Victory Turns to Loss: The Tyler Presidency

Although the Whig victory of 1840 was a milestone in American politics, the triumph of Whig principles was short-lived. William Henry Harrison, who was sixty-eight, died of pneumonia a month after his inauguration. For the first time in American history, the vice president stepped up to the presidency. Not for the last time, important differences between the dead president and his successor reshaped the direction of American politics. John Tyler of Virginia, quickly nicknamed "His Accidency," was a former Democrat who had left the party because he disagreed with Jackson's autocratic style. The Whigs had sought him primarily for his sectional appeal and had not inquired too closely into his political opinions, which turned out to be anti-Whig as well as anti-Jackson.

OVERVIEW | The Second American Party System

Democrats	First organized to elect Andrew Jackson to the presidency in 1828. The Democratic Party spoke for Jeffersonian democracy, expansion, and the freedom of the "common man" from interference from government or from financial monopolies like the Bank of the United States. It found its power base in the rural South and West and among some northern urban workers. The Democratic Party was the majority party from 1828 to 1860.
Whigs	Organized in opposition to Andrew Jackson in the early 1830s. Heir to Federalism, the Whig Party favored a strong role for the national government in the economy (for example, it promoted Henry Clay's American System) and supported active social reform. Its power base lay in the North and Old Northwest among voters who benefited from increased commercialization and among some southern planters and urban merchants. The Whigs won the elections of 1840 and 1848.

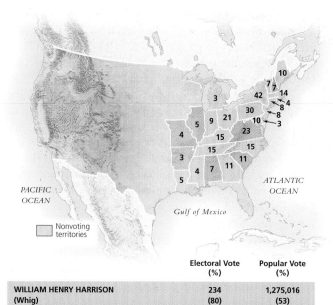

	Electoral Vote (%)	Popular Vote (%)
WILLIAM HENRY HARRISON (Whig)	234 (80)	1,275,016 (53)
Martin Van Buren (Democrat)	60 (20)	1,129,102 (47)

MAP 11.5 The Election of 1840 The Whigs triumphed in the election of 1840 by beating the Democrats at their own game. Whigs could expect to do well in the commercializing areas of New England and the Old Northwest, but their adopted strategy of popular campaigning worked well in the largely rural South and West as well, contributing to Harrison's victory. The Whigs' choice of John Tyler as vice presidential candidate, another strategy designed to appeal to southern voters, backfired when Harrison died and Tyler, who did not share Whig principles, became America's first vice president to succeed to the presidency.

President Tyler vetoed a series of bills embodying all the elements of Henry Clay's American System: tariffs, internal improvements, a new Bank of the United States. In exasperation, congressional Whigs forced Tyler out of the party, and his entire cabinet of Whigs resigned. To replace them, Tyler appointed former Democrats like himself. Thus, the Whig triumph of 1840, one of the clearest victories in American electoral politics, was negated by the stalemate between Tyler and the Whig majority in Congress. The Whigs were to win only one more election, that of 1848.

American Arts and Letters

Jackson's presidency was a defining moment in the development of an American identity. His combination of western belligerency and combative individualism was the strongest statement of American distinctiveness since Thomas Jefferson's agrarianism. Did Jackson speak for all of America? The Whigs did not think so. And the definitions of American identity that were beginning to emerge in popular culture and in intellectual circles were more

complex than the message coming from the White House. Throughout the nation, however, there was a widespread interest in information and literature of all kinds. The Age of the Common Man would prove to be the period when American writers and painters found the national themes that allowed them to produce the first distinctively American literature and art.

Popular Cultures and the Spread of the Written Word

The print revolution, described earlier in connection with political parties, had effects far beyond politics. Newspapers and pamphlets fostered a variety of popular cultures. For western readers, the Crockett almanacs offered a mix of humorous stories and tall tales attributed to Davy Crockett (the boisterous Tennessee "roarer" who died defending the Alamo in 1836). In New York City, the immensely popular "penny papers" (so called from their price) that began appearing in 1833 fostered a distinctive urban culture. These papers, with lurid headlines such as "Double Suicide" and "Secret Tryst," fed the same popular appetite for scandal as did other popular publications. The *Police Gazette* magazine; pamphlets about murder trials, swindlers, and pirates; and temperance dime novels such as *The Inebriate*, written in 1842 by a struggling young newspaperman named Walter (later Walt) Whitman, were read by many. Throughout the country, religious literature was still most widely read, but a small middle-class audience existed for literary magazines and, among women especially, for sentimental magazines and novels.

Accompanying all these changes in print communication was an invention that outsped them all: the telegraph, so innovative that its inventor spent years fruitlessly seeking private funds to back its application. Finally, with financing from the federal government, Samuel F. B. Morse sent his first message—What Hath God Wrought?—from Washington to Baltimore in 1844. Soon messages in Morse code would be transmitted instantaneously across the continent. The impact of this revolutionary invention, the first to separate the message from the speed at which a human messenger could travel, was immediate. The timeliness of information available to the individual, from important national news to the next train's arrival time, vastly increased. Distant events gained new and exciting immediacy. Everyone's horizon and sense of community were widened.

Creating a National American Culture

For all the improvements in communication, the United States was a provincial culture, still looking to Britain for values, standards, and literary offerings, and still mocked by the British. In a famous essay in the *Edinburgh Review* in 1820, Sidney Smith bitingly inquired, "In the four quarters

Read the Document

Davy Crockett, Advice to Politicians (1833) at **www.myhistorylab.com**

A Regular Row in the Backwoods. The 1841 issue of the *Crockett Almanac*, named after the Tennessee backwoodsman made famous by his self-serving tall tales, portrayed a rough rural "sport." Inexpensive comic almanacs combined illustrated jokes on topical subjects with astrological and weather predictions.

of the globe, who reads an American book? or goes to an American play? or looks at an American picture or statue? What does the world yet owe to American physicians or surgeons? What new substances have their chemists discovered?" The answer was nothing—yet.

In the early years of the nineteenth century, eastern seaboard cities actively built the cultural foundation that would nurture American art and literature. Philadelphia's American Philosophical Society, founded by Benjamin Franklin in 1743, boasted a distinguished roster of scientists, including Thomas Jefferson—concurrently its president and president of the United States—and Nicholas Biddle, Jackson's opponent in the Bank War. Culturally, Boston ran a close second to Philadelphia, founding the Massachusetts General Hospital (1811) and the Boston Athenaeum (1807), a gentlemen's library and reading room. Southern cities were much less successful in supporting culture. Charleston had a Literary and Philosophical Society (founded in 1814), but the widely dispersed residences of the southern elite made urban cultural institutions difficult to sustain. Thus, unwittingly, the South ceded cultural leadership to the North.

The cultural picture was much spottier in the West. A few cities, such as Lexington, Kentucky, and Cincinnati, Ohio, had civic cultural institutions, and some transplanted New Englanders maintained connections with New England culture. A group of pioneers in Ames, Ohio, for example, founded a "coonskin library" composed of books purchased from Boston and paid for in coonskins. But most pioneers were at best uninterested and at worst actively hostile to traditional literary culture. This was neither from lack of literacy nor from a failure to read. Newspaper and religious journals both had large readerships in the West: the *Methodist Christian Advocate*, for example, reached 25,000 people yearly (compared with the *North American Review*'s 3,000 readers). The frontier emphasis on the practical was hard to distinguish from anti-intellectualism.

Thus, in the early part of the nineteenth century, the gap between the intellectual and cultural horizons of a wealthy Bostonian and a frontier farmer in Michigan widened. Part of the unfinished task of building a national society was the creation of a national culture that could fill this gap. For writers and artists, the challenge was to find distinctively American themes.

Of the eastern cities, New York produced the first widely recognized American writers. In 1819, Washington Irving published *The Sketch Book*, thus immortalizing Rip Van Winkle and the Headless Horseman. Within a few years, James Fenimore Cooper's Leatherstocking novels (of which *The Last of the Mohicans*, published in 1826, is the best known) achieved wide success in both America and Europe. Cooper's novels established the experience of westward expansion, of which the conquest of the Indians was a vital part, as a serious and distinctive American literary theme.

It was New England, however, that claimed to be the forge of American cultural independence from Europe. As Ralph Waldo Emerson proclaimed in "The American Scholar," a lecture he delivered in 1837 to the Harvard faculty, "Our day of dependence, our long apprenticeship to the learning of other lands, draws to a close." He went on to encourage American writers to find inspiration in the ordinary details of daily life. The stuff of literature, he declared, was to be found in "the familiar, the low . . . the milk in the pan; the ballad in the street; the news of the boat." Immensely popular, Emerson gave more than 1,500 lectures in twenty states between 1833 and 1860. "The American Scholar," his most famous lecture, carried a message of cultural self-sufficiency that Americans were eager to hear.

Artists and Builders

Artists were as successful as novelists in finding American themes. Thomas Cole, who came to America from England in 1818, painted American scenes in the style of

Asher Durand, a member of the Hudson River School of landscape painting, produced this work, *Kindred Spirits*, as a tribute to Thomas Cole, the leader of the school. Cole is one of the figures depicted standing in a romantic wilderness.

SOURCE: Asher Brown Durand, *Kindred Spirits*, 1849. Oil on canvas, 44 × 36 in. Collection of the New York Public Library, Astor, Lenox and Tilden Foundations.

the British romantic school of landscape painting. Cole founded the Hudson River school of American painting, a style and subject matter frankly nationalistic in tone.

The western painters—realists such as Karl Bodmer and George Catlin as well as the romantics who followed them, like Albert Bierstadt and Thomas Moran—drew on the dramatic western landscape and its peoples. Their art was an important contribution to the American sense of the land and to the nation's identity. Catlin, driven by a need to document Indian life before it disappeared,

spent eight years among the tribes of the upper Missouri River. Then he assembled his collection—more than 500 paintings in all—and toured the country from 1837 to 1851 in an unsuccessful attempt to arouse public indignation about the plight of the Indian nations. George Caleb Bingham, an accomplished genre painter, produced somewhat tidied-up scenes of real-life American workers, such as flatboatmen on the Missouri River. All these painters found much to record and to celebrate in American life.

CHRONOLOGY

1819	*Dartmouth College* v. *Woodward*	**1834**	Whig Party organized
1821	Mexican independence from Spain		British abolish slavery in their Caribbean colonies
1824	*Gibbons* v. *Ogden*	**1836**	Jackson issues Specie Circular
	John Quincy Adams elected president by the House of Representatives		Martin Van Buren elected president
1826	First American use of the steam-powered printing press	**1837**	*Charles River Bridge* v. *Warren Bridge*
1828	Congress passes "Tariff of Abominations"		Revolts against Britain in Upper and Lower Canada
	Andrew Jackson elected president		Ralph Waldo Emerson first presents "The American Scholar"
	John C. Calhoun publishes *Exposition and Protest* anonymously		Panic of 1837
1830	Jackson vetoes Maysville Road Bill	**1838**	Cherokee removal along the "Trail of Tears"
	Congress passes Indian Removal Act	**1840**	Whig William Henry Harrison elected president
1832	Nullification Crisis begins		Act of Union merges Upper and Lower Canada
	Jackson vetoes renewal of Bank of the United States charter	**1841**	John Tyler assumes presidency at the death of President Harrison
	Jackson reelected president		
1833	General Antonio Lopez de Santa Anna elected president of Mexico		

The haste and transience of American life are nowhere as obvious as in the architectural record of this era, which is sparse. The monumental neoclassical style (complete with columns) that Jefferson had recommended for official buildings in Washington continued to be favored for public buildings elsewhere and by private concerns trying to project an imposing image, such as banks. But in general, Americans were in too much of a hurry to build for the future, and in balloon-frame construction, they found the perfect technique for the present. Balloon-frame structures—which consist of a basic frame of wooden studs fastened with crosspieces top and bottom—could be put up quickly, cheaply, and without the help of a skilled carpenter. Covering the frame with wooden siding was equally simple, and the resultant dwelling was as strong, although not as well insulated, as a house of solid timber or logs. Balloon-frame construction was first used in Chicago in the 1830s, where it created the city almost instantly. The four-room balloon-frame house, affordable to many who could not have paid for a traditionally built dwelling, became standard in that decade. This was indeed housing for the common man and his family.

Conclusion

Andrew Jackson's presidency witnessed the building of a strong national party system based on nearly universal white manhood suffrage. Sectionalism and localism seemed to have been replaced by a more national consciousness that was clearly expressed in the two national political parties, the Whigs and the Democrats. The Second American Party System created new democratic political communities united by common political opinions and often mobilized by common political resentments.

Culturally, American writers and artists began to establish a distinctive American identity in the arts. But as the key battles of the Jackson presidency—the Nullification Crisis, Indian removal, and the Bank War—showed, the forces of sectionalism resisted the strong nationalizing tendencies of the era. Equally clearly, popular political opinion, once aroused, was not always as controllable as politicians may have wished. As the next chapter will show, economic developments in the North were beginning to create a very different society and electorate from that of the slave South or the rural West.

Review Questions

1. What reasons might a person of the 1820s and 1830s give for opposing universal white manhood suffrage? Suffrage for free African American men? For women of all races?

2. Opponents believed that Andrew Jackson was unsuited in both political experience and temperament to be president of the United States, yet his presidency is considered one of the most influential in American history. Why?

3. Both the Nullification Crisis and Indian removal raised the constitutional issue of the rights of a minority in a nation governed by majority rule. What rights, in your opinion, does a minority have, and what kinds of laws are necessary to defend those rights?

4. Why was the issue of government support for internal improvements so controversial? What *is* the appropriate role for government in economic development?

5. What were the key differences between Whigs and Democrats? What did each party stand for? Who were their supporters? What were the links between each party's programs and party supporters?

6. What distinctive American themes did the writers, artists, and builders of the 1820s and 1830s express in their works? Are they still considered American themes today?

Recommended Reading

Bray Hammond, *Banks and Politics in America* (1957). The classic study of the Bank War and its consequences.

Patrick J. Jung, *The Black Hawk War of 1832* (2007). An up-to-date study of one of the last Indian wars in the eastern United States.

Alexander Keyssar, *The Right to Vote: The Contested History of Democracy in the United States* (2000). A survey that examines the reasons for continual limits on the franchise.

Lynn Hudson Parsons, *The Birth of Modern Politics: Andrew Jackson, John Quincy Adams, and the Election of 1828* (2009). Lively and clearly written, this account of a crucial election pays as much attention to John Quincy Adams as to Jackson.

Alisse Portnoy, *Their Right to Speak: Women's Activism in the Indian and Slave Debates* (2005). Women's political assertion in the two public issues.

David S. Reynolds, *Waking Giant* (2008). A colorful account of turbulent popular and intellectual cultures, 1815–1848.

Robert Remini, *Andrew Jackson and the Source of American Freedom* (1981). An account of Jackson's White House years by his major biographer.

Harry L. Watson, *Liberty and Power: The Politics of Jacksonian America* (1990). An excellent overview of Jacksonian politics.

Sean Wilentz, *The Rise of American Democracy: Jefferson to Lincoln* (2005). A massive political study that traces the different histories of "city" and "country" democracy.

PEARSON myhistorylab™ Connections

Reinforce what you learned in this chapter by studying the many documents, images, maps, review tools, and videos available at www.myhistorylab.com.

Read and Review

✓• Study and Review Chapter 11

•⁞• Read the Document

A Legal Scholar Opposes Spreading the Vote (1821)

An American Senator Opposes Nullification (1830)

A Choctaw Chief Bids Farewell (1832)

Black Hawk, from "The Life of Black Hawk" (1833)

Michel Chevalier, Society, Manner and Politics in the U.S. (1834)

Ballad of General Jackson and the Six Militia Men (1827)

Proclamation Concerning Nullification (1832)

John Quincy Adams, Inaugural Address (1825)

Treaty with the Sioux and Other Tribes (1825)

Andrew Jackson, Veto of the Bank Bill (1832)

Alexis de Tocqueville, Democracy in America (1835)

The Force Bill (1833)

Davy Crockett, Advice to Politicians (1833)

👁 See the Map *Native American Land Cessions to 1829*

Research and Explore

•⁞• Read the Document

Exploring America: American Art

Profile
Davy Crockett

(((•• Hear the Audio

Hear the audio files for Chapter 11 at
www.myhistorylab.com.

12

Industry and the North

1790s–1840s

CHAPTER OUTLINE

Unidentified artist, "Middlesex Company Woolen Mills of Lowell, Massachusetts," ca. 1848. Oil on canvas. American Textile History Museum, Lowell, Mass.

Women Factory Workers Form a Community in Lowell, Massachusetts

In the 1820s and 1830s, young farm women from all over New England flocked to Lowell, Massachusetts, to work a twelve-hour day in one of the first cotton textile factories in America. Living six to eight to a room in nearby boardinghouses, the women of Lowell earned an average of $3 a week. Some also attended inexpensive nighttime lectures or classes. Lowell, considered a model factory town, drew worldwide attention. As one admirer of its educated workers said, Lowell was less a factory than a "philanthropic manufacturing college."

The Boston investors who financed Lowell were businessmen, not philanthropists, but they wanted to keep Lowell free of the dirt, poverty, and social disorder that made English factory towns notorious. Built in 1823, Lowell boasted six neat factory buildings grouped around a central clock tower, the area pleasantly landscaped with flowers, shrubs, and trees. Housing was similarly well ordered: a Georgian mansion for the company agent; trim houses for the overseers; row houses for the mechanics and their families; and boardinghouses, each supervised by a responsible matron, for the workforce that made Lowell famous—young New England farm women.

The choice of young women as factory workers seemed shockingly unconventional. In the 1820s and

AMERICAN Communities

1830s, young unmarried women simply did not live alone; they lived and worked with their parents until they married. In these years of growth and westward expansion, however, America was chronically short of labor, and the Lowell manufacturers were shrewd enough to realize that young farm women were an untapped labor force. For farmers' sons, the lure of acquiring their own farms in the West was much stronger than factory wages, but for their sisters, escaping from rural isolation and earning a little money was an appealing way to spend a few years before marriage. To attract respectable young women, Lowell offered supervision both on the job and at home, with strict rules of conduct, compulsory religious services, cultural opportunities such as concerts and lectures, and cash wages.

When they first arrived in Lowell, the young women were often bewildered by the large numbers of townspeople and embarrassed by their own rural clothing and country ways. The air of the mill was hot, humid, full of cotton lint, and the noise of the machinery—"the buzzing and hissing and whizzing of pulleys and rollers and spindles and flyers"—was constant. It was company policy for senior women to train the newcomers, and often sisters or neighbors who had preceded them to the mill helped them adjust to their new surroundings.

The work itself was simple, consisting largely of knotting broken threads on spinning machines and power looms. Most women, accustomed to the long days of farm work, enjoyed their jobs. One woman wrote home: "The work is not disagreeable. It tried my patience sadly at first, but in general I like it very much. It is easy to do, and does not require very violent exertion, as much of our farm work does."

Textile mills ran on a rigid work schedule with fines or penalties imposed on latecomers and slackers. Power-driven machinery operated at a sustained, uniform pace throughout every mill; human workers had to learn to do the same. This precise work schedule represented the single largest change from preindustrial work habits, and it was the hardest adjustment for the workers. Moreover, each mill positioned one or two male overseers on every floor to make sure the pace was maintained.

Why did young farm women come to Lowell? Some worked out of need, but most regarded Lowell as an opportunity: an escape from rural isolation and from parental supervision, a chance to buy the latest fashions and learn "city ways," to attend lectures and concerts, to save for a dowry, or to pay for an education. As writer Lucy Larcom, one of the most famous workers, said, the women who came to Lowell sought "an opening into freer life." Working side by side and living with six to twelve other women, some of whom might be relatives or friends from home, the Lowell women built a close, supportive community for themselves.

The owners of Lowell made large profits and also drew praise for their carefully managed community, with its intelligent and independent workforce. But their success was short-lived. In the 1830s, facing competition and poor economic conditions, the owners imposed wage cuts and work speedups that their model workforce did not take lightly. Despite the system of paternalistic control at the mills, the close bonds the women forged gave them the courage and solidarity to "turn out" in spontaneous protests, which were, however, unsuccessful in reversing the wage cuts. By 1850, the "philanthropic manufacturing college" was no more. The original Lowell workforce of New England farm girls had been largely replaced by poor Irish immigrants of both sexes, who earned much less than their predecessors. Now Lowell was simply another mill town.

The history of Lowell epitomizes the process by which the North (New England and the Middle Atlantic states) industrialized. A society composed largely of self-sufficient farm families (Jefferson's "yeoman farmers") changed to one of urban wage earners. Industrialization did not occur overnight. Large factories were not common until the 1880s, but long before that decade, most workers had already experienced a fundamental change in their working patterns. Once under way, the market revolution changed how people worked, how they thought, and how they lived: the very basis of community. In the early years of the nineteenth century, northern communities led this transformation, fostering attitudes far different from those prevalent in the agrarian South.

Read the **Document**
A Week at the Mill (1845)
at **www.myhistorylab.com**

Lowell

1. What were the effects of the transportation revolution?

2. What was the market revolution?

3. How did industrialization affect workers in early factories?

4. How did the market revolution change the lives of ordinary people?

5. What were the values of the new middle class?

FOCUS Questions

1790s–1840s

The Transportation Revolution

Between 1800 and 1840, the United States experienced truly revolutionary improvements in transportation. More than any other development, these improvements encouraged Americans to look beyond their local communities to broader ones and to foster the enterprising commercial spirit for which they became so widely known.

Improved transportation had dramatic effects, both on individual mobility and on the economy. By 1840, it was easier for people to move from one locale to another, but, even more remarkably, people now had easy access in their own cities and towns to commercial goods made in distant centers. Thus, even for people who remained in one place, horizons were much broader in 1840 than they had been forty years before. The difference lay in better roads, in improvements in water transport, and in the invention and speedy development of railroads (see Map 12.1).

Roads

In 1800, travel by road was difficult for much of the year. Mud in the spring, dust in the summer, and snow in the winter all made travel by horseback or carriage uncomfortable, slow, and sometimes dangerous. Localities and states tried to improve local roads or contracted with private turnpike companies to build, maintain, and collect tolls on important stretches of road. In general, however, local roads remained poor. The federal government demonstrated its commitment to the improvement of interregional transportation by funding the National Road in 1808, at the time the greatest single federal transportation expense (its eventual cost was $7 million). Stretching from Cumberland, Maryland, to Vandalia, Illinois, almost at the Mississippi River, by 1839, the National Road tied the East and the West together and helped to foster a national community.

Canals and Steamboats

However much they helped the movement of people, the National Road and other roads were unsatisfactory in a commercial sense. Shipments of bulky goods like grain were too slow and expensive by road. Waterborne transportation was much cheaper and still the major commercial link among the Atlantic seaboard states and in the Mississippi–Ohio River system. But before the 1820s, most water routes were north–south or coastal (Boston to Charleston, for example); east–west links were urgently needed. Canals turned out to be the answer.

The Erie Canal—the most famous canal of the era—was the brainchild of New York governor DeWitt Clinton, who envisioned a link between New York City and the Great Lakes through the Hudson River, and a 364-mile-long canal stretching from Albany to Buffalo. When Clinton proposed the canal in 1817, it was derisively called "Clinton's Ditch"; the longest American canal then in existence was only twenty-seven miles long and had taken nine years to build. Nevertheless, Clinton convinced the New York legislature to approve a bond issue for the canal, and investors (New York and British merchants) subscribed to the tune of $7 million, an immense sum for the day.

((•─ **Hear the Audio** *The Erie Canal* at www.myhistorylab.com

Building the canal—40 feet wide, 4 feet deep, 364 miles long, with 83 locks and more than 300 bridges along the way—was a vast engineering and construction challenge. In the early stages, nearby farmers worked for $8 a month, but when malaria hit the workforce in the summer of 1819, many went home. They were replaced by 3,000 Irish contract laborers, who were much more expensive—50 cents a day plus room and board—but more reliable (if they survived). Local people regarded the Irish workers as different and frightening, but the importation of foreign contract

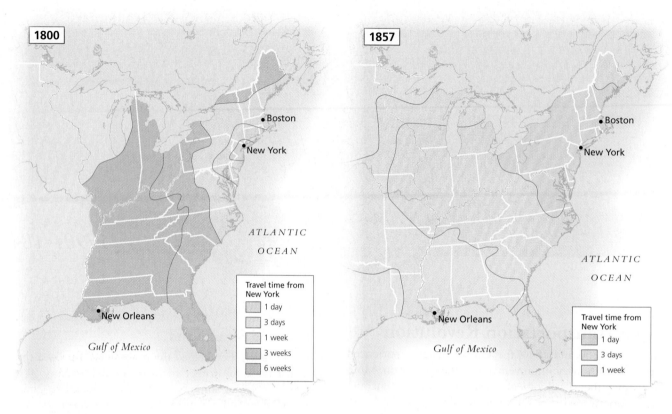

MAP 12.1 Travel Times, 1800 and 1857 The transportation revolution dramatically reduced travel times and vastly expanded everyone's horizons. Improved roads, canals, and the introduction of steamboats and railroads made it easier for Americans to move and made even those who did not move less isolated. Better transportation linked the developing West to the eastern seaboard and fostered a sense of national identity and pride.

labor for this job was a portent of the future. Much of the heavy construction work on later canals and railroads was performed by immigrant labor.

DeWitt Clinton had promised, to general disbelief, that the Erie Canal would be completed in less than ten years, and he made good on his promise. The canal was the wonder of the age. The Erie Canal provided easy passage to and from the interior, both for people and for goods. It drew settlers like a magnet from the East and, increasingly, from overseas: by 1830, some 50,000 people a year were moving west on the canal to the rich farmland of Indiana, Illinois, and territory farther west. Earlier settlers now had a national, indeed an international, market for their produce. Moreover, farm families along the canal began purchasing household goods and cloth, formerly made at home. One of the most dramatic illustrations of the canal's impact was a rapid decline in the production of homespun cloth in the towns and counties along its route, from 16.5 million yards of textiles in 1825, the year the Erie Canal opened, to half that amount ten years later.

••◦ Read the **Document**
Extract from Albany Daily Advertiser (1819) at **www.myhistorylab.com**

Towns along the canal—Utica, Rochester, Buffalo—became instant cities, each an important commercial center in its own right. Perhaps the greatest beneficiary was New York City, which quickly established a commercial and financial supremacy no other American city could match. The Erie Canal decisively turned New York's merchants away from Europe and toward America's own heartland, building both interstate commerce and a feeling of community. As the famous song put it,

You'll always know your neighbor,
You'll always know your pal,
If you've ever navigated
On the Erie Canal.

The phenomenal success of the Erie Canal prompted other states to construct similar waterways to tap the rich interior market. Between 1820 and 1840, $200 million was invested in canal building. No other waterway achieved the success of the Erie, which collected $8.5 million in tolls in its first nine years. Nevertheless, the spurt of canal building ended the geographical isolation of much of the country.

The Erie Canal bustled with commerce almost from the moment of its opening in 1825. Five boats are shown waiting their turn to enter the lock that will raise each of them to the next level of the canal.

SOURCE: Collection of The New-York Historical Society, Negative # 34684.

An even more important improvement in water transportation, especially in the American interior, was the steamboat. Robert Fulton first demonstrated the commercial feasibility of steamboats in 1807, and they were soon operating in the East. Redesigned with more efficient engines and shallower, broader hulls, steamboats transformed commerce on the country's great inland river system: the Ohio, the Mississippi, the Missouri, and their tributaries. Steamboats were extremely dangerous, however; boiler explosions, fires, and sinkings were common, leading to one of the first public demands for regulation of private enterprise in 1838.

The increased river- and canal-borne trade, like the New England shipping boom of a generation earlier, stimulated urban growth and all kinds of commerce. Cities such as Cincinnati, already notable for its rapid growth, experienced a new economic surge. A frontier outpost in 1790, Cincinnati was by the 1830s a center of steamboat manufacture and machine tool production as well as a central shipping point for food for the southern market.

Railroads

Remarkable as all these transportation changes were, the most remarkable was still to come. Railroads, new in 1830 (when the Baltimore and Ohio Railroad opened with thirteen miles of track), grew to an astounding 31,000 miles by 1860. By that date, New England and the Old Northwest had laid a dense network of rails, and several lines had reached west beyond the Mississippi. The South, the least industrialized section of the nation, had fewer railroads. "Railroad mania" surpassed even canal mania, as investors—as many as one-quarter of them British—rushed to profit from the new invention.

Early railroads, like the steamboat, had to overcome many technological and supply problems. For example, locomotives, to generate adequate power, had to be heavy. Heavy locomotives, in turn, required iron rather than wooden rails. The resulting demand forced America's iron industry to modernize (at first, railroad iron was imported from England). Heavy engines also required a solid gravel roadbed and strong wooden ties.

This Currier and Ives print of 1849, *The Express Train*, captures the popular awe at the speed and wonder of the new technology. This "express" probably traveled no more than thirty miles per hour.

The Market Revolution

The market revolution, the most fundamental change American communities had ever experienced, was the outcome of three interrelated developments: the rapid improvements in transportation just described, commercialization, and industrialization. Commercialization involved the replacement of household self-sufficiency and barter with the production of goods for a cash market. And industrialization involved the use of power-driven machinery to produce goods once made by hand.

Watch the Video *Nineteenth-Century Industrialization* at **www.myhistorylab.com**

Arranging steady supplies of both and the labor to lay them was a construction challenge on a new scale. Finally, there were problems of standardization: because so many early railroads were short and local, builders used any gauge (track width) that served their purposes. Thus, gauges varied from place to place, forcing long-haul passengers and freight to change trains frequently. At one time, the trip from Philadelphia to Charleston involved eight gauge changes. It was not until the 1850s that consolidation of local railroads into larger systems began in earnest. But already it was clear that this newest transportation innovation would have far-reaching social consequences.

The Effects of the Transportation Revolution

The new ease of transportation fueled economic growth by making distant markets accessible. The startling successes of innovations such as canals and railroads attracted large capital investments, including significant amounts from foreign investors ($500 million between 1790 and 1861), which fueled further growth.

Every east–west road, canal, and railroad helped to reorient Americans away from the Atlantic and toward the heartland. This new focus was decisive in the creation of national pride and identity. The transportation revolution fostered an optimistic, risk-taking mentality in the United States that stimulated invention and innovation. More than anything, the transportation revolution allowed people to move with unaccustomed ease. Transportation improvements linked Americans in larger communities of interest, beyond the local communities in which they lived. And improved transportation made possible the larger market on which commercialization and industrialization depended (see Map 12.2).

The Accumulation of Capital

In the northern states, the business community was composed largely of merchants in the seaboard cities: Boston, Providence, New York City, Philadelphia, and Baltimore. Many had made substantial profits in the international shipping boom period from 1790 to 1807 (as discussed in Chapter 9). Such extraordinary opportunities attracted enterprising people. John Jacob Astor, who had arrived penniless from Germany in 1784, made his first fortune in the Pacific Northwest fur trade with China and eventually dominated the fur trade in the United States through his American Fur Company. Astor made a second fortune in New York real estate, and when he retired in 1834 with $25 million, he was reputed to be the wealthiest man in America. Many similar stories of success, though not as fabulous as Astor's, demonstrated that risk takers might reap rich rewards in international trade.

When the early years of the nineteenth century posed difficulties for international trade, some of the nation's wealthiest men turned to local investments. In Providence, Rhode Island, Moses Brown and his son-in-law William Almy began to invest some of the profits the Brown family had reaped from a worldwide trade in iron, candles, rum, and African slaves in the new manufacture of cotton textiles. Cincinnati merchants banded together to finance the building of the first steamboats to operate on the Ohio River.

Much of the capital for the new investments came from banks, both those in seaport cities that had been established for the international trade and those, like the Lynn, Massachusetts, Mechanics Bank, founded in 1814 by a group of Lynn's Quaker merchants, that served local clients. An astonishing amount of capital, however, was raised through family connections. In the late eighteenth

MAP 12.2 Commercial Links: Rivers, Canals, Roads, 1830, and Rail Lines, 1850 By 1830, the United States was tied together by a network of roads, canals, and rivers. This transportation revolution fostered a great burst of commercial activity and economic growth. Transportation improvements accelerated the commercialization of agriculture by getting farmers' products to wider, nonlocal markets. Access to wider markets likewise encouraged new textile and other manufacturers to increase their scale of production. By 1850, another revolutionary mode of transportation, the railroad, had emerged as a vital link to the transportation infrastructure.

century, members of the business communities in the seaboard cities had begun to consolidate their position and property by intermarriage. In Boston, such a strong community developed that when Francis Cabot Lowell needed $300,000 in 1813 to build the world's first automated cotton mill in Waltham, Massachusetts (the prototype of the Lowell mills), he had only to turn to his family network.

Southern cotton provided the capital for continuing development. Because Northerners built the nation's ships, controlled the shipping trade, and provided the nation's banking, insurance, and financial services, the astounding growth in southern cotton exports enriched northern merchants almost as much as southern planters. Southerners complained that their combined financial and shipping costs diverted forty cents of every dollar paid for their cotton to Northerners. Profits from cotton shipping provided some of the funds the Boston Associates made available to Francis Cabot Lowell. In another example, New York merchant Anson Phelps invested the profits he made from cotton shipping in iron mines in Pennsylvania and metalworks in Connecticut. Although imperfectly understood at the time, the truth is that the development of northern industry was paid for by southern cotton produced by enslaved African American labor. The surprising wealth that cotton brought to southern planters fostered the market revolution.

Finally, the willingness of American merchants to "think big" and risk their money in the development of a large domestic market was caused in part by American nationalism. Their confidence in a future that did not yet exist was not simply a sober economic calculation but an assertion of pride in the potential of this new and expanding nation.

The Putting-Out System

Initially, the American business community invested not in machinery and factories, but in the "putting-out system" of home manufacture, thereby expanding and transforming it. In this significant departure from preindustrial work, people still produced goods at home, but under the direction of a merchant, who "put out" the raw materials to them, paid them a certain sum per finished piece, and sold the completed item to a distant market. A look at the shoe industry in Lynn, Massachusetts, shows how the putting-out system transformed American manufacturing.

Long a major center of the shoe industry, Lynn, in 1800, produced 400,000 pairs of shoes—enough for every fifth person in the country. Skilled craftsmen in Lynn controlled production through the traditional system of apprenticeship. Apprentices lived with the master craftsman and were treated like members of the family. Commonly, apprentices became journeymen craftsmen, working for wages in the shops of master craftsmen until they had enough capital to set up shop for themselves. In

Lynn, 200 master artisans and their families, including their journeymen and apprentices, worked together in hundreds of small home workshops called "ten-footers" (from their size, about ten feet square). The artisans and journeymen cut the leather, the artisans' wives and daughters did the binding of the upper parts of the shoe, the men stitched the shoe together, and children and apprentices helped where needed. In the early days, the artisan commonly bartered his shoes for needed products. Sometimes an artisan sold his shoes to a larger retailer in Boston or Salem. Although production of shoes in Lynn increased yearly from 1780 to 1810 as markets widened, shoes continued to be manufactured in traditional ways.

The investment of merchant capital in the shoe business changed everything. In Lynn, a small group of Quaker shopkeepers and merchants, connected by family, religious, and business ties, took the lead in reorganizing the trade. Financed by the bank they founded in 1814, Lynn capitalists like Micajah Pratt built large, two-story central workshops to replace the scattered ten-footers. Pratt employed a few skilled craftsmen to cut leather for shoes, but he put out the rest of the shoemaking to less-skilled workers who were no longer connected by family ties. Putting-out workers were paid on a piecework basis, much less than a master craftsman or a journeyman. This arrangement allowed the capitalist to employ much more labor for the same investment than the traditional artisan workshop. Shoe production increased enormously: the largest central shop in 1832 turned out ten times more shoes than the largest shopkeeper had sold in 1789. Gradually the putting-out system and central workshops replaced artisans' shops. Some artisans became wealthy owners of workshops, but most became wage earners, and the apprenticeship system eventually disappeared.

The putting-out system moved the control of production from the individual artisan households to the merchant capitalists, who could now control labor costs, production goals, and shoe styles to fit certain markets. For example, the Lynn trade quickly monopolized the market for cheap boots for southern slaves and western farmers, leaving workshops in other cities to produce shoes for wealthier customers. This specialization of the national market—indeed, even thinking in terms of a national market—was new. Additionally, and most important from the capitalist's point of view, the owner of the business controlled the workers and could cut back or expand the labor force as economic and marketplace conditions warranted. The unaccustomed severity of economic slumps like the Panics of 1819 and 1837 made this flexibility especially desirable.

While the central workshop system prevailed in Lynn and in urban centers like New York City, the putting-out system also fostered a more dispersed form of home production. By 1810, there were an estimated 2,500 so-called outwork weavers in New England, operating handlooms

Industrialization and Rural Life

At first glance, this looks like a typical rural landscape of the well-known genre known as pastoral painting. But look again: what is the locomotive doing there? Its presence must have been a shock to the first viewers, who were familiar with pastoral landscapes but unfamiliar with new inventions like the steam locomotive in this setting. To appreciate its novelty, contrast this painting to the Currier and Ives print in *The Express Train* on p. 312.

George Inness was an American artist who specialized in painting settled and cultivated eastern landscapes. This painting was commissioned by the president of the Delaware Lackawanna and Western Railroad to mark its opening. Inness rose to the challenge of blending a locomotive, double tracks (foreground) and the roundhouse (background) into a rural landscape. However, the railroad committee was not satisfied, demanding that he show all four company locomotives (three are in the background) and that the letters *D.L.&W* be painted on the side of the nearest one. At first Inness refused on artistic grounds, but being in need of money, he finally agreed. The painting is thus one of the first American examples of a "fine art" advertisement. Even at this early date, there was conflict between the demands of art and those of the advertiser.

• **Why do you think the railroad company chose Inness, known for his landscapes, to paint the picture? What kind of statement about the relationship between industrialization and rural life does the painting make?**

SOURCE: LeRoy Ireland, *The Works of George Inness, An Illustrated Catalogue Raisonne* (Austin: University of Texas Press, 1965), p. 28.

This carved and painted figure, designed as a whirligig and trade sign, shows a woman at a spinning wheel. Until the transportation revolution made commercial cloth widely available, spinning was one of the most time-consuming tasks that women and young girls did at home.

in their own homes. Other crafts that rapidly became organized according to the putting-out system were flax and wool spinning, straw braiding, glove making, and the knitting of stockings. For example, the palm-leaf hat industry that supplied farm laborers and slaves in the South and West relied completely on women and children, who braided the straw for the hats at home part-time. Absorbed into families' overall domestic routines, the outwork activity seemed small, but the size of the industry itself was surprising: in 1837, 33,000 Massachusetts women braided palm-leaf hats, whereas only 20,000 worked in the state's cotton textile mills.

The Spread of Commercial Markets

Although the putting-out system meant a loss of independence for artisans such as those in Lynn, Massachusetts, New England farm families liked it. From their point of view, the work could easily be combined with domestic work, and the pay was a new source of income that they could use to purchase mass-produced goods rather than spend the time required to make those things themselves. In this way farm families moved away from the local barter system and into a larger market economy.

Commercialization, or the replacement of barter by a cash economy, did not happen immediately or uniformly throughout the nation. Fixed prices for goods produced by the new principles of specialization and division of labor appeared first along established trade routes. Rural areas in established sections of the country that were remote from trade routes continued in traditional ways (see Seeing History). Strikingly, however, western farming frontiers were commercial from the very start. The existence of a cash market was an important spur to westward expansion.

The Yankee West

Every advance in transportation—better roads, canals, steamboats, railroads—made it easier for farmers to get their produce to market. Improvements in agricultural machinery increased the amount of acreage a farmer could cultivate. These two developments, added to the availability of rich, inexpensive land in the heartland, dramatically changed the Old Northwest. The sudden change from subsistence to commercial agriculture in the Old Northwest is a particularly vivid example of the impact of transportation changes and commercialization.

New Routes West

The impact of the transportation revolution on the Old Northwest was startling. Settlement of the region, ongoing since the 1790s, vastly accelerated and shifted. Before 1830, most migrants had traveled by the Pennsylvania Turnpike or the National Road to settle in the southern part of the region. In the 1830s, after the opening of the Erie Canal, migrants from New England streamed into northern Ohio, Illinois, Indiana, southern Wisconsin, and Michigan and began to reach into Iowa. In the decade of the 1830s, three quarters of a million people migrated to the region, and by 1850 the population of the Old Northwest almost quadrupled.

Migrants of New England origin (Yankees) accounted for at least 40 percent of the population, and they brought with them a distinctive culture that stressed community building. As had been true of the earlier "Yankee Exodus" after the War of 1812 (see Chapter 9), New Englanders immediately established schools, churches, and town government in their new locations. Southern migrants, like their counterparts who migrated to the Old Southwest, were much more likely to rely on kinship ties rather than found community institutions, except for churches. Yankees were different from Southerners in another way: they welcomed commercial agriculture.

Commercial Agriculture in the Old Northwest

The long period of subsistence farming that had characterized colonial New England and the early Ohio Valley frontier before 1830 was superseded by commercial agriculture stimulated by the transportation revolution and by government policy. The easy terms of federal land sales were an important inducement: terms eased from an initial rate of $2.00 per acre for a minimum of 320 acres in 1800 to $1.25 an acre for 80 acres in 1820. Still, this was too much for most settlers to pay all at once and many settlers relied on credit, which was extended by banks, storekeepers, speculators, promoters, and, somewhat later, railroads, which received large grants of federal lands.

The very need for cash to purchase land involved western settlers in commercial agriculture from the beginning. Farmers, and the towns and cities that grew up to supply them, needed access to markets for their crops. Local residents clamored for the canals and railroads (often financed by state as well as private money) that tied the individual farm into national and international commercial networks. Commercial agriculture in turn encouraged regional specialization. Because in each new western area wheat yields were higher than in earlier ones, farmers in older regions were forced to shift away from wheat to other crops. The constant opening of new farmland encouraged mobility: prepared to move on when the price was right, many Yankee farmers regarded their farmland not as a permanent investment but as a speculation. This too marked a difference from colonial and southern attitudes in which permanent ownership of farms, with enough to land to endow one's sons, had always been the goal.

New tools made western farmers unusually productive. John Deere's steel plow (invented in 1837) cut plowing time in half, making cultivation of larger acreages possible. Seed drills were another important advance. But the most remarkable innovation was Cyrus McCormick's reaper, patented in 1834. Previously, harvesting had depended on manpower alone. A man could cut two or three acres of wheat a day with a cradle scythe, but with the horse-drawn reaper, he could cut twelve acres. Western farmers rushed to buy the new machines, confident that increased production would rapidly pay for them. In most years, their confidence was justified. But in bad years, farmers found that their new levels of debt could mean failure and foreclosure. They were richer but more economically vulnerable than they had been before.

This advertisement contrasts farmers harvesting traditionally with a sickle compared to the speed of the mechanized McCormick reaper.

Thus, within a few short years the Old Northwest became the nation's agricultural heartland. In 1859, the region produced 46 percent of the nation's wheat and 33 percent of its corn. Moreover, a steadily increasing amount was exported to foreign markets: from 12 percent in 1820 to 27 percent in 1840 to 70 percent in 1860. While Southerners boasted in 1858 that "Cotton is note the problem of consistent capitalization King," in fact the Old Northwest, not the South, had become the export heart of the national economy.

Transportation Changes Affect Western Cities

The changing fortunes of the region's major cities demonstrate the dramatic effects of improvements in transportation. Before 1830, when the easiest way to move goods and people was by water, Ohioans shipped corn and hogs first by flatboat and later by steamboat down the Ohio and Mississippi Rivers to New Orleans. Cincinnati, the center

of the Ohio trade, earned the nickname "Porkopolis" because of the importance of its slaughterhouses.

After 1830, with the opening of the Erie Canal and canals in Ohio and Illinois, St. Louis became the distribution point for the flood of goods New York merchants sent westward via the canal system. St. Louis became a magnet for migration: in 1849, the year of the California gold rush (see Chapter 14), 60,000 people passed through the city and surprisingly one third of them stayed. Much to the dismay of many rural Missourians, who were of southern origin, at least half of the migrants were Yankees, and 40 percent of the city's merchants were from New York and Boston.

After 1840, with the impact of railroads, the region's distribution system changed again, causing Chicago, barely a dot on the map early in the century, to grow at an incredible rate. By 1860, it had reached a population of 100,000 and, although still smaller than Cincinnati and St. Louis, was clearly destined to become the nation's east–west hub (see Map 12.3).

MAP 12.3A AND 12.3B Commercial Links: The Old Northwest, **1830, 1860** After 1825, the Erie Canal brought streams of migrants to the upper parts of the Old Northwest, where they quickly built roads, canals, and railroads. These maps illustrate the changes in transportation that made their commercial agriculture possible.

The loser in this economic redistribution was New Orleans. As early as 1853, only 30 percent of Old Northwest produce was shipped via New Orleans, while 60 percent was exported via the Erie Canal. Railroads increased the disparity, while at the same time they provided easy transportation to New Englanders who wanted to move west. These new transportation links tied the Old Northwest to New York and New England economically and politically, creating, as one southerner bitterly commented, a "universal Yankee nation" that was a huge factor in the sectional disputes and eventual civil war that were to come (see Chapter 15).

Industrialization Begins

The most dramatic single aspect of the market revolution was industrialization. Even in its earliest stages, industrialization changed the nature of work itself.

British Technology and American Industrialization

It was the third component of the market revolution, industrialization, that brought the greatest changes to personal lives. Begun in Britain in the eighteenth century, industrialization was the result of a series of technological changes in the textile trade. In marked contrast to the putting-out system, in which capitalists had dispersed work into many individual households, industrialization required workers to concentrate in factories and pace themselves to the rhythms of power-driven machinery.

The simplest and quickest way for America to industrialize was to copy the British, but the British, well aware of the value of their machinery, enacted laws forbidding its export and even the emigration of skilled workers. Over the years, however, Americans managed to lure a number of British artisans to the United States.

In 1789, Samuel Slater, who had just finished an apprenticeship in the most up-to-date cotton spinning factory in England, disguised himself as a farm laborer and slipped out of England without even telling his mother good-bye. In Providence, Rhode Island, he met Moses Brown and William Almy, who had been trying without success to duplicate British industrial technology. Having carefully committed the designs to memory before leaving England, Slater promptly built copies of the latest British machinery for Brown and Almy. Slater Mill, as it became known, began operation in 1790. It was the most advanced cotton mill in America.

Following British practice, Slater drew his workforce primarily from among young children (ages seven to twelve) and women, whom he paid much less than the handful of skilled male workers he hired to keep the machines working. The yarn spun at Slater's mill was then put out to local home weavers, who turned it into cloth on hand-looms. As a result, home weaving flourished in areas near the mill, giving families a new opportunity to make money at a task with which they were already familiar.

●▪●▪[Read the **Document**
Biography: Samuel Slater
at **www.myhistorylab.com**

Many other merchants and mechanics followed Slater's lead, and the rivers of New England were soon dotted with mills wherever waterpower could be tapped.

The Lowell Mills

Another way to deal with British competition was to beat the British at their own game. With the intention of designing better machinery, a young Bostonian, Francis Cabot Lowell, made an apparently casual tour of British textile mills in 1810. Lowell made a good impression on his English hosts, who were pleased by his interest and

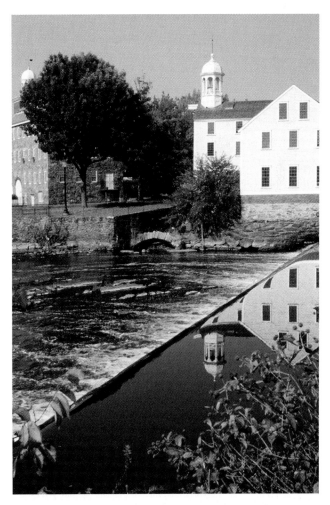

This photograph shows the much restored Slater Mill, the first cotton textile factory in the United States, and the falls that powered its machinery. Built in 1793, the mill—now a National Historic Landmark—is an example of the way early entrepreneurs used the power potential of New England's swiftly flowing streams.

his intelligent questions. They did not know that each night, in his hotel room, Lowell made detailed sketches from memory of the machines he had inspected during the day.

Lowell was more than an industrial spy, however. When he returned to the United States, he went to work with a Boston mechanic, Paul Moody, to improve on the British models. Lowell and Moody not only made the machinery for spinning cotton more efficient, but they also invented a power loom. This was a great advance, for now all aspects of textile manufacture, from the initial cleaning and carding (combing) to the production of finished lengths of cloth, could be gathered together in the same factory. Such a mill required a

much larger capital investment than a small spinning mill such as Slater's, but Lowell's family network gave him access to the needed funds. In 1814, he opened the world's first integrated cotton mill in Waltham, near Boston. It was a great success: in 1815, the Boston Associates (Lowell's partners) made profits of 25 percent, and their efficiency allowed them to survive the intense British competition following the War of 1812. Many smaller New England mills did not survive. The lesson was clear: size mattered.

The Boston Associates took the lesson to heart, and when they moved their enterprise to a new location in 1823, they thought big. They built an entire town at the junction of the Concord and Merrimack Rivers where

MAP 12.4 Lowell, Massachusetts, 1832 This town plan of Lowell, Massachusetts, in 1832, illustrates the comprehensive relationship the owners envisaged between the factories and the workforce. The mills are located on the Merrimack River, while nearby are the boardinghouses for the single young female workers, row houses for the male mechanics and their families, and houses for the overseers. Somewhat farther away is the mansion of the company agent.

the village of East Chelmsford stood, renaming it Lowell in memory of Francis, who had died, still a young man, in 1817. As the opening of this chapter describes, the new industrial community boasted six mills and company housing for all the workers. In 1826, the town had 2,500 inhabitants; ten years later the population was 17,000 (see Map 12.4).

Family Mills

Lowell was unique. Much more common in the early days of industrialization were small rural spinning mills, on the model of Slater's first mill, built on swiftly running streams near existing farm communities. Because the owners of smaller mills often hired entire families, their operations came to be called family mills. The employment pattern at these mills followed that established by Slater at his first mill in 1790. Children aged eight to twelve, whose customary job was "doffing" (changing) bobbins on the spinning machines, made up 50 percent of the workforce. Women and men each made up about 25 percent of the workforce, but men had the most skilled and best-paid jobs.

Relations between these small rural mill communities and the surrounding farming communities were often difficult, as the history of the towns of Dudley and Oxford, Massachusetts, shows. Samuel Slater, now a millionaire, built three small mill communities near these towns in the early years of the nineteenth century. Each consisted of a small factory, a store, and cottages and a boardinghouse for workers. Most of Slater's workers came from outside the Dudley–Oxford area. They were a mixed group—single young farm women of the kind Lowell attracted, the poor and destitute, and workers from other factories looking for better conditions. They rarely stayed long: almost 50 percent of the workforce left every year.

Slater's mills also provided a substantial amount of work for local people, putting out to them both the initial cleaning of the raw cotton and the much more lucrative weaving of the spun yarn. But in spite of this economic link, relations between Slater and his workers on one side and the farmers and shopkeepers of the Dudley and Oxford communities on the other were stormy. They disagreed over the building of mill dams (essential for the mill power supply, these dams sometimes flooded local fields), over taxes, over the upkeep of local roads, and over schools. Residents of Dudley and Oxford became increasingly hostile to Slater's authoritarian control, which they regarded as undemocratic. Their dislike carried over to the workers as well. Disdaining the mill workers for their poverty and transiency, people in the rural communities began

●●►▌**Read** the **Document**

Employers Advertise for Help Wanted in the 1820s at **www.myhistorylab.com**

referring to them as "operatives," making them somehow different in their work roles from themselves. Industrial work thus led to new social distinctions.

"The American System of Manufactures"

Not all American industrial technology was copied from British inventions, for there were many homegrown inventors. Indeed, calling Americans "mechanic[s] by nature," one Frenchman observed that "in Massachusetts and Connecticut there is not a labourer who had not invented a machine or tool." Perhaps the most important invention was the development of standardized parts.

The concept of interchangeable parts, realized first in gun manufacturing, was so unusual that the British soon dubbed it the "American system." In this system, a gun was broken down into its component parts and an exact mold was made for each. All pieces made from the same mold (after being hand filed by inexpensive unskilled laborers) matched a uniform standard. As a result, repairing a gun required only installing a replacement for the

In 1816, Connecticut gunsmith Simeon North did what Eli Whitney had only hoped to do. North produced the first gun with interchangeable parts. North's invention, taken up and improved by the national armories at Springfield and Harpers Ferry, formed the basis of the American system of manufactures.

Two Mill Girls Disagree about Conditions at Lowell

From its very beginnings there was controversy over the conditions for the women (the mill "girls") who worked at Lowell. One positive indicator was the tone of the articles appearing in the *Lowell Offering*, a magazine paid for by the Lowell management but written by the mill girls themselves. The first article, published in 1840, is attributed to Sarah Bagley, who just a few years later became a founding member of the New England Female Labor Reform Association. Five years later, the view of factory life in the second article was first rejected by the *Lowell Offering* as too critical, whereupon it was published as a tract (pamphlet) by the Lowell Female Labor Reform Association.

● **These two statements contradict each other. Who do you believe and how do you explain the contradiction?**

Sarah: The Pleasures of Factory Life

. . . [W]e are quite sure our views of the matter are just—having been engaged as an operative the last four years. Pleasures there are, even in factory life; and we have many, known only to those of like employment. . . . In the mills, we are not so far from God and nature, as many persons might suppose. We cultivate, and enjoy much pleasure in cultivating flowers and plants. A large and beautiful variety of plants I placed around the walls of the rooms, giving them more the appearance of a flower garden than a workshop . . .

> "Pleasures there are, even in factory life; . . ."

Another great source of pleasure is, that by becoming operatives, we are often enabled to assist aged parents who have become too infirm to provide for themselves; or perhaps to educate some orphan brother or sister, and fit them for future usefulness . . .

Another source is found in the fact of our being acquainted with some person or persons that reside in almost every part of the country . . .

Let no one suppose that the "factory girls" are without guardians. We are placed in the care of overseers who feel under moral obligation to look after our interest; and, if we are sick, to acquaint themselves with our situation and wants; and, if need be, to remove us to the Hospital . . .

---

defective part rather than laboriously making a new part or perhaps an entirely new gun, as had been the customary practice.

The concept originated in 1798 from the inventive Eli Whitney, who contracted with the government to make 10,000 rifles in twenty-eight months, an incredibly short period had he been planning to produce each rifle by hand in the traditional way. Whitney's ideas far outran his performance. It took him ten years to fulfill his contract, and even then he had not managed to perfect the production of all the rifle parts. Two other New Englanders, Simeon North and John Hall, created milling machines that could grind parts to the required specifications and brought the concept to fruition, North in 1816 and Hall in 1824. When the system of interchangeable machine-made parts was adopted by the national armory at Springfield, Massachusetts, the Springfield rifle got its name.

America's early lead in interchangeable parts was a substantial source of national pride. As American gunmaker Samuel Colt boasted, "There is nothing that cannot be made by machine." Standardized production quickly revolutionized the manufacture of items as simple as nails and as complicated as clocks. Like the factory system itself, the American system spread slowly. For example, Isaac Singer's sewing machine, first patented in 1851, was not made with fully interchangeable parts until 1873, when the company was already selling 230,000 machines a year. The sewing machine revolutionized the manufacture of clothing, which up to this time had been made by women for their families at home and by hand.

American businesses mass-produced high-quality goods for ordinary people earlier than manufacturers in Britain or any other European country were able to do. The availability of these goods was a practical demonstration of American beliefs in democracy and equality. As historian David Potter has perceptively remarked, "European radical thought is prone to demand that the man of property be stripped of his carriage and his fine clothes. But American radical thought is likely to insist, instead, that the ordinary man is entitled to mass-produced copies, indistinguishable from the originals."

In Lowell, we enjoy abundant means of information, especially in the way of public lectures. The time of lecturing is appointed to suit the convenience of the operatives . . .

And last, though not least, is the pleasure of being associated with the institutions of religion, and thereby availing ourselves of the Library, Bible Class, Sabbath School, and all other means of religious instruction. Most of us, when at home, live in the country, and therefore cannot enjoy these privileges to the same extent; and many of us not at all.

SOURCE: S. G. B., "Pleasures of Factory Life," in *Lowell Offering*, December 1840.

Amelia: Some of the Beauties of Our Factory System—Otherwise, Lowell Slavery

. . . [T]he next beautiful feature which [our toiling maiden] discovers in this *glorious* system is, the long number of hours which she is obliged to spend in the close, unwholesome apartment. It is not enough, like the poor peasant of Ireland or the Russian serf who labors from sun to sun, but during one half of the year, she must still continue to toil on, long after Nature's lamp has ceased to lend its aid . . . she is also through the winter months required to rise, partake of her morning meal, and be at her station in the mill, while the sun is yet sleeping behind the eastern hills; thus working on average, at least twelve hours and three fourths per day, exclusive of the time allotted for her hasty meals, which is in winter simply one half hour at noon—in the spring is allowed the same at morn, and during the summer is added 15 minutes to the half hour at noon. Then too, when she is at last released from her wearisome day's toil, still may she not depart in peace. No! her footsteps must be dogged to see that they do not stray beyond the corporation limits, and she *must*, whether she will or no, be subjected to the manifold inconveniences of a large crowded boarding-house, where, too, the price paid for her accommodation is so utterly insignificant, that it will not ensure to her the common comforts of life; she is obliged to sleep in a small comfortless, half-ventilated apartment containing some half a dozen occupants each, but no matter, *she is an operative*—it is all well enough for her; there is no "abuse" about it; no indeed; so think our employers.

SOURCE: Amelia, "Some of the Beauties of Our Factory System—Otherwise, Lowell Slavery," *Factory Tract Number 1*, Female Labor Reform Association, Lowell, Massachusetts, 1845.

"[T]here is no abuse about it, no indeed; so think our employers."

From Artisan to Worker

The changes wrought by the market revolution had major and lasting effects on ordinary Americans. The proportion of wage laborers in the nation's labor force rose from 12 percent in 1800 to 40 percent by 1860. Most of these workers were employed in the North, and almost half were women, performing piecework in their homes. The young farm woman who worked at Lowell for a year or two, then returned home; the master craftsman in Lynn who expanded his shop with the aid of merchant capital; the home weaver who prospered on outwork from Slater's mill—all were participating, often unknowingly, in fundamental personal and social changes.

Preindustrial Ways of Working

When Lowell began operation, 97 percent of all Americans still lived on farms, and most work was done in or near the home. As had been true in colonial times, the lives of most people were family and community based and depended on local networks of barter and mutual obligation. Work was slow, unscheduled, and task oriented. People did their jobs as they needed to be done, along with the daily household routine. "Home" and "work" were not separate locations or activities but were intermixed. Likewise, in urban areas, skilled craftsmen organized the apprenticeship system in the family-learning model used farms, training apprentices who became journeymen and skilled workers in turn.

In both rural and urban settings, working families were organized along strictly patriarchal lines. The man had unquestioned authority to direct the lives and work of family members and apprentices and to decide on occupations for his sons and marriages for his daughters. His wife had many crucial responsibilities—feeding, clothing, child rearing, taking care of apprentices, and all the other domestic affairs of the household—but in all these duties she was subject to the direction of her husband. Men were heads of families and bosses of artisanal shops; although entire families were engaged in the enterprise, the husband and father was the trained craftsman, and assistance by the family was informal and generally unrecognized.

In 1787, Edward Hicks painted his childhood home, rendering an idealized image of rural harmony that owes more to faith in republican agrarianism than to the artist's accurate memory. The prosperous preindustrial farm had a mixed yield—sheep, cattle, dairy products, and field crops— and had an African American farm worker (perhaps a slave), shown plowing.

SOURCE: *Residence of David Twining*, 1787. Oil on canvas. Abby Aldrich Rockefeller Folk Art Museum, Colonial Williamsburg Foundation, Williamsburg, VA.

Mechanization and Gender

The apprenticeship system was destroyed by the immense increase in productivity made possible by the principles of division of labor and specialization applied in shoe production in Lynn and in other trades elsewhere. For example, in New York by the mid-1820s, tailors and shoemakers were teaching apprentices only a few simple operations, using them as helpers. In almost every trade, apprentices no longer lived with the master's family, and their parents received cash payment for the child's work. Thus, in effect, the apprenticeship system was replaced by child labor.

Industrialization posed a further threat to the status and independence of skilled male workers. In trade after trade, mechanization meant that most tasks could be performed by unskilled labor. For example, the textile mills at Lowell and elsewhere hired a mere handful of skilled mechanics; most of the rest of the workers were unskilled and lower paid. In fact, the work in the textile mills was so simple that children came to form a large part of the workforce. By 1850, in New York City, many formerly skilled trades, including shoemaking, weaving, silversmithing, pottery making, and cabinetmaking, were filled with unskilled, low-paid workers who did one specialized operation or tended machinery. Many former artisans were reduced to performing wage labor for others. Because women were so frequently hired in the putting-out system, male workers began to oppose female participation in the workforce, fearing that it would lower their own wages.

These fears appeared to be confirmed by the experience of women in the new garment industry, which emerged in the 1820s. In New York City, employers began hiring women to sew ready-made clothing, at first rough, unfitted clothing for sailors and southern slaves, but later, overalls and shirts for Westerners, and finer items, such as men's shirts. Most women performed this work at low piecework rates in their homes. Although by 1860, Brooks Brothers, the famous men's clothing firm, had seventy "inside" workers in a model central workshop, the firm relied primarily on putting out sewing to 3,000 women who worked at home.

Soon the low pay and seasonal nature of the industry became notorious. Overcrowding of the market—all women could sew—led to low wages. Women were pushed into the garment trade because they were barred from many occupations considered inappropriate for them, and the oversupply of workers led to wage cutting. To make matters worse, most people believed that "respectable" women did not do factory work (Lowell in its "model" years was the exception that proved the rule), and this disparagement fostered low pay and poor working conditions.

▪▪▪ Read the Document
Female Industrial Association (1825) at **www.myhistorylab.com**

Manufacturers in the garment trade made their profits not from efficient production but by obtaining intensive labor for very low wages. The lower the piece rate, the more each woman, sewing at home, had to produce to earn enough to live. The invention of the sewing machine only made matters worse. Manufacturers dropped their piecework rates still lower, and some women found themselves working fifteen to eighteen hours a day, producing more than they ever had but earning the same pay.

▪▪▪ Read the Document
A New England Factory Issues Regulations for Workers in 1825 at **www.myhistorylab.com**

Time, Work, and Leisure

Preindustrial work had a flexibility that factory work did not, and it took factory workers a while to get accustomed to the constant pace of work. In the early days of

This illustration of seamstresses at work, from *Sartain's Union Magazine*, January 1851, shows an early abuse created by the market revolution. Women workers were crowded into just a few occupations, thereby allowing owners to offer very low wages for very long hours of work. The women in this illustration appear to be gathered together in a central workshop, where they had each other for company. Many other women sewed alone at home, often for even lower wages.

Slater's mill in Rhode Island, workers sometimes took a few hours off to go berry picking or to attend to other business. And when Slater insisted on a twelve-hour day that required candles for night work, one upset father demanded that his children be sent home at sunset, the traditional end of the workday.

Factory workers gradually adjusted to having their lives regulated by the sound of the factory bell, but they did not necessarily become the docile "hands" the owners wanted. Absenteeism was common, accounting for about 15 percent of working hours, and there was much pilfering. Workers were beginning to think of themselves as a separate community whose interests differed from those of owners, and the tyranny of time over their work was certainly one reason for this.

Another adjustment required by the constant pace was that time now had to be divided into two separate activities—work and leisure. In preindustrial times, work and leisure were blended for farmers and artisans. The place of work—often the home—and the pace made it possible to stop and have a chat or a friendly drink with a visitor. Now, however, the separation of home and workplace and the pace of production not only squeezed the fun out of the long workday but also left a smaller proportion of time for leisure activities.

For many workingmen, the favored spot for after-hours and Sunday leisure became the local tavern.

Community-wide celebrations and casual sociability, still common in rural areas, began to be replaced in cities by spectator sports—horse racing, boxing, and (beginning in the 1850s) baseball—and by popular entertainments, such as plays, operas, minstrel shows, concerts, and circuses. Some of these diversions, such as plays and horse racing, appealed to all social classes, but others, like parades, rowdy dance halls, and tavern games like quoits and ninepins were favored working-class amusements. The effect of these changes was to make working-class amusements more distinct, and visible, than they had been before.

Free Labor

Another effect of the market revolution was the transformation of a largely barter system into cash payments. For workers, this change was both unsettling and liberating. On the minus side, workers were no longer part of a settled, orderly, and familiar community. On the plus side, they were now free to labor wherever they could, at whatever wages their skills or their bargaining power could command. That workers took their freedom seriously is evidenced by the very high rate of turnover—50 percent a year—in the New England textile mills.

But if moving on was a sign of increased freedom of opportunity for some workers, for others it was an unwanted consequence of the market revolution. In

TIME TABLE OF THE LOWELL MILLS,
To take effect on and after Oct. 21st, 1851.

The Standard time being that of the meridian of Lowell, as shown by the regulator clock of JOSEPH RAYNES, 43 Central Street.

	From 1st to 10th inclusive.				From 11th to 20th inclusive.				From 21st to last day of month.			
	1st Bell	2d Bell	3d Bell	Eve. Bell	1st Bell	2d Bell	3d Bell	Eve. Bell	1st Bell	2d Bell	3d Bell	Eve. Bell
January,	5.00	6.00	6.50	*7.30	5.00	6 00	6.50	*7.30	5.00	6.00	6.50	*7.30
February,	4.30	5.30	6.40	*7.30	4.30	5.30	6.25	*7.30	4.30	5.30	6.15	*7.30
March,	5.40	6.00		*7.30	5.20	5.40		*7.30	5.05	5.25		6.35
April,	4.45	5.05		6.45	4.30	4.50		6.55	4.30	4.50		7.00
May,	4 30	4.50		7·00	4.30	4.50		7.00	4.30	4.50		7 00
June,	"	"		"	"	"		"	"	"		"
July,	"	"		"	"	"		"	"	"		"
August,	"	"		"	"	"		"	"	"		"
September,	4.40	5.00		6.45	4.50	5.10		6.30	5.00	5.20		*7.30
October,	5.10	5.30		*7.30	5.20	5.40		*7.30	5.35	5.55		*7.30
November,	4.30	5.30	6.10	*7.30	4.30	5.30	6.20	*7.30	5.00	6.00	6.35	*7.30
December,	5.00	6.00	6.45	*7.30	5.00	6.00	6.50	*7.30	5.00	6·00	6.50	*7 30

* Excepting on Saturdays from Sept. 21st to March 20th inclusive, when it is rung at 20 minutes after sunset.

YARD GATES,
Will be opened at ringing of last morning bell, of meal bells, and of evening bells; and kept open Ten minutes.

MILL GATES.
Commence hoisting Mill Gates, Two minutes before commencing work.

WORK COMMENCES,
At Ten minutes after last morning bell, and at Ten minutes after bell which "rings in" from Meals.

BREAKFAST BELLS.
During March "Ring out".........at....7.30 a. m.........."Ring in" at 8:05 a. m.
April 1st to Sept. 20th inclusive.....at....7 00 " " .... " " at 7.35 " "
Sept. 21st to Oct. 31st inclusive.....at....7.30 " " .... " " at 8.05 " "
Remainder of year work commences after Breakfast.

DINNER BELLS.
"Ring out" ....12.30 p. m.........."Ring in".... 1.05 p. m.

In all cases, the *first* stroke of the bell is considered as marking the time.

This timetable from the Lowell Mills illustrates the elaborate time schedules that the cotton textile mills expected their employees to meet. For workers, it was difficult to adjust to the regimentation imposed by clock time, in contrast to the approximate times common to preindustrial work.

New England, for example, many quite prosperous artisans and farmers faced disruptive competition from factory goods and western commercial agriculture. They could remain where they were only if they were willing to become factory workers or, in the case of farmers, to move west and try to become successful commercial farmers themselves.

At the heart of this industrializing economy was the notion of free labor. Originally, "free" referred to individual economic choice—that is, to the right of workers to move to another job rather than be held to a position by customary obligation or the formal contract of apprenticeship or journeyman labor. But "free labor" soon came to encompass as well the range of attitudes—hard work, self-discipline, and a striving for economic independence—that were necessary for success in a competitive, industrializing economy. These were profoundly new and individualistic attitudes.

The spread of the factory system and of the ideology of free labor soon became an issue in the growing political battle between the North and the South over slavery. Southern

defenders of slavery compared their cradle-to-grave responsibility to their slaves with northern employers' "heartless" treatment of their "wage slaves." Certainly the new northern employer assumed less responsibility for individual workers than had the traditional artisan. Although the earliest textile manufacturers, like those at Lowell, provided housing for their workers, workers soon became responsible for their own food and housing. Moreover, northern employers felt no obligation to help or care for old or disabled workers. Southerners were right: this was a heartless system. But Northerners were also right: industrialization was certainly freer than the slave system, freer even than the hierarchical craft system, although it sometimes offered only the freedom to starve.

Early Strikes

Rural women workers led some of the first strikes in American labor history. In 1824, in one of the first of these actions, women workers at a Pawtucket, Rhode Island, textile mill led their coworkers, female and male, out on strike to protest wage cuts and longer hours.

More famous were the strikes led by the women at the model mill at Lowell. The first serious trouble came in 1834, when 800 women participated in a spontaneous turnout to protest a wage cut of 25 percent. The owners were shocked and outraged by the strike, considering it both unfeminine and ungrateful. The workers, however, were bound together by a sense of sisterhood and were protesting not just the attack on their economic independence but also the blow to their position as "daughters of freemen still." As a group of New Hampshire female workers rhetorically asked, "Why [is] there . . . so much want, dependence and misery among us, if forsooth, we are freemen and freewomen?" Nevertheless, the wage cuts were enforced, as were more cuts in 1836, again in the face of a turnout. Many women simply packed their clothes in disgust and returned home to the family farm. Others who remained formed the New England Female Labor Reform Association in 1845, which promptly petitioned the Massachusetts legislature to enact a ten-hour workday. The Massachusetts legislature ignored the ten-hour-day proposal even when presented with a petition in 1846 that had 10,000 signatures, 4,000 from Lowell women. But in 1847, legislators in New Hampshire, responding to a petition from women workers in Nashua who had refused to work after "lighting up" (after dark), made theirs the first state to enact a ten-hour-day law. Maine followed in 1848 and Pennsylvania in 1849. For the first time, thanks to women's pioneering role in factory protests, a group of workers had obtained state legislation improving their working conditions.

Like these strikes, most turnouts by factory workers in the 1830s—male or female—were unsuccessful. Owners, claiming that increasing competition made wage cuts inevitable, were always able to find new workers—Irish immigrants or, after their failed 1837 revolt, French Canadians, for example—who would work at lower wages. The preindustrial notion of a community of interest between owner and workers had broken down and workers, both female and male, began to band together to act on their own behalf (see Communities in Conflict).

The New Middle Class

The market revolution reached into every aspect of life, down to the most personal family decisions. As just described, it changed working life. The market revolution also fundamentally changed the social order, creating a new middle class with distinctive habits and beliefs.

Wealth and Rank

There had always been social divisions in America. Since the early colonial period, planters in the South and merchants in the North had comprised a wealthy elite. Somewhere below the elite but above the mass of people was the "middling sort": a small professional group that included lawyers, ministers, schoolteachers, doctors, public officials, some prosperous farmers, prosperous urban shop keepers and innkeepers, and a few wealthy artisans such as Boston silversmith Paul Revere. "Mechanics and farmers"— artisans and yeoman farmers—made up another large group, and the laboring poor, consisting of ordinary laborers, servants, and marginal farmers, were below them. At the very bottom were the paupers—those dependent on public charity—and the enslaved. This was the "natural" social order that fixed most people in the social rank to which they were born. Although many a male servant in early America aspired to become a small farmer or artisan, he did not usually aspire to become a member of the wealthy elite, nor did serving maids often marry rich men.

The market revolution ended this stable and hierarchical social order, creating the dynamic and unstable one we recognize today: upper, middle, and working classes, whose members all share the hope of climbing as far up the social ladder as they can. This social mobility was new. The expanding opportunities of the market revolution enriched the already rich: by the 1840s, the top 1 percent of the population owned about 40 percent of the nation's wealth. At the other extreme, fully one-third of the population possessed little more than the clothes they wore and some loose change. The major transformation came in the lives of the "middling sort."

The market revolution downgraded many independent artisans. Formerly independent artisans or farmers (or, more frequently, their children) joined the rapidly growing ranks of managers and white-collar workers such as accountants, bank tellers, clerks, bookkeepers, and insurance agents. Occupational opportunities shifted dramatically in just one generation. In Utica, New York, for example, 16 percent of the city's young men held white-collar jobs in 1855, compared with only 6 percent of their fathers. At the same time, 15 percent fewer younger men filled artisanal occupations than older men.

These new white-collar workers owed not only their jobs but also their lifestyles to the new structure and organization of industry. The new economic order demanded certain habits and attitudes of workers: sobriety, responsibility, steadiness, and hard work. Inevitably, employers found themselves not only enforcing these new standards but also adopting them themselves.

Religion and Personal Life

Religion, which had undergone dramatic changes since the 1790s, played a key role in the emergence of the new attitudes. The Second Great Awakening had supplanted the orderly and intellectual Puritan religion of early New England. The new evangelical religious spirit, which stressed the achievement of salvation through personal faith, was more democratic and more enthusiastic than the earlier faith. The concept of original sin, the cornerstone of Puritan belief, was replaced by the optimistic belief that a willingness to be saved was enough to ensure salvation. Conversion and repentance were no longer private, because they now took place in huge revival meetings in which an entire congregation focused on the sinners about to be saved and where group support actively encouraged individual conversion. The converted bore a heavy personal responsibility to demonstrate their faith in their own daily lives through morally respectable behavior. In this way, the new religious feeling fostered individualism and self-discipline.

The Second Great Awakening had its greatest initial success on the western frontier in the 1790s, but by the 1820s, evangelical religion was reaching a new audience: the people whose lives were being changed by the market revolution and who needed help in adjusting to the demands made by the new economic conditions. In 1825, in Utica, New York, and in other towns along the recently opened Erie Canal, evangelist Charles G. Finney began a series of dramatic revival meetings. His spellbinding message reached both rich and poor, converting members of all classes to the new evangelistic religion. In 1830, made famous by these gatherings, Finney was invited by businessmen to preach in Rochester. Finney preached every day for six months—three times on Sundays—and his wife, Lydia, made home visits to the unconverted and mobilized the women of Rochester for the cause. Under the Finneys' guidance and example, prayer meetings were held in schools and businesses, and impromptu religious services were held in people's homes.

Read the Document
Charles Finney, What a Revival of Religion Is (1835) at **www.myhistorylab.com**

Middle-class women in particular carried Finney's message by prayer and pleading to the men of their families, who found that evangelism's stress on self-discipline and individual achievement helped them adjust to new business conditions. The enthusiasm and optimism of evangelism aided what was often a profound personal transformation in the face of the market's stringent new demands. Moreover, it gave businessmen a basis for demanding the same behavior from their workers. Businessmen now argued that traditional paternalism had no role in the new business world. Because achievement depended on individual character, each worker was responsible for making his own way.

The New Middle-Class Family

The economic changes of the market revolution reshaped family roles, first in the middle class and eventually throughout the entire society. As men increasingly concentrated their energies on their careers and occupations, women assumed major new responsibilities for rearing the children and inculcating in them the new attitudes necessary for success in the business world. The division of labor that occurred in industry was reflected in the middle-class home: father the breadwinner, mother the nurturer, working together in partnership to raise successful middle-class children.

When the master craftsman became a small manufacturer, or the small subsistence farmer began to manage a large-scale commercial operation, production moved away from both the family home and its members. Husbands and fathers became managers of paid workers— or workers themselves—and although they were still considered the heads of their households, they spent most of the day away from their homes and families. The husband was no longer the undisputed head of a family unit that combined work and personal life. Their wives, on the other hand, remained at home, where they were still responsible for cooking, cleaning, and other domestic tasks but no longer contributed directly to what had previously been the family enterprise. Instead, women took on a new responsibility, that of providing a quiet, well-ordered, and relaxing refuge from the pressures of the industrial world.

Catharine Beecher's *A Treatise on Domestic Economy*, first published in 1841, became the standard housekeeping guide for a generation of middle-class American women.

●◦●─Read the Document

Catharine Beecher, from A Treatise on Domestic Economy (1841) at **www.myhistorylab.com**

In it, Beecher combined innovative ideas for household design (especially in the kitchen, where she introduced principles of organization) with medical information, child-rearing advice, recipes, and numerous discussions of the mother's moral role in the family. The book clearly filled a need: for many pioneer women, it was the only book besides the Bible that they carried west with them.

As the work roles of middle-class men and women diverged, so did social attitudes about appropriate male and female characteristics and behavior. Men were expected to be steady, industrious, responsible, and painstakingly attentive to their business. They had little choice: in the competitive, uncertain, and rapidly changing business conditions of the early nineteenth century, these qualities were essential for men who hoped to hold their existing positions or to get ahead. In contrast, women were expected to be nurturing, gentle, kind, moral, and selflessly devoted to their families. They were expected to operate within the "woman's sphere"—the home.

The maintenance or achievement of a middle-class lifestyle required the joint efforts of husband and wife. More cooperation between them was called for than in the preindustrial, patriarchal family. The nature of the new, companionate marriage that evolved in response to the market revolution was reflected most clearly in decisions concerning children. Middle-class couples had fewer children than did their predecessors. The dramatic fall in the birthrate during the nineteenth century (from an average of seven children per woman in 1800 to five in 1860) is evidence of conscious decisions about family limitation, first by members of the new middle class and later by working-class families. Few couples used mechanical methods of contraception such as the condom, partly because these were difficult to obtain and partly because most people associated their use with prostitution and the prevention of venereal disease rather than with family planning. Instead, people used birth control methods that relied on mutual consent: coitus interruptus (withdrawal before climax), the rhythm method (intercourse only during the woman's infertile period), and, most often, abstinence or infrequent intercourse.

When mutual efforts at birth control failed, married women often sought a surgical abortion, a new technique that was much more reliable than the folk remedies women had always shared among themselves. Surgical abortions were widely advertised after 1830, and widely used, especially by middle-class married women seeking to limit family size. Some historians estimate that one out of every four pregnancies was aborted in the years from 1840 to 1860 (compared to one in six in 2000). The rising rate of abortion by married women (in other words, its use as birth control) prompted the first legal bans; by 1860, twenty states had outlawed the practice.

Accompanying the interest in family limitation was a redefinition of sexuality. Doctors generally recommended that sexual urges be controlled, but they believed that men would have much more difficulty exercising such control than women, partly because they also believed that women were uninterested in sex. (Women who were visibly interested ran the risk of being considered

This middle-class family group, painted in 1840, illustrates the new importance of children and of the mother–child bond.

SOURCE: Frederick Spencer, *Family Group,* 1840. © Francis G. Mayer/CORBIS.

immoral or "fallen" and thereupon shunned by the middle class.) Medical manuals of the period suggested that it was the task of middle-class women to help their husbands and sons restrain their sexuality by appealing to their higher, moral natures. Although it is always difficult to measure the extent to which the suggestions in advice books were applied in actual practice, it seems that many middle-class women accepted this new and limited definition of their sexuality because of the desire to limit the number of their pregnancies.

Many women of the late eighteenth century wanted to be free of the medical risks and physical debility that too-frequent childbearing brought, but they had little chance of achieving that goal until men became equally interested in family limitation. The rapid change in attitudes toward family size that occurred in the early nineteenth century has been repeated around the world as other societies undergo the dramatic experience of industrialization. It is a striking example of the ways economic changes affect our most private and personal decisions.

Middle-Class Children

Child rearing had been shared in the preindustrial household, boys learning farming or craft skills from their fathers while girls learned domestic skills from their mothers. The children of the new middle class, however, needed a new kind of upbringing, one that involved a long period of nurturing in the beliefs and personal habits necessary for success. Mothers assumed primary responsibility for

this training, in part because fathers were too busy but also because people believed that women's superior qualities of gentleness, morality, and loving watchfulness were essential to the task.

Fathers retained a strong role in major decisions concerning children, but mothers commonly turned to other women for advice on daily matters. Through their churches, women formed maternal associations for help in raising their children to be religious and responsible. In Utica, New York, for example, these extremely popular organizations enabled women to form strong networks sustained by mutual advice and by publications such as *Mother's Magazine*, issued by the Presbyterian Church, and *Mother's Monthly Journal*, put out by the Baptists.

●●●●─Read the Document
Mother's Magazine (1934)
at **www.myhistorylab.com**

Middle-class status required another sharp break with tradition. As late as 1855, artisanal families expected all children over fifteen years to work. Middle-class families, in contrast, sacrificed to keep their sons in school or in training for their chosen professions, and they often housed and fed their sons until the young men had "established" themselves financially and could marry. Mothers took the lead in an important informal activity: making sure their children had friends and contacts that would be useful when they were old enough to consider careers and marriage. Matters such as these, rarely considered by earlier generations living in small communities, now became important in the new middle-class communities of America's towns and cities.

Contrary to the growing myth of the self-made man, middle-class success was not a matter of individual achievement. Instead it was usually based on a family strategy in which fathers provided the money and mothers the nurturance. The reorganization of the family described in this section was successful: from its shelter and support emerged generations of ambitious, responsible, and individualistic middle-class men. But although boys were trained for success, this was not an acceptable goal for their sisters. Women were trained to be the silent "support system" that undergirded male success. And women were also expected to ease the tensions of the transition to new middle-class behavior by acting as models and monitors of traditional values.

Read the Document

A New England Woman Describes the Responsibilities of American Women in 1847 at **www.myhistorylab.com**

Sentimentalism and Transcendentalism

Just as factory workers were forced by the nature of their work to develop new attitudes, so too the new middle class adopted attitudes that suited its new social roles. Two new "isms" soon emerged: sentimentalism, which appealed particularly to women, and transcendentalism, which encouraged men to a new self-reliance.

The individualistic competitiveness brought by the market revolution caused women of the new middle class to place extraordinary emphasis on sincerity and feeling. So-called sentimentalism sprang from nostalgia for the imagined trust and security of the familiar, face-to-face life of the preindustrial village. Sermons, advice manuals, and articles now thundered warnings to young men of the dangers and deceits of urban life and especially of fraudulent "confidence men and painted ladies" who were not what they seemed. Middle-class women were expected to counteract the impersonality and hypocrisy of the business world by the example of their own morality and sincere feeling.

For guidance in this new role, women turned to a new literary form, the sentimental novel. In contrast to older forms like sermons and learned essays, the novel was popular, accessible, and emotionally engrossing. Although denounced by ministers and scholars as frivolous, immoral, and subversive of authority, the novel found a ready audience among American women. Publishers of novels found a lucrative market, one that increased from $2.5 million in 1820 to $12.5 million in 1850. By 1850, *Harper's Magazine* estimated, four-fifths of the reading public were women, and they were reading novels written by women.

To be a "lady novelist" was a new and rather uncomfortably public occupation for women. Several authors, such as Susan Warner, were driven to novel writing when their fathers lost their fortunes in the Panic of 1837. Warner's 1850 novel *The Wide Wide World* went through fourteen editions in two years, and works by other authors

such as Lydia Maria Child, Catherine Sedgwick, and E. D. E. N. Southworth sold in the thousands of copies. Sentimental novels concentrated on private life. Religious feeling, antipathy toward the dog-eat-dog world of the commercial economy, and the need to be prepared for unforeseen troubles were common themes. Although the heroines usually married happily at the end of the story, few novels concentrated on romantic love. Most of these domestic novels, as they were known, presented readers with a vision of responsibility and community based on moral and caring family life.

Although sentimentalism originally sprang from genuine fear of the dangers individualism posed to community trust, it rapidly hardened into a rigid code of etiquette for all occasions. Moments of genuine and deep feeling, such as death, were smothered in elaborate rules concerning condolences, expressions of grief, and appropriate clothing. A widow, for example, was expected to wear "deep mourning" for a year—dresses of dull black fabrics and black bonnets covered with long, thick black veils—and in the following year "half mourning"—shiny black silk dresses, perhaps with trim of gray, violet, or white, and hats without veils. Thus, sentimentalism rapidly became concerned not with feelings but with social codes. Transformed into a set of rules about genteel manners to cover all occasions, sentimentalism itself

Emerson's romantic glorification of nature included the notion of himself as a "transparent eyeball," as he wrote in "Nature" in 1836. This caricature of Emerson is from "Illustrations of the New Philosophy" by Christopher Pearce Cranch.

CHRONOLOGY

1790	Samuel Slater's first mill opens in Rhode Island	**1823**	Lowell mills open
1798	Eli Whitney contracts with the federal government for 10,000 rifles, which he undertakes to produce with interchangeable parts	**1824**	John Hall successfully achieves interchangeable parts at Harpers Ferry armory
			Women lead strike at Pawtucket textile mill
1810	Francis Cabot Lowell tours British textile factories	**1825**	Erie Canal opens
	First steamboat on the Ohio River	**1830**	Baltimore and Ohio Railroad opens
			Charles G. Finney's Rochester revivals
1812	Micajah Pratt begins his own shoe business in Lynn, Massachusetts	**1833**	National Road completed to Columbus, Ohio
1813	Francis Cabot Lowell raises $300,000 to build his first cotton textile factory at Waltham, Massachusetts	**1834**	First strike at Lowell mills
			Cyrus McCormick patents the McCormick reaper
1815	War of 1812 ends; British competition in manufactures resumes	**1837**	John Deere invents steel plow
1817	Erie Canal construction begins	**1841**	Catharine Beecher's *A Treatise on Domestic Economy* published
1818	National Road completed to Wheeling, Virginia (now West Virginia)	**1845**	New England Female Reform Association formed
1820s	Large-scale outwork networks develop in New England		

became a mark of middle-class status. And it became one of the tasks of the middle-class woman to make sure her family conformed to the social code and associated only with other respectable families. In this way, women forged and enforced the distinctive social behavior of the new middle class.

As the new middle class conformed to the rules of sentimental behavior, it also sought a more general intellectual reassurance. Middle-class men, in particular, needed to feel comfortable about their public assertions of individualism and self-interest. One source of reassurance was the philosophy of transcendentalism and its well-known spokesman, Ralph Waldo Emerson. Originally a Unitarian minister, Emerson quit the pulpit in 1832 and became what one might call a secular minister. Famous as a writer and lecturer, he popularized transcendentalism, a romantic philosophical theory claiming that there was an ideal, intuitive reality transcending ordinary life. The best place to achieve that individual intuition of the Universal Being, Emerson suggested, was not in church or in society but alone in the natural world. As he wrote in "Nature" (1836), "Standing on the bare ground—my head bathed by the blithe air, and uplifted into infinite space—all mean egotism vanishes. I become a transparent Eyeball; I am

nothing; I see all; the currents of the Universal Being circulate through me; I am part and parcel of God." The same assertion of individualism rang through Emerson's stirring polemic "Self-Reliance" (1841). Announcing "Whoso would be a man, must be a nonconformist," Emerson urged that "Nothing is at last sacred but the integrity of your own mind." Inspirational but down-to-earth, Emerson was just the philosopher to inspire young businessmen of the 1830s and 1840s to achieve success in a responsible manner.

Emerson's younger friend, Henry David Thoreau, pushed the implications of individualism further than the more conventional Emerson. Determined to live the transcendental ideal of association with nature, Thoreau lived in solitude in a primitive cabin for two years at Walden Pond, near Concord, Massachusetts, confronting "the essential facts of life." His experience was the basis for *Walden* (1854), a penetrating criticism of the spiritual cost of the market revolution. Denouncing the materialism that led "the mass of men [to] lead lives of quiet desperation," Thoreau recommended a simple life of subsistence living that left time for spiritual thought.

Read the Document
Henry David Thoreau, Walden (1854) at **www.myhistorylab.com**

Margaret Fuller, perhaps the most intellectually gifted of the transcendental circle, was patronized by Emerson because she was a woman. She expressed her sense of women's wasted potential in her pathbreaking work *Woman in the Nineteenth Century* (1845). Intellectually and emotionally, however, Fuller achieved liberation only when she moved to Europe and participated in the liberal Italian revolution of 1848. The romantic destiny she sought was tragically fulfilled when she, her Italian husband, and their child died in a shipwreck off the New York coast as they returned to America in 1850.

Although Thoreau and Fuller were too radical for many readers, Emerson's version of the romantic philosophy of transcendentalism, seemingly so at odds with the competitive and impersonal spirit of the market revolution, was in fact an essential component of it. Individualism, or, as Emerson called it, self-reliance, was at the heart of the personal transformation required by the market revolution. Sentimentalism, transcendentalism, and evangelical religion all helped the new middle class to forge values and beliefs that were appropriate to their social roles.

Conclusion

The three transformations of the market revolution—improvements in transportation, commercialization, and industrialization—changed the ways people worked, and in time, changed how they thought.

For most people, the changes were gradual. Until midcentury, the lives of rural people were still determined largely by community events, although the spread of democratic politics and the availability of newspapers and other printed material increased their connection to a larger world. Wage earners made up only 40 percent of the working population in 1860, and factory workers made up an even smaller percentage.

The new middle class was most dramatically affected by the market revolution. All aspects of life, including intimate matters of family organization, gender roles, and the number and raising of children, changed. New values—evangelical religion, sentimentalism, and transcendentalism—helped the members of the new middle class in their adjustment. As the next chapter describes, the nation's cities were the first arena where old and new values collided.

Review Questions

I. What changes in preindustrial life and work were caused by the market revolution?

2. This chapter argues that when people begin doing new kinds of work, their beliefs and attitudes change. Give three examples of such changes described in the chapter. Can you think of other examples?

3. Discuss the opinion offered by historian David Potter that mass production has been an important democratizing force in American politics. Do you agree? Why or why not?

4. Consider the portrait of the nineteenth-century middle-class family offered in this chapter and imagine yourself as a member of such a family. What new aspects of family relations would you welcome? Which would be difficult? Why?

Recommended Reading

Christopher Clark, *The Roots of Rural Capitalism: Western Massachusetts, 1780–1860* (1990). The most thorough examination to date of how the commercial spirit changed rural life.

Alan Dawley, *Class and Community: The Industrial Revolution in Lynn* (1976). A pathbreaking study of the shift from artisanal to wage labor.

Susan E. Gray, *The Yankee West* (1996). Demonstrates the Yankee connection between capitalism and community in lower Michigan.

Daniel Walker Howe, *What Hath God Wrought: The Transformation of America, 1815–1848* (2007). This acclaimed 900-page survey credits technological change as the catalyst of the social, economic, and political transformations of the era.

Paul Johnson, *Sam Patch, the Famous Jumper* (2003). Johnson uses the story of Patch, famous for plunging over Niagara Falls to explore the bumpy transition from independent artisan to wage worker.

Gerard Koeppel, *Bond of Union: Building the Erie Canal and the American Empire* (2009). The most recent account of the epic story of the building of the famous canal.

Mary Ryan, *The Making of the Middle Class* (1981). A study of Utica, New York, demonstrating the role of women in the family strategies of the new middle class.

Charles Sellers, *The Market Revolution: Jacksonian America, 1815–1846* (1991). A synthesis of the political, religious, and economic changes of the period.

George Rogers Taylor, *The Transportation Revolution, 1815–1860* (1951). The indispensable book on all aspects of the American economy during this period.

myhistorylab Connections

Reinforce what you learned in this chapter by studying the many documents, images, maps, review tools, and videos available at www.myhistorylab.com.

Read and Review

✓●─Study and Review Chapter 12

•••─Read the Document

A Week at the Mill (1845)

Extract from Albany Daily Advertiser (1819)

Employers Advertise for Help Wanted in the 1820s

Hodgdon Family Letters Regarding Life in the Mills (1840)

A New England Factory Issues Regulations for Workers in 1825

Female Industrial Association (1825)

Charles Finney, What a Revival of Religion Is (1835)

A New England Woman Describes the Responsibilities of American Women in 1847

Catharine Beecher, from A Treatise on Domestic Economy (1841)

Mother's Magazine (1934)

Henry David Thoreau, Walden (1854)

👁─See the Map

Expanding America and Internal Improvements

Commercial Links: Rivers, Canals, Roads, 1830, and Rail Lines, 1850

Research and Explore

•••─Read the Document

Exploring America: Machinery

Profiles
 DeWitt Clinton
 Charles and Lydia Finney
 Samuel Slater

((●─Hear the Audio *The Erie Canal*

🔊─Watch the Video

Nineteenth-Century Industrialization

Railroads and Expansion

─── ((●─Hear the Audio ───

Hear the audio files for Chapter 12 at
www.myhistorylab.com.

13

Meeting the Challenges
of the New Age

Immigration, Urbanization, Social Reform 1820s–1850s

Great Riot at the Astor Place Opera House, New York, Thursday Evening, May 10, 1849. Publisher: N. Currier, 1849. Museum of the City of New York. The Harry T. Peters Collection. 56.300.377.

Women Reformers of Seneca Falls Respond to the Market Revolution

In the summer of 1848, Charlotte Woodward, a nineteen-year-old glove maker who did outwork in her rural home, saw a small advertisement in an upstate New York newspaper announcing a "convention to discuss the social, civil, and religious condition and rights of woman," to be held at Seneca Falls on July 19 and 20. Woodward persuaded six friends to join her in the forty-mile journey to the convention. "At first we travelled quite alone," she recalled. "But before we had gone many miles we came on other wagon-loads of women, bound in the same direction. As we reached different crossroads we saw wagons coming from every part of the country, and long before we reached Seneca Falls we were a procession."

To the surprise of the convention organizers, almost 300 people—men as well as women—attended the two-day meeting, which focused on the Declaration of Sentiments, a petition for women's rights modeled on the Declaration of Independence. "We hold these truths to be self-evident," it announced: "That all men and women are created equal." As the Declaration of Independence detailed the oppressions King George III had imposed on the colonists, the Declaration of Sentiments detailed, in a series of resolutions, the oppressions men had imposed on women. Men had deprived women of legal rights, of

AMERICAN Communities

335

the right to own their own property, of custody of their children in cases of divorce, of the right to higher education (at that time only Oberlin College and Mount Holyoke Female Seminary admitted women), of full participation in religious worship and activity, and of the right to vote.

The attendees approved all the resolutions unanimously but the last, which a minority found too radical. "Why Lizzie, thee will make us ridiculous!" Quaker Lucretia Mott had exclaimed when Elizabeth Cady Stanton proposed the voting rights measure. Indeed the newspapers reporting on the convention thought the demand for the vote was ridiculously unfeminine. Undeterred, and buoyed by the success of this first women's rights convention, the group promptly planned another convention to reach new supporters and develop strategies to implement their resolutions.

The struggle for women's rights was only one of many reform movements that emerged in the United States in the wake of the economic and social disruptions of the market revolution that deeply affected regions like Seneca Falls. A farming frontier in 1800, it had been drawn into national commerce in 1828, when it was reached by an offshoot of the Erie Canal. It was drawn even further into the modern age when the railroad arrived in 1841. A village of 200 in 1824, Seneca Falls had grown to a town of over 4,000 by 1842. It was now a center for flour milling and manufacturing as well as a hub of the outwork network of which Charlotte Woodward was a part. Swamped by newcomers (among them a growing number of poor Irish Catholics), the inhabitants of Seneca Falls struggled to maintain a sense of community. They formed volunteer organizations of all kinds—religious, civic, social, educational, and recreational. And they became active participants in reform movements seeking to counteract the effects of industrialization, rapid growth, and the influx of newcomers.

Many reformers belonged to liberal religious groups with wide social perspectives. Perhaps a third of those attending the women's rights convention, for example, were members of the Wesleyan Methodist Society of Seneca Falls, which had broken with the national Methodist organization because it would not take a strong stand against slavery. Another quarter was Progressive Quakers of the nearby town of Waterloo, who had broken with their national organization for the same reason. Both groups were outspoken in their belief

in the moral equality of all humankind and in their commitment to social activism. The Wesleyans, for example, resolved in 1847 that "we cannot identify our Christian and moral character with societies where women and colored persons are excluded." Seneca Falls had been the site of a "Temperance Reformation" in the early 1840s, and many attendees at the Women's Rights convention were also active in the temperance movement, a more limited but extremely popular reform cause dedicated to promoting abstinence from alcohol.

The idea for the Women's Rights convention emerged during a meeting in early July 1848 between Lucretia Mott, a Philadelphia Quaker and the nation's best-known woman reformer, and Elizabeth Cady Stanton of Seneca Falls, wife of a well-known anti-slavery orator. Reflecting her many concerns, Mott had just finished a tour of the new penitentiary at Auburn and a nearby Indian reservation and was visiting her sister in Waterloo. Stanton first met Mott in 1840 at the World AntiSlavery Conference in London, where the two women forged bonds after the conference organizers refused to recognize Mott as an official American delegate because she was a woman. In 1848, Stanton renewed her acquaintance with Mott and, in this context of friendship and shared concern for reform, the two began planning the convention.

Stanton and her family had moved from Boston where, she remembered, they had "near neighbors, a new home with all the modern conveniences, and well-trained servants." Living in a house on the outskirts of Seneca Falls, her three children suffering from malaria, she had none of those things. "I now fully understood," she mused,

> the practical difficulties most women had to contend with. . . . The general discontent I felt with woman's portion as wife, mother, housekeeper, physician and spiritual guide, the chaotic conditions into which everything fell without her constant supervision, and the wearied anxious look of the majority of women impressed me with a strong feeling that some active measures should be taken to remedy the wrongs of society in general, and of women in particular.

As she and Mott spoke of the changes that would be necessary to allow women to care for their families but have energy left over to reform "the wrongs of society," the idea of a women's rights convention was born. The women's rights movement that took shape from this convention proved exceptionally long-lasting.

1. What caused the immigration of the 1840s and 1850s, and what were the responses to it?

2. Why were cities so unable to cope with rapid urbanization?

3. What motivated reform movements?

4. What were the origins and political effects of the abolitionist movement?

5. How were women involved in reform efforts?

FOCUS
Questions

1820s–1850s

Stanton, soon to form a working partnership with former temperance worker Susan B. Anthony, devoted the rest of her life to women's rights.

But what of Charlotte Woodward, a local farm girl, unaware of the national reform community? Why was she there? In this age of hopefulness and change, she wanted a better life for herself. She was motivated, she said, by "all the hours that I sat and sewed gloves for a miserable pittance, which, after it was earned, could never be mine." By law and custom, her father, as head of the household, was entitled to her wages. "I wanted to work," she explained, "but I wanted to choose my task and I wanted to collect my wages." The reforming women of Seneca Falls, grouped together on behalf of social improvement, had found in the first women's rights

Seneca Falls

convention a way to speak for the needs of working women such as Charlotte Woodward.

All over the North, in communities like Seneca Falls as well as in cities like New York, Americans gathered together in reform organizations to try to solve the problems that the market revolution posed for work, family life, personal and social values, and urban growth. Through these organizations, local women and men became participants in wider communities of social concern, but in spite of their best efforts, they were rarely able to settle the issues that had brought them together. The aspirations of some, among them women, free blacks, and immigrants, clashed with the social control agendas of other groups. In this fervent atmosphere of reform, many problems were raised but few were resolved.

AMERICAN
Communities

Immigration and the City

Although the market revolution affected all aspects of American life, nowhere was its impact so noticeable as in the cities. And it was primarily in cities that the startlingly large number of new immigrants clustered.

The Growth of Cities

The market revolution dramatically increased the size of America's cities, with the great seaports leading the way. The proportion of America's population living in cities increased from only 7 percent in 1820 to almost 20 percent in 1860, a rate of growth greater than at any other time in the country's history. The nation's five largest cities in 1850 were the same as in 1800, with one exception. New York, Philadelphia, Baltimore, and Boston still topped the list, but New Orleans had edged out Charleston. The rate of urban growth was extraordinary. All four Atlantic seaports grew at least 25 percent each decade between 1800 and 1860, and often much more. New York, which grew from 60,000 in 1800 to 202,600 in 1830 and to more than 1 million in 1860, emerged as the nation's most populous city, its largest port, and its financial center.

Another result of the market revolution was the appearance of "instant" cities at critical points on the new transportation network. Utica, New York, once a frontier trading post, was transformed by the opening of the Erie Canal into a commercial and manufacturing center. Chicago, on the shores of Lake Michigan, was transformed by the coming of the railroad into a major junction for water and rail transport. The city, which emerged as a fur trading center around Fort Dearborn, an army post built in 1803, had become, by the 1850s, a hub of trade boasting grain storage facilities, slaughterhouses, and warehouses of all kinds. Farm implement manufacturers such as Cyrus McCormick built manufacturing plants there to serve the needs of midwestern farmers. By 1860 Chicago had a population of over 100,000, making it the nation's eighth largest city (see Figure 13.1).

Patterns of Immigration

One of the key aspects of urban growth was a surge in immigration to the United States that began in the 1820s and accelerated dramatically after 1830. From an annual figure of about 20,000 in 1831, immigration ballooned to a record 430,000 in 1854 before declining in the years prior to the Civil War. The proportion of immigrants in the population jumped from 1.6 percent in the 1820s to 11.2 percent in 1860. In the nation's cities, the proportion was vastly larger: by 1860, nearly half of New York's population (48 percent) was foreign-born (see Map 13.1).

Most of the immigrants to the United States during this period came from Ireland and Germany. Political unrest and poor economic conditions in Germany and the catastrophic Potato Famine of 1845–49 in Ireland were responsible for an enormous surge in immigration from those countries between 1845 and 1854. The starving, desperate "Famine Irish" who crowded into eastern seaports were America's first large refugee group. Between them, the Germans and the Irish represented the largest influx of non-English immigrants the country had known (many Americans found the Irish dialect as strange as a foreign language). They were also the poorest: most of the Irish arrived destitute. In addition, most of the Irish and half of the Germans were Catholics, an unwelcome novelty that provoked a nativist backlash among some Protestant Americans, including many leaders of national reform movements (see Chapter 15).

It would be a mistake, however, to think that immigration was unwelcome to everyone. Industries needed willing workers, and western states, among them Wisconsin, Iowa, and Minnesota, actively advertised in Europe for settlers. Many of the changes in industry and transportation that accompanied the market revolution would have been impossible without immigrants. Irish contract workers, for example, were essential to the completion of the Erie Canal in 1825. And Irish women and men kept the mills at Lowell operating when the mill operators, facing increasing competition, sought cheaper labor to replace their original labor force of farm women.

Few immigrants found life in the United States pleasant or easy. In addition to the psychological difficulties of

FIGURE 13.1 Urban Growth, 1820–60

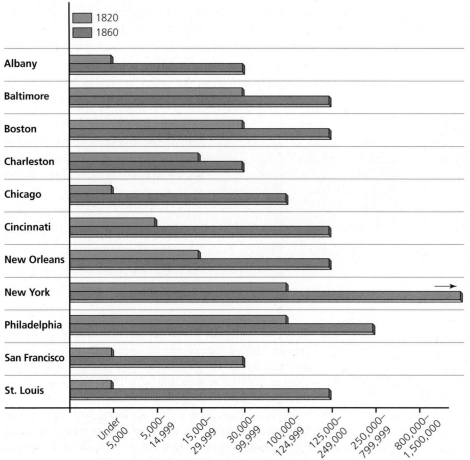

SOURCE: From *Immigrant Life in New York City, 1825–1863* by Robert Ernst. Copyright 1994 by Syracuse University Press. Reprinted by permission.

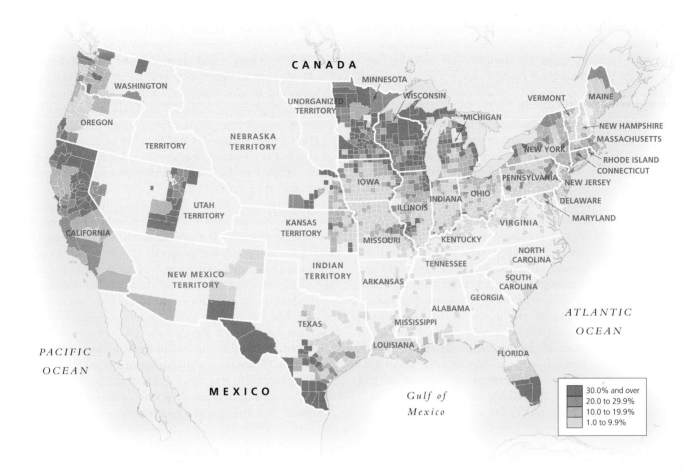

MAP 13.1 Distribution of Foreign-Born Residents of the United States in 1860 The ethnic composition of the American population was increased by Irish and German immigration in the 1840s and 1850s, Chinese immigration to the California gold rush, Mormon recruitment of Scottish and English followers to Utah, and the reclassification of Mexicans after the Mexican-American War as foreigners in what had been their own lands.

leaving a home and familiar ways behind, most immigrants endured harsh living and working conditions. America's cities were unprepared for the social problems posed by large numbers of immigrants.

Irish Immigration

The first major immigrant wave to test American cities was caused by the catastrophic Irish Potato Famine of 1845–49. Throughout Ireland, many native Irish subsisted on small landholdings and a diet of potatoes while working as labor-ers on British-owned farms. Young people who knew they could not hope to own land in Ireland had long looked to America for better opportunities. Indeed, from 1818 to 1845, at least 10,000 Irish emigrated yearly. But in the latter year, Ireland's green fields of potato plants turned black with blight. The British government could not cope with the

●●●—Read the Document

Irish Laborers Get an Endorsement in 1833 at **www.myhistorylab.com**

scale of the disaster. The Irish had two choices: starve or leave. One million people died, and another 1.5 million emigrated, the majority to the United States. Starving, dis-eased (thousands died of typhus during the voyage), and destitute, hundreds of thousands (250,000 in 1851 alone) disembarked in the East Coast ports of New York, Philadelphia, Boston, and Baltimore. Lacking the money to go inland and begin farming, they remained in the cities. Crowded together in miserable housing, desperate for work at any wages, foreign in their religion and pastimes (drinking and fighting, their critics said), tenaciously nationalistic and bitterly anti-British, they created ethnic enclaves of a kind new to American cities.

The largest numbers of Irish came to New York, which managed to absorb them. But Boston, a much smaller and more homogeneous city, was overwhelmed by the Irish influx. By 1850, a quarter of Boston's popula-tion was Irish, most of them recent immigrants. Boston, the home of Puritanism and the center of American intellectualism, did not welcome illiterate Irish Catholic peasants. All over the city, in places of business and in homes normally eager for domestic servants, the signs went up: "No Irish Need Apply."

German Immigration

Germans, like the Irish, had a long history of emigration to America. William Penn, impressed by the industriousness of the Germans, had taken pains to invite them to immigrate to the colony he founded. By 1790, they made up one-third of Pennsylvania's population. The nineteenth-century immigration of Germans began somewhat later and more slowly than that of the Irish, but by 1854 it had surpassed the Irish influx. Some German peasants, like the Irish, were driven from their homeland by potato blight in the mid-1840s. But the typical German immigrant was a small farmer or artisan dislodged by the same market forces at work in America: the industrialization of production and consolidation, and the commercialization of farming. There was also a small group of middle-class liberal intellectuals who left the German states (Germany was not yet a unified nation) after 1848 when attempts at revolution had failed. Among these individuals was Carl Schurz, who rose to become a general in the Union Army, a senator

from Missouri, and secretary of the interior in the administration of Rutherford B. Hayes.

On the whole, German migrants were not as poor as the Irish, and they could afford to move out of the East Coast seaports to other locations. Many Germans made their way up the Mississippi and Ohio valleys, where they settled in Pittsburgh, Cincinnati, St. Louis, and Milwaukee (soon the most German city in the country), and on farms in Ohio, Indiana, Missouri, and Texas. In Texas, the nucleus of a German community began with a Mexican land grant in the 1830s. Few Germans settled either in northeastern cities or in the South.

German agricultural communities took a distinctive form that fostered cultural continuity. Immigrants formed predominantly German towns by clustering, or taking up adjoining land. A small cluster could support German churches, German-language schools, and German customs and thereby attract other Germans, some directly from Europe and some from other parts of the United States. Non-German neighbors often sold out and moved on, but the Germans stayed and improved the land so they could pass it on to the next generation. They used soil conservation practices that were unusual for the time. Persistence paid: German cluster communities exist to this day in Texas, the Midwest, and the Pacific Northwest, and families of

Samuel Waugh's *The Bay and Harbor of New York*, painted in 1855, Castle Garden, New York's first official center for immigrants, receiving a boatload of newcomers from Ireland and perhaps from Germany. Note the anti-Irish caricatures, including the trunk on the right labeled "Pat Murfy for Ameriky." A Chinese junk rides at anchor in the harbor, a reminder that not all immigration in this period was from Europe.

German origin are still the single largest ethnic group in agriculture.

The Chinese in California

Another area attracting immigrants was Gold Rush California, which drew, among others, numbers of Chinese (see Chapter 14). The Chinese who came to California worked in the mines, mostly as independent prospectors. Other miners disliked their industriousness and their clannishness. By the mid-1860s, Chinese workers made up 90 percent of the laborers building the Central Pacific Railroad, replacing more expensive white laborers and sowing the seeds of the long-lasting hostility of American workers toward Chinese. In the meantime, however, San Francisco's Chinatown, the oldest Chinese ethnic enclave in America, became a well-established, thriving community and a refuge in times of anti-Chinese violence.

Ethnic Neighborhoods

Ethnic neighborhoods were not limited to the Chinese. Almost all new immigrants preferred to live in neighborhoods where they could find not only family ties and familiar ways but also community support as they learned how to survive in new surroundings. Isolated partly by their own beliefs (for Catholics fully reciprocated the hatred and fear that Protestants had showed them), Irish immigrants created their own communities in Boston and New York, their major destinations. They raised the money to erect Catholic churches with Irish priests. They established parochial schools with Irish nuns as teachers and sent their children to them in preference to the openly anti-Catholic public schools. They formed mutual aid societies based on kinship or town of origin in Ireland. Men and women formed religious and social clubs, lodges, and brotherhoods and their female auxiliaries. Irishmen manned fire and militia companies as well. This dense network of associations served the same purpose that social welfare organizations do today: providing help in time of need and offering companionship in a hostile environment.

Germans who settled in urban areas also built their own ethnic enclaves—"Little Germanies"—in which they sought to duplicate the rich cultural life of their homeland. Like the Irish, the Germans formed church societies, mutual benefit societies, and fire and militia companies to provide mutual support. Partly because their communities were more prosperous than those of the Irish, the Germans also formed a network of leisure organizations: singing societies, debating and political clubs, concert halls like New York's Beethoven Hall, theaters, *turnvereins* (gymnastics associations), and beer gardens. They published German-language newspapers as well.

Ethnic clustering allowed new immigrants to hold onto aspects of their culture that they valued and to transplant them to American soil. Many native-born Americans, however, viewed ethnic neighborhoods with deep suspicion. The *Boston American* expressed the sentiments of many in 1837 when it remarked:

> Our foreign population are too much in the habit of retaining their own national usages, of associating too exclusively with each other, and living in groups together. It would be the part of wisdom, to ABANDON AT ONCE ALL USAGES AND ASSOCIATIONS WHICH MARK THEM AS FOREIGNERS, and to become in feeling and custom, as well as in privileges and rights, citizens of the United States.

Urban Problems

It was within the new urban environment, with its stimulating and frightening confusion of rapid growth, occupational and ethnic change, and economic competition, that new American political and social forms began to emerge.

New Living Patterns in the Cities

The preindustrial cities of eighteenth-century America had been small and compact "walking cities," in which people, rich and poor, lived near their work in a dense, small-scale housing pattern that fostered neighborliness and the mingling of social classes. The growth caused by immigration changed the character of urban life by sharpening class differences.

Even though per capita income in America is estimated to have doubled between 1800 and 1850, the gap between rich and poor was glaringly apparent in the nation's cities. Differences in income affected every aspect of urban life. Very poor families (about 70 percent of the urban population), including almost all new immigrants, performed unskilled labor in jobs where the future was uncertain at best, lived in cheap rented housing, moved frequently, and depended on more than one income to survive. Artisans and skilled workers with incomes of $500 or more could live adequately, though often in cramped quarters that also served as their shops. A middle-class family with an income of more than $1,000 a year (about 25 percent of the population) could live comfortably in a house of four to six rooms complete with carpeting, wallpaper, and good furniture. The very rich (about 3 percent) built mansions and large town houses and staffed them with many servants. In the summer, they left the cities for country estates or homes at seaside resorts such as Newport, Rhode Island, which attracted wealthy families from all over the country.

Early nineteenth-century cities lacked municipal water supplies, sewers, and garbage collection. People drank water from wells, used outdoor privies that often contaminated the water supply, and threw garbage and slop out the door to be foraged by roaming herds of pigs. Clearly, this was a recipe for disease, and every American city suffered epidemics of sanitation-related diseases such as yellow fever, cholera, and typhus. Philadelphia's yellow fever epidemic of 1793 caused 4,000 deaths and stopped all business with the outside world for more than a month. Major cholera epidemics ravaged New York in 1832 and 1849, and New Orleans suffered repeated episodes of cholera and yellow fever.

Yet the cities were slow to take action. Mostly, this was due to poor understanding of the links between sanitation and disease, but expense was also a factor. Neither New York nor Boston had a public water system until the 1840s. Garbage collection remained a private service, and cities charged property owners for the costs of sewers, water mains, and street paving. Poorer areas of the cities could not afford the costs. When disease struck, wealthier people simply left the cities, leaving the poor to suffer.

Lack of municipal services encouraged residential segregation. Richer people clustered in neighborhoods that had the new amenities. One of New York's first wealthy areas, Gramercy Park, was developed in 1831 by a speculator who transformed what had been Gramercy Farm into "an ornamental private square or park, with carriageways and footwalks." Only purchasers of the surrounding lots had keys to the park; everyone else was excluded. By the 1850s, the middle class began to escape cities completely by moving to the new "streetcar suburbs," named for the new mode of urban transportation that connected these nearby areas to the city itself.

As the middle class left the city, the poor clustered in bad neighborhoods that became known as slums. The worst New York slum in the nineteenth century was Five Points, a stone's throw from City Hall. There, immigrants, free black people, and criminals were crammed into rundown buildings known in the slang of the time as "rookeries."

THE FIVE POINTS IN 1859
Crossing of Baxter [late Orange] Park [late Cross] & Worth [late Anthony] Sts.

The Five Points neighborhood in lower Manhattan illustrates the segregated housing patterns that emerged as New York City experienced rapid growth. Immigrants, free African Americans, the poor, and criminals were crowded together in New York's most notorious slum, while wealthier people moved to more prosperous neighborhoods.

Notorious gangs of thieves and pickpockets with names such as the Plug Uglies and the Shirt Tails dominated the district. Starvation and murder were commonplace.

With the influx of European immigrants after 1830, middle-class Americans increasingly saw slums as the home of strange and foreign people who deserved less than American-born citizens did. In this way, residential patterns came to embody larger issues of class and citizenship. Even disease itself was blamed on immigrants. As banker John Pintard reasoned in 1832, the cholera epidemic of that year must be God's judgment on "the lower classes of intemperate dissolute and filthy people huddled together like swine in their polluted habitations."

Ethnicity in Urban Popular Culture

Immigrants to American cities contributed to a new urban popular culture, with New York, the largest city, leading the way. In the period 1820–60, New York experienced the replacement of artisanal labor by wagework, two serious depressions (1837–43 and 1857), and a vast influx of immigrant labor (see Figure 13.2).

In response to these pressures, working-class amusements became rougher and rowdier. Taverns that served as neighborhood centers of drink and sociability were also frequent centers of brawls and riots. Community groups such as fire engine companies that had once included men of all social classes now attracted rough young laborers who formed their own gangs and defended "their" turf against other gangs. Men in some trades, such as that of butcher, became notorious for starting fights in taverns and grog shops.

Irish immigrants, in particular, faced not only employment discrimination but also persistent cultural denigration. It was common for newspapers of the time to caricature the Irish as monkeys, similar to the way cartoonists portrayed African Americans. The Irish response, which was to insist on their "whiteness," played itself out in urban popular culture in violence and mockery.

Theaters, which had been frequented by men of all social classes, provided another setting for violence. Few women, except for the prostitutes who met their customers in the third tier of the balcony, attended. In the 1820s, a long-standing tradition of small-scale rioting by poorer patrons against unpopular actors began to change into more serious violence. The Astor Place Riot of 1849 began as a theater riot by Irish immigrants and others against a British actor but escalated into a pitched battle between the mob and the militia that left twenty-two dead.

By the 1830s, middle-class and upper-class men withdrew to more respectable theaters to which they could bring their wives and daughters, and workers found new amusements in theaters such as the Lafayette Circus, which featured dancing girls and horseback riders as well as theatrical acts. Another popular urban working-class amusement was the blackface minstrel show. In 1832, Thomas Rice, a young white man in blackface, appeared at a variety show at the Bowery Theater where he sang and danced the song *Jump Jim Crow*. His performance was so wildly popular that he had to repeat it twenty times before the audience would let him go. In this way, the cruel stereotype of the slow-witted slave, Jim Crow, entered American popular culture and Rice himself became one of the best-known blackface minstrels. Blackface minstrel shows were among the most popular American entertainments. White actors (often Irish) blacked their faces and entertained audiences with songs (including the famous "Dixie," written by an Irishman as a blackface song), dances, theatrical skits, and antiblack political jokes. Minstrel shows were a favorite American entertainment for the rest of the nineteenth century.

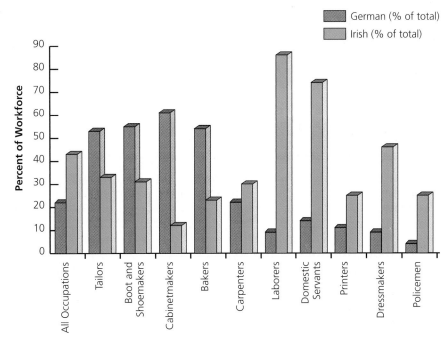

FIGURE 13.2 Participation of Irish and German Immigrants in the New York City Workforce for Selected Occupations, 1855 This chart shows the impact of the new immigrants on the New York's workforce, and the dramatic difference between groups. German workers predominate in the skilled trades, while the Irish are clustered in low-skilled, low paying occupations.

SOURCE: From *The Alcoholic Republic: An American Tradition*, by W. J. Rorabaugh, copyright © 1979 by Oxford University Press, Inc. Used by permission of Oxford University Press, Inc.

IRISH EMIGRANT.

Patrick, (just landing.) "By my Sowl, you're black, old fellow! How long have ye bin here;"

Nigger, (imitatng the brogue.) "Jist three months, my honey!"

Pat. "By the powers, I'll go back to Tipperary in a jiffy! I'd not be so black as that fur all the whiskey in Roscrea!"

This cartoon encounter between a newly arrived Irishman and an African American expresses the fear of many immigrants that they would be treated like blacks and denied the privileges of whiteness.

The Labor Movement and Urban Politics

By the 1830s, the status of artisans and independent craftsmen in the nation's cities had deteriorated. Members of urban workers' associations, increasingly angry over their declining status in the economic and social order, became active defenders of working-class interests in their cities.

Urban worker protest against changing conditions first took the form of party politics. The Workingmen's Party was founded in Philadelphia in 1827, and chapters quickly formed in New York and Boston as well. Using the language of class warfare—"two distinct classes . . .

●●●[Read the Document

Preamble of the Mechanics Union of Trade Associations (1827) at **www.myhistorylab.com**

those that live by their own labor and they that live upon the labor of others"—the "Workies" campaigned for the ten-hour day and the preservation of the small artisanal shop. Jacksonian Democrats were quick to pick up on some of their themes, attracting many Workingmen's votes in 1832, the year Andrew Jackson campaigned against the "monster" Bank of the United States (see Chapter 11).

For their part, the Whigs wooed workers by assuring them that Henry Clay's American System, and tariff protection in particular, would be good for the economy and for workers' jobs. Nevertheless, neither major political party really spoke to the primary need of workers—for well-paid, stable jobs that assured them independence and respect. Unsatisfied with the response of political parties, workers turned to labor organization to achieve their goals.

Between 1833 and 1837, a wave of strikes in New York City cut the remaining ties between master craftsmen and the journeymen who worked for them. In 1833, journeymen carpenters struck for higher wages. Workers in fifteen other trades came to their support, and within a month the strike was won. The lesson was obvious: if skilled workers banded together across craft lines, they could improve their conditions. The same year, representatives from nine different craft groups formed the General Trades Union (GTU) of New York. By 1834, similar groups had sprung up in over a dozen cities—Boston, Louisville, and Cincinnati among them. In 1834 representatives of several local GTUs organized the National Trades Union (NTU). In its founding statement the NTU criticized the "unjustifiable distribution of the wealth of society in the hands of a few individuals," which had created for working people "a humiliating, servile dependency, incompatible with . . . natural equality."

Naturally, employers disagreed with the NTU's criticism of the economic system. In Cincinnati and elsewhere, employers prevailed upon police to arrest strikers even when no violence had occurred. In another case, New York employers took striking journeymen tailors to

SEEING History

P.T. Barnum's Famous "Curiosity:" General Tom Thumb

Phineas T. Barnum opened Barnum's American Museum in New York City in 1842 exhibiting human and animal "curiosities" with inimitable showmanship that was an artful mix of fact and fiction. For example it was a fact that "General" Tom Thumb, one of Barnum's most famous exhibits, was midget who stood 25 inches tall and weighed 15 pounds. But he was not a general: he was a carefully-coached four-year-old boy when Barnum first started exhibiting him in 1842, claiming that he was eleven years old. His real name was Charles Stratton; his father had agreed that Barnum could exhibit his son for $3.00 a week.

Onstage, the tiny general was an instant success. Singing, dancing, and portraying characters as varied as Napoleon, a Scottish highlander, and Cupid, Tom Thumb enjoyed a long, happy, and profitable career under Barnum's tutelage. As a child, he met and performed for Queen Victoria of England. As an adult (he grew to 40 inches) he and his wife (another midget employed by Barnum named Lavinia Warren) were guests of President and Mrs. Lincoln at the White House. He and Barnum enjoyed a long friendship, and Thumb never expressed any feelings of resentment.

Many of Barnum's exhibits *were* outright hoaxes (for example The Feejee Mermaid, and General Washington's nurse who claimed to be 161 years old) but many were persons with physical anomalies (Siamese twins, giants, bearded women, fat boys, and so on) or "exotics" from little-known cultural groups like a family from Burma who appeared "half-naked" in American eyes.

• **Barnum's mixture of fact and fiction was regularly denounced as "humbug," but audiences flocked to his shows. Why? What drew them?**

court in 1836. Judge Ogden Edwards pronounced the strikers guilty of conspiracy and declared unions un-American. He assured the strikers that "the road of advancement is open to all" and that they would do better to strive to be masters themselves rather than "conspire" with their fellow workers. The GTU responded with a mass rally at which Judge Edwards was burned in effigy.

A year later, stunned by the effects of the Panic of 1837, the GTU collapsed. The founding of these general unions, a visible sign of a class-based community of interest among workers, is generally considered to mark the beginning of the American labor movement. However, the early unions included only white men in skilled trades, who made up only a small percentage of all workers. The majority of workers—men in unskilled occupations, all free African Americans, and all women—were excluded.

Although workers were unable to create strong unions or stable political parties that spoke for their economic interests, they were a vital factor in urban politics. As America's cities experienced unprecedented growth, the electorate mushroomed. In New York, for example, the number of voters grew from 20,000 in 1825 to 88,900 in 1855. Furthermore, by 1855 half of the voters were foreign-born. The ease with which new immigrants gained the vote stood in marked contrast to the continuing restrictions on the voting rights of free African American men. Because immigrants clustered in neighborhoods, their impact on politics could be concentrated and manipulated. Legally, three years' residence in the United States was required before one could apply for citizenship, but there was clear evidence of swifter naturalization in large cities with effective political organizations. In New York, for example, the Irish-dominated districts quickly became Democratic Party strongholds. Germans, who were less active politically than the Irish, nevertheless voted heavily for the new Republican Party in the 1850s. Between them, these two new blocs of immigrant voters destroyed the Whig Party that had controlled New York politics before the immigrants arrived.

In New York City, the Tammany Society, begun in the 1780s as a fraternal organization of artisans, slowly evolved into the key organization of the new mass politics. (Named after the Delaware chief mentioned in Chapter 3, the society met in a hall called the Wigwam and elected "sachems" as their officers.) Tammany, which was affiliated with the national Democratic Party, reached voters by using many of the techniques of mass appeal made popular earlier by craft organizations—parades, rallies, popular songs, and party newspapers.

Civic Order

The challenges to middle-class respectability posed by new immigrants and unruly workers were fostered and publicized by the immensely popular "penny papers," which began publication in 1833, and by the rapidly growing number of political papers. This exuberant urban popular culture was unquestionably a part of the same new democratic political spirit that led to the great upsurge in political participation discussed in Chapter 11. And it was the inspiration for some of America's most innovative writers, foremost among them urban journalist, Democratic Party activist, and poet, Walt Whitman, who distilled his passionate love for the variety and commonness of the American people in *Leaves of Grass*, a book of free-verse poems published in 1855. Regarded at the time as scandalous because of its frank language, Whitman's poetry nevertheless captured the driving energy and democratic spirit of the new urban popular culture. In a

rather more sinister way, so did the writings of Edgar Allan Poe, who found the inspiration for his gothic horror stories, such as "The Murders in the Rue Morgue" (1841) and "The Mystery of Marie Roget" (1842), not in Europe (as his titles might suggest) but in contemporary American crimes. Judging from their literature, Americans were apparently fascinated by their own urban violence.

Working-class use of the streets for parades, celebrations, and marches was an established aspect of urban life and perhaps nowhere so much a part of the city as in New Orleans. There, African American bands played in funeral processions, and dances drawing hundreds of slaves were regularly held in Congo Square, while elsewhere Choctaw Indians drummed and respectable middle-class men rang cowbells as they took part in rowdy street serenades in response to unpopular events.

In New York, the prosperous classes were increasingly frightened by the urban poor and by working-class rowdyism. New York City's tradition of New Year's Eve "frolics," in which laborers, apprentices, and other members of the lower classes paraded through the streets playing drums, trumpets, whistles, and other noisemakers, was an example. By 1828, the revelry had been taken over by gangs of young workers from the lower classes, 4,000 strong, who marched through the city, overturning carts, breaking windows, obstructing traffic, and harassing middle-class citizens. In the following year, the city government banned the traditional New Year's Eve parade.

In colonial days, civic disturbances had been handled informally: members of the city watch asked onlookers for whatever assistance was necessary to keep the peace. New York City's first response in the 1820s and 1830s to increasing civic disorder was to hire more city watchmen and to augment them with constables and marshals. When riots occurred, the militia was called, and deaths were increasingly common as they forcibly restrained mobs. Finally, in 1845, the city created a permanent police force with a mandate to keep the poor in order. Southern cities, because of fear of slave disorder, had police forces much earlier. By the 1820s, New Orleans, Charleston, and Savannah had armed and uniformed city guards who patrolled in military fashion.

But even with police forces in place, the pressures of rapid urbanization, immigration, and the market revolution proved to be too much for America's cities. Beginning in the 1830s, a series of urban riots broke out against the two poorest urban groups: Catholics and free black people. As if their miserable living conditions were not enough, Irish immigrants were met with virulent anti-Catholicism. In 1834, rioters burned an Ursuline convent in Charlestown, Massachusetts; in 1844, a Philadelphia mob attacked priests and nuns and vandalized Catholic churches; in 1854, a mob destroyed an Irish neighborhood in Lawrence, Massachusetts. Often the Irish replied in kind—for example, in an 1806 riot in

By 1855, half the voters in New York City were foreign-born. This 1858 engraving of an Irish bar in the Five Points area appeared in the influential *Harper's Weekly*. It expressed the temperance reformers' dislike of immigrants and their drinking habits and the dismay of political reformers that immigrant saloons and taverns were such effective organizing centers for urban political machines.

New York, when they counterattacked a mob that disrupted their Christmas Eve mass in a Catholic church on Augustus Street. But the most common targets of urban violence were free African Americans.

Free African Americans in the Cities

By 1860, there were nearly half a million free African Americans in the United States, constituting about 11 percent of the country's total black population. More than half of all free African Americans lived in the North, mostly in cities, where they competed with immigrants and native-born poor white people for jobs as day laborers and domestic servants. Their relative social position is reflected in statistics on per capita annual income in Boston in the 1850s: $91 for black people and $131 for Irish immigrants compared to $872 for the population at large. Philadelphia and New York had the largest black communities. There were much smaller but still significant black communities in the New England cities of Boston, Providence, and New Haven and in Ohio cities like Cincinnati.

Free African Americans in northern cities faced residential segregation (except for the domestic servants who lived in with white families), pervasive job discrimination, segregated public schools, and severe limitations on their civil rights. In addition to these legal restrictions, there were matters of custom: African Americans of all economic classes endured daily affronts, such as exclusion from public concerts, lectures, and libraries, and segregation or exclusion from public transportation. For example, in Massachusetts—which had the reputation of being more hospitable to black people than any other northern state—the famed African American abolitionist Frederick Douglass was denied admission to a zoo on Boston Common, a public lecture and revival meeting, a restaurant, and a public omnibus, all within the space of a few days.

In common with Irish and German immigrants, African Americans created defenses against the hostile larger society by building their own community structures. They formed associations for aiding the poorest members of the community, for self-improvement, and for socializing. Tired of being insulted by the white press, African American communities supported their own newspapers. The major community organization was the black Baptist or African Methodist Episcopal (AME) church, which served, as one historian put it, as "a place of worship, a social and cultural center, a political meeting

This appealing portrait of a musician, *The Bone Player*, evokes the prevalent stereotype of African Americans as innately musical, but it also clearly portrays a man who is proud of his talent.

SOURCE: William Sidney Morris (American, 1807–1868), *The Bone Player*, 1856. Oil on canvas, 91.76 × 73.98 cm (36⅛ × 29⅛ in.). Courtesy, Museum of Fine Arts, Boston. Bequest of Martha C. Karolik for the M. and M. Karolik Collection of American Paintings. 48.46 Reproduced with permission. Photograph © 2006 Museum of Fine Arts, Boston. All Rights Reserved.

place, a hiding place for fugitives, a training ground for potential community leaders, and one of the few places where blacks could express their true feelings."

Employment prospects for black men deteriorated from 1820 to 1850. Those who had held jobs as skilled artisans were forced from their positions, and their sons denied apprenticeships, by white mechanics and craftsmen who were themselves suffering from the effects of the market revolution. Limited to day labor, African Americans found themselves in direct competition with the new immigrants, especially the Irish, for jobs. On the waterfront, black men lost their jobs as carters and longshoremen to the Irish. One of the few occupations to remain open to them was that of seaman. More than 20 percent of all American sailors in 1850 were black, and over the years, their ranks included an increasing number of runaway slaves. The pay was poor and the conditions miserable, but many black men found more equality aboard ship than they did ashore. Mothers, wives, and daughters worked as domestic servants (in competition with Irishwomen), washerwomen, and seamstresses.

Free African Americans remained committed to their enslaved brethren in the South. In New York, for example, black communities rioted four times—in 1801, 1819,

1826, and 1832—against slave catchers taking escaped slaves back to slavery. But even more frequently, free African Americans were themselves targets of urban violence. An 1829 riot in Cincinnati sent a thousand black people fleeing to Canada in fear for their lives; a three-day riot in Providence in 1831 destroyed an African American district; an 1834 New York riot destroyed a black church, a school, and a dozen homes. Philadelphia, "the City of Brotherly Love," was repeatedly rocked by antiblack riots in the period between 1820 and 1859. Urban riots of all kinds had cost 125 lives by 1840, and more than 1,000 by 1860.

Social Reform Movements

The passion for reform that had become such an important part of the new middle-class thinking was focused on the problems of the nation's cities. As the opening of this chapter describes, the earliest response to the dislocations caused by the market revolution was community based and voluntary. Middle-class people tried to deal with social changes in their communities by joining organizations devoted to reforms. The temperance movement and reforms involving education, prisons and asylums, women's rights, abolitionism, and, above all, the spread of evangelical religion were all concerns of the middle class. The reform message was vastly amplified by inventions such as the steam printing press, which made it possible to publish reform literature in great volume. Soon there were national networks of reform groups.

Religion, Reform, and Social Control

Evangelical religion was fundamental to social reform. Men and women who had been converted to the enthusiastic new faith assumed personal responsibility for making changes in their own lives. Personal reform quickly led to social reform. Religious converts were encouraged in their social activism by such leading revivalists as Charles G. Finney, who preached a doctrine of "perfectionism," claiming it was possible for all Christians to personally understand and live by God's will and thereby become "as perfect as God." Furthermore, Finney predicted, "the complete reformation of the whole world" could be achieved if only enough converts put their efforts into moral reform. This new religious feeling evoked by Finney was intensely hopeful: members of evangelistic religions really did expect to convert the world and create the perfect moral and religious community on earth.

Much of America was swept by this reform-minded religious fervor, and it was the new middle class that set the agenda. Reform efforts arose from the recognition that the traditional methods of small-scale local relief were no longer adequate. In colonial times, families (sometimes at the request of local government) had housed and cared for the ill or incapacitated. Small local almshouses and prisons had housed the poor and the criminal. Reformers now realized that large cities had to make large-scale provisions for social misfits and that institutional rather than private efforts were needed. This thinking was especially true of the institutional reform movements that began in the 1830s, such as the push for insane asylums. At this time, of course, the federal government provided no such relief.

A second characteristic of the reform movements was a belief in the basic goodness of human nature. All reformers believed that the condition of the unfortunate—the poor, the insane, the criminal—would improve in a wholesome environment. Thus, insane asylums were built in rural areas, away from the noise and stress of the cities, and orphanages had strict rules that were meant to encourage discipline and self-reliance. Prison reform carried this sentiment to the extreme. On the theory that bad social influences were largely responsible for crime, some "model" prisons completely isolated prisoners from one another, making them eat, sleep, work, and do required Bible reading in their own cells. The failure of these prisons to achieve dramatic changes for the better in their inmates (a number of isolated prisoners went mad, and some committed suicide) or to reduce crime was one of the first indications that reform was not a simple task.

A third characteristic of the reform movements was their moralistic dogmatism. Reformers were certain they knew what was right and were determined to see their improvements enacted. It was a short step from developing individual self-discipline to imposing discipline on others. The reforms that were proposed thus took the form of social controls. Lazy, sinful, intemperate, or unfit members of society were to be reformed for their own good, whether they wanted to be or not. This attitude was bound to cause controversy; by no means did all Americans share the reformers' beliefs, nor did those for whom it was intended always take kindly to being the targets of the reformers' concern.

Indeed, some aspects of the social reform movements were harmful. The evangelical Protestantism of the reformers promoted a dangerous hostility to Catholic immigrants from Ireland and Germany that, as noted earlier, repeatedly led to urban riots. The temperance movement, in particular, targeted immigrants for their free drinking habits. Seeking uniformity of behavior rather than tolerance, the reformers thus helped to promote the virulent nativism that infected American politics between 1840 and 1860 (see Chapter 15).

Regional and national reform organizations quickly grew from local projects to deal with social problems such as drinking, prostitution, mental illness, and crime. In 1828, for example, Congregationalist minister Lyman Beecher joined other ministers in forming a General Union for Promoting the Observance of the Christian Sabbath; the aim was to prevent business on Sundays. To achieve its goals, the General Union adopted the same methods used by political parties: lobbying, petition drives, fundraising, and special publications. These and other efforts, Beecher said, were all for the purpose of establishing "the moral government of God." Beecher was also

a leader of the anti-Catholic and anti-immigrant movement, warning in 1835 of a "terrific inundation" of Catholics in the West (he meant the Ohio Valley) that threatened American democracy. His vehement sermons warning of the danger contributed to the popular anger that led to the burning of the Charlestown convent in 1834.

In effect, Beecher and similar reformers engaged in political action but remained aloof from direct electoral politics, stressing their religious mission. In any case, sabbatarianism was controversial. Workingmen (who usually worked six days a week) were angered when the General Union forced the Sunday closure of their favorite taverns and were quick to vote against the Whigs, the party perceived to be most sympathetic to reform thinking. But in many new western cities, sabbatarianism divided the business class itself. In Rochester, a city created by the Erie Canal, businessmen who wished to observe Sunday only in religious ways were completely unable to stop the traffic of passenger and freight boats owned by other businessmen. Other reforms likewise muddied the distinction between political and social activity. It is not surprising that women, who were barred from electoral politics but not from moral and social activism, were major supporters of reform.

Education and Women Teachers

Women became deeply involved in reform movements through their churches. It was they who did most of the fundraising for the home missionary societies that were beginning to send the evangelical message worldwide—at first by ministers alone, later by married couples. Nearly every church had a maternal association, where mothers gathered to discuss ways to raise their children as true Christians. These associations reflected a new and more positive definition of childhood. The Puritans had believed that children were born sinful and that their wills had to be broken before they could become godly. Early schools reflected these beliefs: teaching was by rote, and punishment was harsh and physical. Educational reformers, however, tended to believe that children were born innocent and needed gentle nurturing and encouragement if they were to flourish. At home, mothers began to play the central role in child rearing. Outside the home, women helped spread the new public education pioneered by Horace Mann, secretary of the Massachusetts State Board of Education.

Although literacy had long been valued, especially in New England, schooling since colonial times had been a private enterprise and a personal expense. In 1827, Massachusetts pioneered compulsory education by legislating that public schools be supported by public taxes. Soon schooling for white children between the ages of five and nineteen was common, although, especially in rural schools, the term might be only a month or so long.

Read the **Document**

Noted Educator Speaks on Public Schooling in 1848 at **www.myhistorylab.com**

Uniformity in curriculum and teacher training, and the grading of classes by ability—measures pioneered by Horace Mann in the 1830s—quickly caught on in other states. In the North and West (the South lagged far behind), more and more children went to school, and more and more teachers, usually young single women, were hired to teach them.

The spread of public education created the first real career opportunity for women. The great champion of teacher training for women was Catharine Beecher, daughter of Lyman, who clearly saw her efforts as part of the larger work of establishing "the moral government of God." Arguing that women's moral and nurturing nature ideally suited them to be teachers, Beecher campaigned tirelessly on their behalf.

Watch the Video
Who Was Horace Mann and Why Are So Many Schools Named After Him? at **www.myhistorylab.com**

By 1850, women were dominant in primary school teaching, which had come to be regarded as an acceptable occupation for educated young women during the few years between their own schooling and marriage. For some women, teaching was a great adventure; they enthusiastically volunteered to be "schoolmarms" on the distant western frontiers of Wisconsin and Iowa. Still others thought globally. The young women who attended Mary Lyon's Mount Holyoke Female Seminary in Massachusetts, founded in 1837, hoped to be missionary teachers in distant lands. For others, a few years of teaching was quite enough. Low pay (half of what male schoolteachers earned) and strict community supervision (women teachers had to board with families in the community) were probably sufficient to make almost any marriage proposal look appealing.

Temperance

Reformers believed not only that children could be molded but also that adults could change. The largest reform organization of the period, the American Society for the Promotion of Temperance, founded in 1826, boasted more than 200,000 members by the mid-1830s. Dominated by evangelicals, local chapters used revival methods—lurid temperance tracts detailing the evils of alcohol, large prayer and song meetings, and heavy group pressure—to encourage young men to stand up, confess their bad habits, and "take the pledge" not to drink. Here again, women played an important role (see Figure 13.3).

Excessive drinking was a national problem, and it appears to have been mostly a masculine one, for respectable women did not drink in public. (Many did, however, drink alcohol-based patent medicines. Lydia Pinkham's Vegetable Compound, marketed for "female complaints," was 19 percent alcohol.) Men drank hard cider and liquor—whiskey, rum—in abundance. Traditionally, drinking had been a basic part of men's working lives. It concluded occasions as formal as the

Winslow Homer's famous painting, *The Country School* (1871), illustrates the central role of young women in education. Homer's painting is both affectionate and realistic, showing the idealism of the young teacher at the same time showing the barefoot condition of many of her pupils.

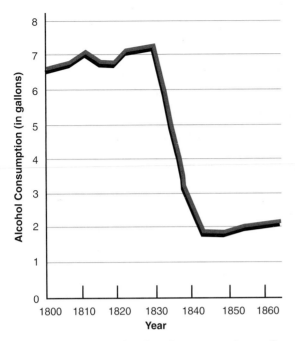

FIGURE 13.3 Per Capita Consumption of Alcohol, 1800–60 The underlying cause of the dramatic fall in alcohol consumption during the 1830s was the changing nature of work brought about by the market revolution. Contributing factors were the shock of the Panic of 1837 and the untiring efforts of temperance reformers.

SOURCE: W. J. Rorabaugh, *The Alcoholic Republic: An American Tradition* (New York: Oxford University Press, 1979).

signing of a contract and accompanied such informal activities as card games. Drink was a staple offering at political speeches, rallies, and elections. In the old artisanal workshops, drinking had been a customary pastime. Much of the drinking was well within the bounds of sociability, but the widespread use must have encouraged drunkenness.

There were many reasons to support temperance. Heavy-drinking men hurt their families economically by spending their wages on drink. Women had no recourse: the laws of the time gave men complete financial control of the household, and divorce was difficult as well as socially unacceptable. Excessive drinking also led to violence and crime, both within the family and in the larger society.

But there were other reasons. The new middle class, preoccupied with respectability, morality, and efficiency, found the old easygoing drinking ways unacceptable. Much of the new industrial machinery was dangerous and workers needed to be sober to be safe. As work patterns changed, employers banned alcohol at work and increasingly considered drinking men not only unreliable but also immoral. Temperance became a social and political issue. Whigs, who embraced the new morality, favored it; Democrats, who in northern cities consisted increasingly

of immigrant workers, were opposed. Both German and Irish immigrants valued the social drinking that occurred in beer gardens and saloons and were hostile to temperance reform.

The Panic of 1837 affected the temperance movement. Whereas most temperance crusaders in the 1820s had been members of the middle class, the long depression of 1837–43 prompted artisans and skilled workers to give up or at least cut down substantially on drinking. Forming associations known as Washington Temperance Societies, these workers spread the word that temperance was the workingman's best chance to survive economically and to maintain his independence. Their wives, gathered together in Martha Washington Societies, were frequently even more committed to temperance than their husbands.

By the mid-1840s, alcohol consumption had been more than halved, to less than two gallons per capita, about the level of today. Concern over drinking would remain constant throughout the nineteenth century and into the twentieth.

Watch the Video
Drinking and the Temperance Movement in Nineteenth-Century America at **www.myhistorylab.com**

Moral Reform, Asylums, and Prisons

Alcohol was not the only "social evil" that reform groups attacked. Another was prostitution, which was common in the nation's port cities. The customary approach of evangelical reformers was to "rescue" prostitutes, offering them the salvation of religion, prayer, and temporary shelter. The success rate was not very high. As an alternative to prostitution, reformers usually offered domestic work, a low-paying and restrictive occupation that many women scorned. Nevertheless, campaigns against prostitution, generally organized by women, continued throughout the nineteenth century.

One of the earliest and most effective antiprostitution groups was the Female Moral Reform Society. Founded by evangelical women in New York in 1834 (the first president was Lydia Finney), it boasted 445 affiliates throughout the country by 1840. The societies quickly realized that prostitution was not as much a moral as an economic issue and moved to organize charity and work for poor women and orphans. They also took direct action against the patrons of prostitutes by printing their names in local papers and then successfully lobbied the New York state legislature for criminal penalties against the male clients as well as the women themselves.

Another dramatic example of reform was the asylum movement, spearheaded by the evangelist Dorothea Dix. In 1843, Dix horrified the Massachusetts state legislature with the results of her several years of study of the conditions to which insane women were subjected. She described in lurid detail how the women were

This Currier and Ives lithograph, *The Drunkard's Progress*, dramatically conveys the message that the first glass leads the drinker inevitably to alcoholism and finally to the grave, while his wife and child (shown under the arch) suffer.

incarcerated with ordinary criminals, locked up in "cages, closets, stalls, pens! Chained, naked, beaten with rods, and lashed into obedience!" Dix's efforts led to the establishment of a state asylum for the insane in Massachusetts and to similar institutions in other states. By 1860, twenty-eight states had public institutions for the insane.

Other reformers were active in related causes, such as prison reform and the establishment of orphanages, homes of refuge, and hospitals. Model penitentiaries were built in Auburn and Ossining (known as "Sing Sing"), New York, and in Philadelphia and Pittsburgh. Characterized by strict order and discipline, these prisons were supposed to reform rather than simply incarcerate their inmates, but their regimes of silence and isolation caused despair more often than rehabilitation.

Utopianism and Mormonism

Amid all the political activism and reform fervor of the 1830s, a few people chose to escape into utopian communities and new religions. The upstate New York area along the Erie Canal was the seedbed for this movement, just as it was for

See the Map
Utopian Communities before the Civil War at
www.myhistorylab.com

evangelical revivals and reform movements like the Seneca Falls convention. The area was so notable for its reform enthusiasm that it has been called "the Burned-Over District," a reference to the waves of reform that swept through like forest fires (see Map 13.2).

Apocalyptic religions tend to spring up in places experiencing rapid social change. The Erie Canal region, which experienced the full impact of the market revolution in the early nineteenth century, was such a place. A second catalyst is hard times, and the prolonged depression that began with the Panic of 1837 led some people to embrace a belief in imminent catastrophe. The Millerites (named for their founder, William Miller) believed that the Second Coming of Christ would occur on October 22, 1843. In anticipation, members of the church sold their belongings and bought white robes for their ascension to heaven. When the Day of Judgment did not take place as expected, most of Miller's followers drifted away. But a small group persisted. Revising their expectations, they formed the core of the Seventh-Day Adventist faith, which is still active today.

The Shakers, founded by "Mother" Ann Lee in 1774, were the oldest utopian group. An offshoot of the Quakers, the Shakers espoused a radical social philosophy that called for the abolition of the traditional family in

- Mormons
- Millerites
- Fourierists
- Antislavery churches
- 1831 revivals

Lake Ontario

Rochester

Utica

Seneca Falls

Waterloo

Lake Erie

MAP 13.2 Reform Movements in the Burned-Over District The so-called
Burned-Over District, the region of New York State most changed by the opening of the Erie Canal, was
a seedbed of religious and reform movements. The Mormon Church originated there and utopian groups
and sects like the Millerites and the Fourierists thrived. Charles G. Finney held some of his most successful
evangelical revivals in the district. Antislavery feeling was common in the region, and the women's rights
movement began at Seneca Falls.

SOURCE: Reprinted from *Whitney R. Cross, The Burned-Over District: The Social and Intellectual History of Enthusiastic
Religion in Western New York, 1800–1850.* Copyright © 1950 by Cornell University. Used with permission of the
publisher, Cornell University Press.

favor of a family of brothers and sisters joined in equal fellowship. Despite its insistence on celibacy, the Shaker
movement grew between 1820 and 1830, eventually
reaching twenty settlements in eight states with a total
membership of 6,000. The Shakers' simple and highly
structured lifestyle, their isolation from the changing
world, and their belief in equality drew new followers,
especially among women. In contrast, another utopian
community, the Oneida Community, became notorious
for its sexual freedom. Founded by John Humphrey Noyes
in 1848, the Oneida community, like the Shaker community, viewed itself as one family.
But rather than celibacy, members
practiced "complex marriage," a
system of highly regulated group
sexual activity. Only "spiritually advanced" males (Noyes
himself and a few others) could father children, who were

•••─[Read the Document

*Visit to the Shakers,
Lowell Offering (1841)* at
www.myhistorylab.com

raised communally. These practices gave the sect a notorious reputation as a den of "free love" and "socialism," preventing Noyes from increasing its membership beyond 200.

Still other forthrightly socialist communities flourished briefly. New Harmony, Indiana, founded by the
famous Scottish industrialist Robert Owen in 1825, was
to be a manufacturing community
without poverty and unemployment. The community survived only
three years. Faring little better were
the "phalanxes," huge communal buildings structured on
the socialist theories of the French thinker Charles Fourier.
Based on his belief that there was a rational way to divide
work, Fourier suggested, for example, that children would
make the best garbage collectors because they didn't mind
dirt! The rapid failure of these socialist communities was
due largely to inadequate planning and organization.

•••─[Read the Document

*O. A. Brownson, Brook
Farm (1842)* at
www.myhistorylab.com

Another reason may have been, as Louisa May Alcott suggested in her satirical reminiscence, *Transcendental Wild Oats*, that the women were left to do all the work while the men philosophized.

The most successful of the nineteenth-century communitarian movements was also a product of the Burned-Over District. In 1830, a young man named Joseph Smith founded the Church of Jesus Christ of Latter-Day Saints, based on the teachings of the Book of Mormon, which he claimed to have received from an angel in a vision. Initially Mormonism, as the new religion became known, seemed little different from the many other new religious groups and utopian communities of the time. But under the benevolent authority of its patriarch, Joseph Smith, it rapidly gained distinction for its extraordinary unity. Close cooperation and hard work made the Mormon community successful, attracting both new followers and the animosity of neighbors, who resented Mormon exclusiveness and economic success.

The Mormons were harassed in New York and driven west to Ohio and then Missouri. Finally they seemed to find an ideal home in Nauvoo, Illinois, where in 1839 they built a model community, achieving almost complete self-government and isolation from non-Mormon neighbors. But in 1844, dissension within the community over Joseph Smith's new doctrine of polygamy (marriage between one man and more than one woman simultaneously) gave outsiders a chance to intervene. Smith and his brother were arrested peacefully but were killed by a mob from which their jailers failed to protect them. The beleaguered Mormon community decided to move beyond reach of harm. Led by Brigham Young, the Mormons migrated in 1846 to the Great Salt Lake in present-day Utah. After several lean years (once, a grasshopper plague was stopped by the providential arrival of sea gulls, who ate the insects), the Mormon method of communal settlement proved successful. Their hopes of isolation were dashed, however, by the California Gold Rush of 1849 (see Chapter 14).

Antislavery and Abolitionism

The antislavery feeling that was to play such an important role in the politics of the 1840s and 1850s also had its roots in the religious reform movements that began in the 1820s and 1830s. Three groups—free African Americans, Quakers, and militant white reformers—worked to bring an end to slavery, but each in different ways. Their efforts eventually turned a minor reform movement into the dominant political issue of the day.

African Americans against Slavery

For free African Americans, the resistance to slavery was fundamental; organized antislavery groups dated to the 1790s. By 1830, there were at least fifty African American abolitionist societies in the North. These organizations held yearly national conventions, where famous African American abolitionists such as Frederick Douglass, Harriet Tubman, and Sojourner Truth spoke. The first African American newspaper, founded in 1827 by John Russwurm and Samuel Cornish, announced its antislavery position in its title, *Freedom's Journal*, and its position in the famous opening lines of the first issue: "for too long others have spoken for us."

In 1829, David Walker, a free African American in Boston, wrote a widely distributed pamphlet, *Appeal to the Colored Citizens of the World*, that encouraged slave rebellion. "We must and shall be free . . . in spite of you," Walker warned whites. "And woe, woe will be it to you if we have to obtain our freedom by fighting." White Southerners blamed pamphlets such as these and the militant articles of African American journalists for stirring up trouble among southern slaves and, in particular, for Nat Turner's revolt in 1831. The vehemence of white southern reaction testifies to the courage of that handful of determined free African Americans who persisted in speaking for their enslaved brothers and sisters long before most white Northerners even noticed. For example, African American activist Maria Stewart lectured on abolition and religion to large public meetings in Boston in the early 1830s, years before the Grimké sisters, who were white, became notorious for giving public speeches to mixed audiences of men and women.

Read the Document
National Convention of Colored People, Report on Abolition (1847) at **www.myhistorylab.com**

Read the Document
An African American Abolitionist Advocates Racial Action in 1829 at **www.myhistorylab.com**

The American Colonization Society

The first national attempt to "solve" the problem of slavery was a plan for gradual emancipation of slaves (with compensation to their owners) and their resettlement in Africa. This plan was the work of the American Colonization Society, formed in 1817 by northern religious reformers (Quakers prominent among them) and a number of southern slave owners, most from the Upper South and the border states (Kentuckian Henry Clay was a supporter). The American Colonization Society was remarkably ineffective; by 1830, it had managed to send only 1,400 black people to a colony in Liberia, West Africa. Critics pointed out that more slaves were born in a week than the society sent back to Africa in a year. And the reaction of free African Americans was emphatic: "We are natives of this country," an African American minister in New York pointed out. Then he added bitterly, "We only ask that we be treated as well as foreigners."

White Abolitionists

The third and best-known group of antislavery reformers was headed by William Lloyd Garrison. In 1831, deeply influenced by those black activists he called his "good colored friends," Garrison broke with the gradualist persuaders of the American Colonization Society and began publishing his own paper, the *Liberator*. Garrison's new "immediatist" tactic was to mount a sweeping crusade condemning slavery as sinful and demanding its immediate abolition. Garrison's crusade, like evangelical religion, was personal and moral. In reality, Garrison did not

Read the **Document**

William Lloyd Garrison, First Issue of the Liberator (1831) at
www.myhistorylab.com

expect that all slaves would be freed immediately, but he did want and expect everyone to acknowledge the immorality of slavery. On the other hand, Garrison took the truly radical step of demanding full social equality for African Americans, referring to them individually as "a man and a brother" and "a woman and a sister." Garrison's determination electrified the antislavery movement, but his inability to compromise limited his effectiveness as a leader.

Garrison's moral vehemence radicalized northern antislavery religious groups. Theodore Weld, an evangelical minister, joined Garrison in 1833 in forming the American Anti-Slavery Society. The following year, Weld encouraged a group of students at Lane Theological Seminary in Cincinnati to form an antislavery society. When the seminary's president, Lyman Beecher, sought to suppress it, the students moved en masse to Oberlin College in northern Ohio, where they were joined by revivalist Charles Finney, who became president of the college. Oberlin soon became known as the most liberal college in the country, not only for its antislavery stance but for its acceptance of African American students and of women students as well.

Moral horror over slavery deeply engaged many Northerners in the abolitionist movement. They flocked to hear firsthand accounts of slavery by Frederick Douglass and Sojourner Truth and by the white sisters from South Carolina, Angelina and Sarah Grimké. Northerners eagerly read slave narratives and books such as Theodore Weld's 1839 treatise *American Slavery As It Is* (based in part on the recollections of Angelina Grimké, whom Weld had married), which provided graphic details of abuse under slavery.

The style of abolitionist writings and speeches was similar to the oratorical style of the religious revivalists. Northern abolitionists believed that a full description of the evils of slavery would force southern slave owners to confront their wrongdoing and lead to a true act of repentance—freeing their slaves. They were confrontational, denunciatory, and personal in their message, much like the evangelical preachers. Southerners, however, regarded abolitionist attacks as libelous and abusive.

Abolitionists adopted another tactic of revivalists and temperance workers when, to enhance their powers of persuasion, they began to publish great numbers of antislavery tracts. In 1835 alone, they mailed more than a million pieces of antislavery literature to southern states. This tactic also drew a backlash: southern legislatures banned

abolitionist literature, encouraged the harassment and abuse of anyone distributing it, and looked the other way when (as in South Carolina) proslavery mobs seized and burned it. The Georgia legislature even offered a $5,000 reward to anyone who would kidnap William Lloyd Garrison and bring him to the South to stand trial for inciting rebellion. Most serious, the majority of southern states reacted by toughening laws concerning emancipation, freedom of movement, and all aspects of slave behavior. Hoping to prevent the spread of the abolitionist message, most southern states reinforced laws making it a crime to teach a slave how to read. Ironically, then, the immediate impact of abolitionism in the South was to stifle dissent and make the lives of slaves harder.

Even in the North, controversy over abolitionism was common. Some places were prone to anti-abolitionist violence. The Ohio Valley, settled largely by Southerners, was one such place, as were northern cities experiencing the strains of rapid growth, such as Philadelphia. Immigrant Irish, who found themselves pitted against free black people for jobs, were often violently anti-abolitionist. A tactic that abolitionists borrowed from revivalists—holding large and emotional meetings—opened the door to mob action. Crowds of people often disrupted such meetings, especially those addressed by Theodore Weld, whose oratorical style earned him the title of "the Most Mobbed Man in the United States." William Lloyd Garrison was stoned, dragged through the streets, and on one occasion almost hanged by a Boston mob. In a three-day New York riot of 1834, abolitionist Arthur Tappan's home and store were sacked at the same time that black churches and homes were damaged and free blacks attacked. In 1837, antislavery editor Elijah P. Lovejoy of Alton, Illinois, was killed and his press destroyed.

Abolitionism and Politics

Abolitionism began as a social movement but soon intersected with sectional interests and became a national political issue. In the 1830s, massive abolitionist petition drives gathered a total of nearly 700,000 petitions requesting the abolition of slavery and the slave trade in the District of Columbia but were rebuffed by Congress. At southern insistence and with President Andrew Jackson's approval, Congress passed a "gag rule" in 1836 that prohibited discussion of antislavery petitions.

Many Northerners viewed the gag rule and censorship of the mails, which Southerners saw as necessary defenses against abolitionist frenzy, as alarming threats to free speech. First among them was Massachusetts representative John Quincy Adams, the only former president ever to serve in Congress after leaving the executive branch. Adams so publicly and persistently denounced the gag rule as a violation of the constitutional right to petition that it was repealed in 1844. Less well-known Northerners, like the thousands of women who canvassed their neighborhoods with petitions, made personal commitments to abolitionism that they did not intend to abandon.

John Quincy Adams was also a key figure in the abolitionists' one undoubted victory, the fight to free the fifty-three slaves on the Spanish ship *Amistad* and return them to Africa. Although the Africans successfully mutinied against the *Amistad*'s crew in 1839, when the ship was found in American waters, a legal battle over their "ownership" ensued, during which the Africans themselves were held in jail. Prominent abolitionists, notably Lewis Tappan, financed the legal fight, which went all the way to the Supreme Court, where Adams won the case for the *Amistad* defendants against the American government, which supported the Spanish claim.

Although abolitionist groups raised the nation's emotional temperature, they failed to achieve the moral unity they had hoped for, and they began to splinter. Frederick Douglass and William Lloyd Garrison parted ways when Douglass, refusing to be limited to a simple recital of his life as a slave, began to make specific suggestions for improvements in the lives of free African Americans.

When Douglass chose the path of political action, Garrison denounced him as "ungrateful."

Douglass and other free African Americans worked under persistent discrimination, even from antislavery whites; some of the latter refused to hire black people or to meet with them as equals. For example, some Philadelphia Quaker meetings, though devoted to the antislavery cause, maintained segregated seating for black people in their churches. While many white reformers eagerly pressed for civil equality for African Americans, they did not accept the idea of social equality. On the other hand, black and white "stations" worked closely in the risky enterprise of passing fugitive slaves north over the famous Underground Railroad, as the various routes by which slaves made their way to freedom were called. Contrary to abolitionist legend, however, it was free African Americans, rather than white people, who played the major part in helping the fugitives.

In 1840, the abolitionist movement formally split. The majority moved toward party politics (which Garrison abhorred), founding the Liberty Party and choosing James G. Birney (whom Theodore Weld had converted to abolitionism) as their presidential candidate. Thus, the abolitionist movement, which began as an effort at moral reform, took its first major step into politics, and this step in turn led to the formation of the Republican Party in the 1850s and to the Civil War (see Chapter 15).

For one particular group of antislavery reformers, the abolitionist movement opened up new possibilities for

The different dates of these two widely used antislavery images are important. The title page of Thomas Branagan's 1807 book includes an already commonly used image at the time of a male slave. The engraving of a chained female slave was made by Patrick Reason, a black artist, in 1835. The accompanying message saying "Am I Not a Woman and a Sister?" spoke particularly to white female abolitionists in the North, who were just becoming active in antislavery movements in the 1830s.

In 1837, white abolitionist Elijah P. Lovejoy had placed the press he used to print his antislavery newspaper in an Alton, Illinois, warehouse in order to protect the press against a mob. This contemporary woodcut depicts the mob's attack on the warehouse. Lovejoy died defending it.

men kept sneaking into the talks, and soon the sisters found themselves speaking to mixed gatherings. The meetings got larger and larger, and the sisters became the first well-known female public speakers in America. In 1837 Angelina Grimké became the first woman to address a meeting of the Massachusetts state legislature (Sarah Bagley, the Lowell worker, was the second).

The Grimké sisters were criticized for speaking because they were women. A letter from a group of ministers cited the Bible in reprimanding the sisters for stepping out of "woman's proper sphere" of silence and subordination. Sarah Grimké answered the ministers in her 1838 *Letters on the Equality of the Sexes and the Condition of Women*, claiming that "men and women were CREATED EQUAL. . . . Whatever is right for a man to do, is right for woman." She followed with this ringing assertion: "I seek no favors for my sex. I surrender not our claim to equality. All I ask of our brethren is, that they will take their feet from off our necks and permit us to stand upright on that ground which God designed us to occupy" (see Communities in Conflict).

Not all female assertiveness was as dramatic as Sarah Grimké's, but women in the antislavery movement found it a constant struggle to be heard. Some solved the problem of male dominance by forming their own groups, like the Philadelphia Female Anti-Slavery Society. In the antislavery movement and other reform groups as well, men accorded women a secondary role, even when—as was frequently the case—women constituted a majority of the members.

action. Through their participation in antislavery activity, some women came to a vivid realization of the social constraints on their activism.

The Women's Rights Movement

American women, without the vote or a role in party politics, found a field of activity in social reform movements. There was scarcely a reform movement in which women were not actively involved. The majority of women did not participate in these activities, for they were fully occupied with housekeeping and child rearing (families with five children were the average). A few women—mostly members of the new middle class, who could afford servants—had the time and energy to look beyond their immediate tasks. Touched by the religious revival, these women enthusiastically joined reform movements. Led thereby to challenge social restrictions, some, such as the Grimké sisters, found that their commitment carried them beyond the limits of what was considered acceptable activity for women.

Watch the Video
The Women's Rights Movement in Nineteenth-Century America at
www.myhistorylab.com

The Grimké Sisters

Sarah and Angelina Grimké, members of a prominent South Carolina slaveholding family, rejected slavery out of religious conviction and moved north to join a Quaker community near Philadelphia. In the 1830s, these two sisters found themselves drawn into the growing antislavery agitation in the North. Because they knew about slavery firsthand, they were in great demand as speakers. At first they spoke to "parlor meetings" of women only, as was considered proper. But interested

Women's Rights

The Seneca Falls Convention of 1848, the first women's rights convention in American history, was an outgrowth of almost twenty years of female activity in social reform. As described in the chapter opener, the long agenda of rights was drawn directly from the discrimination many women had experienced in social reform groups. Every year after 1848, women gathered to hold women's rights conventions and to work for political, legal, and social equality. Over the years, in response to persistent lobbying, states passed property laws more favorable to women, and altered divorce laws to allow women to retain custody of children. Teaching positions in higher education opened up to women, as did jobs in some other occupations, and women gained the vote in some states, beginning with Wyoming

Read the Document
Sojourner Truth, Address to Woman's Rights Convention (1851) at
www.myhistorylab.com

When Women Speak Up

When white abolitionist women like Angelina Grimké, Abby Kelly, and Lucretia Mott began to speak about slavery to audiences of both women and men ("promiscuous assemblies" as they were called), many people objected, among them the clergymen who issued a Pastoral Letter in 1837. This pastoral letter famously evoked Sarah Grimké's vehement assertion of equality: "Whatever is right for a man to do, is right for woman." But ridicule was another reaction, as the rhyming response by abolitionist Maria Weston Chapman illustrates.

• **In 1837, Maria Weston Chapman chose to respond to the pastoral letter with humor. What other responses might be appropriate?**

The Pastoral Letter Condemns Women in Public Life

We invite your attention to the dangers which at present seem to threaten the female character with wide-spread and permanent injury. The appropriate duties and influence of woman are clearly stated in the New Testament. Those duties and that influence are unobtrusive and private, but the source of mighty power. When the mild, dependent, softening influences of woman upon the sternness of man's opinions are fully exercised, society feels the effects of it in a thousand forms. The power of woman is in her dependence, flowing from the consciousness of the weakness which God has given her for her protection. . . .

> "The power of woman is in her dependence . . . ."

But when she assumes the place and tone of man as a public reformer, our care and protection of her seem unnecessary; we put ourselves in self-defence against her; she yields the power which God has

Territory in 1869. In 1920, seventy-two years after universal woman suffrage was first proposed at Seneca Falls, a woman's right to vote was at last guaranteed in the Nineteenth Amendment to the Constitution.

Historians have only recently realized how much the reform movements of this "Age of the Common Man" were due to the efforts of the "common woman." Women played a vital role in all the social movements of the day. In doing so, they implicitly challenged the popular notion of separate spheres for men and women—the public world for him, home and family for her. The separate spheres argument, although it heaped praise on women for their allegedly superior moral qualities, was meant to exclude them from political life. The reforms discussed in this chapter show clearly that women reformers believed they had a right and a duty to propose solutions for the moral and social problems of the day. Empowered by their own religious beliefs and activism, the Seneca Falls reformers spoke for all American women when they demanded an end to the unfair restrictions they suffered as women.

A CONVENTION OF HEMMERS AND STIT HERS HELD AT LYNN, FEB. 28, FOR ADOPTING A LIST OF PRICES; MRS. E. HALL, PRESIDING.—(See page 284.)

Women's gatherings, like the first women's rights convention in Seneca Falls in 1848, and this meeting of strikers in Lynn in 1860, were indicators of widespread female activism.

given her for her protection, and her character becomes unnatural. If the vine, whose strength and beauty is to lean upon the trellis-work, and thus conceal its clusters, thinks to assume the independence and the overshadowing nature of the elm, it will not only cease to bear fruit, but follow shame and dishonor into the dust. We can not, therefore, but regret the mistaken conduct of those who encourage females to bear a persuasive and ostentatious part in measures of reform, and countenance not those of that sex who so far forget themselves as to itinerate in the character of public lecturers and teachers.

The Abolitionist Maria Weston Chapman's Rhyming Response

"The Times That Try Men's Souls"

Confusion has seized us, and all things go wrong, The women have leaped from "their spheres."

And, instead of fixed stars, shoot as comets along,

And are setting the world by the ears!
In courses erratic they're wheeling through space,
In brainless confusion and meaningless chase.

. . .

They've taken a notion to speak for themselves,
And are wielding the tongue and the pen;
They've mounted the rostrum; the termagant elves,
And—oh horrid!—are talking to men!

. . .

SOURCE: Pastoral Letter and Chapman poem quoted in Elizabeth Cady Stanton, Susan B. Anthony, and Matilda Joslyn Gage, eds., *History of Woman Suffrage*, Vol. I, (1889) pp. 81–82.

"The women have leaped from 'their spheres.'"

Conclusion

Beginning in the 1820s, the market revolution changed the size and social order of America's preindustrial cities and towns. Immigration, dramatically rapid population growth, and changes in working life and class structure created a host of new urban problems ranging from sanitation to civic order. These changes occurred so rapidly that they seemed overwhelming. Former face-to-face methods of social control no longer worked. To fill the gap, new kinds of associations—the political party, the religious crusade, the reform cause, the union movement—sprang up. These associations were new manifestations of the deep human desire for social connection, for continuity, and—especially in the growing cities—for social order. A striking aspect of these associations was the uncompromising nature of the attitudes and beliefs on which they were based. Most groups were formed of like-minded people who wanted to impose their will on others. Such intolerance boded ill for the future. If political parties, religious bodies, and reform groups were to splinter along sectional lines (as happened in the 1850s), political compromise would be very difficult. In the meantime, however, Americans came to terms with the market revolution by engaging in a passion for improvement. As a perceptive foreign observer, Francis Grund noted, "Americans love their country not as it is but as it will be."

Review Questions

1. What impact did the new immigration of the 1840s and 1850s have on American cities?

2. Why did urbanization produce so many problems?

3. What motivated the social reformers of the period? Were they benevolent helpers or dictatorial social controllers? Study several reform causes and discuss similarities and differences among them.

4. Abolitionism differed little from other reforms in its tactics, but the effects of antislavery activism were politically explosive. Why was this so?

5. Women were active members of almost every reform group. What reasons might women have given for their unusual degree of participation?

Recommended Reading

Fergus M. Bordewich, *Bound for Canaan: The Underground Railroad and the War for the Soul of America* (2005) An engrossing account of the nation's first racially integrated, religiously motivated movement for racial justice.

Eric Burin, *Slavery and the Peculiar Solution: A History of the American Colonization Society* (2005). Explains the failure of the notion that slavery could simply be deported away.

CHRONOLOGY

1817	American Colonization Society founded
1820s	Shaker colonies grow
1825	New Harmony founded, fails three years later
1826	American Society for the Promotion of Temperance founded
1827	Workingmen's Party founded in Philadelphia
	Freedom's Journal begins publication
	Public school movement begins in Massachusetts
1829	David Walker's *Appeal to the Colored Citizens of the World* is published
1830	Joseph Smith founds Church of Jesus Christ of Latter-Day Saints (Mormon Church)
	Charles G. Finney's revivals in Rochester
1831	William Lloyd Garrison begins publishing antislavery newspaper, the *Liberator*
1832	Immigration begins to increase
1833	American Anti-Slavery Society founded by William Lloyd Garrison and Theodore Weld
1834	First Female Moral Reform Society founded in New York
	National Trades Union formed
1836	Congress passes "gag rule" to prevent discussion of antislavery petitions
1837	Antislavery editor Elijah P. Lovejoy killed
	Angelina Grimké addresses Massachusetts legislature
	Sarah Grimké writes *Letters on the Equality of the Sexes and the Condition of Women*
	Panic begins seven-year depression
1839	Theodore Weld publishes *American Slavery As It Is*
1840s	New York and Boston complete public water systems
1840	Liberty Party founded
1843	Millerites await the end of the world
	Dorothea Dix spearheads asylum reform movement
1844	Mormon leader Joseph Smith killed by mob
1845	New York creates city police force
	Beginning of Irish Potato Famine and mass Irish immigration into the United States
1846	Mormons begin migration to the Great Salt Lake
1848	Women's Rights Convention at Seneca Falls
	John Noyes founds Oneida Community

Scott Gac, *Singing for Freedom: The Hutchinson Family Singers and the Nineteenth-Century Culture of Reform* (2007). Uses the story of the protest songs of this musical antislavery family to explore the role of popular entertainment in an age of reform.

James Oliver Horton and Lois E. Horton, *In Hope of Liberty: Culture, Community and Protest among Northern Free Blacks, 1700–1860* (1997). A fine portrait that adds the perspective of change over time to earlier studies.

Mary Kelley, *Learning to Stand and Speak: Women, Education, and Public Life in America's Republic* (2006). The centrality of education to women's growing role in civic life.

Philip B. Kunhardt, Jr, et al, *P. T. Barnum, America's Greatest Showman* (1995) There are other, more analytical accounts, but this has colorful descriptions and many pictures.

Sally McMillen, *Seneca Falls and the Origins of the Woman's Rights Movement* (2008). A comprehensive overview of the history of the women's rights movement in the nineteenth century.

Richard S. Newman, *The Transformation of American Abolitionism: Fighting Slavery in the Early Republic* (2002). Compares antislavery societies in Massachusetts and Philadelphia and credits black abolitionists as originators of "immediatism."

Mary Ryan, *Civic Wars: Democracy and Public Life in the American City during the Nineteenth Century* (1997). A study of New York, New Orleans, and San Francisco that argues that urban popular culture was "meeting-place democracy" in action.

Deborah Van Broekhoven, *The Devotion of These Women: Rhode Island in the Antislavery Network* (2002). Shows how informal women's activities sustained antislavery protest at the local level.

Margaret Washington, *Sojourner Truth's America* (2009) A full scale life and times of an influential figure.

PEARSON myhistorylab Connections

Reinforce what you learned in this chapter by studying the many documents,
images, maps, review tools, and videos available at www.myhistorylab.com.

Read and Review

✓● Study and Review   Chapter 13

●●● Read the Document

Elizabeth Cady Stanton, Declaration of Sentiments (1848)

Irish Laborers Get an Endorsement in 1833

Preamble of the Mechanics Union of Trade Associations (1827)

Noted Educator Speaks on Public Schooling in 1848

Visit to the Shakers, Lowell Offering (1841)

O. A. Brownson, Brook Farm (1842)

An African American Abolitionist Advocates Racial Action in 1829

William Lloyd Garrison, First Issue of the Liberator (1831)

Sojourner Truth, Address to Woman's Rights Convention (1851)

National Convention of Colored People, Report on Abolition (1847)

◉ See the Map *Utopian Communities before the Civil War*

Research and Explore

●●● Read the Document

Exploring America: Angelina Grimké

Profiles
  Mother Ann Lee
  Walt Whitman

◉ Watch the Video

Religious Troublemakers of the 19th Century

Drinking and the Temperance Movement in Nineteenth-Century America

Who was Horace Mann and why are so many schools named after him?

The Women's Rights Movement in Nineteenth-Century America

((●● Hear the **Audio**

Hear the audio files for Chapter 13 at
www.myhistorylab.com.

14

Chapter 14 at www.myhistorylab.com

((•─Hear the Audio

The Territorial Expansion
of the United States 1830s–1850s

Emigrant Wagons Waiting to Cross the Missouri River. Painting by William Henry Jackson.

Texans and Tejanos "Remember the Alamo!"

For thirteen days in February and March 1836, a force of 187 Texans held the mission fortress known as the Alamo against a siege by 5,000 Mexican troops under General Antonio López de Santa Anna, president of Mexico. Santa Anna had come north to subdue rebellious Texas, the northernmost part of the Mexican province of Coahuila y Tejas, and to place it under central authority. On March 6 he ordered a final assault, and in brutal fighting that claimed over 1,500 Mexican lives, his army took the mission. All the defenders were killed, including Commander William Travis and the well-known frontiersmen Jim Bowie and Davy Crockett. It was a crushing defeat for the Texans. But the cry "Remember the Alamo!" rallied their remaining forces, which, less than two months later, routed the Mexican army and forced Santa Anna to grant Texas independence from Mexico. Today, the Alamo is one of the most cherished historic sites in the United States.

But memory is selective: within a generation of the uprising, few remembered that many Tejanos, Spanish-speaking people born in Texas, had joined with American settlers fighting for Texas independence. During the 1820s, the Mexican government had authorized several American colonies, concentrated in the central and eastern portions of the huge Texas territory and managed by *empresarios* (land agents) like Stephen F. Austin. These settler communities consisted mostly of farmers from the Mississippi Valley, who introduced slavery and cotton growing to the rich soil of coastal and upland Texas.

The Tejano community, descended from eighteenth-century Spanish and Mexican settlers, included wealthy *rancheros* who raised cattle on the shortgrass prairies of southern Texas, as well as the cowboys known as *vaqueros* and the *peónes*, or poor tenant farmers. Although there was relatively little contact between the Americans and Tejanos, their leaders interacted in San Antonio, the center of regional government. The Tejano elite, enthusiastic about American plans for the economic development of Texas, welcomed the American immigrants. Many Americans married into elite Tejano families, who hoped that by thus assimilating and sharing power with the Americans, they could not only maintain but also strengthen their community.

The Mexican state, however, was politically and socially unstable during these first years after its successful revolt against Spain in 1821. Liberals favored a loose federal union, conservatives a strong central state. As a northern frontier province, Texas did not have the benefits of statehood; as a result most Tejanos found themselves taking the liberal side in the struggle, opting for more local control over government activities. When, in 1828, the conservative centralists came to power in Mexico City and decided the Americans had too much influence in Texas, many Tejanos rose up with the Americans in opposition. In 1832, the Tejano elite of San Antonio and many prominent *rancheros* favored provincial autonomy and a strong role for the Americans.

As Santa Anna's army approached from the south, the wealthy *ranchero* Juan Nepomuceno Seguín, one of the leaders of the San Antonio community, recruited a company of Tejano volunteers and joined the American force inside the walls of the Alamo. During the siege, Commander Travis sent Seguín and some of his men for reinforcements. Stopped by Mexican troops on his way across the lines, Seguín called out, *"¡Somos paisanos!"* ("We are countrymen!"), confusing the guards just long enough for Seguín and his men to make their escape despite the hail of gunfire that quickly ensued. Seguín returned from his unsuccessful mission to find

⬤⬤─Read the Document

A Tejano Describes the Beginning of the Texas Revolution in 1835–36 at **www.myhistorylab.com**

the burned bodies of the Alamo defenders, including seven San Antonio Tejanos. *"Texas será libre!"* ("Texas shall be free!") Seguín called out as he directed the burial of the Alamo defenders. In April, Seguín led a regiment of Tejanos in the decisive battle of San Jacinto that won independence for Texas.

Pleased with independence, Tejanos played an important political role in the new Republic of Texas at first. The liberal Lorenzo de Zavala was chosen vice president, and Seguín became the mayor of San Antonio. But soon things began to change, illustrating a recurring pattern in the American occupation of new lands—a striking shift in the relations between different cultures in frontier areas. Most commonly, in the initial stage newcomers blended with native peoples, creating a "frontier of inclusion." The first hunters, trappers, and traders on every American frontier—west of the Appalachians, in the Southwest, and in the Far West—married into the local community and tried to learn native ways. Outnumbered Americans adapted to local societies as a matter of simple survival.

A second stage occurred when the number of Americans increased and they began occupying more and more land or, as in California, "rushing" in great numbers to mine gold, overrunning native communities. This unstable period usually resulted in warfare along with rapidly growing hostility and racial prejudice—all of which were largely absent in earlier days.

A third stage of stable settlement occurred when the native community had been completely "removed" or isolated. In this "frontier of exclusion," racial mixing was rare. In Texas, American settlers—initially invited in by Mexicans and Tejanos—developed an anti-Mexican passion, regarding all Spanish speakers as their Mexican enemies rather than their Tejano allies. Tejanos were attacked and forced from their homes; some of their villages were burned to the ground. "On the pretext that they were Mexicans," Seguín wrote, Americans treated Tejanos "worse than brutes. . . . My countrymen ran to me for protection against the assaults or exactions of these adventurers." But even in his capacity as mayor, Seguín could do little, and in 1842, he and his family, like hundreds of other Tejano families, fled south to Mexico in fear for their lives.

Spanish-speaking communities in Texas, and later in New Mexico and California, like the communities of Indians throughout the West, became

1. What was manifest destiny?

2. What were the major differences between the Oregon, Texas, and California frontiers?

3. What were the most important consequences of the Mexican–American War?

4. What was the link between expansion and slavery?

5. What were the issues in the election of 1848?

FOCUS Questions

1830s–1850s

conquered peoples. "White folks and Mexicans were never made to live together," a Texas woman told a traveler a few years after the revolution. "The Mexicans had no business here," she said, and the Americans might "just have to get together and drive them all out of the country." The descendants of the first European settlers of the American Southwest had become foreigners in the land their people had lived in for two centuries.

For Americans, westward expansion has always meant the establishment of American communities in new territory. In the nineteenth century, this establishment was marked by an intolerance of diversity. Frontiers in Oregon, Texas, and California differed in their details, but the movement from inclusion to exclusion occurred everywhere: as communities were established, the "other" people were either removed, as in the case of American Indians, or subjected, as with the Tejanos. This is one example of how the word "community" has had different meanings at different times in American history.

AMERICAN Communities

San Antonio

Exploring the West

There seemed to be no stopping the expansion of the American people. By 1840, they had occupied all of the land east of the Mississippi River and had organized all of it (except for Florida and Wisconsin) into states. Less than sixty years after the United States gained its independence, the majority of its population lived west of the original thirteen states.

The speed and success of this expansion were a source of deep national pride that whetted appetites for further expansion. Many Americans looked eagerly westward to the vast unsettled reaches of the Louisiana Purchase: to Texas, Santa Fé, to trade with Mexico, and even to the Far West, where New England sea captains had been trading for furs since the 1780s. By 1848, the United States had gained all of these coveted western lands. This chapter examines the way the United States became a continental nation, forming many frontier communities in the process. Exploring the vast continent of North America and gaining an understanding of its geography took several centuries and the efforts of many people.

The Fur Trade

The fur trade, which flourished from the 1670s to the 1840s, was an important spur to exploration on the North American continent. In the 1670s, the British Hudson's Bay Company and its French Canadian rival, Montreal's North West Company, began exploring beyond the Great Lakes in the Canadian West in search of beaver pelts. Indeed, Alexander Mackenzie of the North West Company reached the Pacific Ocean in 1793, becoming the first European to make a transcontinental crossing of North America. Traders and trappers for both companies depended on the goodwill and cooperation of the native

The artist Alfred Jacob Miller, a careful observer of the western fur trade, shows a mountain man and his Indian wife in his 1837 *Bourgeois Walker and His Wife*. Walker and his wife worked together to trap and prepare beaver pelts for market, as did other European men and their Indian wives.

SOURCE: Alfred Jacob Miller, *Bourgeois Walker and His Wife*, 1837. Watercolor. 37.1940.78. The Walters Art Museum, Baltimore.

peoples of the region. From the marriages of European men with native women arose a distinctive mixed-race group, the "métis" (French for "mixed").

Not until the 1820s were American companies able to challenge British dominance of the trans-Mississippi fur trade. In 1824, William Henry Ashley of the Rocky Mountain Fur Company instituted the "rendezvous" system. This was a yearly trade fair, held deep in the Rocky Mountains (Green River and Jackson Hole were favored locations), to which trappers brought their catch of furs. These yearly fur rendezvous were modeled on traditional Indian trade gatherings, such as the one at the Mandan villages on the upper Missouri River and the huge gathering that took place every year at Celilo Falls on the Columbia River. The fur rendezvous was a boisterous, polyglot, many-day affair at which trappers of many nationalities—Americans and Indian peoples, French Canadians, and métis, as well as Mexicans from Santa Fé and Taos—gathered to trade, drink, and gamble.

Most American trappers, like the British and French before them, sought accommodation and friendship with Indian peoples: nearly half of them contracted long-lasting marriages with Indian women, who not only helped in the trapping and curing of furs but also acted as vital diplomatic links between the white and Indian worlds. One legendary trapper adapted so well that he became a Crow chief: the African American Jim Beckwourth, who married a Crow woman and was accepted into her tribe.

For all its adventure, the American fur trade was short-lived. By the 1840s, the population of beaver in western streams was virtually destroyed, and the day of the mountain man was over. But with daring journeys like

that of Jedediah Smith, the first American to enter California over the Sierra Nevada Mountains, the mountain men had helped forge a clear picture of western geography. Soon permanent settlers would follow the trails they had blazed.

Government-Sponsored Exploration

Following the lead of fur trade explorers like Alexander Mackenzie, David Thompson and others, the federal government played a major role in the exploration and development of the U.S. West. The exploratory and scientific aspects of the Lewis and Clark expedition in 1804–06 set a precedent for many government-financed quasi-military expeditions. In 1806 and 1807, Lieutenant Zebulon Pike led an expedition to the Rocky Mountains in Colorado. Major Stephen Long's exploration and mapping of the Great Plains in the years 1819–20 was part of a show of force meant to frighten British fur trappers out of the West. Then, in 1843 and 1844, another military explorer, John C. Frémont, mapped the overland trails to Oregon and California. In the 1850s, the Pacific Railroad surveys explored possible transcontinental railroad routes (see Map 14.1).

Beginning with Long's expedition, the results of these surveys were published by the government, complete with maps, illustrations, and, after the Civil War, photographs. These publications fed a strong popular appetite for pictures of the breathtaking scenery of the Far West and information about its inhabitants. Artists like Karl Bodmer and George Catlin produced stunning portraits of American Indians. And landscape artists like Thomas Moran and Albert Bierstadt painted grand (and sometimes fanciful) pictures of spectacular western

Legend:
- Mackenzie, 1793
- Lewis and Clark, 1804–06
- Zebulon Pike, 1806–07
- Fraser, 1808
- Thompson, 1810–11
- Stephen Long, 1819–20
- Jedediah Smith, 1822–30

MAP 14.1 Exploration of the Continent, 1804–30 Members of British fur trading companies like Alexander Mackenzie and David Thompson led the way in exploration. Lewis and Clark's "voyage of discovery" of 1804–06 was the first of many U.S. government-sponsored western military expeditions. Lieutenant Zebulon Pike crossed the Great Plains in 1806, followed by Major Stephen Long in 1819–20. Meanwhile, American fur trappers, among them the much-traveled Jedediah Smith, became well acquainted with the Far West as they hunted beaver for their pelts.

mountains. These images of the American West made a powerful contribution to the emerging American self-image. American pride in the land—the biggest of this, the longest of that, the most spectacular of something else—was founded on the images brought home by government surveyors and explorers.

In the wake of the pathfinders came hundreds of government geologists and botanists as well as the surveyors who mapped and plotted the West for settlement according to the Land Ordinance of 1785. The basic pattern of land survey and sale established by these measures (see Chapter 7) was followed all the way to the Pacific Ocean. The federal government sold the western public lands at low prices. The federal government also shouldered the expense of Indian removal by making long-term commitments to compensate the Indian people themselves and supporting the forts and soldiers whose task was to maintain peace between settlers and Indian peoples in newly opened areas.

Expansion and Indian Policy

While American artists were painting the way of life of western Indian peoples, eastern Indian tribes were being removed from their homelands to Indian Territory (present-day Oklahoma, Kansas, and Nebraska), a region widely regarded as unfarmable and popularly known as the Great American Desert. The justification for this western removal, as Thomas Jefferson had explained early in the century, was the creation of a space where Indian people could live undisturbed by white people while they slowly adjusted to "civilized" ways. But the government officials who negotiated the removals failed to predict the tremendous speed at which white people would settle the West (see Map 14.2).

Encroachment on Indian Territory was not long in coming. The territory was crossed by the Santa Fé Trail, established in 1821; in the 1840s, the northern part was crossed by the heavily traveled Overland Trails to California, Oregon, and the Mormon community in Utah. In 1854, the government abolished the northern half of Indian Territory, establishing the Kansas and Nebraska Territories in its place and opening them to immediate white settlement. The tribes of the area—the Potawatomis, Wyandots, Kickapoos, Sauks, Foxes, Delawares, Shawnees, Kaskaskias, Peorias, Piankashaws, Weas, Miamis, Omahas, Otos, and Missouris—signed treaties accepting either vastly reduced reservations or allotments. Those who accepted allotments—sections of private land—often sold them, under pressure, to white people. Thus, many of the Indian people who had hoped for independence and escape from white pressures in Indian Territory lost both their autonomy and their tribal identity.

The people in the southern part of Indian Territory, in what is now Oklahoma, fared somewhat better. Those members of the southern tribes—the Cherokees, Chickasaws, Choctaws, Creeks, and Seminoles—who had survived the trauma of forcible removal from the Southeast in the 1830s, quickly created impressive new communities. The five tribes divided up the territory and established self-governing nations with their own schools and churches. The societies they created were not so different from the American societies from which they had been expelled. The five tribes even carried slavery west with them: an elite economic group established plantations and shipped their cotton to New Orleans like other Southerners. Until after the Civil War, these southern tribes were able to withstand outside pressures and remain the self-governing communities that treaties had assured them they would be.

The Politics of Expansion

America's rapid expansion had many consequences, but perhaps the most significant was that it reinforced Americans' sense of themselves as pioneering people. Ever since the time of Daniel Boone, venturing into the wilderness has held a special place in the American imagination and been seen almost as a right.

Manifest Destiny, an Expansionist Ideology

How did Americans justify their restless expansionism? After all, the United States was already a very large country with much undeveloped land. To push beyond existing boundaries was to risk war with Great Britain, which claimed the Pacific Northwest, and with Mexico, which held what is now Texas, New Mexico, Arizona, Utah, Nevada, California, and part of Colorado. Undertaking such a conquest required a rationale.

In 1845, newspaperman John O'Sullivan provided it. It was, he wrote, "our manifest destiny to overspread the continent allotted by Providence for the free development of our yearly multiplying millions." Sullivan argued that Americans had a God-given right to bring the benefits of American democracy to other, more backward peoples—meaning Mexicans and Indians—by force, if necessary. The notion of manifest destiny summed up the powerful combination of pride in what America had achieved and missionary zeal and racist attitudes toward other peoples that lay behind the thinking of many expansionists. Americans were proud of their rapid development: the surge in population, the remarkable canals and railroads, the grand scale of the American enterprise. Why shouldn't America be even bigger?

Expansionism was deeply tied to national politics. O'Sullivan, whose "manifest destiny" became the expansionist watchword, was not a neutral observer: he was the editor of the *Democratic Review*, a party newspaper. Most Democrats were wholehearted supporters of expansion,

●●●[Read the Document

A Newspaper Man Declares the "Manifest Destiny" of the United States in 1845 at **www.myhistorylab.com**

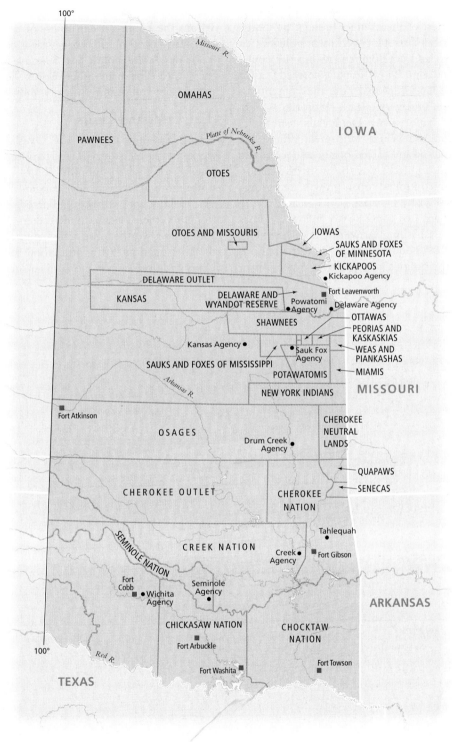

MAP 14.2 Indian Territory before the Kansas–Nebraska Act of 1854
Indian Territory lay west of Arkansas, Missouri, and Iowa and east of Mexican Territory. Most of the Indian peoples who lived there in the 1830s and the 1840s had been "removed" from east of the Mississippi River. The southern part (now Oklahoma) was inhabited by peoples from the Old Southwest: the Cherokees, Chickasaws, Choctaws, Creeks, and Seminoles. North of that in what is now Kansas and Nebraska lived peoples who had been removed from the Old Northwest. All these Indian peoples had trouble adjusting not only to a new climate and a new way of life but also to the close proximity of some Indian tribes who were their traditional enemies.

whereas many Whigs (especially in the North) opposed it. Whigs welcomed most of the changes brought by industrialization but advocated strong government policies that would guide growth and development within the country's existing boundaries. They feared (correctly, as it turned out) that expansion would raise the contentious issue of the extension of slavery to new territories.

On the other hand, many Democrats feared the industrialization that the Whigs welcomed. Where the Whigs saw economic progress, Democrats saw economic depression (the Panic of 1837 was the worst the nation had experienced), uncontrolled urban growth, and growing social unrest. For many Democrats, the answer to the nation's social ills was to continue to follow Thomas Jefferson's vision of establishing agriculture in the new territories in order to counterbalance industrialization. Another factor in the political struggle over expansion in

the 1840s was that many Democrats were Southerners, for whom the continual expansion of cotton-growing lands was a matter of social faith as well as economic necessity.

These were politicians' reasons. The average farmer moved west for many other reasons: land hunger, national pride, plain and simple curiosity, and a sense of adventure.

The Overland Trails

The 2,000-mile trip on the Overland Trails from the banks of the Missouri River to Oregon and California usually took seven months, sometimes more. Travel was slow, dangerous, tedious, and exhausting. Forced to lighten their loads as animals died and winter weather threatened, pioneers often arrived at their destinations with little food and few belongings. Uprooted from family and familiar surroundings, pioneers

Read the Document
Francis Parkman, The Oregon Trail (1847) at **www.myhistorylab.com**

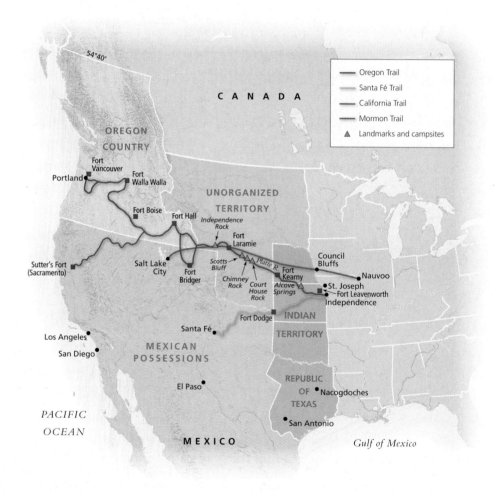

MAP 14.3 The Overland Trails, 1840 All the great trails west started at the Missouri River. The Oregon, California, and Mormon Trails followed the Platte River into Wyoming, crossed South Pass, and divided in western Wyoming. The much harsher Santa Fé Trail stretched 900 miles southwest across the Great Plains. All of the trails crossed Indian Territory and, to greater or lesser extent, Mexican possessions as well.

FERRIAGE of the PLATTE.
above the mouth of Deer Ck.
July 20, 1849

J. Goldsborough Bruff, one of thousands who rushed to California for gold in 1849, sketched several wagons being ferried over the Platte River. The need for individuals to cooperate is obvious. Less obvious in this sketch is the danger: men and livestock often drowned trying to ford western rivers.

faced the prospect of being, in the poignant and much-used biblical phrase, "strangers in a strange land." Yet despite the risks, settlers streamed west: 5,000 to Oregon by 1845 and about 3,000 to California by 1848 (before the discovery of gold) (see Map 14.3).

Pioneers had many motives for making the trip. Glowing reports from Oregon's Willamette Valley, for example, seemed to promise economic opportunity and healthy surroundings, an alluring combination to farmers in the malaria-prone Midwest who had been hard hit by the Panic of 1837. But rational motives do not tell the whole story. Many men were motivated by a sense of adventure, by a desire to experience the unknown, or, using a common nineteenth century term for an unequalled experience, they wanted to "see the elephant."

Few pioneers traveled alone, partly because they feared Indian attack (which was rare) but largely because they needed help fording rivers or crossing mountains with heavy wagons. Most Oregon pioneers traveled with their families but usually also joined a larger group, forming a "train." In the earliest years, when the route was still uncertain, trains hired "pilots," generally former fur trappers. Often the men of the wagon train drew up semimilitary constitutions, electing a leader. Democratic as this process appeared, not everyone was willing to obey the leader, and many trains experienced dissension and breakups along the trail. But in essence, all pioneers—men, women, and children—were part of a

Read the Document
Elizabeth Dixon Smith Geer, Oregon Trail Journal (1847, 1848) at **www.myhistorylab.com**

new, westward-moving community in which they had to accept both the advantages and disadvantages of community membership.

Wagon trains started westward as soon as the prairies were green (thus ensuring feed for the livestock). The daily routine was quickly established. Men took care of the moving equipment and the animals, while the women cooked and kept track of the children. Slowly, at a rate of about fifteen miles a day, the wagon trains moved west until they reached Oregon or California. In addition to tedium and exhaustion, wagon trains were beset by such trail hazards as illness and accident. Danger from Indian attack, which all pioneers feared, was actually very small. It appears that unprovoked white attacks on Indians were more common than the reverse. In contrast, cholera killed at least a thousand people a year in 1849 and in the early 1850s, when it was common along sections of the trail along the Platte River. Spread by contaminated water, cholera caused vomiting and diarrhea, which in turn led to extreme dehydration and death, often in one night.

In the afflicted regions, trailside graves were a frequent and grim sight. Drownings were not uncommon, nor were accidental ax wounds or shootings, and children sometimes fell out of wagons and were run over. The members of the wagon train community provided support for survivors: men helped widows drive their wagons onward, women nursed and tended babies whose mothers were dead, and at least one parentless family, the seven Sager children, were brought to Oregon in safety.

By 1860, almost 300,000 people had traveled the Overland Trails to Oregon or California. Ruts from the wagon wheels can be seen in a number of places along the route even today. In 1869, the completion of the transcontinental railroad marked the end of the wagon train era (see Figure 14.1).

Oregon

The American settlement of Oregon provides a capsule example of the stages of frontier development. The first contacts between the region's Indian peoples and Europeans were commercial. Spanish, British, Russian, and American ships traded for sea otter skins from the 1780s to about 1810. Subsequently, land-based groups scoured the region for beaver skins as well. In this first "frontier of inclusion" there were frequent contacts, many of them sexual, between Indians and Europeans.

Both Great Britain and the United States claimed the Oregon Country by right of discovery, but in the Convention of 1818, the two nations agreed to occupy it jointly, postponing a final decision on its disposition. In reality, the British clearly dominated the region. In 1824, the Hudson's Bay Company consolidated Britain's position by establishing a major fur trading post at Fort Vancouver, on the banks of the Columbia River. Like all fur-trading ventures, the post exemplified the racial

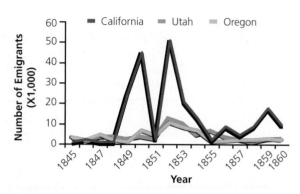

FIGURE 14.1 Overland Emigration to Oregon, California, and Utah, 1840–60 Before 1849, the westward migration consisted primarily of family groups going to Oregon or Utah. The discovery of gold in California dramatically changed the migration: through 1854, most migrants were single men "rushing" to California, which remained the favored destination up until 1860. Over the twenty-year period from 1840 to 1860, the Overland Trails were transformed from difficult and dangerous routes to well-marked and well-served thorough-fares.

SOURCE: From *The Plains Across: The Overland Emigrants and the Trans-Mississippi West, 1840-60.* Copyright 1979 by Board of Trustees of the University of Illinois. Used with permission of the University of Illinois Press.

mixing of a "frontier of inclusion." Fort Vancouver housed a polyglot population of eastern Indians (Delawares and Iroquois), local Chinook Indians, French and métis from Canada, British traders, and Hawaiians. But the effect of the fur trade on native tribes in Oregon was catastrophic; suffering the fate of all Indian peoples after their initial contact with Europeans, they were decimated by European diseases.

The first permanent European settlers in Oregon were retired fur trappers and their Indian wives and families. The next to arrive were Protestant and Catholic missionaries, among them Methodist Jason Lee in 1834, Congregationalists Marcus and Narcissa Whitman in 1836, Franciscan priests Frances Blanchet and Modeste Demers in 1838, and Jesuit Pierre-Jean De Smet in 1840. None of these missionaries was very successful. Epidemics had taken the lives of many of the region's peoples, and those who were left were disinclined to give up their nomadic life and settle down as the missionaries wanted them to do.

Finally, in the 1840s, came the Midwest farmers who would make up the majority of Oregon's permanent settlers, carried on the wave of enthusiasm known as "Oregon fever" and lured by free land and patriotism. By 1845, Oregon boasted 5,000 American settlers, most of them living in the Willamette Valley and laying claim to lands to which they had as yet no legal right, because neither Britain nor the

Read the Document

Mariah and Stephen King to their Their Family (1846) at **www.myhistorylab.com**

United States had concluded land treaties with Oregon's Indian peoples. Their arrival signaled Oregon's transition away from a "frontier of inclusion."

Joint occupancy of Oregon by the Americans and the British continued until 1846. Initially, a peaceful outcome seemed doubtful. In his campaign for president in 1844, President James K. Polk coined the belligerent slogan "Fifty-four Forty or Fight," suggesting that the United States would go to war if it didn't get control of all the territory south of 54°40' north latitude, the border between Russian Alaska and British Canada. Once elected, however, Polk was willing to compromise. In June 1846, Britain and the United States concluded a treaty establishing the 49th parallel as the U.S.–Canada border but leaving the island of Vancouver in British hands. The British then quietly wound up their declining fur trade in the region. In 1849, the Hudson's Bay Company closed Fort Vancouver and moved its operations to Victoria,

thus ending the Pacific Northwest's largely successful experience with joint occupancy. Oregon's Donation Land Claim Act of 1850 codified the practice of giving 320 acres to each white male aged eighteen or over and 640 acres to each married couple to settle in the territory (African Americans, Hawaiians, and American Indians were excluded).

The white settlers realized that they had to forge strong community bonds if they hoped to survive on their distant frontier. Cooperation and mutual aid were the rule. In the earliest years, American settlers got vital help from the Hudson's Bay Company, even though its director, Dr. John McLoughlin, had been ordered by the British government not to encourage American settlement. McLoughlin disregarded his orders, motivated both by sympathy for the plight of the newcomers and by a keen sense of the dangers his enterprise would face if he were outnumbered by angry Americans.

This view of Fort Vancouver on the Columbia River in the 1840s shows established agriculture and thriving commerce, indicated by the large sailing ship on the river, which is probably the Hudson's Bay Company yearly supply ship from England. It was a scene like this that led Narcissa Whitman to call Fort Vancouver "the New York of the Pacific."

Until well into the 1850s, residents organized yearly parties that traveled back along the last stretches of the Oregon Trail to help straggling parties making their way to the territory. Kinship networks were strong and vital: many pioneers came to join family who had migrated before them. Food sharing and mutual labor were essential in the early years when crop and live-stock loss to weather or natural predators was common. Help, even to total strangers, was customary in times of illness or death.

Relations with the small and unthreatening disease-thinned local Indian tribes were generally peaceful until 1847, when Cayuse Indians killed the missionaries Marcus and Narcissa Whitman. Their deaths triggered a series of "wars" against the remaining native people. A "frontier of exclusion" had been achieved. Nonetheless, the process by which Oregon became part of the United States (it was admitted as a state in 1859) was relatively peaceful, especially when compared with American expansion into the Spanish provinces of New Mexico and Texas.

The Santa Fé Trade

Commerce with Santa Fé, first settled by colonists from Mexico in 1609, and the center of the Spanish frontier province of New Mexico, had long been desired by American traders. But Spain had forcefully resisted American penetration. For example, Lieutenant Zebulon Pike's Great Plains and Rocky Mountain exploration of 1806–07 ended ignominiously with his capture by Spanish soldiers.

When Mexico gained its independence from Spain in 1821, this exclusionary policy changed. American traders were now welcome in Santa Fé, but the trip over the legendary Santa Fé Trail from Independence, Missouri, was a forbidding 900 miles of arid plains, deserts, and mountains. On the Santa Fé Trail, unlike the Oregon Trail, there was serious danger of Indian attack, for neither the Comanches nor the Apaches of the southern high plains tolerated trespassers. In 1825, at the urging of Senator Benton and others, Congress voted federal protection for the Santa Fé Trail, even though much of it lay in Mexican territory. The number of people venturing west in the trading caravans increased yearly because the profits were so great (the first American trader to reach Santa Fé, William Becknell, realized a 1,000 percent profit). By the 1840s, a few hundred American trappers and traders (called *extranjeros*, or "foreigners") lived permanently in New Mexico. In Santa Fé, some American merchants married daughters of important local families, suggesting the start of the inclusive stage of frontier contact.

Settlements and trading posts soon grew up along the long Santa Fé Trail. One of the most famous was Bent's Fort, on the Arkansas River in what is now eastern Colorado, which did a brisk trade in beaver skins and buffalo robes. Like most trading posts, it had a multi-ethnic population. In the 1840s, the occupants included housekeeper Josefa Tafoya of Taos, whose husband was a carpenter from Pennsylvania; an African American cook; a French tailor from New Orleans; Mexican muleteers; and a number of Indian women, including the two Cheyenne women who were the (successive) wives of William Bent, cofounder of the fort. This racially mixed existence was characteristic of all early trading frontiers, but another western frontier, the American agricultural settlement in Texas, was different from the start.

Mexican Texas

In 1821, when Mexico gained its independence from Spain, there were 2,240 Tejano (Spanish-speaking) residents of Texas. Established in 1716 as a buffer against possible French attack on New Spain, the main Texas settlements of Nacogdoches, Goliad, and San Antonio remained small, far-flung frontier outposts (see Chapter 5). As was customary throughout New Spain, communities were organized around three centers: missions and *presidios* (forts), which formed the nuclei of towns, and the large cattle-raising *ranchos* on which rural living depended. The most colorful figures were *mestizo* (mixed-blood) *vaqueros*, renowned for their horsemanship; Americanization of their name made "buckaroos" of the American cowboys to whom they later taught their skills. Most Tejanos were small farmers or common laborers who led hardscrabble frontier lives. But all Tejanos, rich and poor, faced the constant threat of raids by Comanche Indians.

Legendary warriors, the Comanches raided the small Texas settlements at will and even struck deep into Mexico itself. Once they raided so far south that they saw brightly plumed birds (parrots) and "tiny men with tails" (monkeys); apparently they had reached the tropical Yucatán. The nomadic Comanches followed the immense buffalo herds on which they depended for food and clothing. Their relentless raids on the Texas settlements rose from a determination to hold onto this rich buffalo territory, for the buffalo provided all that they wanted. They had no interest in being converted by mission priests or incorporated into mixed-race trading communities.

Americans in Texas

In 1821, seeking to increase the strength of its buffer zone between the heart of Mexico and the marauding Comanches, the Mexican government granted Moses Austin of Missouri an area of 18,000 square miles within the territory of Texas. Moses died shortly thereafter, and the grant was taken up by his son Stephen F. Austin, who became the first American *empresario* (land agent). From the beginning, the American settlement of Texas differed markedly from that of other frontiers. Elsewhere, Americans frequently settled on land to which Indian peoples still held title, or, as in the case of Oregon, they occupied lands to which other countries also made claim. In contrast, the Texas settlement

Painted by George Catlin in about 1834, this scene, *Commanche Village Life*, shows how the everyday life of the Comanches was tied to buffalo. The women in the foreground are scraping buffalo hide, and buffalo meat can be seen drying on racks. The men and boys may be planning their next buffalo hunt.

was fully legal: Austin and other empresarios owned their lands as a result of formal contracts with the Mexican government. In exchange, Austin agreed that he and his colonists would become Mexican citizens and would adopt the Catholic religion. It is difficult to say which of these two provisions was the more remarkable, for most nineteenth-century Americans defined their Americanness in terms of citizenship and the Protestant religion.

Insisting that "no frontiersman who has no other occupation than that of hunter will be received—no drunkard, no gambler, no profane swearer, no idler," Austin chose instead prosperous southern slave owners eager to expand the lands devoted to cotton. Soon Americans (including African American slaves, to whose presence the Mexican government turned a blind eye) outnumbered Tejanos by nearly two to one: in 1830, there were an estimated 7,000 Americans and 4,000 Tejanos living in Texas.

The Austin settlement of 1821 was followed by others, twenty-six in all, concentrating in the fertile river bottoms of eastern Texas (along the Sabine River) and south central Texas (the Brazos and the Colorado Rivers). These large settlements were highly organized farming enterprises whose principal crop was cotton, grown by African American slave labor and sold in the international market. By the early 1830s, Americans in Texas, ignoring the border between Mexican Texas and the United States, were sending an estimated $500,000 worth of goods (mostly cotton) yearly to New Orleans for export.

Austin's colonists and those who settled later were predominantly Southerners who viewed Texas as a natural extension of the cotton frontier in Mississippi and Louisiana. These settlers created "enclaves" (self-contained communities) that had little contact with Tejanos or Indian peoples. In fact, although they lived in Mexican territory, most Americans never bothered to learn Spanish. Nor, in spite of Austin's promises, did they become Mexican citizens or adopt the Catholic religion. Yet, because of the nature of agreements made by the empresarios, the Americans could not set up local American-style governments like the one created by settlers in Oregon. Like the immigrants who flooded into East Coast cities (see Chapter 13), the Americans in Texas were immigrants to another country—but one to which they did not intend to adapt.

For a brief period, Texas was big enough to hold three communities: Comanche, Tejano, and American. The nomadic Comanches rode the high plains of northern and western Texas, raiding settlements primarily for horses. The Tejanos maintained their ranchos and missions mostly in the South, while American farmers occupied the eastern and south central sections. Each group would fight to hold its land: the Comanches, their rich hunting grounds; the Mexicans, their towns and ranchos; and the newcomers, the Americans, their rich land grants.

The balance among the three communities in Texas was broken in 1828, when centrists gained control of the government in Mexico City and, in a dramatic shift of policy, decided to exercise firm control over the northern province. As the Mexican government restricted American immigration, outlawed slavery, levied customs duties and taxes, and planned other measures, Americans seethed and talked of rebellion. Bolstering their cause were as many as 20,000 additional Americans, many of them openly expansionist, who flooded into Texas after 1830. These most recent settlers did not intend to become Mexican citizens. Instead, they planned to take over Texas.

Many of the post-1830 immigrants were vehemently anti-Mexican. Statements of racial superiority were commonplace, and even Stephen Austin wrote in 1836 that he saw the Texas conflict as one of barbarism on the part of "a

1820 Spanish province

1840 Republic

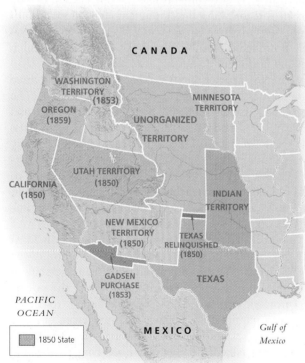

1850 State

MAP 14.4 Texas: From Mexican Province to U.S. State In the space of twenty years, Texas changed shape three times. Initially part of the Mexican province of Coahuila y Tejas, it became the Republic of Texas in 1836, following the Texas Revolt, and was annexed to the United States in that form in 1845. Finally, in the Compromise of 1850 following the Mexican-American War, it took its present shape.

mongrel Spanish-Indian and negro race, against civilization and the Anglo-American race."

Between 1830 and 1836, in spite of the mediation efforts of Austin (who was imprisoned for eighteen months by the Mexican government for his pains), the mood on both the Mexican and the American-Texan sides became more belligerent. In the fall of 1835, war finally broke out, and a volunteer American and Tejano army assembled. After the disastrous defeat at the Alamo described in the chapter opener, Mexican general and president Antonio López de Santa Anna led his army in pursuit of the remaining army of American and Tejano volunteers commanded by General Sam Houston.

On April 21, 1836, at the San Jacinto River in eastern Texas, Santa Anna thought he had Houston trapped at last. Confident of victory against the exhausted Texans, Santa Anna's army rested in the afternoon, failing even to post sentries. Although Houston advised against it, Houston's men voted to attack immediately rather than wait till the next morning. Shouting "Remember the Alamo!" for the first time, the Texans completely surprised their opponents and won an overwhelming victory. On May 14, 1836, Santa Anna signed a treaty fixing the southern boundary of the newly independent Republic of Texas at the Rio Grande. The Mexican Congress, however, repudiated the treaty and refused to recognize Texan independence (see Map 14.4).

The Republic of Texas

The Republic of Texas was unexpectedly rebuffed in another quarter as well. The U.S. Congress refused to grant it statehood when, in 1837, Texas applied for admission to the Union. Petitions opposing the admission of a fourteenth slave state (there were then thirteen free states) poured into Congress. Congressman (and former president) John Quincy Adams of Massachusetts led the opposition to the admission of Texas. Congress debated and ultimately dropped the Texas application.

The unresolved conflict with Mexico put heavy stress on American–Tejano relations. As before, ambitious Anglos married into the Tejano elite, which made it easier for those Tejano families to adjust to the changes in law and commerce that the Americans quickly enacted. But following a temporary recapture of San Antonio by Mexican forces in 1842, positions hardened. Many more of the Tejano elite fled to Mexico, and Americans discussed banishing or imprisoning all Tejanos until the border issue was settled. This was, of course, impossible. Culturally, San Antonio remained a Mexican city long after the Americans had declared independence. The Americans in the Republic of Texas were struggling to reconcile American ideals of democracy with the reality of subordinating those with a prior claim, the Tejanos, to the status of a conquered people.

American control over the other Texas residents, the Indians, was also slow in coming. The Comanches still rode the high plains of northern and western Texas. West of the Rio Grande, equally fierce Apache bands were in control. Both groups soon learned to distrust American promises to stay out of their territory, and they did not hesitate to raid settlements and to kill trespassers. Not until after the Civil War and major campaigns by the U.S. Army were these fierce Indian tribes conquered.

Texans continued to press for annexation to the United States, while at the same time seeking recognition and support from Great Britain. The idea of an independent and expansionist republic on its southern border that might gain the support of America's traditional enemy alarmed many Americans. Annexation thus became an urgent matter of national politics. This issue also added to the troubles of a governing Whig Party that was already deeply divided by the policies of John Tyler, who had become president by default when William Harrison died in office (see Chapter 11). Tyler raised the issue of annexation in 1844, hoping thereby to ensure his reelection, but the strategy backfired. Presenting the annexation treaty to Congress, Secretary of State John Calhoun awakened sectional fears by connecting Texas with the urgent need of southern slave owners to extend slavery.

In a storm of antislavery protest, Whigs rejected the treaty proposed by their own president and ejected Tyler himself from the party. In his place, they chose Henry Clay, the party's longtime standard-bearer, as their presidential candidate. Clay took a noncommittal stance on Texas, favoring annexation, but only if Mexico approved. Since Mexico's emphatic disapproval was well known, Clay's position was widely interpreted as a politician's effort not to alienate voters on either side of the fence.

In contrast, in the Democratic Party, wholehearted and outspoken expansionists seized control. Sweeping aside their own senior politician, Van Buren, who like Clay tried to remain uncommitted, the Democrats nominated their first "dark horse" candidate, James K. Polk of Tennessee. Democrats enthusiastically endorsed Polk's platform, which called for "the re-occupation of Oregon and the re-annexation of Texas at the earliest practicable period."

Polk won the 1844 election by the narrow margin of 40,000 popular votes (although he gained 170 electoral votes to Clay's 105). An ominous portent for the Whigs was the showing of James G. Birney of the Liberty Party, who polled 62,000 votes, largely from northern antislavery Whigs. Nevertheless, the 1844 election was widely interpreted as a mandate for expansion. Thereupon, John Tyler, in one of his last actions as president, pushed through Congress a joint resolution (which did not require the two-thirds approval by the Senate necessary for treaties) for the annexation of Texas. When Texas entered the Union in December 1845, it was the twenty-eighth state and the fifteenth slave state.

The Mexican-American War

James K. Polk lived up to his expansive campaign promises. In 1846, he peacefully added Oregon south of the 49th parallel to the United States; in 1848, following the Mexican-American War, he acquired Mexico's northern provinces of California and New Mexico as well. Thus, with the annexation of Texas, the United States, in the short space of three years, had added 1.5 million square miles of territory, an increase of nearly 70 percent. Polk was indeed the "manifest destiny" president.

Read the Document
James K. Polk, First Inaugural Address (1845) at **www.myhistorylab.com**

Origins of the War

In the spring of 1846, just as the controversy over Oregon was drawing to a peaceful conclusion, tensions with Mexico grew more serious. Because the United States supported the Texas claim of all land north of the Rio Grande, it became embroiled in a border dispute with Mexico. In June 1845, Polk sent General Zachary Taylor to Texas, and by October a force of 3,500 Americans was on the Nueces River with orders to defend Texas in the event of a Mexican invasion.

Polk had something bigger than border protection in mind. He coveted the continent clear to the Pacific Ocean. At the same time that he sent Taylor to Texas, Polk secretly

Watch the Video
The Annexation of Texas at **www.myhistorylab.com**

instructed the Pacific naval squadron to seize the California ports if Mexico declared war. He also wrote the American consul in Monterey, Thomas Larkin, that a peaceful takeover of California by its residents—Spanish Mexicans and Americans alike—would not be unwelcome.

Meanwhile, in November 1845, Polk sent a secret envoy, John Slidell, to Mexico with an offer of $30 million or more for the Rio Grande border in Texas and Mexico's provinces of New Mexico and California. When the Mexican government refused even to receive Slidell, an angry Polk ordered General Taylor and his forces south to the Rio Grande, into the territory that Mexicans claimed as their soil. In April 1846, a brief skirmish between American and Mexican soldiers broke out in the disputed zone. Polk seized on the event, sending a war message to Congress: "Mexico has passed the boundary of the United States, has invaded our territory and shed American blood upon American soil. . . . War exists, and, notwithstanding all our efforts to avoid it, exists by the act of Mexico herself." This claim of President Polk's was, of course, contrary to fact. On May 13, 1846, Congress declared war on Mexico (see Map 14.5).

See the Map
The Mexican-American War at
www.myhistorylab.com

Mr. Polk's War

From the beginning, the Mexican–American War was politically divisive. Whig critics in Congress, among them a gawky young congressman from Illinois named Abraham Lincoln, questioned Polk's account of the border incident. They accused the president of misleading Congress and of maneuvering the country into an unnecessary war. The history of congressional concern over the way presidents

LANDING OF THE AMERICAN FORCES UNDER GEN⁺ SCOTT
AT VERA CRUZ MARCH 9ᵗʰ 1847.

General Winfield Scott's amphibious attack on the Mexican coastal city of Veracruz in March 1847 was greeted with wide popular acclaim in the United States. It was the first successful amphibious attack in U.S. military history. Popular interest in the battles of the Mexican-American War was fed by illustrations such as this in newspapers and magazines.

MAP 14.5 The Mexican-American War, 1846–48 The Mexican-American War began with an advance by U.S. forces into the disputed area between the Nueces River and the Rio Grande in Texas. The war's major battles were fought by General Zachary Taylor in northern Mexico and General Winfield Scott in Veracruz and Mexico City. Meanwhile Colonel Stephen Kearny secured New Mexico and, with the help of the U.S. Navy and John C. Frémont's troops, California.

have exercised their war powers begins here. The issue would again be prominent, for example, during the Vietnam War, in the Reagan years, and in the questions about the reasons for war with Iraq in 2003. As the Mexican-American War dragged on and casualties and costs mounted—13,000 Americans and 50,000 Mexicans died and the United States spent $97 million—opposition increased, especially among northern antislavery Whigs.

Many Northerners asked why Polk had been willing to settle for only a part of Oregon but was so eager to pursue a war for slave territory. Thus, expansionist dreams served to fuel sectional antagonisms.

The northern states witnessed both mass and individual protests against the war. In Massachusetts, the legislature passed a resolution condemning Polk's declaration of war as unconstitutional, and philosopher–writer Henry

David Thoreau went to jail rather than pay the taxes he believed would support the war effort. (Thoreau's dramatic gesture was undercut by his aunt, who paid his fine after he had spent only one night in jail.) Thoreau then wrote his classic essay "Civil Disobedience," justifying the individual's moral duty to oppose an immoral government. In the early twentieth century, the Indian nationalist Mohandas Gandhi used Thoreau's essay to justify his campaign of "passive resistance" against British imperial rule in India. In turn, Martin Luther King Jr. and others used Gandhi's model of civil disobedience as a basis for their activities in the American civil rights movement of the 1950s and 1960s.

A New Englander Calls for Civil Disobedience to Protest the Mexican War at www.myhistorylab.com

Whigs termed the war with Mexico "Mr. Polk's War," but the charge was not just a Whig jibe. Although he lacked a military background, Polk assumed the overall planning of the war's strategy (a practice that the critical Mr. Lincoln was to follow in the Civil War). By his personal attention to the coordination of civilian political goals and military requirements, Polk gave a new and expanded definition to the role of the president as commander in chief during wartime. By the end of 1846, the northern provinces that Polk had coveted were secured, but contrary to his expectations, Mexico refused to negotiate. In February 1847, General Santa Anna of Alamo fame attacked the American troops led by General Taylor at Buena Vista but was repulsed by Taylor's small force. A month later, in March 1847, General Winfield Scott launched an amphibious attack on the coastal city of Veracruz and rapidly captured it. Americans celebrated these twin victories joyously, but they were to be the last easy victories of the war. It took Scott six months of brutal fighting against stubborn Mexican resistance on the battlefield and harassing guerrilla raids to force his way to Mexico City. American troops reacted bitterly to their high casualty rates, retaliating against Mexican citizens with acts of murder, robbery, and rape. General Scott himself admitted that his troops had "committed atrocities to make Heaven weep and every American of Christian morals blush for his country." In September, Scott took Mexico City, and Mexican resistance came to an end.

With the American army went a special envoy, Nicholas Trist, who delivered Polk's terms for peace. In the Treaty of Guadalupe Hidalgo, signed February 2, 1848, Mexico ceded its northern provinces of California and New Mexico (which included present-day Arizona, Utah, Nevada, and part of Colorado) and accepted the Rio Grande as the boundary of Texas. The United States agreed to pay Mexico $15 million and assume about $2 million in individual claims against that nation.

When Trist returned to Washington with the treaty, however, Polk was furious. He had actually recalled Trist after Scott's sweeping victory, intending to send a new envoy with greater demands, but Trist had ignored the recall order. "All Mexico!" had become the phrase widely used by those in favor of further expansion, Polk among them. But two very different groups opposed further expansion. The first group, composed of northern Whigs, included such notables as Ralph Waldo Emerson, who grimly warned, United States will conquer Mexico, but it will be as the man swallows arsenic, which brings him down in turn. Mexico will poison us." The second group was composed of Southerners who realized that Mexicans could not be kept as conquered people but would have to be offered territorial government as Louisiana had been offered in 1804. Senator John C. Calhoun of South Carolina, leading the opposition, warned against admitting "colored and mixed-breed" Mexicans "on an equality with people of the United States." Bowing to these political protests, Polk reluctantly accepted the treaty. A later addition, the $10 million Gadsden Purchase of parts of present-day New Mexico and Arizona, added another 30,000 square miles to the United States in 1853. This purchase, made to facilitate a southern transcontinental railroad route through arid borderland, was a far cry from the rich heartland of Mexico that Polk had hoped to annex (see Map 14.6).

The Press and Popular War Enthusiasm

The Mexican-American War was the first war in which regular, on-the-scene reporting by representatives of the press caught the mass of ordinary citizens up in the war's daily events. Thanks to the recently invented telegraph, newspapers could get the latest news from their reporters, who were among the world's first war correspondents. The "penny press," with more than a decade's experience of reporting urban crime and scandals, was quick to realize that the public's appetite for sensational war news was apparently insatiable. For the first time in American history, accounts by journalists, and not the opinions of politicians, became the major shapers of popular attitudes toward a war. From beginning to end, news of the war stirred unprecedented popular excitement (see Seeing History).

The reports from the battlefield united Americans in a new way: they became part of a temporary but highly emotional community linked by newsprint and buttressed by public gatherings. In the spring of 1846, news of Zachary Taylor's victory at Palo Alto prompted the largest meeting ever held in the cotton textile town of Lowell, Massachusetts. In May 1847, New York City celebrated the twin victories at Veracruz and Buena Vista with fireworks, illuminations, and a "grand procession" estimated at 400,000 people. Generals Taylor and Scott became overnight heroes, and in time, both became presidential candidates. Exciting, sobering, and terrible, war news had a deep hold on the popular imagination. It was a lesson newspaper publishers never forgot.

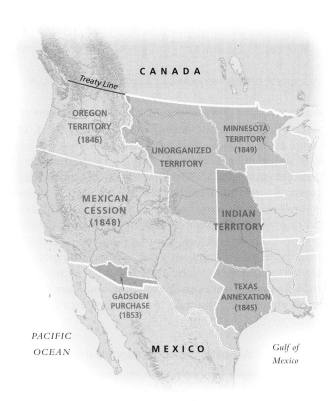

MAP 14.6 Territory Added, 1845–53 James K. Polk was elected president in 1844 on an expansionist platform. He lived up to most of his campaign rhetoric by gaining the Oregon Country (to the 49th parallel) peacefully from the British, Texas by the presidential action of his predecessor John Tyler, and present-day California, Arizona, Nevada, Utah, New Mexico, and part of Colorado by war with Mexico. In the short space of three years, the size of the United States grew by 70 percent. In 1853, the Gadsden Purchase added another 30,000 square miles.

California and the Gold Rush

In the early 1840s, California was inhabited by many semino-madic Indian tribes whose people numbered approximately 50,000. There were also some 7,000 *Californios*, descendants of the Spanish-Mexican pioneers who had begun to settle in 1769. Even American annexation at the end of the Mexican-American War changed little for the handful of Americans on this remote frontier. But then came the gold rush of 1849, which changed California permanently.

Russian–Californio Trade

The first outsiders to penetrate the isolation of Spanish California were not Americans but Russians. Evading Spanish regulations, Californios traded with the Russian American Fur Company in Sitka, Alaska. A mutually beneficial barter of California food for iron tools and woven cloth from Russia was established in 1806. This arrangement became even brisker after the Russians settled Fort Ross (near present-day Mendocino) in 1812 and led in time to regular trade with Mission San Rafael and Mission Sonoma. That the Russians in Alaska, so far from their own capital, were better supplied with manufactured goods than the Californios is an index of the latter's isolation.

When Mexico became independent in 1821, the California trade was thrown open to ships of all nations. Nevertheless, Californios continued their special relationship with the Russians, exempting them from the taxes and inspections that they required of Americans. However, agricultural productivity declined after 1832, when the Mexican government ordered the secularization of the California missions, and the Russians regretfully turned to the rich farms of the Hudson's Bay Company in the Pacific Northwest for their food supply. In 1841, they sold Fort Ross, and the Russian–Californio connection came to an end.

Read the Document
Richard Henry Dana, Two Years before the Mast (1840) at **www.myhistorylab.com**

Early American Settlement

It was Johann Augustus Sutter, a Swiss who had settled in California in 1839, becoming a Mexican citizen, who served as a focal point for American settlement in the 1840s. Sutter held a magnificent land grant in the Sacramento Valley. At the center of his holdings was Sutter's Fort, a walled compound that was part living quarters and part supply shop for his vast cattle ranch, which was run largely on forced Indian labor. In the 1840s, Sutter offered valuable support to the handful of American overlanders who chose California over Oregon, the destination preferred by most pioneers. Most of these Americans, keenly aware that they were interlopers in Mexican territory, settled near Sutter in California's Central Valley, away from the Californio clustered along the coast.

The 1840s' immigrants made little effort to intermarry with the Californios or to conform to Spanish ways. They were bent on taking over the territory. In June 1846, these Americans banded together at Sonoma in the Bear Flag Revolt (so called because their flag bore a bear emblem), declaring independence from Mexico. The American takeover of California was not confirmed until the Treaty of Guadalupe Hidalgo in 1848. In the meantime, California was regarded by most Americans merely as a remote, sparsely populated frontier, albeit one with splendid potential. Polk and other expansionists coveted the magnificent harbors in San Diego and San Francisco as the basis for Pacific trade with Asia, but in 1848 this prospect was still only a dream.

Gold!

In January 1848, carpenter James Marshall noticed small flakes of gold in the millrace at Sutter's Mill (present-day Coloma). Soon he and all the rest of John Sutter's

SEEING History

War News from Mexico

The unprecedented immediacy of the news reporting from the battlefields of the Mexican-American War, transmitted for the first time by telegraph, is captured in this painting by the American artist Richard Caton Woodville, painted in 1848 (the year the war ended). Woodville was one of a number of genre painters who enlivened their depictions of everyday life and ordinary people by focusing on political debates or dramatic moments like the one shown here.

Almost every aspect of this painting is political commentary. The central figure in the painting is standing on the porch of the American Hotel reading the latest war news to the crowd of men gathered around him from a cheap "penny paper" full of sensational stories, war news, and lithographs of battle scenes from the war. Although the audience seems deeply engaged, the range of expressions reminds the viewer that the war was very divisive, with many antislavery Northerners in outright opposition. The placement of the African American man at a lower level on the step is a clear statement of his exclusion from political participation. Don't overlook the woman leaning out of the window on the right side of the painting. She too is excluded from politics but is obviously just as interested and concerned as the men. Woodville's inclusion of the black child in a white smock seems to be an ambiguous statement about the impact of the Mexican-American War on slavery.

• **Are you surprised at the extent of political commentary in this painting? Are paintings an appropriate media for political opinion?**

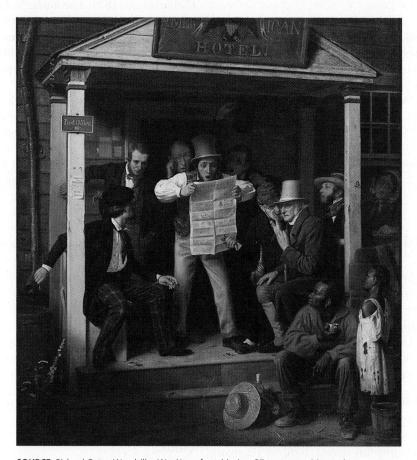

SOURCE: Richard Caton Woodville, *War News from Mexico*, Oil on canvas. Manovgian Foundation on loan to the National Gallery of Art, Washington, DC. © Board of Trustees, National Gallery of Art, Washington.

employees were panning for gold in California's streams. But not until the autumn of 1848 did the East Coast hear the first rumors about the discovery of gold in California. The reports were confirmed in mid-November when an army courier arrived in Washington carrying a tea caddy full of gold dust and nuggets. The spirit of excitement and adventure so recently aroused by the Mexican-American War was now directed toward California, the new El Dorado. Thousands left farms and jobs and headed west, by land and by sea, to make their fortune. Later known as "forty-niners" for the year the gold rush began in earnest, these people came from all parts of the United States—and indeed, from all over the world. They transformed what had been a quiet ranching paradise into a teeming and tumultuous community in search of wealth in California's rivers and streams.

Eighty percent of the forty-niners were Americans. They came from every state. The gold rush was an eye-opening expansion of their horizons for the many who had known only their hometown folks before. The second largest group of migrants was from nearby Mexico and the western coast of Latin America (13 percent). The remainder came from Europe and Asia (see Figure 14.2).

The presence of Chinese miners surprised many Americans. Several hundred Chinese arrived in California in 1849 and 1850, and in 1852 more than 20,000 landed in San Francisco hoping to share in the wealth of "Gum Sam" (Golden Mountain). Most came, like the Americans, as temporary sojourners, intending to return home as soon as they made some money. Again, like most of the American miners, the majority of Chinese were men who left their wives at home. Dressed in their distinctive blue cotton shirts, baggy pants, and broad-brimmed hats, and with long queues hanging down their backs, hardworking Chinese miners soon became a familiar sight in the gold

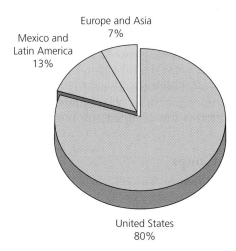

FIGURE 14.2 Where the Forty-Niners Came From Americans drawn to the California gold rush of 1849 encountered a more diverse population than most had previously known. Nearly as novel to them as the 20 percent from foreign countries was the regional variety from within the United States itself.

fields, as did the presence of "Chinatowns." The distinctive appearance of the Chinese, added to the threat of economic competition that they posed, quickly aroused American hostility. A special tax was imposed on foreign miners in 1852, and in the 1870s, Chinese immigration was sharply curtailed.

In 1849, as the gold rush began in earnest, San Francisco, the major entry port and supply point, sprang to life. From a settlement of 1,000 in 1848, it grew to a city of 35,000 in 1850. This surge suggested that the real money to be made in California was not in panning for gold but in feeding, clothing, housing, provisioning, and

This drawing of the bar of a gambling saloon in San Francisco in 1855 shows the effects of the gold rush on California. Men from all parts of the world are gathered at this elegant bar in the large cosmopolitan city of San Francisco, which had been only a small trading post before gold was discovered in 1849.

SOURCE: Frank Marryat, *The Bar of a Gambling Saloon*, published 1855. Lithograph. Collection of the New-York Historical Society, New York City.

entertaining the miners. Among the first to learn that lesson was the German Jewish immigrant Levi Strauss, who sold so many tough work pants to miners that his name became synonymous with his product. The white population of California jumped from an estimated pre–gold rush figure of 11,000 to more than 100,000 by 1852. California was admitted into the Union as a state in 1850.

Mining Camps

As had occurred in San Francisco, most mining camps boomed almost instantly to life, but unlike San Francisco, they were empty again within a few years. In spite of the aura of glamour that surrounds the names of the famous camps—Poker Flat, Angels Camp, Whiskey Bar, Placerville, Mariposa—they were generally dirty and dreary places. Most miners lived in tents or hovels, unwilling to take time from mining to build themselves decent quarters. They cooked monotonous meals of beans, bread, and bacon or, if they had money, bought meals at expensive restaurants and boardinghouses (where the table might be no more than a plank over two flour barrels). They led a cheerless, uncomfortable, and unhealthy existence, especially during the long, rainy winter months, with few distractions apart from the saloon, the gambling hall, and the prostitute's bed (see Map 14.7).

Read the Document

Edward Gould Buffum, from Six Months in the Gold Mines (1850) at **www.myhistorylab.com**

Most miners were young, unmarried, and unsuccessful. Only a small percentage ever struck it rich in California. Gold deposits that were accessible with pick and shovel were soon exhausted, and the deeper deposits required capital and machinery. Increasingly, those who stayed on in California had to give up the status of independent miners and become wage earners for large mining concerns.

As in San Francisco, a more reliable way to earn money in the camps was to supply the miners. Every mining community had its saloonkeepers, gamblers, prostitutes, merchants, and restaurateurs. Like the miners themselves, these people were transients, always ready to pick up and move at the word of a new gold strike. The majority of women in the early mining camps were prostitutes. Some grew rich or married respectably, but most died young of drugs, venereal disease, or violence. Most of the other women were hardworking wives of miners, and in this predominantly male society, they made good money doing domestic work by keeping boardinghouses, cooking, and doing laundry.

Partly because few people put any effort into building communities—they were too busy seeking gold—violence was endemic in mining areas, and much of it was racial. Discrimination, especially against Chinese, Mexicans, and African Americans, was common. Frequently miners' claims were "jumped": thieves would rob them of the gold

MAP 14.7 California in the Gold Rush This map shows the major gold camps along the mother lode in the western foothills of the Sierra Nevada Mountains. Gold seekers reached the camps by crossing the Sierra Nevada near Placerville on the Overland Trail or by sea via San Francisco. The main area of Spanish-Mexican settlement, the coastal region between Monterey and Los Angeles, was remote from the goldfields.

SOURCE: From *The Historical Atlas of California* by Warren A. Beck and Ynez Hasse. Copyright 1974 University of Oklahoma Press. Reprinted by permission.

they had accumulated, kill them, or chase them away, and then file their own claim for the victims' strike. Or unscrupulous miners might use the law to their advantage to secure the claims of others without violence—for example, by taking advantage of the prohibitively high mining tax on foreigners.

In the end, most mining camps were at best temporary communities. The gold "played out" and people moved on, leaving ghost towns behind. By the mid-1850s, the immediate effects of the gold rush had passed. California had a booming population, a thriving agriculture, and a corporate mining industry. The gold rush also

Chinese first came to California in 1849 attracted by the gold rush. Frequently, however, they were forced off their claims by intolerant whites. Rather than enjoy an equal chance in the goldfields, they were often forced to work as servants or in other menial occupations.

left California with a population that was larger, more affluent, and (in urban San Francisco) more culturally sophisticated than that in other newly settled territories. And it was significantly more multicultural than the rest of the nation, for many of the Chinese and Mexicans, as well as immigrants from many European countries, remained in California after the gold rush subsided. But the gold rush left some permanent scars, and not just on the foothills landscape: the virtual extermination of the California Indian peoples, the dispossession of many Californios who were legally deprived of their land grants, and the growth of racial animosity toward the Chinese in particular. The major characteristics of the mining frontier, evident first in the California gold rush and repeated many times thereafter in similar gold rushes in Colorado, Montana, Idaho, South Dakota, Arizona, and Alaska were a lack of stable communities and a worsening of racial tensions.

The Politics of Manifest Destiny

In three short years, from 1845 to 1848, the territory of the United States grew an incredible 70 percent, and a continental nation took shape. This expansion, pushed by economic desires and feelings of American cultural superiority, led directly to the emergence of the divisive issue of slavery as the dominant issue in national politics.

The Wilmot Proviso

In 1846, almost all the northern members of the Whig Party opposed Democratic president James Polk's belligerent expansionism on antislavery grounds. Northern Whigs correctly feared that expansion would reopen the issue of slavery in the territories. But the outpouring of popular enthusiasm for the Mexican-American War convinced most Whig congressmen that they needed to vote military appropriations for the war in spite of their misgivings.

Ironically, it was not the Whigs but a freshman Democratic congressman from Pennsylvania, David Wilmot, who opened the door to sectional controversy over expansion. In August 1846, only a few short months after the beginning of the Mexican-American War, Wilmot proposed, in an amendment to a military appropriations bill, that slavery be banned in all the territories acquired from Mexico. He was ready, Wilmot said, to "sustain the institutions of the South as they exist" but not to extend them. In the debate and voting that followed, something new and ominous occurred: southern Whigs joined southern Democrats to vote against the measure, while Northerners of both parties supported it. Sectional interest had triumphed over party loyalty. Wilmot's Proviso triggered the first breakdown of the national party system and reopened the debate about the place of slavery in the future of the nation.

OVERVIEW | Expansion Causes the First Splits in the Second American Party System

1844	Whigs reject President John Tyler's move to annex Texas and expel him from the Whig Party.
	Southern Democrats choose expansionist James K. Polk as their presidential candidate, passing over Martin Van Buren, who is against expansion.
	Liberty Party runs abolitionist James Birney for president, attracting northern antislavery Whigs.
1846	The Wilmot Proviso, proposing to ban slavery in the territories that might be gained in the Mexican-American War, splits both parties: southern Whigs and Democrats oppose the measure; northern Whigs and Democrats support it.
1848	The new Free-Soil Party runs northern Democrat Martin Van Buren for president, gaining 10 percent of the vote from abolitionists, antislavery Whigs, and some northern Democrats. This strong showing by a third party causes Democrat Lewis Cass to lose the electoral votes of New York and Pennsylvania, allowing the Whig Zachary Taylor to win.

The Wilmot Proviso was so controversial that it was deleted from the necessary military appropriations bills during the Mexican-American War. But in 1848, following the Treaty of Guadalupe Hidalgo, the question of the expansion of slavery could no longer be avoided or postponed. Antislavery advocates from the North argued with proslavery Southerners in a debate that was much more prolonged and bitter than in the Missouri Crisis debate of 1819. Civility quickly wore thin: threats were uttered and fistfights broke out on the floor of the House of Representatives. The Wilmot Proviso posed a fundamental challenge to both parties. Neither the Democrats nor the Whigs could take a strong stand on the amendment because neither party could get its northern and southern wings to agree (see Communities in Conflict).

The Free-Soil Movement

Why did David Wilmot propose this controversial measure? Wilmot, a northern Democrat, was propelled not by ideology but by the pressure of practical politics. The dramatic rise of the Liberty Party, founded in 1840 by abolitionists, threatened to take votes away from both the Whig and the Democratic parties. The Liberty Party won 62,000 votes in the 1844 presidential election, all in the North. This was more than enough to deny victory to the Whig candidate, Henry Clay.

The Liberty Party took an uncompromising stance against slavery. The party proposed to prohibit the admission of slave states to the Union, end slavery in the District of Columbia, and abolish the interstate slave trade that was vital to the expansion of cotton growing into the Old Southwest. Liberty Party members also favored denying office to all slaveholders (a proposal that would have robbed all the southern states of their senators). Liberty Party doctrine was too uncompromising for the mass of northern voters, who immediately realized that the southern states would leave the Union before accepting it. Still, as the 1844 vote indicated, many Northerners opposed slavery. From this sentiment, the Free-Soil Party was born.

The free-soil argument was a calculated adjustment of abolitionist principles to practical politics. It shifted the focus from the question of the morality of slavery to the ways in which slavery posed a threat to northern expansion. The free-soil doctrine thus established a direct link between expansion, which most Americans supported, and sectional politics.

Free-soilers were willing to allow slavery to continue in the existing slave states because they supported the Union, not because they approved of slavery. They were unwilling, however, to allow the extension of slavery to new and unorganized territory. If the South were successful in extending slavery, they argued, northern farmers who moved west would find themselves competing at an economic disadvantage with large planters using slave labor. Free-soilers also insisted that the northern values of freedom and individualism would be destroyed if the slave-based southern labor system were allowed to spread.

Many free-soilers really meant "anti-black" when they said "antislavery." They proposed to ban all African American people from the new territories (a step that four states—Indiana, Illinois, Iowa, and Oregon—took but did not always enforce). William Lloyd Garrison promptly denounced the free-soil doctrine as "whitemanism," a racist effort to make the territories white. There was much truth to his charge: most Northerners were unwilling to consider social equality for African Americans, free or slave. Banning all black people from the western territories seemed a simple solution.

The Election of 1848

A swirl of emotions—pride, expansionism, sectionalism, abolitionism, free-soil sentiment—surrounded the election of 1848. The issues raised by the Wilmot Proviso remained to be resolved, and every candidate had to have an answer to the question of whether slavery should be admitted in the new territories.

Lewis Cass of Michigan, the Democratic nominee for president (Polk, in poor health, declined to run for a second term), proposed to apply the doctrine of popular sovereignty to the crucial slave–free issue. Popular sovereignty was based on the accepted constitutional principle that decisions about slavery (like, for example, rules about suffrage)

In 1848, the Whigs nominated a hero of the Mexican-American War, General Zachary Taylor, who ran on his military exploits. In this campaign poster, every letter of Taylor's name is decorated with scenes from the recent war, which had seized the popular imagination in a way no previous conflict had done.

should be made at the state rather than the national level. In reality, popular sovereignty was an admission of the national failure to resolve sectional differences. It simply shifted decision making on the crucial issue of the expansion of slavery from national politicians to the members of territorial and state legislatures, who, belonging to different parties, were in as much disagreement as members of Congress and just as unable to resolve it.

Moreover, the doctrine of popular sovereignty was deliberately vague about when a territory would choose its status. Would it do so during the territorial stage or at the point of applying for statehood? Clearly, this question was crucial, for no slave owner would invest in new land if the territory could later be declared free, and no abolitionist would move to a territory that was destined to become a slave state. Cass hoped his ambiguity on this point would win him votes in both North and South.

For their part, the Whigs passed over perennial candidate Henry Clay and turned to a war hero, General Zachary Taylor. Taylor, a Louisiana slaveholder, refused to take a position on the Wilmot Proviso, allowing both northern and southern voters to hope that he agreed with them. Privately, Taylor opposed the expansion of slavery. In public, he evaded the issue by running as a war hero and a national leader who was above sectional politics.

The deliberate vagueness of the two major candidates displeased many northern voters. An uneasy mixture of disaffected Democrats (among them David Wilmot) and Whigs joined former Liberty Party voters to support the candidate of the Free-Soil Party, former president Martin Van Buren. Van Buren, angry at the Democratic Party for passing him over in 1844 and displeased with the growing southern dominance of the Democratic Party, ran as a spoiler. He knew he could not win the election, but he could divide the Democrats. In the end, Van Buren garnered 10 percent of the vote (all in the North). The vote for the Free-Soil Party cost Cass the electoral votes of New York and Pennsylvania, and General Zachary Taylor won the election with only 47 percent of the popular vote. This was the second election after 1840 that the Whigs had won by running a war hero who could duck hard questions by claiming to be above politics. Uncannily, history was to repeat itself: Taylor, like William Henry Harrison, died before his term was completed, and the chance he offered to maintain national unity—if ever it existed—was lost.

Conclusion

In the decade of the 1840s, westward expansion took many forms, from relatively peaceful settlement in Oregon, to war with Mexico over Texas, to the overwhelming numbers of gold rushers who changed California forever. Most of these frontiers—in Oregon, New Mexico, and California—began as frontiers of inclusion, in which small numbers of Americans were eager for trade, accommodation, and intermarriage with the original inhabitants. Texas, with its agricultural enclaves, was the exception to this pattern. Yet on every frontier, as the number of American settlers increased, so did the sentiment for exclusion, so that by 1850, whatever their origins, the far-flung American continental settlements were more similar than different, and the success of manifest destiny seemed overwhelming.

COMMUNITIES *in* CONFLICT

The Sectional Split over the Expansion of Slavery

David Wilmot's proviso was deceptively short, simply stating that "neither slavery nor involuntary servitude shall ever exist" in any territory gained from Mexico, but it provoked a thundering response from Senator John C. Calhoun, the South's spokesman. Wilmot then replied, equally defiant. Years later, looking back on the polarized positions of Wilmot, Calhoun, and their supporters, Senator Thomas Hart Benton mused:

> Truly the abolitionists and the nullifiers were necessary to each other—the two halves of a pair of shears, neither of which could cut until joined together. Then the map of the Union was in danger; for in their conjunction, that map was cloth between the edges of the shears.

• **In his "shears" image, is Senator Benton saying that one side or the other ought to have refused to engage with the other, or that the engagement, thus begun with Wilmot's Proviso, was irreconcilable?**

John C. Calhoun: Let Us Be Done with Compromises

Sir, there is no mistaking the signs of the times; and it is high time that the Southern States, the slaveholding States, should inquire what is now their relative strength in this Union. . . . Already we are in a minority in the other House, in the electoral college, and I may say, in every department of this government, except at present in the Senate of the United States. . . . [Thus we] have at present only one position in the government, by which we may make any resistance to this aggressive policy which has been declared against the South. . . . [And more free states are likely to be admitted so that in a few years.] How will we then stand? There will be but fourteen on the part of the South—we are to be fixed, limited, and forever—and twenty-eight on the part of the non-slaveholding States! Double our number! . . . We shall be at the entire mercy of the non-slaveholding States. Can we look to their justice and regard for our interests? I ask, can we rely on that?

Now sir, I put again the solemn question—does the Constitution afford any remedy? . . . How then do we stand in reference to this

> "We shall be at the entire mercy of the non-slaveholding States."

The election of 1848, virtually a referendum on manifest destiny, yielded ironic results. James K. Polk, who presided over the unprecedented expansion, did not run for a second term and, thus, the Democratic Party gained no electoral victory to match the military one. The electorate that had been so thrilled by the war news voted for a war hero—who led the anti-expansionist Whig Party. The election was decided by Martin Van Buren, the Free-Soil candidate who voiced the sentiments of the abolitionists, a reform group that had been insignificant just a few years before. The amazing expansion achieved by the Mexican–American War—America's manifest destiny—made the United States a continental nation but stirred up the issue that was to tear it apart. Sectional rivalries and fears now dominated every aspect of politics. Expansion, once a force for unity, now divided the nation into Northerners and Southerners, who could not agree on the community they shared—the federal Union.

Review Questions

1. Define and discuss the concept of manifest destiny.

2. Trace the different ways in which the frontiers in Oregon, Texas, and California moved from frontiers of inclusion to frontiers of exclusion.

3. Take different sides (Whig and Democrat) and debate the issues raised by the Mexican–American War.

4. The California gold rush was an unprecedented scramble for riches. What were its effects on its participants, on California, and on the nation as a whole?

5. Referring to Chapter 13, compare the positions of the Liberty Party and the Free-Soil Party. Examine the factors that made the free-soil doctrine politically so acceptable and abolitionism so controversial.

territorial question—this public domain of ours? Why, sir, what is it? It is the common property of the States of this Union. . . . Sir, these territories are the property of the States united; held jointly for their common use. And is it consistent with justice, that any portion of the partners, outnumbering another portion, shall oust them of this common property of theirs—shall pass any law which shall proscribe the citizens of other portions of the Union from emigrating with their property to the territories of the United States?

Let us be done with compromises. Let us go back and stand upon the Constitution!

David Wilmot Replies: Defeat Today Will But Arouse the Teeming Millions

I ask not that slavery be abolished. I demand that this government preserve the integrity of *free territory* against the aggressions of slavery—against its wrongful usurpations. Sir, I was in favor of the annexation of Texas. I supported it with my whole influence and strength. I was willing to take Texas as she was. . . . Slavery existed in Texas—planted there, it is true, in defiance of law; still, it existed . . . the whole of Texas has been given up to slavery. The Democracy of the North, almost to a man, went for annexation. Yes, sir, here was an empire larger than France given up to slavery. Shall further concessions be made by the North? Shall we give up free territory, the inheritance of free labor? Must we yield this, also? Never, sir, never, until we ourselves are fit to be slaves. . . . Defeat! Sir, there can be no defeat. Defeat to-day will but arouse the teeming millions of the North, and lead to a more decisive and triumphant victory tomorrow.

SOURCES: Thomas Hart Benton, *Thirty Years' View . . . 1820 to 1850* (New York: D. Appleton and Company, 1854–56), Vol. II, p. 695.
Clyde N. Wilson and Shirley Bright Cook, eds., *The Papers of John C. Calhoun*, Vol. XXIV, 1846–47, pp. 169–174.
Charles Buxton Goin, *David Wilmot, Free Soiler: A Biography of the Great Advocate of the Wilmot Proviso* (New York: D. Appleton and Company, 1924), p. 167.

"Shall further concessions be made by the North? . . . Never, sir, never . . ."

Recommended Reading

Maria Raquél Casas, *Married to a Daughter of the Land: Spanish Mexican Women and Interethnic Marriage in California, 1820–1880* (2007). Argues that intermarriage did not lead to Anglo cultural dominance because intermarried Californias and their children remained culturally Spanish Mexican.

Paul Foos, *A Short, Offhand, Killing Affair: Soldiers and Social Conflict During the Mexican-American War* (2002). The lives and attitudes of ordinary American soldiers.

Pekka Hämäläinen, *The Comanche Empire* (2008). A perspective-changing book that shows how the Comanches became the dominant force on the Southern Plains.

Albert Hurtado, *John Sutter: A Life on the North American Frontier* (2006). A life and times that views Sutter as a major player in the history of California.

Susan Johnson, *Roaring Camp: The Social World of the California Gold Rush* (2000). A beautifully written study of the varieties of mining camp experience.

Paul D. Lack, *The Texas Revolutionary Experience: A Political and Social History, 1835–1836* (1992). A political and social history that stresses the chaotic and discordant nature of the Texas Revolt.

Robert W. Merry, *A Country of Vast Designs: James K. Polk, the Mexican War, and the Conquest of the American Continent* (2009). A major reconsideration of the politics of the Polk administration and the Mexican American War.

Walter Nugent, *Habits of Empire: A History of American Expansion* (2008). A sweeping overview that traces expansionism from 1782 to the present day.

Raul A. Ramos, *Beyond the Alamo: Forging Mexican Ethnicity in San Antonio, 1821-1861* (2008). The transition from political dominance to political minority.

CHRONOLOGY

1609	First Spanish settlement in New Mexico
1670s	British and French Canadians begin fur trade in western Canada
1716	First Spanish settlements in Texas
1769	First Spanish settlement in California
1780s	New England ships begin sea otter trade in Pacific Northwest
1793	Alexander Mackenzie of the North West Company reaches the Pacific Ocean.
1803	Louisiana Purchase
1804–06	Lewis and Clark expedition
1806	Russian–Californio trade begins
1806–07	Zebulon Pike's expedition across the Great Plains to the Rocky Mountains
1819–20	Stephen Long's expedition across the Great Plains
1821	Hudson's Bay Company gains dominance of western fur trade
	Mexico seizes independence from Spain
	Santa Fé Trail opens, soon protected by U.S. military
	Stephen F. Austin becomes first American empresario in Texas
1824	First fur rendezvous sponsored by Rocky Mountain Fur Company
	Hudson's Bay Company establishes Fort Vancouver in Oregon Country
1830	Indian Removal Act moves eastern Indians to Indian Territory
1833–34	Prince Maximilian and artist Karl Bodmer visit Plains Indians
1834	Jason Lee establishes first mission in Oregon Country
1835	Texas revolts against Mexico
1836	Battles of the Alamo and San Jacinto
	Republic of Texas formed
1843–44	John C. Frémont maps trails to Oregon and California
1844	Democrat James K. Polk elected president on an expansionist platform
1845	Texas annexed to the United States as a slave state
	John O'Sullivan coins the phrase "manifest destiny"
1846	Oregon question settled peacefully with Britain
	Mexican-American War begins
	Bear Flag Revolt in California
	Wilmot Proviso
1847	Cayuse War begins in Oregon
	Americans win battles of Buena Vista, Veracruz, and Mexico City
1848	Treaty of Guadalupe Hidalgo
	Free-Soil Party captures 10 percent of the popular vote in the North
	General Zachary Taylor, a Whig, elected president
1849	California gold rush

PEARSON myhistorylab Connections

Reinforce what you learned in this chapter by studying the many documents, images, maps, review tools, and videos available at www.myhistorylab.com.

Read and Review

✓● Study and Review Chapter 14

●●● Read the Document

A Tejano Describes the Beginning of the Texas Revolution in 1835-36

William Barret Travis, Letter from the Alamo (1836)

A Newspaper Man Declares the "Manifest Destiny" of the United States in 1845

Francis Parkman, The Oregon Trail (1847)

Elizabeth Dixon Smith Geer, Oregon Trail Journal (1847, 1848)

Mariah and Stephen King to their Family (1846)

James K. Polk, First Inaugural Address (1845)

Richard Henry Dana, Two Years before the Mast (1840)

Edward Gould Buffum, from Six Months in the Gold Mines (1850)

((●● Hear the Audio *A New Englander Calls for Civil Disobedience to Protest the Mexican War*

◉● See the Map *The Mexican-American War*

Research and Explore

●●● Read the Document

Exploring America: The Unwelcome Mat

Whose History Is It: Remembering the Alamo

Profiles
Jim Beckwourth
Juan Seguin

◉● Watch the Video *The Annexation of Texas*

((●● Hear the Audio

Hear the audio files for Chapter 14 at
www.myhistorylab.com.

15

Chapter 15 at www.myhistorylab.com

((•—[Hear the Audio

The Coming Crisis
the 1850s

Grand procession of Wide-Awakes at New York on the evening of October 3, 1860. Courtesy of the Library of Congress.

Illinois Communities Debate Slavery

AMERICAN Communities

On seven occasions through the late summer and autumn of 1858, in seven small Illinois towns, thousands of farmers and townspeople put aside their daily routines, climbed into carriages, farm wagons, and carts, and converged on their local town green. Entertained by brass bands, pageantry, and vast quantities of food and local gossip, they waited impatiently for the main event, the chance to take part in the Lincoln–Douglas debate on the most urgent question of the day—slavery.

"The prairies are on fire," announced the *New York Evening Post* correspondent who covered the debates. "It is astonishing how deep an interest in politics these people take." The reason was clear: by 1858, the American nation was in political crisis. The decade-long effort to solve the problem of the future of slavery had failed. For most of this time, Washington politicians trying to build broad national parties with policies acceptable to voters in both the North and the South had done their best not to talk about slavery. That the Lincoln–Douglas debates were devoted to one issue alone—slavery and the future of the Union—showed how serious matters had become.

Democratic Senator Stephen A. Douglas of Illinois and his Republican challenger, Springfield lawyer

393

Abraham Lincoln, presented their views in three hours of closely reasoned argument. But they did not speak alone. Cheers, boos, groans, and shouted questions from active, engaged listeners punctuated all seven of the now famous confrontations between the two men. Thus, the Lincoln–Douglas debates were community events in which Illinois citizens—who, as did Americans everywhere, held varying political beliefs—took part. Some individuals were proslavery, some antislavery, and many were undecided, but all were agreed that democratic politics gave them the means to air their opinions, to resolve their differences, and to assess the candidates who were running for a Senate seat from Illinois.

Stephen Douglas was the leading Democratic contender for the 1860 presidential nomination, but before he could mount a campaign for national office, he had first to win reelection to the Illinois seat he had held in the U.S. Senate for twelve years. His vote against allowing slavery in Kansas had alienated him from the strong southern wing of his own party and had put him in direct conflict with its top leader, President James Buchanan. Because the crisis of the Union was so severe and Douglas's role so pivotal, his reelection campaign clearly previewed the 1860 presidential election. For the sake of its future, the Republican Party had to field a strong opponent: it found its candidate in Abraham Lincoln.

Lincoln had represented Illinois in the House of Representatives in the 1840s but had lost political support in 1848 because he had opposed the Mexican-American War. Developing a prosperous Springfield law practice, he had been an influential member of the Illinois Republican Party since its founding in 1856. Although he had entered political life as a Whig, Lincoln was radicalized by the issue of the extension of slavery. Even though his wife's family were Kentucky slave owners, Lincoln's commitment to freedom and his resistance to the spread of slavery had now become absolute: for him, freedom and the Union were inseparable.

Much less known than Douglas, Lincoln was the underdog in the 1858 Senate race. As they squared off in each of the seven Illinois towns, Douglas and Lincoln were an amusing sight. Douglas was short and his build was very square; his nickname was the "Little Giant." Lincoln, on

Read the Document

The Lincoln-Douglas Debates (1858) at **www.myhistorylab.com**

the other hand, was very tall and very thin. Both were eloquent and powerful speakers. In every town, audiences of 10,000 to 15,000 listened attentively and responded vocally to each speaker's long and thought-packed arguments.

Douglas had many strengths going into the debates. He spoke for the Union, he claimed, pointing out that the Democratic Party was a national party whereas the Republican Party was only sectional. He repeatedly appealed to the racism of much of his audience with declarations such as, "I would not blot out the great inalienable rights of the white men for all the negroes that ever existed!" Calling his opponent a "Black Republican," he implied that Lincoln and his party favored the social equality of whites and blacks, even race mixing.

Lincoln did not believe in the social equality of the races, but he did believe wholeheartedly that slavery was a moral wrong. Pledging the Republican Party to the "ultimate extinction" of slavery, Lincoln continually warned that Douglas's position would lead to the opposite result: the spread of slavery everywhere. Although in this argument Lincoln was addressing the northern fear of an expansionist "slave power," he strove at the same time to present himself as a moderate. He did not favor the breakup of the Union, but he never wavered from his antislavery stance.

The first of the seven debates, held in Ottawa, in northern Illinois, on Saturday, August 21, 1858, showed not only the seriousness but also the exuberance of the democratic politics of the time. By early morning, the town was jammed with people. The clouds of dust raised by carriages driving to Ottawa, one observer complained, turned the town into "a vast smoke house." By one o'clock, the town square was filled to overflowing, and the debate enthralled an estimated 12,000 people. Ottawa was pro-Republican, and the audience heckled Douglas unmercifully. At the second debate, a week later in Freeport, Douglas's use of the phrase "Black Republicans" drew angry shouts of "White, white" from the crowd. But as the debates moved south in the state, where Democrats predominated, the tables were turned, and Lincoln sometimes had to plead for a chance to be heard.

Although Douglas won the 1858 senatorial election in Illinois, the acclaim that Lincoln gained in the famous debates helped establish the Republicans'

1. Why did people in the North and the South tend to see the issue of slavery so differently?

2. Why were the politicians of the 1850s unable to find a lasting political compromise on the issue of slavery?

3. What was the intent of the Compromise of 1850?

4. What explains the end of the Second American Party System and the rise of the Republican Party?

5. Why did the South secede following the Republican Party victory in the election of 1860?

FOCUS Questions

the 1850s

claim to be the only party capable of stopping the spread of slavery and made Lincoln himself a strong contender for the Republican presidential nomination in 1860. But the true winners of the Lincoln–Douglas debates were the people of Illinois who gathered peacefully to discuss the most serious issue of their time. The young German immigrant Carl Schurz, who attended the Quincy debate, was deeply impressed by its democratic character. He noted, "There was no end of cheering and shouting and jostling on the streets of Quincy that day. But in spite of the excitement created by the political contest, the crowds remained very good-natured, and the occasional jibes flung from one side to the other were uniformly received with a laugh."

—Illinois

The Lincoln–Douglas debates are famous for their demonstration of the widespread public belief in commonality and community to resolve disagreements. Unfortunately, differences that could be resolved through conversation and friendship in the local community were less easy to resolve at the national level. In the highly charged and highly public political atmosphere of Congress, politicians struggled in vain to find compromises to hold the national community together.

AMERICAN Communities

America in 1850

The swift victory in the Mexican-American War, topped by the "prize" of California gold discussed in Chapter 14, bolstered American national pride and self-confidence. Certainly, the America of 1850 was a very different nation from the republic of 1800. Geographic expansion, population increase, economic development, and the changes wrought by the market revolution had transformed the struggling new nation. Economically, culturally, and politically Americans had forged a strong sense of national identity.

Expansion and Growth

America was now a much larger nation than it had been in 1800. Through war and diplomacy, the country had grown to continental dimensions, more than tripling in size from 890,000 to 3 million square miles. Its population had increased enormously from 5.3 million in 1800 to more than 23 million, 4 million of whom were African American slaves and 2 million new immigrants, largely from Germany and Ireland. Comprising just sixteen states in 1800, America in 1850 had thirty-one states, and more than half of the population lived west of the Appalachians. America's cities had undergone the most rapid half century of growth they were ever to experience (see Map 15.1).

America was also much richer: it is estimated that real per capita income doubled between 1800 and 1850, moving the nation decisively out of the "developing" category. Southern cotton, which had contributed so much to American economic growth, continued to be the nation's principal export, but it was no longer the major influence on the domestic economy. The growth of manufacturing

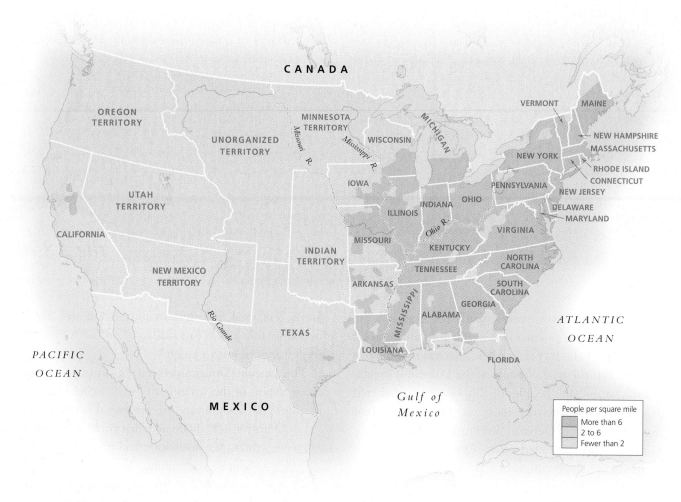

MAP 15.1 U.S. Population and Settlement, 1850 By 1850, the United States was a continental nation. Its people, whom Thomas Jefferson had once thought would not reach the Mississippi River for forty generations, had not only passed the river but also leapfrogged to the West Coast. In comparison to the America of 1800 (see Map 9.1 on p. 222), the growth was astounding.

in the Northeast and the rapid opening up of rich farmlands in the Midwest had serious domestic implications. As the South's share of responsibility for economic growth waned, so did its political importance—at least in the eyes of many Northerners. Thus, the very success of the United States both in geographic expansion and in economic development served to undermine the role of the South in national politics and to hasten the day of open conflict between the slave South and the free-labor North and Midwest.

Politics, Culture, and National Identity

The notion of "manifest destiny" first expressed in the expansionist fervor of the 1840s was based on a widespread belief among Americans in the superiority of their democracy. This belief was a unifying theme in a growing sense of national identity and the new middle-class values, institutions, and culture that supported it. Since the

turn of the century, American writers had struggled to find distinctive American themes, and these efforts bore fruit in the 1850s in the burst of creative activity termed the "American Renaissance." Newspapers, magazines, and communication improvements of all kinds created a national audience for the American scholars and writers who emerged during this decade.

During the American Renaissance, American writers pioneered new literary forms. Nathaniel Hawthorne, in works like "Young Goodman Brown" (1835), raised the short story to a distinctive American literary form. Poets like Walt Whitman and Emily Dickinson experimented with unrhymed and "off-rhyme" verse. Henry David Thoreau published *Walden* in 1854. A pastoral celebration of his life at Walden Pond, in Concord, Massachusetts, the essay was also a searching meditation on the cost to the individual of the loss of contact with nature that was a consequence of the market revolution.

Indeed, although the midcentury popular mood was one of self-congratulation, most of the writers of the American Renaissance were social critics. In *The Scarlet Letter* (1850) and *The House of the Seven Gables* (1851), Nathaniel Hawthorne brilliantly exposed the repressive and hypocritical aspects of Puritan New England in the colonial period and the often impossible moral choices faced by individuals. Hawthorne's friend Herman Melville, in his great work *Moby-Dick* (1851), used the story of Captain Ahab's obsessive search for the white whale to write a profound study of the nature of good and evil and a critique of American society in the 1850s. The strongest social critique, however, was Frederick Douglass's starkly simple autobiography, *Narrative of the Life of Frederick Douglass* (1845), which told of his brutal life as a slave.

The most successful American novel of the midnineteenth century was also about the great issue of the day—slavery. In writing *Uncle Tom's Cabin*, Harriet Beecher Stowe combined the literary style of the popular women's domestic novels of the time (discussed in Chapter 12) with vivid details of slavery culled from firsthand accounts by northern abolitionists and escaped slaves. Stowe, the daughter of the reforming clergyman Lyman Beecher, had married a Congregational minister and had herself long been active in antislavery work. Her famous novel told a poignant story of the Christ-like slave Uncle Tom, who patiently endured the cruel treatment of an evil white overseer, Simon Legree.

●▪●[Read the **Document**
A New England Writer Portrays Slavery in 1852 at **www.myhistorylab.com**

Published in 1851, it was a runaway best seller. More than 300,000 copies were sold in the first year, and within ten years, the book had sold more than 2 million copies, becoming the all-time American best seller in proportion to population. Turned into a play that remained popular throughout the nineteenth century, *Uncle Tom's Cabin* reached an even wider audience. Scenes from the novel such as that of Eliza carrying her son across the ice-choked Ohio River to freedom, Tom weeping for his children as he was sold south, and the death of little Eva are among the best-known passages in all of American literature. *Uncle Tom's Cabin* was more than a heart-tugging story: it was a call to action. In 1863, when Harriet Beecher Stowe was introduced to Abraham Lincoln, the president is said to have remarked, "So you're the little woman who wrote the book that made this great war!"

Cracks in National Unity

Stowe's novel clearly spoke to the growing concern of the American people. The year 1850 opened to the most serious political crisis the United States had ever known. The issue raised by the 1846 Wilmot Proviso—whether slavery should be extended to the new territories—could no longer be ignored (see Chapter 14). Furthermore, California, made rich and populous by the gold rush, applied for statehood in 1850, thereby reopening the issue of the balance between slave and free states.

The Compromise of 1850

The Compromise of 1850 was actually five separate bills (lacking a majority for a comprehensive measure), embodying three separate compromises.

First, California was admitted as a free state, but the status of the remaining former

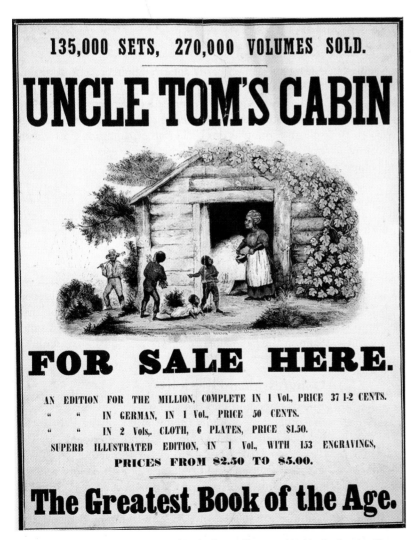

135,000 SETS, 270,000 VOLUMES SOLD.

UNCLE TOM'S CABIN

FOR SALE HERE.

AN EDITION FOR THE MILLION, COMPLETE IN 1 Vol., PRICE 37 1-2 CENTS.
"   "   IN GERMAN, IN 1 Vol., PRICE 50 CENTS.
"   "   IN 2 Vols., CLOTH, 6 PLATES, PRICE $1.50.
SUPERB ILLUSTRATED EDITION, IN 1 Vol., WITH 153 ENGRAVINGS,
PRICES FROM $2.50 TO $5.00.

The Greatest Book of the Age.

This poster advertises *Uncle Tom's Cabin*, the best-selling novel by Harriet Beecher Stowe. The poignant story of long-suffering African American slaves had an immense impact on Northern popular opinion, swaying it decisively against slavery. In that respect, the poster's boast, "The Greatest Book of the Age," was correct.

OVERVIEW | The Great Sectional Compromises

1820	Missouri Compromise	Admits Missouri to the Union as a slave state and Maine as a free state; prohibits slavery in the rest of the Louisiana Purchase Territory north of 36°30′.
		Territory Covered: The entire territory of the Louisiana Purchase, exclusive of the state of Louisiana, which had been admitted to the Union in 1812.
1850	Compromise of 1850	Admits California to the Union as a free state, settles the borders of Texas (a slave state); sets no conditions concerning slavery for the rest of the territory acquired from Mexico. Enacts national Fugitive Slave Law.
		Territory Covered: The territory that had been part of Mexico before the end of the Mexican-American War and the Treaty of Guadalupe Hidalgo (1848): part of Texas, California, Utah Territory (now Utah, Nevada, and part of Colorado), and New Mexico Territory (now New Mexico and Arizona).

Mexican possessions was left to be decided by popular sovereignty (a vote of the territory's inhabitants) when they applied for statehood. Utah's application for statehood was not accepted until 1896 because of controversy over the Mormon practice of polygamy. The result was, for the time being, fifteen slave states and sixteen free states. Second, Texas (a slave state) was required to cede land to New Mexico Territory (free or slave status undecided). In return, the federal government assumed $10 million of debts Texas had incurred before it became a state. Finally, the slave trade, but not slavery itself, was ended in the District of Columbia, but a stronger fugitive slave law, to be enforced in all states, was enacted (see Map 15.2).

Read the Document
Daniel Webster, Speech to the U.S. Senate (1850) at **www.myhistorylab.com**

See the Map
The Compromise of 1850 at **www.myhistorylab.com**

Jubilation and relief greeted the news that compromise had been achieved, but analysis of the votes on the five bills that made up the compromise revealed no consistent majority. The sectional splits within each party that had existed before the compromise remained. Antislavery northern Whigs and proslavery southern Democrats, each the larger wing of their party, were the least willing to compromise.

Political Parties Split over Slavery

The Second American Party System, forged in the great controversies of Andrew Jackson's presidency (see Chapter 11), was a national party system. At a time when the ordinary person still had very strong sectional loyalties, the mass political party created a national community of like-minded voters. Yet, by the election of 1848, sectional interests were eroding the political "glue" in both parties.

Although each party still appeared united, sectional fissures ran deep.

Political splits were preceded by divisions in other social institutions. Disagreements about slavery had already split the country's great religious organizations into northern and southern groups: the Presbyterians in 1837, the Methodists in 1844, and the Baptists in 1845. (Some of these splits turned out to be permanent. The Southern Baptist Convention, for example, is still a separate body.) Theodore Weld, the abolitionist leader, saw these splits as inevitable: "Events . . . have for years been silently but without a moment's pause, settling the basis of two great parties, the nucleus of one slavery, of the other, freedom." Indeed, the abolitionists had been posing this simple yet uncompromising choice between slavery and freedom since the 1830s. Moreover, they had been insisting on a compelling distinction: as Liberty Party spokesman Salmon P. Chase said, "Freedom is national; slavery only is local and sectional."

Congressional Divisions

But was freedom national and slavery sectional, or was it the other way around? In the midst of the debate that preceded the Compromise of 1850, President Zachary Taylor died of acute gastroenteritis, caused by a hasty snack of fruit and cold milk at a Fourth of July celebration. A bluff military man, Taylor had been prepared to follow Andrew Jackson's precedent during the Nullification Crisis of 1832 and simply demand that Southern dissidents compromise. Vice President Millard Fillmore, who assumed the presidency, was a much weaker man who did not seize the opportunity for presidential action.

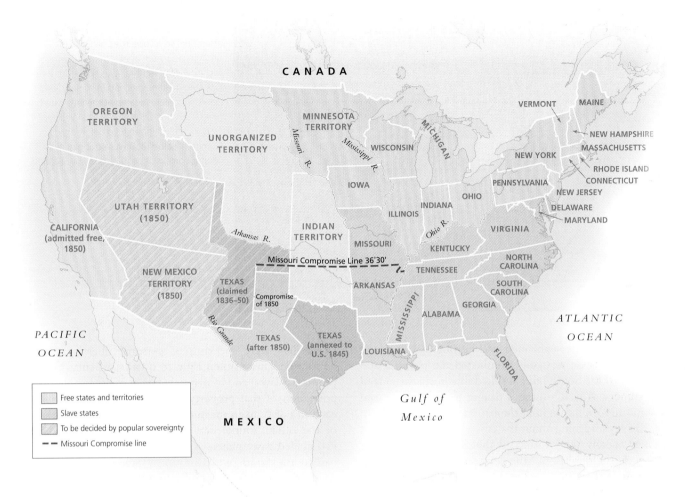

MAP 15.2 The Compromise of 1850 The Compromise of 1850, messier and more awkward than the Missouri Compromise of 1820, reflected heightened sectional tensions. California was admitted as a free state, the borders of Texas were settled, and the status of the rest of the former Mexican territory was left to be decided later by popular sovereignty. No consistent majority voted for the five separate bills that made up the compromise.

And Southerners, personified by John C. Calhoun, were unwilling to compromise. Calhoun, who had uncompromisingly spoken for the slave South since the Nullification Crisis in 1828 (see Chapter 11) insisted that the states' rights doctrine was necessary to protect the legitimate rights of a minority in a democratic system governed by majority rule. Now in 1850 Calhoun broadened his argument to insist that Congress did not have a constitutional right to prohibit slavery in the territories. The territories, he said, were the common property of all the states, North and South, and slave owners had a constitutional right to the protection of their property wherever they moved.

Calhoun's position on the territories quickly became Southern dogma: anything less than full access to the territories was unconstitutional. As Congressman Robert Toombs of Georgia put the case in 1850, the choice was stark: "Give us our just rights and we are ready to stand by the Union. Refuse [them] and for one, I will strike for independence." Calhoun, Toombs, and other Southerners were insisting that slavery had to be national.

Calhoun's failing health served to make his ultimatum all the more ominous. He brought an aura of death with him as he sat on the Senate floor for the last time, listening to the speech that he was too ill to read for himself. He died less than a month later, still insisting on the right of the South to secede if necessary to preserve its way of life.

The Southern threat to secede confirmed for many Northerners the warnings of antislavery leaders that they were endangered by a menacing "slave power." Liberty Party leader James Birney, in a speech in 1844, was the first to add this phrase to the nation's political vocabulary. "The

In 1850, the three men who had long represented America's three major regions attempted to resolve the political crisis brought on by the application of California for statehood. Henry Clay is speaking; John C. Calhoun stands second from right; and Daniel Webster is seated at the left, with his head in his hand. Both Clay and Webster were ill, and Calhoun died before the Compromise of 1850 was arranged by a younger group of politicians led by Stephen A. Douglas.

slave power," Birney explained, was a group of aristocratic slave owners who not only dominated the political and social life of the South but conspired to control the federal government as well, posing a danger to free speech and free institutions throughout the nation.

Birney's warning about the "slave power" in 1844 had seemed merely the overheated rhetoric of an extremist group of abolitionists. But the defensive Southern political strategies of the 1850s convinced an increasing number of Northern voters that "the slave power" did in fact exist. The long-standing proslavery strategy of maintaining supremacy in the Senate by having at least as many slave as free states admitted to the Union (a plan that required slavery expansion) now looked like a conspiracy by sectional interests to control national politics. In Northern eyes, the South became a demonic monolith that threatened the national government.

Two Communities, Two Perspectives

Ironically, it was their common commitment to expansion that made the argument between Northerners and Southerners so irreconcilable. Southerners had been the strongest supporters of the Mexican-American War, and they still hoped to expand into Cuba. On the other hand, although many Northern Whigs had opposed the Mexican-American War, most did so for antislavery reasons, not because they opposed expansion. The strong showing of the Free-Soil Party (which evolved out of the Liberty Party) in the election of 1848 (getting 10 percent of the popular vote) was proof of that. Basically, both North and South believed in manifest destiny, but each on its own terms.

Similarly, both North and South used the language of basic rights and liberties in the debate over expansion. But

free-soilers were speaking of personal liberty, whereas Southerners meant their right to own a particular kind of property (slaves) and to maintain a way of life based on the possession of that property. In defending its own rights, each side had taken measures that infringed on the rights of the other. Southerners pointed out that abolitionists had libeled slave owners as a class and that they had bombarded the South with unwanted literature, abused the right of petition to Congress, incited slaves to rebellion, and actively helped slaves to escape. For their part, Northerners accused slave owners of censorship of the mails; imposition of the "gag rule" (repealed in 1844), which prohibited any petition against slavery from being read to or discussed by Congress; suppression of free speech in the South; and, of course, commission of the moral wrong of enslaving others in the first place.

By 1850, North and South had created fixed stereotypes of the other. To antislavery Northerners, the South was an economic backwater dominated by a small slave-owning aristocracy that lived off the profits of forced labor and deprived poor whites of their democratic rights and the fruits of honest work. The slave system was not only immoral but also a drag on the entire nation, for, in the words of Senator William Seward of New York, it subverted the "intelligence, vigor and energy" that were essential for national growth.

Things looked very different through Southern eyes. Far from being economically backward, the South, through its export of cotton, was, according to Southerners, the great engine of national economic growth from which the North benefited. Slavery was not only a blessing to an inferior race but also the cornerstone of democracy, for it ensured the freedom and independence of all white men without entailing the bitter class divisions that marked the North. Slave own-ers accused Northern manufacturers of hypocrisy for practicing "wage slavery" without the paternal benevo-lence they claimed to bestow on their slaves. The North, James Henry Hammond of South Carolina charged, had eliminated the "name [of slavery], but not the thing," for "your whole hireling class of manual laborers and 'oper-atives' . . . are essentially slaves" (see Communities in Conflict, Chapter 10).

By the early 1850s, these vastly different visions of the North and the South—the result of many years of political controversy—had become fixed, and the chances of national reconciliation increasingly slim. Over the course of the decade, many Americans came to believe that the place of slavery in the nation's life had to be permanently settled. And they increasingly wondered whether their two sectional communities—one slave, one free—could continue to be part of a uni-tary national one.

In the country as a whole, the feeling was that the Compromise of 1850 had solved the question of slavery in the territories. The *Philadelphia Pennsylvanian* was confi-dent that "peace and tranquility" had been ensured, and the *Louisville Journal* said that a weight seemed to have been lifted from the heart of America. But many Southerners felt that their only real gain in the contested compromise was the Fugitive Slave Law, which quickly turned out to be an inflammatory measure.

The Fugitive Slave Law

From the early days of their movement, Northern aboli-tionists had urged slaves to escape, promising assistance and support when they reached the North. Some free African Americans had given far more than verbal support, and most escaped slaves found their most reliable help within Northern free black communities. Northerners had long been appalled by professional slave catchers, who zealously seized African Americans in the North and took them south into slavery again. Most abhorrent in Northern eyes was that captured black people were at the mercy of slave catchers because they had no legal right to defend them-selves. In more than one case, a free African American was captured in his own community and helplessly shipped into slavery.

As a result of stories like this, nine Northern states passed personal liberty laws between 1842 and 1850, serv-ing notice that they would not cooperate with federal recapture efforts. These laws enraged Southerners, who had long been convinced that all Northerners, not just abolitionists, were actively hindering efforts to reclaim their escaped slaves.

The Fugitive Slave Law, enacted in 1850, dramati-cally increased the power of slave owners to capture escaped slaves. The full authority of the federal govern-ment now supported slave owners, and although fugitives

were guaranteed a hearing before a federal commis-sioner, they were not allowed to testify on their own behalf. Furthermore, the new law imposed federal penalties on citi-zens who protected or assisted fugitives or who did not cooper-ate in their return. A number of free Northern blacks, estimated at 30,000 to 40,000, emigrated to Canada to avoid the possibility of capture.

Read the **Document**
Benjamin Drew, from Narratives of Fugitive Slaves in Canada (1855) at www.myhistorylab.com

In Boston, the center of the American abolitionist movement, reaction to the Fugitive Slave Law was fierce. When an escaped slave named Shadrach Minkins was seized in February 1851, a group of African American men broke into the courtroom, overwhelmed the federal marshals, seized Minkins, and sent him safely to Canada. The action had community support and a Massachusetts jury defiantly refused to convict the perpetrators.

In the most famous Boston case, a biracial group of armed abolitionists led by Unitarian clergyman Thomas

JD9512 Recaptured Slave circa 1854
Anthony Burns (1834 - 1862) surrounded by scenes of his capture. He was arrested in Boston in May 1854 on a charge of theft. Recognised as a fugitive slave, his return to Virginia was the cause of riots. After he was bought out of slavery, he later became pastor of a Negro baptist church in St. Catherine's Canada.
PHOTO: HULTON GETTY / LIAISON AGENCY

Escaped slave Anthony Burns, shown here surrounded by scenes of his capture in 1854, was the cause of Boston's greatest protest against the Fugitive Slave Law. The injustice of his trial and shipment back to the South converted many Bostonians to the antislavery cause.

Wentworth Higginson stormed the federal courthouse in 1854 in an attempt to save escaped slave Anthony Burns. The rescue effort failed, and a federal deputy marshal was killed. President Pierce sent marines, cavalry, and artillery to Boston to reinforce the guard over Burns and ordered a federal ship to be ready to deliver the fugitive back into slavery. When the effort by defense lawyers to argue for Burns's freedom failed, Bostonians raised money to buy his freedom. But the U.S. attorney, ordered by the president to enforce the Fugitive Slave Law in all circumstances, blocked the purchase. The case was lost, and Burns was marched to the docks through streets lined with sorrowing abolitionists. Buildings were shrouded in black and draped with American flags hanging upside down, while bells tolled as if for a funeral.

The Burns case radicalized many Northerners. Conservative Whig George Hilliard wrote to a friend, "When it was all over, and I was left alone in my office, I put my face in my hands and wept. I could do nothing less." During the 1850s, 322 black fugitives were sent back into slavery; only 11 were declared free.

In this volatile atmosphere, escaped African Americans wrote and lectured bravely on behalf of freedom. Frederick Douglass, the most famous and eloquent of the fugitive slaves, spoke out fearlessly in support of armed resistance. Openly active in the underground network that helped slaves reach safety in Canada, Douglass himself had been constantly in danger of capture until his friends bought his freedom in 1847. Harriet Jacobs, who escaped to the North after seven years in hiding in the South, wrote bitterly in her *Incidents in the Life of a Slave Girl* (1861) that "I was, in fact, a slave in New York, as subject to slave laws as I had been in a slave state . . . I had been chased during half my life, and it seemed as if the chase was never to end." Threatened by owners who came north for her, Jacobs was forced into hiding while Northern white friends arranged her purchase. "A gentleman near me said, 'It's true; I have seen the bill of sale.' 'The bill of sale!' Those words struck me like a blow. So I was sold at last! A human being sold in the free city of New York!"

●●▶ Read the Document
Harriet Jacobs, Incidents in the Life of a Slave Girl (1861) at
www.myhistorylab.com

The Fugitive Slave Law made slavery national and forced Northern communities to confront the full meaning of slavery. Although most people were still unwilling to grant social equality to the free African Americans who lived in the Northern states, more and more had come to believe that the institution of slavery was wrong. The strong Northern reaction against the Fugitive Slave Law also had consequences in the South. Northern protests against the Fugitive Slave Law bred suspicion in the South and encouraged secessionist thinking. These new currents of public opinion were reflected in the election of 1852.

CAUTION!!
COLORED PEOPLE
OF BOSTON, ONE & ALL,
You are hereby respectfully CAUTIONED and advised, to avoid conversing with the
Watchmen and Police Officers of Boston,
For since the recent ORDER OF THE MAYOR & ALDERMEN, they are empowered to act as
KIDNAPPERS
AND
Slave Catchers,
And they have already been actually employed in KIDNAPPING, CATCHING, AND KEEPING SLAVES. Therefore, if you value your LIBERTY, and the *Welfare of the Fugitives* among you, *Shun* them in every possible manner, as so many *HOUNDS* on the track of the most unfortunate of your race.
Keep a Sharp Look Out for KIDNAPPERS, and have TOP EYE open.
APRIL 24, 1851.

This handbill warning free African Americans of danger circulated in Boston following the first of the infamous recaptures under the Fugitive Slave Law, that of Thomas Sims in 1851.

The Election of 1852

The first sign of the weakening of the national party system in 1852 was the difficulty both parties experienced at their nominating conventions. After fifty-two ballots General Winfield Scott (a military hero like two of the party's previous three candidates), rather than the sitting President Fillmore, was nominated. Many Southern Whigs were permanently alienated by the choice; although Whigs were still elected to Congress from the South, their loyalty to the national party was strained to the breaking point. The Whigs never again fielded a presidential candidate.

The Democrats had a wider variety of candidates: Lewis Cass of popular sovereignty fame; Stephen Douglas, architect of the Compromise of 1850; and James Buchanan, described as a "northern man with southern principles." Cass, Douglas, and Buchanan competed for forty-nine ballots, each strong enough to block the others but not strong enough to win. Finally, the party turned to a handsome, affable nonentity, Franklin Pierce of New Hampshire, who was thought to have Southern sympathies. Uniting on a platform pledging "faithful execution" of all parts of the Compromise of 1850, including the Fugitive Slave Law, Democrats polled well in the South and in the North. Most Democrats who had voted for the Free-Soil Party in 1848 voted for Pierce. So, in record numbers, did immigrant Irish and German voters, who were eligible for citizenship after three years' residence. The strong immigrant vote for Pierce was a sign of the strength of Democratic Party organizations in Northern cities. Voter turnout was below 70 percent, lower than it had been since 1836.

"Young America": The Politics of Expansion

Pierce entered the White House in 1853 on a wave of good feeling. Massachusetts Whig Amos Lawrence reported, "Never since Washington has an administration commenced with the hearty [good] will of so large a portion of the country." This goodwill was soon strained by Pierce's support for the expansionist adventures of the "Young America" movement.

The "Young America" movement began as a group of writers and politicians in the New York Democratic Party who believed in the democratic and nationalistic promise of "manifest destiny" (a term coined by one of their members, John O'Sullivan). By the 1850s, however, their lofty goals had shrunk to a desire to conquer Central America and Cuba. Young America expansionists had glanced covetously southward since the end of the Mexican-American War. During the Pierce administration, several private "filibusters" (from the Spanish *filibustero*, meaning an "adventurer" or "pirate") invaded Caribbean and Central American countries, usually with the declared intention of extending slave territory. The best-known filibuster, William Walker, led not one but three invasions of Nicaragua. In 1855, Walker became ruler of the country and encouraged settlement by Southern slave owners, but he was unseated by a regional revolt in 1857. His subsequent efforts to regain control of the country failed, and in his last attempt, he was captured and executed by firing squad in Honduras.

The Pierce administration, not directly involved in the filibustering, *was* deeply involved in an effort to obtain Cuba. In 1854, Pierce authorized his minister to Spain, Pierre Soulé, to try to force the unwilling Spanish to sell Cuba for $130 million. Soulé met in Ostend, Belgium, with the American ministers to France and England, John Mason and James Buchanan, to compose the offer, which was a mixture of cajolements and threats. At first appealing to Spain to recognize the deep affinities between the Cubans and American Southerners that made them "one people with one destiny," the document went on to threaten to "wrest" Cuba from Spain if necessary. This amazing document, which became known as the Ostend

Manifesto, was supposed to be secret but was soon leaked to the press. Deeply embarrassed, the Pierce administration was forced to repudiate it.

In another expansionist gesture in another direction, President Franklin Pierce dispatched Commodore Matthew Perry across the Pacific to Japan, a nation famous for its insularity and hostility to outsiders. The mission resulted in 1854 in a commercial treaty that opened Japan to American trade. Perry's feat caused a newspaper in tiny Olympia, Washington, to boast, "We shall have the boundless Pacific for a market in manifest destiny. We were born to command it."

Overall, however, the complicity between the Pierce administration and proslavery expansionists was foolhardy and lost the Northern goodwill with which it had begun. The sectional crisis that preceded the Compromise of 1850 had made obvious the danger of reopening the territorial issue. Ironically, it was not the Young America expansionists but the prime mover of the Compromise of 1850, Stephen A. Douglas, who reignited the sectional struggle over slavery expansion.

The Crisis of the National Party System

In 1854, Douglas introduced the Kansas-Nebraska Act, proposing to open those lands that had been the northern part of Indian Territory to American settlers under the principle of popular sovereignty. He thereby reopened the question of slavery in the territories. Douglas knew he was taking a political risk, but he believed he could satisfy both his expansionist aims and his presidential ambitions. He was wrong: he pushed the national party system into crisis, first killing the Whigs and then destroying the Democrats.

The Kansas-Nebraska Act

In a stunning example of the expansionist pressures generated by the market revolution, Stephen Douglas introduced the Kansas-Nebraska Act to further the construction of a transcontinental railroad across what was still considered the "Great American Desert" to California. Douglas wanted the rail line to terminate in Chicago, in his own state of Illinois, rather than in the rival St. Louis, but for that to happen, the land west of Iowa and Missouri had to be organized into territories (the first step toward statehood). To get Congress to agree to the organization of the territories, however, Douglas needed the votes of Southern Democrats, who were unwilling to support him unless the territories were open to slavery.

Douglas thought he was solving his problem by proposing that the status of slavery in the new territories be governed by the principle of popular sovereignty. Democratic politicians had favored this democratic-sounding slogan, vague enough to appeal to both proslavery and antislavery voters, ever since 1848. Douglas

A Japanese painting shows Commodore Matthew Perry landing in Japan in 1853. The commercial treaty Perry signed with the Japanese government, which opened a formerly closed country to American trade, was viewed in the United States as another fruit of manifest destiny.

SOURCE: *The Landing of Commodore Perry in Japan in 1853.* (Detail) Japanese, Edo period, 19th century. Handscroll; ink and color on paper, 10 7/8 × 211 1/8 in. (27.6 × 536.3 cm). Museum of Fine Arts, Boston. William Sturgis Bigelow Collection, RES.11.6054. Photograph © 2006 Museum of Fine Arts, Boston.

thought Southerners would support his bill because of its popular sovereignty provision and Northerners because it

⊙ See the Map
The Kansas-Nebraska Act at **www.myhistorylab.com**
favored a northern route for the transcontinental railroad. Douglas chose also to downplay the price he had to pay for Southern support—by allowing the possibility of slavery in the new territories, his bill in effect repealed the Missouri Compromise of 1820, which barred slavery north of latitude 36°30′ (see Map 15.3).

The Kansas-Nebraska bill passed, but it badly strained the major political parties. Southern Whigs voted with Southern Democrats in favor of the measure; Northern Whigs rejected it absolutely, creating an irreconcilable split that left Whigs unable to field a presidential candidate in 1856. The damage to the Democratic Party was almost as great. In the congressional elections of 1854, Northern Democrats lost two-thirds of their seats (a drop from ninety-one to twenty-five), giving the Southern Democrats (who were solidly in favor of slavery extension) the dominant voice both in Congress and within the party.

Douglas had committed one of the greatest miscalculations in American political history. A storm of protest arose throughout the North. More than 300 large anti-Nebraska rallies occurred during congressional consideration of the bill, and the anger did not subside. Douglas, who confidently believed that "the people of the North will sustain the measure when they come to understand

it," found himself shouted down more than once at public rallies when he tried to explain the bill.

The Kansas-Nebraska bill shifted a crucial sector of Northern opinion: the wealthy merchants, bankers, and manufacturers, known as the "Cotton Whigs," who had economic ties with Southern slave owners and had always disapproved of abolitionist activity. Convinced that the bill would encourage antislavery feeling in the North, Cotton Whigs urged Southern politicians to vote against it, only to be ignored. Passage of the Kansas-Nebraska Act convinced many Northern Whigs that compromise with the South was impossible.

In Kansas in 1854, hasty treaties were concluded with the Indian tribes who owned the land. Some, such as the Kickapoos, Shawnees, Sauks, and Foxes, agreed to relocate to small reservations. Others, like the Delawares, Weas, and Iowas, agreed to sell their lands to whites. Still others, such as the Cheyennes and Sioux, kept the western part of Kansas Territory (now Colorado)—until gold was discovered there in 1859. Once the treaties were signed, both proslavery and antislavery white settlers began to pour in, and the battle was on.

"Bleeding Kansas"

The first to claim land in Kansas were residents of nearby Missouri, itself a slave state. Missourians took up land claims, established proslavery strongholds such as the towns of Leavenworth, Kickapoo, and Atchison, and repeatedly and

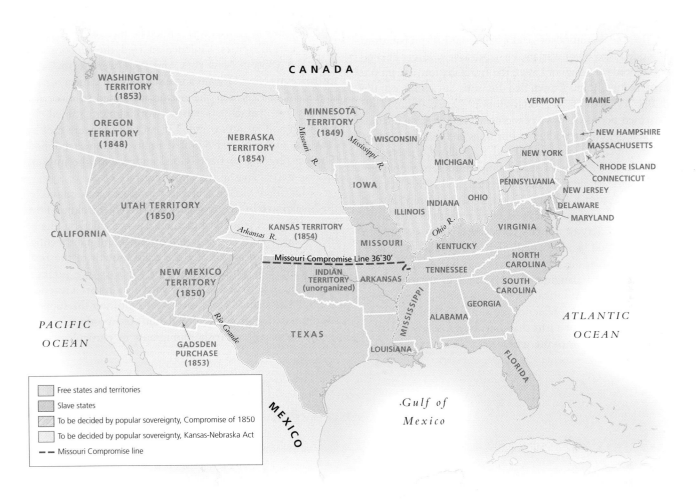

MAP 15.3 The Kansas–Nebraska Act, 1854 The Kansas–Nebraska Act, proposed by Steven A. Douglas in 1854, opened the central and northern Great Plains to settlement. The act had two major faults: it robbed Indian peoples of half the territory guaranteed to them by treaty and, because it repealed the Missouri Compromise line, it opened up the lands to warring proslavery and antislavery factions.

blatantly swamped Kansas elections with Missouri votes. In 1855, in the second of several notoriously fraudulent elections, 6,307 ballots were cast in a territory that had fewer than 3,000 eligible voters. Most of the proslavery votes were cast by "border ruffians," as they proudly called themselves, from Missouri. These were frontiersmen, fond of boasting that they could "scream louder, jump higher, shoot closer, get drunker at night and wake up soberer in the morning than any man this side of the Rocky Mountains."

Northerners quickly responded. The first party of New Englanders arrived in the summer of 1854 and established the free-soil town of Lawrence, named for former "Cotton Whig" Amos Lawrence, who financed them. More than a thousand others had joined them by the following summer. Many Northern migrants were free-soilers, and many were religious reformers as well. The

contrast of values between them and the border ruffians was almost total. When nondrinking William Phillips stiffly refused a friendly offer of a drink from a Missourian, the border ruffian burst out, "That's just it! This thing of temperance and abolitionism and the Emigrant Aid Society are all the same kind of thing."

Kansas soon became a bloody battleground as the two factions struggled to secure the mandate of "popular sovereignty." Free-soilers in Lawrence received shipments of heavy crates, innocuously marked "BOOKS" but actually containing Sharps repeating rifles, sent by eastern supporters. For their part, the border ruffians—already heavily armed, with Bowie knives in their boots, revolvers at their waists, rifles slung from their shoulders, and swords at their sides—called for reinforcements. Senator David Atchison of Missouri exhorted Alabamans: "Let your young men come forth to Missouri and Kansas! Let them come well armed!"

In the summer of 1856, these lethal preparations exploded into open warfare. First, proslavery forces burned and looted the town of Lawrence. In retaliation, a grim old man named John Brown led his sons in a raid on the proslavery settlers of Pottawatomie Creek, killing five unarmed people. A wave of violence ensued. Armed bands roamed the countryside, and burnings and killings became commonplace. John Brown and his followers were just one of many bands of marauding murderers who were never arrested, never brought to trial, and never stopped from committing further violence. Peaceful residents of large sections of rural Kansas were repeatedly forced to flee to the safety of military forts when rumors of one or another armed band reached them.

The rest of the nation watched in horror as the residents of Kansas slaughtered each other in the pursuit of sectional goals. Americans' pride in their nation's great achievements was threatened by the endless violence in one small part—but a part that increasingly seemed to represent the divisions of the whole.

The Politics of Nativism

The violence in Kansas was echoed by increasing violence in the nation's cities. Violence marred the elections of 1854 and 1856 in New York, and there were serious disturbances in New Orleans and elsewhere. In Chicago, riots started in 1855, when the mayor attempted to close the saloons on Sunday. German workingmen joined by Irishmen and Swedes paraded in protest and were met by 200 men of the National Guard, militia, and special police. The ensuing "Lager Beer Riots" ended with the imposition of martial law on the entire city.

This urban violence, like that in Kansas, was caused by the breakdown of the two-party system. The breakup of the Whig Party left a political vacuum that was filled by one of the strongest bursts of nativism, or anti-immigrant feeling, in American history, and by the rapid growth of the new American Party, which formed in 1850 to give political expression to nativism. The new party was in part a reaction to the Democratic Party's success in capturing the support of the rapidly growing population of mostly Catholic foreign-born voters. Irish immigrants in particular voted

Lawrence, the center of free-soil sentiment in Kansas, was burned and looted by proslavery opponents in 1856. Events like this, perpetrated by pro- and antislavery forces alike, earned the territory the name, "Bleeding Kansas."

Brooks Beats Sumner

In a violent episode on the floor of the U.S. Senate in 1856, Senator Charles Sumner of Massachusetts suffered permanent injury when Congressman Preston Brooks of South Carolina beat him so hard with his cane that it broke. A few days earlier, Sumner had given an insulting antislavery speech in which he had singled out for ridicule Senator Andrew Butler of South Carolina. Senator Butler was Preston Brooks's uncle; in Brooks's mind, he was simply avenging an intolerable affront to his uncle's honor.

So far had the behavioral codes of North and South diverged that each man found his own action perfectly justifiable and the action of the other outrageous. Their attitudes were mirrored in their respective sections. Protest rallies were held in most northern cities; Sumner himself received sympathy letters from hundreds of strangers, all expressing indignation, as one writer put it, over "the most foul, most damnable and dastardly attack," and sympathetic illustrations like this one appeared in northern papers. In contrast, southern newspapers almost unanimously supported Brooks, regarding it as a well-deserved whipping for an intolerable insult. A group of Charleston merchants even bought Brooks a new cane inscribed: "Hit him again."

- **Is violence always a threat to democracy?**
- **Are there situations where it is justified?**
- **Is this one of those occasions?**

SOUTHERN CHIVALRY — ARGUMENT versus CLUB'S.

The Debate over Immigration

Briefly, in the early 1850s, the Know-Nothing Party rode the wave of widespread public apprehension about the new immigrants to political success. The following expression of views, first from a nativist, J. Wayne Laurens, and second from Senator William H. Seward, a leader of the new Republican Party, debated the nature of American citizenship.

• **Debates over immigration continue to this day, in much the same terms that Laurens and Seward argued in the 1850s. What does this continuing debate suggest about the nature of Americanism?**

From *The Crisis, or, the Enemies of America Unmasked*

Many of our leading statesmen have recently declared that no foreigner should be naturalized till he has resided in this country twenty-one years. But we care for no man's authority in so plain a case. The thing is self-evident. Americans should rule America; and the voters are really the rulers. None but a native born American would ever have been allowed to vote, if justice had been done, from the beginning. The franchise should have been held sacred. Let those vote, whose vote is already legalized. But when we come to revise the naturalization laws, . . . let us make thorough work of it, and in future grant the privilege of voting to no man who was not born on the American soil. We have had enough of artificial naturalizing. In all future time, let nature do the naturalizing herself. Then there will be no mistake, and no false swearing. Foreigners will cease to perjure themselves in order to acquire the privilege of fighting at the polls, and the interests of peace and good morals will be promoted . . . Let no American born citizen vote for a foreigner or for a man who will appoint foreigners to office, and the thing is done. We shall thus rid ourselves of the greatest evil with which this country was ever cursed.

> "We have had enough of artificial naturalizing . . . "

Democratic, both in reaction to Whig hostility (as in Boston) and because of their own antiblack prejudices. Frequently in competition with free African Americans for low-paying jobs, Irish immigrants were more likely to share the attitudes of Southerners than those of abolitionists.

The reformist and individualistic attitudes of many Whigs inclined them toward nativism. Many Whigs disapproved of the new immigrants because they were poor, Catholic, and often disdainful of the temperance movement. Moreover, nativist Whigs held immigration to be solely responsible for the increases in crime and the rising cost of relief for the poor that accompanied the astoundingly rapid urban growth of the 1830s and 1840s (see Chapter 13).

Nativism drew former Whigs, especially young men in white-collar and skilled blue-collar occupations, to the new American Party. At the core of the party were several secret fraternal societies open only to native-born Protestants who pledged never to vote for a Catholic, on the grounds that all Catholics took their orders straight from the pope in Rome. When questioned about their beliefs, party members maintained secrecy by answering, "I know nothing"—hence, the popular name for American Party members, the Know-Nothings. Publicly, the party proposed a twenty-one-year residency requirement before foreigners could vote and a head tax that would "restrain the most worthless and vicious of foreign emigrants from debarking on our shores."

Know-Nothings scored startling victories in Northern state elections in 1854, winning control of the legislature in Massachusetts and polling 40 percent of the vote in Pennsylvania. But in the 1850s, no party could ignore slavery, and in 1855, the American Party split into Northern (antislavery) and Southern (proslavery) wings. Soon after this split, many people who had voted for the Know-Nothings shifted their support to another new party, one that combined many characteristics of the Whigs with a westward-looking, expansionist, free-soil policy. This was the Republican Party, founded in 1854.

There has been a great deal of talk about liberality towards foreign nations. But what foreign nation has ever shown any liberality toward us? Why should we import voters, when we are permitted to export none? They want a free trade in voters corresponding with their free trade in other things, giving to them all the advantage and to us none whatever.

SOURCE: J. Wayne Laurens, *The Crisis, or, the Enemies of America Unmasked* (Philadelphia: G.D. Miller, 1855), pp. 34–35.

Remarks by Senator William Seward during a Senate debate about the Know Nothing "creed":

. . . It is my purpose to say nothing of the Know-Nothings, because of the Know-Nothings, as I have already stated, I know nothing at all. [*Laughter*] I am stating what purports to be the creed which comprehends all the articles of this principle of opposing foreign immigration. I need not discriminate here in favor of those principles which are national, those which are just, and those which are American. I need not point them out, and show which they are. It is sufficient for me to say that, in my judgment, every thing is un-American which makes a distinction, of whatever kind, in this country, between the native-born American and him whose lot is directed to be cast here by an overruling Providence, and who renounces his allegiance to a foreign land, and swears fealty to the country which adopts him.

I am an American citizen. So was my father, before me. Those who can trace their lineage further than I can, may be able to throw further back into antiquity the period when they, by their progenitors, were foreigners and aliens. I cannot certainly carry my genealogy back far enough to know whether it was more than three generations.

Why should I exclude the foreigner to-day? He is only what every American citizen, or his ancestor, was at some time or other. If he be an alien, he is, in the course of one, two, three, four, or five years, to become what we all are, American citizens. Sir, something has been said about loyalty. I desire to know where and when the foreigners, the aliens, in this country, have shown less loyalty to their Government, and to its institutions, than the native citizens?

SOURCE: Senator William H. Seward, *Congressional Globe/United States Congress* (Washington, Blair and Rives, 1854) 33rd Congress, July 12, 1854.

"The foreigner today . . . is only what every American citizen was . . ."

The Republican Party and the Election of 1856

Many constituencies found room in the new Republican Party. Its supporters included many former Northern Whigs who opposed slavery absolutely, many Free-Soil Party supporters who opposed the expansion of slavery but were willing to tolerate it in the South, and many Northern reformers concerned about temperance and Catholicism. The Republicans also attracted the economic core of the old Whig Party—the merchants and industrialists who wanted a strong national government to promote economic growth by supporting a protective tariff, transportation improvements, and cheap land for western farmers. In quieter times, it would have taken this party a while to sort out all its differences and become a true political community. But because of the sectional crisis, the fledgling party nearly won its very first presidential election.

The immediate question facing the nation in 1856 was which new party, the Know-Nothings or the Republicans, would emerge the stronger. But the more important question was whether the Democratic Party could hold together. The two strongest contenders for the Democratic nomination were President Pierce and Stephen A. Douglas. Douglas had proposed the Kansas-Nebraska Act and Pierce had actively supported it. Both men, therefore, had the support of the southern wing of the party. But it was precisely their support of this act that made Northerners oppose both of them. The Kansas-Nebraska Act's divisive effect on the Democratic Party now became clear: no one who had voted on the bill, either for or against, could satisfy both wings of the party. A compromise candidate was found in James Buchanan of Pennsylvania, the "northern man with southern principles." Luckily for him, he had been ambassador to Great Britain at the time of the Kansas-Nebraska Act and, thus, had not had to commit himself.

This nighttime meeting of supporters of the Know-Nothing Party in New York City was dramatically spotlighted by a new device borrowed from the theater, an incandescent calcium light, popularly called a limelight.

The election of 1856 appeared to be a three-way contest that pitted Buchanan against explorer John C. Frémont of the Republican Party and the American (Know-Nothing) Party's candidate, former president Millard Fillmore (see Map 15.4).

In fact, the election was two separate contests, one in the North and one in the South. The Northern race was between Buchanan and Frémont, the Southern one between Buchanan and Fillmore. Frémont's name appeared on the ballot in only four southern states, all in the Upper South, and even there he polled almost no votes. Fillmore attracted more than 40 percent of the vote in ten slave states. Frémont decisively defeated Buchanan in the North, winning eleven of sixteen free states. Buchanan, however, won the election with only 45 percent of the popular vote, because he was the only national candidate. But the Republicans, after studying the election returns, claimed "victorious defeat," for they realized that in 1860, the addition of just two more northern states to their total would mean victory. Furthermore, the Republican Party had clearly defeated the American Party in the battle to win designation as a major party. These were grounds for great optimism—and great concern—for the Republican Party was a sectional, rather than a national, party; it drew almost all its support from the North. Southerners viewed its very existence as an attack on their vital interests. Thus, the rapid rise of the Republicans posed a growing threat to national unity.

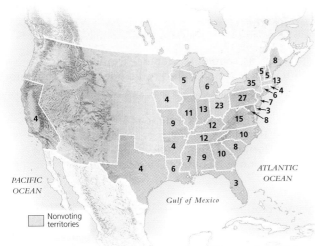

	Electoral Vote (%)	Popular Vote (%)
JAMES BUCHANAN (Democrat)	174 (59)	1,832,955 (45)
John C. Frémont (Republican)	114 (39)	1,339,932 (33)
Millard Fillmore (American)	8 (3)	871,731 (22)

MAP 15.4 The Election of 1856 Because three parties contested the 1856 election, Democrat James Buchanan was a minority president. Although Buchanan alone had national support, Republican John Frémont won most of the free states, and Millard Fillmore of the American Party gained 40 percent of the vote in most of the slave states.

The Differences Deepen

Although James Buchanan firmly believed that he alone could hold together a nation so split by hatred and violence, his self-confidence outran his abilities. He was so deeply indebted to the strong southern wing of the Democratic Party that he could not take the impartial actions necessary to heal "Bleeding Kansas." And his support for a momentous prosouthern decision by the Supreme Court further aggravated sectional differences.

The *Dred Scott* Decision

In *Dred Scott* v. *Sandford*, decided on March 6, 1857, two days after James Buchanan was sworn in, a Southern-dominated Supreme Court attempted—and failed—to solve the political controversy over slavery. Dred Scott had been a slave all his life. His owner, army surgeon John Emerson, had taken Scott on his military assignments during the 1830s to Illinois (a free state) and Wisconsin Territory (a free territory, north of the Missouri Compromise line). During that time, Scott married another slave, Harriet, and their daughter Eliza was born

in free territory. Emerson and the Scotts then returned to Missouri (a slave state) and there, in 1846, Dred Scott sued for his freedom and that of his wife and his daughter born in Wisconsin Territory (who as women had no legal standing of their own) on the grounds that residence in free lands had made them free. It took eleven years for the case to reach the Supreme Court, and by then its importance was obvious to everyone.

Chief Justice Roger B. Taney, of Maryland, seventy-nine years old, hard of hearing and failing of sight, insisted on reading his majority opinion in its entirety, a process that took four excruciating hours. Declaring the Missouri Compromise unconstitutional, Taney asserted that the federal government had no right to interfere with the free movement of property throughout the territories. Taney was in effect making John C. Calhoun's states' rights position, always considered an extremist Southern position, the law of the land (see Chapter 14, Communities in Conflict). He then dismissed the *Dred Scott* case on the grounds that only citizens could bring suits before federal courts and that black people—slave or free—were not citizens. With this bold judicial intervention into the most heated issue of the day, Taney intended to settle the controversy over the expansion of slavery once and for all. Instead, he inflamed the conflict.

Read the Document
Opinion of the Supreme Court for Dred Scott v. Sanford (1857) at **www.myhistorylab.com**

The five Southern members of the Supreme Court concurred in Taney's decision, as did one Northerner, Robert C. Grier. Historians have found that President-elect Buchanan had pressured Grier, a fellow Pennsylvanian, to support the majority. Two of the three other Northerners vigorously dissented, and the last voiced other objections. This was clearly a sectional decision, and the response to it was sectional. Southerners expressed great satisfaction and strong support for the Court. The *Georgia Constitutionalist* announced, "Southern opinion upon the subject of southern slavery . . . is now the supreme law of the land . . . and opposition to southern opinion upon this subject is now opposition to the Constitution, and morally treason against the Government."

Northerners disagreed. Many were so troubled by the *Dred Scott* decision that, for the first time, they found themselves seriously questioning the power of the Supreme Court to establish the "law of the land." The New York legislature passed a resolution declaring that the Supreme Court had lost the confidence and respect of the people of that state and another resolution refusing to allow slavery within its borders "in any form or under any pretense, or for any time, however short." New York Republicans also proposed an equal suffrage amendment for free African Americans, who were largely disenfranchised by a stringent property qualification for voting. But this was too liberal for the state's voters, who defeated it. This racist attitude

OVERVIEW | Political Parties Split and Realign

Whig Party	Ran its last presidential candidate in 1852. The candidate, General Winfield Scott, alienated many Southern Whigs, and the party was so split it could not field a candidate in 1856.
Democratic Party	Remained a national party through 1856, but Buchanan's actions as president made Southern domination of the party so clear that many Northern Democrats were alienated. Stephen Douglas, running as a Northern Democrat in 1860, won 29 percent of the popular vote; John Breckinridge, running as a Southern Democrat, won 18 percent.
Liberty Party	Antislavery party; ran James G. Birney for president in 1844. He won 62,000 votes, largely from Northern antislavery Whigs.
Free-Soil Party	Ran Martin Van Buren, former Democratic president, in 1848. Gained 10 percent of the popular vote, largely from Whigs but also from some Northern Democrats.
American (Know-Nothing) Party	Nativist party made striking gains in 1854 congressional elections, attracting both Northern and Southern Whigs. In 1856, its presidential candidate, Millard Fillmore, won 21 percent of the popular vote.
Republican Party	Founded in 1854. Attracted many Northern Whigs and Northern Democrats. Presidential candidate John C. Frémont won 33 percent of the popular vote in 1856; in 1860, Abraham Lincoln won 40 percent and was elected in a four-way race.

was a bitter blow to free African Americans in the North. Frederick Douglass was so disheartened that he seriously considered immigrating to Haiti.

For the Republican Party, the *Dred Scott* decision represented a formidable challenge. By invalidating the Missouri Compromise, the decision swept away the free-soil foundation of the party. But to directly challenge a Supreme Court decision was a weighty matter. The most sensational Republican counterattack—made by both Abraham Lincoln and William Seward—was the accusation that President Buchanan had conspired with the Southern Supreme Court justices to subvert the American political system by withholding the decision until after the presidential election. Lincoln also raised the frightening possibility that "the next *Dred Scott* decision" would legalize slavery even in free states that abhorred it. President Buchanan's response to events in Kansas, including the drafting of a proslavery constitution, also stoked sectional antagonisms.

Watch the Video
Dred Scott and the Crises that Led to the Civil War at www.myhistorylab.com

The Lecompton Constitution

In Kansas, the doctrine of popular sovereignty led to continuing civil strife and the political travesty of two territorial governments. The first election of officers to a territorial government in 1855 produced a lopsided proslavery outcome that was clearly the result of illegal voting by Missouri border ruffians. Free-soilers protested by forming their own government, giving Kansas both a proslavery territorial legislature in Lecompton and a free-soil government in Topeka.

Free-soil voters boycotted a June 1857 election of representatives to a convention called to write a constitution for the territory once it reached statehood. As a result, the convention had a proslavery majority that wrote the proslavery Lecompton constitution and then applied to Congress for admission to the Union under its terms. In the meantime, in October, free-soil voters had participated in relatively honest elections for the territorial legislature, elections that returned a clear free-soil majority. Nevertheless, Buchanan, in the single most disastrous mistake of his administration, endorsed the proslavery constitution, because he feared the loss of the support of Southern Democrats. It seemed that Kansas would enter the Union as a sixteenth slave state, making the number of slave and free states equal.

Unexpected congressional opposition came from none other than Stephen Douglas, author of the legislation that had begun the Kansas troubles in 1854. Now, in 1857, in what was surely the bravest step of his political career, Douglas opposed the Lecompton constitution on the grounds that it violated the principle of popular sovereignty.

These sympathetic portraits of Harriet and Dred Scott and their daughters in 1857 helped to shape the Northern reaction to the Supreme Court's decision that denied the Scotts' claim to freedom. The infamous *Dred Scott* decision was intended to resolve the issue of slavery expansion but instead heightened angry feelings in both North and South.

He insisted that the Lecompton constitution must be voted on by Kansas voters in honest elections. Defying James Buchanan, the president of his own party, Douglas voted with the majority in Congress in April 1858 to refuse admission to Kansas under the Lecompton constitution. In a new referendum, the people of Kansas also rejected the Lecompton constitution, 11,300 to 1,788. Kansas was finally admitted as a free state in January 1861.

The defeat of the Lecompton constitution did not come easily. There was more bloodshed in Kansas. There was more violence in Congress: a free-for-all involving almost thirty congressmen broke out in the House late one night after an exchange of insults between Republicans and Southern Democrats. And the Democratic Party was breaking apart. Douglas had intended to preserve the Democrats as a national party, but instead he lost the support of the southern wing. Summing up these events, Congressman Alexander Stephens of Georgia wrote glumly to his brother: "All things here are tending my mind to the conclusion that the Union cannot and will not last long."

The Panic of 1857

Adding to the growing political tensions was the short, but sharp, depression of 1857 and 1858. Technology played a part. In August 1857, the failure of an Ohio investment

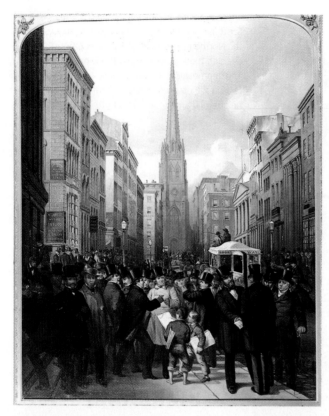

This painting by Charles G. Rosenberg and James H. Cafferty shows a worried crowd exchanging the latest news on Wall Street during the Panic of 1857. This was the first economic depression in which the telegraph played a part by carrying bad financial news in the West to New York much more rapidly than in the past.

house—the kind of event that had formerly taken weeks to be widely known—was the subject of a news story flashed immediately over telegraph wires to Wall Street and other financial markets. A wave of panic selling ensued, leading to business failures and slowdowns that threw thousands out of work. The major cause of the panic was a sharp, but temporary, downturn in agricultural exports to Britain, and recovery was well under way by early 1859.

Because it affected cotton exports less than northern exports, the Panic of 1857 was less harmful to the South than to the North. Southerners took this as proof of the superiority of their economic system to the free-labor system of the North, and some could not resist the chance to gloat. Senator James Henry Hammond of South Carolina drove home the point in his celebrated "King Cotton" speech of March 1858:

> When the abuse of credit had destroyed credit and annihilated confidence; when thousands of the strongest commercial houses in the world were coming down . . . when you came to a deadlock, and revolutions were threatened, what brought you up?

> . . . We have poured in upon you one million six hundred thousand bales of cotton just at the moment to save you from destruction . . . We have sold it for $65,000,000, and saved you.

It seemed that all matters of political discussion were being drawn into the sectional dispute. The next step toward disunion was an act of violence perpetrated by the grim abolitionist from Kansas, John Brown.

John Brown's Raid

In the heated political mood of the late 1850s, some improbable people became heroes. None was more improbable than John Brown, the self-appointed avenger who had slaughtered unarmed proslavery men in Kansas in 1856. In 1859, Brown proposed a wild scheme to raid the South and start a general slave uprising. He believed, as did most Northern abolitionists, that discontent among Southern slaves was so great that such an uprising needed only a spark to get going. Significantly, free African Americans—among them Frederick Douglass—did not support Brown, thinking his plan to raid the federal arsenal at Harpers Ferry, Virginia, was doomed to failure. They were right. On October 16, 1859, Brown led a group of twenty-two white and African American men against the arsenal. However, he had made no provision for escape. Even more incredible, he had made no effort to notify the Virginia slaves whose uprising it was supposed to initiate. In less than a day, the raid was over. Eight of Brown's men (including two of his sons) were dead, no slaves had joined the fight, and Brown himself was captured. Moving quickly to prevent a lynching by local mobs, the state of Virginia tried and convicted Brown (while he was still weak from the wounds of battle) of treason, murder, and fomenting insurrection.

Brown's death by hanging on December 2, 1859, was marked throughout northern communities with public rites of mourning not seen since the death of George Washington. Church bells tolled, buildings were draped in black, ministers preached sermons, prayer meetings were held, abolitionists issued eulogies. Ralph Waldo Emerson said that Brown would "make the gallows as glorious as the cross," and Henry David Thoreau called him "an angel of light." Naturally, not all Northerners supported Brown's action. Northern Democrats and conservative opinion generally repudiated him. But many people, while rejecting Brown's raid, increasingly supported the antislavery cause that he represented.

Brown's raid shocked the South because it aroused the fear of slave rebellion. Southerners believed that Northern abolitionists were provoking slave revolts, a suspicion apparently confirmed when documents captured at Harpers

Read the Document
An Abolitionist is Given the Death Sentence in 1859 at **www.myhistorylab.com**

Read the Document
John Brown's Address before Sentencing (1859) at **www.myhistorylab.com**

In a contemporary engraving, John Brown and his followers are shown trapped inside the armory at Harpers Ferry in October 1859. Captured, tried, and executed, Brown was regarded as a martyr in the North and a terrorist in the South.

Ferry revealed that Brown had the financial support of half a dozen members of the Northern elite. These "Secret Six"—Gerrit Smith, George Stearns, Franklin Sanborn, Thomas Wentworth Higginson, Theodore Parker, and Samuel Gridley Howe—had been willing to finance armed attacks on the slave system.

Even more shocking to Southerners than the raid itself was the extent of Northern mourning for Brown's death. Although the Republican Party disavowed Brown's actions, Southerners simply did not believe the party's statements. Senator Robert Toombs of Georgia warned that the South would "never permit this Federal government to pass into the traitorous hands of the Black Republican party." Talk of secession as the only possible response became common throughout the South.

The South Secedes

By 1860, sectional differences had caused one national party, the Whigs, to collapse. The second national party, the Democrats, stood on the brink of dissolution. Not only the politicians but also ordinary people in both the North and the South were coming to believe there was no way to avoid what in 1858 William Seward (once a Whig, now a Republican) had called an "irrepressible conflict."

The Election of 1860

The split of the Democratic Party into northern and southern wings that had occurred during President Buchanan's tenure became official at the Democratic nominating conventions in 1860. The party convened first in Charleston, South Carolina, the center of secessionist agitation. It was the worst possible location in which to attempt to reach unity. Although Stephen Douglas had the support of the plurality of delegates, he did not have the two-thirds majority necessary for nomination. As the price of their support, Southerners insisted that Douglas support a federal slave code—a guarantee that slavery would be protected in the territories. Douglas could not agree without violating his own belief in popular sovereignty and losing his Northern support.

After ten days, fifty-nine ballots, and two Southern walkouts, the convention ended where it had begun: deadlocked. Northern supporters of Douglas were angry and bitter: "I never heard Abolitionists talk more uncharitably and rancorously of the people of the South than the Douglas men," one reporter wrote. "They say they do not care a damn where the South goes."

In June, the Democrats met again in Baltimore. The Douglasites, recognizing the need for a united party, were

OVERVIEW | The Irrepressible Conflict

1776	**Declaration of Independence**	Thomas Jefferson's denunciation of slavery deleted from the final version.
1787	**Northwest Ordinance**	Slavery prohibited in the Northwest Territory (north of the Ohio River).
1787	**Constitution**	Slavery unmentioned but acknowledged in Article I, Section 2, counting three-fifths of all African Americans, slave and free, in a state's population; and in Article I, Section 9, which barred Congress from prohibiting the international slave trade for twenty years.
1803	**Louisiana Purchase**	Louisiana admitted as a slave state in 1812; no decision about the rest of Louisiana Purchase.
1820	**Missouri Compromise**	Missouri admitted as a slave state, but slavery prohibited in Louisiana Purchase north of 36°30'.
1846	**Wilmot Proviso**	Proposal to prohibit slavery in territory that might be gained in Mexican-American War causes splits in national parties.
1850	**Compromise of 1850**	California admitted as free state; Texas (already admitted in 1845) is a slave state; the rest of Mexican Cession to be decided by popular sovereignty. Ends the slave trade in the District of Columbia, but a stronger Fugitive Slave Law, leading to a number of violent recaptures, arouses Northern antislavery opinion.
1854	**Kansas-Nebraska Act**	At the urging of Stephen A. Douglas, Congress opens Kansas and Nebraska Territories for settlement under popular sovereignty. Open warfare between proslavery and antislavery factions breaks out in Kansas.
1857	**Lecompton Constitution**	President James Buchanan's decision to admit Kansas to the Union with a proslavery constitution is defeated in Congress.
1857	**_Dred Scott_ Decision**	The Supreme Court's denial of Dred Scott's case for freedom is welcomed in the South, condemned in the North. After years of avoidance by politicians, slavery and the future of the Union is the sole topic of the debates.
1858	**The Lincoln–Douglas Debates**	The first open, extended debate between leading politicians about the place of slavery in the Union.
1859	**John Brown's Raid and Execution**	Northern support for John Brown shocks the South.
1860	**Democratic Party Nominating Conventions**	The Democrats are unable to agree on a candidate; two candidates, one Northern (Stephen A. Douglas) and one Southern (John C. Breckinridge) split the party and the vote, thus allowing Republican Abraham Lincoln to win.

eager to compromise wherever they could, but most Southern Democrats were not. More than a third of the delegates bolted. Later, holding a convention of their own, they nominated Buchanan's vice president, John C. Breckinridge of Kentucky. The remaining two-thirds of the Democrats nominated Douglas, but everyone knew that a Republican victory was inevitable. To make matters worse, some Southern Whigs joined with some border-state nativists to form the Constitutional Union Party, which nominated John Bell of Tennessee.

Republican strategy was built on the lessons of the 1856 "victorious defeat." The Republicans planned to carry all the states Frémont had won, plus Pennsylvania, Illinois, and Indiana. The two leading Republican contenders were Senator William H. Seward of New York and Abraham Lincoln of Illinois. Seward, the party's best-known figure, had enemies among party moderates, who thought he was too radical, and among nativists with whom he had clashed in the New York Whig Party (See Communities in Conflict). Lincoln, on the other hand, appeared new, impressive, more moderate than Seward, and certain to carry Illinois. Lincoln won the nomination on the third ballot.

The election of 1860 presented voters with one of the clearest choices in American history. On the key issue of slavery, Breckinridge supported its extension to the territories; Lincoln stood firmly for its exclusion. Douglas attempted to hold the middle ground with his principle of popular sovereignty; Bell vaguely favored compromise as well. The Republicans offered other platform planks designed to appeal to Northern voters: support for a homestead act (free western lands), for a transcontinental railroad, for other internal improvements, and for a higher tariff.

Although they spoke clearly against the extension of slavery, Republicans sought to dispel their radical abolitionist image. The Republican platform condemned John Brown's raid as "the gravest of crimes," repeatedly denied that Republicans favored the social equality of black people, and strenuously affirmed that they sought to preserve the Union. In reality, Republicans simply did not believe the South would secede if Lincoln won. In this, the Republicans were not alone; few Northerners believed Southern threats—Southerners had threatened too many times before.

The only candidate who spoke urgently and openly about the impending threat of secession was Douglas. Breaking with convention, Douglas campaigned personally, in both the North and, bravely, in the hostile South, warning of the danger of dissolution and presenting himself as the only truly national candidate. Realizing his own chances for election were slight, he told his private secretary, "Mr. Lincoln is the next President. We must try to save the Union. I will go South."

In accordance with tradition, Lincoln did not campaign for himself, but many other Republicans spoke for him. The Republicans did not campaign in the South; Breckinridge did not campaign in the North. Each side was, therefore, free to believe the worst about the other. The mood in the Deep South was close to mass hysteria. Rumors of slave revolts—in Texas, Alabama, and South Carolina—swept the region, and vigilance committees sprang up to counter the supposed threat. In the South Carolina up-country, the question of secession dominated races for the state legislature. Candidates, such as A. S. Wallace of York, who advocated "patriotic forbearance" if Lincoln won, were soundly defeated. The very passion and excitement of the election campaign moved Southerners toward extremism. Even the weather—the worst drought and heat wave the South had known for years—contributed to the tension.

The election of 1860 produced the second highest voter turnout in U.S. history (81.2 percent, topped only by 81.8 percent in 1876). The election turned out to be two regional contests: Breckinridge versus Bell in the South, Lincoln versus Douglas in the North. Breckinridge carried eleven slave states with 18 percent of the popular vote; Bell carried Virginia, Tennessee, and Kentucky with 13 percent of the popular vote. Lincoln won all eighteen of the free states (he split New Jersey with Douglas) and almost 40 percent of the popular vote. Douglas carried only Missouri but gained nearly 30 percent of the popular vote. Lincoln's electoral vote total was overwhelming: 180 to a combined 123 for the other three candidates. But although Lincoln had won 54 percent of the vote in the northern states, his name had not even appeared on the ballot in ten southern states. The true winner of the 1860 election was sectionalism (see Map 15.5).

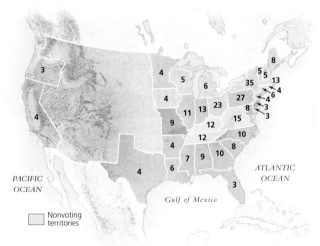

	Electoral Vote (%)	Popular Vote (%)
ABRAHAM LINCOLN (Republican)	180 (59)	1,865,593 (40)
John C. Breckinridge (Southern Democrat)	72 (24)	848,356 (18)
John Bell (Constitutional Union)	39 (13)	592,906 (13)
Stephen A. Douglas (Northern Democrat)	12 (4)	1,382,713 (29)
States that Republicans lost in 1856, won in 1860		

MAP 15.5 The Election of 1860 The election of 1860 was a sectional election. Lincoln won no votes in the South, Breckinridge none in the North. The contest in the North was between Lincoln and Douglas, and although Lincoln swept the electoral vote, Douglas's popular vote was uncomfortably close. The large number of Northern Democratic voters opposed to Lincoln was a source of political trouble for him during the Civil War.

The South Leaves the Union

The results of the election shocked Southerners. They were humiliated and frightened by the prospect of becoming a permanent minority in a political system dominated by a party pledged to the elimination of slavery. In Southern eyes, the Republican triumph meant they would become unequal partners in the federal enterprise, their way of life (the slave system) existing on borrowed time. Mary Boykin Chesnut, member of a well-connected South Carolina family, confided to her diary, "The die is cast—no more vain regrets—sad forebodings are useless. The stake is life or death."

The governors of South Carolina, Alabama, and Mississippi, each of whom had committed his state to secession if Lincoln were elected, immediately issued calls for special state conventions. At the same time, calls went out to southern communities to form vigilance committees and volunteer militia companies. Cooperationists (the term used for those opposed to immediate secession) were either intimidated into silence or simply left behind by the speed of events.

On December 20, 1860, a state convention in South Carolina, accompanied by all the hoopla and excitement of bands, fireworks displays, and huge rallies, voted unanimously to secede from the Union. In the weeks that followed, conventions in six other southern states (Mississippi, Florida, Alabama, Georgia, Louisiana, and Texas) followed suit, with the support, on average, of 80 percent of their delegates. There was genuine division of opinion in the Deep South, especially in Georgia and Alabama, along customary up-country–low-country lines. Yeoman farmers who did not own slaves and workers in the cities of the South were most likely to favor compromise with the North. But secessionists constantly reminded both groups that the Republican victory would lead to the emancipation of the slaves and the end of white privilege. And all Southerners, most of whom were deeply loyal to their state and region, believed that Northerners threatened their way of life. Throughout the South, secession occurred because Southerners no longer believed they had a choice.

In every state that seceded, the joyous scenes of South Carolina were repeated as the decisiveness of action replaced the long years of anxiety and tension. People danced in the streets, most believing the North had no choice but to accept secession peacefully. They ignored the fact that eight other slave states—Delaware, Maryland, Kentucky, Missouri, Virginia, North Carolina, Tennessee, and Arkansas—had not acted, though the latter four states did secede after war broke out (see Map 15.6).

◆◆ Read the Document

South Carolina Declaration of the Causes of Secession (1860) at **www.myhistorylab.com**

Just as Republicans had miscalculated in thinking Southern threats a mere bluff, so secessionists now miscalculated in believing they would be able to leave the Union in peace.

The North's Political Options

What should the North do? President Buchanan, indecisive as always, did nothing. The decision thus rested with Abraham Lincoln, even before he officially became president. One possibility was compromise, and many proposals were suggested, ranging from full adoption of the Breckinridge campaign platform to reinstatement of the Missouri Compromise line. Lincoln cautiously refused them all, making it clear that he would not compromise on the extension of slavery, which was the South's key demand. He hoped, by appearing firm but moderate, to

This special edition of the *Charleston Mercury* was issued on December 20, 1860, the day South Carolina voted to secede from the Union.

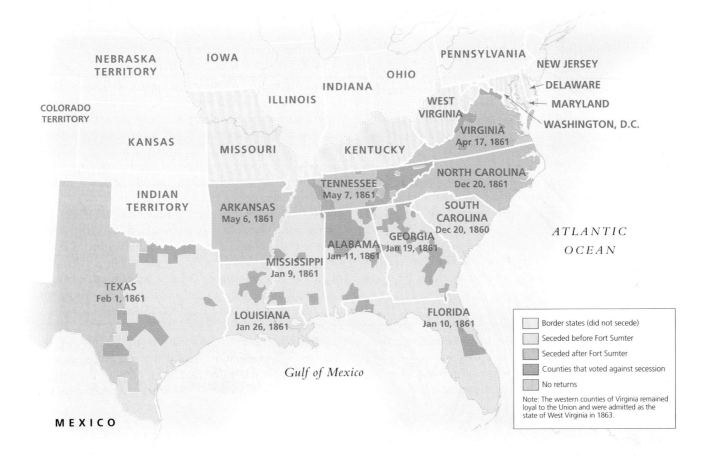

MAP 15.6 The South Secedes The southern states that would constitute the Confederacy seceded in two stages. The states of the Lower South seceded before Lincoln took office. Arkansas and three states of the Upper South—Virginia, North Carolina, and Tennessee—waited until after the South fired on Fort Sumter. And four border slave states—Delaware, Maryland, Kentucky, and Missouri—chose not to secede. Every southern state (except South Carolina) was divided on the issue of secession, generally along up-country–low-country lines. In Virginia, this division was so extreme that West Virginia split off to become a separate nonslave state admitted to the Union in 1863.

discourage additional southern states from seceding, while giving pro-Union Southerners time to organize. He succeeded in his first aim but not in the second. Lincoln and most of the Republican Party had seriously overestimated the strength of pro-Union sentiment in the South.

A second possibility, suggested by Horace Greeley of the *New York Tribune*, was to let the seven seceding states "go in peace." This is what many secessionists expected, but too many Northerners—including Lincoln himself—believed in the Union for this to happen. As Lincoln said, what was at stake was "the necessity of proving that

popular government is not an absurdity. We must settle this question now, whether in a free government the minority have the right to break up the government whenever they choose." At stake was all the accumulated American pride in the federal government as a model for democracies the world over.

The third possibility was force, and this was the crux of the dilemma. Although he believed their action was wrong, Lincoln was loath to go to war to force the seceding states back into the Union. On the other hand, he refused to give up federal powers over military forts and customs posts in the South. These were precisely the powers the seceding states had to command if they were to function as an independent nation. A confrontation was bound to come.

Establishment of the Confederacy

In February, delegates from the seven seceding states met in Montgomery, Alabama, and created the Confederate States of America. They wrote a constitution that was identical to the Constitution of the United States, with a few crucial exceptions: it strongly supported states' rights and made the abolition of slavery practically impossible. These two clauses did much to define the Confederate enterprise. It was difficult to avoid the conclusion that the new Confederacy was defined by the Southern dependence on slave labor. L. W. Spratt of South Carolina confessed as much in 1859: "We stand committed to the South, but we stand more vitally committed to the cause of slavery. It is, indeed, to be doubted whether the South [has] any cause apart from the institution which affects her."

The Montgomery convention chose Jefferson Davis of Mississippi as president and Alexander Stephens of Georgia as vice president of the new nation. Both men were known as moderates. Davis, a slave owner who had been a general in the Mexican-American War and secretary of war in the Pierce administration, and who was currently a senator from Mississippi, had expressed his own uncertainties by retaining his Senate seat for two weeks after Mississippi seceded. Stephens, a former leader in the Whig Party, had been a cooperationist delegate to Georgia's convention, where he urged that secession not be undertaken hastily.

The choice of moderates was deliberate, for the strategy of the new Confederate state was to argue that secession was a normal, responsible, and expectable course of action, and nothing for the North to get upset about. This was the theme that President Jefferson Davis of the Confederate States of America struck in his Inaugural Address, delivered to a crowd of 10,000 from the steps of the State Capitol at Montgomery, Alabama, on February 18, 1861. "We have changed the constituent parts," Davis said, "but not the system of our Government." Secession was a legal and peaceful step that, Davis said, quoting from the Declaration of Independence, "illustrates the American idea that governments rest on the consent of the governed . . . and that it is the right of the people to alter or abolish them at will whenever they become destructive of the ends for which they were established." Davis concluded, "Obstacles may retard, but they cannot long prevent, the progress of a movement sanctified by its justice and sustained by a virtuous people." This impressive inaugural prompted a deeply moved correspondent for the *New York Herald* to report, "God does not permit evil to be done with such earnest solemnity, such all-pervading trust in His Providence, as was exhibited by the whole people on that day."

Lincoln's Inauguration

The country as a whole waited to see what Abraham Lincoln would do, which at first appeared to be very little. In Springfield, Lincoln refused to issue public statements before his inaugural (although he sent many private messages to Congress and to key military officers), for fear of making a delicate situation worse. Similarly, during a twelve-day whistle-stopping railroad trip east from Springfield, he was careful to say nothing controversial. Eastern intellectuals, already suspicious of a mere "prairie lawyer," were not impressed. Finally, hard evidence of an assassination plot forced Lincoln to abandon his whistle-stops at Harrisburg and, protected by Pinkerton detectives, he traveled incognito into Washington, "like a thief in the night," as he complained. These signs of moderation and caution did not appeal to an American public with a penchant for electing military heroes. Americans wanted leadership and action.

Lincoln continued, however, to offer nonbelligerent firmness and moderation. And at the end of his Inaugural Address on March 4, 1861, as he stood ringed by federal troops called out in case of a Confederate attack, the new president offered unexpected eloquence:

> I am loath to close. We are not enemies, but friends. We must not be enemies. Though passion may have strained, it must not break our bonds of affection. The mystic chords of memory, stretching from every battlefield, and patriot grave, to every living heart and hearthstone, all over this broad land, will yet swell the chorus of the Union, when again touched, as surely they will be, by the better angels of our nature.

Conclusion

Americans had much to boast about in 1850. Their nation was vastly larger, richer, and more powerful than it had been in 1800. But the issue of slavery was slowly dividing the North and the South, two communities with similar origins and many common bonds. The following decade was marked by frantic efforts at political compromise, beginning with the Compromise of 1850, continuing with the Kansas-Nebraska Act of 1854, and culminating in the Supreme Court's 1859 decision in the *Dred Scott* case. Increasingly, the ordinary people of the two regions demanded resolution of the crisis. The two great parties of the Second American Party System, the Democrats and the Whigs, unable to find a solution, were

CHRONOLOGY

1820	Missouri Compromise
1828–32	Nullification Crisis
1846	Wilmot Proviso
1848	Treaty of Guadalupe Hidalgo ends Mexican-American War
	Zachary Taylor elected president
	Free-Soil Party formed
1849	California and Utah seek admission to the Union as free states
1850	Compromise of 1850
	California admitted as a free state
	American (Know-Nothing) Party formed
	Zachary Taylor dies; Millard Fillmore becomes president
1851	North reacts to Fugitive Slave Law
	Harriet Beecher Stowe's *Uncle Tom's Cabin* published
1852	Franklin Pierce elected president
1854	Ostend Manifesto
	Kansas-Nebraska Act
	Treaties with Indians in northern part of Indian Territory renegotiated
	Republican Party formed as Whig Party dissolves

1855	William Walker leads his first filibustering expedition to Nicaragua
1856	Burning and looting of Lawrence, Kansas
	John Brown leads Pottawatomie massacre
	Attack on Senator Charles Sumner
	James Buchanan elected president
1857	*Dred Scott* decision
	President Buchanan accepts proslavery Lecompton constitution in Kansas
	Panic of 1857
1858	Congress rejects Lecompton constitution
	Lincoln–Douglas debates
1859	John Brown's raid on Harpers Ferry
1860	Four parties run presidential candidates
	Abraham Lincoln elected president
	South Carolina secedes from Union
1861	Six other Deep South states secede
	Confederate States of America formed
	Lincoln takes office

destroyed. Two new sectional parties—the Republican Party and a Southern party devoted to the defense of slavery—fought the 1860 election, but Southerners refused to accept the national verdict. Politics had failed: the issue of slavery was irreconcilable. The only remaining recourse was war. But although Americans were divided, they were still one people. That made the war, when it came, all the more terrible.

Review Questions

1. What aspects of the remarkable economic development of the United States in the first half of the nineteenth century contributed to the sectional crisis of the 1850s?

2. How might the violent efforts by abolitionists to free escaped slaves who had been recaptured and the

federal armed enforcement of the Fugitive Slave Law have been viewed differently by northern merchants (the so-called Cotton Whigs), Irish immigrants, and abolitionists?

3. Consider the course of events in "Bloody Kansas" from Douglas's Kansas-Nebraska Act to the congressional rejection of the Lecompton constitution. Were these events the inevitable result of the political impasse in Washington, or could other decisions have been made that would have changed the outcome?

4. The nativism of the 1850s that surfaced so strongly in the Know-Nothing Party was eclipsed by the crisis over slavery. But nativist sentiment has been a recurring theme in American politics. Discuss why it was strong in the 1850s and why it has emerged periodically since then.

5. Evaluate the character and actions of John Brown. Was he the hero proclaimed by Northern supporters or the terrorist condemned by the South?

6. Imagine that you lived in Illinois, home state to both Douglas and Lincoln, in 1860. How would you have voted in the presidential election, and why?

Recommended Reading

Orville Vernon Burton, *The Age of Lincoln* (2007). A very readable political and cultural account of the years 1830–1900 and Lincoln's central role in them.

Nicole Etcheson, *Bleeding Kansas: Contested Liberty in the Civil War Era* (2004). A look at the Kansas issue from the perspective of white settlers.

Don E. Fehrenbacher, *The Dred Scott Case: Its Significance in American Law and Politics* (1978). A major study by the leading historian on this controversial decision.

William W. Freehling, *The Road to Disunion,* vol.2: *Sessionists Triumphant, 1854–1861* (2007). The concluding volume of the author's intensive study of the politics of secession.

Robert E. May, *Manifest Destiny's Underworld: Filibustering in Antebellum America* (2002). A study of the activities and attitudes toward the adventurers.

Russell McClintock, *Lincoln and the Decision for War: The Northern Response to Secession* (2008). Examines the crucial months, November 1860 to May 1861.

David S. Reynolds, *John Brown, Abolitionist* (2005). Argues that Brown's extremism became the Civil War norm.

Elizabeth Varon, *Disunion! The Coming of the American Civil War, 1789-1859* (2008). Traces the deep causes of the Civil War to the ongoing conflict between concepts of "union" and "liberty."

PEARSON myhistorylab Connections

Reinforce what you learned in this chapter by studying the many documents, images, maps, review tools, and videos available at www.myhistorylab.com.

Read and Review

✓ Study and Review Chapter 15

Read the Document

The Lincoln-Douglas Debates of 1858

A New England Writer Portrays Slavery in 1852

Daniel Webster, Speech to the U.S. Senate (1850)

Benjamin Drew, from Narratives of Fugitive Slaves in Canada (1855)

Harriet Jacobs, Incidents in the Life of a Slave Girl (1861)

Opinion of the Supreme Court for Dred Scott *v. Sanford (1857)*

An Abolitionist is Given the Death Sentence in 1859

John Brown's Address before Sentencing (1859)

South Carolina Declaration of the Causes of Secession (1860)

See the Map

The Compromise of 1850

The Kansas-Nebraska Act

Research and Explore

Read the Document

Exploring America: Anthony Burns

Profiles
Dred and Harriet Scott
John Brown

Watch the Video

Dred Scott and the Crises that Led to the Civil War

Harriet Beecher Stowe and the Making of Uncle Tom's Cabin

((•— Hear the Audio

Hear the audio files for Chapter 15 at
www.myhistorylab.com.

The Civil War

1861–1865

CHAPTER OUTLINE

Homer, Winslow (1836–1910). Prisoners from the Front. 1866. Oil on canvas, 24 × 38 in. (61 × 96.5 cm).
Gift of Mrs. Frank B. Por. The Metropolitan Museum of Art, New York, NY, U.S.A. Image copyright © The
Metropolitan Museum of Art / Art Resource, NY.

Mother Bickerdyke Connects Northern Communities to Their Boys at War

In May 1861, the Reverend Edward Beecher interrupted his customary Sunday service at Brick Congregational Church in Galesburg, Illinois, to read a disturbing letter to the congregation. Two months earlier, Galesburg had proudly sent 500 of its young men off to join the Union army. They had not yet been in battle. Yet, the letter reported, an alarming number were dying of diseases caused by inadequate food, medical care, and sanitation at the crowded military camp in Cairo, Illinois. Most army doctors were surgeons trained to operate and amputate on the battlefield. They were not prepared to treat soldiers sick with dysentery, pneumonia, typhoid, measles—all serious, frequently fatal diseases that could often be cured with careful nursing. The letter writer, appalled by the squalor and misery he saw around him, complained of abuses by the army. The Union army, however, was overwhelmed with the task of readying recruits for battle and had made few provisions for their health when they were not in combat.

The shocked and grieving members of Beecher's congregation quickly decided to send not only supplies but also one of their number to inspect the conditions

AMERICAN Communities

at the Cairo camp and to take action. In spite of warnings that army regulations excluded women from encampments, the congregation voted to send their most qualified member, Mary Ann Bickerdyke, a middle-aged widow who made her living as a "botanic physician." This simple gesture of community concern launched a remarkable Civil War career.

"Mother" Bickerdyke, as she was called, let nothing stand in the way of helping her "boys." When she arrived in Cairo, she immediately set to work cleaning the hospital tents and the soldiers themselves, and finding and cooking nourishing food for them. The hospital director, who resented her interference, ordered her to leave, but she blandly continued her work. When he reported her to the commanding officer, General Benjamin Prentiss, she quickly convinced the general to let her stay. "I talked sense to him," she later said.

From a peacetime point of view, what Mother Bickerdyke was doing was not unusual. Every civilian hospital had a matron who made sure patients were supplied with clean bed linen and bandages and were fed the proper convalescent diet. But in the context of the war—the sheer number of soldiers, the constant need to set up new field hospitals and commandeer scarce food for an army on the move—it was unusual indeed and required an unusual person. A plainspoken, hardworking woman, totally unfazed by rank or tender masculine egos, Mother Bickerdyke single-mindedly devoted herself to what she called "the Lord's work." The ordinary soldiers loved her; wise generals supported her. Once, when an indignant officer's wife complained about Bickerdyke's rudeness, General William Tecumseh Sherman joked, "You've picked the one person around here who outranks me. If you want to lodge a complaint against her, you'll have to take it to President Lincoln."

Other communities all over the North rallied to make up for the Army's shortcomings with supplies and assistance. By their actions, Mother Bickerdyke and others like her exposed the War Department's inability to meet the needs of the nation's first mass army. The efforts of women on the local level—for example, to make clothing for men from their communities who had gone off to the war—quickly took on national dimensions. The Women's Central Association of Relief (WCAR), whose organizers were mostly reformers in the abolitionist, temperance,

and education movements, eventually had 7,000 chapters throughout the North. Its volunteers raised funds, made and collected food, clothes, medicine, bandages, and more than 250,000 quilts and comforters, and sent them to army camps and hospitals. All told, association chapters supplied an estimated $15 million worth of goods to the Union troops.

In June 1861, responding to requests by officials of the WCAR for formal recognition of the organization, President Abraham Lincoln created the United States Sanitary Commission and gave it the power to investigate and advise the Medical Bureau. The commission's more than 500 "sanitary inspectors" (usually men) instructed soldiers in such matters as water supply, placement of latrines, and safe cooking.

●●[Read the Document
U.S. Sanitary Commission, Sketch of Its Purposes (1864) at **www.myhistorylab.com**

Although at first she worked independently and remained suspicious of all organizations (and even of many other relief workers), in 1862 Mother Bickerdyke became an official agent of "the Sanitary," as it was known. Mother Bickerdyke was an unequaled fundraiser. In speaking tours throughout Illinois, she touched her female listeners with moving stories of wounded boys whom she had cared for as if they were her own sons. Her words to men were more forceful. It was a man's business to fight, she said. If he was too old or ill to fight with a gun, he should fight with his dollars. With the help of Bickerdyke's blunt appeals, the Sanitary raised $50 million for the Union war effort.

As the Civil War continued, Mother Bickerdyke became a key figure in the medical support for General Ulysses S. Grant's campaigns along the Mississippi River. She was with the army at Shiloh, and as Grant slowly fought his way to Vicksburg, she set up convalescent hospitals in Memphis. Grant authorized her to commandeer any army wagons she needed to transport supplies. Between fifty and seventy "contrabands" (escaped former slaves) worked on her laundry crew. On the civilian side, the Sanitary Commission authorized her to draw on its supply depots in Memphis, Cairo, Chicago, and elsewhere. In a practical sense a vital "middlewoman" between the home front and the battlefield, she was also, in a symbolic and emotional sense, a stand-in for all mothers who had sent their sons to war.

1. What advantages did the North possess at the outset of the Civil War?

2. How did the power of the federal government expand as the war progressed?

3. What successes did the South enjoy in the early years of the war?

4. How did the end of slavery affect the war efforts of the North and South?

5. What impact did the war have on Northern political, economic, and social life? and on the same aspects of Southern life?

6. How did Grant and Sherman exemplify a new war strategy?

FOCUS Questions

1861–1865

The Civil War was a national tragedy, ripping apart the political fabric of the country and causing more casualties than any other war in the nation's history. The death toll of approximately 620,000 exceeded the number of dead in all the other wars from the Revolution through the Vietnam War. Yet in another sense, it was a community triumph. Local communities directly supported and sustained their soldiers on a massive scale in unprecedented ways. As national unity failed, the strength of local communities, symbolized by Mother Bickerdyke, endured.

Illinois

AMERICAN Communities

Communities Mobilize for War

A neutral observer in March 1861 might have seen ominous similarities. Two nations—the United States of America (shorn of seven states in the Deep South) and the Confederate States of America—each blamed the other for the breakup of the Union. Two new presidents—Abraham Lincoln and Jefferson Davis—each faced the challenging task of building and maintaining national unity. Two regions—North and South—scorned each other and boasted of their own superiority. But the most important similarity was not yet apparent: both sides were unprepared for the ordeal that lay ahead.

Watch the Video
What Caused the Civil War? at
www.myhistorylab.com

Fort Sumter: The War Begins

Fort Sumter, a federal military installation, sat on an island at the entrance to Charleston harbor. So long as it remained in Union hands, Charleston, the center of secessionist sentiment, would be immobilized. Thus, it was hardly surprising that Fort Sumter would provide President Lincoln with his first crisis.

With the fort dangerously low on supplies, Lincoln had to decide whether to abandon it or risk the fight that might ensue if he ordered it resupplied. On April 6, 1861, Lincoln took cautious and careful action, notifying the governor of South Carolina that he was sending a relief force to the fort carrying only food and no military supplies. Now the decision rested with Jefferson Davis, who opted for decisive action. On April 10, he ordered General P. G. T. Beauregard to demand the surrender of Fort Sumter and to attack it if the garrison did not comply. On April 12, as Lincoln's relief force neared Charleston harbor, Beauregard opened fire. Two days later, the defenders surrendered and the Confederate Stars and Bars rose over Fort Sumter. The people of Charleston celebrated wildly. "I did not know," wrote Mary Boykin Chesnut in her diary, "that one could live such days of excitement."

Even before the attack on Fort Sumter, the Confederate Congress had authorized a volunteer army of 100,000 men to serve for twelve months. There was no difficulty finding volunteers. Men flocked to enlist, and their communities sent them off in ceremonies featuring bands, bonfires, and belligerent oratory. The cry of "On to

Washington!" was raised throughout the South, and orators confidently predicted that the city would be captured and the war concluded within sixty days. For these early recruits, war was a patriotic adventure.

The "thunderclap of Sumter" startled the North into an angry response. The apathy and uncertainty that had prevailed since Lincoln's election disappeared, to be replaced by strong feelings of patriotism. As New Yorker George Templeton Strong recorded in his diary, "God be praised for the unity of feeling here! It is beyond, very far beyond, anything I hoped for." On April 15, Lincoln issued a proclamation calling for 75,000 state militiamen to serve in the federal army for ninety days. Enlistment offices were swamped with so many enthusiastic volunteers that men were sent home. Free African Americans, among the most eager to serve, were turned away: this was not yet a war for or by black people.

The mobilization in Chester, Pennsylvania, was typical of the Northern response to the outbreak of war. A patriotic rally was held at which a company of volunteers (the first of many from the region) calling themselves the "Union Blues" were mustered into the Ninth Regiment of Pennsylvania Volunteers amid cheers and band music. As they marched off to Washington (the gathering place for the Union army), companies of home guards were organized by the men who remained behind. Within a month, the women of Chester had organized a countywide system of war relief that sent a stream of clothing, blankets, bandages, and other supplies to the local troops and provided assistance to their families at home. Such relief organizations, some formally organized, some informal, emerged in every community, North and South, that sent soldiers off to the Civil War. These organizations not only played a vital role in supplying the troops, but they also maintained the human, local link on which so many soldiers depended. In this sense, every American community accompanied its young men to war.

The Border States

The first secession, between December 20, 1860, and February 1, 1861, had taken seven Deep South states out of the Union. Now, in April, the firing on Fort Sumter and Lincoln's call for state militias forced the other Southern states to take sides. Courted—and pressured—by both North and South, four states of the Upper South (Virginia, Arkansas, Tennessee, and North Carolina) joined the original seven in April and May 1861. Virginia's secession tipped the other three toward the Confederacy. The capital of the Confederacy was now moved to Richmond. This meant that the two capitals—Richmond and Washington—were less than 100 miles apart.

This Currier and Ives lithograph shows the opening moment of the Civil War. On April 12, 1861, Confederate General P.G.T. Beauregard ordered the shelling of Fort Sumter in Charleston harbor. Two days later, Union Major Robert Anderson surrendered, and mobilization began for what turned out to be the most devastating war in American history.

This patriotic painting shows the departure of New York's Seventh Regiment for Washington in mid-April of 1861. Stirring scenes like this occurred across the nation following "the thunderclap of Sumter" as communities mobilized for war.

SOURCE: George Hayward (American, born England, 1800–1872?), *Departure of the 7th Regiment, N.Y.S.M., April 19, 1861*, April 19, 1861. Graphite pencil, transparent and opaque watercolor on paper, Sheet: 36.7 × 51.3 cm (14 ⅞₆ × 20 ⅜₆ in.). Museum of Fine Arts, Boston, M. and M. Karolik Collection of American Watercolors and Drawings, 1800–1875, 51.2785. Photograph © 2006 Museum of Fine Arts, Boston.

Still undecided was the loyalty of the northernmost tier of slave-owning states: Missouri, Kentucky, Maryland, and Delaware. Each controlled vital strategic assets. Missouri not only bordered the Mississippi River but also controlled the routes to the west. Kentucky controlled the Ohio River. The main railroad link with the West ran through Maryland and the hill region of western Virginia (which split from Virginia to become the free state of West Virginia in 1863). Delaware controlled access to Philadelphia. Finally, were Maryland to secede, the nation's capital would be completely surrounded by Confederate territory.

Delaware was loyal to the Union (less than 2 percent of its population were slaves), but Maryland's loyalty was divided, as an ugly incident on April 19 showed. When the Sixth Massachusetts Regiment marched through Baltimore, a hostile crowd of 10,000 Southern sympathizers, carrying Confederate flags, pelted the troops with bricks, paving stones, and bullets. Finally, in desperation, the troops fired on the crowd, killing twelve people and wounding others. In retaliation, Southern sympathizers burned the railroad bridges to the North and destroyed the telegraph line to Washington, cutting off communication between the capital and the rest of the Union for six days.

Lincoln's response was swift and stern. He stationed Union troops along Maryland's crucial railroads, declared martial law in Baltimore, and arrested the suspected ringleaders of the pro-Confederate mob and held them without trial. Thus was Maryland's loyalty to the Union ensured. The arrests in Maryland were the first of a number of violations of basic civil rights during the war, all of which the president justified on the basis of national security.

An even bloodier division occurred in Missouri, where old foes from "Bleeding Kansas" faced off. The proslavery governor and most of the legislature fled to Arkansas, where they declared a Confederate state government in exile, while Unionists remained in control in St. Louis. Consequently, Missouri was plagued by guerrilla battles throughout the war. In Kentucky, division took the form of a huge illegal trade with the

Confederacy through neighboring Tennessee, to which Lincoln, determined to keep Kentucky in the Union, turned a blind eye.

That Delaware, Maryland, Missouri, and Kentucky chose to stay in the Union was a severe blow to the Confederacy. Among them, the four states could have added 45 percent to the white population and military manpower of the Confederacy and 80 percent to its manufacturing capacity. Almost as damaging, the decision of four slave states to stay in the Union punched a huge hole in the Confederate argument that the Southern states were forced to secede to protect their right to own slaves.

The Battle of Bull Run

Once sides had been chosen and the initial flush of enthusiasm had passed, the nature of the war, and the mistaken notions about it, soon became clear. The event that shattered the illusions was the First Battle of Bull Run, at Bull Run Creek near Manassas in Virginia in July 1861. Confident of a quick victory, a Union army of 35,000 men marched south, crying "On to Richmond!" So lighthearted and unprepared was the Washington community that the troops were accompanied not only by journalists but also by a crowd of politicians and sightseers. At first the Union troops held their ground against the 25,000 Confederate troops commanded by General P. G. T. Beauregard (of Fort Sumter fame). But when 2,300 fresh Confederate troops arrived as reinforcements, the untrained Northern troops broke ranks in an

uncontrolled retreat that swept up the frightened sightseers as well. Soldiers and civilians alike retreated in disarray all the way to Washington.

The Relative Strengths of North and South

Bull Run was sobering—and prophetic. The Civil War was the most lethal military conflict in American history, leaving a legacy of devastation on the battlefield and desolation at home. It claimed the lives of nearly 620,000 soldiers, more than the First and Second World Wars combined. One out of every four soldiers who fought in the war never returned home.

Overall, in terms of both population and productive capacity, the Union seemed to have a commanding edge over the Confederacy. The North had two and a half times the South's population (22 million to 9 million, of whom 3.5 million were slaves) and enjoyed an even greater advantage in industrial capacity (nine times that of the South). The North produced almost all of the nation's firearms (97 percent), had 71 percent of its railroad mileage, and produced 94 percent of its cloth and 90 percent of its footwear. The North seemed able to feed, clothe, arm, and transport all the soldiers it chose. These advantages were ultimately to prove decisive: by the end of the war, the Union had managed to field and equip more than 2 million soldiers as compared to the Confederacy's 800,000. But in the short term, the South had important assets to counter the advantage of the North (see Figure 16.1).

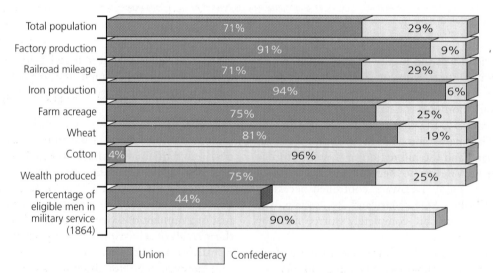

FIGURE 16.1 Comparative Resources, North and South, 1861 As this chart shows, the North far surpassed the South in the resources necessary to support a large, long war. Initially, however, these strengths made little difference in a struggle that began as a traditional war of maneuver in which the South held the defensive advantage. Only slowly did the Civil War become a modern war in which all the resources of society, including the property and lives of civilians, were mobilized for battle.

SOURCE: From *The Times Atlas of World History* Copyright © 1978, Hammond. Reprinted by permission of the publisher.

The first was the nature of the struggle. For the South, this was a defensive war, in which the basic principle of the defense of home and community united almost all white citizens, regardless of their views about slavery. The North would have to invade the South and then control it against guerrilla opposition in order to win.

Second, the military disparity was less extreme than it appeared. Although the North had manpower, its troops were mostly untrained. The professional federal army numbered only 16,000, and most of its experience had been gained in small Indian wars. Moreover, the South, because of its tradition of honor and belligerence, appeared to have an advantage in military leaders, the most notable of which was Robert E. Lee. Offered command of the Union army by President Lincoln, Lee hesitated but finally decided to follow his native state, Virginia, into the Confederacy.

Finally, it was widely believed that slavery would work to the South's advantage, for slaves could continue to do the vital plantation work while their masters went off to war. But above all, the South had the weapon of cotton. Because of the crucial role of cotton in industrialization, Southerners were confident that the British and French need for Southern cotton would soon bring those countries to recognize the Confederacy as a separate nation.

The Governments Organize for War

The Civil War forced the federal government to assume powers unimaginable just a few years before. Abraham Lincoln took as his primary task leading and unifying the nation in his role as commander in chief. He found the challenge almost insurmountable. Jefferson Davis's challenge was even greater. He had to create a Confederate nation out of a loose grouping of eleven states, each believing strongly in states' rights. Yet in the Confederacy, as in the Union, the conduct of the war required central direction.

Lincoln Takes Charge

Lincoln's first task as president was to assert control over his own cabinet. Because he had few national contacts outside the Republican Party, Lincoln chose to staff his cabinet with other Republicans, including, most unusually, several who had been his rivals for the presidential nomination. On one hand, Secretary of State William Seward, widely regarded as the leader of the Republican Party, at first expected to "manage" Lincoln as he had Zachary Taylor in 1848, but he soon became the president's willing partner. On the other hand, Treasury Secretary Salmon P. Chase, a staunch abolitionist,

adamantly opposed concessions to the South and considered Lincoln too conciliatory; he remained a vocal and dangerous critic. That the Republican Party was a not-quite-jelled mix of former Whigs, abolitionists, moderate free-soilers, and even some prowar Democrats made Lincoln's task as party leader much more difficult than it might otherwise have been.

After the fall of Fort Sumter, military necessity prompted Lincoln to call up the state militias, order a naval blockade of the South, and vastly expand the military budget. Breaking with precedent, he took these actions without congressional sanction because Congress was not in session. Military necessity—the need to hold the border states—likewise prompted other early actions, such as the suspension of *habeas corpus* and the acceptance of Kentucky's ambiguous neutrality. Over howls of protest from abolitionists, the president also repudiated an unauthorized declaration issued by General John C. Frémont, military commander in Missouri, in August 1861 that would have freed Missouri's slaves. Lincoln feared that such an action would lead to the secession of Kentucky and Maryland.

Although James K. Polk had assumed responsibility for overall American military strategy during the Mexican-American War (see Chapter 14), Lincoln was the first president to act as commander in chief in both a practical and a symbolic way. He actively directed military policy, because he realized that a civil war presented problems different from those of a foreign war of conquest. Lincoln wanted above all to persuade the South to rejoin the Union, and his every military order was dictated by the hope of eventual reconciliation—hence, his caution and his acute sense of the role of public opinion. At the same time, he presided over a vast expansion of the powers of the federal government.

Expanding the Power of the Federal Government

The greatest expansion in government power during the war was in the War Department, which by early 1862 was faced with the unprecedented challenge of feeding, clothing, and arming 700,000 Union soldiers. Initially, the government relied on the individual states to equip and supply their vastly expanded militias. But the size of the Union army and the complexity of fully supplying it demanded constant efforts at all levels—government, state, and community—throughout the war. Thus, in the matter of procurement and supply, as in mobilization, the battlefront was related to the home front on a scale that Americans had not previously experienced.

The need for money for the vast war effort was pressing. Treasury Secretary Chase worked closely with Congress to develop ways to finance the war. They naturally turned to the nation's economic experts—private bankers, merchants, and managers of large businesses. With the help of Philadelphia financier Jay Cooke, the Treasury used patriotic appeals to sell war bonds to ordinary people in amounts as small as $50. Cooke sold $400 million in bonds, taking for himself what he considered a "fair commission." By the war's end, the United States had borrowed $2.6 billion for the war effort, the first example in American history of the mass financing of war.

Most radical of all was Chase's decision—which was authorized only after a bitter congressional fight—to print and distribute Treasury notes (paper money). Until then, the money in circulation had been a mixture of coins and state bank notes issued by 1,500 different state banks. The Legal Tender Act of February 1862 created a national currency. Because of its color, the paper bank notes were popularly known as "greenbacks." In 1863, Congress passed the National Bank Act, which prohibited state banks from issuing their own notes and forced them to apply for federal charters. The switch to a national currency was widely recognized as a major step toward centralization of economic power in the hands of the federal government. Such a measure would have been unthinkable if Southern Democrats had still been part of the national government.

The absence of Southern Democrats also made possible passage of a number of Republican economic measures not directly related to the war.

Although the outbreak of war overshadowed everything else, the Republican Party in Congress was determined to fulfill its campaign pledge of a comprehensive program of economic development. Republicans quickly passed the Morrill Tariff Act (1861); by 1864, this and subsequent measures had raised tariffs to more than double their prewar rate. In 1862 and 1864, Congress created two federally chartered corporations to build a transcontinental railroad—the Union Pacific Railroad Company, to lay track westward from Omaha, and the Central Pacific, to lay track eastward from California—thus fulfilling the dreams of the many expansionists who believed America's economic future lay in trade with Asia across the Pacific Ocean. Two other measures, both passed in 1862, had long been sought by Westerners. The Homestead Act gave 160 acres of public land to any citizen who agreed to live on the land for five years, improve it by building a house and cultivating some of the land, and pay a small fee. The

●●●[**Read** the **Document**

Homestead Act of 1862
at **www.myhistorylab.com**

This photograph, taken a month before his inauguration, shows Lincoln looking presidential. It was clearly intended to reassure a public still doubtful about his abilities.

Morrill Land Grant Act gave states public land that would allow them to finance land-grant colleges offering education to ordinary citizens in practical skills such as agriculture, engineering, and military science. Coupled with this act, the establishment of a federal Department of Agriculture in 1862 gave American farmers a big push toward modern commercial agriculture.

These were powerful nationalizing forces, connecting ordinary people to the federal government in new ways. The enactment of the Republican program increased the role of the federal government in national life. Although many of the executive war powers lapsed when the battles ended, the accumulation of strength by the federal government was never reversed.

Diplomatic Objectives

To Secretary of State William Seward fell the job of making sure that Britain and France did not extend diplomatic recognition to the Confederacy. Although Southerners had been certain that King Cotton would gain them European support, they were wrong. British public opinion, which had strongly supported the abolition of slavery within the British Empire in the 1830s, would not now countenance the recognition of a new nation based on slavery. British cotton manufacturers found economic alternatives, first using up their backlog of Southern cotton and then turning to Egypt and India for new supplies. In spite of Union protests, however, both Britain and France did allow Confederate vessels to use their ports, and British shipyards sold six ships to the Confederacy. But in 1863, when the Confederacy commissioned Britain's Laird shipyard to build two ironclad ships with pointed prows for ramming Union ships, the Union threatened war, and the British government made sure that the Laird ironclads were never delivered. Seward had wanted to Challenge Britain earlier, in 1861, when the Union seized two Confederate diplomats from the British steamer *Trent*, but Lincoln had overruled him, cautioning, "One war at a time." Seward agreed to release the Confederate envoys, thus defusing the crisis.

Nonbelligerence was also the Union response in 1861, when a bankrupt Mexico suffered the conquest by France. This was a serious violation of Mexican independence, just the kind of European intervention the Monroe Doctrine had been formulated to prevent (see Chapter 9). Mexican forces repelled the French troops on May 5, 1862. Ever since, Mexico has celebrated *El Cinco de Mayo*, although France eventually prevailed and installed the Austrian archduke Maximilian as emperor.

Fearing that France might recognize the Confederacy or invade Texas, Seward had to content himself with refusing to recognize the new Mexican government. Although the goal of Seward's diplomacy—preventing recognition of the Confederacy by the European powers—was always

clear, its achievement was uncertain for more than two years. Northern fears and Southern hopes seesawed with the fortunes of battle. Not until the victories at Vicksburg and Gettysburg in July 1863 could Seward be reasonably confident of success.

Jefferson Davis Tries to Unify the Confederacy

Although Jefferson Davis had held national cabinet rank (as secretary of war under President Franklin Pierce), had experience as an administrator, and was a former military man (none of which was true of Abraham Lincoln), he was unable to hold the Confederacy together. Perhaps no one could have.

Davis's first cabinet of six men, appointed in February 1861, included a representative from each of the states of the first secession except Mississippi, which was represented by Davis himself. This careful attention to the equality of the states pointed to the fundamental problem Davis was unable to overcome. A shared belief in states' rights—that is, in their own autonomy—was a poor basis on which to build a unified nation. Although Davis saw the need for unity, he was unable to impose it. Soon his style of leadership—micromanagement—angered his generals, alienated cabinet members, and gave Southern governors reason to resist his orders. After the first flush of patriotism had passed, the Confederacy never lived up to its hope of becoming a unified nation.

Contradictions of Southern Nationalism

The failure of "cotton diplomacy" was a crushing blow. White Southerners were stunned that Britain and France would not recognize their claim to independence. Well into 1863, the South hoped that a decisive battlefield victory would change the minds of cautious Europeans. In the meantime, plantations continued to grow cotton, but the South withheld it from market, in the hope that lack of raw material for their textile mills would lead the British and French to recognize the Confederacy. In 1862, when the Confederacy ended the embargo and began to ship its great surplus, the world price of cotton plunged. Then too, the Union naval blockade, weak at first, began to take effect. Cotton turned out to be not so powerful a diplomatic weapon after all.

Perhaps the greatest Southern failure was in the area of finances. At first, the Confederate government tried to raise money from the states, but governors refused to impose new taxes. By the time uniform taxes were levied in 1863, it was too late. Heavy borrowing and the printing of great sums of paper money produced runaway inflation (a ruinous rate of 9,000 percent by 1865, compared with 80 percent in the North). Inflation, in turn, caused incalculable damage to morale and prospects for unity.

After the initial surge of volunteers, enlistment in the military fell off, as it did in the North also. In April 1862, the Confederate Congress passed the first draft law in American history, and the Union Congress followed suit in March 1863. The Southern law declared that all able-bodied men between eighteen and thirty-five were eligible for three years of military service. Purchase of substitutes was allowed, as in the North, but in the South the price was uncontrolled, rising eventually to $10,000 in Confederate money. The most disliked part of the draft law was a provision exempting one white man on each plantation with twenty or more slaves. This provision not only seemed to disprove the earlier claim that slavery freed white men to fight, but also it aroused class resentments. A bitter phrase of the time complained, "It's a rich man's war but a poor man's fight."

In the early days of the war, Jefferson Davis successfully mobilized feelings of regional identity and patriotism.

Many Southerners felt part of a beleaguered region that had been forced to resist Northern tyranny. But most felt loyalty to their own state and local communities, not to a Confederate nation. The strong belief in states' rights and aristocratic privilege undermined the Confederate cause. Some Southern governors resisted potentially unifying actions such as moving militias outside their home states. Broader measures, such as general taxation, were widely evaded by rich and poor alike.

The inequitable draft was only one of many things that convinced the ordinary people of the South that this was a war for privileged slave owners, not for them. With its leaders and citizens fearing (perhaps correctly) that centralization would destroy what was distinctively Southern, the Confederacy was unable to mobilize the resources—financial, human, and otherwise—that might have prevented its destruction by Northern armies.

This painting by William C. Washington, *Jackson Entering the City of Winchester*, shows the dashing Confederate General "Stonewall" Jackson saving the Virginia town from Union capture in 1862. Jackson and other Confederate generals evoked fierce loyalty to the Confederacy. Unfortunately, by the time this victory was commemorated, Jackson himself was dead from wounds caused by friendly fire at the Battle of Chancellorsville in May of 1863.

SOURCE: William Washington, *Stonewall Jackson Entering the City of Winchester, Virginia.* Oil painting. Valentine Museum Library, Richmond, Virginia.

The Fighting through 1862

Just as political decisions were often driven by military necessity, the basic Northern and Southern military strategies were affected by political considerations as much as by military ones. The initial policy of limited war, thought to be the best route to ultimate reconciliation, ran into difficulties because of the public's impatience for victories. But victories, as the mounting slaughter made clear, were not easy to achieve.

The War in Northern Virginia

The initial Northern strategy, dubbed by critics the Anaconda Plan (after the constrictor snake), envisaged slowly squeezing the South with a blockade at sea and on the Mississippi River. Proposed by the general-in-chief, Winfield Scott, a native of Virginia, it avoided invasion and conquest in the hope that a strained South would recognize the inevitability of defeat and thus surrender. Lincoln accepted the basics of the plan, but public clamor for a fight pushed him to agree to the disastrous Battle of

Bull Run and then to a major buildup of Union troops in northern Virginia under General George B. McClellan (see Map 16.1).

Dashing in appearance, McClellan was extremely cautious in battle. In March 1862, after almost a year spent drilling the raw Union recruits and after repeated exhortations by an impatient Lincoln, McClellan committed 120,000 troops to what became known as the Peninsular campaign. The objective was to capture Richmond, the Confederate capital. McClellan had his troops and their supplies ferried in 400 ships from Washington to Fortress Monroe, near the mouth of the James River, an effort that took three weeks. Inching up the James Peninsula toward Richmond, he tried to avoid battle, hoping his overwhelming numbers would convince the South to surrender.

In a series of battles known as the Seven Days, Robert E. Lee boldly counterattacked, repeatedly catching McClellan off guard. Taking heavy losses as well as inflicting them, Lee drove McClellan back. In August, Lee routed another Union army, commanded

The contrast between the hope and valor of these young Southern volunteer soldiers, photographed shortly before the First Battle of Bull Run, and the later advertisements for substitutes (at right), is marked. Southern exemptions for slave owners and lavish payment for substitutes increasingly bred resentment among the ordinary people of the South.

SOURCE: Cook Collection. Valentine Museum Library/Richmond History Center.

SUBSTITUTE NOTICES.

WANTED—A SUBSTITUTE for a conscript, to serve during the war. Any good man over the age of 35 years, not a resident of Virginia, or a foreigner, may hear of a good situation by calling at Mr. GEORGE BAGBY'S office, Shockoe Slip, to-day, between the hours of 9 and 11 A. M. [jy 9—1t*] A COUNTRYMAN.

WANTED—Two SUBSTITUTES—one for artillery, the other for infantry or cavalry service. Also, to sell, a trained, thoroughbred cavalry HORSE. Apply to DR. BROOCKS, Corner Main and 12th streets, or to T. T. BROOCKS, jy 9—3t* Petersburg, Va.

WANTED—Immediately, a SUBSTITUTE. A man over 35 years old, or under 18, can get a good price by making immediate application to Room No. 50, Monument Hotel, or by addressing "J. W.," through Richmond P. O. jy 9—1t*

WANTED—A SUBSTITUTE, to go into the 24th North Carolina State troops, for which a liberal price will be paid. Apply to me at Dispatch office this evening at 4 o'clock P. M. jy 9—1t* R. R. MOORE.

WANTED—A SUBSTITUTE, to go in a first-rate Georgia company of infantry, under the heroic Jackson. A gentleman whose health is impaired, will give a fair price for a substitute. Apply immediately at ROOM, No. 13, Post-Office Department, third story, between the hours of 10 and 3 o'clock. jy 9—6t*

WANTED—Two SUBSTITUTES for the war. A good bonus will be given. None need apply except those exempt from Conscript. Apply to-day at GEORGE I. HERRING'S, jy 9—1t* Grocery store, No. 56 Main st.

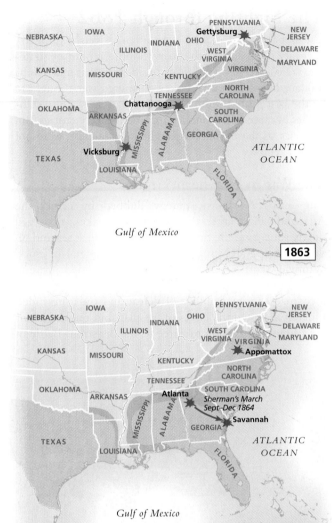

MAP 16.1 Overall Strategy of the Civil War

The initial Northern strategy for subduing the South entailed strangling it by a blockade at sea and obtaining control of the Mississippi River. But at the end of 1862, it was clear that the South's defensive strategy could only be broken by the invasion of Southern territory. In 1864, Sherman's "March to the Sea" and Grant's hammering tactics in northern Virginia brought the war home to the South. Lee's surrender to Grant at Appomattox Courthouse on April 9, 1865, ended the bloodiest war in the nation's history.

by General John Pope, at the Second Battle of Bull Rull (Second Manassas). Lincoln, alarmed at the threat to Washington and disappointed by McClellan's inaction, ordered him to abandon the Peninsular campaign and return to the capital.

Jefferson Davis, like Abraham Lincoln, was an active commander in chief. And like Lincoln, he responded to a public that clamored for more action than a strictly defensive war entailed. After the Seven Days victories, Davis

See the Map

The Civil War, Part I: 1861–1862 at **www.myhistorylab.com**

supported a Confederate march into Maryland. At the same time, he issued a proclamation urging the people of Maryland to make a separate peace. But in the brutal battle of Antietam on September 17, 1862, which claimed more than 5,000 dead and 19,000 wounded, McClellan's army checked Lee's advance. Lee retreated to Virginia, inflicting terrible losses

on Northern troops at Fredericksburg when they again made a thrust toward Richmond in December 1862. The war in northern Virginia was stalemated: neither side was strong enough to win, but each was too strong to be defeated (see Map 16.2).

Shiloh and the War for the Mississippi

Although most public attention was focused on the fighting in Virginia, battles in Tennessee and along the Mississippi River proved to be the key to eventual Union victory. The rising military figure in the West was Ulysses S. Grant, who had once resigned from the service because of a drinking problem. Reenlisting as a colonel after the fall of Fort Sumter, Grant was promoted to brigadier general within two months. In February 1862, Grant captured Fort Henry and Fort Donelson, on the Tennessee and Cumberland Rivers, establishing Union control of much

MAP 16.2 Major Battles in the East, 1861–62
Northern Virginia was the most crucial and the most constant theater of
battle. The prizes were the two opposing capitals, Washington and
Richmond, only 70 miles apart. By the summer of 1862, George B.
McClellan, famously cautious, had achieved only stalemate in the Peninsular
campaign. He did, however, turn back Robert E. Lee at Antietam in
September.

of Tennessee and forcing Confederate troops to retreat
into northern Mississippi.

Moving south with 28,000 men, Grant met a
40,000-man Confederate force commanded by General
Albert Sidney Johnston at Shiloh Church in April 1862.
Seriously outnumbered on the first day, Grant's forces
were reinforced by the arrival of 35,000 troops under the
command of General Don Carlos Buell. After two days of
bitter and bloody fighting in the rain, the Confederates
withdrew. The losses on both sides were enormous: the
North lost 13,000 men, the South 11,000, including

General Johnston, who bled to death. Nevertheless, Union
forces kept moving, capturing Memphis in June and beginning a campaign to eventually capture Vicksburg, "the
Gibraltar of the Mississippi." Grant and other Union generals faced strong Confederate resistance, and progress was
slow. Earlier that year, naval forces under Admiral David
Farragut had captured New Orleans and then continued
up the Mississippi River. By the end of 1862, it was clearly
only a matter of time before the entire river would be in
Union hands. Arkansas, Louisiana, and Texas would then be
cut off from the rest of the Confederacy (see Map 16.3).

MAP 16.3 Major Battles in the Interior, 1862–63
Ulysses S. Grant waged a mobile war, winning at Fort Henry and Fort Donelson in Tennessee in February 1862, at Shiloh in April, and capturing Memphis in June. He then laid siege to Vicksburg, as Admiral David Farragut captured New Orleans and began to advance up the Mississippi River.

The War in the Trans–Mississippi West

Although only one western state, Texas, seceded from the Union, the Civil War was fought in small ways in many parts of the West. Southern hopes for the extension of slavery into the Southwest were reignited by the war, and the just-announced discovery of gold in Colorado impelled the Confederacy to attempt to capture it. Texans mounted an attack on New Mexico, which they had long coveted, and kept their eyes on the larger prizes of Arizona and California. A Confederate force led by General Henry H. Sibley occupied Santa Fé and Albuquerque early in 1862 without resistance, thus posing a serious threat to the entire Southwest. Confederate hopes were dashed, however, by a ragtag group of 950 miners and adventurers organized into the first Colorado Volunteer Infantry

Regiment. After an epic march of 400 miles from Denver, which was completed in thirteen days despite snow and high winds, the Colorado militia stopped the unsuspecting Confederate troops in the Battle of Glorieta Pass on March 26–28, 1862. This dashing action, coupled with the efforts of California militias to safeguard Arizona and Utah from seizure by Confederate sympathizers, secured the Far West for the Union.

Other military action in the West was less decisive. The chronic fighting along the Kansas–Missouri border set a record for brutality when Confederate William Quantrill's Raiders made a predawn attack on Lawrence, Kansas, in August 1863, massacring 150 inhabitants and burning the town. Another civil war took place in Indian Territory, south of Kansas. The southern Indian tribes who had been removed there from the Old Southwest in the 1830s included many who were still bitter over the horrors of their removal by federal troops, and they sympathized with the Confederacy. The Confederacy actively sought Indian support by offering Indian people representation in the Confederate Congress. Consequently, many Indians fought for the South, among them Stand Watie, who became a Confederate military officer. Union victories at Pea Ridge (in northwestern Arkansas) in 1862 and near Fort Gibson (in Indian Territory) in 1863 secured the area for the Union but did little to stop dissension among the Indian groups themselves. After the Civil War, the victorious federal government used the tribes' wartime support for the Confederacy as a justification for demanding further land cessions.

Elsewhere in the West, other groups of Indians found themselves caught up in the wider war. An uprising by the Santee Sioux in Minnesota occurred in August 1862, just as McClellan conceded defeat in the Peninsular campaign in Virginia. Alarmed whites, certain that the uprising was a Confederate plot, ignored legitimate Sioux grievances and responded in kind to Sioux ferocity. In little more than a month, 500 to 800 white settlers and an even greater number of Sioux were killed. Thirty-eight Indians were hanged in a mass execution in Mankato on December 26, 1862, and subsequently all Sioux were expelled from Minnesota. In 1863, U.S. Army Colonel Kit Carson invaded Navajo country in Arizona in retaliation for Indian raids on U.S. troops. Eight thousand Navajos were forced on the brutal "Long Walk" to Bosque Redondo on the Pecos River in New Mexico, where they were held prisoner until a treaty between the United States and the Navajos was signed in 1868.

The hostilities in the West showed that no part of the country, and none of its inhabitants, could remain untouched by the Civil War.

The Naval War

The Union's naval blockade of the South, intended to cut off commerce between the Confederacy and the rest of the world, was initially unsuccessful. The U.S. Navy had only thirty-three ships with which to blockade 189 ports along 3,500 miles of coastline. Southern blockade runners evaded Union ships with ease: only an estimated one-eighth of all Confederate shipping was stopped in 1862. Beginning in 1863, however, as the Union navy became larger, the blockade began to take effect. In 1864, a third of the blockade runners were captured, and in 1865, half of them. As a result, fewer and fewer supplies reached the South.

North and South also engaged in a brief duel featuring the revolutionary new technology of ironcladding. The Confederacy refitted a scuttled Union vessel, the *Merrimac*, with iron plating and renamed it the *Virginia*.

On March 8, 1862, as McClellan began his Peninsular campaign, the *Virginia* steamed out of Norfolk harbor to challenge the Union blockade. The iron plating protected the *Virginia* from the fire of the Union ships, which found themselves defenseless against its ram and its powerful guns. Two Union ships went down, and the blockade seemed about to be broken. But the North had an experimental ironclad of its own, the *Monitor*, which was waiting for the *Virginia* when it emerged from port on March 9. The ungainly *Monitor* was the ship of the future, for it had a revolving turret, a basic component of battleships to come. The historic duel between these first two ironclads was inconclusive, and they were of little consequence for the rest of the war. But this brief duel prefigured the naval and land battles of the world wars of the twentieth century as much as did the massing of huge armies on the battlefield.

For the Union, the most successful naval operation in the first two years of the war was not the blockade but the seizing of exposed coastal areas. The Sea Islands of South Carolina were taken, as were some of the North Carolina islands and Fort Pulaski, which commanded the harbor of Savannah, Georgia. Most damaging to the South was the capture of New Orleans.

The Black Response

The capture of Port Royal in the South Carolina Sea Islands in 1861 was important for another reason. Whites fled at the Union advance, but 10,000 slaves greeted the troops with jubilation and shouts of gratitude. Union troops had unwittingly freed these slaves in advance of any official Union policy on the status of slaves in captured territory.

Early in the war, an irate Southerner who saw three of his slaves disappear behind Union lines at Fortress Monroe, Virginia, demanded the return of his property, citing the Fugitive Slave Law. The Union commander, Benjamin Butler, replied that the Fugitive Slave Law no longer applied and that the escaped slaves were "contraband of war." News of Butler's decision spread rapidly among the slaves in the region of Fortress Monroe. Two days later, eight runaway slaves appeared; the next day, fifty-nine black men and women arrived at the fort. Union commanders had found an effective way to rob the South of its basic workforce. The "contrabands," as they were known, were put to work building fortifications and doing other useful work in Northern camps. Washington, DC, became a refuge for contraband blacks, who crowded into the capital to join the free black people who lived there (at 9,000 people, they were one of the largest urban black populations outside the Confederacy).

Read the **Document**
A Civil War Nurse Writes of Conditions of Freed Slaves (1864) at **www.myhistorylab.com**

The Death of Slavery

As Union troops drove deeper into the South, the black response grew. When Union General William Tecumseh Sherman marched his army through Georgia in 1864, 18,000 slaves—entire families, people of all ages—flocked to the Union lines. By the war's end, nearly a million black people, fully a quarter of all the slaves in the South, had "voted with their feet" for the Union. The overwhelming response of black slaves to the Union advance changed the nature of the war. As increasing numbers of slaves flocked to Union lines, the conclusion that the South refused to face was unmistakable: the southern war to defend the slave system did not have the support of the slaves themselves. Any Northern policy that ignored the issue of slavery and the wishes of the slaves themselves was unrealistic.

The Politics of Emancipation

In 1862, as the issue of slavery loomed ever larger, Abraham Lincoln, acutely aware of divided Northern opinion, inched his way toward a declaration of emancipation. Lincoln was correct to be worried about opinion in the North. Before the war, within the Republican Party, only a small group of abolitionists had favored freeing the slaves. Most Republicans were more concerned about the expansion of slavery than they were about the lives of slaves themselves. For their part, most Northern Democrats were openly antiblack. Irish workers in northern cities had rioted against free African Americans, with whom they often competed for jobs. There was also the question of what would become of slaves who were freed. Northern Democrats effectively played on racial fears in the 1862 congressional elections, warning that freed slaves would pour into northern cities and take jobs from white laborers.

Nevertheless, the necessities of war demanded that Lincoln adopt a policy to end slavery. Even as Radical Republicans chafed at Lincoln's slow pace, he was edging toward a new position. Following the Union victory at Antietam in September 1862, Lincoln issued a preliminary decree: unless the rebellious states returned to the Union by January 1, 1863, he would declare their slaves "forever free." Although Lincoln did not expect the Confederate States to surrender because of his proclamation, the decree increased the pressure on the South by directly linking the slave system to the war effort. Thus, the freedom of black people became part of the struggle. Frederick Douglass, the voice of black America, wrote, "We shout for joy that we live to record this righteous decree."

Read the Document
Abraham Lincoln to Horace Greeley (1862) at www.myhistorylab.com

On January 1, 1863, Lincoln duly issued the final Emancipation Proclamation, which turned out to be less than sweeping. The proclamation freed the slaves in the areas of rebellion—the areas the Union did not control—but specifically exempted slaves in the border states and in former Confederate areas conquered by the Union. Lincoln's purpose was to meet the abolitionist demand for a war against slavery while not losing the support of conservatives, especially in the border states. But the proclamation was so equivocal that Lincoln's own secretary of state, William Seward, remarked sarcastically, "We show our sympathy with slavery by emancipating slaves where we cannot reach them and holding them in bondage where we can set them free."

One group greeted the Emancipation Proclamation with open celebration. On New Year's Day, hundreds of African Americans gathered outside the White House and cheered the president. They called to him, as pastor Henry M. Turner recalled, that "if he would come out of that palace, they would hug him to death." Free African Americans predicted that the news would encourage Southern slaves either to flee to Union lines or refuse to work for their masters. Both of these things were already happening as African Americans seized on wartime changes to reshape white–black relations in the South. In one sense, then, the Emancipation Proclamation simply gave a name to a process already in motion.

Hear the Audio
Free at Last at www.myhistorylab.com

Abolitionists set about moving Lincoln beyond his careful stance in the Emancipation Proclamation. Reformers such as Elizabeth Cady Stanton and Susan B. Anthony lobbied and petitioned for a constitutional amendment outlawing slavery. Congress, at Lincoln's urging, approved and sent to the states a statement banning slavery throughout the United States. Quickly ratified by the Union states in 1865, the statement became the Thirteenth Amendment to the Constitution. (The Southern states, being in a state of rebellion, could not vote.) Lincoln's firm support for this amendment is a good indicator of his true feelings about slavery when he was freed of the kinds of military and political considerations necessarily taken into account in the Emancipation Proclamation.

Black Fighting Men

As part of the Emancipation Proclamation, Lincoln gave his support for the first time to the recruitment of black soldiers. Early in the war, eager black volunteers had been bitterly disappointed at being turned away. Many, like Robert Fitzgerald, a free African American from Pennsylvania, found other ways to serve the Union cause. Fitzgerald first drove a wagon and mule for the Quartermaster Corps, and later, in spite of persistent seasickness, he served in the Union navy. After the Emancipation Proclamation, however, Fitzgerald was able to do what he had wanted to do all along: be a soldier. He enlisted in the Fifth Massachusetts Cavalry, a regiment that, like all the units in which black soldiers served, was 100 percent African American but commanded by white officers (see Seeing History).

This dramatic illustration shows the text of the Emancipation Proclamation and Abraham Lincoln, flanked by the allegorical figures of Justice and Liberty. The glorification of Lincoln as "The Great Emancipator" has obscured the record of his cautious actions before January 1, 1863.

SEEING History

Come and Join Us Brothers

This is a recruitment poster for the Massachusetts 54th Infantry regiment, one of the first official black regiments in the U.S. Army. Organized in March 1863, the 600-man unit led the charge against Fort Wagner, South Carolina, in July, resulting in 116 deaths, including that of the white commanding officer, Colonel Robert Gould Shaw, and many casualties. The bravery of the recruits at Fort Wagner and in other battles changed the minds of many Union officers, who had previously disparaged the fighting abilities of African Americans.

A general belief in African American inferiority was rampant in the North, but the army service of black men made a dent in white racism. Massachusetts enacted the first law forbidding discrimination against African Americans in public facilities. Some major cities, among them San Francisco, Cincinnati, Cleveland, and New York, desegregated their streetcars. Some states—Ohio, California, Illinois—repealed statutes that had barred black people from testifying in court or serving on juries.

• **Frederick Douglass said, "Once let the black man get upon his person the brass letters, U.S., let him get an eagle on his button and a musket on his shoulder and bullets in his pocket," Douglass continued, and "there is no power on earth that can deny that he has earned the right to citizenship." Was Douglass right?**

SOURCE: E. Sachse and Company, "The Shackle Broken by the Genius of Freedom," Baltimore, Md.; 1874, Chicago Historical Society.

In Fitzgerald's company of eighty-three men, half came from slave states and had run away to enlist; the other half came mostly from the North but also from Canada, the West Indies, and France. Other regiments had volunteers from Africa. The proportion of volunteers from the loyal border states (where slavery was still legal) was upwards of 25 percent—a lethal blow to the slave system in those states.

After a scant two months of training, Fitzgerald's company was sent on to Washington and then to battle in northern Virginia. Uncertain of the reception they would receive in Northern cities with their history of antiblack riots, Fitzgerald and his comrades were pleasantly surprised. "We are cheered in every town we pass through," he wrote in his diary. "I was surprised to see a great many white people weeping as the train moved South." White people had reason to cheer: black volunteers, eager and willing to fight, made up 10 percent of the Union army. Nearly 200,000 African Americans (one out of every five black males in the nation) served in the Union army or navy. A fifth of them—37,000—died defending their own freedom and the Union.

Military service was something no black man could take lightly. African American soldiers faced prejudice within the army and had to prove themselves in battle. Moreover, the Confederates hated and feared African American troops and threatened to treat any captured black soldier as an escaped slave subject to execution. On at least one occasion, the threats were carried out. In 1864, Confederate soldiers massacred 262 black soldiers at Fort Pillow, Tennessee, after they had surrendered. Although large-scale episodes such as this were rare (especially after President Lincoln threatened retaliation), smaller ones were not. On duty near Petersburg, Virginia, Robert Fitzgerald's company lost a picket to Confederate hatred: wounded in the leg, he was unable to escape from Confederate soldiers, who smashed his skull with their musket butts.

Another extraordinary part of the story of the African American soldiers was their reception by black people in the South, who were overjoyed at the sight of armed black men, many of them former slaves themselves, wearing the uniform of the Union army. As his regiment entered Wilmington, North Carolina, one soldier wrote, "Men and women, old and young, were running throughout the streets, shouting and praising God. We could then truly see what we have been fighting for."

●◦●┌[**Read** the **Document**
*An African American
Soldier Writes to the
President Appealing for
Equality in 1863 at*
www.myhistorylab.com

African American soldiers were not treated equally by the Union army. They were segregated in camp, given the worst jobs, and paid less than white soldiers ($10 a month rather than $13). Although they might not be able to do much about the other kinds of discrimination, the men of the Fifty-fourth Massachusetts found an unusual way to protest their unequal pay: they refused to accept it, preferring to serve the army for free until it decided to treat them as free men. The protest was effective; in June 1864, the War Department equalized the wages of black and white soldiers.

The Front Lines and the Home Front

Civil War soldiers wrote millions of letters home, more proportionately than in any American war. Their letters and the ones they received in return were links between the front lines and the home front, between the soldiers and their home communities. They are a testament to the patriotism of both Union and Confederate troops, for the story they tell is frequently one of slaughter and horror.

The Toll of War

In spite of early hopes for war without excessive casualties, Civil War battles were appallingly deadly (see Figure 16.2). One reason was technology: improved weapons, particularly modern rifles, had much greater range and accuracy than the smooth-bore muskets they replaced. As Ulysses Grant observed, "At a distance of a few hundred yards, a man could fire at you all day [with a musket] without your finding out." The new Springfield and Enfield rifles were accurate for a quarter of a mile or more.

Civil War generals, however, were slow to adjust to this new reality. Almost all Union and Confederate generals remained committed to the conventional military doctrine of massed infantry offensives that they had learned in their military classes at West Point. Part of this strategy had been to "soften up" a defensive line with artillery before an infantry assault, but now the range of the new rifles made artillery itself vulnerable to attack. As a result, generals relied less on "softening up" than on immense numbers of infantrymen, hoping that enough of them would survive the withering rifle fire to overwhelm the enemy line. Enormous casualties were a consequence of this basic strategy.

Medical ignorance was another factor in the casualty rate. Because the use of antiseptic procedures was in its infancy, men often died because minor wounds became infected. Gangrene was a common cause of death. Disease was an even more frequent killer, taking twice as many men as were lost in battle. The overcrowded and unsanitary conditions of many camps were breeding grounds for smallpox, dysentery, typhoid, pneumonia, and, in the summer, malaria.

Both North and South were completely unprepared to handle the supply and health needs of their large armies. Twenty-four hours after the battle of Shiloh, most of the wounded still lay on the field in the rain. Many

Battles, by date	Union	Confederacy	Total
Fort Donelson 2/13–16/1862 Tennessee	2,832	16,623	19,455
Shiloh 4/6–7/1862 Tennessee	13,047	10,694	23,741
2nd Manassas 8/29–30/1862 Virginia	16,054	9,197	25,251
Antietam 9/17/1862 Maryland	12,410	13,723	26,134
Stone's River 12/31/1862 Tennessee	12,906	11,739	24,645
Chancellorsville 5/1–4/1863 Virginia	17,278	12,821	30,099
Gettysburg 7/1–3/1863 Maryland	23,049	28,063	51,112
Chickamagua 9/19–20/1863 Georgia	16,170	18,454	34,624
Wilderness 5/5–7/1864 Virginia	17,666	7,750	24,624
Spotsylvania 5/8–19/1864 Virginia	18,399	9,000	27,399

Casualities in thousands: 0 4,000 8,000 12,000 16,000 20,000 24,000 28,000 32,000 36,000 40,000 44,000 48,000 52,000 56,000 60,000

FIGURE 16.2 The Casualties Mount Up This chart of the ten costliest battles of the Civil War shows the relentless toll of casualties (killed, wounded, missing, captured) on both the Union and Confederate sides.

died of exposure; some, unable to help themselves, drowned. There was no overall system for recording the war dead, or for their burial. Relatives were often forced to travel to battlefields to search, frequently in vain, for the bodies of their loved ones. Nor were the combatants prepared to deal with masses of war prisoners, as the shocking example of the Confederate prison camp at Andersonville in northern Georgia demonstrated. Andersonville was an open stockade with no shade or shelter, erected early in 1864 to hold 10,000 Northern prisoners. But by midsummer, it held 33,000. During the worst weeks of that summer, 100 prisoners died of disease, exposure, or malnutrition each day.

Army Nurses

There was also an urgent need for skilled nurses to care for wounded and convalescent soldiers. Nursing within a family context was widely considered to be women's work. Caring for sick family members was a key domestic responsibility for women, and most had considerable experience with it. But taking care of strange men in hospitals was another thing. There were strong objections that such work was "unseemly" for respectable women.

Under the pressure of wartime necessity, and over the objections of most army doctors—who resented the challenge to their authority from people no different

than their daughters or wives—women became army nurses. Hospital nursing, previously considered a job only disreputable women would undertake, now became a suitable vocation for middle-class women. Under the leadership of veteran reformer Dorothea Dix of the asylum movement, and in cooperation with the Sanitary Commission (and with the vocal support of Mother Bickerdyke), by the war's end more than 3,000 Northern women had worked as paid army nurses and many more as volunteers. Although women had made important advances, most army nurses and medical support staff were men.

Southern women were also active in nursing and otherwise aiding soldiers, though the South never boasted a single large-scale organization like the Sanitary Commission. The women of Richmond volunteered when they found the war on their doorstep in the summer of 1862. During the Seven Days Battles, thousands of wounded poured into Richmond; many died in the streets, because there was no room for them in hospitals. Richmond women first established informal "roadside hospitals" to meet the need, and their activities expanded from there. As in the North, middle-class women at first faced strong resistance from army doctors and even their

•••─[Read the **Document**

Clara Barton, Memoirs about Medical Life at the Battlefield (1862) at **www.myhistorylab.com**

Nurse Ann Bell tending to wounded soldiers in a Union hospital.

own families, who believed that a field hospital was "no place for a refined lady."

Kate Cumming of Mobile, who nursed in Corinth, Mississippi, after the Battle of Shiloh, faced down such reproofs, though she confided to her diary that nursing wounded men was very difficult: "Nothing that I had ever heard or read had given me the faintest idea of the horrors witnessed here." She and her companion nurses persisted and became an important part of the Confederate medical services. For Southern women, who had been much less active in the public life of their communities than their Northern reforming sisters, this Civil War activity marked an important break with prewar tradition.

The Life of the Common Soldier

The conditions experienced by the eager young volunteers of the Union and Confederate armies included massive, terrifying, and bloody battles, apparently unending, with no sign of victory in sight. Soldiers suffered from the uncertainty of supply, which left troops, especially in the South, without uniforms, tents, and sometimes even food. They endured long marches over muddy, rutted roads while carrying packs weighing fifty or sixty pounds. Disease was rampant in their dirty, verminous, and unsanitary camps, and hospitals were so dreadful that more men left them dead than alive. As a result, desertion was common: an estimated one of every nine Confederate soldiers and one of every seven Union soldiers deserted. Unauthorized absence was another problem. At Antietam, Robert E. Lee estimated that unauthorized absence reduced his strength by a third to a half.

Wartime Politics

In the earliest days of the war, Northerners had joined together in support of the war effort. Democrat Stephen A. Douglas, Lincoln's defeated rival, paid a visit to the White House to offer Lincoln his support, then traveled home to Illinois, where he addressed a huge rally of Democrats in Chicago: "There can be no neutrals in this war, only patriots—or traitors!" Within a month, Douglas was dead at age forty-eight. By 1862, Democrats had split into two factions: the War Democrats and the Peace Democrats, derogatorily called "Copperheads" (from the poisonous snake).

Despite the split in the party in 1860 and the secession of the South, the Democratic Party remained a powerful force in Northern politics. It had received 44 percent of the popular vote in the North in the 1860 election, and its united opposition to the emancipation of slaves explains much of Lincoln's equivocal action on this issue. But the Peace Democrats went far beyond opposition to emancipation, denouncing the draft, martial law, and the high-handed actions of "King Abraham."

The leader of the Copperheads, Clement Vallandigham, a former Ohio congressman, advocated an armistice and a negotiated peace that would "look only to the welfare, peace and safety of the white race, without reference to the effect that settlement may have on the African." Western Democrats, he threatened, might form their own union with the South, excluding New England with its radical abolitionists and high-tariff industrialists. Indeed, in the fall and winter of 1862–63 rumors swirled that the Northwest was ready to secede. Lincoln could not afford to take these threats and rumors lightly.

COMMUNITIES *in* CONFLICT

The Limits of Civil Liberties in Wartime

On May 5, 1863, Clement Vallandigham, the nation's most outspoken "Copperhead," was arrested at his home in Dayton, Ohio, on the charge of traitorous speech. Immediately brought before a military court, he was speedily convicted and sentenced to imprisonment, a sentence that Lincoln himself changed to banishment. Vallandigham's arrest caused a riot in his hometown of Dayton, a storm of protest from Democratic newspapers, and Democratic "indignation" rallies in many cities. Lincoln responded seriously and extensively to the protests, taking the time to compose a careful statement that was published in the *New York Tribune* on June 15, 1863.

• **Which side of this argument do you favor? What should be the limits of free speech in wartime?**

The Press Supports Vallandigham

"A crime has been committed against the most vital right of the poor and the rich, the humble and the exalted—the right to think, to speak, to live. When this thing is consummated, then plainly before the American people does Abraham Lincoln stand—the murderer of the nation. The plea of military or governmental necessity is a flimsy screen that will command no respect. No necessity can justify the monstrous outrage." *Dubuque Herald*, May 14, 1863.

"Let us remind Lincoln that Caesar had his Brutus and Charles the First his Cromwell. Let us also remind the George the Third of the present day that he, too, may have his Cromwell or his Brutus." Orator at the New York indignation rally, quoted in *New York Herald*, May 19, 1863.

"Vallandigham was arrested for no crime known to law, sentenced to a punishment never heard of in any free country, and arbitrarily changed by the President to one not

> **"Vallandigham was arrested for no crime known to law. . . ."**

In 1862, Lincoln proclaimed that all people who discouraged enlistments in the army or otherwise engaged in disloyal practices would be subject to martial law. More than 13,000 people, most of them deserters and war profiteers, were arrested, tried in military courts, and imprisoned. Some, however, were convicted in military courts on charges of "declaring sympathy for the enemy." One of them was Vallandigham himself, who courted arrest but was denied the chance of martyrdom when Lincoln exiled him to the Confederacy rather than to jail. (Ironically, the Confederacy did not want him and quickly sent him to Canada.) Lincoln rejected all protests, claiming that his arbitrary actions were necessary for national security (see Communities in Conflict).

Lincoln also faced challenges from the radical faction of his own party. As the war continued, the Radicals gained strength: it was they who pushed for emancipation in the early days of the war and for harsh treatment of the defeated South after it ended. The most troublesome Radical was Salmon P. Chase, who in December 1862 caused a cabinet crisis when he encouraged Senate Republicans to complain that Secretary of State William Seward was "lukewarm" in his support for emancipation. This Radical challenge was a portent of the party's difficulties after the war, which Lincoln did not live to see—or prevent.

Economic and Social Strains on the North

Wartime needs caused a surge in Northern economic growth, but the gains were unequally distributed. Early in the war, some industries suffered: textile manufacturers could not get cotton, and shoe factories that had made cheap shoes for slaves were without a market. But other industries boomed—boot making, shipbuilding, and the manufacture of woolen goods such as blankets and uniforms, to give just three examples. Coal mining expanded, as did ironmaking, especially the manufacture of iron rails for railroads. Agricultural goods were in great demand, promoting further mechanization of farming. The McCormick brothers grew rich from sales of their reapers in part because women, left to tend the family farm while the men went to war, could manage the demanding task of harvesting if they had mechanized equipment.

Meeting wartime needs enriched some people honestly, but speculators and profiteers also flourished, as they have in every war. By the end of the war, government contracts had exceeded $1 billion. Not all of this business was free from corruption. New wealth was evident in every northern city. Many people were appalled at the spectacle of wealth in the midst of wartime suffering. Still, some of the new wealth went to good causes. Of the more than $3 million raised by the female volunteers of recognized in the Constitution." Henry N. Walker, *Detroit Free Press*, August 26, 1863.

Lincoln Responds

Mr. Vallandigham avows his hostility to the war on the part of the Union; and his arrest was made because he was laboring, with some effect, to prevent the raising of troops; to encourage desertions from the army; and to leave the rebellion without an adequate military force to suppress it. He was not arrested because he was damaging the political prospects of the Administration, or the personal interests of the commanding general, but because he was damaging the army, upon the existence and vigor of which the life of the nation depends. He is warring upon the military, and this gave the military constitutional jurisdiction to lay hands upon him. If Mr. Vallandigham was not damaging the military power of the country, then his arrest was made on mistake of fact, which I would be glad to correct on reasonably satisfactory evidence.

Long experience has shown that armies can not be maintained unless desertion shall be punished by the severe penalty of death. The case requires, and the law and the Constitution sanction this punishment. Must I shoot a simple-minded soldier boy who deserts, while I must not touch a hair of a wily agitator who induces him to desert? This is not the less injurious when effected by getting a father, or brother, or friend, into a public meeting, and there working upon his feelings till he is persuaded to write the soldier boy that he is fighting in a bad cause, for a wicked administration

> "[H]is arrest was made because he was damaging the army. . . ."

of a contemptible Government, too weak to arrest and punish him if he shall desert. I think that in such a case, to silence the agitation and save the boy, is not only constitutional but withal a great mercy.

---

the United States Sanitary Commission, some came from gala Sanitary Fairs designed to attract those with money to spend.

For most people, however, the war brought the day-to-day hardship of inflation. During the four years of the war, the North suffered an inflation rate of 80 percent, or nearly 15 percent a year. This annual rate, three times what is generally considered tolerable, did much to inflame social tensions. Wages rose only half as much as prices, and workers responded by joining unions and striking. Manufacturers, bitterly opposed to unions, freely hired strikebreakers (many of whom were African Americans, women, or immigrants) and formed organizations of their own to prevent further unionization and to blacklist union organizers. Thus, both capital and labor moved far beyond the small, localized confrontations of the early industrial period. The formation of large-scale organizations, fostered by wartime demand, laid the groundwork for the national battle between workers and manufacturers that would dominate the last part of the nineteenth century.

Another major source of social tension was conscription. The Union introduced a draft in March 1863. Especially unpopular was a provision in the draft law that allowed the hiring of substitutes or the payment of a commutation fee of $300. Substitutes were mostly recent

immigrants who had not yet filed for citizenship and were thus not yet eligible to be drafted. It is estimated that immigrants (some of whom were citizens) made up 20 percent of the Union army. Substitution had been accepted in all previous European and American wars. It was so common that President Lincoln, though overage, tried to set an example by paying for a substitute himself. The Democratic Party, however, made substitution an inflammatory issue. Pointing out that $300 was almost a year's wages for an unskilled laborer, they appealed to popular resentment by calling the draft law "aristocratic legislation" and to fear, by running headlines such as "Three Hundred Dollars or Your Life."

As practiced in the local communities, conscription was indeed often marred by favoritism and prejudice. Local officials called up many more poor than rich men and selected a higher proportion of immigrants than non-immigrants. In reality, however, only 7 percent of all men called to serve actually did so. About 25 percent hired a substitute, another 45 percent were exempted for "cause" (usually health reasons), and another 20 to 25 percent simply failed to report to the community draft office. Nevertheless, by 1863, many Northern urban workers believed that the slogan "a rich man's war but a poor man's fight," though coined in the South, applied to them as well.

The New York City Draft Riots

In the spring of 1863, there were protests against the draft throughout the North. Riots and disturbances broke out in many cities, and several federal enrollment officers were killed. The greatest trouble occurred in New York City between July 13 and July 16, 1863, where a wave of working-class looting, fighting, and lynching claimed the lives of 105 people, many of them African American. The rioting, the worst up to that time in American history, was quelled only when five units of the U.S. Army were rushed from the battlefield at Gettysburg, where they had been fighting Confederates the week before.

Read the Document

The New York Times Prints Opinion on the New York Draft Riots in 1863 at **www.myhistorylab.com**

The riots had several causes. Anger at the draft and racial prejudice were what most contemporaries saw. From a historical perspective, however, the riots were at least as much about the urban growth and tensions described in Chapter 13. The Civil War made urban problems worse and heightened the visible contrast between the lives of the rich and those of the poor. These tensions exploded, but were not solved, during those hot days in the summer of 1863.

Ironically, African American men, a favorite target of the rioters' anger, were a major force in easing the national crisis over the draft. Though they had been barred from service until 1863, in the later stages of the war African American volunteers filled much of the manpower gap that the controversial draft was meant to address.

The Failure of Southern Nationalism

The war brought even greater changes to the South. As in the North, war needs led to expansion and centralization of government control over the economy, often in the face of protest by governors who favored states' rights. The expansion of government brought sudden urbanization, a new experience for the predominantly rural South. The population of Richmond, the Confederate capital, almost tripled, in large part because the Confederate bureaucracy grew to 70,000 people. Because of the need for military manpower, a good part of the Confederate bureaucracy consisted of women, who were referred to as "government girls." All of this—government control, urban growth, women in the paid workforce—was new to Southerners, and not all of it was welcomed.

Even more than in the North, the voracious need for soldiers fostered class antagonisms. When small yeoman farmers went off to war, their wives and families struggled to farm on their own, without the help of mechanization, which they could not afford, and without the help of slaves, which they had never owned. But wealthy men could be exempted from the draft if they had more than twenty slaves. Furthermore, many upper-class Southerners—at least 50,000—avoided military service by paying liberally ($5,000 and more) for substitutes. Worst of all was the starvation. The North's blockade and the breakdown of the South's transportation system restricted the availability of food in the South, and these problems were vastly magnified by runaway inflation. Prices in the South rose by an unbelievable 9,000 percent from 1861 to 1865. Speculation and hoarding by the rich made matters even worse. In the spring of 1863, food riots broke out in four Georgia cities (Atlanta among them) and in North Carolina. In Richmond, more than a thousand people, mostly women, broke into bakeries and snatched loaves of bread, crying "Bread! Bread! Our children are starving while the rich roll in wealth!"

Increasingly, the ordinary people of the South, preoccupied with staying alive, refused to pay taxes, to provide food, or to serve in the army. Soldiers were drawn home by the desperation of their families as well as by the discouraging course of the war. By January 1865, the desertion rate had climbed to 8 percent a month.

At the same time, the life of the Southern ruling class was irrevocably altered by the changing nature of slavery. By the end

A black man is lynched during the New York City Draft Riots in July 1863. Free black people and their institutions were major victims of the worst rioting in American history until then. The riots were more than a protest against the draft; they were also an outburst of frustration over urban problems that had been festering for decades.

of the war, one-quarter of all slaves had fled to the Union lines, and those who remained often stood in a different relationship to their owners. As white masters and overseers left to join the army, white women were left behind on the plantation to cope with shortages, grow crops, and manage the labor of slaves. Lacking the patriarchal authority of their husbands, white women found that white–black relationships shifted, sometimes drastically (as when slaves fled) and sometimes more subtly. Slaves increasingly made their own decisions about when and how they would work, and they refused to accept the punishments that would have accompanied this insubordination in prewar years. One black woman, implored by her mistress not to reveal the location of a trunk of money and silver plate when the invading Yankees arrived, looked her in the eye and said, "Mistress, I can't lie over that; you bought that silver plate when you sold my three children."

Peace movements in the South were motivated by a confused mixture of realism, war weariness, and the animosity of those who supported states' rights and opposed Jefferson Davis. The anti-Davis faction was led by his own vice president, Alexander Stephens, who early in 1864 suggested a negotiated peace. Peace sentiment was especially strong in North Carolina, where more than a hundred public meetings in support of negotiations were held in the summer of 1863. Davis would have none of it, and he commanded enough votes in the Confederate Congress to enforce his will and to suggest that peace sentiment was traitorous.

The Tide Turns

As Lincoln's timing of the Emancipation Proclamation showed, by 1863 the nature of the war was changing. The proclamation freeing the slaves struck directly at the Southern home front and the civilian workforce. That same year, the nature of the battlefield war changed as well. The Civil War became the first total war.

The Turning Point of 1863

In the summer of 1863, the moment finally arrived when the North could begin to hope for victory. But for the Union army, the year opened with stalemate in the East and slow and costly progress in the West. For the South, 1863 represented its highest hopes for military success and for diplomatic recognition by Britain or France.

Attempting to break the stalemate in northern Virginia, General Joseph "Fighting Joe" Hooker and a Union army of 130,000 men attacked a Confederate army half that size at Chancellorsville in May. In response, Robert E. Lee daringly divided his forces, sending General Thomas "Stonewall" Jackson and 30,000 men on a day-long flanking movement that caught the Union troops by surprise. Chancellorsville was a great Confederate victory; there were 17,000 Union losses. However, Confederate losses were also great: 13,000 men, representing more than 20 percent of Lee's army.

Though weakened, Lee moved to the attack. In June, in his second and most dangerous single thrust into Union territory, he moved north into Maryland and Pennsylvania. His purpose was as much political as military: he hoped that a great Confederate victory would lead Britain and France to intervene in the war and demand a negotiated peace. The ensuing Battle of Gettysburg, July 1–3, 1863, was another horrible slaughter. On the last day, Lee sent 15,000 men, commanded by George Pickett, to attack the heavily defended Union center. The charge was suicidal. When the Union forces opened fire at 200 yards, one Southern officer reported, "Pickett's division just seemed to melt away. . . . Nothing but stragglers came back."

Lee retreated from the field, leaving more than one-third of his army behind—28,000 men killed, wounded, or missing. Union general George Meade elected not to pursue with his battered Union army (23,000 casualties). "We had them in our grasp," Lincoln said in bitter frustration. "We had only to stretch forth our arms and they were ours. And nothing I could say or do could make the Army move." Nevertheless, Lee's great gamble had failed; he never again mounted a major offensive (see Map 16.4).

The next day, July 4, 1863, Ulysses S. Grant took Vicksburg, Mississippi, after a costly siege. The combined news of Gettysburg and Vicksburg dissuaded Britain and France from recognizing the Confederacy and checked the Northern peace movement. It also tightened the North's grip on the South, for the Union now controlled the entire Mississippi River. In November, Generals Grant and Sherman broke the Confederate hold on Chattanooga, Tennessee, thereby opening the way to Atlanta.

Grant and Sherman

In March 1864, President Lincoln called Grant east and appointed him general-in-chief of all the Union forces. Lincoln's critics were appalled. Grant was an uncouth Westerner (like the president) and (unlike the president) was rumored to have a drinking problem. Lincoln replied that if he knew the general's brand of whiskey, he would send a barrel of it to every commander in the Union army.

Grant devised a plan of strangulation and annihilation. While he took on Lee in northern Virginia, he sent General William Tecumseh Sherman to defeat Confederate general Joe Johnston's Army of Tennessee, which was

Read the Document

John Dooley, Passages from His Journal (1863) at www.myhistorylab.com

See the Map

The Civil War, Part II: 1863–1865 at www.myhistorylab.com

MAP 16.4 The Turning Point, 1863 In June, Lee boldly struck north into Maryland and Pennsylvania, hoping for a victory that would cause Britain and France to demand a negotiated peace on Confederate terms. Instead, he lost the hard-fought battle of Gettysburg, July 1–3. The very next day, Grant's long siege of Vicksburg succeeded. These two great Fourth of July victories turned the tide in favor of the Union. The Confederates never again mounted a major offensive. Total Union control of the Mississippi now exposed the Lower South to attack.

defending the approach to Atlanta. Both Grant and Sherman exemplified the new kind of warfare. They aimed to inflict maximum damage on the fabric of Southern life, hoping that the South would choose to surrender rather than face total destruction. This decision to broaden the war so that it directly affected civilians was new in American military history and prefigured the total wars of the twentieth century.

In northern Virginia, Grant pursued a policy of destroying civilian supplies. He said he "regarded it as humane to both sides to protect the persons of those found at their homes, but to consume everything that could be used to support or supply armies." One of those supports was slaves. Grant welcomed fleeing slaves to Union lines and encouraged army efforts to put them to work or enlist them as soldiers. He also cooperated with the efforts of groups like the New England Freedmen's Aid Society, which sent Northern volunteers (many of them women) into Union-occupied parts of the South to educate former slaves. The Freedmen's Bureau, authorized by Congress in March 1865, continued this work into Reconstruction. One of the Northern teachers who went south in 1866 to work for the bureau was Robert Fitzgerald, the former soldier.

The most famous example of the new strategy of total war was General Sherman's 1864 march through Georgia. Sherman captured Atlanta on September 2, 1864, and the rest of Georgia now lay open to him. In November, Sherman set out to march the 285 miles to the coastal city of Savannah, living off the land and destroying everything in his path. His military purpose was to tighten the noose around Robert E. Lee's army in northern Virginia by cutting off Mississippi, Alabama, and Georgia from the rest of the Confederacy. But his second purpose, openly stated, was to "make war so terrible" to the people of the South, to "make them so sick of war that generations would pass away before they would again appeal to it." Accordingly, he told his men to seize, burn, or destroy everything in their path (but, significantly, not to harm civilians).

◆◆◆ Read the Document

William T. Sherman, The March through Georgia (1875) at **www.myhistorylab.com**

It was estimated that Sherman's army did $100 million worth of damage. "They say no living thing is found in Sherman's track," Mary Boykin Chesnut wrote, "only chimneys, like telegraph poles, to carry the news of [his] attack backwards."

Terrifying to white Southern civilians, Sherman was initially hostile to black Southerners as well. In the interests of speed and efficiency, his army turned away many of the 18,000 slaves who flocked to it in Georgia, causing a number to be recaptured and reenslaved. This callous action caused such a scandal in Washington that Secretary of War Edwin Stanton arranged a special meeting in Georgia with Sherman and twenty African American ministers who spoke for the freed slaves. This meeting in itself was extraordinary: no one had ever before asked slaves what they wanted. Equally extraordinary was Sherman's response in Special Field Order 15, issued in January 1865: he set aside more than 400,000 acres of Confederate land to be given to the freed slaves in forty-acre parcels. This was war of a kind that white Southerners had never imagined.

The 1864 Election

The war complicated the 1864 presidential election. Lincoln was renominated during a period when the war was going badly. Opposed by the Radicals, who thought he was too conciliatory toward the South, and by Republican conservatives, who disapproved of the Emancipation Proclamation, Lincoln had little support within his own party.

In contrast, the Democrats had an appealing candidate: General George McClellan, a war hero (always a favorite with American voters) who was known to be sympathetic to the South. Democrats played shamelessly on the racist fears of the urban working class, accusing Republicans of being "negro-lovers" and warning that racial mixing lay ahead.

A deeply depressed Lincoln fully expected to lose the election. "I am going to be beaten," he told an army officer in August 1864, "and unless some great change takes place badly beaten." A great change did take place: Sherman captured Atlanta on September 2. Jubilation swept the North: some cities celebrated with 100-gun salutes. Lincoln won the election with 55 percent of the popular vote. Seventy-eight percent of the soldiers voted for him rather than for their former commander. Ordinary people and war-weary soldiers had voted to continue a difficult and divisive conflict. The election was important evidence of Northern support for Lincoln's policy of unconditional surrender for the South. There would be no negotiated peace; the war would continue.

Nearing the End

As Sherman devastated the lower South, Grant was locked in struggle with Lee in northern Virginia. Grant did not favor subtle strategies. He bluntly said, "The art of war is simple enough. Find out where your enemy is. Get at him as soon as you can. Strike at him as hard as you can, and keep moving on." Following this plan, Grant eventually hammered Lee into submission but at enormous cost. Lee

This striking photograph by Thomas C. Roche shows a dead Confederate soldier, killed at Petersburg on April 3, 1865, only six days before the surrender at Appomattox. The new medium of photography conveyed the horror of the war with a gruesome reality to the American public.

had learned the art of defensive warfare (his troops called him "the King of Spades" because he made them dig trenches so often), and he inflicted heavy losses on the Union army in a succession of bloody encounters in the spring and summer of 1864: almost 18,000 at the battle of the Wilderness, more than 8,000 at Spotsylvania, and 12,000 at Cold Harbor. At Cold Harbor, Union troops wrote their names and addresses on scraps of paper and pinned them to their backs, so certain were they of being killed or wounded in battle.

Grim and terrible as Grant's strategy was, it proved effective. Rather than pulling back after his failed assaults, he kept moving south, finally settling in for a prolonged siege of Lee's forces at Petersburg. The North's great advantage in population finally began to tell. There were more Union soldiers to replace those lost in battle, but there were no more white Confederates (see Map 16.5).

In desperation, the South turned to what had hitherto been unthinkable: arming slaves to serve as soldiers in the Confederate army. But—and this was the bitter irony—the African American soldiers and their families would have to be promised freedom or they would desert to the Union at the first chance they had. Even though Davis's proposal had the support of General Robert E. Lee, the Confederate Congress balked at first. As one member candidly admitted, "If slaves make good soldiers our whole theory of slavery is wrong." Finally, on March 13, the Confederate Congress authorized a draft of black soldiers—without mentioning freedom. Although two regiments of African American soldiers were immediately organized in Richmond, it was too late. The South never had to publicly acknowledge the paradox of having to offer slaves freedom so that they would fight to defend slavery.

By the spring of 1865, public support for the war simply disintegrated in the South. Starvation, inflation, dissension, and the prospect of military defeat were too much. In February, Jefferson Davis sent his vice president, Alexander Stephens, to negotiate terms at a peace conference at Hampton Roads. Lincoln would not countenance anything less than full surrender, although he did offer gradual emancipation with compensation for slave owners. Davis, however, insisted on Southern independence at all costs. Consequently, the Hampton Roads conference failed and

MAP 16.5 The Final Battles in Virginia, 1864–65
In the war's final phase early in 1865, Sherman closed one arm of a pincers by marching north from Savannah, while Grant attacked Lee's last defensive positions in Petersburg and Richmond. Lee retreated from them on April 2 and surrendered at Appomattox Court House on April 9, 1865.

Hear the Audio

When This Cruel War Is Over at
www.myhistorylab.com

Southern resistance faded away. In March 1865, Mary Boykin Chesnut recorded in her diary: "I am sure our army is silently dispersing. Men are going the wrong way all the time. They slip by now with no songs nor shouts. They have given the thing up."

Appomattox

In the spring of 1865, Lee and his remaining troops, outnumbered two to one, still held Petersburg and Richmond. Starving, short of ammunition, and losing men in battle or to desertion every day, Lee retreated from Petersburg on April 2. The Confederate government fled Richmond, stripping and burning the city. Seven days later, Lee and his 25,000 troops surrendered to Grant at Appomattox Court House. Grant treated Lee with great respect and set a historic precedent by giving the Confederate troops parole. This meant they could not subsequently be prosecuted for treason. Grant then sent the starving army on its way with three days' rations for every man. Jefferson Davis, who had hoped to set up a new government in Texas, was captured in Georgia on May 10. The war was finally over.

Watch the Video

The Meaning of the Civil War for Americans at
www.myhistorylab.com

Sensing that the war was near its end, Abraham Lincoln visited Grant's troops when Lee withdrew from Petersburg on April 2. Thus it was that Lincoln came to visit Richmond, and to sit briefly in Jefferson Davis's presidential office, soon after Davis had left it. As Lincoln walked the streets of the burned and pillaged city, black people poured out to see him and surround him, shouting "Glory to God! Glory! Glory! Glory!" Lincoln in turn, said to Admiral David Porter: "Thank God I have lived to see this. It seems to me that I have been dreaming a horrid dream for four years, and now the nightmare is gone."

Death of a President

Lincoln had only the briefest time to savor the victory. On the night of April 14, President and Mrs. Lincoln went to Ford's Theater in Washington. There Lincoln was shot at point-blank range by John Wilkes Booth, a Confederate sympathizer. He died the next day. After a week of observances in Washington, Lincoln's coffin was loaded on a funeral train that slowly carried him back to Springfield. All along the railroad route, day and night, in small towns and large, people gathered to see the train pass and to pay their last respects. At that moment, the Washington community and the larger Union community were one and the same.

The nation as a whole was left with Lincoln's vision for the coming peace, expressed in the unforgettable words of his Second Inaugural Address:

> With malice toward none, with charity for all, with firmness in the right as God gives us to see the right, let us strive on to finish the work we are in, to bind up the nation's wounds, to care for him who shall have borne the battle and for his widow and his orphan, to do all which may achieve and cherish a just and lasting peace among ourselves and with all nations.

The 55th Massachusetts Colored Regiment is shown entering Charleston, February 21, 1865, greeted by happy crowds of African Americans. For white Charlestonians, the sight of victorious black troops in the cockpit of the Confederacy was devastating.

THE FUNERAL OF PRESIDENT LINCOLN, NEW YORK, APRIL 25TH 1865.

PASSING UNION SQUARE.

Lincoln's funeral cortege in New York City, April 25, 1865, just one of the many ceremonies that marked
Lincoln's final trip to Springfield, Illinois, his burying place.

Conclusion

In 1865, a divided people were forcibly reunited by battle.
Their nation, the United States of America, had been permanently changed by civil war. Devastating losses among
the young men of the country—the greatest such losses the
nation was ever to suffer—would affect not only their families but also all of postwar society. Politically, the deepest
irony of the Civil War was that only by fighting it had
America become completely a nation. For it was the war
that broke down local isolation. Ordinary citizens in local
communities, North and South, developed a national perspective as they sent their sons and brothers to be soldiers,
their daughters to be nurses and teachers. Then, too, the
federal government, vastly strengthened by wartime necessity, reached the lives of ordinary citizens more than ever
before. The question now was whether this strengthened
but divided national community, forged in battle, could
create a just peace.

Review Questions

1. At the outset of the Civil War, what were the relative
    advantages of the North and the South, and how did
    they affect the final outcome?

2. In the absence of the Southern Democrats, in the
    early 1860s, the new Republican Congress was able
    to pass a number of party measures with little oppo-
    sition. What do these measures tell you about the
    historical roots of the Republican Party? More gen-
    erally, how do you think we should view legislation
    passed in the absence of the customary opposition,
    debate, and compromise?

3. The greatest problem facing Jefferson Davis and the
    Confederacy was the need to develop a true feeling
    of nationalism. Can the failure of this effort be
    blamed on Davis's weakness as a leader alone, or are
    there other causes?

CHRONOLOGY

1861   March: Morrill Tariff Act

April: Fort Sumter falls; war begins

April: Mobilization begins

April–May: Virginia, Arkansas, Tennessee, and North Carolina secede

June: United States Sanitary Commission established

July: First Battle of Bull Run

December: French troops arrive in Mexico, followed by British and Spanish forces in January

1862   February: Legal Tender Act

February: Battles of Fort Henry and Fort Donelson

March: Battle of Pea Ridge

March: Battle of the *Monitor* and the *Merrimack* (renamed the *Virginia*)

March–August: George B. McClellan's Peninsular campaign

March: Battle of Glorieta Pass

April: Battle of Shiloh

April: Confederate Conscription Act

April: David Farragut captures New Orleans

May: *El Cinqo de Mayo*: Mexican troops repel French invaders

May: Homestead Act

June–July: Seven Days Battles

July: Pacific Railway Act

July: Morrill Land Grant Act

August: Santee Sioux Uprising, Minnesota

September: Battle of Antietam

December: Battle of Fredericksburg

1863   January: Emancipation Proclamation

February: National Bank Act

March: Draft introduced in the North

March: Colonel Kit Carson sends 8,000 Navajos on the "Long Walk" to Bosque Redondo, New Mexico Territory

April: Richmond bread riot

May: Battle of Chancellorsville

June: French occupy Mexico City

July: Battle of Gettysburg

July: Surrender of Vicksburg

July: New York City Draft Riots

November: Battle of Chattanooga

November: Union troops capture Brownsville, Texas

1864   March: Ulysses S. Grant becomes general-in-chief of Union forces

April: Fort Pillow massacre

May: Battle of the Wilderness

May: Battle of Spotsylvania

June: Battle of Cold Harbor

June: Maximilian becomes Emperor of Mexico

September: Atlanta falls

October: St. Albans incident

November: Abraham Lincoln reelected president

November–December: William Tecumseh Sherman's march to the sea

1865   April: Richmond falls

April: Robert E. Lee surrenders at Appomattox

April: Lincoln assassinated

December: Thirteenth Amendment to the Constitution becomes law

4. In what ways can it be said that the actions of African Americans, both slave and free, came to determine the course of the Civil War?

5. Wars always have unexpected consequences. List some of those consequences both for soldiers and for civilians in the North and in the South.

6. Today Abraham Lincoln is considered one of our greatest presidents, but he did not enjoy such approval at the time. List and evaluate some of the contemporary criticisms of Lincoln.

Recommended Reading

Paul D. Escott, *"What Shall We Do with the Negro?" Lincoln, White Racism, and Civil War America* (2009). A survey of contemporary newspapers, magazines, and books about the future of African Americans after slavery reveals the depth of white racism.

Drew Gilpin Faust, *This Republic of Suffering: Death and the American Civil War* (2008). The acclaimed book that assesses the cost of Civil War deaths on the American people.

Jacqueline Jones, *Saving Savannah: The City and the Civil War* (2008). A compelling picture of Savannah's African American community, before, during, and after the Civil War.

Stephanie McCurry, *Confederate Reckoning* (2010). A compelling account of the revolt of Southern slaves and poor white women against the ideals of the Confederacy.

Robert Tracy McKenzie, *Lincolnites and Rebels: A Divided Town in the American Civil War* (2006). Presents Knoxville, TN, as a civil war within a Civil War.

James McPherson, *Battle Cry of Freedom* (1988). The highly readable standard account of the Civil War.

Jeremy Neely, *The Border between Them: Violence and Reconciliation on the Kansas-Missouri Line* (2007). Begins before Anglo settlement and continues through the bloody Civil War years.

Nina Silbar, *Daughters of the Union: Northern Women Fight the Civil War* (2005). Argues that women found a new sense of self and citizenship in wartime.

Andrew Ward, *The Slaves' War: The Civil War in the Words of Former Slaves* (2009). Gathers sources to provide a new perspective.

Jennifer L. Weber, *Copperheads: The Rise and Fall of Lincoln's Opponents in the North* (2006). An even-handed new study.

Keith P. Wilson, *Campfires of Freedom: The Camp Life of Black Soldiers during the Civil War* (2002). Camp life examined to show the soldiers' personal transition from slavery to freedom.

PEARSON
myhistorylab Connections

Reinforce what you learned in this chapter by studying the many documents, images, maps, review tools, and videos available at www.myhistorylab.com.

Read and Review

✓• Study and Review Chapter 16

••• Read the Document

U.S. Sanitary Commission, Sketch of Its Purposes (1864)

Homestead Act of 1862

Elizabeth Keckley, Four Years in the White House (1868)

Abraham Lincoln to Horace Greeley (1862)

Clara Barton, Memoirs about Medical Life at the Battlefield (1862)

An African American Soldier Writes to the President Appealing for Equality in 1863

A Civil War Nurse Writes of Conditions of Freed Slaves (1864)

The New York Times Prints Opinion on the New York Draft Riots in 1863

John Dooley, Passages from His Journal (1863)

William T. Sherman, The March through Georgia (1875)

👁 See the Map

The Civil War, Part I: 1861–1862

The Civil War, Part II: 1863–1865

Research and Explore

••• Read the Document

A Nation Divided: The Civil War

Exploring America: Fort Pillow Massacre

Profiles
Judah Benjamin
Louisa Schuyler

((•• Hear the Audio

Free at Last

When This Cruel War Is Over

👁 Watch the Video

The Civil War

What Caused the Civil War?

The Meaning of the Civil War for Americans

((•• Hear the Audio

Hear the audio files for Chapter 16 at
www.myhistorylab.com.

17

((•–[Hear the Audio

Reconstruction

1863–1877

CHAPTER OUTLINE

Theodor Kaufmann (1814–1896), *On to Liberty*, 1867. Oil on canvas, 36 × 56 in (91.4 × 142.2 cm). Runaway slaves escaping through the woods. Art Resource/Metropolitan Museum of Art.

Hale County, Alabama: From Slavery to Freedom in a Black Belt Community

On a bright Saturday morning in May 1867, 4,000 former slaves streamed into the town of Greensboro, bustling seat of Hale County in west-central Alabama. They came to hear speeches from two delegates to a recent freedmen's convention in Mobile and to find out about the political status of black people under the Reconstruction Act just passed by Congress. Tensions mounted in the days following this unprecedented gathering, as military authorities began supervising voter registration for elections to the upcoming constitutional convention that would rewrite the laws of Alabama. On June 13, John Orrick, a local white, confronted Alex Webb, a politically active freedman, on the streets of Greensboro. Webb had recently been appointed a voter registrar for the district. Orrick swore he would never be registered by a black man and shot Webb dead. Hundreds of armed and angry freedmen formed a posse to search for Orrick but failed to find him. Galvanized by Webb's murder, 500 local freedmen formed a chapter of the Union League, the Republican Party's organizational arm in the South. The chapter functioned as both a militia company and a forum to agitate for political rights.

Violent political encounters between black people and white people were common in southern communities

459

in the wake of the Civil War. Communities throughout the South struggled over the meaning of freedom in ways that reflected their particular circumstances. The 4 million freed people constituted roughly one-third of the total southern population, but the black–white ratio in individual communities varied enormously. In some places, the Union army had been a strong presence during the war, hastening the collapse of the slave system and encouraging experiments in free labor. Other areas had remained relatively untouched by the fighting. In some areas, small farms prevailed; in others, including Hale County, large plantations dominated economic and political life.

West-central Alabama had emerged as a fertile center of cotton production just two decades before the Civil War. There, African Americans, as throughout the South's black belt, constituted more than three-quarters of the population. With the arrival of federal troops in the spring of 1865, African Americans in Hale County, like their counterparts elsewhere, began to challenge the traditional organization of plantation labor.

One owner, Henry Watson, found that his entire workforce had deserted him at the end of 1865. "I am in the midst of a large and fertile cotton growing country," Watson wrote to a partner. "Many plantations are entirely without labor, many plantations have insufficient labor, and upon none are the laborers doing their former accustomed work." Black women refused to work in the fields, preferring to stay home with their children and tend garden plots. Nor would male field hands do any work, such as caring for hogs, that did not directly increase their share of the cotton crop.

Above all, freed people wanted more autonomy. Overseers and owners grudgingly allowed them to work the land "in families," letting them choose their own supervisors and find their own provisions. The result was a shift from the gang labor characteristic of the antebellum period, in which large groups of slaves worked under the harsh and constant supervision of white overseers, to the sharecropping system, in which African American families worked small plots of land in exchange for a small share of the crop. This shift represented less of a victory for newly freed African Americans than a defeat for plantation owners, who resented even the limited economic independence it forced them to concede to their black workforce.

Only a small fraction—perhaps 15 percent—of African American families were fortunate enough to be able to buy land. The majority settled for some version of sharecropping, while others managed to rent land from owners, becoming tenant farmers. Still, planters throughout Hale County had to change the old routines of plantation labor. Local African Americans also organized politically. In 1866, Congress had passed the Civil Rights Act and sent the Fourteenth Amendment to the Constitution to the states for ratification; both promised full citizenship rights to former slaves. Hale County freedmen joined the Republican Party and local Union League chapters. They used their new political power to press for better labor contracts, demand greater autonomy for the black workforce, and agitate for the more radical goal of land confiscation and redistribution. "The colored people are very anxious to get land of their own to live upon independently; and they want money to buy stock to make crops," reported one black Union League organizer. "The only way to get these necessaries is to give our votes to the [Republican] party." Two Hale County former slaves, Brister Reese and James K. Green, won election to the Alabama state legislature in 1869.

It was not long before these economic and political gains prompted a white counterattack. In the spring of 1868, the Ku Klux Klan—a secret organization devoted to terrorizing and intimidating African Americans and their white Republican allies—came to Hale County. Disguised in white sheets, armed with guns and whips, and making nighttime raids on horseback, Klansmen flogged, beat, and murdered freed people. They intimidated voters and silenced political activists. Planters used Klan terror to dissuade former slaves from leaving plantations or organizing for higher wages. With the passage of the Ku Klux Klan Act in 1871, the federal government cracked down on the Klan, breaking its power temporarily in parts of the former Confederacy. But no serious effort was made to stop Klan terror in the west Alabama black belt, and planters there succeeded in reestablishing much of their social and political control.

The events in Hale County illustrate the struggles that beset communities throughout the South during the Reconstruction era after the Civil War. The destruction of slavery and the Confederacy forced African Americans and white people to renegotiate their old roles. These community battles both shaped and were shaped by the

1. What were the competing political plans for reconstructing the defeated Confederacy?

2. How did African Americans negotiate the difficult transition from slavery to freedom?

3. What were the most important political and social legacies of Reconstruction in the southern states?

4. How did economic and political transformations in the North reflect another side of Reconstruction?

FOCUS Questions

1863–1877

victorious and newly expansive federal government in Washington. But the new arrangements of both political power sharing and the organization of labor had to be worked out within local communities. In the end, Reconstruction was only

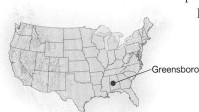
Greensboro

partially successful. Not until the "Second Reconstruction" of the twentieth-century civil rights movement would the descendants of Hale County's African Americans begin to enjoy the full fruits of freedom—and even then not without challenge.

AMERICAN Communities

The Politics of Reconstruction

When General Robert E. Lee's men stacked their guns at Appomattox, the bloodiest war in American history ended. More than 600,000 soldiers had died during the four years of fighting, 360,000 Union and 260,000 Confederate. Another 275,000 Union and 190,000 Confederate troops had been wounded. Although President Abraham Lincoln insisted early on that the purpose of the war was to preserve the Union, by 1863 it had evolved as well into a struggle for African American liberation. Indeed, the political, economic, and moral issues posed by slavery were the root cause of the Civil War, and the war ultimately destroyed slavery, although not racism, once and for all.

The Civil War also settled the constitutional crisis provoked by the secession of the Confederacy and its justification in appeals to states' rights. The name "United States" would from then on be understood as a singular rather than a plural noun, signaling an important change in the meaning of American nationality. The old notion of the United States as a voluntary union of sovereign states gave way to the new reality of a single nation, in which the federal government took precedence over the individual states. The key historical developments of the Reconstruction era revolved around precisely how the newly strengthened national government would define its relationship with the defeated Confederate states and the 4 million newly freed slaves.

The Defeated South

The white South paid an extremely high price for secession, war, and defeat. In addition to the battlefield casualties, the Confederate states sustained deep material and psychological wounds. Much of the best agricultural land was laid waste, including the rich fields of northern Virginia, the Shenandoah Valley, and large sections of Tennessee, Mississippi, Georgia, and South Carolina. Many towns and cities—including Richmond, Atlanta, and Columbia, South Carolina—were in ruins. By 1865, the South's most precious commodities, cotton and African American slaves, no longer were measures of wealth and prestige. Retreating Confederates destroyed most of the South's cotton to prevent its capture by federal troops. What remained was confiscated by Union agents as contraband of war. The former slaves, many of whom had fled to Union lines during the latter stages of the war, were determined to chart their own course in the reconstructed South as free men and women.

Emancipation proved the bitterest pill for white Southerners to swallow, especially the planter elite. Conquered and degraded, and in their view robbed of their slave property, white people responded by regarding African Americans, more than ever, as inferior to

•• Read the Document

Confederate Song, "I'm a Good Old Rebel" (1866) at **www.myhistorylab.com**

themselves. In the antebellum South, white skin had defined a social bond that transcended economic class. It gave even the poorest white a badge of superiority over even the most skilled slave or prosperous free African American. Emancipation, however, forced white people to redefine their world. The specter of political power and social equality for African Americans made racial order the consuming passion of most white Southerners during the Reconstruction years. In fact, racism can be seen as

one of the major forces driving Reconstruction and, ultimately, undermining it.

Abraham Lincoln's Plan

By late 1863, Union military victories had convinced President Lincoln of the need to fashion a plan for the reconstruction of the South (see Chapter 16). Lincoln based his reconstruction program on bringing the seceded states back into the Union as quickly as possible. His Proclamation of Amnesty and Reconstruction of December 1863 offered "full pardon" and the restoration of property, not including slaves, to white Southerners willing to swear an oath of allegiance to the United States and its laws, including the Emancipation Proclamation. Prominent Confederate military and civil leaders were excluded from Lincoln's offer, though he indicated that he would freely pardon them.

The president also proposed that when the number of any Confederate state's voters who took the oath of allegiance reached 10 percent of the number who had voted

"Decorating the Graves of Rebel Soldiers," *Harper's Weekly,* August 17, 1867. After the Civil War, both Southerners and Northerners created public mourning ceremonies honoring fallen soldiers. Women led the memorial movement in the South that, by establishing cemeteries and erecting monuments, offered the first cultural expression of the Confederate tradition. This engraving depicts citizens of Richmond, Virginia, decorating thousands of Confederate graves with flowers at the Hollywood Memorial Cemetery on the James River. A local women's group raised enough funds to transfer over 16,000 Confederate dead from northern cemeteries for reburial in Richmond.

in the election of 1860, this group could establish a state government that Lincoln would recognize as legitimate. Fundamental to this Ten Percent Plan was that the reconstructed governments accept the abolition of slavery. Lincoln's plan was designed less as a blueprint for reconstruction than as a way to shorten the war and gain white people's support for emancipation.

Lincoln's amnesty proclamation angered those Republicans—known as Radical Republicans—who advocated not only equal rights for the freedmen but also a tougher stance toward the white South. In July 1864, Senator Benjamin F. Wade of Ohio and Congressman Henry W. Davis of Maryland, both Radicals, proposed a harsher alternative to the Ten Percent Plan. The Wade–Davis bill required 50 percent of a seceding state's white male citizens to take a loyalty oath before elections could be held for a convention to rewrite the state's constitution. The Radical Republicans saw reconstruction as a chance to effect a fundamental transformation of southern society. They thus wanted to delay the process until war's end and to limit participation to a small number of southern Unionists. Lincoln viewed Reconstruction as part of the larger effort to win the war and abolish slavery. He wanted to weaken the Confederacy by creating new state governments that could win broad support from southern white people. The Wade–Davis bill threatened his efforts to build political consensus within the southern states. Lincoln, therefore, pocket-vetoed the bill by refusing to sign it within ten days of the adjournment of Congress.

As Union armies occupied parts of the South, commanders improvised a variety of arrangements involving confiscated plantations and the African American labor force. For example, in 1862 General Benjamin F. Butler began a policy of transforming slaves on Louisiana sugar plantations into wage laborers under the close supervision of occupying federal troops. Butler's policy required slaves to remain on the estates of loyal planters, where they would receive wages according to a fixed schedule, as well as food and medical care for the aged and sick. Abandoned plantations would be leased to northern investors.

In January 1865, General William T. Sherman issued Special Field Order 15, setting aside the Sea Islands off the Georgia coast and a portion of the South Carolina Lowcountry rice fields for the exclusive settlement of freed people. Each family would receive forty acres of land and the loan of mules from the army—the origin, perhaps, of the famous call for "forty acres and a mule" that would soon capture the imagination of African Americans throughout the South. Sherman's intent was not to revolutionize southern society but to relieve the demands placed on his army by the thousands of impoverished African Americans who followed his march to the sea. By the summer of 1865 some 40,000 freed people, eager to take advantage of the general's order, had been settled on 400,000 acres of "Sherman land."

Photography pioneer Timothy O'Sullivan took this portrait of a multigenerational African American family on the J. J. Smith plantation in Beaufort, South Carolina, in 1862. Many white plantation owners in the area had fled, allowing slaves like these to begin an early transition to freedom before the end of the Civil War.

Conflicts within the Republican Party prevented the development of a systematic land distribution program. Still, Lincoln and the Republican Congress supported other measures to aid the emancipated slaves. In March 1865 Congress established the Freedmen's Bureau. Along with providing food, clothing, and fuel to destitute former slaves, the bureau was charged with supervising and managing "all the abandoned lands in the South and the control of all subjects relating to refugees and freedmen." The act that established the bureau also stated that forty acres of abandoned or confiscated land could be leased to freed slaves or white Unionists, who would have an option to purchase after three years and "such title thereto as the United States can convey."

On the evening of April 14, 1865, while attending the theater in Washington, President Lincoln was shot by John Wilkes Booth and died of his wounds several hours later. At the time of his assassination, Lincoln's reconstruction policy remained unsettled and incomplete. In its broad outlines, the president's plans had seemed to favor a speedy restoration of the southern states to the Union and a minimum of federal intervention in their affairs. But with his death the specifics of postwar Reconstruction had to be hammered out by a new president, Andrew Johnson of Tennessee, a man whose personality, political background,

Read the **Document**
Carl Schurz, Report on the Condition of the South (1865) at **www.myhistorylab.com**

and racist leanings put him at odds with the Republican-controlled Congress.

Andrew Johnson and Presidential Reconstruction

Andrew Johnson, a Democrat and former slaveholder, was a most unlikely successor to the martyred Lincoln. Throughout his career, Johnson had championed yeoman farmers and viewed the South's plantation aristocrats with contempt. He was the only southern member of the U.S. Senate to remain loyal to the Union, and he held the planter elite responsible for secession and defeat. In 1862, Lincoln appointed Johnson to the difficult post of military governor of Tennessee. There he successfully began wartime Reconstruction and cultivated Unionist support in the mountainous eastern districts of that state.

In 1864, the Republicans, in an appeal to northern and border state "War Democrats," nominated Johnson for vice president. But despite Johnson's success in Tennessee and in the 1864 campaign, many Radical Republicans distrusted him, and the hardscrabble Tennessean remained a political outsider in Republican circles. In the immediate aftermath of Lincoln's murder, however, Johnson appeared to side with those Radical Republicans who sought to treat the South as a conquered territory. Any support for Johnson quickly faded as the new president's policies unfolded. Johnson defined Reconstruction as the province of the executive, not the legislative branch, and he planned to restore the Union as quickly as possible. He blamed individual Southerners—the planter elite—rather than entire states for leading the South down the disastrous road to secession. In line with this philosophy, Johnson outlined mild terms for reentry to the Union.

In the spring of 1865, Johnson granted amnesty and pardon, including restoration of property rights except slaves, to all Confederates who pledged loyalty to the Union and support for emancipation. Fourteen classes of Southerners, mostly major Confederate officials and wealthy landowners, were excluded. But these men could apply individually for presidential pardons. (During his tenure Johnson pardoned roughly 90 percent of those who applied.) Significantly, Johnson instituted this plan while Congress was not in session.

By the autumn of 1865, ten of the eleven Confederate states claimed to have met Johnson's requirements to reenter the Union. On December 6, 1865, in his first annual message to Congress, the president declared the "restoration" of the Union virtually complete. But a serious division within the federal government was taking shape, for the Congress was not about to allow the president free rein in determining the conditions of southern readmission.

Andrew Johnson used the term "restoration" rather than "reconstruction." A lifelong Democrat with ambitions to be elected president on his own in 1868,

Johnson hoped to build a new political coalition composed of northern Democrats, conservative Republicans, and southern Unionists. Firmly committed to white supremacy, he opposed political rights for the freedmen. Johnson's open sympathy for his fellow white Southerners, his antiblack bias, and his determination to control the course of Reconstruction placed him on a collision course with the powerful Radical wing of the Republican Party.

Free Labor and the Radical Republican Vision

Most Radicals were men whose careers had been shaped by the slavery controversy. One of the most effective rhetorical weapons used against slavery and its spread had been the ideal of a society based upon free labor. The model of free individuals, competing equally in the labor market and enjoying equal political rights, formed the core of this worldview. Equality of opportunity created a more fluid social structure where, as Abraham Lincoln had noted, "There is not of necessity any such thing as a free hired laborer being fixed in that condition."

Radicals now looked to reconstruct southern society along these same lines, backed by the power of the national government. They argued that once free labor, universal education, and equal rights were implanted in the South, that region would be able to share in the North's material wealth, progress, and social mobility. Representative George W. Julian of Indiana typified the Radical vision for the South. He called for elimination of the region's large plantations, arguing that the South needed to develop "small farms, thrifty tillage, free schools, social independence, flourishing manufactures and the arts, respect for honest labor, and equality of political rights." In the most far-reaching proposal, Representative Thaddeus Stevens of Pennsylvania called for the confiscation of 400 million acres belonging to the wealthiest 10 percent of Southerners to be redistributed to black and white yeomen and northern land buyers. "The whole fabric of Southern society must be changed," Stevens told Pennsylvania Republicans in September 1865, "and never can it be done if this opportunity is lost. How can republican institutions, free schools, free churches, free social intercourse exist in a mingled community of nabobs and serfs?"

Northern Republicans were especially outraged by the stringent "black codes" passed by South Carolina, Mississippi, Louisiana, and other states. These were designed to restrict the freedom of the black labor force and keep freed people as close to slave status as possible. Laborers who left their jobs before contracts expired would forfeit wages already earned and be subject to arrest by any white citizen. Vagrancy, very broadly defined, was punishable by fines and

"Office of the Freedmen's Bureau, Memphis, Tennessee," *Harper's Weekly*, June 2, 1866. Established by Congress in 1865, the Freedmen's Bureau provided economic, educational, and legal assistance to former slaves in the post–Civil War years. Bureau agents were often called on to settle disputes between black and white Southerners over wages, labor contracts, political rights, and violence. Although most southern whites only grudgingly acknowledged the bureau's legitimacy, freed people gained important legal and psychological support through testimony at public hearings like this one.

involuntary plantation labor. Apprenticeship clauses obliged black children to work without pay for employers. Some states attempted to bar African Americans from land ownership. Other laws specifically denied African Americans equality with white people in civil rights, excluding them from juries and prohibiting interracial marriages. The black codes underscored the unwillingness of white Southerners to accept freedom for African Americans

The Radicals, although not a majority of their party, were joined by moderate Republicans as growing numbers of Northerners grew suspicious of white southern intransigence and the denial of political rights to freedmen When the Thirty-ninth Congress convened in December 1865, the large Republican majority prevented the seating of the white Southerners elected to Congress under President Johnson's provisional state governments. Republicans also established the Joint Committee on Reconstruction. After hearing extensive testimony from a broad range of witnesses, it concluded that not only were old Confederates back in power in the South but also that black codes and racial violence required increased protection for African Americans.

In the spring of 1866, Congress passed two important bills designed to aid African Americans. The landmark Civil Rights bill, which bestowed full citizenship on African Americans, overturned the 1857 *Dred Scott* decision and the black codes. It defined all persons born in the United States (except Indian peoples) as national citizens, and it enumerated various rights, including the rights to make and enforce contracts, to sue, to give evidence, and to buy and sell property. Under this bill, African Americans acquired "full and equal benefit of all laws and proceedings for the security of person and property as is enjoyed by white citizens."

Congress also voted to enlarge the scope of the Freedmen's Bureau, empowering it to build schools and pay teachers, and also to establish courts to prosecute those charged with depriving African Americans of their civil rights. The bureau achieved important, if limited, success in aiding African Americans. Bureau-run schools helped lay the foundation for southern public education. The bureau's network of courts allowed freed people to bring suits against white people in disputes involving violence, nonpayment of wages, or unfair division of crops. The very existence of courts hearing public testimony by African Americans provided an important psychological challenge to traditional notions of white racial domination.

But an angry President Johnson vetoed both of these bills. In opposing the Civil Rights bill, Johnson denounced the assertion of national power to protect African American civil rights, claiming it was a "stride toward centralization, and the concentration of all legislative powers in the national Government." But Johnson's intemperate attacks on the Radicals—he damned them as traitors unwilling to restore the Union—united moderate and Radical Republicans and they succeeded in overriding the vetoes. Congressional Republicans, led by the Radical faction, were now unified in challenging the president's power to direct Reconstruction and in using national authority to define and protect the rights of citizens.

In June 1866, fearful that the Civil Rights Act might be declared unconstitutional, and eager to settle the basis for the seating of southern representatives, Congress passed the Fourteenth Amendment. The amendment defined national citizenship to include former slaves ("all persons born or naturalized in the United States") and prohibited the states from violating the privileges of citizens without due process of law. It also empowered Congress to reduce the representation of any state that denied suffrage to males over twenty-one. Republicans adopted the Fourteenth Amendment as their platform for the 1866 congressional elections and suggested that southern states would have to ratify it as a condition of readmission. President Johnson, meanwhile, took to the stump in August to support conservative Democratic and Republican candidates. His unrestrained speeches often degenerated into harangues, alienating many voters and aiding the Republican cause.

For their part, the Republicans skillfully portrayed Johnson and northern Democrats as disloyal and white Southerners as unregenerate. Republicans began an effective campaign tradition known as "waving the bloody shirt"—reminding northern voters of the hundreds of thousands of Yankee soldiers left dead or maimed by the war. In the November 1866 elections, the Republicans increased their majority in both the House and the Senate and gained control of all the northern states. The stage was now set for a battle between the president and Congress. Was it to be Johnson's "restoration" or Congressional Reconstruction?

Congressional Reconstruction and the Impeachment Crisis

United against Johnson, moderate and Radical Republicans took control of Reconstruction early in 1867. In March, Congress passed the First Reconstruction Act over Johnson's veto. This act divided the South into five military districts subject to martial law. To achieve restoration, southern states were first required to call new constitutional conventions, elected by universal manhood suffrage. Once these states had drafted new constitutions, guaranteed African American voting rights, and ratified the Fourteenth Amendment, they were eligible for readmission to the Union. Supplementary legislation, also passed over the president's veto, invalidated the provisional governments established by Johnson, empowered the military to administer voter registration, and required an oath of loyalty to the United States (see Map 17.1).

⊙ **See the Map**
Reconstruction at
www.myhistorylab.com

Congress also passed several laws aimed at limiting Johnson's power. One of these, the Tenure of Office Act, stipulated that any officeholder appointed by the president with the Senate's advice and consent could not be removed until the Senate had approved a successor. In

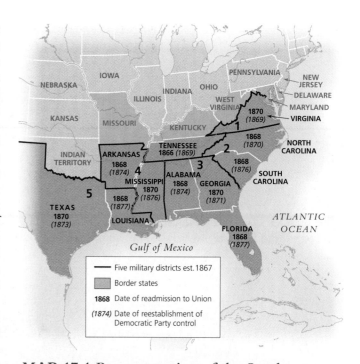

MAP 17.1 Reconstruction of the South, 1866–77 Dates for the readmission of former Confederate states to the Union and the return of Democrats to power varied according to the specific political situations in those states.

this way, congressional leaders could protect Republicans, such as Secretary of War Edwin M. Stanton, entrusted with implementing Congressional Reconstruction. In August 1867, with Congress adjourned, Johnson suspended Stanton and appointed General Ulysses S. Grant interim secretary of war. This move enabled the president to remove generals in the field that he judged to be too radical and replace them with men who were sympathetic to his own views. It also served as a challenge to the Tenure of Office Act. In January 1868, when the Senate overruled Stanton's suspension, Grant broke openly with Johnson and vacated the office. Stanton resumed his position and barricaded himself in his office when Johnson attempted to remove him once again.

Outraged by Johnson's relentless obstructionism, and seizing upon his violation of the Tenure of Office Act as a pretext, moderate and Radical Republicans in the House of Representatives again joined forces and voted to impeach the president by a vote of 126 to 47 on February 24, 1868, charging him with eleven counts of high crimes and misdemeanors. To ensure the support of moderate Republicans, the articles of impeachment focused on violations of the Tenure of Office Act. The case against Johnson would have to be made on the basis of willful violation of the law. Left unstated were the Republicans' real reasons for wanting the president removed: Johnson's political views and his opposition to the Reconstruction Acts.

An influential group of moderate Senate Republicans feared the damage a conviction might do to the constitutional separation of powers. They also worried about the political and economic policies that might be pursued by Benjamin Wade, the president pro tem of the Senate and a leader of the Radical Republicans, who, because there was no vice president, would succeed to the presidency if Johnson were removed from office. Behind the scenes during his Senate trial, Johnson agreed to abide by the Reconstruction Acts. In May, the Senate voted 35 for conviction, 19 for acquittal—one vote shy of the two-thirds necessary for removal from office. Johnson's narrow acquittal established the precedent that only criminal actions by a president—not political disagreements—warranted removal from office.

The Election of 1868

By the summer of 1868, seven former Confederate states (Alabama, Arkansas, Florida, Louisiana, North Carolina, South Carolina, and Tennessee) had ratified the revised constitutions, elected Republican governments, and ratified the Fourteenth Amendment. They had thereby earned readmission to the Union. In 1868 Republicans nominated Ulysses S. Grant, the North's foremost military hero, as their nominee for President. Grant enjoyed tremendous popularity after the war, especially when he broke with Johnson. Totally lacking in political experience, Grant admitted, after receiving the nomination, that he had been forced into it in spite of himself.

Significantly, at the very moment that the South was being forced to enfranchise former slaves as a prerequisite for readmission to the Union, the Republicans rejected a campaign plank endorsing black suffrage in the North. State referendums calling for black suffrage failed in eight northern states between 1865 and 1868, succeeding only in Iowa and Minnesota. The Democrats, determined to reverse Congressional Reconstruction, nominated Horatio Seymour, former governor of New York and a longtime foe of emancipation and supporter of states' rights.

Read the **Document**

History Bookshelf: Ulysses S. Grant, Memoirs (1886) at **www.myhistorylab.com**

The Fifteenth Amendment, ratified in 1870, stipulated that the right to vote could not be denied "on account of race, color, or previous condition of servitude." This illustration expressed the optimism and hopes of African Americans generated by this consitutional landmark aimed at protecting black political rights. Note the various political figures (Abraham Lincoln, John Brown, Frederick Douglass) and movements (abolitionism, black education) invoked here, providing a sense of how the amendment ended a long historical struggle.

The Ku Klux Klan emerged as a potent instrument of terror (see the opening of this chapter). In Louisiana, Arkansas, Georgia, and South Carolina, the Klan threatened, whipped, and murdered black and white Republicans to prevent them from voting. This terrorism enabled the Democrats to carry Georgia and Louisiana, but it ultimately cost the Democrats votes in the North. In the final tally, Grant carried twenty-six of the thirty-four states for an Electoral College victory of 214 to 80. Significantly, more than 500,000 African American voters cast their ballots for Grant, demonstrating their overwhelming support for the Republican Party. The Republicans also retained large majorities in both houses of Congress.

In February 1869, Congress passed the Fifteenth Amendment, providing that "the right of citizens of the United States to vote shall not be denied or abridged on account of race, color, or previous condition of servitude." To enhance the chances of ratification, Congress required the four remaining unreconstructed states—Mississippi, Georgia, Texas, and Virginia—to ratify both the Fourteenth and Fifteenth Amendments before readmission. They did so

and rejoined the Union in early 1870. The Fifteenth Amendment was ratified in February 1870. In the narrow sense of simply readmitting the former Confederate states to the Union, Reconstruction was complete.

Woman Suffrage and Reconstruction

Many women's rights advocates had long been active in the abolitionist movement. The Fourteenth and Fifteenth Amendments, which granted citizenship and the vote to freedmen, both inspired and frustrated these activists. Insisting that the causes of the African American vote and the women's vote were linked, Elizabeth Cady Stanton, Susan B. Anthony, and Lucy Stone founded the American Equal Rights Association in 1866. The group launched a series of lobbying and petition campaigns to remove racial and sexual restrictions on voting from state constitutions. Throughout the nation, the old abolitionist organizations and the Republican Party emphasized passage of the Fourteenth and Fifteenth Amendments and withdrew funds and support from the cause of woman suffrage. Disagreements over these amendments divided suffragists for decades.

This contemporary colored engraving depicts a meeting of the National Woman Suffrage Association in Chicago, c.1870. The suffrage campaign attracted many middle class women into political activism for the first time.

OVERVIEW	Reconstruction Amendments to the Constitution, 1865–1870	

Amendment and Date Passed by Congress	Main Provisions	Ratification Process (3/4 of all States Including Ex-Confederate States Required)
13 (January 1865)	• Prohibited slavery in the United States	December 1865 (27 states, including 8 southern states)
14 (June 1866)	• Conferred national citizenship on all persons born or naturalized in the United States • Reduced state representation in Congress proportionally for any state disfranchising male citizens • Denied former Confederates the right to hold state or national office • Repudiated Confederate debt	July 1868 (after Congress made ratification a prerequisite for readmission of ex-Confederate states to the Union)
15 (February 1869)	• Prohibited denial of suffrage because of race, color, or previous condition of servitude	March 1870 (ratification required for readmission of Virginia, Texas, Mississippi, and Georgia)

The radical wing, led by Stanton and Anthony, opposed the Fifteenth Amendment, arguing that ratification would establish an "aristocracy of sex," enfranchising all men while leaving women without political privileges. They argued for a Sixteenth Amendment that would secure the vote for women. Other women's rights activists, including Lucy Stone and Frederick Douglass, asserted that "this hour belongs to the Negro." They feared a debate over woman suffrage at the national level would jeopardize passage of the two amendments.

By 1869 woman suffragists had split into two competing organizations: the moderate American Woman Suffrage Association (AWSA), which sought the support of men, and the more radical all-female National Woman Suffrage Association (NWSA). For the NWSA, the vote represented only one part of a broad spectrum of goals inherited from the Declaration of Sentiments manifesto adopted at the first women's rights convention held in 1848 at Seneca Falls, New York (see Chapter 13).

Although women did not win the vote in this period, they did establish an independent suffrage movement that eventually drew millions of women into political life. The NWSA in particular demonstrated that self-government and democratic participation in the public sphere were crucial for women's emancipation. The failure of woman suffrage after the Civil War was less a result of factional fighting than of the larger defeat of Radical Reconstruction and the ideal of expanded citizenship.

The Meaning of Freedom

For nearly 4 million slaves, freedom arrived in various ways in different parts of the South. In many areas, slavery had collapsed long before Lee's surrender at Appomattox. In regions far removed from the presence of federal troops, African Americans did not learn of slavery's end until the spring of 1865. There were thousands of sharply contrasting stories, many of which revealed the need for freed slaves to confront their owners. One Virginia slave, hired out to another family during the war, had been working in the fields when a friend told her she was now free. "Is dat so?" she exclaimed. Dropping her hoe, she ran the seven miles to her old place, confronted her former mistress, and shouted, "I'se free! Yes, I'se free! Ain't got to work fo' you no mo'." But regardless of specific regional circumstances, the meaning of "freedom" would be contested for years to come. The deep desire for independence from white control formed the underlying aspiration of newly freed slaves. For their part, most southern white people sought to restrict the boundaries of that independence. As individuals and as members of communities transformed by emancipation, former slaves struggled to establish economic, political, and cultural autonomy. They built on the twin pillars of slave culture—the family and the church—to consolidate and expand African American institutions and thereby laid the foundation for the modern African American community.

Moving About

The first impulse of many emancipated slaves was to test their freedom. The simplest, most obvious way to do this

Read the Document

Jourdon Anderson to His Former Master (1865) at **www.myhistorylab.com**

involved leaving home. Throughout the summer and fall of 1865, observers in the South noted enormous numbers of freed people on the move. One former slave squatting in an abandoned tent outside Selma, Alabama, explained his feeling to a northern journalist: "I's want to be free man, cum when I please, and nobody say nuffin to me, nor order me roun'." When urged to stay on with the South Carolina family she had served for years as a cook, a slave woman replied firmly: "No, Miss, I must go. If I stay here I'll never know I am free."

Yet many who left their old neighborhoods returned soon afterward to seek work in the general vicinity or even on the plantation they had left. Many wanted to separate themselves from former owners, but not from familial ties and friendships. Others moved away altogether, seeking jobs in nearby towns and cities. Many former slaves left predominantly white counties, where they felt more vulnerable and isolated, for new lives in the relative comfort of predominantly black communities. In most southern states, there was a significant population shift toward black belt plantation counties and towns after the war. Many African Americans, attracted by schools, churches, and fraternal societies as well as the army, preferred the city. Between 1865 and 1870, the African American population of the South's ten largest cities doubled, while the white population increased by only 10 percent.

Disgruntled planters had difficulty accepting African American independence. During slavery, they had expected obedience, submission, and loyalty from African Americans. Now many could not understand why so many former slaves wanted to leave, despite urgent pleas to continue working at the old place. The deference and humility white people expected from African Americans could no longer be taken for granted. Indeed, many freed people went out of their way to reject the old subservience. Moving about freely was one way of doing this, as was refusing to tip one's hat to white people, ignoring former masters or mistresses in the streets, and refusing to step aside on sidewalks. When freed people staged parades, dances, and picnics to celebrate their new freedom, as they did, for example, when commemorating the Emancipation Proclamation, white people invariably condemned them angrily for "insolence," "outrageous spectacles," or "putting on airs."

African American Families, Churches, and Schools

Emancipation allowed freed people to strengthen family ties. For many former slaves, freedom meant the opportunity to find long-lost family members. To track down these relatives, freed people trekked to faraway places, put ads in newspapers, sought the help of Freedmen's Bureau agents, and questioned anyone who might have information about loved ones. Many thousands of family reunions, each with its own story, took place after the war. One North Carolina slave, who had seen his parents separated by sale, recalled many years later what for him had been the most significant aspect of freedom. "I has got thirteen great-gran' chilluns an' I know whar dey ever'one am. In slavery times dey'd have been on de block long time ago." Thousands of African American couples who had lived together under slavery streamed to military and civilian authorities and demanded to be legally married. By 1870, the two-parent household was the norm for a large majority of African Americans.

For many freed people, the attempt to find lost relatives dragged on for years. Searches often proved frustrating, exhausting, and ultimately disappointing. Some "reunions" ended painfully with the discovery that spouses had found new partners and started new families.

Emancipation brought changes to gender roles within the African American family as well. By serving in the Union army, African American men played a more direct role than women in the fight for freedom. In the political sphere, black men could now serve on juries, vote, and hold office; black women, like their white counterparts, could not. Freedmen's Bureau agents designated the husband as household head and established lower wage scales for women laborers. African American editors, preachers, and politicians regularly quoted the biblical injunction that wives submit to their husbands.

African American men asserted their male authority, denied under slavery, by insisting their wives work at home instead of in the fields. African American women generally wanted to devote more time than they had under slavery to caring for their children and to performing such domestic chores as cooking, sewing, gardening, and laundering. Yet African American women continued to work outside the home, engaging in seasonal field labor for wages or working a family's rented plot. Most rural black families barely eked out a living and, thus, the labor of every family member was essential to survival. The key difference from slave times was that African American families themselves, not white masters and overseers, decided when and where women and children worked.

The creation of separate African American churches proved the most lasting and important element of the energetic institution building that went on in postemancipation

An overflow congregation crowds into Richmond's First African Baptist Church in 1874. Despite their poverty, freed people struggled to save money, buy land, and erect new buildings as they organized hundreds of new black churches during Reconstruction. As the most important African American institution outside the family, the black church, in addition to tending to spiritual needs, played a key role in the educational and political life of the community.

years. Before the Civil War, southern Protestant churches had relegated slaves and free African Americans to second-class membership. Black worshipers were required to sit in the back during services, they were denied any role in church governance, and they were excluded from Sunday schools. Even in larger cities, where all-black congregations sometimes built their own churches, the law required white pastors.

In communities around the South, African Americans now pooled their resources to buy land and build their own churches. Before these structures were completed, they might hold services in a railroad boxcar, where Atlanta's First Baptist Church began, or in an outdoor arbor, the original site of the First Baptist Church of Memphis. Churches became the center not only for religious life but also for many other activities that defined the African American community: schools, picnics, festivals, and political meetings. The church became the first social institution fully controlled by African Americans. In nearly every community, ministers, respected for their speaking and organizational skills, were among the most

influential leaders. By 1877, the great majority of black Southerners had withdrawn from white-dominated churches. In South Carolina, for example, only a few hundred black Methodists attended biracial churches, down from over 40,000 in 1865. Black Baptist churches, with their decentralized and democratic structure and more emotional services, attracted the greatest number of freed people. By the end of Reconstruction, the vast majority of African American Christians belonged to black Baptist or Methodist churches.

The rapid spread of schools reflected African Americans' thirst for self-improvement. Southern states had prohibited education for slaves. But many free black people managed to attend school, and a few slaves had been able to educate themselves. Still, over 90 percent of the South's adult African American population was illiterate in 1860. Access to education thus became a central part of the meaning of freedom. Freedmen's Bureau agents repeatedly expressed amazement at the number of makeshift classrooms organized by African Americans in rural areas. A bureau officer described these "wayside schools": "A negro riding on a loaded wagon, or sitting on a hack waiting for a train, or by the cabin door, is often seen, book in hand delving after the rudiments of knowledge. A group on the platform of a depot, after carefully conning an old spelling book, resolves itself into a class."

African American communities received important educational aid from outside organizations. By 1869, the Freedmen's Bureau was supervising nearly 3,000 schools serving over 150,000 students throughout the South. Over half of the roughly 3,300 teachers in these schools were African Americans, many of whom had been free before the Civil War. Other teachers included dedicated northern white women, volunteers sponsored by the American Missionary Association (AMA). The bureau and the AMA also assisted in the founding of several black colleges, including Tougaloo, Hampton, and Fisk, designed to train black teachers. Black self-help proved crucial to the education effort. Throughout the South in 1865 and 1866, African Americans raised money to build schoolhouses, buy supplies, and pay teachers. Black artisans donated labor for construction, and black families offered room and board to teachers.

Land and Labor After Slavery

Most newly emancipated African Americans aspired to quit the plantations and to make new lives for themselves. Some freed people did find jobs in railroad building, mining, ranching, or construction work. Others raised subsistence crops and tended vegetable gardens as squatters. White planters, however, tried to retain African Americans as permanent agricultural laborers. Restricting the employment of former slaves was an important goal of the black codes. For example, South Carolina legislation in 1865 provided that "no person of color shall pursue or practice the art, trade, or business of an artisan, mechanic, or shopkeeper, or any other trade employment, or business, besides that of husbandry, or that of a servant under contract for service or labor" without a special and costly permit.

The majority of African Americans hoped to become self-sufficient farmers. Many former slaves believed they were entitled to the land they had worked throughout their lives. General Oliver O. Howard, chief commissioner of the Freedmen's Bureau, observed that many "supposed that the Government [would] divide among them the lands of the conquered owners, and furnish them with all that might be necessary to begin life as an independent farmer." This perception was not merely a wishful fantasy. Frequent reference in the Congress and the press to the question of land distribution made the idea of "forty acres and a mule" not just a pipe dream but a matter of serious public debate. But by 1866, the federal government had already pulled back from the various wartime experiments involving the breaking up of large plantations and the leasing of small plots to individual families. President Johnson directed General Howard of the Freedmen's Bureau to evict tens of thousands of freed people settled on confiscated and abandoned land in southeastern Virginia, southern Louisiana, and the Georgia and South Carolina Lowcountry.

In communities throughout the South, freed people and their former masters negotiated new arrangements for organizing agricultural labor. In Hale County, Alabama, for example, local black farmhands contracted to work on Henry Watson's plantation in 1866 deserted him when they angrily discovered that their small share of the crop left them in debt. Local Union League activists encouraged newly freed slaves to remain independent of white farmers, and political agitation for freedmen's rights encouraged them to push for better working conditions as well. Yet few owners would sell or even rent land to blacks. Watson, desperate for field hands, finally agreed to subdivide his plantation and rent it to freedmen, who would work under their own supervision without overseers. Black families left the old slave quarters and began building cabins scattered around the plantation. By 1868, Watson was convinced that black farmers made good tenants; like many other landowners, he grudgingly accepted greater independence for black families in exchange for a more stable labor force. By 1869, as one Hale County correspondent reported, "Many planters have turned their stock, teams, and every facility to farming, over to the negroes, and only require an amount of toll for the use of the land" (see Map 17.2).

By the late 1860s, sharecropping and tenant farming had emerged as the dominant form of working the land. Sharecropping represented a compromise between planters and former slaves. Under sharecropping arrangements that were usually very detailed, individual families contracted with landowners to be responsible for a specific plot. Large plantations were thus broken into family-sized farms. Generally, sharecropper families received one-third of the year's crop if the owner furnished implements, seed, and draft animals or one-half if they provided their own supplies. African Americans preferred sharecropping to gang labor, as it allowed families to set their own hours and tasks and offered freedom from white supervision and control. For planters, the system stabilized the workforce by requiring sharecroppers to remain until the harvest and to employ all family members. It also offered a way around the chronic shortage of cash and credit that plagued the postwar South. Freed people did not aspire to sharecropping. Owning land outright or tenant farming (renting land) were both more desirable. But though black sharecroppers clearly enjoyed more autonomy than in the past, the vast

Read the Document

A Sharecrop Contract (1882) at **www.myhistorylab.com**

MAP 17.2 The Barrow Plantation, Oglethorpe County, Georgia, 1860 and 1881 (approx. 2,000 acres) These two maps, based on drawings from *Scribner's Monthly*, April 1881, show some of the changes brought by emancipation. In 1860, the plantation's entire black population lived in the communal slave quarters, right next to the white master's house. In 1881, black sharecropper and tenant families lived on individual plots, spread out across the land. The former slaves had also built their own school and church.

majority never achieved economic independence or land ownership. They remained a largely subordinate agricultural labor force.

The Origins of African American Politics

Hundreds of African American delegates, selected by local meetings or churches, attended statewide political conventions held throughout the South in 1865 and 1866. Previously free African Americans, as well as black ministers, artisans, and veterans of the Union army, tended to dominate these proceedings, setting a pattern that would

hold throughout Reconstruction. Convention debates sometimes reflected the tensions within African American communities, such as friction between poorer former slaves and better-off free black people, or between lighter- and darker-skinned African Americans. But most of these state gatherings concentrated on passing resolutions on issues that united all African Americans. The central concerns were suffrage and equality before the law.

The passage of the First Reconstruction Act in 1867 encouraged even more political activity among African Americans. The military started registering the South's electorate, ultimately enrolling approximately 735,000 black

Changing Images of Reconstruction

After the Civil War, northern journalists and illustrators went south to describe Reconstruction in action. They took a keen interest in how the newly freed slaves were reshaping local and national politics. A drawing by *Harper's Weekly* illustrator William L. Sheppard titled "Electioneering in the South" clearly approved of the freedmen's exercise of their new citizenship rights. "Does any man seriously doubt," the caption asked, "whether it is better for this vast population to be sinking deeper and deeper in ignorance and servility, or rising into general intelligence and self-respect? They can not be pariahs; they can not be peons; they must be slaves or citizens."

Thomas Nast was the nation's best-known political cartoonist during the 1860s and 1870s. During the Civil War he strongly supported the Union cause and the aspirations of the newly freed slaves. But by 1876, like many Northerners originally sympathetic to guaranteeing blacks full political and civil rights, Nast had turned away from the early ideals of Reconstruction. Nast used grotesque racial caricature to depict southern African Americans and northern Irish immigrants as undeserving of the right to vote. The aftermath of the disputed 1876 presidential election included charges of widespread vote fraud from both Republicans and Democrats. Nast's view—published in *Harper's Weekly* in December 1876, while the election's outcome was still in doubt—reflected concerns among many middle-class Northerners that the nation's political system was tainted by the manipulation of "ignorant" voters in both the South and the North.

• How does the portrayal of the larger African American community in "Electioneering in the South" reflect the political point being made?

• What do the caricatures in "The Ignorant Vote" suggest about Reconstruction era ideas about the meaning of "whiteness"?

and 635,000 white voters in the ten unreconstructed states. Five states—Alabama, Florida, Louisiana, Mississippi, and South Carolina—had black electoral majorities. Fewer than half the registered white voters participated in the elections for state constitutional conventions in 1867 and 1868. In contrast, four-fifths of the registered black voters cast ballots in these elections. Much of this new African American political activism was channeled through local Union League chapters throughout the South. However, as the fate of Alex Webb in Hale County, Alabama, again makes clear, few whites welcomed this activism.

Begun during the war as a northern, largely white middle-class patriotic club, the Union League now became the political voice of the former slaves. Union League chapters brought together local African Americans, soldiers, and Freedmen's Bureau agents to demand the vote and an end to legal discrimination against African Americans. It brought out African American voters, instructed freedmen in the rights and duties of citizenship, and promoted Republican candidates. Not surprisingly, newly enfranchised freedmen voted Republican and formed the core of the Republican Party in the South. For most ordinary African Americans, politics was inseparable from economic issues, especially the land question. Grassroots political organizations frequently intervened in local disputes with planters over the terms of labor contracts. African American political groups closely followed the congressional debates over Reconstruction policy and agitated for land confiscation and distribution. Perhaps most important, politics was the only arena where black and white Southerners might engage each other on an equal basis.

Read the **Document**
Address from the Colored Citizens of Norfolk, VA (1865) at **www.myhistorylab.com**

"The First Vote," *Harper's Weekly*, November 16, 1867, reflected the optimism felt by much of the northern public as former slaves began to vote for the first time. The caption noted that freedmen went to the ballot box "not with expressions of exultation or of defiance of their old masters and present opponents depicted on their countenances, but looking serious and solemn and determined."

Southern Politics and Society

By the summer of 1868, when the South had returned to the Union, the majority of Republicans believed the task of Reconstruction to be finished. Ultimately, they put their faith in a political solution to the problems facing the vanquished South. That meant nurturing a viable two-party system in the southern states, where no Republican Party had ever existed. If that could be accomplished, Republicans and Democrats would compete for votes, offices, and influence, just as they did in northern states. Most Republican congressmen were moderates, conceiving Reconstruction in limited terms. They rejected radical calls for confiscation and redistribution of land, as well as permanent military rule of the South. The Reconstruction Acts of 1867 and 1868 laid out the requirements for the readmission of southern states, along with the procedures for forming and electing new governments.

Yet over the next decade, the political structure created in the southern states proved too restricted and fragile to sustain itself. To most southern whites, the active participation of African Americans in politics seemed extremely dangerous. Federal troops were needed to protect Republican governments and their supporters from violent opposition. Congressional action to monitor southern elections and protect black voting rights became routine. Despite initial successes, southern Republicanism proved an unstable coalition of often conflicting elements, unable to sustain effective power for very long. By 1877, Democrats had regained political control of all the former Confederate states.

Southern Republicans

Three major groups composed the fledgling Republican coalition in the postwar South. African American voters made up a large majority of southern Republicans throughout the Reconstruction era. Yet African Americans outnumbered whites in only three southern states; Republicans would have to attract white support to win elections and sustain power.

A second group consisted of white Northerners, derisively called "carpetbaggers" by native white Southerners. Most carpetbaggers combined a desire for personal gain with a commitment to reform the "unprogressive" South by developing its material resources and introducing Yankee institutions, such as free labor and free public schools. Most were veterans of the Union army who stayed in the South after the war. Others included Freedmen's Bureau agents and businessmen who had invested capital in cotton plantations and other enterprises.

Carpetbaggers tended to be well educated and from the middle class. Albert Morgan, for example, was an army veteran from Ohio who settled in Mississippi after the war. When he and his brother failed at running a cotton plantation and sawmill, Morgan became active in Republican politics as a way to earn a living. He won election to the state constitutional convention, became a power in the state legislature, and risked his life to keep the Republican organization alive in the Mississippi Delta region. Although they made up a tiny percentage of the population, carpetbaggers played a disproportionately large role in southern politics. They won a large share of Reconstruction offices, particularly in Florida, South Carolina, and Louisiana and in areas with large African American constituencies.

The third major group of southern Republicans was the native whites pejoratively termed "scalawags." They had even more diverse backgrounds and motives than the northern-born Republicans. Some were prominent prewar Whigs who saw the Republican Party as their best chance to regain political influence. Others viewed the party as an agent of modernization and economic expansion. "Yankees and Yankee notions are just what we want in this country," argued Thomas Settle of North Carolina. "We want their capital to build factories and workshops. We want their intelligence, their energy and enterprise." Loyalists during the war and traditional enemies of the planter elite (most were small farmers), these white Southerners looked to the Republican Party for help in settling old scores and relief from debt and wartime devastation.

Southern Republicanism also reflected prewar political divisions. Its influence was greatest in those regions that had long resisted the political and economic power of the plantation elite. Thus, southern Republicans could dominate the mountainous areas of western North Carolina, eastern Tennessee, northern Georgia, and southwestern Virginia as much as Democrats controlled other areas. Yet few white Southerners identified with the political and economic aspirations of African Americans. Moderate elements more concerned with maintaining white control of the party, and encouraging economic investment in the region, outnumbered and defeated "confiscation radicals" who focused on obtaining land for African Americans.

Reconstructing the States: A Mixed Record

With the old Confederate leaders barred from political participation, and with carpetbaggers and newly enfranchised African Americans representing many of the plantation districts, Republicans managed to dominate the ten southern constitutional conventions from 1867 to 1869. Most of these conventions produced constitutions that expanded democracy and the public role of the state. The new documents guaranteed the political and civil rights of African Americans, and they abolished property qualifications for officeholding and jury service as well as imprisonment for debt. They created the first state-funded systems of education in the South to be administered by state commissioners. The new constitutions also mandated establishment of orphanages, penitentiaries, and homes for the insane. In 1868, only three years after the end of the war, Republicans came to power in most of the southern states. By 1869, new constitutions had been ratified in all the old Confederate states.

Republican governments in the South faced a continual crisis of legitimacy that limited their ability to legislate change. They had to balance reform against the need to gain acceptance, especially by white Southerners. Their achievements were thus mixed. In the realm of race relations there was a clear thrust toward equal rights and against discrimination. Republican legislatures followed up the federal Civil Rights Act of 1866 with various antidiscrimination clauses in new constitutions and laws prescribing harsh penalties for civil rights violations.

Segregation, though, became the norm in public school systems. African American leaders often accepted segregation because they feared that insistence on integrated education would jeopardize funding for the new school systems. Segregation in railroad cars and other public places was more objectionable. By the early 1870s, as black influence and assertiveness grew, laws guaranteeing equal access to transportation and public accommodation were passed in many states. By and large, though, such civil rights laws were difficult to enforce in local communities.

In economic matters, Republican governments failed to fulfill African Americans' hopes of obtaining land. Few former slaves possessed the cash to buy land in the open market, and they looked to the state for help. Republicans tried to weaken the plantation system and promote black ownership by raising taxes on land. Yet even when state governments seized land for nonpayment of taxes, the property was never used to help create black homesteads.

Republican leaders envisioned promoting northern-style capitalist development—factories, large towns, and diversified agriculture—through state aid. Much Republican state lawmaking was devoted to encouraging railroad construction. But in spite of all the new laws, it proved impossible to attract significant amounts of northern and European investment capital. The obsession with railroads withdrew resources from education and other programs. As in the North, it also opened the doors to widespread corruption and bribery of public officials. Railroad failures eroded public confidence in the Republicans' ability to govern.

White Resistance and "Redemption"

The emergence of a Republican Party in the reconstructed South brought two parties, but not a two-party system, to the region. The opponents of Reconstruction,

The Ku Klux Klan emerged as a potent political and social force during Reconstruction, terrorizing freed people and their white allies. An 1868 Klan warning threatens Louisiana governor Henry C. Warmoth with death. Warmoth, an Illinois-born "carpetbagger," was the state's first Republican governor. Two Alabama Klansmen, photographed in 1868, wear white hoods to hide their identities.

the Democrats, refused to acknowledge Republicans' right to participate in southern political life. Republicans were split between those who urged conciliation in an effort to gain white acceptance and those who emphasized consolidating the party under the protection of the military.

From its founding in 1868 through the early 1870s, the Ku Klux Klan waged an ongoing terrorist campaign against Reconstruction governments and local leaders. Just as the institution of slavery had depended on violence and the threat of violence, the Klan acted as a kind of guerrilla military force in the service of the Democratic Party, the planter class, and all those who sought the restoration of white supremacy. It employed a wide array of terror tactics: destroying ballot boxes, issuing death threats, beating and murdering politically active blacks and their white allies. Freedmen and their allies sometimes resisted the Klan. In Hale County, Alabama, Union Leaguers set up a warning system using buglers to signal the activities of Klan raiders. But violence and intimidation decimated Union League leadership in the countryside by 1869.

In October 1870, after Republicans carried Laurens County in South Carolina, bands of white people drove 150 African Americans from their homes and murdered thirteen white and black Republican activists. In March 1871, three African Americans were arrested in Meridian, Mississippi, for giving "incendiary" speeches. At their court hearing, Klansmen killed two of the defendants and the Republican judge, and thirty more African Americans were murdered in a day of rioting. The single bloodiest episode of Reconstruction era violence took place in Colfax, Louisiana, on Easter Sunday 1873. Nearly 100 African Americans were murdered after they failed to hold a besieged courthouse during a contested election.

Southern Republicans looked to Washington for help. In 1870 and 1871, Congress passed three Enforcement Acts designed to counter racial terrorism. These declared that interference with voting was a federal offense. The acts provided for federal supervision of voting and authorized the president to send the army and to suspend the writ of habeas corpus in districts declared to be in a state of insurrection. The most sweeping measure was the Ku Klux Klan Act of April 1871, which made the violent infringement of civil and political rights a federal crime punishable by the national government. By the election of 1872, the federal government's intervention had helped break the Klan and restore a semblance of law and order.

The Civil Rights Act of 1875 outlawed racial discrimination in theaters, hotels, railroads, and other public places. But the law proved more an assertion of principle than a direct federal intervention in southern affairs. Enforcement required African Americans to take their cases to the federal courts, a costly and time-consuming procedure.

As wartime idealism faded, northern Republicans became less inclined toward direct intervention in southern affairs. They had enough trouble retaining political control in the North. In 1874, the Democrats gained a majority in the House of Representatives for the first time since 1856. Key northern states also began to fall to the Democrats. Northern Republicans slowly abandoned the freedmen and their white allies in the South. Southern Democrats were also able to exploit a deepening fiscal crisis by blaming Republicans for excessive extension of public credit and the sharp increase in tax rates.

Gradually, conservative Democrats "redeemed" one state after another. Virginia and Tennessee led the way in 1869, North Carolina in 1870, Georgia in 1871, Texas in 1873, and Alabama and Arkansas in 1874. In Mississippi, white conservatives employed violence and intimidation to wrest control in 1875 and "redeemed" the state the following year. Republican infighting in Louisiana in 1873 and 1874 led to a series of contested election results, including bloody clashes between black militia and armed whites, and finally to "redemption" by the Democrats in 1877.

Several Supreme Court rulings involving the Fourteenth and Fifteenth Amendments effectively constrained federal protection of African American civil rights. In the so-called Slaughterhouse cases of 1873, the Court issued its first ruling on the Fourteenth Amendment. The cases involved a Louisiana charter that gave a New Orleans meatpacking company a monopoly over the city's butchering business on the grounds of protecting public health. A rival group of butchers had sued, claiming the law violated the Fourteenth Amendment, which prohibited states from depriving any person of life, liberty, or property without due process of law. The Court held that the Fourteenth Amendment protected only the former slaves, not butchers, and that it protected only national citizenship rights, not the regulatory powers of states. It separated national citizenship from state citizenship and declared that most of the rights that Americans enjoyed on a daily basis—freedom of speech, fair trials, the right to sit on juries, protection from unreasonable searches, and the right to vote—were under the control of state law. The ruling in effect denied the original intent of the Fourteenth Amendment—to protect against state infringement of national citizenship rights as spelled out in the Bill of Rights.

Three other decisions curtailed federal protection of black civil rights. In *United States* v. *Reese* (1876) and *United States* v. *Cruikshank* (1876), the Court restricted congressional power to enforce the Ku Klux Klan Act. Future prosecution would depend on the states rather than on federal authorities. In these rulings, the Court held that the Fourteenth Amendment extended the federal power to protect civil rights only in cases involving discrimination by states; discrimination by individuals or groups was not covered. The Court also ruled that the Fifteenth Amendment did not guarantee a citizen's right to vote; it only barred certain specific grounds for denying suffrage—"race, color, or previous condition of servitude." This interpretation opened the door for southern states to disenfranchise African Americans for allegedly nonracial reasons. States back under Democratic control began to limit African American voting by passing laws restricting voter eligibility through poll taxes and property requirements.

Finally, in the 1883 Civil Rights Cases decision, the Court declared the Civil Rights Act of 1875 unconstitutional, holding that the Fourteenth Amendment gave Congress the power to outlaw discrimination by states but not by private individuals. The majority opinion held that black people must no longer "be the special favorite of the laws." Together, these Supreme Court decisions marked the end of federal attempts to protect African American rights until well into the next century.

King Cotton: Sharecroppers, Tenants, and the Southern Environment

The Republicans' vision of a "New South" remade along the lines of the northern economy failed to materialize. Instead, the South declined into the country's poorest agricultural region. Unlike midwestern and western farm towns burgeoning from trade in wheat, corn, and livestock, Southern communities found themselves almost entirely dependent on the price of one commodity. In the post–Civil War years, "King Cotton" expanded its realm, as greater numbers of small white farmers found themselves forced to switch from subsistence crops to growing cotton for the market (see Map 17.3).

A chronic shortage of capital and banking institutions made local merchants and planters the sole source of credit. They advanced loans and supplies to small owners, tenant farmers, and sharecroppers in exchange for a lien, or claim, on the year's cotton crop. They often charged extremely high interest rates on advances, while marking up the prices of the goods sold in their stores. Taking advantage of the high illiteracy rates among poor Southerners, landlords and merchants easily altered their books to inflate the figures. At the end of the year, sharecroppers and tenants found themselves deep in debt to stores for seed, supplies, and clothing. Despite hard work and even bountiful harvests, few small farmers could escape from heavy debt. The spread of the "crop lien" system as the South's main form of agricultural credit forced more and more farmers into cotton growing.

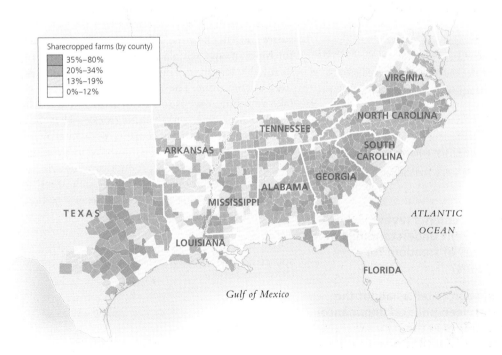

MAP 17.3 Southern Sharecropping and the Cotton Belt, 1880 The economic depression of the 1870s forced increasing numbers of southern farmers, both white and black, into sharecropping arrangements. Sharecropping was most pervasive in the cotton belt regions of South Carolina, Georgia, Alabama, Mississippi, and eastern Texas.

The Ku Klux Klan in Alabama

During Reconstruction the Ku Klux Klan (KKK) claimed as many as 12,000 members in Alabama, or about one in every nine white male voters. The KKK enjoyed deep and widespread support from many whites, including women and children, who viewed the Klan as the protector of white supremacy and a weapon against the Republican Party. Democratic newspapers routinely printed favorable accounts of Klan activities, as well as pro-Klan advertisements, songs, and jokes—and threats directed at intended Klan victims. The following excerpt from a sympathetic newspaper report of Klan activities in the central Alabama town of Florence was published in the *Shelby County Guide* on December 3, 1868.

African Americans and their Republican allies, however, experienced the Klan as a terrorist organization responsible for murder, beatings, arson, and violent intimidation aimed at preventing African American political organizing and economic advancement. This view is vividly presented in a first-person account of Klan terror given by George Houston, an ex-slave and tailor, who had been elected to represent Sumter County in the Alabama state legislature. Houston had helped organize a Union League chapter and actively registered black voters. After local Klansmen wounded his son and broke down the door to his house, Houston grabbed his gun and shot back. In this testimony to a congressional committee investigating the KKK's terrorist campaign, he describes the immediate scene and the campaign to intimidate him.

• **How do the documents reveal profoundly different understandings of the consequences of freedom for African Americans?**

• **What do the sources tell us about the connections between political dominance and economic power in the Reconstruction era South?**

Movements of the Mystic Klan, from the *Shelby County Guide*, December 3, 1868

About a week ago Saturday night the Ku Klux came into town to regulate matters. They were here from eleven p.m. to three o'clock a.m.—five hundred in all. They shot one very bad Negro, putting six balls through his head. Many heard the noise, but did not know what was going on. They also hung three or four Negroes nearly dead, and whipped others severely in order to make them tell them about their nightly meetings, and what their object was in holding the same; also, as to who their leaders were. They made a clean breast of the whole matter, telling everything. The strongest thing about these Ku Klux was that they did not hesitate to unmask themselves when asked to do so; and out of the whole party none were identified.—Every one who saw them says their horses were more beautiful than, and far superior to, any in the country round about. They spoke but little but always to a purpose. They went to several stores and knocked; the doors were opened at once. They then called for rope, and at each place a coil was rolled out to them. They cut it in suitable length to hang a man with. No one asked for money and they offered none. They did not disturb any one else, nor did they take any thing except some few Enfield rifles which were found in possession of some very bad Negroes.—They called on the revenue officer and passed a few remarks with him. What transpired is not known, but it has made a great improvement in his conversation. The visitants advent has been productive of much good and benefit to the community, though all regret such steps should have to be resorted to, every one says "give us peace," and really I believe them to be truly sincere.

> **"They shot one very bad Negro. . . . [T]hey also hung three or four . . . nearly dead. . . ."**

SOURCE: Reprinted with permission from the Alabama Department of Archives and History, Montgomery, Alabama

George Houston's Testimony, Montgomery, October 17, 1871

Q: **How many were there in the crowd that attacked your house?**

A. I can't tell. It looked like a great many men. It was starlight and before day. There was a good deal of cursing after they got shot and broke down my door. The reason they were afraid to come in was, I think, because that shot was fired. They didn't come back.

Q: **Did you notice whether they were disguised?**

A. Only the one that I shot at. He looked like he was wrapped up in some white cloth; it looked so by starlight. That is all I could see.

Q: **Had you any trouble with your neighbors?**

A. Nothing more than some talk that I didn't like from some wealthy men of the county. One of them had come to me, and told me if I turned against them they would turn against me. They looked upon me as being the prominent Negro of the county. I know the men that told me that thing very well. It was in a dry goods store in that town.

Q: **What did they want you to do?**

A. They wanted me to deny what was called the Union League. They had understood I belonged to it. The reason they took a great fancy to me was, I was a tailor in that place. My master had learned me this trade on account of my health and crippleness when I was a slave. I had run a shop for sixteen years there. They came to me, and said I made my living off of them and not off of the damned niggers, and if I turned against them they would turn against me. I said my belonging to the Union League didn't do them any harm. They said, 'Yes, it does.' I said, 'It's only to teach our ignorant colored men.' This was our talk privately, and this was only a few months before I was shot. That is all I could assign for the cause of it, and taking the fact that the other colored men were shot down just before, and I was a representative of that county. There was a public meeting; we had made some public speeches, some white and some black men, and I told them I was opposed to this.

Q: **Opposed to what?**

A. Opposed to colored men being shot down like dogs, when I knew that the officers of the county could stop it. I told the sheriff that to his face. If they took exceptions to me on that account, that is all I can tell, for I was raised there, and they never could put a scratch of a pen against me before, and nothing else could they have taken from it except that I tried

> "[I was] opposed to colored men being shot down like dogs."

to hold up the men that had been shot down by violence; some at night, some by daylight; some were found in the stock pools with their guts cut out. All this came to my ears and the other men's ears.

Q: **How many colored men were assassinated in that county?**

A. I think eight or nine, before I was shot, were killed dead, according to the accounts of the white men and black men I got through the county. I stop at eight or nine, but I really think there were a few more.

Q: **Is the bullet there now in the leg?**

A. Yes sir; and it will stay there until God Almighty takes it out. I had a doctor fifteen minutes probing to get that out. The ball went through my child's flesh, too. My child had to go fifteen miles to his grandfather and I had to suffer and go off. I had to sacrifice my property. And yet I am a Republican, and I will die one. I say the Republican Party freed me, and I will die on top of it. I don't care who is pleased. I vote every time. I was register of my county, and my master sent in and lent me his pistols to carry around my waist when I was register, to protect myself against my enemies. I am a Republican today, and if the Republican Party can't do me any good, I will never turn against it. I can work in the cotton patch and work at my trade, and get along without any benefit from my party, and so I will stick to the Republican Party and die in it.

SOURCE: "Affairs in Insurrectionary States: Report and Minority Reviews, Alabama, vol. 2," *Senate Reports*, 42nd Congress, 2nd Session, vol. 2, pt. 9, no. 41.

As the "crop lien" system spread, and as more and more farmers turned to cotton growing as the only way to obtain credit, expanding production depressed prices. Competition from new cotton centers in the world market, such as Egypt and India, accelerated the downward spiral. As cotton prices declined alarmingly, to roughly eleven cents per pound in 1875 to five cents by the early 1890s, per capita wealth in the South fell steadily, equaling only one-third that of the East, Midwest, or West by the 1890s. Small farmers caught up in a vicious cycle of low cotton prices, debt, and dwindling food crops found their old ideal of independence sacrificed to the cruel logic of the cotton market.

To obtain precious credit, most southern farmers, both black and white, found themselves forced to produce cotton for market and, thus, became enmeshed in the debt-ridden crop lien system. In traditional cotton-producing areas, especially the black belt, landless farmers growing cotton had replaced slaves growing cotton. In the Upcountry and newer areas of cultivation, cotton-dominated commercial agriculture, with landless tenants

Read the Document

James T. Rapier, Testimony Before U.S. Senate (1880) at **www.myhistorylab.com**

and sharecroppers as the main workforce, had replaced the more diversified subsistence economy of the antebellum era. These patterns hardened throughout the late nineteenth century. By 1900, roughly half of the South's 2,620,000 farms were operated by tenants, who rented land, or sharecroppers, who pledged a portion of the crop to owners in exchange for some combination of work animals, seed, and tools. Over one-third of the white farmers and nearly three-quarters of the African American farmers in the cotton states were tenants or sharecroppers. Large parts of the southern landscape would remain defined by this system well into the twentieth century: small farms operated by families who did not own their land, mired in desperate poverty and debt.

Reconstructing the North

Abraham Lincoln liked to cite his own rise as proof of the superiority of the northern system of "free labor" over slavery. "There is no permanent class of hired laborers amongst us," Lincoln asserted. "Twenty-five years ago, I was a hired laborer. The hired laborer of yesterday, labors on his own account today; and will hire others to labor for him tomorrow. Advancement—improvement in condition—is the order of things in a society of equals." But the triumph of the North brought with it fundamental changes in the economy, labor relations, and politics that brought Lincoln's ideal vision into question. The spread of the factory system, the growth of large and powerful corporations, and the rapid expansion of capitalist enterprise all hastened the development of a large unskilled and routinized workforce. Rather than becoming independent producers, more and more

workers found themselves consigned permanently to wage labor.

The old Republican ideal of a society bound by a harmony of interests had become overshadowed by a grimmer reality of class conflict. A violent national railroad strike in 1877 was broken only with the direct intervention of federal troops. That conflict struck many Americans as a turning point. Northern society, like the society of the South, appeared more hierarchical than equal.

The Age of Capital

In the decade following Appomattox, the North's economy continued the industrial boom begun during the Civil War. By 1873, America's industrial production had grown 75 percent over the 1865 level. By that time, too, the number of nonagricultural workers in the North had surpassed the number of farmers. Between 1860 and 1880, the number of wage earners in manufacturing and construction more than doubled, from 2 million to over 4 million. Only Great Britain boasted a larger manufacturing economy than the United States. During the same period, nearly 3 million immigrants arrived in America, almost all of whom settled in the North and West.

The railroad business both symbolized and advanced the new industrial order. Shortly before the Civil War, enthusiasm mounted for a transcontinental line. Private companies took on the huge and expensive job of construction, but the federal government funded the project, providing the largest subsidy in American history. The Pacific Railway Act of 1862 granted the Union Pacific and the Central Pacific rights to a broad swath of land extending from Omaha, Nebraska, to Sacramento, California. An 1864 act bestowed a subsidy of $15,000 per mile of track laid over smooth plains country and varying larger amounts up to $48,000 per mile in the foothills and mountains of the Far West. The Union Pacific employed gangs of Irish American and African American workers to lay track heading west from Omaha.

Meanwhile the Central Pacific, pushing east from California, had a tougher time finding workers, and began recruiting thousands of men from China. In 1868, the Senate ratified the Burlingame Treaty, giving Chinese the right to emigrate to the United States, while specifying that "nothing contained herein shall be held to confer naturalization." The right to work in America, in other words, did not bestow any right to citizenship. Some 12,000 Chinese laborers (about 90 percent of the workforce) bore the brunt of the difficult conditions in the Sierra Nevada where blizzards, landslides, and steep rock faces took an awful toll. Chinese workers earned a reputation for toughness and efficiency. "If we found we were in a hurry for a job of work," wrote one of the Central Pacific's superintendents, "it was better to put on Chinese at once." Working in baskets suspended by ropes, Chinese laborers chipped away at solid granite walls and became

Chinese immigrants, like these section gang workers, provided labor and skills critical to the successful completion of the first transcontinental railroad. This photo was taken in Promontory Point, Utah Territory, in 1869.

expert in the use of nitroglycerin for blasting through the mountains. But after completion of the transcontinental line threw thousands of Chinese railroad workers onto the California labor market, the open-door immigration pledge in the Burlingame Treaty would soon be eclipsed by a virulent tide of anti-Chinese agitation among western politicians and labor unions. In 1882, Congress passed the Chinese Exclusion Act, suspending any further Chinese immigration for ten years.

On May 10, 1869, Leland Stanford, the former governor of California and president of the Central Pacific Railroad, traveled to Promontory Point in Utah Territory to hammer a ceremonial golden spike, marking the finish of the first transcontinental line. Other railroads went up with less fanfare. The Southern Pacific, chartered by the state of California, stretched from San Francisco to Los Angeles, and on through Arizona and New Mexico to connections with New Orleans. The Atchison, Topeka, and Santa Fe reached the Pacific in 1887 by way of a southerly route across the Rocky Mountains. The Great

Northern, one of the few lines financed by private capital, extended west from St. Paul, Minnesota, to Washington's Puget Sound.

Railroad corporations became America's first big businesses. Railroads required huge outlays of investment capital, and their growth increased the economic power of banks and investment houses centered in Wall Street. Bankers often gained seats on the boards of directors of railroad companies, and their access to capital sometimes gave them the real control of the corporations. By the early 1870s the Pennsylvania Railroad was the nation's largest single company with more than 20,000 employees. A small group of railroad executives, including Cornelius Vanderbilt, Jay Gould, Collis P. Huntington, and James J. Hill, amassed unheard-of fortunes. When he died in 1877, Vanderbilt left his son $100 million. By comparison, a decent annual wage for working a six-day week was around $350.

Some of the nation's most prominent politicians routinely accepted railroad largesse. Republican Senator

William M. Stewart of Nevada, a member of the Committee on Pacific Railroads, received a gift of 50,000 acres of land from the Central Pacific for his services. The worst scandal of the Grant administration grew out of corruption involving railroad promotion. As a way of diverting funds for the building of the Union Pacific Railroad, an inner circle of Union Pacific stockholders created the dummy Crédit Mobilier construction company. In return for political favors, a group of prominent Republicans received stock in the company. When the scandal broke in 1872, it politically ruined Vice President Schuyler Colfax and led to the censure of two congressmen.

Other industries also boomed in this period, especially those engaged in extracting minerals and processing natural resources. Railroad growth stimulated expansion in the production of coal, iron, stone, and lumber, and these also received significant government aid. For example, under the National Mineral Act of 1866, mining companies received millions of acres of free public land. Oil refining enjoyed a huge expansion in the 1860s and 1870s. As with railroads, an early period of fierce competition soon gave way to concentration. By the late 1870s, John D. Rockefeller's Standard Oil Company controlled almost 90 percent of the nation's oil-refining capacity.

Liberal Republicans and the Election of 1872

With the rapid growth of large-scale, capital-intensive enterprises, Republicans increasingly identified with the interests of business rather than the rights of freedmen or the antebellum ideology of "free labor." State Republican parties now organized themselves around the spoils of federal patronage rather than grand causes such as preserving the Union or ending slavery. Republicans had no monopoly on political scandal. In 1871 New York City newspapers reported the shocking story of how Democratic Party boss William M. Tweed and his friends had systematically stolen tens of millions from the city treasury. But to many the scandal represented only the most extreme case of the routine corruption that now plagued American political life.

By the end of President Grant's first term, a large number of disaffected Republicans sought an alternative. The Liberal Republicans, as they called themselves, emphasized the doctrines of classical economics. They called for a return to limited government, arguing that bribery, scandal, and high taxes all flowed from excessive state interference in the economy.

Liberal Republicans were also suspicious of expanding democracy. They believed that politics ought to be the province of "the best men"—educated and well-to-do men like themselves, devoted to the "science of government."

They proposed civil service reform as the best way to break the hold of party machines on patronage.

Although most Liberal Republicans had enthusiastically supported abolition, the Union cause, and equal rights for freedmen, they now opposed continued federal intervention in the South. The national government had done all it could for the former slaves; they must now take care of themselves. In the spring of 1872, a diverse collection of Liberal Republicans nominated Horace Greeley to run for president. A longtime foe of the Democratic Party, Greeley nonetheless won that party's presidential nomination as well. All Americans, Greeley urged, must put the Civil War behind them and "clasp hands across the bloody chasm."

Grant easily defeated Greeley, carrying every state in the North and winning 56 percent of the popular vote. But the 1872 election accelerated the trend toward federal abandonment of African American citizenship rights. The Liberal Republicans quickly faded as an organized political force. But their ideas helped define a growing conservative consciousness among the northern public. Their agenda included retreat from the ideal of racial justice, hostility toward trade unions, suspicion of immigrant and working-class political power, celebration of competitive individualism, and opposition to government intervention in economic affairs.

The Depression of 1873

In the fall of 1873, the postwar boom came to an abrupt halt as a severe financial panic triggered a deep economic depression. The collapse resulted from commercial overexpansion, especially speculative investing in the nation's railroad system. By 1876, half the nation's railroads had defaulted on their bonds. Over the next two years more than 100 banks folded and 18,000 businesses shut their doors. The depression that began in 1873 lasted sixty-five months—the longest economic contraction in the nation's history until then.

The human toll was enormous. As factories began to close across the nation, the unemployment rate soared to about 15 percent. In many cities the jobless rate was much higher; roughly one-quarter of New York City workers were unemployed in 1874. Many thousands of men took to the road in search of work, and the "tramp" emerged as a new and menacing figure on the social landscape. The Pennsylvania Bureau of Labor Statistics noted that never before had "so many of the working classes, skilled and unskilled been moving from place to place seeking employment that was not to be had." Farmers were also hard hit by the depression. Agricultural output continued to grow, but prices and land values fell sharply. As prices for their crops fell, farmers had a more difficult time repaying their fixed loan obligations; many sank deeper into debt.

"The Tramp," *Harper's Weekly*, September 2, 1876. The depression that began in 1873 forced many thousands of unemployed workers to go "on the tramp" in search of jobs. Men wandered from town to town, walking or riding railroad cars, desperate for a chance to work for wages or simply for room and board. The "tramp" became a powerful symbol of the misery caused by industrial depression and, as in this drawing, an image that evoked fear and nervousness among the nation's middle class.

Mass meetings of workers in New York and other cities issued calls to government officials to create jobs through public works. But these appeals were rejected. Indeed, many business leaders and political figures denounced even meager efforts at charity. They saw the depression as a natural, if painful, part of the business cycle, one that would allow only the strongest enterprises (and workers) to survive. The depression of the 1870s prompted workers and farmers to question the old free-labor ideology that celebrated a harmony of interests in northern society. More people voiced anger at and distrust of large corporations that exercised great economic power from outside their communities

The Electoral Crisis of 1876

With the economy mired in depression, Democrats looked forward to capturing the White House in 1876. New scandals plaguing the Grant administration also weakened the Republican Party. In 1875, a conspiracy surfaced between distillers and U.S. revenue agents to cheat the government out of millions in tax revenues. The government secured indictments against more than

200 members of this "Whiskey Ring," including Orville E. Babcock, Grant's private secretary. Though acquitted, thanks to Grant's intervention, Babcock resigned in disgrace. In 1876, Secretary of War William W. Belknap was impeached for receiving bribes for the sale of trading posts in Indian Territory, and he resigned to avoid conviction.

Democrats nominated Governor Samuel J. Tilden of New York, who brought impeccable reform credentials to his candidacy. In 1871 he had helped expose and prosecute the "Tweed Ring" in New York City. As governor he had toppled the "Canal Ring," a graft-ridden scheme involving inflated contracts for repairs on the Erie Canal. In their platform, the Democrats linked the issue of corruption to an attack on Reconstruction policies. They blamed the Republicans for instituting "a corrupt centralism."

Republican nominee Rutherford B. Hayes, governor of Ohio, also sought the high ground. As a lawyer in Cincinnati he had defended runaway slaves. Later he had distinguished himself as a general in the Union army. Hayes promised, if elected, to support an efficient civil service system, to vigorously prosecute officials who betrayed the public trust, and to introduce a system of free universal education.

On an election day marred by widespread vote fraud and violent intimidation, Tilden received 250,000 more popular votes than Hayes. But Republicans refused to concede victory, challenging the vote totals in the electoral college. Tilden garnered 184 uncontested electoral votes, one shy of the majority required to win, while Hayes received 165 (see Map 17.4).

The problem centered on twenty disputed votes from Florida, Louisiana, South Carolina, and Oregon. In each of the three southern states two sets of electoral votes were returned. In Oregon, which Hayes had unquestionably carried, the Democratic governor nevertheless replaced a disputed Republican elector with a Democrat.

The crisis was unprecedented. In January 1877, Congress moved to settle the deadlock, establishing an Electoral Commission composed of five senators, five representatives, and five Supreme Court justices; eight were Republicans and seven were Democrats. The commission voted along strict partisan lines to award all the contested electoral votes to Hayes. Outraged by this decision, Democratic congressmen threatened a filibuster to block Hayes's inauguration. Violence and stalemate were avoided when Democrats and Republicans struck a compromise in February. In return for Hayes's ascendance to the presidency, the Republicans promised to appropriate more money for southern internal improvements, to appoint a Southerner to Hayes's cabinet, and to pursue a policy of noninterference ("home rule") in southern affairs.

Shortly after assuming office, Hayes ordered removal of the remaining federal troops in Louisiana and South Carolina. Without this military presence to sustain them, the Republican governors of those two states quickly lost power to Democrats. "Home rule" meant Republican abandonment of freed people, Radicals, carpetbaggers, and scalawags. It also effectively nullified the Fourteenth and Fifteenth Amendments and the Civil Rights Act of 1866. The Compromise of 1877 completed repudiation of the idea, born during the Civil War and pursued during Congressional Reconstruction, of a powerful federal government protecting the rights of all American citizens.

Conclusion

Reconstruction succeeded in the limited political sense of reuniting a nation torn apart by the Civil War. The Radical Republican vision, emphasizing racial justice, equal civil and political rights guaranteed by the Fourteenth and Fifteenth Amendments, and a new southern economy organized around independent small farmers, never enjoyed the support of the majority of its party or the northern public. By 1877, the political force of these ideals was spent and the national retreat from them nearly complete.

The end of Reconstruction left the way open for the return of white domination in the South. The freed people's political and civil equality proved only temporary. It would take a "Second Reconstruction," the civil rights movement of the next century, to establish full black citizenship rights once and for all. The federal government's failure to pursue land reform left former slaves without the economic independence needed for full emancipation. Yet the newly autonomous black family, along with black-controlled churches, schools, and other social institutions, provided the foundations for the modern African American community. If the federal government was not yet fully committed to protecting equal rights in local communities, the Reconstruction Era at least pointed to how that goal might be achieved. Even as the federal government retreated from the defense of equal rights for black people, it took a more aggressive stance as the protector of business interests. The Hayes administration responded decisively to one of the worst outbreaks of class violence in American history by dispatching federal troops to several northern cities to break the Great Railroad Strike of 1877. In the aftermath of Reconstruction, the struggle between capital and labor had clearly replaced "the southern question" as the number one political issue of the day. "The overwhelming labor question has dwarfed all other questions into nothing," wrote an Ohio Republican. "We have home questions enough to occupy attention now."

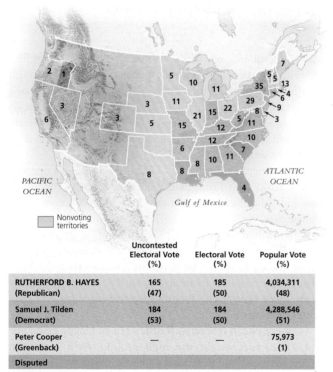

	Uncontested Electoral Vote (%)	Electoral Vote (%)	Popular Vote (%)
RUTHERFORD B. HAYES (Republican)	165 (47)	185 (50)	4,034,311 (48)
Samuel J. Tilden (Democrat)	184 (53)	184 (50)	4,288,546 (51)
Peter Cooper (Greenback)	—	—	75,973 (1)
Disputed			

Nonvoting territories

MAP 17.4 The Election of 1876 The presidential election of 1876 left the nation without a clear-cut winner.

CHRONOLOGY

1865	Freedmen's Bureau established
	Abraham Lincoln assassinated
	Andrew Johnson begins Presidential Reconstruction
	Black codes begin to be enacted in southern states
	Thirteenth Amendment ratified
1866	Civil Rights Act passed
	Congress approves Fourteenth Amendment
	Ku Klux Klan founded
1867	Reconstruction Acts, passed over President Johnson's veto, begin
	Congressional Reconstruction
	Tenure of Office Act
	Southern states call constitutional conventions
1868	President Johnson impeached by the House but acquitted in Senate trial
	Fourteenth Amendment ratified
	Most Southern states readmitted to the Union
	Ulysses S. Grant elected president
1869	Congress approves Fifteenth Amendment
	Union Pacific and Central Pacific tracks meet at Promontory Point in Utah Territory
	Suffragists split into National Woman Suffrage Association and American Woman Suffrage Association
1870	Fifteenth Amendment ratified
1871	Ku Klux Klan Act passed
	"Tweed Ring" in New York City exposed
1872	Liberal Republicans break with Grant and Radicals, nominate Horace Greeley for president
	Crédit Mobilier scandal
	Grant reelected president
1873	Financial panic and beginning of economic depression
	Slaughterhouse Cases
1874	Democrats gain control of House for first time since 1856
1875	Civil Rights Act
1876	Disputed election between Samuel Tilden and Rutherford B. Hayes
1877	Electoral Commission elects Hayes president
	President Hayes dispatches federal troops to break Great Railroad Strike and withdraws last remaining federal troops from the South

Review Questions

1. How did various visions of a "reconstructed" South differ? How did these visions reflect the old political and social divisions that had led to the Civil War?

2. What key changes did emancipation make in the political and economic status of African Americans? Discuss the expansion of citizenship rights in the post–Civil War years. To what extent did women share in the gains made by African Americans?

3. What role did such institutions as the family, the church, the schools, and the political parties play in the African American transition to freedom?

4. How did white Southerners attempt to limit the freedom of former slaves? How did these efforts succeed, and how did they fail?

5. Evaluate the achievements and failures of Reconstruction governments in the southern states.

6. What were the crucial economic changes occurring in the North and South during the Reconstruction era?

Recommended Reading

David W. Blight, *Race and Reunion: The Civil War in American Memory* (2001). An elegantly written and deeply researched inquiry into how Americans "remembered" the Civil War in the half-century after Appomattox, arguing that sectional reconciliation came at the cost of racial division.

Thomas J. Brown, ed., *Reconstructions: New Perspectives on the Postbellum United States* (2006). A wide-ranging collection of essays that explores Reconstruction from a broadly national perspective, including economic, political, and cultural impacts.

Jane Dailey, *Before Jim Crow: The Politics of Race in Postemancipation Virginia* (2000). A fine study that focuses on the tension between the drive to establish white supremacy and the struggle for biracial coalitions in post–Civil War Virginia politics.

Michael W. Fitzgerald, *Splendid Failure: Postwar Reconstruction in the American South* (2007). A beautifully written one-volume overview of Reconstruction, focusing on national politics and the slow but steady capitulation of Republican leaders to white supremacist public opinion in the North and South.

Eric Foner, *Forever Free: The Story of Emancipation and Reconstruction* (2005). An excellent, brief, one-volume overview that condenses Foner's more comprehensive work on Reconstruction. It also includes several striking "visual essays" by Joshua Brown, documenting the changes in visual representations of African Americans in popular media of the era.

Eric Foner, *Reconstruction: America's Unfinished Revolution, 1863–1877* (1988). The most comprehensive and thoroughly researched overview of the Reconstruction era.

Steven Hahn, *A Nation Under Our Feet: Black Political Struggles in the Rural South from Slavery to the Great Migration* (2003). This Pulitzer Prize–winning history includes excellent chapters detailing the political activism of recently freed slaves and the violent resistance they encountered throughout the rural South.

Charles Lane, *The Day Freedom Died: The Colfax Massacre, the Supreme Court, and the Betrayal of Reconstruction* (2008). A riveting narrative account of the era's single worst incident of racist violence, along with its legal and political aftermath.

Elizabeth Regosin, *Freedom's Promise: Ex-Slave Families and Citizenship in the Age of Emancipation* (2002). A thoughtful analysis of how freedmen and freedwomen asserted familial relationships as a means to claiming citizenship rights after emancipation, based on research into federal pension applications made by dependent survivors of Civil War soldiers.

Scott Reynolds Nelson, *Iron Confederacies: Southern Railways, Klan Violence, and Reconstruction* (1999). Pathbreaking analysis of how conservative southern and northern business interests rebuilt the South's railroad system and also achieved enormous political power within individual states.

Mark Wahlgren Summers, *A Dangerous Stir: Fear, Paranoia, and the Making of Reconstruction* (2009). A thoughtful new interpretation by a leading scholar of nineteenth-century politics, emphasizing how deep-seated, often unreasonable fears of conspiracy and revolution dominated much of the era's political discourse.

PEARSON myhistorylab Connections

Reinforce what you learned in this chapter by studying the many documents, images, maps, review tools, and videos available at www.myhistorylab.com.

Read and Review

✓• Study and Review Chapter 17

•••• Read the Document

Confederate Song, "I'm a Good Old Rebel" (1866)

Carl Schurz, Report on the Condition of the South (1865)

Mississippi Black Code (1865)

Jourdon Anderson to His Former Master (1865)

A Sharecrop Contract (1882)

Address from the Colored Citizens of Norfolk, VA (1865)

James T. Rapier, Testimony Before U.S. Senate (1880)

👁️ See the Map Reconstruction

Research and Explore

•••• Read the Document

Exploring America: Did Reconstruction Work for the Freed People?

Profiles
   Tunis Campbell
   Nathan Bedford Forrest

History Bookshelf: Ulysses S. Grant, Memoirs (1886)

Whose History Is it?: Flying the Stars and Bars: The Contested Meaning of the Confederate Flag

Watch the Video

Reconstruction in Texas

The Promise and Failure of Reconstruction

Trials of Racial Identity in Nineteenth-Century America

((•• Hear the Audio

Hear the audio files for Chapter 17 at
www.myhistorylab.com.

APPENDIX

THE DECLARATION OF INDEPENDENCE

When in the course of human events it becomes necessary for one people to dissolve the political bands which have connected them with another and to assume, among the powers of the earth, the separate and equal station to which the laws of nature and of nature's God entitle them, a decent respect to the opinions of mankind requires that they should declare the causes which impel them to the separation.

We hold these truths to be self-evident, that all men are created equal; that they are endowed by their Creator with certain unalienable rights; that among these are life, liberty, and the pursuit of happiness. That, to secure these rights, governments are instituted among men, deriving their just powers from the consent of the governed; that, whenever any form of government becomes destructive of these ends, it is the right of the people to alter or to abolish it, and to institute a new government, laying its foundation on such principles, and organizing its powers in such form, as to them shall seem most likely to effect their safety and happiness. Prudence, indeed, will dictate that governments long established should not be changed for light and transient causes; and, accordingly, all experience hath shown that mankind are more disposed to suffer, while evils are sufferable, than to right themselves by abolishing the forms to which they are accustomed. But when a long train of abuses and usurpations, pursuing invariably the same object, evinces a design to reduce them under absolute despotism, it is their right, it is their duty, to throw off such government and to provide new guards for their future security. Such has been the patient sufferance of these colonies, and such is now the necessity which constrains them to alter their former systems of government. The history of the present King of Great Britain is a history of repeated injuries and usurpations, all having, in direct object, the establishment of an absolute tyranny over these States. To prove this, let facts be submitted to a candid world:

He has refused his assent to laws the most wholesome and necessary for the public good.

He has forbidden his governors to pass laws of immediate and pressing importance, unless suspended in their operation till his assent should be obtained; and, when so suspended, he has utterly neglected to attend to them.

He has refused to pass other laws for the accommodation of large districts of people, unless those people would relinquish the right of representation in the legislature, a right inestimable to them and formidable to tyrants only.

He has called together legislative bodies at places unusual, uncomfortable, and distant from the depository of their public records, for the sole purpose of fatiguing them into compliance with his measures.

He has dissolved representative houses, repeatedly for opposing, with manly firmness, his invasions on the rights of the people.

He has refused, for a long time after such dissolutions, to cause others to be elected; whereby the legislative powers, incapable of annihilation, have returned to the people at large for their exercise; the state remaining, in the meantime, exposed to all the danger of invasion from without and convulsions within.

He has endeavored to prevent the population of these States; for that purpose, obstructing the laws for naturalization of foreigners, refusing to pass others to encourage their migration hither, and raising the conditions of new appropriations of lands.

He has obstructed the administration of justice by refusing his assent to laws for establishing judiciary powers.

He has made judges dependent on his will alone for the tenure of their offices and the amount and payment of their salaries.

He has erected a multitude of new offices and sent hither swarms of officers to harass our people and eat out their substance.

He has kept among us, in time of peace, standing armies, without the consent of our legislatures.

He has affected to render the military independent of, and superior to, the civil power.

He has combined with others to subject us to a jurisdiction foreign to our Constitution and unacknowledged by our laws, giving his assent to their acts of pretended legislation—

For quartering large bodies of armed troops among us;

For protecting them by mock trial, from punishment for any murders which they should commit on the inhabitants of these States;

For cutting off our trade with all parts of the world;

For imposing taxes on us without our consent;

For depriving us, in many cases, of the benefit of trial by jury;

For transporting us beyond seas to be tried for pretended offences;

For abolishing the free system of English laws in a neighboring province, establishing therein an arbitrary government, and enlarging its boundaries, so as to render it at once an example and fit instrument for introducing the same absolute rule into these colonies;

For taking away our charters, abolishing our most valuable laws, and altering, fundamentally, the powers of our governments.

For suspending our own legislatures and declaring themselves invested with power to legislate for us in all cases whatsoever.

He has abdicated government here by declaring us out of his protection and waging war against us.

He has plundered our seas, ravaged our coasts, burnt our towns, and destroyed the lives of our people.

He is, at this time, transporting large armies of foreign mercenaries to complete the works of death, desolation, and tyranny already begun with circumstances of cruelty and perfidy scarcely paralleled in the most barbarous ages, and totally unworthy the head of a civilized nation.

He has constrained our fellow citizens, taken captive on the high seas, to bear arms against their country, to become the executioners of their friends and brethren, or to fall themselves by their hands.

He has excited domestic insurrections amongst us and has endeavored to bring on the inhabitants of our frontiers, the merciless Indian savages, whose known rule of warfare is an undistinguished destruction of all ages, sexes, and conditions.

In every stage of these oppressions, we have petitioned for redress in the most humble terms; our repeated petitions have been answered only by repeated injury. A prince whose character is thus marked by every act which may define a tyrant is unfit to be the ruler of a free people.

Nor have we been wanting in attention to our British brethren. We have warned them, from time to time, of attempts made by their legislature to extend an unwarrantable jurisdiction over us. We have reminded them of the circumstances of our emigration and settlement here. We have appealed to their native justice and magnanimity, and we have conjured them, by the ties of our common kindred, to

disavow these usurpations, which would inevitably interrupt our connections and correspondence. They, too, have been deaf to the voice of justice and consanguinity. We must, therefore, acquiesce in the necessity which denounces our separation, and hold them, as we hold the rest of mankind, enemies in war, in peace, friends.

We, therefore, the representatives of the United States of America, in general Congress assembled, appealing to the Supreme Judge of the world for the rectitude of our intentions, do, in the name and by the authority of the good people of these colonies, solemnly publish and declare, that these united colonies are, and of right ought to be, free and independent states: that they are absolved from all allegiance to the British Crown, and that all political connection between them and the state of Great Britain is, and ought to be, totally dissolved; and that, as free and independent states, they have full power to levy war, conclude peace, contract alliances, establish commerce, and to do all other acts and things which independent states may of right do. And, for the support of this declaration, with a firm reliance on the protection of Divine Providence, we mutually pledge to each other our lives, our fortunes, and our sacred honor.

THE ARTICLES OF CONFEDERATION AND PERPETUAL UNION*

Between the states of New Hampshire, Massachusetts-bay Rhode Island and Providence Plantations, Connecticut, New York, New Jersey, Pennsylvania, Delaware, Maryland, Virginia, North Carolina, South Carolina, and Georgia.

Article 1

The Stile of this Confederacy shall be "The United States of America."

Article 2

Each state retains its sovereignty, freedom, and independence, and every power, jurisdiction, and right, which is not by this Confederation expressly delegated to the United States, in Congress assembled.

Article 3

The said States hereby severally enter into a firm league of friendship with each other, for their common defense, the security of their liberties, and their mutual and general welfare, binding themselves to assist each other, against all force offered to, or attacks made upon them, or any of them, on account of religion, sovereignty, trade, or any other pretense whatever.

Article 4

The better to secure and perpetuate mutual friendship and intercourse among the people of the different States in this Union, the free inhabitants of each of these States,

paupers, vagabonds, and fugitives from justice excepted, shall be entitled to all privileges and immunities of free citizens in the several States; and the people of each State shall have free ingress and regress to and from any other State, and shall enjoy therein all the privileges of trade and commerce, subject to the same duties, impositions, and restrictions as the inhabitants thereof respectively, provided that such restrictions shall not extend so far as to prevent the removal of property imported into any State, to any other State of which the owner is an inhabitant; provided also that no imposition, duties or restriction shall be laid by any State, on the property of the United States, or either of them.

If any person guilty of, or charged with, treason, felony, or other high misdemeanor in any State, shall flee from justice, and be found in any of the United States, he shall, upon demand of the Governor or executive power of the State from which he fled, be delivered up and removed to the State having jurisdiction of his offense.

Full faith and credit shall be given in each of these States to the records, acts, and judicial proceedings of the courts and magistrates of every other State.

Article 5

For the most convenient management of the general interests of the United States, delegates shall be annually appointed in such manner as the legislatures of each State shall direct, to meet in Congress on the first Monday in November, in every year, with a power reserved to each State to recall its delegates, or any of them, at any time within the year, and to send others in their stead for the remainder of the year.

No State shall be represented in Congress by less than two, nor by more than seven members; and no person

*Agreed to in Congress November 15, 1777; ratified March 1781.

shall be capable of being a delegate for more than three years in any term of six years; nor shall any person, being a delegate, be capable of holding any office under the United States, for which he, or another for his benefit, receives any salary, fees or emolument of any kind.

Each State shall maintain its own delegates in a meeting of the States, and while they act as members of the committee of the States.

In determining questions in the United States in Congress assembled, each State shall have one vote.

Freedom of speech and debate in Congress shall not be impeached or questioned in any court or place out of Congress, and the members of Congress shall be protected in their persons from arrests or imprisonments, during the time of their going to and from, and attendence on Congress, except for treason, felony, or breach of the peace.

Article 6

No State, without the consent of the United States in Congress assembled, shall send any embassy to, or receive any embassy from, or enter into any conference, agreement, alliance or treaty with any King, Prince or State; nor shall any person holding any office of profit or trust under the United States, or any of them, accept any present, emolument, office or title of any kind whatever from any King, Prince or foreign State; nor shall the United States in Congress assembled, or any of them, grant any title of nobility.

No two or more States shall enter into any treaty, confederation or alliance whatever between them, without the consent of the United States in Congress assembled, specifying accurately the purposes for which the same is to be entered into, and how long it shall continue.

No State shall lay any imposts or duties, which may interfere with any stipulations in treaties, entered into by the United States in Congress assembled, with any King, Prince or State, in pursuance of any treaties already proposed by Congress, to the courts of France and Spain.

No vessel of war shall be kept up in time of peace by any State, except such number only, as shall be deemed necessary by the United States in Congress assembled, for the defense of such State, or its trade; nor shall any body of forces be kept up by any State in time of peace, except such number only, as in the judgement of the United States in Congress assembled, shall be deemed requisite to garrison the forts necessary for the defense of such State; but every State shall always keep up a well-regulated and disciplined militia, sufficiently armed and accoutered, and shall provide and constantly have ready for use, in public stores, a due number of filed pieces and tents, and a proper quantity of arms, ammunition and camp equipage.

No State shall engage in any war without the consent of the United States in Congress assembled, unless such State be actually invaded by enemies, or shall have received certain advice of a resolution being formed by some nation of Indians to invade such State, and the danger is so imminent as not to admit of a delay, till the United States in Congress assembled can be consulted; nor shall any State grant commissions to any ships or vessels of war, nor letters of marque or reprisal, except it be after a declaration of war by the United States in Congress assembled, and then only against the King-dom or State and the subjects thereof, against which war has been so declared, and under such regulations as shall be established by the United States in Congress assembled, unless such State be infested by pirates, in which case vessels of war may be fitted out for that occasion, and kept so long as the danger shall continue, or until the United States in Congress assembled shall determine otherwise.

Article 7

When land forces are raised by any State for the common defense, all officers of or under the rank of colonel, shall be appointed by the legislature of each State respectively, by whom such forces shall be raised, or in such manner as such State shall direct, and all vacancies shall be filled up by the State which first made the appointment.

Article 8

All charges of war, and all other expenses that shall be incurred for the common defense or general welfare, and allowed by the United States in Congress assembled, shall be defrayed out of a common treasury, which shall be supplied by the several States in proportion to the value of all land within each State, granted to or surveyed for any person, as such land and the buildings and improvements thereon shall be estimated according to such mode as the United States in Congress assembled, shall from time to time direct and appoint.

The taxes for paying that proportion shall be laid and levied by the authority and direction of the legislatures of the several States within the time agreed upon by the United States in Congress assembled.

Article 9

The United States in Congress assembled, shall have the sole and exclusive right and power of determining on peace and war, except in the cases mentioned in the sixth article; of sending and receiving ambassadors; entering into treaties and alliances, provided that no treaty of commerce shall be made whereby the legislative power of the respective States shall be restrained from imposing such imposts and duties on foreigners, as their own people are subjected to, or from prohibiting the exportation or importation of any species of goods or commodities whatsoever; of establishing rules for deciding in all cases, what captures on land or water shall be legal, and in what manner prizes taken by land or naval forces in the service of the United States shall be divided or appropriated; of granting letters of marque and reprisal in times of peace; appointing courts for the trial of piracies and felonies committed on the high seas and establishing courts for receiving and determining finally appeals in all cases of captures, provided that no member of Congress shall be appointed a judge of any of the said courts.

The United States in Congress assembled shall also be the last resort on appeal in all disputes and differences now subsisting or that hereafter may arise between two or more States concerning boundary, jurisdiction or any other causes whatever; which authority shall always be exercised in the manner following. Whenever the legislative or executive authority or lawful agent of any State in controversy with another shall present a petition to Congress stating the matter in question and praying for a hearing, notice thereof shall be given by order of Congress to the legislative or executive authority of the other State in controversy, and a day assigned for the appearance of the parties by their lawful agents, who shall then be directed to appoint by joint consent, commissioners or judges to constitute a court for hearing and determining the matter in question: but if they cannot agree, Congress shall name three persons out of each of the United States, and from the list of such persons each party shall alternately strike out one, the petitioners beginning, until the number shall be reduced to thirteen; and from that number not less than seven, nor more than nine names as Congress shall direct, shall in the presence of Congress be drawn out by lot, and the persons whose names shall be so drawn or any five of them, shall be commissioners or judges, to hear and finally determine the controversy, so always as a major part of the judges who shall hear the cause shall agree in the determination: and if either party shall neglect to attend at the day appointed, without showing reasons, which Congress shall judge sufficient, or being present shall refuse to strike, the Congress shall proceed to nominate three persons out of each State, and the secretary of Congress shall strike in behalf of such party absent or refusing; and the judgement and sentence of the court to be appointed, in the manner before prescribed, shall be final and conclusive; and if any of the parties shall refuse to submit to the authority of such court, or to appear or defend their claim or cause, the court shall nevertheless proceed to pronounce sentence, or judgement, which shall in like manner be final and decisive, the judgement or sentence and other proceedings being in either case transmitted to Congress, and lodged among the acts of Congress for the security of the parties concerned: provided that every commissioner, before he sits in judgement, shall take an oath to be administered by one of the judges of the supreme or superior court of the State, where the cause shall be tried, "well and truly to hear and determine the matter in question, according to the best of his judgement, without favor, affection or hope of reward:" provided also, that no State shall be deprived of territory for the benefit of the United States.

All controversies concerning the private right of soil claimed under different grants of two or more States, whose jurisdictions as they may respect such lands, and the States which passed such grants are adjusted, the said grants or either of them being at the same time claimed to have originated antecedent to such settlement of jurisdiction, shall on the petition of either party to the Congress of the United States, be finally determined as near as may be in the same manner as is before prescribed for deciding disputes respecting territorial jurisdiction between different States.

The United States in Congress assembled shall also have the sole and exclusive right and power of regulating the alloy and value of coin struck by their own authority, or by that of the respective States; fixing the standards of weights and measures throughout the United States; regulating the trade and managing all affairs with the Indians not members of any of the States; provided that the legislative right of any State within its own limits be not infringed or violated; establishing or regulating post offices from one State to another, throughout all the United States, and exacting such postage on the papers passing through the same as may be requisite to defray the expenses of the said office; appointing all officers of the land forces in the service of the United States, excepting regimental officers; appointing all the officers of the naval forces, and commissioning all officers whatever in the service of the United States; making rules for the government and regulation of the said land and naval forces, and directing their operations.

The United States in Congress assembled shall have authority to appoint a committee, to sit in the recess of Congress, to be denominated "A Committee of the States," and to consist of one delegate from each State; and to appoint such other committees and civil officers as may be necessary for managing the general affairs of the United States under their direction; to appoint one of their members to preside, provided that no person be allowed to serve in the office of president more than one year in any term of three years; to ascertain the necessary sums of money to be raised for the service of the United States, and to appropriate and apply the same for defraying the public expenses; to borrow money, or emit bills on the credit of the United States, transmitting every half year to the respective States an account of the sums of money so borrowed or emitted; to build and equip a navy; to agree upon the number of land forces, and to make requisitions from each State for its quota, in proportion to the number of white inhabitants in such State; which requisition shall be binding, and thereupon the legislature of each State shall appoint the regimental officers, raise the men and cloath, arm and equip them in a soldierlike manner, at the expense of the United States; and the officers and men so cloathed, armed and equipped shall march to the place appointed, and within the time agreed on by the United States in Congress assembled; but if the United States in Congress assembled shall, on consideration of circumstances judge proper that any State should not raise men, or should raise a smaller number of men than the quota thereof, such extra number shall be raised, officered, cloathed, armed and equipped in the same manner as the quota of each State, unless the legislature of such State shall judge that such extra number cannot be safely spared out in the same, in which case they shall raise, officer, cloath, arm and equip as many of such extra number as they judge can be safely spared. And the officers and men so cloathed, armed, and equipped, shall march to the place appointed, and within the time agreed on by the United States in Congress assembled.

The United States in Congress assembled shall never engage in a war, nor grant letters of marque or reprisal in time of peace, nor enter into any treaties or alliances, nor coin money, nor regulate the value thereof, nor ascertain the sums and expenses necessary for the defense and welfare of the United States, or any of them, nor emit bills, nor borrow money on the credit of the United States, nor appropriate money, nor agree upon the number of vessels of war, to be built or purchased, or the number of land or sea forces to be raised, nor appoint a commander in chief of the army or navy, unless nine States assent to the same: nor shall a question on any other point, except for adjourning from day to day be determined, unless by the votes of the majority of the United States in Congress assembled.

The Congress of the United States shall have power to adjourn to any time within the year, and to any place within the United States, so that no period of adjournment be for a longer duration than the space of six months, and shall publish the journal of their proceedings monthly, except such parts thereof relating to treaties, alliances or military operations, as in their judge-ment require secrecy; and the yeas and nays of the delegates of each State on any question shall be entered on the journal, when it is desired by any delegates of a State, or any of them, at his or their request shall be furnished with a transcript of the said journal, except such parts as are above excepted, to lay before the legislatures of the several States.

Article 10

The Committee of the States, or any nine of them, shall be authorized to execute, in the recess of Congress, such of the powers of Congress as the United States in Congress assembled, by the consent of the nine States, shall from time to time think expedient to vest them with; provided that no power be delegated to the said Committee, for the exercise of which, by the Articles of Confederation, the voice of nine States in the Congress of the United States assembled is requisite.

Article 11

Canada acceding to this confederation, and adjoining in the measures of the United States, shall be admitted into, and entitled to all the advantages of this Union; but no other colony shall be admitted into the same, unless such admission be agreed to by nine States.

Article 12

All bills of credit emitted, monies borrowed, and debts contracted by, or under the authority of Congress, before the assembling of the United States, in pursuance of the present confederation, shall be deemed and considered as a charge against the United States, for payment and satisfaction whereof the said United States, and the public faith are hereby solemnly pledged.

Article 13

Every State shall abide by the determination of the United States in Congress assembled, on all questions which by this confederation are submitted to them. And the Articles of this Confederation shall be inviolably observed by every State, and the Union shall be perpetual; nor shall any alteration at any time hereafter be made in any of them; unless such alteration be agreed to in a Congress of the United States, and be afterwards confirmed by the legislatures of every State.

These articles shall be proposed to the legislatures of all the United States, to be considered, and if approved of by them, they are advised to authorize their delegates to ratify the same in the Congress of the United States; which being done, the same shall become conclusive.

THE CONSTITUTION OF THE UNITED STATES OF AMERICA

We the people of the United States, in order to form a more perfect union, establish justice, insure domestic tranquillity, provide for the common defense, promote the general welfare, and secure the blessings of liberty to ourselves and our posterity, do ordain and establish this Constitution for the United States of America.

Article I

Section 1. All legislative powers herein granted shall be vested in a Congress of the United States, which shall consist of a Senate and House of Representatives.

Section 2. 1. The House of Representatives shall be composed of members chosen every second year by the people of the several States, and the electors in each State shall have the qualifications requisite for electors of the most numerous branch of the State legislature.

2. No person shall be a representative who shall not have attained to the age of twenty-five years, and been seven years a citizen of the United States, and who shall not, when elected, be an inhabitant of that State in which he shall be chosen.

3. Representatives and direct taxes[1] shall be apportioned among the several States which may be included within this Union, according to their respective numbers, which shall be determined by adding to the whole number of free persons, including those bound to service for a term

of years, and excluding Indians not taxed, three fifths of all other persons.[2] The actual enumeration shall be made within three years after the first meeting of the Congress of the United States, and within every subsequent term of ten years, in such manner as they shall by law direct. The number of representatives shall not exceed one for every thirty thousand, but each State shall have at least one representative; and until such enumeration shall be made, the State of New Hampshire shall be entitled to choose three, Massachusetts eight, Rhode Island and Providence Plantations one, Connecticut five, New York six, New Jersey four, Pennsylvania eight, Delaware one, Maryland six, Virginia ten, North Carolina five, South Carolina five, and Georgia three.

4. When vacancies happen in the representation from any State, the executive authority thereof shall issue writs of election to fill such vacancies.

5. The House of Representatives shall choose their speaker and other officers; and shall have the sole power of impeachment.

Section 3. 1. The Senate of the United States shall be composed of two senators from each State, chosen by the legislature thereof,[3] for six years; and each senator shall have one vote.

2. Immediately after they shall be assembled in consequence of the first election, they shall be divided as equally as may be into three classes. The seats of the senators of the first class shall be vacated at the expiration of the second year,

[1]See the Sixteenth Amendment.

[2]See the Fourteenth Amendment.
[3]See the Seventeenth Amendment.

of the second class at the expiration of the fourth year, and of the third class at the expiration of the sixth year, so that one third may be chosen every second year; and if vacancies happen by resignation, or otherwise, during the recess of the legislature of any State, the executive thereof may make temporary appointments until the next meeting of the legislature, which shall then fill such vacancies.[4]

3. No person shall be a senator who shall not have attained to the age of thirty years, and been nine years a citizen of the United States, and who shall not, when elected, be an inhabitant of that State for which he shall be chosen.

4. The Vice President of the United States shall be President of the Senate, but shall have no vote, unless they be equally divided.

5. The Senate shall choose their other officers, and also a president pro tempore, in the absence of the Vice President, or when he shall exercise the office of the President of the United States.

6. The Senate shall have the sole power to try all impeachments. When sitting for that purpose, they shall be on oath or affirmation. When the President of the United States is tried, the chief justice shall preside: and no person shall be convicted without the concurrence of two thirds of the members present.

7. Judgment in cases of impeachment shall not extend further than to removal from office, and disqualification to hold and enjoy any office of honor, trust or profit under the United States: but the party convicted shall nevertheless be liable and subject to indictment, trial, judgment and punishment, according to law.

Section 4. 1. The times, places, and manner of holding elections for senators and representatives, shall be prescribed in each State by the legislature thereof; but the Congress may at any time by law make or alter such regulations, except as to the places of choosing senators.

2. The Congress shall assemble at least once in every year, and such meeting shall be on the first Monday in December, unless they shall by law appoint a different day.

Section 5. 1. Each House shall be the judge of the elections, returns and qualifications of its own members, and a majority of each shall constitute a quorum to do business; but a smaller number may adjourn from day to day, and may be authorized to compel the attendance of absent members, in such manner, and under such penalties as each House may provide.

2. Each House may determine the rules of its proceedings, punish its members for disorderly behavior, and, with the concurrence of two thirds, expel a member.

3. Each House shall keep a journal of its proceedings, and from time to time publish the same, excepting such parts as may in their judgment require secrecy; and the yeas and nays of the members of either House on any question shall, at the desire of one fifth of those present, be entered on the journal.

4. Neither House, during the session of Congress, shall, without the consent of the other, adjourn for more than three days, nor to any other place than that in which the two Houses shall be sitting.

Section 6. 1. The senators and representatives shall receive a compensation for their services, to be ascertained by law, and paid out of the Treasury of the United States. They shall in all cases, except treason, felony, and breach of the peace, be privileged from arrest during their attendance at the session of their respective Houses, and in going to and returning from the same; and for any speech or debate in either House, they shall not be questioned in any other place.

2. No senator or representative shall, during the time for which he was elected, be appointed to any civil office under the authority of the United States, which shall have been created, or the emoluments whereof shall have been increased, during such time; and no person holding any office under the United States shall be a member of either House during his continuance in office.

Section 7. 1. All bills for raising revenue shall originate in the House of Representatives; but the Senate may propose or concur with amendments as on other bills.

2. Every bill which shall have passed the House of Representatives and the Senate, shall, before it become a law, be presented to the President of the United States; If he approves he shall sign it, but if not he shall return it, with his objections, to that House in which it shall have originated, who shall enter the objections at large on their journal, and proceed to reconsider it. If after such reconsideration two thirds of that House shall agree to pass the bill, it shall be sent, together with the objections, to the other House, by which it shall likewise be reconsidered, and if approved by two thirds of that House, it shall become a law. But in all such cases the votes of both Houses shall be determined by yeas and nays, and the names of the persons voting for and against the bill shall be entered on the journal of each House respectively. If any bill shall not be returned by the President within ten days (Sundays excepted) after it shall have been presented to him, the same shall be a law, in like manner as if he had signed it, unless the Congress by their adjournment prevent its return, in which case it shall not be a law.

3. Every order, resolution, or vote to which the concurrence of the Senate and the House of Representatives may be necessary (except on a question of adjournment) shall be presented to the President of the United States; and before the same shall take effect, shall be approved by him, or being disapproved by him, shall be repassed by two thirds of the Senate and House of Representatives, according to the rules and limitations prescribed in the case of a bill.

Section 8. The Congress shall have the power

1. To lay and collect taxes, duties, imposts, and excises, to pay the debts and provide for the common defense and general welfare of the United States; but all duties, imposts, and excises shall be uniform throughout the United States.

2. To borrow money on the credit of the United States;

3. To regulate commerce with foreign nations, and among the several States, and with the Indian tribes;

4. To establish a uniform rule of naturalization, and uniform laws on the subject of bankruptcies throughout the United States;

5. To coin money, regulate the value thereof, and of foreign coin, and fix the standard of weights and measures;

6. To provide for the punishment of counterfeiting the securities and current coin of the United States;

7. To establish post offices and post roads;

---

[4]See the Seventeenth Amendment.

8. To promote the progress of science and useful arts, by securing for limited times to authors and inventors the exclusive right to their respective writings and discoveries;

9. To constitute tribunals inferior to the Supreme Court;

10. To define and punish piracies and felonies committed on the high seas, and offenses against the law of nations;

11. To declare war, grant letters of marque and reprisal, and make rules concerning captures on land and water;

12. To raise and support armies, but no appropriation of money to that use shall be for a longer term than two years;

13. To provide and maintain a navy;

14. To make rules for the government and regulation of the land and naval forces;

15. To provide for calling forth the militia to execute the laws of the Union, suppress insurrections and repel invasions;

16. To provide for organizing, arming, and disciplining the militia, and for governing such part of them as may be employed in the service of the United States, reserving to the States respectively, the appointment of the officers, and the authority of training the militia according to the discipline prescribed by Congress;

17. To exercise exclusive legislation in all cases whatsoever, over such district (not exceeding ten miles square) as may, by cession of particular States, and the acceptance of Congress, become the seat of the government of the United States, and to exercise like authority over all places purchased by the consent of the legislature of the State in which the same shall be, for the erection of forts, magazines, arsenals, dockyards, and other needful buildings; and

18. To make all laws which shall be necessary and proper for carrying into execution the foregoing powers, and all other powers vested by this Constitution in the government of the United States, or any department or officer thereof.

Section 9. 1. The migration or importation of such persons as any of the States now existing shall think proper to admit, shall not be prohibited by the Congress prior to the year one thousand eight hundred and eight, but a tax or duty may be imposed on such importation, not exceeding ten dollars for each person.

2. The privilege of the writ of habeas corpus shall not be suspended, unless when in cases of rebellion or invasion the public safety may require it.

3. No bill of attainder or ex post facto law shall be passed.

4. No capitation, or other direct, tax shall be laid, unless in proportion to the census or enumeration hereinbefore directed to be taken.[5]

5. No tax or duty shall be laid on articles exported from any State.

6. No preference shall be given by any regulation of commerce or revenue to the ports of one State over those of another: nor shall vessels bound to, or from, one State be obliged to enter, clear, or pay duties in another.

7. No money shall be drawn from the treasury, but in consequence of appropriations made by law; and a regular statement and account of the receipts and expenditures of all public money shall be published from time to time.

8. No title of nobility shall be granted by the United States: and no person holding any office of profit or trust under them, shall, without the consent of the Congress, accept of any present, emolument, office, or title, of any kind whatever, from any king, prince, or foreign State.

Section 10. 1. No State shall enter into any treaty, alliance, or confederation; grant letters of marque and reprisal; coin money; emit bills of credit; make any thing but gold and silver coin a tender in payment of debts; pass any bill of attainder, ex post facto law, or law impairing the obligation of contracts, or grant, any title of nobility.

2. No State shall, without the consent of the Congress, lay any imposts or duties on imports or exports, except what may be absolutely necessary for executing its inspection laws: and the net produce of all duties and imposts laid by any State on imports or exports, shall be for the use of the treasury of the United States; and all such laws shall be subject to the revision and control of the Congress.

3. No State shall, without the consent of the Congress, lay any duty of tonnage, keep troops, or ships of war in time of peace, enter into any agreement or compact with another State, or with a foreign power, or engage in war, unless actually invaded, or in such imminent danger as will not admit of delay.

Article II

Section 1. 1. The executive power shall be vested in a President of the United States of America. He shall hold his office during the term of four years, and, together with the Vice President, chosen for the same term, be elected, as follows:

2. Each State shall appoint, in such manner as the legislature thereof may direct, a number of electors, equal to the whole number of senators and representatives to which the State may be entitled in the Congress: but no senator or representative, or person holding any office of trust or profit under the United States, shall be appointed an elector.

The electors shall meet in their respective States, and vote by ballot for two persons, of whom one at least shall not be an inhabitant of the same State with themselves. And they shall make a list of all the persons voted for, and of the number of votes for each; which list they shall sign and certify, and transmit sealed to the seat of the government of the United States, directed to the president of the Senate. The president of the Senate shall, in the presence of the Senate and House of Representatives, open all the certificates, and the votes shall then be counted. The person having the greatest number of votes shall be the President, if such number be a majority of the whole number of electors appointed; and if there be more than one who have such majority, and have an equal number of votes, then the House of Representatives shall immediately choose by ballot one of them for President; and if no person have a majority, then from the five highest on the list the said House shall in like manner choose the President. But in choosing the President, the votes shall be taken by States, the representation from each State having one vote; a quorum for this purpose shall consist of a member or members from two thirds of the States, and a majority of all the States shall be necessary to a choice. In every case after the choice of the President, the

---

[5]See the Sixteenth Amendment.

person having the greatest number of votes of the electors shall be the Vice President. But if there should remain two or more who have equal votes, the Senate shall choose from them by ballot the Vice President.[6]

3. The Congress may determine the time of choosing the electors, and the day on which they shall give their votes; which day shall be the same throughout the United States.

4. No person except a natural born citizen, or a citizen of the United States, at the time of the adoption of this Constitution, shall be eligible to the office of President; neither shall any person be eligible to the office who shall not have attained to the age of thirty-five years, and been fourteen years a resident within the United States.

5. In case of the removal of the President from office, or of his death, resignation, or inability to discharge the powers and duties of the said office, the same shall devolve on the Vice President, and the congress may by law provide for the case of removal, death, resignation or inability, both of the President and Vice President, declaring what officer shall then act as President, and such officer shall act accordingly until the disability be removed, or a President shall be elected.

6. The President shall, at stated times, receive for his services a compensation which shall neither be increased nor diminished during the period for which he shall have been elected, and he shall not receive within that period any other emolument from the United States, or any of them.

7. Before he enter on the execution of his office, he shall take the following oath or affirmation:—"I do solemnly swear (or affirm) that I will faithfully execute the office of President of the United States, and will to the best of my ability, preserve, protect and defend the Constitution of the United States."

Section 2. 1. The President shall be commander in chief of the army and navy of the United States, and of the militia of the several States, when called into the actual service of the United States; he may require the opinion in writing, of the principal officer in each of the executive departments, upon any subject relating to the duties of their respective offices, and he shall have power to grant reprieves and pardons for offenses against the United States, except in cases of impeachment.

2. He shall have power, by and with the advice and consent of the Senate, to make treaties, provided two thirds of the senators present concur; and he shall nominate, and by and with the advice and consent of the Senate, shall appoint ambassadors, other public ministers and consuls, judges of the Supreme Court, and all other officers of the United States, whose appointments are not herein otherwise provided for, and which shall be established by law; but the Congress may by law vest the appointment of such inferior officers, as they think proper, in the President alone, in the courts of laws, or in the heads of departments.

3. The President shall have power to fill up all vacancies that may happen during the recess of the Senate, by granting commissions which shall expire at the end of their next session.

Section 3. He shall from time to time give to the Congress information of the state of the Union, and recommend to their consideration such measures as he shall judge necessary and expedient; he may, on extraordinary occasions, convene both Houses, or either of them, and in case of disagreement between them with respect to the time of adjournment, he may adjourn them to such time as he shall think proper; he shall receive ambassadors and other public ministers; he shall take care that the laws be faithfully executed, and shall commission all the officers of the United States.

Section 4. The President, Vice President, and all civil officers of the United States, shall be removed from office on impeachment for, and conviction of, treason, bribery, or other high crimes and misdemeanors.

Article III

Section 1. The judicial power of the United States shall be vested in one Supreme Court, and in such inferior courts as the Congress may from time to time ordain and establish. The judges, both of the Supreme and inferior courts, shall hold their offices during good behavior, and shall, at stated times, receive for their services, a compensation, which shall not be diminished during their continuance in office.

Section 2. 1. The judicial power shall extend to all cases, in law and equity, arising under this Constitution, the laws of the United States, and treaties made, or which shall be made, under their authority;—to all cases of admiralty and maritime jurisdiction;—to controversies to which the United States shall be a party;[7]—to controversies between two or more States;—between a State and citizens of another State;—between citizens of different States;—between citizens of the same State claiming lands under grants of different States, and between a State, or the citizens thereof, and foreign States, citizens or subjects.

2. In all cases affecting ambassadors, other public ministers and consuls, and those in which a State shall be party, the Supreme Court shall have original jurisdiction. In all the other cases before mentioned, the Supreme Court shall have appellate jurisdiction, both as to law and fact, with such exceptions, and under such regulations as the Congress shall make.

3. The trial of all crimes, except in cases of impeachment, shall be by jury; and such trial shall be held in the State where the said crimes shall have been committed; but when not committed within any State, the trial shall be such place or places as the congress may by law have directed.

Section 3. 1. Treason against the United States shall consist only in levying war against them, or in adhering to their enemies, giving them aid and comfort. No person shall be convicted of treason unless on the testimony of two witnesses to the same overt act, or on confession in open court.

2. The Congress shall have power to declare the punishment of treason, but no attainder of treason shall work corruption of blood, or forfeiture except during the life of the person attained.

---

[6]Superseded by the Twelfth Amendment.

[7]See the Eleventh Amendment.

Article IV

Section 1. Full faith and credit shall be given in each State to the public acts, records, and judicial proceedings of every other State. And the Congress may by general laws prescribe the manner in which such acts, records and proceedings shall be proved, and the effect thereof.

Section 2. 1. The citizens of each State shall be entitled to all privileges and immunities of citizens in the several States.[8]

2. A person charged in any State with treason, felony, or other crime, who shall flee from justice, and be found in another State, shall on demand of the executive authority of the State from which he fled, be delivered up to be removed to the State having jurisdiction of the crime.

3. No person held to service or labor in one State under the laws thereof, escaping into another, shall, in consequence of any law or regulation therein, be discharged from such service or labor, but shall be delivered up on claim of the party to whom such service or labor may be due.[9]

Section 3. 1. New States may be admitted by the Congress into this Union; but no new State shall be formed or erected within the jurisdiction of any other State, nor any State be formed by the junction of two or more States, or parts of States, without the consent of the legislatures of the States concerned as well as of the Congress.

2. The Congress shall have power to dispose of and make all needful rules and regulations respecting the territory or other property belonging to the United States; and nothing in this Constitution shall be so construed as to prejudice any claims of the United States, or of any particular State.

Section 4. The United States shall guarantee to every State in this Union a republican form of government, and shall protect each of them against invasion; and on application of the legislature, or of the executive (when the legislature cannot be convened) against domestic violence.

Article V

The Congress, whenever two thirds of both Houses shall deem it necessary, shall propose amendments to this Constitution, or, on the application of the legislatures of two thirds of the several States, shall call a convention for proposing amendments, which in either case shall be valid to all intents and purposes, as part of this Constitution, when ratified by the legislatures of three fourths of the several States, or by conventions in three fourths thereof, as the one or the other mode of ratification may be proposed by the Congress; Provided that no amendment which may be made prior to the year one thousand eight hundred and eight shall in any manner affect the first and fourth clauses in the ninth section of the first article; and that no State, without its consent, shall be deprived of its equal suffrage in the Senate.

Article VI

1. All debts contracted and engagements entered into, before the adoption of this Constitution, shall be as valid against the United States under this Constitution, as under the Confederation.[10]

2. This Constitution, and the laws of the United States which shall be made in pursuance thereof; and all treaties made, or which shall be made, under the authority of the United States, shall be the supreme law of the land; and the judges in every State shall be bound thereby, any thing in the Constitution or laws of any State to the contrary notwithstanding.

3. The senators and representatives before mentioned, and the members of the several State legislatures, and all executive and judicial officers, both of the United States and of the several States, shall be bound by oath or affirmation to support this Constitution; but no religious test shall ever be required as a qualification to any office or public trust under the United States.

Article VII

The ratification of the conventions of nine States shall be sufficient for the establishment of this Constitution between the States so ratifying the same.

Done in Convention by the unanimous consent of the States present the seventeenth day of September in the year of our Lord one thousand seven hundred and eighty-seven, and of the independence of the United States of America the twelfth. In witness whereof we have hereunto subscribed our names.

[Signatories' names omitted]

★ ★ ★

Articles in addition to, and amendment of, the Constitution of the United States of America, proposed by Congress, and ratified by the legislatures of the several States, pursuant to the fifth article of the original Constitution.

Amendment I [First ten amendments ratified December 15, 1791]

Congress shall make no law respecting an establishment of religion, or prohibiting the free exercise thereof; or abridging the freedom of speech, or of the press; or the right of the people peaceably to assemble, and to petition the government for a redress of grievances.

Amendment II

A well regulated militia, being necessary to the security of a free State, the right of the people to keep and bear arms, shall not be infringed.

Amendment III

No soldier shall, in time of peace be quartered in any house, without the consent of the owner, nor in time of war, but in a manner to be prescribed by law.

Amendment IV

The right of the people to be secure in their persons, houses, papers, and effects, against unreasonable searches

---

[8]See the Fourteenth Amendment, Sec. 1.
[9]See the Thirteenth Amendment.

[10]See the Fourteenth Amendment, Sec. 4.

and seizures, shall not be violated, and no warrants shall issue, but upon probable cause, supported by oath or affirmation, and particularly describing the place to be searched, and the persons or things to be seized.

Amendment V

No person shall be held to answer for a capital or otherwise infamous crime, unless on a presentment or indictment of a grand jury, except in cases arising in the land or naval forces, or in the militia, when in actual service in time of war or public danger; nor shall any person be subject for the same offense to be twice put in jeopardy of life or limb; nor shall be compelled in any criminal case to be a witness against himself, nor be deprived of life, liberty, or property, without due process of law; nor shall private property be taken for public use, without just compensation.

Amendment VI

In all criminal prosecutions, the accused shall enjoy the right to a speedy and public trial, by an impartial jury of the State and district wherein the crime shall have been committed, which district shall have been previously ascertained by law, and to be informed of the nature and cause of the accusation; to be confronted with the witnesses against him; to have compulsory process for obtaining witnesses in his favor, and to have the assistance of counsel for his defense.

Amendment VII

In suits at common law, where the value in controversy shall exceed twenty dollars, the right of trial by jury shall be preserved, and no fact tried by a jury shall be otherwise reexamined in any court of the United States, than according to the rules of the common law.

Amendment VIII

Excessive bail shall not be required, nor excessive fines imposed, nor cruel and unusual punishments inflicted.

Amendment IX

The enumeration in the Constitution of certain rights shall not be construed to deny or disparage others retained by the people.

Amendment X

The powers not delegated to the United States by the Constitution, nor prohibited by it to the States, are reserved to the States respectively, or to the people.

Amendment XI [January 8, 1798]

The judicial power of the United States shall not be construed to extend to any suit in law or equity, commended or prosecuted against one of the United States by citizens of another State, or by citizens or subjects of any foreign State.

Amendment XII [September 25, 1804]

The electors shall meet in their respective States, and vote by ballot for President and Vice President, one of whom, at least, shall not be an inhabitant of the same State with themselves; they shall name in their ballots the person voted for as President, and in distinct ballots the person voted for as Vice President, and they shall make distinct lists of all persons voted for as President and of all persons voted for as Vice President, and of the number of votes for each, which lists they shall sign and certify, and transmit sealed to the seat of the government of the United States, directed to the President of the Senate;—The President of the Senate shall, in the presence of the Senate and House of Representatives, open all the certificates and the votes shall then be counted;—The person having the greatest number of votes for President, shall be the President, if such number be a majority of the whole number of electors appointed; and if no person have such majority, then from the persons having the highest numbers not exceeding three on the list of those voted for as President, the House of Representatives shall choose immediately, by ballot, the President. But in choosing the President, the votes shall be taken by States, the representation from each State having one vote; a quorum for this purpose shall consist of a member or members from two thirds of the States, and a majority of all the States shall be necessary to a choice. And if the House of Representatives shall not choose a President whenever the right of choice shall devolve upon them, before the fourth day of March next following, then the Vice President shall act as President, as in the case of the death or other constitutional disability of the President. The person having the greatest number of votes as Vice President shall be the Vice President, if such number be a majority of the whole number of electors appointed, and if no person have a majority, then from the two highest numbers on the list, the Senate shall choose the Vice President; a quorum for the purpose shall consist of two thirds of the whole number of Senators, and a majority of the whole number shall be necessary to a choice. But no person constitutionally ineligible to the office of President shall be eligible to that of Vice President of the United States.

Amendment XIII [December 18, 1865]

Section 1. Neither slavery nor involuntary servitude, except as a punishment for crime whereof the party shall have been duly convicted, shall exist within the United States, or any place subject to their jurisdiction.

Section 2. Congress shall have power to enforce this article by appropriate legislation.

Amendment XIV [July 28, 1868]

Section 1. All persons born or naturalized in the United States, and subject to the jurisdiction thereof, are citizens of the United States and of the State wherein they reside. No State shall make or enforce any law which shall abridge the privileges or immunities of citizens of the United States; nor shall any State deprive any person of life, liberty, or property, without due process of law; nor deny to any person within its jurisdiction the equal protection of the laws.

Section 2. Representatives shall be apportioned among the several States according to their respective numbers, counting the whole number of persons in each State, excluding Indians not taxed. But when the right to vote at any election for the choice of electors for President and Vice President of the United States, representatives in Congress, the executive and judicial officers of a State, or the members of the legislature thereof, is denied to any of the male inhabitants of such State, being twenty-one years of age, and citizens of the United States, or in any way abridged, except for participating in rebellion, or other crime, the basis of representation there shall be reduced in the proportion which the number of such male citizens shall bear to the whole number of male citizens twenty-one years of age in such State.

Section 3. No person shall be a senator or representative in Congress, or elector of President and Vice President, or hold any office, civil or military, under the United States, or under any State, who having previously taken an oath, as a member of Congress, or as an officer of the United States, or as a member of any State legislature, or as an executive or judicial officer of any State, to support the Constitution of the United States, shall have engaged in insurrection or rebellion against the same, or given aid or comfort to the enemies thereof. But Congress may by a vote of two thirds of each House, remove such disability.

Section 4. The validity of the public debt of the United States, authorized by law, including debts incurred for payment of pensions and bounties for services in suppressing insurrection or rebellion; shall not be questioned. But neither the United States nor any State shall assume or pay any debt or obligation incurred in aid of insurrection or rebellion against the United States, or any claim for the loss or emancipation of any slave; but all such debts, obligations, and claims shall be held illegal and void.

Section 5. The Congress shall have the power to enforce, by appropriate legislation, the provisions of this article.

Amendment XV [March 30, 1870]

Section 1. The right of citizens of the United States to vote shall not be denied or abridged by the United States or by any State on account of race, color, or previous condition of servitude.

Section 2. The Congress shall have power to enforce this article by appropriate legislation.

Amendment XVI [February 25, 1913]

The Congress shall have power to lay and collect taxes on incomes, from whatever source derived, without apportionment among the several States, and without regard to any census or enumeration.

Amendment XVII [May 31, 1913]

The Senate of the United States shall be composed of two senators from each State, elected by the people thereof, for six years; and each senator shall have one vote. The electors in each State shall have the qualifications requisite for electors of the most numerous branch of the State legislature.

When vacancies happen in the representation of any State in the Senate, the executive authority of such State shall issue writs of election to fill such vacancies: Provided, That the legislature of any State may empower the executive thereof to make temporary appointments until the people fill the vacancies by election as the legislature may direct.

This amendment shall not be so construed as to affect the election or term of any senator chosen before it becomes valid as part of the Constitution.

Amendment XVIII[11] [January 29, 1919]

After one year from the ratification of this article, the manufacture, sale, or transportation of intoxicating liquors within, the importation thereof into, or the exportation thereof from the United States and all territory subject to the jurisdiction thereof for beverage purposes is thereby prohibited.

The Congress and the several States shall have concurrent power to enforce this article by appropriate legislation.

This article shall be inoperative unless it shall have been ratified as an amendment to the Constitution by the legislatures of the several States, as provided in the constitution, within seven years from the date of the submission hereof to the States by Congress.

Amendment XIX [August 26, 1920]

The right of citizens of the United States to vote shall not be denied or abridged by the United States or by any State on account of sex.

Congress shall have the power to enforce this article by appropriate legislation.

Amendment XX [January 23, 1933]

Section 1. The terms of the President and Vice President shall end at noon on the 20th day of January and the terms of Senators and Representatives at noon on the 3d day of January, of the years in which such terms would have ended if this article had not been ratified; and the terms of their successors shall then begin.

Section 2. The Congress shall assemble at least once in every year, and such meeting shall begin at noon on the 3d day of January, unless they shall by law appoint a different day.

Section 3. If, at the time fixed for the beginning of the term of President, the President-elect shall have died, the Vice President-elect shall become President. If a President shall not have been chosen before the time fixed for the beginning of his term, or if the President-elect shall have failed to qualify, then the Vice President-elect shall act as President until a President shall have qualified; and the Congress may by law provide for the case wherein neither a President-elect nor a Vice President-elect shall have qualified, declaring who shall then act as President, or the manner in which one who is to act shall be selected, and such person shall act accordingly until a President or Vice President shall have qualified.

Section 4. The Congress may by law provide for the case of the death of any of the persons from whom, the

---

[11]Repealed by the Twenty-first Amendment

House of Representatives may choose a President whenever the right of choice shall have devolved upon them, and for the case of the death of any of the persons from whom the Senate may choose a Vice President whenever the right of choice shall have devolved upon them.

Section 5. Sections 1 and 2 shall take effect on the 15th day of October following the ratification of this article.

Section 6. This article shall be inoperative unless it shall have been ratified as an amendment to the Constitution by the legislatures of three-fourths of the several States within seven years from the date of its submission.

Amendment XXI [December 5, 1933]

Section 1. The Eighteenth Article of amendment to the Constitution of the United States is hereby repealed.

Section 2. The transportation or importation into any State, Territory, or possession of the United States for delivery or use therein of intoxicating liquors in violation of the laws thereof, is hereby prohibited.

Section 3. This article shall be inoperative unless it shall have been ratified as an amendment to the Constitution by conventions in the several States, as provided in the Constitution, within seven years from the date of the submission thereof to the States by the Congress.

Amendment XXII [March 1, 1951]

No person shall be elected to the office of the President more than twice, and no person who has held the office of President, or acted as President, for more than two years of a term to which some other person was elected President shall be elected to the office of the President more than once.

But this article shall not apply to any person holding the office of President when this article was proposed by the Congress, and shall not prevent any person who may be holding the office of President, or acting as President, during the term within which this article becomes operative from holding the office of President or acting as President during the remainder of such term.

This article shall be inoperative unless it shall have been ratified as an amendment to the Constitution by the legislatures of three-fourths of the several States within seven years from the date of its submission to the States by the Congress.

Amendment XXIII [March 29, 1961]

Section 1. The District constituting the seat of Government of the United States shall appoint in such manner as the Congress may direct.

A number of electors of President and Vice President equal to the whole number of Senators and Representa-tives in Congress to which the District would be entitled if it were a State, but in no event more than the least populous State; they shall be in addition to those appointed by the States, but they shall be considered, for the purposes of the election of President and Vice President, to be electors appointed by a State; and they shall meet in the District and perform such duties as provided by the twelfth article of amendment.

Section 2. The Congress shall have power to enforce this article by appropriate legislation.

Amendment XXIV [January 23, 1964]

Section 1. The right of citizens of the United States to vote in any primary or other election for President or Vice President, for electors for President or Vice President, or for Senator or Representative in Congress, shall not be denied or abridged by the United States or any State by reason of failure to pay any poll tax or other tax.

Section 2. The Congress shall have power to enforce this article by appropriate legislation.

Amendment XXV [February 10, 1967]

Section 1. In case of the removal of the President from office or of his death or resignation, the Vice President shall become President.

Section 2. Whenever there is a vacancy in the office of the Vice President, the President shall nominate a Vice President who shall take office upon confirmation by a majority of both Houses of Congress.

Section 3. Whenever the President transmits to the President pro tempore of the Senate and the Speaker of the House of Representatives his written declaration that he is unable to discharge the powers and duties of his office, and until he transmits to them a written declaration to the contrary, such powers and duties shall be discharged by the Vice President as Acting President.

Section 4. Whenever the Vice President and a majority of either the principal officers of the executive departments or of such other body as Congress may by law provide, transmit to the President pro tempore of the Senate and the Speaker of the House of Representatives their written declaration that the President is unable to discharge the powers and duties of his office, the Vice President shall immediately assume the powers and duties of the office as Acting President.

Thereafter, when the President transmits to the President pro tempore of the Senate and the Speaker of the House of Representatives his written declaration that no inability exists, he shall resume the powers and duties of his office unless the Vice President and a majority of either the principal officers of the executive departments or of such other body as Congress may by law provide, transmit within four days to the President pro tempore of the Senate and the Speaker of the House of Representatives their written declaration that the President is unable to discharge the powers and duties of his office. Thereupon Congress shall decide the issue, assembling within forty-eight hours for that purpose if not in session. If the Congress, within twenty-one days after receipt of the latter written declaration, or, if Congress is not in session, within twenty-one days after Congress is required to assemble, determines by two-thirds vote of both Houses that the President is unable to discharge the powers and duties of his office, the Vice President shall continue to discharge the same as Acting President; otherwise, the President shall resume the powers and duties of his office.

Amendment XXVI [June 30, 1971]

Section 1. The right of citizens of the United States who are eighteen years of age or older to vote shall not be denied or abridged by the United States or by any State on account of age.

    Section 2. The Congress shall have power to enforce this article by appropriate legislation.

Amendment XXVII[12] *[May 7, 1992]*

    No law, varying the compensation for services of the Senators and Representatives, shall take effect until an election of Representatives shall have intervened.

[12]James Madison proposed this amendment in 1789 together with the ten amendments that were adopted as the Bill of Rights, but it failed to win ratification at the time. Congress, however, had set no deadline for its ratification, and over the years—particularly in the 1980s and 1990s—many states voted to add it to the Constitution. With the ratification of Michigan in 1992 it passed the threshold of 3/4ths of the states required for adoption, but because the process took more than 200 years, its validity remains in doubt.

•◦•—[Read the Document

Admission of States to the Union
Demographics of the United States

PRESIDENTS AND VICE PRESIDENTS

1. George Washington (1789)
   John Adams (1789)

2. John Adams (1797)
   Thomas Jefferson (1797)

3. Thomas Jefferson (1801)
   Aaron Burr (1801)
   George Clinton (1805)

4. James Madison (1809)
   George Clinton (1809)
   Elbridge Gerry (1813)

5. James Monroe (1817)
   Daniel D. Thompkins (1817)

6. John Quincy Adams (1825)
   John C. Calhoun (1825)

7. Andrew Jackson (1829)
   John C. Calhoun (1829)
   Martin Van Buren (1833)

8. Martin Van Buren (1837)
   Richard M. Johnson (1837)

9. William H. Harrison (1841)
   John Tyler (1841)

10. John Tyler (1841)

11. James K. Polk (1845)
    George M. Dallas (1845)

12. Zachary Taylor (1849)
    Millard Fillmore (1849)

13. Millard Fillmore (1850)

14. Franklin Pierce (1853)
    William R. King (1853)

15. James Buchanan (1857)
    John C. Breckinridge (1857)

16. Abraham Lincoln (1861)
    Hannibal Hamlin (1861)
    Andrew Johnson (1865)

17. Andrew Johnson (1865)

18. Ulysses S. Grant (1869)
    Schuyler Colfax (1869)
    Henry Wilson (1873)

19. Rutherford B. Hayes (1877)
    William A. Wheeler (1877)

20. James A. Garfield (1881)
    Chester A. Arthur (1881)

21. Chester A. Arthur (1881)

22. Grover Cleveland (1885)
    T. A. Hendricks (1885)

23. Benjamin Harrison (1889)
    Levi P. Morgan (1889)

24. Grover Cleveland (1893)
    Adlai E. Stevenson (1893)

25. William McKinley (1897)
    Garret A. Hobart (1897)
    Theodore Roosevelt (1901)

26. Theodore Roosevelt (1901)
    Charles Fairbanks (1905)

27. William H. Taft (1909)
    James S. Sherman (1909)

28. Woodrow Wilson (1913)
    Thomas R. Marshall (1913)

29. Warren G. Harding (1921)
    Calvin Coolidge (1921)

30. Calvin Coolidge (1923)
    Charles G. Dawes (1925)

31. Herbert C. Hoover (1929)
    Charles Curtis (1929)

32. Franklin D. Roosevelt (1933)
    John Nance Garner (1933)
    Henry A. Wallace (1941)
    Harry S. Truman (1945)

33. Harry S. Truman (1945)
    Alben W. Barkley (1949)

34. Dwight D. Eisenhower (1953)
    Richard M. Nixon (1953)

35. John F. Kennedy (1961)
    Lyndon B. Johnson (1961)

36. Lyndon B. Johnson (1963)
    Hubert H. Humphrey (1965)

37. Richard M. Nixon (1969)
    Spiro T. Agnew (1969)
    Gerald R. Ford (1973)

38. Gerald R. Ford (1974)
    Nelson A. Rockefeller (1974)

39. James E. Carter Jr. (1977)
    Walter F. Mondale (1977)

40. Ronald W. Reagan (1981)
    George H. Bush (1981)

41. George H. Bush (1989)
    James D. Quayle III (1989)

42. William J. Clinton (1993)
    Albert Gore (1993)

43. George W. Bush (2001)
    Richard Cheney (2001)

44. Barack H. Obama (2009)
    Joseph Biden (2009)

PRESIDENTIAL ELECTIONS

Year	Number of States	Candidates	Party	Popular Vote*	Electoral Vote[†]	Percentage of Popular Vote*
1789	11	GEORGE WASHINGTON	No party designations		69	
		John Adams			34	
		Other Candidates			35	
1792	15	GEORGE WASHINGTON	No party designations		132	
		John Adams			77	
		George Clinton			50	
		Other Candidates			5	
1796	16	JOHN ADAMS	Federalist		71	
		Thomas Jefferson	Democratic-Republican		68	
		Thomas Pinckney	Federalist		59	
		Aaron Burr	Democratic-Republican		30	
		Other Candidates			48	
1800	16	THOMAS JEFFERSON	Democratic-Republican		73	
		Aaron Burr	Democratic-Republican		73	
		John Adams	Federalist		65	
		Charles C. Pinckney	Federalist		64	
		John Jay	Federalist		1	
1804	17	THOMAS JEFFERSON	Democratic-Republican		162	
		Charles C. Pinckney	Federalist		14	
1808	17	JAMES MADISON	Democratic-Republican		122	
		Charles C. Pinckney	Federalist		47	
		George Clinton	Democratic-Republican		6	
1812	18	JAMES MADISON	Democratic-Republican		128	
		DeWitt Clinton	Federalist		89	
1816	19	JAMES MONROE	Democratic-Republican		183	
		Rufus King	Federalist		34	
1820	24	JAMES MONROE	Democratic-Republican		231	
		John Quincy Adams	Independent-Republican		1	
1824	24	JOHN QUINCY ADAMS	Democratic-Republican	108,740	84	30.5
		Andrew Jackson	Democratic-Republican	153,544	99	43.1
		William H. Crawford	Democratic-Republican	46,618	41	13.1
		Henry Clay	Democratic-Republican	47,136	37	13.2
1828	24	ANDREW JACKSON	Democrat	647,286	178	56.0
		John Quincy Adams	National-Republican	508,064	83	44.0
1832	24	ANDREW JACKSON	Democrat	687,502	219	55.0
		Henry Clay	National-Republican	530,189	49	42.4
		William Wirt	Anti-Masonic	33,108	7	
		John Floyd	National-Republican		11	2.6

*Percentage of popular vote given for any election year may not total 100 percent because candidates receiving less than 1 percent of the popular vote have been omitted.

[†]Prior to the passage of the Twelfth Amendment in 1904, the electoral college voted for two presidential candidates; the runner-up became Vice-President. Data from *Historical Statistics of the United States, Colonial Times to 1957* (1961), pp. 682–683, and *The World Almanac*.

PRESIDENTIAL ELECTIONS (continued)

Year	Number of States	Candidates	Party	Popular Vote	Electoral Vote	Percentage of Popular Vote
1836	26	MARTIN VAN BUREN	Democrat	765,483	170	50.9
		William H. Harrison	Whig		73	
		Hugh L. White	Whig		26	
		Daniel Webster	Whig	739,795	14	49.1
		W. P. Mangum	Whig		11	
1840	26	WILLIAM H. HARRISON	Whig	1,274,624	234	53.1
		Martin Van Buren	Democrat	1,127,781	60	46.9
1844	26	JAMES K. POLK	Democrat	1,338,464	170	49.6
		Henry Clay	Whig	1,300,097	105	48.1
		James G. Birney	Liberty	62,300		2.3
1848	30	ZACHARY TAYLOR	Whig	1,360,967	163	47.4
		Lewis Cass	Democrat	1,222,342	127	42.5
		Martin Van Buren	Free-Soil	291,263		10.1
1852	31	FRANKLIN PIERCE	Democrat	1,601,117	254	50.9
		Winfield Scott	Whig	1,385,453	42	44.1
		John P. Hale	Free-Soil	155,825		5.0
1856	31	JAMES BUCHANAN	Democrat	1,832,955	174	45.3
		John C. Frémont	Republican	1,339,932	114	33.1
		Millard Fillmore	American ("Know Nothing")	871,731	8	21.6
1860	33	ABRAHAM LINCOLN	Republican	1,865,593	180	39.8
		Stephen A. Douglas	Democrat	1,382,713	12	29.5
		John C. Breckinridge	Democrat	848,356	72	18.1
		John Bell	Constitutional Union	592,906	39	12.6
1864	36	ABRAHAM LINCOLN	Republican	2,206,938	212	55.0
		George B. McClellan	Democrat	1,803,787	21	45.0
1868	37	ULYSSES S. GRANT	Republican	3,013,421	214	52.7
		Horatio Seymour	Democrat	2,706,829	80	47.3
1872	37	ULYSSES S. GRANT	Republican	3,596,745	286	55.6
		Horace Greeley	Democrat	2,843,446		*43.9
1876	38	RUTHERFORD B. HAYES	Republican	4,036,572	185	48.0
		Samuel J. Tilden	Democrat	4,284,020	184	51.0
1880	38	JAMES A. GARFIELD	Republican	4,453,295	214	48.5
		Winfield S. Hancock	Democrat	4,414,082	155	48.1
		James B. Weaver	Greenback-Labor	308,578		3.4
1884	38	GROVER CLEVELAND	Democrat	4,879,507	219	48.5
		James G. Blaine	Republican	4,850,293	182	48.2
		Benjamin F. Butler	Greenback-Labor	175,370		1.8
		John P. St. John	Prohibition	150,369		1.5

*Because of the death of Greeley, Democratic electors scattered their votes.

PRESIDENTIAL ELECTIONS (continued)

Year	Number of States	Candidates	Party	Popular Vote	Electoral Vote	Percentage of Popular Vote
1888	38	BENJAMIN HARRISON	Republican	5,447,129	233	47.9
		Grover Cleveland	Democrat	5,537,857	168	48.6
		Clinton B. Fisk	Prohibition	249,506		2.2
		Anson J. Streeter	Union Labor	146,935		1.3
1892	44	GROVER CLEVELAND	Democrat	5,555,426	277	46.1
		Benjamin Harrison	Republican	5,182,690	145	43.0
		James B. Weaver	People's	1,029,846	22	8.5
		John Bidwell	Prohibition	264,133		2.2
1896	45	WILLIAM MCKINLEY	Republican	7,102,246	271	51.1
		William J. Bryan	Democrat	6,492,559	176	47.7
1900	45	WILLIAM MCKINLEY	Republican	7,218,491	292	51.7
		William J. Bryan	Democrat; Populist	6,356,734	155	45.5
		John C. Woolley	Prohibition	208,914		1.5
1904	45	THEODORE ROOSEVELT	Republican	7,628,461	336	57.4
		Alton B. Parker	Democrat	5,084,223	140	37.6
		Eugene V. Debs	Socialist	402,283		3.0
		Silas C. Swallow	Prohibition	258,536		1.9
1908	46	WILLIAM H. TAFT	Republican	7,675,320	321	51.6
		William J. Bryan	Democrat	6,412,294	162	43.1
		Eugene V. Debs	Socialist	420,793		2.8
		Eugene W. Chafin	Prohibition	253,840		1.7
1912	48	WOODROW WILSON	Democrat	6,296,547	435	41.9
		Theodore Roosevelt	Progressive	4,118,571	88	27.4
		William H. Taft	Republican	3,486,720	8	23.2
		Eugene V. Debs	Socialist	900,672		6.0
		Eugene W. Chafin	Prohibition	206,275		1.4
1916	48	WOODROW WILSON	Democrat	9,127,695	277	49.4
		Charles E. Hughes	Republican	8,533,507	254	46.2
		A. L. Benson	Socialist	585,113		3.2
		J. Frank Hanly	Prohibition	220,506		1.2
1920	48	WARREN G. HARDING	Republican	16,143,407	404	60.4
		James M. Cox	Democrat	9,130,328	127	34.2
		Eugene V. Debs	Socialist	919,799		3.4
		P. P. Christensen	Farmer–Labor	265,411		1.0
1924	48	CALVIN COOLIDGE	Republican	15,718,211	382	54.0
		John W. Davis	Democrat	8,385,283	136	28.8
		Robert M. La Follette	Progressive	4,831,289	13	16.6
1928	48	HERBERT C. HOOVER	Republican	21,391,993	444	58.2
		Alfred E. Smith	Democrat	15,016,169	87	40.9
1932	48	FRANKLIN D. ROOSEVELT	Democrat	22,809,638	472	57.4
		Herbert C. Hoover	Republican	15,758,901	59	39.7
		Norman Thomas	Socialist	881,951		2.2

PRESIDENTIAL ELECTIONS (continued)

Year	Number of States	Candidates	Party	Popular Vote	Electoral Vote	Percentage of Popular Vote
1936	48	FRANKLIN D. ROOSEVELT	Democrat	27,752,869	523	60.8
		Alfred M. Landon	Republican	16,674,665	8	36.5
		William Lemke	Union	882,479		1.9
1940	48	FRANKLIN D. ROOSEVELT	Democrat	27,307,819	449	54.8
		Wendell L. Willkie	Republican	22,321,018	82	44.8
1944	48	FRANKLIN D. ROOSEVELT	Democrat	25,606,585	432	53.5
		Thomas E. Dewey	Republican	22,014,745	99	46.0
1948	48	HARRY S TRUMAN	Democrat	24,105,812	303	49.5
		Thomas E. Dewey	Republican	21,970,065	189	45.1
		J. Strom Thurmond	States' Rights	1,169,063	39	2.4
		Henry A. Wallace	Progressive	1,157,172		2.4
1952	48	DWIGHT D. EISENHOWER	Republican	33,936,234	442	55.1
		Adlai E. Stevenson	Democrat	27,314,992	89	44.4
1956	48	DWIGHT D. EISENHOWER	Republican	35,590,472	457 ★	57.6
		Adlai E. Stevenson	Democrat	26,022,752	73	42.1
1960	50	JOHN F. KENNEDY	Democrat	34,227,096	303 †	49.9
		Richard M. Nixon	Republican	34,108,546	219	49.6
1964	50	LYNDON B. JOHNSON	Democrat	42,676,220	486	61.3
		Barry M. Goldwater	Republican	26,860,314	52	38.5
1968	50	RICHARD M. NIXON	Republican	31,785,480	301	43.4
		Hubert H. Humphrey	Democrat	31,275,165	191	42.7
		George C. Wallace	American Independent	9,906,473	46	13.5
1972	50	RICHARD M. NIXON‡	Republican	47,165,234	520	60.6
		George S. McGovern	Democrat	29,168,110	17	37.5
1976	50	JAMES E. CARTER JR.	Democrat	40,828,929	297	50.1
		Gerald R. Ford	Republican	39,148,940	240	47.9
		Eugene McCarthy	Independent	739,256		
1980	50	RONALD W. REAGAN	Republican	43,201,220	489	50.9
		James E. Carter Jr.	Democrat	34,913,332	49	41.2
		John B. Anderson	Independent	5,581,379		
1984	50	RONALD W. REAGAN	Republican	53,428,357	525	59.0
		Walter F. Mondale	Democrat	36,930,923	13	41.0
1988	50	GEORGE H. W. BUSH	Republican	48,901,046	426	53.4
		Michael Dukakis	Democrat	41,809,030	111	45.6
1992	50	WILLIAM J. CLINTON	Democrat	43,728,275	370	43.2
		George H. W. Bush	Republican	38,167,416	168	37.7
		H. Ross Perot	United We Stand, America	19,237,247		19.0

★Walter B. Jones received 1 electoral vote.

†Harry F. Byrd received 15 electoral votes.

‡Resigned August 9, 1974: Vice President Gerald R. Ford became President.

PRESIDENTIAL ELECTIONS (continued)

Year	Number of States	Candidates	Party	Popular Vote	Electoral Vote	Percentage of Popular Vote
1996	50	WILLIAM J. CLINTON	Democrat	45,590,703	379	49.0
		Robert Dole	Republican	37,816,307	159	41.0
		H. Ross Perot	Reform	7,874,283		8.0
2000	50	GEORGE W. BUSH	Republican	50,459,624	271	47.9
		Albert Gore	Democrat	51,003,328	266	49.4
		Ralph Nader	Green	2,882,985	0	2.7
2004	50	GEORGE W. BUSH	Republican	59,117,523	286	51.1
		John Kerry	Democrat	55,557,584	252	48.0
		Ralph Nader	Green	405,623	0	0.3
2008	50	BARACK H. OBAMA	Democrat	69,456,897	365	52.9
		John McCain	Republican	59,934,814	173	45.7

BIBLIOGRAPHY

CHAPTER 1

Settling the Continent

Larry D. Agenbroad, et al., eds., *Megafauna and Man* (1990)

John Bierhorst, ed., *The Red Swan: Myths and Tales of the American Indians* (1976)

Robson Bonnichsen and Karen L. Turnmire, *Ice Age People of North America: Environments, Origins, and Adaptations* (1999)

Michael H. Crawford, *The Origins of Native Americans: Evidence from Anthropological Genetics* (1998)

Tom D. Dillehay, *The Settling of the Americas: A New Prehistory* (2000)

E. James Dixon, *Bones, Boats, and Bison: Archaeology and the First Colonization of Western North America* (2000)

Richard Erdoes and Alfonso Ortiz, eds., *American Indian Myths and Legends* (1984)

Guy Gibbon, *Archaeology of Prehistoric Native America: An Encyclopedia* (1998)

Lee Eldridge Huddleston, *Origins of the American Indians: European Concepts, 1492–1729* (1967)

George Kubler, *Esthetic Recognition of Ancient Amerindian Art* (1991)

Hanns J. Prem, *The Ancient Americas: A Brief History and Guide to Research* (1997)

Heather Anne Pringle, *In Search of Ancient North America: An Archaeological Journey to Forgotten Cultures* (1996)

Richard F. Townsend, ed., *The Ancient Americas: Art from Sacred Landscapes* (1992)

Frederick Hadleigh West, ed., *American Beginnings: The Prehistory and Palaeoecology of Beringia* (1996)

New Ways of Living on the Land

Kenneth M. Ames and Herbert D. G. Mascher, *Peoples of the Northwest Coast: Their Archaeology and Prehistory* (2000)

Leonard W. Blake and Hugh C. Cutler, *Plants from the Past* (2001)

David S. Brose, et al., *Ancient Art of the American Woodland Indians* (1985)

Thomas E. Emerson, et al., eds. *Late Woodland Societies: Tradition and Transformation Across the Midcontinent* (2000)

Richard I. Ford, ed., *Prehistoric Food Production in North America* (1985)

Sarah W. Neusius, *Foraging, Collecting, and Harvesting: Archaic Period Subsistence and Settlement in the Eastern Woodlands* (1986)

James L. Phillips and James A. Brown, eds., *Archaic Hunters and Gatherers in the American Midwest* (1983)

Richard H. Steckel and Jerome C. Rose, *The Backbone of History: Health and Nutrition in the Western Hemisphere* (2002)

The Development of Farming

Frances R. Berdan, *The Aztecs of Central Mexico* (1982)

David S. Brose and N'omi Greber, eds., *Hopewell Archaeology* (1979)

David Carrasco, et al., eds., *Mesoamerica's Classic Heritage: From Teotihuacan to the Aztecs* (2000)

William S. Dancey and Paul J Pacheco, eds., *Ohio Hopewell Community Organization* (1997)

Emil W. Haury, *The Hohokam* (1976)

Ted Hirschfield, *Middle Mississippians: Encounters with the Prehistoric Amerindians* (1996)

Rosemary Joyce, *Gender and Power in Prehispanic Mesoamerica* (2000)

William F. Keegan, ed., *Emergent Horticultural Economies of the Eastern Woodlands* (1987)

R. Barry Lewis and Charles Stout, eds., *Mississippian Towns and Sacred Spaces* (1998)

George R. Milner, *The Cahokia Chiefdom: The Archaeology of a Mississippian Society* (1998)

Warren King Moorehead, *The Cahokia Mounds* (2000)

Barker H. Morrow and V. B. Price, eds., *Anasazi Architecture and American Design* (1997)

Timothy R. Pauketat and Thomas E. Emerson, eds., *Cahokia: Domination and Ideology in the Mississippian World* (1997)

Stephen Plog, *Ancient Peoples of the American Southwest* (1998)

Paul F. Reed, ed., *Foundations of Anasazi Culture: The Basketmaker-Pueblo Transition* (2000)

Bruce D. Smith, *The Mississippian Emergence* (1990)

David E. Stuart, *Anasazi America: Seventeen Centuries on the Road from Center Place* (2000)

Christy G. Turner, *Man Corn: Cannibalism and Violence in the Prehistoric American Southwest* (2000)

W. H. Wills, *Early Prehistoric Agriculture* (1988)

Biloine W. Young and Melvin L. Fowler, *Cahokia, The Great Native American Metropolis* (2000)

Cultural Regions of North America on the Eve of Colonization

Michael A. Adler, ed., *The Prehistoric Pueblo World, A.D. 1150–1350* (1996)

Kenneth M. Ames and Herbert D. G. Mascher, *Peoples of the Northwest Coast: Their Archaeology and Prehistory* (2000)

Elizabeth M. Brunfiel and John W. Fox, *Factional Competition and Political Development in the New World* (1993)

Catherine M. Cameron, *Hopi Dwellings: Architecture at Oryi* (1999)

Lyle Campbell and Marianne Mithun, eds., *The Languages of Native America* (1979)

Paul H. Carlson, *The Plains Indians* (1999)

James Taylor Carson, *Searching for the Bright Path: The Mississippi Choctaws from Prehistory to Removal* (1999)

May Castleberry, *The New World's Old World: Photographic Views of Ancient America* (2003)

Cheryl Claassen and Rosemary A. Joyce, eds., *Women in Prehistory: North America and Mesoamerica* (1997)

Olive P. Dickason, *Canada's First Nations: A History of Founding Peoples* (1992)

Lynn H. Gamble, *The Chumash World at European Contact: Power, Trade, and Feasting among Complex Hunter-Gatherers* (2008)

Michelle Hegmon, ed., *The Archaeology of Regional Interaction: Religion, Warfare, and Exchange Across the American Southwest* (1999)

June Helm, *The People of Denendah: Ethnohistory of the Indians of Canada's Northwest Territories* (2000)

David P. Henige, *Numbers from Nowhere: The American Indian Contact Population Debate* (1998)

David LaVere, *The Caddo Chiefdoms: Caddo Economics and Politics, 700–1835* (1998)

Steven A. LeBlanc, *Prehistoric Warfare in the American Southwest* (1999)

Stephen H. Lekson, *The Chaco Meridian: Centers of Political Power in the Ancient Southwest* (1999)

Jill E. Neitzel, ed., *Great Towns and Regional Politics: In the Prehistoric American Southwest and Southeast* (1999)

Mallory McCane O'Connor, *Lost Cities of the Ancient Southeast* (1995)

Alfonso Ortiz, ed., *New Perspectives on the Pueblos* (1972)

Howard S. Russell, *Indian New England Before the Mayflower* (1980)

Frank G. Speck, *Penobscot Man* (1940)

Bruce Trigger, *The Children of Aataentsic: A History of the Huron People to 1660* (1976)

CHAPTER 2

The Expansion of Europe

Thomas Bender, *A Nation among Nations: America's Place in World History* (2006)

James M. Blaut, *1492: The Debate on Colonialism, Eurocentrism, and History* (1992)

Fernand Braudel, *The Mediterranean and the Mediterranean World in the Age of Philip II* (1972)

Carol Cipolla, *Before the Industrial Revolution: European Society and Economy, 1100–1700* (1976)

Patrick Collinson, *The Religion of Protestants: The Church in English Society, 1559–1625* (1982)

Andre Gunder Frank, *World Accumulation, 1492–1789* (1978)

Giancarlo Masini and Iacopo Gari, *How Florence Invented America: Vespucci, Verranzano, and Mazzei and Their Contribution to the Conception of the New World* (1998)

Douglass North, *The Rise of the Western World: A New Economic History* (1973)

José Casas Pardo, ed., *Economic Effects of the European Expansion, 1492–1824* (1992)

J. H. Parry, *The Age of Reconnaissance* (1963)

———, *Europe and a Wider World: The Establishment of the European Hegemony: Trade and Expansion in the Age of the Renaissance* (1966)

Geoffrey Vaughn Scannell, *The First Imperial Age: European Overseas Expansion c. 1400–1715* (1989)

The Spanish in the Americas

Jorge Cañizares-Esguerra, *Puritan Conquistadors: Iberianizing the Atlantic, 1550–1700* (2006)

Fredi Chiapelli, ed., *First Images of America: The Impact of the New World on the Old* (1976)

Kathleen Deagan and José María Cruxent, *Columbus's Outpost among the Taínos: Spain and America at La Isabela, 1493–1498* (2002)

Henry F. Dobyns, *Their Number Become Thinned: Native American Population Dynamics in Eastern North America* (1983)

J. H. Elliott, *The Old World and the New, 1492–1650* (1970)

J. H. Elliott, *Spain, Europe, and the Wider World, 1500–1800* (2009)

Alejandro de la Fuente, *Havana and the Atlantic in the Sixteenth Century* (2008)

Anthony Grafton, *New Worlds, Ancient Texts: The Power of Tradition and the Shock of Discovery* (1992)

John H. Hann, *A History of the Timucua Indians and Missions* (1996)

Paul E. Hoffman, *Florida's Frontiers* (2002)

Hugh Honour, *New Golden Land: European Images of America from the Discoveries to the Present Time* (1975)

Charles Hudson and Carmen Chaves Tesser, eds., *The Forgotten Centuries: Indians and Europeans in the American South, 1521–1704* (1994)

René Jara and Nicholas Spadaccini, eds., *Amerindian Images and the Legacy of Columbus* (1992)

Elizabeth A. H. John, *Storms Brewed in Other Men's Worlds: The Confrontation of Indians, Spanish, and French in the Southwest, 1540–1795* (1975)

Henry Kamen, *Spain's Road to Empire: The Making of a World Power, 1492–1763* (2002)

Susan Kellogg, *Weaving the Past: A History of Latin America's Indigenous Women from the Prehispanic Period to the Present* (2005)

James Lang, *Conquest and Commerce: Spain and England in the Americas* (1975)

James Lockhart and Stuart B. Schwartz, *Early Latin America: A History of Colonial Spanish America and Brazil* (1983)

Albert Mauncy, *Sixteenth-Century St. Augustine: The People and Their Homes* (1997)

Jerald T. Milanich, *Laboring in the Fields of the Lord: Spanish Missions and Southeastern Indians* (1999)

Jerald T. Milanich and Charles Hudson, *Hernando de Soto and the Indians of Florida* (1993)

James Howlett O'Donnell III, *Southeastern Frontiers: Europeans, Africans, and American Indians, 1513–1840: A Critical Bibliography* (1982)

Edmundo O'Gorman, *The Invention of America: An Inquiry into the Historical Nature of the New World and the Meaning of its History* (1961)

Stuart B. Schwartz, *Victors and Vanquished: Spanish and Nahua Views of the Conquest of Mexico* (2000)

Stuart B. Schwartz, *All Can Be Saved: Religious Tolerance and Salvation in the Iberian Atlantic World* (2008)

Hugh Thomas, *Rivers of Gold: The Rise of the Spanish Empire, from Columbus to Magellan* (2004)

Northern Explorations and Encounters

Alfred Goldsworthy Bailey, *The Conflict of European and Eastern Algonkian Cultures, 1504–1700* (1969)

Peter T. Bradley, *British Maritime Enterprise in the New World: From the Late Fifteenth to the Mid-Eighteenth Century* (1999)

Carl Bridenbaugh, *Vexed and Troubled Englishmen, 1590–1642* (1968)

Nicholas Canny, *Making Ireland British, 1580–1650* (2001)

Susan Danforth, *Encountering the New World, 1493–1800* (1991)

Philip J. Deloria and Neal Salisbury, eds., *A Companion to American Indian History* (2002)

G. R. Elton, *England under the Tudors* (1974)

Andrew Fitzmaurice, *Humanism and America: An Intellectual History of English Colonization, 1500–1625* (2003)

C. H. George and Katherine George, *The Protestant Mind of the English Reformation* (1961)

John Guy, *Tudor England* (1988)

Neil Kamil, *Fortress of the Soul: Violence, Metaphysics, and Material Life in the Huguenots' New World, 1517–1751* (2005)

Paul Kelton, *Epidemics and Enslavement: Biological Catastrophe in the Native Southeast, 1492–1715* (2007)

R. J. Knecht, *The French Civil Wars, 1562–1598* (2000)

Karen Ordahl Kupperman, *Indians and English: Facing Off in Early America* (2000)

Peter Laslett, *The World We Have Lost* (1965)

Anthony McFarlane, *The British in the Americas, 1480–1815* (1994)

Ken MacMillan, *Sovereignty and Possession in the English New World: The Legal Foundations of Empire, 1576–1640* (2006)

Peter C. Mancall, *Hakluyt's Promise: An Elizabethan's Obsession for an English America* (2007)

Lee Miller, *Roanoke: Solving the Mystery of England's Lost Colony* (2000)

James S. Pritchard, *In Search of Empire: The French in the Americas, 1670–1730* (2004)

David B. Quinn, *North America from Earliest Discovery to First Settlements* (1977)

———, *The Roanoke Voyages, 1584–1590*, 2 vols. (1955)

Bernard W. Sheehan, *Savagism and Civility: Indians and Englishmen in Colonial Virginia* (1980)

Kim Sloan, *A New World: England's First View of America* (2007)

Russell Thornton, *American Indian Holocaust and Survival* (1987)

Margo Todd, ed., *Reformation to Revolution: Politics and Religion in Early Modern England* (1995)

Marcel Trudel, *The Beginnings of New France, 1524–1663* (1973)

Keith Wrightson, *English Society, 1580–1680* (1982)

Biography

Miles H. Davidson, *Columbus Then and Now: A Life Reexamined* (1997)

Harry Kelsey, *Sir Francis Drake: The Queen's Pirate* (1998)

Carole Levin, *The Heart and Stomach of a King: Elizabeth I and the Politics of Sex and Power* (1994)

Richard Lee Marks, *Cortés: The Great Adventurer and the Fate of Aztec Mexico* (1993)

James McDermott, *Martin Frobisher: Elizabethan Privateer* (2001)

Edmund S. Morgan, *American Heroes: Profiles of Men and Women Who Shaped Early America* (2009)

Andrés Reséndez, *A Land So Strange: The Epic Journey of Cabeza de Vaca* (2007)

P. E. Russell, *Prince Henry the Navigator: A Life* (2000)

David Starkey, *Elizabeth: The Struggle for the Throne* (2000)

Camilla Townsend, *Malintzin's Choices: An Indian Woman in the Conquest of Mexico* (2006)

David M. Traboulay, *Columbus and Las Casas: The Conquest and Christianization of America, 1492–1566* (1994)

Henry Raup Wagner, *The Life and Writings of Bartolomé de las Casas* (1967)

CHAPTER 3
Spain and Its Competitors in North America

Gary Clayton Anderson, *The Indian Southwest, 1580–1830: Ethnogenesis and Reinvention* (1999)

James Axtell, *The Invasion Within: The Contest of Culture in Colonial North America* (1985)

Denys Delâge, *Bitter Feast: Amerindians and Europeans in Northeastern North America, 1600–64* (1993)

W. J. Eccles, *The Canadian Frontier, 1534–1760* (1983)

Carl J. Ekberg, *French Roots in the Illinois Country: The Mississippi Frontier in Colonial Times* (1998)

Eric Hinderaker and Peter C. Mancall, *At the Edge of Empire: The Backcountry in British North America* (2003)

J. R. Jones, *The Anglo–Dutch Wars of the Seventeenth Century* (1996)

Robert L. Kapitzke, *Religion, Power, and Politics in Colonial St. Augustine* (2001)

Cathy D. Matson, *Merchants and Empire: Trading in Colonial New York* (1998)

Donna Merwick, *The Shame and the Sorrow: Dutch-Amerindian Encounters in New Netherland* (2006)

Peter Moogk, *La Nouvelle France: The Making of French Canada, a Cultural History* (2000)

Daniel Paul, *We Were Not the Savages: A Mi'kmaq Perspective on the Collision Between European and Native American Civilizations* (2000)

Oliver Rink, *Holland on the Hudson: An Economic and Social History of Dutch New York* (1986)

Benjamin Schmidt, *Innocence Abroad: The Dutch Imagination and the New World, 1570–1670* (2001)

Irene Silverblatt, *Modern Inquisitions: Peru and the Colonial Origins of the Civilized World* (2004)

Sylvia Van Kirk, *Many Tender Ties: Women in Fur-Trade Society in Western Canada, 1670–1870* (1999)

England in the Chesapeake

Robert Appelbaum and John Wood Sweet, eds., *Envisioning an English Empire: Jamestown and the Making of the North Atlantic World* (2005)

Warren M. Billings, *A Little Parliament: The Virginia General Assembly in the Seventeenth Century* (2004)

Edward L. Bond, *Damned Souls in a Tobacco Colony: Religion in Seventeenth-Century Virginia* (2000)

Kathleen M. Brown, *Good Wives, Nasty Wenches, and Anxious Patriarchs: Gender, Race, and Power in Colonial Virginia* (1996)

Wesley F. Craven, *White, Red, and Black: The Seventeenth Century Virginian* (1971)

Frederic W. Gleach, *Powhatan's World and Colonial Virginia: A Conflict of Cultures* (1997)

April Lee Hatfield, *Atlantic Virginia: Intercolonial Relations in the Seventeenth Century* (2004)

Ronald Hoffman, *Princes of Ireland, Planters of Maryland: A Carroll Saga, 1500–1782* (2000)

James Horn, *A Land as God Made It: Jamestown and the Birth of America* (2005)

William M. Kelso, *Jamestown: The Buried Truth* (2006)

John D. Krugler, *English and Catholic: The Lords Baltimore in the Seventeenth Century* (2004)

Karen Ordahl Kupperman, *Settling with the Indians: The Meeting of English and Indian Cultures in America, 1580–1640* (1980)

Karen Ordahl Kupperman, *The Jamestown Project* (2007)

Gloria L. Main, *Tobacco Colony: Life in Early Maryland, 1650–1720* (1982)

Peter C. Mancall, ed., *The Atlantic World and Virginia, 1550–1624* (2007)

Michael Leroy Oberg, *Dominion and Civility: English Imperialism and Native America, 1585–1685* (1999)

John Ruston Pagan, *Anne Orthwood's Bastard: Sex and Law in Early Virginia* (2003)

The New England Colonies

Elinor Abbot, *Our Company Increases Apace: History, Language, and Social Identity in Early Colonial Andover, Massachusetts* (2007)

Douglas Anderson, *William Bradford's Books: Of Plimmoth Plantation and the Printed Word* (2003)

Richard Archer, *Fissures in the Rock: New England in the Seventeenth Century* (2001)

David Grayson Allen, *In English Ways: The Movement of Societies and the Transferal of English Local Law and Custom* (1981)

Bernard Bailyn, *The New England Merchants in the Seventeenth Century* (1955)

Carl Bridenbaugh, *Fat Mutton and Liberty of Conscience: Society in Rhode Island, 1636–1690* (1974)

Kristina Bross, *Dry Bones and Indian Sermons: Praying Indians and Colonial American Identity* (2004)

James P. Byrd Jr., *The Challenges of Roger Williams: Religious Liberty, Violent Persecution, and the Bible* (2002)

Colin G. Calloway and Neal Salisbury, eds., *Reinterpreting New England Indians and the Colonial Experience* (2003)

Joyce E. Chaplin, *Subject Matter: Technology, the Body, and Science on the Anglo–American Frontier, 1500–1676* (2001)

Joseph A. Conforti, *Saints and Strangers: New England in British North America* (2006)

David Cressy, *Coming Over: Migration and Communication between England and New England in the Seventeenth Century* (1987)

William Cronon, *Changes in the Land: Indians, Colonists, and the Ecology of New England* (1983)

John Demos, *A Little Commonwealth: Family Life in Plymouth Colony* (1970)

Richard Godbeer, *Escaping Salem: The Other Witch Hunt of 1692* (2004)

David D. Hall, ed., *Puritans in the New World: A Critical Anthology* (2004)

Timothy Hall, *Separating Church and State: Roger Williams and Religious Liberty* (1998)

Francis Jennings, *The Invasion of America: Indians, Colonialism, and the Cant of Conquest* (1975)

Carol F. Karlsen, *The Devil in the Shape of a Woman: Witchcraft in Colonial New England* (1987)

Benjamin W. Labaree, *America and the Sea: A Maritime History* (1998)

Amy Scrager Lang, *Prophetic Women: Anne Hutchinson and the Problem of Dissent in the Literature of New England* (1987)

Mary Beth Norton, *In the Devil's Snare: The Salem Witchcraft Crisis of 1692* (2002)

Ann Marie Plane, *Colonial Intimacies: Indian Marriage in Early New England* (2000)

Bianca Premo, *Children of the Father King: Youth, Authority, and Legal Minority in Colonial Lima* (2005)

Jenny Hale Pulsipher, *Subjects unto the Same King: Indians, English, and the Contest for Authority in Colonial New England* (2006)

Elizabeth Reis, *Damned Women: Sinners and Witches in Puritan New England* (1997)

Patricia E. Rubertone, *Grave Undertakings: An Archaeology of Roger Williams and the Narragansett Indians* (2001)

Neal Salisbury, *Manitou and Providence: Indians, Europeans, and the Making of New England* (1982)

David J. Silverman, *Faith and Boundaries: Colonists, Christianity, and Community among the Wampanoag Indians of Martha's Vineyard, 1600–1871* (2005)

Rebecca J. Tannenbaum, *The Healer's Calling: Women and Medicine in Early New England* (2002)

Teresa A. Toulouse, *The Captive's Position: Female Narrative, Male Identity, and Royal Authority in Colonial New England* (2007)

David A. Weir, *Early New England: A Covenanted Society* (2005)

The Restoration Colonies

Wesley F. Craven, *The Southern Colonies in the Seventeenth Century, 1607–1689* (1949)

Michael Kammen, *Colonial New York: A History* (1975)

Sung Bok Kim, *Landlord and Tenant in Colonial New York: Manorial Society, 1664–1775* (1978)

H. T. Merrens, *Colonial North Carolina* (1964)

Donna Merwick, *Death of a Notary: Conquest and Change in Colonial New York* (1999)

Gary B. Nash, *Quakers and Politics: Pennsylvania, 1681–1726* (1968)

M. Eugene Sirmans, *Colonial South Carolina: A Political History, 1663–1763* (1966)

Jack M. Sosin, *English America and the Restoration Monarchy of Charles II: Transatlantic Politics, Commerce, and Kinship* (1980)

Barry Aron Vann, *In Search of Ulster-Scots Land: The Birth and Geotheological Imagings of a Transatlantic People, 1603–1703* (2008)

Conflict and War

Thomas J. Archdeacon, *New York City, 1664–1710* (1976)

Paul Boyer and Stephen Nissenbaum, *Salem Possessed* (1974)

Colin G. Calloway, ed., *After King Philip's War: Presence and Persistence in Indian New England* (1997)

Guy Chet, *Conquering the American Wilderness: The Triumph of European Warfare in the Colonial Northeast* (2003)

Eveline Cruickshanks, *The Glorious Revolution* (2000)

James D. Drake, *King Philip's War: Civil War in New England, 1675–1676* (1999)

Ramón A. Gutiérrez, *When Jesus Came, the Corn Mothers Went Away: Marriage, Sexuality, and Power in New Mexico, 1500–1846* (1991)

Richard R. Johnson, *Adjustment to Empire: The New England Colonies, 1675–1715* (1981)

D. W. Jordan, *Maryland's Revolution of Government, 1689–1692* (1974)

Karen Ordahl Kupperman, *Indians and English: Facing Off in Early America* (2000)

Almon Wheeler Lauber, *Indian Slavery in Colonial Times within the Present Limits of the United States* (1913)

Jill Lepore, *The Name of War: King Philip's War and the Origins of American Identity* (1998)

David S. Lovejoy, *The Glorious Revolution in America* (1972)

Robert W. Preucel, ed., *Archaeologies of the Pueblo Revolt: Identity, Meaning, and Renewal in the Pueblo World* (2002)

Nancy Shoemaker, *A Strange Likeness: Becoming Red and White in Eighteenth-Century North America* (2004)

Wilcomb E. Washburn, *The Governor and the Rebel: A History of Bacon's Rebellion in Virginia* (1957)

Stephen S. Webb, *1676: The End of American Independence* (1980)

Biography

Paula Gunn Allen, *Pocahontas: Medicine Woman, Spy, Entrepreneur, Diplomat* (2003)

Francis J. Bremer, *John Winthrop: America's Forgotten Founding Father* (2003)

David Hackett Fischer, *Champlain's Dream* (2008)

Mary K. Geiter, *William Penn* (2000)

Allan Greer, *Mohawk Saint: Catherine Tekakwitha and the Jesuits* (2005)

J. A. Leo Lemay, *The American Dream of Captain John Smith* (1991)

Peter C. Mancall, *Fatal Journey: The Final Expedition of Henry Hudson* (2009)

Edmund S. Morgan, *Puritan Dilemma: The Story of John Winthrop* (1958)

Michael Leroy Oberg, *Uncas: First of the Mohegans* (2003)

Ann Sanford, *Anne Bradstreet, the Worldly Puritan* (1974)

Marc Simmons, *The Last Conquistador: Juan de Oñate and the Settling of the Far Southwest* (1991)

Camilla Townsend, *Pocahontas and the Powhatan Dilemma* (2004)

Alvin Gardner Weeks, *Massasoit of the Pokanokets* (1919)

Michael P. Winship, *The Times and Trials of Anne Hutchinson: Puritans Divided* (2005)

CHAPTER 4

The African Slave Trade

Jay Coughtry, *The Notorious Triangle: Rhode Island and the African Slave Trade, 1799–1807* (1981)

Philip D. Curtin, *Economic Change in Precolonial Africa: Senegambia in the Era of the Slave Trade* (1975)

Basil Davidson, *The African Slave Trade* (1980)

Benedict G. Der, *The Slave Trade in Northern Ghana* (1998)

Elizabeth Donnan, ed., *Documents Illustrative of the History of the Slave Trade to America,* 4 vols. (1930–35)

Madge Dresser, *Slavery Obscured: The Social History of the Slave Trade in an English Provincial Port* (2001)

David Eltis, et al., eds., *Slavery in the Development of the Americas* (2004)

Eli Faber, *Jews, Slaves, and the Slave Trade: Setting the Record Straight* (1998)

Philip Gould, *Barbaric Traffic: Commerce and Antislavery in the Eighteenth-Century Atlantic World* (2003)

Robert W. Harms, *The Diligent: A Voyage through the Worlds of the Slave Trade* (2001)

Saidiya V. Hartman, *Lose Your Mother: A Journey along the Atlantic Slave Route* (2007)

J. E. Inikori, *Forced Migration: The Impact of the Export Slave Trade on African Societies* (1982)

Robert W. July, *A History of the African People* (1992)

Herbert S. Klein, *The Middle Passage: Comparative Studies in the Atlantic Slave Trade* (1978)

Robin Law, *The Slave Coast of West Africa, 1550–1750: The Impact of the Atlantic Slave Trade on an African Society* (1991)

Paul E. Lovejoy, ed., *Africans in Bondage: Studies in Slavery and the Slave Trade* (1986)

Daniel P. Mannix and Malcolm Crowley, *Black Cargoes: A History of the Atlantic Slave Trade* (1962)

David Northrup, ed., *The Atlantic Slave Trade* (1994)

J. A. Rawley, *The Transatlantic Slave Trade* (1981)

Edward Reynolds, *Stand the Storm: A History of the Atlantic Slave Trade* (1985)

A. C. de C. M. Saunders, *A Social History of Black Slaves and Freemen in Portugal, 1441–1555* (1982)

Stephanie E. Smallwood, *Saltwater Slavery: A Middle Passage from Africa to American Diaspora* (2007)

Randy J. Sparks, *Two Princes of Calabar: An Eighteenth-Century Atlantic Odyssey* (2004)

Jon Vogt, *Portuguese Rule on the Gold Coast, 1469–1682* (1979)

James Walvin, *Making the Black Atlantic: Britain and the African Diaspora* (2000)

The Development of North American Slave Societies

L. R. Bailey, *Indian Slave Trade in the Southwest: A Study of Slave-Taking and the Traffic in Indian Captives* (1966)

Ira Berlin, *Generations of Captivity: A History of African-American Slaves* (2003)

T. H. Breen and Stephen Innes, *"Myne Owne Ground": Race and Freedom on Virginia's Eastern Shore* (1980)

James F. Brooks, *Captives and Cousins: Slavery, Kinship, and Community in the Southwest Borderlands* (2002)

David S. Cecelski, *The Waterman's Song: Slavery and Freedom in Maritime North Carolina* (2001)

Verner W. Crane, *The Southern Frontier, 1670–1732* (1929)

Mariana L. R. Dantas, *Black Townsmen: Urban Slavery and Freedom in the Eighteenth-Century Americas* (2008)

Richard S. Dunn, *Sugar and Slaves: The Rise of the Planter Class in the English West Indies, 1624–1713* (1972)

S. Max Edelson, *Plantation Enterprise in Colonial South Carolina* (2006)

David Eltis, *The Rise of African Slavery in the Americas* (2000)

Sharla M. Fett, *Working Cures: Healing, Health, and Power on Southern Slave Plantations* (2002)

Laura Foner and Eugene D. Genovese, eds., *Slavery in the New World: A Reader in Comparative History* (1969)

Thelma Wills Foote, *Black and White Manhattan: The History of Racial Formation in Colonial New York City* (2004)

Allan Gallay, *The Indian Slave Trade: The Rise of the English Empire in the American South, 1670–1717* (2002)

Leslie M. Harris, *In the Shadow of Slavery: African Americans in New York City, 1626–1863* (2003)

Graham Russell Hodges, *Root and Branch: African Americans in New York and East Jersey, 1613–1863* (1999)

Thomas N. Ingersoll, *Mammon and Manon in Early New Orleans: The First Slave Society in the Deep South, 1718–1819* (1999)

Charles Joyner, *Down by the Riverside: A South Carolina Slave Community* (1984)

Alan Kulikoff, *Tobacco and Slaves: The Development of Southern Cultures in the Chesapeake, 1680–1800* (1986)

Jane Landers, *Black Society in Spanish Florida* (1999)

Daniel Littlefield, *Rice and Slaves: Ethnicity and the Slave Trade in Colonial South Carolina* (1981)

Paul E. Lovejoy, *Transformations in Slavery: A History of Slavery in Africa* (1983)

Edgar J. McManus, *Black Bondage in the North* (1973)

Gary B. Nash, *Red, White, and Black: The Peoples of Early North America* (1992)

Julia Floyd Smith, *Slavery and Rice Culture in Low Country Georgia, 1750–1860* (1985)

Peter H. Wood, *Black Majority: Negroes in Colonial South Carolina from 1670 through the Stone Rebellion* (1974)

African to African American

John B. Boles, *Black Southerners, 1619–1869* (1984)

Alex Bontemps, *The Punished Self: Surviving Slavery in the Colonial South* (2001)

Sylviane A. Diouf, *Servants of Allah: African Muslims Enslaved in the Americas* (1998)

John Hope Franklin and Loren Schweniger, *Runaway Slaves: Rebels in the Plantation* (1999)

Michael Gomez, *Exchanging Our Country Marks: The Transformation of African Identities in the Colonial and Antebellum South* (1998)

Annette Gordon-Reed, *Thomas Jefferson and Sally Hemings: An American Controversy* (1997)

Herbert G. Gutman, *The Black Family in Slavery and Freedom, 1750–1925* (1976)

Gwendolyn Midlo Hall, *Slavery and African Ethnicities in the Americas: Restoring the Links* (2005)

Joseph E. Harris, ed., *Global Dimensions of the African Diaspora* (1982)

Jill Lepore, *New York Burning: Liberty, Slavery, and Conspiracy in Eighteenth-Century Manhattan* (2005)

Jennifer L. Morgan, *Laboring Women: Reproduction and Gender in New World Slavery* (2004)

Gerald W. Mullin, *Flight and Rebellion: Slave Resistance in Eighteenth-Century Virginia* (1972)

Orlando Patterson, *Slavery and Social Death: A Comparative Study* (1982)

Jon E. Sensbach, *Rebecca's Revival: Creating Black Christianity in the Atlantic World* (2005)

Mark M. Smith, *Mastered by the Clock: Time, Slavery, and Freedom in the American South* (1997)

Sterling Stuckey, *Slave Culture: Nationalist Theory and the Foundations of Black America* (1987)

V. B. Thompson, *The Making of the African Diaspora in the Americas, 1441–1900* (1984)

Slavery and Empire

Joyce O. Appleby, *Economic Thought and Ideology in Seventeenth-Century England* (1978)

Heather Cateau and S. H. H. Carrington, eds., *Capitalism and Slavery Fifty Years Later: Eric Eustace Williams—A Reassessment of the Man and His Work* (2000)

Peter A. Coclanis, ed., *The Atlantic Economy during the Seventeenth and Eighteenth Centuries: Organization, Operation, Practice, and Personnel* (2005)

Andy Doolen, *Fugitive Empire: Locating Early American Imperialism* (2005)

Eugene Genovese and Elizabeth Fox-Genovese, *Fruits of Merchant Capital: Slavery and Bourgeois Property in the Rise and Expansion of Capitalism* (1983)

E. J. Hobsbawn, *Industry and Empire: The Making of Modern English Society, 1750 to the Present Day* (1968)

Joseph E. Inikori, *Africans and the Industrial Revolution in England: A Study in International Trade and Economic Development* (2002)

Michael Kammen, *Empire and Interest: The American Colonies and the Politics of Mercantilism* (1970)

Cathy Matson, ed., *The Economy of Early America: Historical Perspectives and New Directions* (2006)

John J. McCusker and Russell R. Menard, *The Economy of British America, 1607–1787* (1985)

John J. McCusker and Kenneth Morgan, eds., *The Early Modern Atlantic Economy* (2001)

Barbara L. Solow, ed., *Slavery and the Rise of the Atlantic System* (1991)

Eric Williams, *Capitalism and Slavery* (1944)

Slavery and Freedom

David Brion Davis, *The Problem of Slavery in Western Culture* (1966)

Carl N. Degler, *Neither Black nor White: Slavery and Race Relations in Brazil and the United States* (1971)

Edmund S. Morgan, *American Slavery, American Freedom: The Ordeal of Colonial Virginia* (1975)

Joel Williamson, *New People: Miscegenation and Mulattoes in the United States* (1980)

Biography

Vincent Carretta, *Equiano, the African: Biography of a Self-Made Man* (2005)

Philip D. Curtin, ed., *Africa Remembered: Narratives of West Africans from the Era of the Slave Trade* (1967)

Paul Edwards, ed., *The Interesting Narrative of the Life of Olaudah Equiano, or Gustavus Vassa, the African, written by himself* (1987)

James B. Hedges, *The Browns of Providence Plantation* (1952)

Kenneth A. Lockridge, *The Diary and Life of William Byrd II of Virginia, 1674–1744* (1987)

Thomas P. Slaughter, *The Beautiful Soul of John Woolman, Apostle of Abolition* (2008)

Phinizy Spalding, *Oglethorpe in America* (1977)

CHAPTER 5

North American Regions

Patricia Albers and Beatrice Medicine, eds., *The Hidden Half: Studies of Plains Indian Women* (1983)

Stephen Conrad Ausband, *Byrd's Line: A Natural History* (2002)

Kenneth J. Banks, *Chasing Empire across the Sea: Communications and the State in the French Atlantic, 1713–1763* (2002)

Carole Blackburn, *Harvest of Souls: The Jesuit Missions and Colonialism in North America, 1632–1650* (2000)

Bradley G. Bond, ed., *French Colonial Louisiana and the Atlantic World* (2005)

Trevor Burnard, *Creole Gentlemen: The Maryland Elite, 1691–1776* (2002)

Richard L. Bushman, *From Puritan to Yankee: Character and the Social Order in Connecticut, 1690–1765* (1967)

David Bussiert and Steven G. Reinhardt, eds., *Creolization in the Americas* (2000)

Edward D. Castillo, ed., *Native American Perspectives on the Hispanic Colonization of Alta California* (1992)

Andrew R. L. Cayton and Frederika J. Teute, eds., *Contact Points: American Frontiers from the Mohawk Valley to the Mississippi, 1750–1830* (1998)

Cornelia Hughes Dayton, *Women before the Bar: Gender, Law, and Society in Connecticut, 1639–1789* (1995)

John Demos, *The Unredeemed Captive: A Family Story from Early America* (1994)

Brian Leigh Dunnigan, *Frontier Metropolis: Picturing Early Detroit, 1701–1838* (2001)

Kathleen DuVal, *The Native Ground: Indians and Colonists in the Heart of the Continent* (2006)

Carville Earle, *The American Way: A Geographical History of Crisis and Recovery* (2003)

Robbie Ethridge, *Creek Country: The Creek Indians and Their World* (2003)

John C. Ewers, *The Horse in Blackfoot Indian Culture* (1955)

David Hackett Fischer and James C. Kelly, *Bound Away: Virginia and the Westward Movement* (2000)

Kirsten Fischer, *Suspect Relations: Sex, Race, and Resistance in Colonial North Carolina* (2002)

Joseph W. Glass, *The Pennsylvania Culture Region: A View from the Barn* (1986)

Evan Haefeli and Kevin Sweeney, *Captors and Captives: The 1704 French and Indian Raid on Deerfield* (2003)

Thomas Hallock, *From the Fallen Tree: Frontier Narratives, Environmental Politics, and the Roots of a National Pastoral, 1749–1826* (2003)

Robert F. Heizer, *The Destruction of California Indians* (1974)

Christine Leigh Heyrman, *Commerce and Culture: The Maritime Communities of Colonial Massachusetts* (1984)

Warren R. Hofstra, *The Planting of New Virginia: Settlement and Landscape in the Shenandoah Valley* (2004)

Daniel J. Hulsebosch, *Constituting Empire: New York and the Transformation of Constitutionalism in the Atlantic World, 1664–1830* (2005)

Donald A. Hutslar, *The Architecture of Migration: Log Construction in the Ohio Country, 1750–1850* (1986)

Rhys Isaac, *Worlds of Experience: Communities in Colonial Virginia* (1987)

Robert H. Jackson, *Indian Population Decline: The Missions of Northwestern New Spain, 1687–1840* (1994)

———, *From Savages to Subjects: Missions in the History of the American Southwest* (2000)

Francis Jennings, *The Ambiguous Iroquois Empire* (1984)

Terry G. Jordan and Matti Kaups, *The American Backwoods Frontier: An Ethnic and Ecological Interpretation* (1988)

Lyle Kohler, *A Search for Power: "The Weaker Sex" in Seventeenth-Century New England, 1650–1750* (1982)

James T. Lemon, *The Best Poor Man's Country: A Geographical Study of Early Southeastern Pennsylvania* (1972)

Kenneth Lockridge, *Literacy in Colonial New England* (1974)

Martha McCollough, *Three Nations, One Place: A Comparative Ethnohistory of Social Change among the Comanches and Hasinais during Spain's Colonial Era, 1689–1821* (2004)

James H. Merrell, *The Indians' New World: Catawbas and Their Neighbors from European Contact through the Era of Removal* (1989)

———, *Into the American Woods: Negotiators on the Pennsylvania Frontier* (1999)

Jane T. Merritt, *At the Crossroads: Indians and Empires on a Mid-Atlantic Frontier, 1700–1763* (2003)

Peter N. Moore, *World of Toil and Strife: Community Transformation in Backcountry South Carolina, 1750–1805* (2007)

Gary B. Nash, *The Urban Crucible* (1979)

Steven J. Oatis, *A Colonial Complex: South Carolina's Frontiers in the Era of the Yamasee War, 1680–1730* (2004)

William A. Pencak and Daniel K. Richter, eds., *Friends and Enemies in Penn's Woods: Indians, Colonists, and the Racial Construction of Pennsylvania* (2004)

Jacqueline Peterson and Jennifer S. H. Brown, eds., *The New Peoples: Being and Becoming Métis in North America* (1985)

Daniel K. Richter, *The Ordeal of the Longhouse: The Peoples of the Iroquois League in the Era of European Colonization* (1992)

S. Scott Rohrer, *Hope's Promise: Religion and Acculturation in the Southern Backcountry* (2005)

Darrett B. Rutman and Anita H. Rutman, *A Place in Time: Middlesex County, Virginia, 1650–1750* (1984)

Marylynn Salmon, *Women and the Law of Property in Early America* (1986)

Sally Schwartz, *A Mixed Multitude: The Struggle for Toleration in Colonial Pennsylvania* (1987)

William S. Simmons, *Spirit of the New England Tribes: Indian History and Folklore, 1620–1984* (1986)

Daniel Blake Smith, *Inside the Great House: Planter Family Life in Eighteenth-Century Chesapeake Society* (1980)

Jewel L. Spangler, *Virginians Reborn: Anglican Monopoly, Evangelical Dissent, and the Rise of the Baptists in the Late Eighteenth Century* (2008)

Linda L. Sturtz, *Within Her Power: Propertied Women in Colonial Virginia* (2002)

Margaret Connell Szasz, *Scottish Highlanders and Native Americans: Indigenous Education in the Eighteenth-Century Atlantic World* (2007)

Laurel T. Ulrich, *Good Wives: Image and Reality in the Lives of Women in Northern New England, 1650–1750* (1982)

Daniel H. Usner Jr., *Indians, Settlers, and Slaves in a Frontier Exchange Economy: The Lower Mississippi Valley before 1783* (1992)

David J. Weber, *Bárbaros: Spaniards and Their Savages in the Age of Enlightenment* (2005)

Kathleen Wilson, *The Island Race: Englishness, Empire, and Gender in the Eighteenth Century* (2003)

Bradford J. Wood, *This Remote Part of the World: Regional Formation in Lower Cape Fear, North Carolina, 1725–1775* (2004)

Diverging Social and Political Patterns

Bernard Bailyn, *The Peopling of British North America: An Introduction* (1986)

Linda Baumgarten, *What Clothes Reveal: The Language of Clothing in Colonial and Federal America* (2002)

Richard R. Beeman, *The Varieties of Political Experience in Eighteenth-Century America* (2004)

Mary Sarah Bilder, *The Transatlantic Constitution: Colonial Legal Culture and the Empire* (2004)

Ruth H. Bloch, *Gender and Morality in Anglo-American Culture, 1650–1800* (2003)

James E. Block, *Nation of Agents: The American Path to a Modern Self and Society* (2002)

Bruce C. Daniels, ed., *Power and Status: Essays on Officeholding in Colonial America* (1986)

Robert J. Dinkin, *Voting in Provincial America: A Study of Elections in the Thirteen Colonies, 1680–1776* (1977)

A. Roger Ekirch, *Bound for America: The Transportation of British Convicts to the Colonies, 1718–1775* (1987)

Jay Gitlin, *The Bourgeois Frontier: French Towns, French Traders, and American Expansion* (2009)

Patrick Griffin, *The People with No Name: Ireland's Ulster Scots, America's Scots Irish, and the Creation of a British Atlantic World, 1689-1764* (2001)

Catherine Kerrison, *Claiming the Pen: Women and Intellectual Life in the Early American South* (2006)

Carla Gardina Pestana and Sharon V. Salinger, eds., *Inequality in Early America* (1999)

Thomas L. Purvis, *Proprietors, Patronage, and Paper Money: Legislative Politics in New Jersey, 1703–1776* (1986)

Sharon V. Salinger, *"To Serve Well and Faithfully": Labor and Indentured Servants in Pennsylvania, 1682–1800* (1987)

The Cultural Transformation of British North America

Eve Tavor Bannet, *Empire of Letters: Letter Manuals and Transatlantic Correspondence, 1680–1820* (2005)

Linda Baumgarten, *What Clothes Reveal: The Language of Clothing in Colonial and Federal America: The Colonial Williamsburg Collection* (2002)

Patricia U. Bonomi, *Under the Cope of Heaven: Religion, Society, and Politics in Colonial America* (1986)

Henry Steele Commager, *The Empire of Reason: How Europe Imagined and America Realized the Enlightenment* (1977)

Patricia Crain, *The Story of A: The Alphabetization of America from "The New England Primer" to "The Scarlet Letter"* (2000)

James Delbourgo, *A Most Amazing Scene of Wonders: Electricity and Enlightenment in Early America* (2006)

John Demos, *Circles and Lines: The Shape of Life in Early America* (2004)

Sara S. Gronim, *Everyday Nature: Knowledge of the Natural World in Colonial New York* (2007)

Nancy Isenberg and Andrew Burstein, eds., *Mortal Remains: Death in Early America* (2003)

Thomas S. Kidd, *The Great Awakening: The Roots of Evangelical Christianity in Colonial America* (2007)

David W. Kling and Douglas A. Sweeney, eds., *Jonathan Edwards at Home and Abroad: Historical Memories, Cultural Movements, Global Horizons* (2003)

Frank Lambert, *Inventing the "Great Awakening"* (1999)

Ned C. Landsman, *From Colonials to Provincials: American Thought and Culture, 1680–1760* (1997)

Jackson Turner Main, *The Social Structure of Revolutionary America* (1965)

Ann Smart Martin, *Buying into the World of Goods: Early Consumers in Backcountry Virginia* (2008)

E. Jennifer Monaghan, *Learning to Read and Write in Colonial America* (2005)

Barbara B. Oberg and Harry S. Stout, eds., *Benjamin Franklin, Jonathan Edwards, and the Representation of American Culture* (1993)

Susan Scott Parrish, *American Curiosity: Cultures of Natural History in the Colonial British Atlantic World* (2006)

Amy Plantinga Pauw, *The Supreme Harmony of All: The Trinitarian Theology of Jonathan Edwards* (2002)

Mark A. Peterson, *The Price of Redemption: The Spiritual Economy of Puritan New England* (1997)

Nina Reid-Mahoney, *Philadelphia's Enlightenment, 1740–1800: Kingdom of Christ, Empire of Reason* (2001)

Frank Shuffelton, ed., *The American Enlightenment* (1993)

Biography

Elaine G. Breslaw, *Dr. Alexander Hamilton and Provincial America: Expanding the Orbit of Scottish Culture* (2008)

Robert E. Brown, *Jonathan Edwards and the Bible* (2002)

Patricia Cleary, *Elizabeth Murray: A Woman's Pursuit of Independence in Eighteenth-Century America* (2000)

Verner W. Crane, *Benjamin Franklin and a Rising People* (1952)

Philip F. Gura, *Jonathan Edwards: America's Evangelical* (2005)

Harry Kelsey, *Juan Rodriguez Cabrillo* (1986)

Gerald R. McDermott, *Jonathan Edwards Confronts the Gods* (2000)

Robert Middlekauff, *The Mathers: Three Generations of Puritan Intellectuals, 1596–1728* (1999)

Martin J. Morgado, *Junípero Serra's Legacy* (1987)

Harry S. Stout, *The Divine Dramatist: George Whitefield and the Rise of Modern Evangelicalism* (1991)

Laurel Ulrich, *A Midwife's Tale: The Life of Martha Ballard, Based on Her Diary, 1785–1812* (1990)

CHAPTER 6

The Seven Years' War in America

Fred Anderson, *A People's Army: Massachusetts Soldiers and Society in the Seven Years' War* (1984)

Frank W. Brecher, *Losing a Continent: France's North American Policy, 1753–1763* (1998)

Stephen Brumwell, *Redcoats: The British Soldier and War in the Americas, 1755–1763* (2002)

Colin G. Calloway, *The Scratch of a Pen: 1763 and the Transformation of America* (2006)

David Dixon, *Never Come to Peace Again: Pontiac's Uprising and the Fate of the British Empire in North America* (2005)

Gregory Evans Dowd, *War Under Heaven: Pontiac, the Indian Nations, and the British Empire* (2002)

John Mack Faragher, *A Great and Noble Scheme: The Tragic Story of the Expulsion of the French Acadians from Their American Homeland* (2005)

Sylvia R. Frey, *The British Soldier in America: A Social History of Military Life in the Colonial Period* (1981)

Kevin Kenny, *Peaceable Kingdom Lost: The Paxton Boys and the Destruction of William Penn's Holy Experiment* (2009)

Dougles E. Leach, *Roots of Conflict: British Armed Forces and Colonial Americans, 1677–1763* (1986)

Richard Middleton, *The Bells of Victory: The Pitt–Newcastle Ministry and the Conduct of the Seven Years' War, 1757–1762* (1985)

Robert C. Newbold, *The Albany Congress and Plan of Union of 1754* (1955)

John Oliphant, *Peace and War on the Anglo-Cherokee Frontier, 1756–63* (2001)

William Pencak, *War, Politics, and Revolution in Provincial Massachusetts* (1981)

Tom Pocock, *Battle for Empire: The Very First World War, 1756–63* (1998)

Alan Rogers, *Empire and Liberty* (1974)

David Curtis Skaggs and Larry L. Nelson, eds., *The Sixty Years' War for the Great Lakes, 1754–1814* (2001)

Matthew C. Ward, *Breaking the Backcountry: The Seven Years' War in Virginia and Pennsylvania, 1754–1765* (2003)

Noel T. St. John Williams, *Redcoats along the Hudson* (1997)

Richard White, *The Middle Ground: Indians, Empires, and Republics in the Great Lakes Region, 1650–1815* (1991)

Imperial Crisis in British North America

Stuart Andrews, *The Rediscovery of America: Transatlantic Crosscurrents in an Age of Revolution* (1998)

Thomas C. Barrow, *Trade and Empire: The British Customs Service in Colonial America* (1967)

Don Cook, *The Long Fuse: How England Lost the American Colonies, 1760–1785* (1995)

Theodore Draper, *A Struggle for Power: The American Revolution* (1996)

Marc Egnal, *A Mighty Empire: The Origins of the American Revolution* (1988)

Eliga H. Gould, *The Persistence of Empire: British Political Culture in the Age of the American Revolution* (2000)

Woody Holton, *Forced Founders: Indians, Debtors, Slaves, and the Making of the American Revolution in Virginia* (1999)

Alice Hanson Jones, *The Wealth of a Nation to Be* (1980)

John J. McCusker, *Rum and the American Revolution* (1989)

Philip James McFarland, *The Brave Bostonians: Hutchinson, Quincy, Franklin, and the Coming of the American Revolution* (1998)

Robert W. T. Martin, *The Free and Open Press: The Founding of American Democratic Press Liberty, 1640–1800* (2001)

J. G. A. Pocock, *The Machiavellian Moment: Florentine Political Thought and the Atlantic Republican Tradition* (1975)

William Lowell Putnam, *John Peter Zenger and the Fundamental Freedom* (1997)

Ray Raphael, *First American Revolution: Before Lexington and Concord* (2002)

Caroline Robbins, *The Eighteenth-Century Commonwealthman* (1959)

Arthur M. Schlesinger, *The Colonial Merchants and the American Revolution* (1917)

John W. Tyler, *Smugglers and Patriots: Boston Merchants and the Advent of the American Revolution* (1986)

Carl Ubbelohde, *The Vice-Admiralty Courts and the American Revolution* (1960)

Kathleen Wilson, *Island Race: Englishness, Empire, and Gender in the Eighteenth Century* (2003)

From Resistance to Rebellion

David Ammerman, *In the Common Cause: American Response to the Coercive Acts of 1774* (1974)

T. H. Breen, *Tobacco Culture: The Mentality of the Great Tidewater Planters on the Eve of Revolution* (1985)

Richard D. Brown, *Revolutionary Politics in Massachusetts: The Boston Committee of Correspondence and the Towns, 1772–1774* (1970)

Richard L. Bushman, *King and People in Provincial Massachusetts* (1985)

Benjamin L. Carp, *Rebels Rising: Cities and the American Revolution* (2007)

H. Trevor Colbourn, *The Lamp of Experience: Whig History and the Intellectual Origins of the American Revolution* (1965)

Light Townsend Cummins, *Spanish Observers and the American Revolution, 1775–1783* (1991)

Derek Davis, *Religion and the Continental Congress, 1774–1789: Contributions to Original Intent* (2000)

Bernard Donoughue, *British Politics and the American Revolution: The Path to War, 1773–1775* (1964)

Gregory T. Edgar, *Reluctant Break with Britain: From Stamp Act to Bunker Hill* (1997)

Jack P. Greene, *Understanding the American Revolution: Issues and Actors* (1995)

John R. Howe, *Language and Political Meaning in Revolutionary America* (2004)

Benjamin W. Labaree, *The Boston Tea Party* (1974)

Pauline Maier, *From Resistance to Rebellion* (1972)

Peter C. Messer, *Stories of Independence: Identity, Ideology, and History in Eighteenth-Century America* (2005)

Edmund S. Morgan, *The Birth of the Republic, 1763–1789* (1956)

Jackson O'Shaughnessy, *An Empire Divided: The American Revolution and the British Caribbean* (2000)

Ray Raphael, *First American Revolution: Before Lexington and Concord* (2002)

John Shy, *Toward Lexington: The Role of the British Army in the Coming of the American Revolution* (1965)

Peter David Garner Thomas, *Tea Party to Independence: The Third Phase of the American Revolution, 1773–1776* (1991)

David Waldstreicher, *Runaway America: Benjamin Franklin, Slavery, and the American Revolution* (2004)

Lee Ward, *The Politics of Liberty in England and Revolutionary America* (2004)

Morton White, *The Philosophy of the American Revolution* (1978)

Gary Wills, *Inventing America* (1978)

Biography

John K. Alexander, *Samuel Adams: America's Revolutionary Politician* (2002)

Bernard Bailyn, *The Ordeal of Thomas Hutchinson* (1974)

Della Gray Barthelmas, *The Signers of the Declaration of Independence* (1997)

Richard R. Beeman, *Patrick Henry: A Biography* (1974)

Jeremy Black, *Pitt the Elder* (1992)

John Brooke, *King George III* (1974)

John E. Ferling, *The Loyalist Mind: Joseph Galloway and the American Revolution* (1977)

———, *Setting the World Ablaze: Washington, Adams, and Jefferson and the American Revolution* (2000)

William M. Fowler, Jr., *The Baron of Beacon Hill: A Biography of John Hancock* (1979)

———, *Samuel Adams: Radical Puritan* (1997)

Rhys Isaac, *Landon Carter's Uneasy Kingdom: Revolution and Rebellion on a Virginia Plantation* (2004)

Keith Krawczynski, *William Henry Drayton: South Carolina Revolutionary Patriot* (2001)

Edward Larkin, *Thomas Paine and the Literature of Revolution* (2005)

J. A. Leo Lemay, *The Life of Benjamin Franklin*, 2 vols. (2006)

David A. McCants, *Patrick Henry, the Orator* (1990)

Edmund S. Morgan, *Benjamin Franklin* (2002)

Colin Nicolson, *"Infamas Govener" Francis Bernard and the Origins of the American Revolution* (2001)

Peter Shaw, *The Character of John Adams* (1976)

Peter D. G. Thomas, *Lord North* (1974)

Andrew S. Walmsley, *Thomas Hutchinson and the Origins of the American Revolution* (1999)

Gordon S. Wood, *Americanization of Benjamin Franklin* (2004)

CHAPTER 7
The War for Independence

Ian Barnes, *The Historical Atlas of the American Revolution* (2000)

Thomas Bender, *A Nation among Nations: America's Place in World History* (2006)

Ira Berlin and Ronald Hoffman, eds., *Slavery and Freedom in the Age of the American Revolution* (1983)

Wayne Bodle, *Valley Forge Winter: Civilians and Soldiers in War* (2002)

T.H. Breen, *Marketplace of Revolution: How Consumer Politics Shaped American Independence* (2004)

Jacqueline Barbara Carr, *After the Siege: A Social History of Boston, 1775–1800* (2005)

Charles E. Claghorn, *Women Patriots of the American Revolution* (1991)

Stephen Conway, *British Isles and the War of American Independence* (2000)

Lawrence D. Cress, *Citizens in Arms: The Army and the Militia in American Society to the War of 1812* (1982)

Paul Finkleman, ed., *Slavery, Revolutionary America, and the New Nation* (1989)

David Hackett Fischer, *Washington's Crossing* (2004)

William M. Fowler Jr., *Rebels Under Sail: The American Navy During the Revolution* (1976)

Francis Fox, *Sweet Land of Liberty: The Ordeal of the American Revolution in Northampton County, Pennsylvania* (2000)

Paul A. Gilje, *Liberty on the Waterfront: American Maritime Culture in the Age of Revolution* (2003)

Joseph T. Glatthaar and James Kirby Martin, *Forgotten Allies: The Oneida Indians and the American Revolution* (2006)

Eliga H. Gould and Peter S. Onuf, eds., *Empire and Nation: The American Revolution in the Atlantic World* (2005)

Barbara Graymont, *The Iroquois in the American Revolution* (1972)

Patrick Griffin, *American Leviathan: Empire, Nation, and the Revolutionary Frontier* (2007)

Leslie Hall, *Land and Allegiance in Revolutionary Georgia* (2001)

Phillip Hamilton, *The Making and Unmaking of a Revolutionary Family: The Tuckers of Virginia, 1752–1830* (2003)

David C. Hendrickson, *Peace Pact: The Lost World of the American Founding* (2003)

Ronald Hoffman and Peter J. Albert, eds., *Arms and Independence: The Military Character of the American Revolution* (1984)

———, eds., *Women in the Age of the American Revolution* (1989)

Ronald Hoffman and Thad W. Tate, eds., *An Uncivil War: The Southern Backcountry during the American Revolution* (1985)

Francis Jennings, *The Creation of America: Through Revolution to Empire* (2000)

Mark E. Kann, *A Republic of Men: The American Founders, Gendered Language, and Patriarchial Politics* (1998)

Cynthia A. Kierner, *Southern Women in Revolution, 1776–1800* (1998)

Wim Klooster, *Revolutions in the Atlantic World: A Comparative History* (2009)

Gregory T. Knouff, *The Soldier's Revolution: Pennsylvanians in Arms and the Forging of Early American Identity* (2004)

Arthur S. Lefkowitz, *The Long Retreat: The Calamitous American Defense of New Jersey, 1776* (1999)

Michael A. McDonnell, *The Politics of War: Race, Class, and Conflict in Revolutionary Virginia* (2007)

Paul B. Moyer, *Wild Yankees: The Struggle for Independence along Pennsylvania's Revolutionary Frontier* (2007)

Paul C. Nagel, *The Adams Women: Abigail and Louise Adams, Their Sisters and Daughters* (1987)

Gary B. Nash, *Race and Revolution* (1990)

Mary Beth Norton, *The British Americans: The Loyalist Exiles in England, 1774–1789* (1972)

Mary Beth Norton, *Liberty's Daughters: The Revolutionary Experience of American Women, 1750–1800* (1980)

Greg O'Brien, *Choctaws in a Revolutionary Age, 1750–1830* (2002)

James O'Donnell, *Southern Indians in the American Revolution* (1973)

Andrew Jackson O'Shaughnessy, *An Empire Divided: The American Revolution and the British Caribbean* (2000)

Anne M. Ousterhout, *The Most Learned Woman in America: A Life of Elizabeth Graeme Fergusson* (2004)

Howard W. Peckham, *The Toll of Independence: Engagements and Battle Casualties of the American Revolution* (1974)

Elizabeth Perkins, *Border Life: Experience and Memory in the Revolutionary Ohio Valley* (1998)

Jim Piecuch, *Three Peoples, One King: Loyalists, Indians, and Slaves in the Revolutionary South, 1775–1782* (2008)

Benjamin Quarles, *The Negro in the American Revolution*, rev. ed. (1996)

John Resch and Walter Sargent, eds., *War and Society in the American Revolution: Mobilization and Home Fronts* (2007)

Liam Riordan, *Many Identities, One Nation: The Revolution and Its Legacy in the Mid-Atlantic* (2007)

David Lee Russell, *The American Revolution in the Southern Colonies* (2000)

Andrew Stockley, *Britain and France at the Birth of America: The European Powers and the Peace Negotiations of 1782–1783* (2001)

Judith L. Van Buskirk, *Generous Enemies: Patriots and Loyalists in Revolutionary New York* (2002)

James W. St. G. Walker, *The Black Loyalists* (1976)

Anthony F. C. Wallace, *The Death and Rebirth of the Seneca* (1970)

Betty Wood, *Gender, Race, and Rank in a Revolutionary Age: The Georgia Lowcountry, 1750–1820* (2000)

Alfred F. Young, ed., *The American Revolution: Explorations in American Radicalism* (1976)

The United States in Congress Assembled

Joyce Appleby, *Inheriting the Revolution: The First Generation of Americans* (2000)

Richard Beeman, et al., eds., *Beyond Confederation: Origins of the Constitution and American National Identity* (1987)

E. Wayne Carp, *To Starve the Army at Pleasure: Continental Army Administration and American Political Culture, 1774–1783* (1984)

E. J. Ferguson, *The Power of the Purse: A History of American Public Finance, 1776–1790* (1960)

John Ferling, *A Leap in the Dark: The Struggle to Create the American Republic* (2003)

Calvin C. Jillson, *Congressional Dynamics: Structure, Coordination, and Choice in the First American Congress, 1774–1789* (1994)

Jackson Turner Main, *Political Parties before the Constitution* (1973)

Jack N. Rakove, *The Beginnings of National Politics: An Interpretive History of the Continental Congress* (1979)

Gerald Sourzh, *Benjamin Franklin and American Foreign Policy* (1969)

Gordon S. Wood, *The Creation of the American Republic, 1776–1787* (1969)

Revolutionary Politics in the States

Willi Paul Adams, *The First American Constitutions: Republican Ideology and the Making of the State Constitutions* (1980)

Roger H. Brown, *Redeeming the Republic: Federalists, Taxation, and the Origins of the Constitution* (1993)

Thomas J. Humphrey, *Land and Liberty: Hudson Valley Riots in the Age of Revolution* (2004)

Donald S. Lutz, *Popular Consent and Popular Control: Whig Political Theory in the Early State Constitutions* (1980)

Jackson Turner Main, *The Sovereign States, 1775–1789* (1973)

Liam Riordan, *Many Identities, One Nation: The Revolution and Its Legacy in the Mid-Atlantic* (2007)

Laurel Thatcher Ulrich, *The Age of Homespun: Objects and Stories in the Creation of an American Myth* (2001)

Biography

William Howard Adams, *Gouverneur Morris: An Independent Life* (2003)

Silvio A. Bedini, *The Life of Benjamin Banneker* (1972)

Patricia Cleary, *Elizabeth Murray: A Woman's Pursuit of Independence in Eighteenth-Century America* (2000)

Kate Davies, *Catharine Macaulay and Mercy Otis Warren: The Revolutionary Atlantic and the Politics of Gender* (2005)

Joseph J. Ellis, *His Excellency: George Washington* (2004)

John Mack Faragher, *Daniel Boone: The Life and Legend of an American Pioneer* (1992)

Douglas Southall Freeman, *George Washington*, 7 vols. (1948–57)

Lowell Hayes Harrison, *George Rogers Clark and the War in the West* (1976)

John W. Hartmann, *The American Partisan: Henry Lee and the Struggle for Independence, 1776–1780* (2000)

Don Higginbotham, ed., *George Washington Reconsidered* (2001)

Isabel Thompson Kelsay, *Joseph Brant, 1743–1807: Man of Two Worlds* (1984)

James Kirby Martin, *Benedict Arnold, Revolutionary Hero* (1997)

Gregory D. Massey, *John Laurens and the American Revolution* (2000)

J. Kent McGaughy, *Richard Henry Lee of Virginia: A Portrait of an American Revolutionary* (2004)

David Paul Nelson, *General Sir Guy Carleton, Lord Dorchester: Solider-Statesman of Early British Canada* (2000)

William Henry Robinson, *Phillis Wheatley and Her Writings* (1984)

John Saillant, *Black Puritan, Black Republican: The Life and Thought of Lemuel Haynes, 1753–1833* (2003)

Susan Burgess Shenstone, *So Obstinately Loyal: James Moody, 1744–1809* (2000)

Harlow Giles Unger, *Lafayette* (2002)

Henry Wiencek, *Imperfect God: George Washington, His Slaves, and the Creation of America* (2003)

Julie Winch, *A Gentleman of Color: The Life of James Forten* (2002)

Alfred F. Young, *Masquerade: The Life and Times of Deborah Sampson, Continental Soldier* (2004)

Rosemarie Zagarri, *A Woman's Dilemma: Mercy Otis Warren and the American Revolution* (1995)

CHAPTER 8

The Crisis of the 1780s

Terry Bouton, *Taming Democracy: "The People," the Founders, and the Troubled Ending of the Ameri can Revolution* (2007)

Keith L. Dougherty, *Collective Action Under the Articles of Confederation* (2001)

Ronald Hoffman and Peter J. Albert, eds., *Soverign States in an Age of Uncertainty* (1982)

Robert A. Gross, eds., *In Debt to Shays: The Bicentennial of an Agrarian Rebellion* (1993)

Merrill Jensen, *The New Nation: A History of the United States during the Confederation, 1781–1789* (1950)

Bruce H. Mann, *Republic of Debtors: Bankruptcy in the Age of American Independence* (2002)

David P. Szatmary, *Shays' Rebellion: The Making of an Agrarian Insurrection* (1980)

The New Constitution

Douglass Adair, *Fame and the Founding Fathers*, ed. Trevor Colbourn (1974)

Akhil Reed Amar, *America's Constitution: A Biography* (2005)

Bernard Bailyn, *To Begin the World Anew: The Genius and Ambiguities of the American Founders* (2003)

Charles A. Beard, *An Economic Interpretation of the Constitution of the United States* (1913)

Saul Cornell, *The Other Founders: Anti-Federalism and the Dissenting Tradition in America, 1788–1828* (1999)

Saul Cornell, *A Well-Regulated Militia: The Founding Fathers and the Origins of Gun Control in America* (2006)

Robert A. Dahl, *How Democratic Is the American Constitution?* (2003)

Max M. Edling, *A Revolution in Favor of Government: Origins of the U.S. Constitution and the Making of the American State* (2003)

Max Farrand, ed., *Records of the Federal Convention of 1787*, 4 vols. (1911–37)

Paul Finkelman, *Slavery and the Founders: Race and Liberty in the Age of Jefferson* (2001)

David C. Hendrickson, *Peace Pact: The Lost World of the American Founding* (2003)

John P. Kaminski and Gaspare J. Saladino, eds., *The Documentary History of the Ratification of the Constitution* (1982)

Leonard W. Levy, *Origins of the Bill of Rights* (1999)

Robert A. McGuire, *To Form a More Perfect Union: A New Economic Interpretation of the United States Constitution* (2003)

James H. Read, *Power Versus Liberty: Madison, Hamilton, Wilson, and Jefferson* (2000)

David Brian Robertson, *The Constitution and America's Destiny* (2005)

Gary Rosen, *American Compact: James Madison and the Problem of Founding* (1999)

David J. Siemers, *Ratifying the Republic: Antifederalists and Federalists in Constitutional Time* (2002)

Herbert J. Storing, ed., *The Complete Anti-Federalist*, 7 vols. (1981)

H. Richard Uviller and William G. Merkel, *The Militia and the Right to Arms, or, How the Second Amendment Fell Silent* (2002)

David Waldstreicher, *Slavery's Constitution: From Revolution to Ratification* (2009)

The New Nation

Kenneth R. Bowling and Donald R. Kennon, eds., *Neither Separate Nor Equal: Congress in the 1790s* (2000)

Collin G. Calloway, *Crown and Calumet: British-Indian Relations, 1783–1815* (1987)

Noble E. Cunningham, *Jefferson vs. Hamilton: Confrontations That Shaped a Nation* (2000)

Wilbur Edel, *Kekionga! The Worst Defeat in the History of the U.S. Army* (1997)

Todd Estes, *The Jay Treaty Debate, Public Opinion, and the Evolution of Early American Political Culture* (2006)

Ronald L. Hatzenbuehler, *"I Tremble for My Country": Thomas Jefferson and the Virginia Gentry* (2006)

James Horn et al., eds., *Revolution of 1800: Democracy, Race, and the New Republic* (2002)

Edward S. Kaplan, *The Bank of the United States and the American Economy* (1999)

Peter McNamara, *Political Economy and Statesmanship: Smith, Hamilton, and the Foundation of the Commercial Republic* (1998)

David Andrew Nichols, *Red Gentlemen and White Savages: Indians, Federalists, and the Search for Order on the American Frontier* (2008)

Mark J. Rozell, et al., eds., *George Washington and the Origins of the American Presidency* (2000)

Garrett Ward Sheldon, *The Political Philosophy of James Madison* (2001)

Wiley Sword, *President Washington's Indian War: The Struggle for the Old Northwest, 1790–1795* (1985)

Alan Taylor, *The Divided Ground: Indians, Settlers, and the Northern Borderland of the American Revolution* (2006)

Edward L. Widmer, *Ark of the Liberties: America and the World* (2008)

Eva Sheppard Wolf, *Race and Liberty in the New Nation: Emancipation in Virginia from the Revolution to Nat Turner's Rebellion (2006)*

Federalists and Democratic-Republicans

Bruce Ackerman, *The Failure of the Founding Fathers: Jefferson, Marshall, and the Rise of Presidential Democracy* (2005)

Doron Ben-Atar and Barbara B. Oberg, eds., *Federalists Reconsidered* (1998)

William N. Chambers, *Political Parties in a New Nation: The American Experience, 1776–1809* (1963)

Alexander De Conde, *The Quasi-War: Politics and Diplomacy of the Undeclared War with France, 1797–1801* (1966)

John Ferling, *Adams vs. Jefferson: The Tumultuous Election of 1800* (2004)

Cynthia A. Kierner, *Scandal at Bizarre: Rumor and Reputation in Jefferson's America* (2004)

Andrew Lenner, *The Federal Principle in American Politics, 1790–1833* (2001)

Forrest McDonald, *States' Rights and the Union: Imperium in Imperio, 1776–1876* (2000)

Paul Douglas Newman, *Fries's Rebellion: The Enduring Struggle for the American Revolution* (2004)

Michael A. Palmer, *Stoddert's War: Naval Operations During the Quasi-War with France, 1798–1801* (2000)

James H. Read, *Power versus Liberty: Madison, Hamilton, Wilson, and Jefferson* (2000)

Andrew W. Robertson, *The Language of Democracy: Political Rhetoric in the United States and Britain, 1790–1900* (1995)

James Roger Sharp, *American Politics in the Early Republic: The New Nation in Crisis* (1993)

Darren Staloff, *Hamilton, Adams, Jefferson: The Politics of Enlightenment and the American Founding* (2005)

David Waldsteicher, *In the Midst of Perpetual Fetes: The Making of American Nationalism, 1776–1820* (1997)

Karl-Friedrich Walling, *Republican Empire: Alexander Hamilton on War and Free Government* (1999)

Garry Wills, *Negro President: Jefferson and the Slave Power* (2003)

Robert E. Wright, *The First Wall Street: Chestnut Street, Philadelphia, and the Birth of American Finance* (2005)

"The Rising Glory of America"

Philip Barnard, Mark L. Kamrath, and Stephen Shapiro, eds., *Revising Charles Brockden Brown: Culture, Politics, and Sexuality in the Early Republic* (2004)

Steven Blakemore, *Joel Barlow's Columbiad: A Bicentennial Reading* (2007)

Martha Tomhave Blauvelt, *The Work of the Heart: Young Women and Emotion, 1780–1830* (2007)

R. A. Burchell, ed., *The End of Anglo–America: Historical Essays in the Study of Cultural Divergence* (1991)

Andrew Burstein, *Sentimental Democracy: The Evolution of America's Romantic Self-Image* (1999)

Susan Branson, *These Fiery Frenchified Dames: Women and Political Culture in Early National Philadelphia* (2001)

Joanna Brooks and John Saillant, eds., *"Face Zion Forward": First Writers of the Black Atlantic, 1785–1798* (2002)

Robert A. Ferguson, *Reading the Early Republic* (2004)

Ellen Fernandez-Sacco, *Spectacular Masculinities: The Museums of Peale, Baker, and Bowen in the Early Republic* (1998)

Catherine O'Donnell Kaplan, *Men of Letters in the Early Republic: Cultivating Forums of Citizenship* (2008)

Mary Kelley, *Learning to Stand and Speak: Women, Education, and Public Life in America's Republic* (2006)

Linda Kerber, *Women of the Republic: Intellect and Ideology in Revolutionary America* (1980)

Jill Lepore, *A Is for American: Letters and Other Characters in the Newly United States* (2002)

Sandra F. VanBurkleo, *"Belonging to the World": Women's Rights and American Constitutional Culture* (2001)

Karen A. Weyler, *Intricate Relations: Sexual and Economic Desire in American Fiction, 1789–1814* (2004)

Biography

Gay Wilson Allen, *St. John de Crèvecoeur: The Life of an American Farmer* (1987)

Aleine Austin, *Matthew Lyon, "New Man" of the Democratic Revolution, 1749–1822* (1981)

Lance Banning, *The Sacred Fire of Liberty: James Madison and the Founding of the Federal Republic* (1995)

R. B. Bernstein, *Thomas Jefferson* (2003)

Richard Brookhiser, *Alexander Hamilton, American* (1999)

Harvey Lewis Carter, *The Life and Times of Little Turtle: First Sagamore of the Wabash* (1987)

Ron Chernow, *Alexander Hamilton* (2004)

Helen A. Cooper, *John Trumbull: The Hand and Spirit of a Painter* (1982)

John Patrick Diggins, *John Adams* (2003)

Dorinda Evans, *The Genius of Gilbert Stuart* (1999)

Roger G. Kennedy, *Burr, Hamilton, and Jefferson: A Study in Character* (2000)

James Haw, *John and Edward Rutledge of South Carolina* (1997)

Don Higginbotham, *George Washington: Uniting a Nation* (2002)

Lawrence S. Kaplan, *Alexander Hamilton: Ambivalent Anglophile* (2002)

Stephen F. Knott, *Alexander Hamilton and the Persistence of Myth* (2002)

David McCullough, *John Adams* (2001)

Marty D. Matthews, *Forgotten Founder: The Life and Times of Charles Pinckney* (2004)

David Micklethwait, *Noah Webster and the American Dictionary* (2000)

Jules David Prown, *John Singleton Copley* (1966)

William M. S. Rasmussen and Robert S. Tilton, *George Washington: The Man Behind the Myths* (1999)

Sheila L. Skemp, *Judith Sargent Murray: A Brief Biography with Documents* (1998)

K. Alan Synder, *Defining Noah Webster: Mind and Morals in the Early Republic* (1990)

Harlow G. Unger, *Noah Webster: The Life and Times of an American Patriot* (1998)

Wil Verhoeven, *Gilbert Imlay: Citizen of the World* (2008)

David C. Ward, *Charles Willson Peale: Art and Selfhood in the Early Republic* (2004)

Garry Wills, *James Madison* (2002)

Mason Locke Weems, *The Life of Washington,* ed. Marcus Cunliffe (1962)

CHAPTER 9

North American Communities from Coast to Coast

James Gibson, *Imperial Russia in Frontier America* (1976)

Marcel Giraud, *A History of French Louisiana, 1698–1715* (1974)

Barbara Sweetland Smith and Redmond Barnett, eds., *Russian America* (1990)

David Weber, *The Spanish Frontier in North America* (1993)

The National Economy

W. Eliot Brownlee, *Dynamics of Ascent: A History of the American Economy* (1979)

Stuart Bruchey, *The Roots of American Economic Growth, 1607–1861* (1965)

Curtis P. Nettels, *The Emergence of a National Economy, 1775–1815* (1962)

Douglass C. North, *The Economic Growth of the United States, 1790–1860* (1966)

The Jefferson Presidency

Henry Adams, *The United States in 1800* (1955)

Catharine Allgor, *Parlor Politics: In Which the Ladies of Washington Help Build a City and a Government* (2000)

Catharine Allgor, *Parlor Politics: In Which the Ladies of Washington Help Build a City and a Government* (2000)

Stephen E. Ambrose, *Undaunted Courage: Meriwether Lewis, Thomas Jefferson, and the Opening of the American West* (1996)

Robert Lowry Clinton, *Marbury v. Madison and Judicial Review* (1989)

Noble E. Cunningham, *The Jeffersonian Republicans and Power: Party Operations, 1801–1809* (1963)

George Drago, *Jefferson's Louisiana: Politics and the Clash of Legal Traditions* (1975)

Joseph J. Ellis, *American Sphinx: The Character of Thomas Jefferson* (1998)

James Horn, Jan Ellen Lewis, and Peter S. Onuf, eds., *The Revolution of 1800: Democracy, Race and the New Republic* (2002)

Jon Kukla, *A Wilderness So Immense: The Louisiana Purchase and the Destiny of America* (2003)

Frank Lambert, *The Barbary Wars: American Independence in the Atlantic World* (2005)

Larry E. Morris, *The Fate of the Corps: What Became of the Lewis and Clark Explorers After the Expedition* (2004)

Peter S. Onuf., *Jefferson's Empire* (2000)

James Ronda, *Lewis and Clark among the Indians* (1984)

Burton Spivak, *Jefferson's English Crisis: Commerce, Embargo, and the Republican Revolution* (1979)

Robert W. Tucker and David Hendrickson, *Empire of Liberty: The Statecraft of Thomas Jefferson* (1990)

G. Edward White, *The Marshall Court and Cultural Change, 1815–1835,* abridged ed. (1991)

James S. Young, *The Washington Community, 1800–1828* (1966)

Renewed Imperial Rivalry in North America

Henry Warner Bowden, *American Indians and Christian Missions: Studies in Cultural Conflict* (1981)

Gregory Evans Dowd, *A Spirited Resistance: The North American Indian Struggle for Unity, 1745–1815*

R. David Edmunds, *Tecumseh and the Quest for Indian Leadership* (1984)

Donald Hickey, *The War of 1812: A Forgotten Conflict* (1989)

Reginald Horsman, *Expansion and American Indian Policy, 1783–1812* (1967)

Drew R. McCoy, *The Last of the Fathers: James Madison and the Republican Legacy* (1989)

Francis Paul Prucha, *The Great Father: The United States Government and the American Indians,* 2 vols. (1984)

Ian W. Toll, *Six Frigates: The Epic History of the Founding of the U.S. Navy* (2006)

Defining the Boundaries

John Boles, *Religion in Antebellum Kentucky* (1976)

Andrew Cayton, *The Frontier Republic: Ideology and Politics in the Ohio Country, 1789–1812* (1986)

———, *Frontier Indiana* (1996)

George Dangerfield, *The Era of Good Feelings* (1952)

John Mack Faragher, *Sugar Creek* (1987)

Anita Shafer Goodstein, *Nashville, 1780–1860: From Frontier to City* (1989)

John Craig Hammond, *Slavery, Freedom and Expansion in the Early American West* (2007)

Christine Leigh Heyrman, *Southern Cross: The Beginnings of the Bible Belt* (1997)

Walter LaFeber, ed., *John Quincy Adams and the American Continental Empire* (1965)

Walter Nugent, *Habits of Empire: A History of American Expansion* (2008)

Malcolm J. Rohrbough, *The Land Office Business* (1968)

———, *The Trans-Appalachian Frontier: Peoples, Societies, and Institutions, 1775–1850* (1978)

C. Edward Skeen, *1816: America Rising* (2003)

Richard Slotkin, *Regeneration through Violence: The Mythology of the American Frontier* (1973)

Richard C. Wade, *The Urban Frontier: The Rise of Western Cities, 1790–1850* (1973)

CHAPTER 10

King Cotton and Southern Expansion

Bruce Levine, *Half Slave and Half Free: The Roots of Civil War* (1992)

Daniel S. Dupre, *Transforming the Cotton Frontier, Madison County, Alabama, 1800–1840* (1997)

Robert W. Fogel and Stanley Engerman, *Time on the Cross: The Economics of American Negro Slavery* (1974)

Robert Gudmestad, *A Troublesome Commerce: The Transformation of the Interstate Slave Trade* (2002)

Joseph P. Reidy, *From Slavery to Agrarian Capitalism in the Cotton Plantation South: Central Georgia, 1800–1880* (1992)

Adam Rothman, *Slave Country: American Expansion and the Origins of the Deep South* (2005)

Michael Tadman, *Speculators and Slaves: Masters, Traders, and Slaves in the South South* (1989)

Gavin Wright, *The Political Economy of the Cotton South: Households, Markets, and Wealth in the Nineteenth Century* (1978)

Slavery and African American Communities

Ira Berlin and Philip D. Morgan, eds., *Cultivation and Culture: Labor and the Shaping of Slave Life in the Americas* (1993)

John Blassingame, *The Slave Community,* rev. ed. (1979)

Thomas C. Buchanan, *Black Life on the Mississippi: Slaves, Free Blacks, and the Western Steamboat World* (2004)

Stephanie Camp, *Closer to Freedom: Enslaved Women and Everyday Resistance in the Plantation South* (2004)

Randolph B. Campbell, *An Empire for Slavery: The Peculiar Institution in Texas, 1821–1865* (1989)

Charles B. Dew, *Bond of Iron: Master and Slave at Buffalo Forge* (1994)

Douglas Egerton, *Gabriel's Rebellion: The Virginia Slave Conspiracies of 1800 and 1802* (1993)

Barbara Field, *Slavery on the Middle Ground: Maryland during the Nineteenth Century* (1985)

Eugene D. Genovese, *From Rebellion to Revolution: Afro-American Slave Revolts in the Making of the Modern World* (1979)

Jean M. Humez, *Harriet Tubman: The Life and Life Stories* (2003)

Walter Johnson, *Soul By Soul: Inside the Antebellum Slave Market* (1999)

Charles Joyner, *Down by the Riverside: A South Carolina Slave Community* (1984)

Lawrence W. Levine, *Black Culture and Black Consciousness: Afro-American Folk Thought from Slavery to Freedom* (1977)

Ann Patton Malone, *Sweet Chariot: Slave Family and Household Structure in Nineteenth-Century Louisiana* (1992)

Dylan Penningroth, *The Claims of Kinfolk: African American Property and Community in the Nineteenth Century South* (2003)

Albert Raboteau, *Slave Religion: The "Invisible Institution" in the Antebellum South* (1978)

Marie Jenkins Schwartz, *Born in Bondage: Growing Up Enslaved in the Antebellum South* (2001)

Marie Jenkins Schwartz, *Birthing a Slave: Motherhood and Medicine in the Antebellum South* (2006)

Kenneth Stampp, *The Peculiar Institution* (1956)

Brenda Stevenson, *Life in Black and White: Family and Community in the Slave South* (1996)

Sterling Stuckey, *Slave Culture: Nationalist Theory and the Foundation of Black America* (1987)

Richard C. Wade, *Slavery in the Cities: The South 1820–1860* (1964)

Deborah Gray White, *Arn't I a Woman?* (1985)

Yeomen, Planters, and the Defense of Slavery

David T. Bailey, *Shadow on the Church: Southwestern Evangelical Religion and the Issue of Slavery, 1783–1860* (1985)

Charles C. Bolton, *Poor Whites of the Antebellum South: Tenants and Laborers in Central North and Northern Mississippi* (1994)

F. N. Boney, *Southerners All* (1990)

Bill Cecil-Fronsman, *Common White: Class and Culture in Antebellum North Carolina* (1992)

Erskine Clarke, *Dwelling Place: A Plantation Epic* (2005)

William J. Cooper, *The South and the Politics of Slavery, 1829–1856* (1978)

Clement Eaton, *The Freedom of Thought Struggle in the Old South* (1964)

Drew Gilpin Faust, ed., *The Ideology of Slavery: Proslavery Thought in the Antebellum South, 1830–1860* (1981)

———, *James Henry Hammond and the Old South* (1982)

Lacy K. Ford, Jr., *Origins of Southern Radicalism: The South Carolina Upcountry, 1800–1860* (1988)

Elizabeth Fox-Genovese, *Within the Plantation Household* (1988)

Jean Friedman, *The Enclosed Garden: Women and Community in the Evangelical South, 1830–1900* (1985)

Annette Gordon-Reed, *The Hemingses of Monticello: An American Family* (2008)

J. William Harris, *Plain Folk and Gentry in a Slave Society: White Liberty and Black Slavery in Augusta's Hinterlands* (1985)

Donald P. McNeilly, *The Old South Frontier: Cotton Plantations and the Formation of Arkansas Society, 1819–1861* (2000)

Christopher Morris, *Becoming Southern: The Evolution of a Way of Life, Warren County and Vicksburg, Mississippi, 1770–1860* (1995)

Michael O'Brien, *Conjectures of Order: Intellectual Life and the American South* (2004)

Joshua Rothman, *Notorious in the Neighborhood: Sex and Families Across the Color Line in Virginia, 1787–1861* (2003)

Michael Wayne, *Death of an Overseer* (2001)

Jonathan Daniel Wells, *The Origins of the Southern Middle Class, 1800–1861* (2004)

Bertram Wyatt-Brown, *Southern Honor: Ethics and Behavior in the Old South* (1982)

Jeffrey Robert Young, *Domesticating Slavery: The Master Class in Georgia and South Carolina, 1670–1837* (1999)

CHAPTER 11

The New Democratic Politics and Jackson Presidency

Glenn C. Altschuler and Stuart M. Blumin, *Rude Republic: Americans and Their Politics in the Nineteenth Century* (2000)

William L. Anderson, *Cherokee Removal: Before and After* (1991)

Anne M. Boylan, *The Origins of Women's Activism: New York and Boston 1797–1840* (2002)

Steven C. Bullock, *Revolutionary Brotherhood: Freemasonry and the Transformation of the American Social Order, 1730–1840* (1996)

Donald B. Cole, *The Presidency of Andrew Jackson* (2003)

John Ehle, *Trail of Tears* (1988)

Ronald P. Formisano, *The Transformation of Political Culture: Massachusetts Parties, 1790s–1840s* (1983)

William W. Freehling, *Prelude to Civil War* (1966)

John Lauritz Larson, *Internal Improvement: National Public Works and the Promise of Popular Government in the Early United States* (2001)

Lucy Maddox, *Removals: Nineteenth-Century American Literature and the Politics of Indian Affairs* (1991)

Simon Newman, *Parades and the Politics of the Street* (1997)

Arthur M. Schlesinger Jr., *The Age of Jackson* (1945)

John Ward, *Andrew Jackson: Symbol for an Age* (1955)

Chilton Williamson, *American Suffrage: From Property to Democracy, 1760–1860* (1960)

Alan Taylor, *William Cooper's Town: Power and Persuasion on the Frontier of the Early American Republic* (1995)

The Rise of the Whigs and the Second American Party System

Michael Holt, *The Rise and Fall of the American Whig Party* (1999)

Daniel W. Howe, *The Political Culture of the American Whigs* (1980)

Lawrence F. Kohl, *The Politics of Individualism: Parties and the American Character in the Jacksonian Era* (1989)

Richard P. McCormick, *The Second American Party System: Party Formation in the Jacksonian Era* (1966)

Joel H. Sibley, *The Partisan Imperative: The Dynamics of American Politics before the Civil War* (1985)

American Arts and Letters

Richard D. Brown, *Knowledge Is Power: The Diffusion of Information in Early America, 1700–1865* (1989)

Cathy N. Davidson, *Revolution and the Word: The Rise of the Novel in America* (1986)

Nathan O. Hatch, *The Democratization of American Christianity* (1989)

Jean V. Matthews, *Toward A New Society: American Thought and Culture, 1800–1830* (1991)

Barbara Novak, *Nature and Culture: American Landscape Painting 1825–1875* (1982)

Kenneth Silverman, *Lightening Man: The Accursed Life of Samuel F.B. Morse* (2003)

Gwendolyn Wright, *Building the Dream: A Social History of Housing in America* (1981)

CHAPTER 12

The Transportation Revolution

Peter L. Bernstein, *Wedding of the Waters: The Erie Canal and the Making of a Great Nation* (2005)

Clarence Danhof, *Changes in Agriculture: The Northern United States, 1820–1870* (1969)

E. M. Dodd, *American Business Corporations until 1860* (1954)

Albert Fishlow, *American Railroads and the Transformation of the Ante-Bellum Economy* (1965)

Paul W. Gates, *The Farmer's Age: Agriculture. 1815–1860* (1966)

John Denis Haeger, *The Investment Frontier: New York Businessmen and the Economic Development of the Old Northwest* (1981)

Oscar Handlin and Mary Handlin, *Commonwealth: A Study of the Role of Government in the American Economy: Massachusetts, 1774–1861* (1947)

Morton J. Horwitz, *The Transformation of American Law, 1780–1860* (1977)

Karl Raitz, ed., *The National Road* (1995)

Ronald E. Shaw, *Canals for a Nation: The Canal Era in the United States, 1790–1860* (1990)

Carol Sheriff, *The Artificial River: The Erie Canal and the Paradox of Progress, 1817–1862* (1996)

Peter Way, *Common Labour: Workers and the Digging of North American Canals, 1780–1860* (1993)

The Market Revolution

Jeffrey S. Adler, *Yankee Merchants and the Making of the Urban West* (1991)

Ian R. Bartky, *Selling the True Time: Nineteenth-Century Timekeeping in America* (2000)

Martin Bruegel, *Farm, Shop, Landing: The Rise of a Market Society in the Hudson Valley, 1780–1860* (2002)

Thomas C. Cochran, *Frontiers of Change: Early Industrialism in America* (1981)

Robert F. Dalzell Jr., *Enterprising Elite: The Boston Associates and the World They Made* (1987)

Thomas Dublin, *Women at Work: The Transformation of Work and Community in Lowell, Massachusetts, 1826–1860* (1979)

———, *Transforming Women's Work: New England Lives in the Industrial Revolution* (1994)

David Houndshell, *From the American System to Mass Production, 1800–1932* (1984)

David J. Jeremy, *Transatlantic Industrial Revolution: The Diffusion of Textile Technology between Britain and America* (1981)

Paul Johnson, *A Shopkeeper's Millennium: Society and Revivals in Rochester, New York, 1815–1837* (1978)

Bruce Laurie, *Artisans into Workers: Labor in Nineteenth-Century America* (1989)

Walter Licht, *Industrializing America: The Nineteenth Century* (1995)

Merritt R. Smith, *Harpers Ferry Armory and the New Technology* (1977)

Melvyn Stokes and Stephen Conway, eds., *The Market Revolution in America: Social, Political and Religious Expressions 1800–1880* (1996)

Barbara Tucker, *Samuel Slater and the Origins of the American Textile Industry, 1790–1860* (1984)

From Artisan to Worker

Mary H. Blewett, *Men, Women, and Work: Class, Gender, and Protest in the New England Shoe Industry, 1780–1910* (1988)

Paul G. Faler, *Mechanics and Manufacturers in the Early Industrial Revolution: Lynn, Massachusetts* (1981)

Michael H. Glickstein, *Concepts of Free Labor in Antebellum America* (1991)

Joan M. Jensen, *Loosening the Bonds: Mid-Atlantic Farm Women, 1750–1850* (1986)

Bruce Laurie, *Working People of Philadelphia, 1800–1850* (1980)

W. J. Rorabaugh, *The Craft Apprentice: From Franklin to the Machine Age in America* (1986)

A New Social Order

Stuart M. Blumin, *The Emergence of the Middle Class: Social Experience in the American City* (1989)

Jeanne Boydston, *Home and Work* (1990)

Janet Farrell Brodie, *Contraception and Abortion in Nineteenth-Century America* (1994)

Nancy E. Cott, *The Bonds of Womanhood: "Woman's Sphere" in New England, 1780–1835* (1977)

Anthony F. C. Wallace, *Rockdale: The Growth of an American Village in the Early Industrial Revolution* (1977)

Middle-Class Culture

Barbara A. Bardes and Suzanne Gossett, *Declarations of Independence: Women and Political Power in Nineteenth-Century American Fiction* (1990)

Karen Halttunen, *Confidence Men and Painted Women: A Study of Middle-Class Culture in America* (1982)

John F. Kasson, *Rudeness and Civility: Manners in Nineteenth-Century America* (1990)

Walter Benn Michaels and Donald E. Pease, eds., *The American Renaissance Reconsidered* (1985)

Lewis Perry, *Intellectual Life in America* (1984)

Ann Rose, *Transcendentalism as a Social Movement* (1981)

Steven J. Ross, *Workers on the Edge: Work, Leisure and Politics in Industrializing Cincinnati, 1788–1890* (1985)

Richard Teichgraeber III, *Sublime Thoughts/Penny Wisdom: Situating Emerson and Thoreau in the American Market* (1995)

Jane Tompkins, *Sensational Designs: The Cultural World of American Fiction, 1790–1860* (1986)

CHAPTER 13

Immigration and Ethnicity

Oscar Handlin, *The Uprooted* (1951; 2nd ed. 1973)

Noel Ignatiev, *How the Irish Became White* (1995)

Kerby A. Miller, *Emigrants and Exiles: Ireland and the Irish Exodus to North America* (1985)

Stanley Nadel, *Little Germany: Ethnicity, Religion, and Class in New York City, 1845–1880* (1990)

David Roediger, *The Wages of Whiteness* (1991)

Dennis P. Ryan, *Beyond the Ballot Box: A Social History of the Boston Irish, 1845–1917* (1989)

Urban America

Oliver E. Allen, *The Tiger: The Rise and Fall of Tammany Hall* (1995)

W. Jeffrey Bolster, *Black Jacks: African American Seamen in the Age of Sail* (1997)

Paul Boyer, *Urban Masses and the Moral Order in America, 1820–1920* (1978)

Amy Bridges, *A City in the Republic: Antebellum New York and the Origins of Machine Politics* (1984)

John Duffy, *The Sanitarians* (1990)

Paul A. Gilje, *The Road to Mobocracy: Popular Disorder in New York City, 1763–1834* (1987)

David Grimsted, *American Mobbing, 1828–1865: Toward Civil War* (1998)

Herbert G. Gutman, *Work, Culture, and Society in Industrializing America: Essays in American Working-Class History* (1976)

James Oliver Horton, *Free People of Color: Inside the African American Community* (1993)

Gerard T. Koeppel, *Water for Gotham* (2000)

W.T. Lhaman, Jr., *Jump Jim Crow* (2003)

Gary B. Nash, *Forging Freedom: Philadelphia's Black Community, 1720–1840* (1988)

Benjamin Reiss, *The Showman and the Slave: Race, Death and Memory in Barnum's America* (2001)

Charles E. Rosenberg, *The Cholera Years* (1962)

Dennis C. Rousey, *Policing the Southern City, New Orleans 1805–1889* (1997)

Sam Bass Warner, *The Private City: Philadelphia in Three Periods of Its Growth* (1968)

Religion, Reform, and Utopianism

Arthur Bestor, *Backwoods Utopias* (1950)

Richard Lyman Bushman, *Joseph Smith: Rough Stone Rolling* (2006)

Lawrence Cremin, *American Education: The National Experience, 1783–1861*

Whitney R. Cross, *The Burned-Over District: The Social and Intellectual History of Enthusiastic Religion in Western New York, 1800–1850* (1950)

Barbara Epstein, *The Politics of Domesticity: Women, Evangelism, and Temperance in Nineteenth Century America* (1981)

Lori D. Ginzberg, *Women and the Work of Benevolence: Morality, Politics, and Class in the Nineteenth-Century United States* (1990)

Carl F. Kaestle, *Pillars of the Republic: Common Schools and American Society, 1780–1860* (1983)

W. J. Rorabaugh, *The Alcoholic Republic: An American Tradition* (1979)

David Rothman, *The Discovery of the Asylum: Social Order and Disorder in the New Republic* (1971)

Abolitionism

Fergus M. Bordewich, *Bound for Canaan: The Underground Railroad and the War for the Soul of America* (2005)

Eric Burin, *Slavery and the Peculiar Solution: A History of the American Colonization Society* (2005)

David Brion Davis, *The Problem of Slavery in the Age of Revolution, 1770–1823* (1975)

Frederick Douglass, *The Narrative of the Life of Frederick Douglass, An American Slave* (1845)

Peter P. Hinks, *To Awaken My Afflicted Brethren: David Walker and the Problem of Antebellum Slave Resistance* (1997)

Howard Jones, *Mutiny on the* Amistad (1987)

Jean Fagan Yellin, *Women and Sisters: The Antislavery Feminists in American Culture* (1989)

Women's Rights

Ellen C. DuBois, *Feminism and Suffrage: The Emergence of an Independent Women's Movement in America, 1848–1869* (1978)

Phillip B. Kunhardt, Jr., et al., *P.T. Barnum, America's Greatest Showman* (1995)

Gerda Lerner, *The Grimké Sisters from South Carolina: Pioneers for Women's Rights and Abolition* (1967)

Nancy Lusignan Schultz, *Fire and Roses* (2000)

Kathryn Sklar, *Catharine Beecher: A Study in American Domesticity* (1973)

Sandra S. Weber, *Special History Study, Women's Rights National Historical Park, Seneca Falls, New York* (1985)

Margaret Washington, *Sojourner Truth's America* (2009)

CHAPTER 14

Exploration and Expansion

Jennifer S. H. Brown, *Strangers in Blood: Fur Trade Company Families in Indian Country* (1980)

William H. Goetzmann, *Army Exploration in the American West, 1803–1863* (1959)

William H. Goetzmann and William N. Goetzmann, *The West of the Imagination* (1986)

Norman A. Graebner, *Empire on the Pacific: A Study in American Continental Expansion* (1955)

LeRoy R. Hafen, ed., *The Mountain Men and the Fur Trade of the Far West*, 10 vols. (1968–72)

Sam W. Haynes, *James Polk and the Expansionist Impulse,* (1997)

Thomas R. Hietala, *Manifest Design: Anxious Aggrandizement in Late Jacksonian America* (1985)

Reginald Horsman, *Race and Manifest Destiny* (1981)

Theodore J. Karaminski, *Fur Trade and Exploration: Opening of the Far Northwest, 1821–1852* (1983)

Patricia Nelson Limerick, *The Legacy of Conquest: The Unbroken Past of the Unbroken West* (1987)

Frederick Merk, *Manifest Destiny and Mission in American History: A Reinterpretation* (1963)

———, *History of the Westward Movement* (1978)

Dale Morgan, *Jedediah Smith and the Opening of the West* (1982)

Peter Nabakov, ed., *Native American Testimony: An Anthology of Indian and White Relations* (1978)

James P. Ronda, *Astoria and Empire* (1990)

Charles G. Sellers, *James K. Polk: Jacksonian, 1795–1843* (1957)

———, *James K. Polk: Continentalist, 1843–1846* (1966)

Henry Nash Smith, *Virgin Land: The American West as Symbol and Myth* (1950)

Edward H. Spicer, *Cycles of Conquest: The Impact of Spain, Mexico, and the United States on the Indians of the Southwest, 1533–1960* (1981)

Robert A. Trennert, *Alternative to Extinction: Federal Indian Policy and the Beginnings of the Reservation System, 1846–1851* (1975)

Sylvia Van Kirk, *"Many Tender Ties": Women in Fur Trade Society in Western Canada, 1670–1870* (1980)

Albert K. Weinberg, *Manifest Destiny: A Study of Nationalist Expansionism in American History* (1957)

Peter Booth Wiley with Korogi Ichiro, *Yankees in the Land of the Gods: Commodore Perry and the Opening of Japan* (1990)

David J. Wishart, *The Fur Trade of the American West, 1807–1840: A Geographic Synthesis* (1979)

California and Oregon

John W. Caughey, *The California Gold Rush* (1975)

Sucheng Chan, *This Bittersweet Soil: The Chinese in California Agriculture 1860–1910* (1987)

Malcolm Clark Jr., *Eden Seekers: The Settlement of Oregon, 1818–1862* (1981)

Douglas H. Daniels, *Pioneer Urbanites: A Social and Cultural History of Black San Francisco* (1980)

John Mack Faragher, *Women and Men on the Overland Trail* (1979)

James R. Gibson, *Farming the Frontier: The Agricultural Opening of Oregon Country, 1786–1846* (1985)

Ramon Gutierrez and Richard J. Orsi, *Contested Eden: California Before the Gold Rush* (1998)

Albert L. Hurtado, *Indian Survival on the California Frontier* (1988)

Julie Roy Jeffrey, *Frontier Women: Civilizing The West? 1840–1860* (1998)

———, *Converting the West: A Biography of Narcissa Whitman* (1991)

Marquis James, *The Raven: The Story of Sam Houston* (1929)

David Johnson, *Founding the Far West: California, Oregon, and Nevada, 1840–1890* (1992)

Alvin Josephy, *The Nez Percé and the Opening of the Northwest* (1965)

Rodman W. Paul, *California Gold: The Beginning of Mining in the Far West* (1974)

Leonard Pitt, *The Decline of the Californios: A Social History of the Spanish-Speaking Californians, 1846–1890* (1966)

James J. Rawls, *Indians of California: The Changing Image* (1984)

Brian Roberts, *American Alchemy: The California Gold Rush and Middle-Class Culture* (2000)

Malcolm Rohrbough, *Days of Gold: The California Gold Rush and the American Nation* (2001)

Kevin Starr, *Americans and the California Dream, 1850–1915* (1973)

———, and Richard J. Orsei., eds., *Rooted in Barbarous Soil: People, Culture and Community in Gold Rush California* (2000)

John I. Unruh Jr., *The Plains Across: Overland Emigrants and the Trans–Mississippi West, 1840–1860* (1979)

Texas and the Mexican–American War

K. Jack Bauer, *The Mexican War, 1846–1848* (1974)

William C. Binkley, *The Texas Revolution* (1952)

Gene M. Brack, *Mexico Views Manifest Destiny* (1976)

Holly Beachley Brear, *Inherit the Alamo: Myth and Ritual at an American Shrine* (1995)

Donald E. Chipman, *Spanish Texas, 1519–1821* (1992)

Seymour Conner and Odie Faulk, *North America Divided: The Mexican War, 1846–1848* (1971)

Arnoldo De León, *They Called Them Greasers: Anglo Attitudes toward Mexicans in Texas, 1821–1900* (1983)

———, *The Tejano Community 1836–1900* (1982)

John S. D. Eisenhower, *So Far from God: The U.S. War with Mexico 1846–1848* (1989)

Neil Harlow, *California Conquered: War and Peace on the Pacific, 1846–1850* (1982)

Timothy J. Henderson, *A Glorious Defeat: Mexico and Its War with the United States* (2007)

Robert W. Johannsen, *To the Halls of the Montezumas: The Mexican War in the American Imagination* (1985)

Ernest McPherson Lander Jr., *Reluctant Imperialist: Calhoun, South Carolina, and the Mexican War* (1980)

Timothy Matovina, *Tejano Religion and Ethnicity: San Antonio, 1921–1860* (1995)

Frederick Merk, *Slavery and the Annexation of Texas* (1972)

David Montejano, *Anglos and Mexicans in the Making of Texas, 1836–1986* (1987)

Stanley Noyes, *Los Comanches: The Horse People, 1751–1845* (1994)

David Pletcher, *The Diplomacy of Annexation: Texas, Oregon, and the Mexican War* (1973)

Andreas V. Reichstein, *Rise of the Lone Star: The Making of Texas* (1989)

Randy Roberts and James S. Olson, *A Line in the Sand: The Alamo in Blood and Memory* (2001)

Malcolm Rohrbough, *Days of Gold: The California Gold Rush* (1997)

Susan Scholwer, *Alamo Images: Changing Perceptions of a Texas Experience* (1985)

John H. Schroeder, *Mr. Polk's War: American Opposition and Dissent, 1846–1848* (1971)

Otis A. Singletary, *The Mexican War* (1960)

Jésus F. de la Teja, *San Antonio de Béxar: A Community on New Spain's Northern Frontier* (1995)

David J. Weber, *The Mexican Frontier, 1821–1846: The American Southwest under Mexico* (1982)

The Politics of Manifest Destiny

Chaplain W. Morrison, *Democratic Politics and Sectionalism: The Wilmot Proviso Controversy* (1967)

Michael Morrison, *Slavery and the American West: The Eclipse of Manifest Destiny and the Coming of the Civil War* (1997)

Joseph G. Raybeck, *Free Soil: The Election of 1848* (1970)

Joel H. Sibley, *The Shrine of Party: Congressional Voting Behavior, 1841–1852* (1967)

———, *Storm Over Texas: The Annexation Controversy and the Road to Civil War* (2005)

CHAPTER 15

The Crisis over Slavery

Richard H. Abbott, *Cotton and Capital: Boston Businessmen and Antislavery Reform, 1854–1868* (1991)

Orville Vernon Burton, *The Age of Lincoln* (2007)

Gary Collison, *Shadrach Minkins: From Fugitive Slave to Citizen* (1997)

W. Ehrlich, *They Have No Rights: Dred Scott's Struggle for Freedom* (1979)

Eric Foner, *Free Soil, Free Labor, Free Men: The Ideology of the Republican Party before the Civil War* (1970)

C. C. Goen, *Broken Churches, Broken Nation* (1985)

Thomas F. Grossett, *Uncle Tom's Cabin and American Culture* (1985)

William A. Link, *Roots of Secession: Slavery and Politics in Antebellum Virginia* (2003)

Robert E. May, *Manifest Destiny's Underworld: Filibustering in Antebellum America* (2002)

William Lee Miller, *Arguing About Slavery: The Great Battle in the United States Congress* (1996)

H. Craig Miner and William E. Unrau, *The End of Indian Kansas* (1978)

Stephen Oates, *To Purge This Land with Blood: A Biography of John Brown* (1970)

Leonard L. Richards, *The Slave Power: The Free North and Southern Domination, 1780–1860* (2000)

Anne C. Rose, *Voices of the Marketplace: American Thought and Culture, 1830–1860* (1995)

J. Rossbach, *Ambivalent Conspirators: John Brown, the Secret Six and a Theory of Black Political Violence* (1982)

Thomas P. Slaughter, *Bloody Dawn: The Christiana Riots and Racial Violence in the Antebellum North* (1991)

Kenneth M. Stampp, *America in 1857: A Nation on the Brink* (1990)

John Stauffer, *The Black Hearts of Men: Radical Abolitionists and the Transformation of Race* (2001)

Albert Von Frank, *The Trials of Anthony Burns: Freedom and Slavery in Emerson's Boston* (1998)

Edward L. Widmer, *Young America: The Flowering of Democracy in New York City* (1999)

Gerald W. Wolff, *The Kansas-Nebraska Bill: Party, Section, and the Coming of the Civil War* (1977)

Bertram Wyatt-Brown, *Yankee Saints and Southern Sinners* (1985)

The Crisis of the National Party System

Tyler Anbinder, *Nativism and Slavery: The Northern Know-Nothings and the Politics of the 1850s* (1992)

J. H. Baker, *Affairs of Party: The Political Culture of Northern Democrats in the Mid-Nineteenth Century* (1983)

Robert F. Engs and Randall M. Miller, eds., *The Birth of the Grand Old Party* (2002)

Ronald Formisano, *The Birth of Mass Political Parties: Michigan, 1827–1861* (1971)

William E. Gienapp, *The Origins of the Republican Party, 1852–1856* (1987)

Michael Holt, *The Political Crisis of the 1850s* (1978)

Robert W. Johannsen, *The Lincoln-Douglas Debates* (1965)

John Mayfield, *Rehearsal for Republicanism: Free Soil and the Politics of Antislavery* (1980)

The South Secedes

William. L. Barney, *The Road to Secession* (1972)

William. L. Barney, *The Secessionist Impulse: Alabama and Mississippi in 1860* (1974)

Charles H. Brown, *Agents of Manifest Destiny: The Lives and Times of the Filibusters* (1980)

Steven A. Channing, *Crisis of Fear: Secession in South Carolina* (1970)

William J. Cooper, *The South and the Politics of Slavery* (1978)

Avery O. Craven, *The Growth of Southern Nationalism 1848–1861* (1953)

William W. Freehling, *The Road to Disunion*, Vol. I: *Secessionists at Bay, 1776–1854* (1991)

———, *The Road to Disunion*, Vol II: *Secessionists Triumphant* (2007)

Michael P. Johnson, *Secession and Conservatism in the Lower South: The Social and Ideological Bases of Secession in Georgia, 1860–1861* (1983)

Robert E. May, *The Southern Dream of a Caribbean Empire, 1854–1861* (1973)

John McCardell, *The Idea of a Southern Nation: Southern Nationalists and Southern Nationalism, 1830–1861* (1979)

K. M. Stampp, *And the War Came: The North and the Secession Crisis 1860–1861* (1950)

Joe A. Stout, *The Liberators: Filibustering Expeditions into Mexico, 1848–1862, and the Last Thrust of Manifest Destiny* (1973)

Ronald L. Takaki, *A Proslavery Crusade: The Agitation to Reopen the African Slave Trade* (1971)

J. Mills Thornton, *Politics and Power in a Slavery Society* (1978)

Eric H. Walter, *The Fire-Eaters* (1992)

Elizabeth Varon, *Disunion! The Coming of the American Civil War, 1789–1859* (2008)

CHAPTER 16

The Lincoln Presidency and the Northern Home Front

Jeanie Attie, *Patriotic Toil: Northern Women and the American Civil War* (1998)

Edward Ayers, *In the Presence of Mine Enemies: War in the Heart of America, 1859–1863* (2003)

Richard Franklin Bensel, *Yankee Leviathan: The Origins of Central State Authority in America, 1859–1877* (1991)

Joan Cashin, *The War Was You and Me: Civilians in the American Civil War* (2002)

Paul A. Cimbala and Randall M. Miller, *Union Soldiers and the Northern Home Front: Wartime Experiences, Postwar Adjustments* (2002)

George M. Frederickson, *The Inner Civil War: Northern Intellectuals and the Crisis of the Union* (1965)

J. Matthew Gallman, *The North Fights the Civil War: The Home Front* (1994)

Doris Kearns Goodwin, *Team of Rivals: The Political Genius of Abraham Lincoln* (2005)

Frank L. Klement, *The Limits of Dissent: Clement L. Vallandigham and the Civil War* (1970)

Ernest A. McKay, *The Civil War and New York City* (1990)

James M. McPherson, *Abraham Lincoln and the Second American Revolution* (1990)

Mark E. Neely, *The Fate of Liberty: Abraham Lincoln and Civil Liberties* (1991)

Thomas H. O'Connor, *Civil War Boston: Homefront and Battlefield* (1997)

Phillip Shaw Paludan, *The Presidency of Abraham Lincoln* (1994)

———, *"A People's Contest": The Union at War, 1861–1865* (1988)

Heather Cox Richardson, *The Greatest Nation of the Earth: Republican Economic Policies during the Civil War* (1997)

Anne C. Rose, *Victorian America and the Civil War* (1992)

Joel Sibley, *A Respectable Minority: The Democratic Party in the Civil War Era, 1860–1868* (1977)

Lyde Cullen Sizer, *The Political Work of Northern Women Writers and the Civil War* (2000)

Jennifer L. Weber, *Copperheads: The Rise and Fall of Lincoln's Opponents in the North* (2006)

Bell I. Wiley, *The Life of Johnny Reb* (1943)

———, *The Life of Billy Yank* (1952)

The Death of Slavery

Ira Berlin et al. eds., *Freedom, A Documentary History of Emancipation, 1861–1867,* Series 1, Volume I: *The Destruction of Slavery* (1985)

———, eds., *Freedom, A Documentary History of Emancipation, 1861–1867,* Series 1, Volume II: *The Wartime Genesis of Free Labor: The Upper South* (1993)

———, eds. *Freedom, A Documentary History of Emancipation, 1861–1867,* Series 1, Volume III: *The Wartime Genesis of Free Labor: The Lower South* (1990)

———, eds. *Freedom, A Documentary History of Emancipation, 1861–1867,* Series 2: *The Black Military Experience* (1988)

John Hope Franklin, *The Emancipation Proclamation* (1963)

Willie Lee Rose, *Rehearsal for Reconstruction: The Port Royal Experiment* (1964)

The Confederacy and the Southern Home Front

Steven V. Ash, *When the Yankees Came: Conflict and Chaos in the Occupied South 1861–1865* (1995)

William Blair, *Virginia's Private War: Feeding Body and Soul in the Confederacy, 1861–1865* (1998)

Joan Cashin, *First Lady of the Confederacy: Varina Davis's Civil War* (2006)

Daniel W. Crofts, *Reluctant Confederates: Upper South Unionists in the Secession Crisis* (1989)

William C. Davis, *"A Government of Our Own": The Making of the Confederacy* (1994)

Wayne K. Durrill, *War of Another Kind: A Southern Community in the Great Rebellion* (1990)

Laura F. Edwards, *Scarlett Doesn't Live Here Anymore: Southern Women in the Civil War Era* (2000)

Drew Gilpin Faust, *The Creation of Confederate Nationalism* (1988)

———, *The Confederate Republic: A Revolution against Politics* (1994)

William W. Freehling, *The South vs. The South: How Anti-Confederate Southerners Shaped the Course of the Civil War*

James L. Roark, *Masters without Slaves: Southern Planters in the Civil War and Reconstruction* (1978)

William Rogers, *Confederate Home Front: Montgomery During the Civil War* (1999)

Jonathan Dean Sarris, *A Separate Civil War: Communities in Conflict in the Mountain South* (2006)

Daniel E. Sutherland, *Seasons of War: The Ordeal of a Confederate Community 1861–1865* (1995)

Frank Towers, *The Urban South and the Coming of the Civil War* (2004)

LeeAnn Whites, *The Civil War as a Crisis in Gender: Augusta, Georgia, 1860–1890* (1995)

David Williams, Teresa Crisp Williams, and David Carlson, *Plain Folk in a Rich Man's War: Class and Dissent in Confederate Georgia* (2002)

The Fighting

Michael Barton, *Good Men: The Character of Civil War Soldiers* (1981)

Ken Burns, *The Civil War* (1990)

Bruce Catton, *A Stillness at Appomattox* (1953)

David Eocher, *The Longest Night* (2001)

Shelby Foote, *The Civil War: A Narrative,* 3 vols. (1958–1974)

Joseph T. Glatthaar, *Forged in Battle: The Civil War Alliance of Black Soldiers and White Officers* (1990)

———, *The March to the Sea and Beyond: Sherman's Troops in the Savannah and Carolinas Campaign* (1985)

Mark Grimsley, *The Hard Hand of War: Union Policy toward Southern Civilians, 1861–1865* (1995)

Edward Hagerman, *The American Civil War and the Origins of Modern Warfare* (1988)

Alvin Josephy, *The Civil War in the West* (1992)

Bruce Levine, *Confederate Emancipation: Southern Plans to Free and Arm Slave During the Civil War* (2006)

Gerald F. Linderman, *Embattled Courage: The Experience of Combat in the American Civil War* (1987)

James M. McPherson, *Battle Cry of Freedom: The Civil War Era* (1988)

———, *The Atlas of the Civil War* (1994)

Edwin S. Redkey, ed., *A Grand Army of Black Men: Letters from African-American Soldiers in the Union Army, 1861–1865* (1992)

Charles Royster, *The Destructive War: William Tecumseh Sherman, Stonewall Jackson, and the Americans* (1991)

John David Smith, ed., *Black Soldiers in Blue: African American Troops in the Civil War Era* (2002)

CHAPTER 17

The Politics of Reconstruction

Richard H. Abbott, *The Republican Party and the South, 1855–1877* (1986)

Bruce E. Baker, *What Reconstruction Meant: Historical Memory in the American South* (2008)

Herman Belz, *Emancipation and Equal Rights* (1978)

Michael Les Benedict, *A Compromise of Principle: Congressional Republicans and Reconstruction* (1974)

————, *The Impeachment and Trial of Andrew Johnson* (1973)

Michael Kent Curtis, *No State Shall Abridge: The Fourteenth Amendment and the Bill of Rights* (1990)

Ellen Carol DuBois, *Feminism and Suffrage* (1978)

Laura F. Edwards, *Gendered Strife & Confusion: The Political Culture of Reconstruction* (1997)

William C. Harris, *With Charity for All: Lincoln and the Restoration of the Union* (1997)

Robert Kaczorowski, *The Politics of Judicial Interpretation: The Federal Courts, Department of Justice, and Civil Rights, 1866–1876* (1985)

James McPherson, *Ordeal by Fire: The Civil War and Reconstruction* (1982)

Michael Perman, *Emancipation and Reconstruction, 1862–1879* (1987)

Brooks D. Simpson, *The Reconstruction Presidents* (1998)

Kenneth M. Stampp, *The Era of Reconstruction, 1865–1877* (1965)

The Meaning of Freedom

Ira Berlin et al., eds., *Freedom: A Documentary History*, 3 vols. (1985–1991)

Paul A Cimbala and Randall M. Miller, eds., *The Freedmen's Bureau and Reconstruction.* (1999)

W. E. B. DuBois, *Black Reconstruction* (1935)

Carol Faulkner, *Women's Radical Reconstruction: The Freedmen's Aid Movement* (2004)

Barbara J. Fields, *Slavery and Freedom on the Middle Ground* (1985)

Eric Foner, *Freedom's Lawmakers: A Directory of Black Officeholders during Reconstruction* (1996)

Noralee Frankel, *Freedom's Women: Black Women and Families in Civil War Era Mississippi* (1999)

Herbert G. Gutman, *The Black Family in Slavery and Freedom* (1976)

Sharon Ann Holt, *Making Freedom Pay: North Carolina Freedpeople Working for Themselves, 1865–1900* (2000)

Richard Hume and Jerry Gough, *Black Carpetbaggers and Scalawags: The Constitutional Conventions of Radical Reconstruction* (2008)

Leon Litwack, *Been in the Storm So Long: The Aftermath of Slavery* (1975)

Lynda J. Morgan, *Emancipation in Virginia's Tobacco Belt* (1992)

Nell Irvin Painter, *Exodusters* (1977)

Howard N. Rabinowitz, *Race Relations in the Urban South, 1865–1890* (1978)

Roger L. Ransom and Richard Sutch, *One Kind of Freedom: The Economic Consequences of Emancipation* (1977)

Edward Royce, *The Origins of Southern Sharecropping* (1993)

Leslie A. Schwalm, *A Hard Fight for We: Women's Transition from Slavery to Freedom in South Carolina* (1997)

Southern Politics and Society

James A. Baggett, *The Scalawags: Southern Dissenters in the Civil War and Reconstruction* (2003)

Nancy Bercaw, *Gendered Freedoms: Race, Rights, and the Politics of the Household in the Delta, 1861–1875* (2003)

Pamela Brandwein, *Reconstructing Reconstruction: The Supreme Court and the Production of Historical Truth* (1999)

Charles W. Calhoun, *Conceiving a New Republic: The Republican Party and the Southern Question, 1869–1900* (2006)

Dan T. Carter, *When the War Was Over: The Failure of Self Reconstruction in the South, 1865–1877* (1985)

Richard N. Current, *Those Terrible Carpetbaggers* (1988)

Michael W. Fitzgerald, *The Union League Movement in the Deep South* (1989)

Stephen Hahn, *The Roots of Southern Populism* (1983)

Sally McMillen, *To Raise Up the South: Sunday Schools in Black and White Churches, 1865–1915* (2001)

Scott Reynolds Nelson, *Iron Confederacies: Southern Railroads, Klan Violence, and Reconstruction* (1999)

Michael S. Perman, *The Road to Redemption: Southern Politics, 1868–1979* (1984)

Daniel W. Stowell, *Rebuilding Zion: The Religious Reconstruction of the South, 1863–1877* (1998)

Allen W. Trelease, *White Terror: The Ku Klux Klan Conspiracy and Southern Reconstruction* (1971)

Richard Valelly, *The Two Reconstructions: The Struggle for Black Enfranchisement* (2004)

Jonathan M. Wiener, *Social Origins of the New South* (1978)

Reconstructing the North

Stephen Buechler, *The Transformation of the Woman Suffrage Movement* (1986)

Morton Keller, *Affairs of State* (1977)

David Montgomery, *Beyond Equality: Labor and the Radical Republicans, 1862–1872* (1967)

Keith I. Polakoff, *The Politics of Inertia: The Election of 1876 and the End of Reconstruction* (1973)

Heather Cox Richardson, *The Death of Reconstruction: Race, Labor, and Politics in the Post Civil War North, 1865–1901* (2001)

————, *West From Appomattox: The Reconstruction of America After the Civil War* (2007)

Andrew Slap, *The Doom of Reconstruction: The Liberal Republicans in the Civil War Era* (2006)

Amy Dru Stanley, *From Bondage to Contract: Wage Labor, Marriage, and the Market in the Age of Slave Emancipation* (1998)

Mark W. Summers, *Railroads, Reconstruction, and the Gospel of Prosperity* (1984)

———, *The Era of Good Stealings* (1993)

Xi Wang, *The Trial of Democracy: Black Suffrage and Northern Republicans, 1860–1910* (1997)

C. Vann Woodward, *Reunion and Reaction: The Compromise of 1877 and the End of Reconstruction* (1956)

Biography

Kenneth D. Ackerman, *Boss Tweed* (2005)

Philip Dray, *Capitol Men: The Epic Story of Reconstruction Through the Lives of the First Black Congressmen* (2008)

Stephen Kantrowitz, *Ben Tillman and the Reconstruction of White Supremacy* (2000)

William S. McFeely, *Frederick Douglass* (1989)

———, *Grant: A Biography* (1981)

———, *Yankee Stepfather: General O. O. Howard and the Freedmen* (1968)

Hans L. Trefousse, *Andrew Johnson* (1989)

———, *Thaddeus Stevens: Nineteenth Century Egalitarian* (1997)

CREDITS

Text, Tables, Maps and Figures

Chapter 1 **Page 12:** "Corn Mother" from AMERICAN INDIAN MYTHS AND LEGENDS by Richard Erdoes and Alfonso Ortiz, copyright © 1984 by Richard Erdoes and Alfonso Ortiz. Used by permission of Pantheon Books, a division of Random House, Inc.

Chapter 4 **Figure 4.1:** From *Voyages: The Trans-Atlantic Slave Trade Database*. http://www.slavevoyages.org (accessed 2010). **Figure 4.2:** From *Time on the Cross: The Economics of American Negro Slavery*, by Robert William Fogel and Stanley L. Engerman. Copyright © 1974 by Robert William Fogel and Stanley L. Engerman. Used by permission of W. W. Norton & Company, Inc. **Figure 4.3:** From *Shipping, Maritime Trade and the Economic Development of Colonial America*, James J. Shepherd, and Gary M. Walton, Eds. Copyright © 1972 Cambridge University Press. Reprinted with the permission of Cambridge University Press **Page 84:** William Snelgrave, *A New Account of Some Parts of Guinea, and the Slave Trade* (1734). **Page 85:** Olaudah Equiano, *The Interesting Narrative of the Life of Olaudah Equiano, or Gus-tavus Vassa, the African, Written by Himself* (1789).

Chapter 5 **Figure 5.1:** *Historical Statistics of the United States* (Washington, DC: Government Printing Office, 1976), 1168. **Figure 5.2:** From "The European Ancestry of the United States Population," by Thomas L. Purvis. *William and Mary Quarterly* 61 (1984): 85–101. Reprinted by permission of the William and Mary Quarterly. **Figure 5.3:** From "The Distribution of Wealth in Eighteenth-Century America," by James Lemon and Gary Nash. *Journal of Social History* 2 (1968):1–24. Reprinted by permission of the George Mason University Press.

Chapter 8 **Figure 8.1:** From "How Much Is That in Real Money?" *Proceedings of the American Antiquarian Society*, N.S. 102 (1992): 297–359. Copyright © 1992 American Antiquarian Society. Courtesy of American Antiquarian Society. Used by permission.

Chapter 9 **Figure 9.2:** From Riegel, R., AMERICA MOVES WEST 5th Edition. © 1971 Wadsworth, a part of Cengage Learning, Inc. Reproduced by permission. www.cengage.com/permissions.

Chapter 10 **Figure 10.1:** From *Atlas of Antebellum Southern Agriculture*, by Sam B. Hilliard. (Baton Rouge: Louisiana State University Press, 1984), pp. 67–71. Copyright © 1984 Louisiana State University Press. Reprinted by permission. **Map 10.2:** From *Atlas of Antebellum Southern Agriculture*, by Sam B. Hilliard. (Baton Rouge: Louisiana State University Press, 1984), pp. 67–71. Copyright © 1984 Louisiana State University Press. Reprinted by permission. **Map 10.3:** From *Historical Atlas of the United States* (Washington, DC: National Geographic Society, 1988). Copyright © 1988 National Geographic Society. Reprinted by permission.

Chapter 11 **Figure 11.1:** From *The Right to Vote*, by Alexander Keyssar. Copyright © 2009 Alexander Keyssar. Reprinted by permission of Basic Books, a member of the Perseus Books Group.

Chapter 12 **Figure 12.1:** Reprinted from Thomas Dublin, *Transforming Women's Work: New England Lives in the Industrial Revolution*. Copyright © 1994 by Thomas Dublin. Used by permission of the Publisher, Cornell University Press.

Chapter 13 **Figure 13.2:** From *Immigrant Life in New York City, 1825–1863* by Robert Ernst. Copyright 1994 by Syracuse University Press. Reprinted by permission. **Map 13.2:** Reprinted from Whitney R. Cross, *The Burned-Over District: The Social and Intellectual History of Enthusiastic Religion in Western New York, 1800–1850*. Copyright © 1950 by Cornell University. Used with permission of the publisher, Cornell University Press.

Chapter 14 **Figure 14.1:** From *The Plains Across: The Overland Emigrants and the Trans-Mississippi West, 1840–60*. Copyright 1979 by Board of Trustees of the University of Illinois. Used with permission of the University of Illinois Press.

Chapter 16 **Figure 16.1:** From *The Times Atlas of World History*. Copyright © 1978, Hammond. Reprinted by permission of the publisher.

Chapter 17 **Page 480:** Reprinted with permission from the Alabama Department of Archives and History, Montgomery, Alabama **Page 481:** "Affairs in Insurrectionary States: Report and Minority Reviews, Alabama, vol. 2," *Senate Reports*, 42nd Congress, 2nd Session, vol. 2, pt. 9, no. 41.

Photos

Chapter 1 **Chapter Opener:** Cahokia Mounds State Historic Site, painting by Michael Hampshire. **Page 5:** James Chatters/Agence France Presse/Getty Images **Page 7:** © Warren Morgan/CORBIS All Rights Reserved **Page 9:** Courtesy of the Denver Museum of Nature and Science **Page 12:** Image #1739-3, courtesy the Library, American Museum of Natural History. **Page 13:** Mimbres black on white bowl, with painted representations of man and woman under a blanket. Grant County, New Mexico. Diam. 26.7 cm. Courtesy National Museum of the American Indian, Smithsonian Institution, 24/3198 **Page 14:** David Muench/CORBIS- NY **Page 15:** © Tony Linck/SuperStock **Page 16:** "Nursing Mother Effigy Bottle." From the Whelpley Collection at the St. Louis Science Center. Photograph © 1985 the Detroit Institute of Arts/The Bridgeman Art Library, NY **Page 18:** Bayerische Staatsbibliothek Munchen...Rar. 5k. **Page 21:** Neg. No. 324281, Photographed by Rota, Engraving by DeBry. American Museum of Natural History Library. **Page 22:** Courtesy of the Library of Congress **Page 23:** Ashmolean Museum, Oxford, England, U.K.

Chapter 2 **Chapter Opener:** The French, under the command of Jean Ribault, discover the River of May (St Johns River) in Florida on 1 May 1562: colored engraving, 1591, by Theodor de Bry after a now lost drawing by Jacques Le Moyne de Morgues. The Granger Collection. **Page 30:** October, from Tres Riches Heures du Duc de Berry. Musee Conde, Chantilly/Bridgeman-Giraudon, Art Resource, NY **Page 32:** © National Maritime Museum Picture Library, London, England. Neg. #E5555-3 **Page 33:** Beinecke Rare Book and Manuscript Library, Yale University **Page 34:** The Granger Collection **Page 36:** Beinecke Rare Book and Manuscript Library, Yale University **Page 37:** De Bry engraving of Spanish attack on native village **Page 42:** Beinecke Rare Book and Manuscript Library, Yale University **Page 43:** Olive and Arthur Kelsall/Nova Scotia Museum **Page 44:** Jacques Le Moyne, "Rene de Loudonniere and Chief Athore," 1564. Gouache and metallic pigments on vellum. Print Collection, The New York Public Library, New York. The New York Public Library/Art Resource, NY **Page 45:** "Elizabeth I", Armada portrait, c. 1588 (oil on panel) by English School (C16th) Private Collection/The Bridgeman Art Library, London/New York.

Chapter 3 **Chapter Opener:** Beinecke Rare Book and Manuscript Library, Yale University **Page 53:** Lowell Georgia/CORBIS- NY **Page 55:** Library of Congress **Page 57:** Courtesy of the Library of Congress **Page 58:** From Samuel de Champlain, Les Voyages, Paris, 1613. Illustration opp. pg. 232. Rare Books Division, The New York Public Library, Astor Lenox and Tilden Foundations. The New York Public Library/Art Resource, NY **Page 59 (top):** Beinecke Rare Book and Manuscript Library, Yale University **Page 59 (bottom):** The Granger Collection **Page 62:** Courtesy, American Antiquarian Society **Page 63:** Courtesy of The John Carter Brown Library, at Brown University. **Page 66:** The Freake-Gibbs Painter (American, Active 1670), "David, Joanna, and Abigail Mason," 1670. Oil on canvas, 39 ½ × 42 ½ in.; Frame: 42 ¾ × 45 ½ × 1 ½ in. Fine Arts Museums of San Francisco, Gift of Mr. and Mrs. John D. Rockefeller 3rd to The Fine Arts Museums of San Francisco, 1979.7.3 **Page 68 (top):** Fort New Amsterdam, New York, 1651. Engraving. Collection of The New-York Historical Society, 77354d **Page 68 (bottom):** Courtesy of The Historical Society of Pennsylvania Collection, Atwater Kent Museum of Philadelphia. **Page 70:** "Courtesy of the Osher Map Library, University of Southern Maine."

Chapter 4 **Chapter Opener:** © Dorling Kindersley, Courtesy of the Wilberforce House Museum, Hull **Page 78:** The Granger Collection **Page 79:** Beinecke Rare Book and Manuscript Library, Yale University **Page 82 (top):** Bibliotheque de L'Arsenal, Paris, France/The Bridgeman Art Library **Page 82 (bottom):** Royal Albert Memorial Museum, Exeter, Devon, UK/Bridgeman Art Library **Page 83:** The Granger Collection, New York **Page 86:** The Granger Collection, New York **Page 88:** Thomas Coram, "View of Mulberry Street, House and Street." Oil on paper, 10 × 17.6 cm. Gibbes Museum of Art/Carolina Art Association. 68.18.01 **Page 90:** John F. Watson, "Annals of Philadelphia," being a collection of memoirs, anecdotes, & incidents of Philadelphia. The London Coffee House. The Library Company of Philadelphia **Page 92:** Abby Aldrich Rockefeller Folk Art Museum, The Colonial Williamsburg Foundation, Williamsburg, VA. **Page 94:** Thomas Moran (American, 1837-1926), "Slave Hunt, Dismal Swamp, Virginia", 1862. Gift of Laura A. Clubb, 1947.8.44. ©2008 The Philbrook Museum of Art, Inc., Tulsa,

Chapter 14 **Chapter Opener:** Scotts Bluff National Monument **Page 366:** Alfred Jacob Miller, "Bourgeois Walker and His Wife," 1837. Watercolor. 37.1940.78. The Walters Art Museum, Baltimore. **Page 371:** Joseph Goldsborough Bruff/Superstock Royalty Free **Page 373:** "Fort Vancouver," artist unknown, ca. 1845–1848. Paul Kane Collection. WA MSS 278. Yale Collection of Western Americana, Beinecke Rare Book and Manuscript Library **Page 375:** Smithsonian American Art Museum, Washington, D.C./Art Resource, NY **Page 378:** Courtesy of the Library of Congress **Page 382:** Richard Caton Woodville, "War News from Mexico," Oil on canvas. Manovgian Foundation on loan to the National Gallery of Art, Washington, DC. © Board of Trustees, National Gallery of Art, Washington. **Page 383:** Frank Marryat, "The Bar of a Gambling Saloon," published 1855. Lithograph. Collection of The New-York Historical Society, New York City. **Page 385:** Courtesy of the California History Room, California State Library, Sacramento, California. **Page 387:** The Granger Collection, New York.

Chapter 15 **Chapter Opener:** Courtesy of the Library of Congress **Page 397:** © Bettmann/CORBIS **Page 400:** Getty Images Inc. - Hulton Archive Photos **Page 401:** [Photographer]/Hulton Archive/Getty Images **Page 402:** Courtesy of the Library of Congress **Page 404:** "The Landing of Commodore Perry in Japan in 1853." (Detail) Japanese, Edo period, 19th century. Handscroll; ink and color on paper, 10 7/8 × 211 1/8 in. (27.6 × 536.3 cm). Museum of Fine Arts, Boston. William Sturgis Bigelow Collection, RES.11.6054. Photograph ©2006 Museum of Fine Arts, Boston. **Page 406:** Kansas State Historical Society **Page 410:** Getty Images - Bambu Productions **Page 413:** ©CORBIS **Page 414:** Museum of the City of New York **Page 415:** The Granger Collection **Page 418:** Getty Images Inc. - Hulton Archive Photos.

Chapter 16 **Chapter Opener:** Homer, Winslow (1836–1910). Prisoners from the Front. 1866. Oil on canvas, 24 × 38 in. (61 × 96.5 cm). Gift of Mrs. Frank B. Por. The Metropolitan Museum of Art, New York, NY, U.S.A. Image copyright © The Metropolitan Museum of Art/Art Resource, NY. **Page 428:** The Granger Collection, New York **Page 429:** George Hayward (American, born England, 1800–1872?), "Departure of the 7th Regiment, N.Y.S.M., April 19, 1861," April 19, 1861. Graphite pencil, transparent and opaque watercolor on paper, Sheet: 36.7 × 51.3 cm (14 7/16 × 20 3/16 in.). Museum of Fine Arts, Boston, M. and M. Karolik Collection of American Watercolors and Drawings, 1800–1875, 51.2785. Photograph © 2006 Museum of Fine Arts, Boston. **Page 432:** CORBIS- NY **Page 434:** William Washington, "Stonewall Jackson Entering the City of Winchester, Virginia." Oil painting. Valentine Museum Library, Richmond, Virginia. **Page 435 (left):** Cook Collection. Valentine Museum Library/Richmond History Center **Page 435 (right)** **Page 441:** Courtesy of The Library of Congress **Page 445:** Center of Military History, U.S. Army **Page 448:** Culver Pictures, Inc. **Page 451:** Courtesy of the Library of Congress **Page 453:** Harper's Weekly, March 18, 1865. Courtesy of William C. Hine. **Page 454:** Library of Congress.

Chapter 17 **Chapter Opener:** Theodor Kaufmann (1814–1896), *On to Liberty*, 1867. Oil on canvas, 36 × 56 in (91.4 × 142.2 cm). Runaway slaves escaping through the woods. Art Resource/Metropolitan Museum of Art. **Page 462:** The Granger Collection, New York. **Page 463:** CORBIS- NY **Page 465:** Library of Congress **Page 467:** Courtesy of the Library of Congress **Page 468:** The Granger Collection, New York. **Page 471:** The Granger Collection **Page 475:** The Granger Collection, New York. **Page 477:** From The Henry Clay Warmoth Papers # 752, Southern Historical Collection, Wilson Library, University of North Carolina at Chapel Hill.

INDEX

Hutchinson, Thomas, 145, 149, 169–170
Hylton v. United States, 203

I

Ice Age, 6, 7
Immigrants/immigration
 Chinese, 341, 383, 385, 482–483
 in cities, 337–341
 to colonies, 119–121
 ethnic neighborhoods and, 341
 German, 338, 340–341, 343, 346
 Irish, 338, 339–340, 343, 344
 nativism and, 408
 patterns of, in 1800s, 338–339
 urban popular culture and, 343
 voting by, 346
Imperialism. *See also* Expansion, U.S.
Imports, 244–245
Incidents in the Life of a Slave Girl (Jacobs), 402
Indentured servants, 60, 119
Independence. *See also* American
  Revolution
 debate over, 156–157
 Declaration of, 159, 160
 negotiation of, 179–180
India, 139
Indian Country, 140–141
Indian Intercourse Act, 234
Indian peoples. *See also specific tribes*
 American Revolution and, 173–175
 ancient, 7–9
 Asian migration of, 5–7
 British and, 235–236, 238–240
 chiefs, primary function of, 12
 cities of, 3–4, 11–12, 15, 19
 during Civil War, 438–449
 culture areas and trade networks, 8
 Desert culture, 9
 diversity of, 4–5
 division of labor among, 12–13
 in eighteenth century, 108–109
 European diseases and, 28, 35, 36–37, 40,
   52, 63, 108
 European stereotypes of, 18, 58
 farming by, 4, 10–15, 17
 first contacts between Europeans and, 28,
   33, 42–43, 61
 forest efficiency, 9, 21
 fur trade and, 365–366
 gift-giving to, 140
 hunting traditions, 8–9
 images of, 46
 kinship systems, 12
 land of, 140–141, 182, 205–206, 234

missionaries and, 111, 232–233
 myths of, 10–11
 of Northeast, 22–23
 of Old Southwest, 254
 origins of, 5–7
 origins of foodways and, 10–11
 origins of tribal names, 19
 population decline of, 36–37, 108
 precolonial population of, 16–17
 Puritans and, 62–63
 relations between colonies and, 56–59,
   62–63
 religion of, 52
 removal of, 254
 resistance to westward expansion by,
   234–236
 Seven Years' War and, 136, 138–139
 slavery and, 34, 40–41, 88
 of South, 19–21
 of Southwest, 17, 19, 20
 Spanish and, 33–42
 technology of, 15
 term for, 4
 in thirteenth century, 3–4
 trade between Europeans and, 43
 treaties with, 141, 182, 205–206, 209,
   234, 368
 U.S. policy toward, 205–206, 234–235,
   292–294
 warfare among, 15–16, 22
 War of 1812 and, 237–240
 wars between colonists and, 69–70, 140
 western expansion and, 368
Indian removal, 292–294
Indian Removal Act, 292
Indian Territory, 254, 292, 368, 369
Indigo, 88
Industrialization
 beginning of, 319–323
 British technology and American, 319
 gender and, 324
 mass production and, 322
 middle class and, 327–332
 in North, 482–484
 politics and, 370
 rural life and, 315
Industry
 American system of manufactures, 321–322
 growth of, 395–396
 in North, 306–332
 putting-out system, 314, 316
 slavery and, 254–255
 in South, 267
 textile, 319–321

Inflation
 during Civil War, 447
 post-Revolutionary, 195, 196
Influenza, 36
Infrastructure, 294–295
Inheritance law, 187
Inoculation controversy, 126–127
Insane asylums, 349, 351–352
Intercourse Act, 205, 234
Internal slave trade, 255–258
Intolerable Acts, 134, 143, 151
Inuits, 7
Irish Catholics, 46
Irish immigrants, 338, 339–340, 343, 344,
   346, 406, 408
Iron Act, 97
Iroquois Five Nation Confederacy, 20, 22,
   54, 70, 108, 136, 173
Iroquois Indians, 20, 22
Irrigation systems, 13
Irving, Washington, 301
Isabel (queen), 32, 33
Italy
 city-states of, 30

J

Jackson, Andrew, 283
 Bank War and, 296–297
 election of 1824 and, 285
 election of 1828 and, 286–287
 Indian removal and, 292–294
 Kitchen Cabinet of, 288
 Nullification crisis and, 291–292
 presidency of, 287–297
 War of 1812 and, 239–240
Jackson, Thomas "Stonewall," 449
Jackson Entering the City of Winchester
   (Washington), 434
Jacobs, Harriet, 402
Jamaica, 34
James I, 61
James II, 70–71
Jamestown, 56–57
Japan
 trade with, 403
Jay, John, 152, 179, 182, 203, 209
Jay's Treaty, 209, 210
Jefferson, Thomas
 committees of correspondence and, 149
 Declaration of Independence and, 160
 election of 1796 and, 210
 election of 1800 and, 212, 213
 foreign policy of, 205, 231–233
 Indian policy and, 234

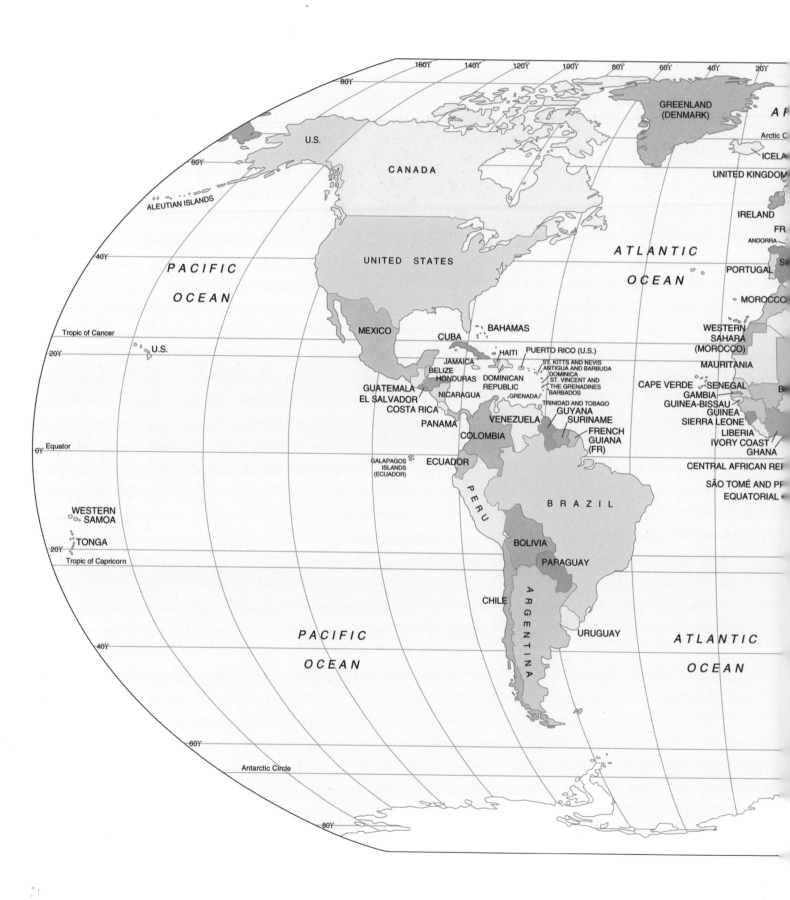

PACIFIC
OCEAN

ALEUTIAN ISLANDS

U.S.

CANADA

UNITED STATES

Tropic of Cancer

20Y

U.S.

MEXICO

BAHAMAS

CUBA

HAITI

PUERTO RICO (U.S.)

JAMAICA

BELIZE

HONDURAS

GUATEMALA

EL SALVADOR

NICARAGUA

COSTA RICA

PANAMA

COLOMBIA

VENEZUELA

ST. KITTS AND NEVIS
ANTIGUA AND BARBUDA
DOMINICA
ST. VINCENT AND
THE GRENADINES
BARBADOS

GRENADA

TRINIDAD AND TOBAGO

GUYANA

SURINAME

FRENCH
GUIANA
(FR)

DOMINICAN
REPUBLIC

GALAPAGOS
ISLANDS
(ECUADOR)

ECUADOR

PERU

BRAZIL

0Y Equator

WESTERN
SAMOA

TONGA

20Y

Tropic of Capricorn

BOLIVIA

PARAGUAY

CHILE

ARGENTINA

URUGUAY

PACIFIC

OCEAN

40Y

ATLANTIC

OCEAN

60Y

Antarctic Circle

80Y

GREENLAND
(DENMARK)

Arctic C

ICELA

UNITED KINGDOM

IRELAND

FR

ANDORRA

PORTUGAL

MOROCCO

WESTERN
SAHARA
(MOROCCO)

MAURITANIA

CAPE VERDE

SENEGAL

GAMBIA

GUINEA-BISSAU

GUINEA

SIERRA LEONE

LIBERIA

IVORY COAST

GHANA

CENTRAL AFRICAN REF

SÃO TOMÉ AND PF

EQUATORIAL

ATLANTIC

OCEAN

ATLANTIC

OCEAN

160Y 140Y 120Y 100Y 80Y 60Y 40Y 20Y

80Y

60Y

40Y

A

OCEAN

SWEDEN
FINLAND
ESTONIA
LATVIA
LITHUANIA
BELARUS
RMANY POLAND
CZECH REPUBLIC
SLOVAK REPUBLIC
SLOVENIA
HUNGARY
CROATIA
UKRAINE
MOLDOVA
AUS.
ROMANIA
ITALY
BOSNIA-HERZEGOVINA
SERBIA
BULGARIA GEORGIA
ALBANIA
MACEDONIA
GREECE TURKEY ARMENIA
MALTA
CYPRUS
TUNISIA
LEBANON
SYRIA
AZERBAIJAN
ISRAEL
IRAQ IRAN
LIBYA
JORDAN
EGYPT
BAHRAIN
KUWAIT
QATAR
SAUDI
ARABIA
NIGER
OMAN
UNITED
ARAB
EMIRATES
CHAD
ERITREA
YEMEN
ERIA
SUDAN
AMEROON
UGANDA
ETHIOPIA
DJIBOUTI
RWANDA
SOMALIA
BURUNDI
KENYA
Democratic
Republic
of Congo
TANZANIA
ANGOLA
MALAWI
COMOROS
ZAMBIA
MOZAMBIQUE
MADAGASCAR
NAMIBIA
BOTSWANA
ZIMBABWE
SWAZILAND
SOUTH
AFRICA
LESOTHO

RUSSIAN FEDERATION

KAZAKHSTAN
MONGOLIA
NORTH
KOREA
UZBEKISTAN
KYRGYZSTAN
JAPAN
PACIFIC
TURKMENISTAN
TAJIKISTAN
SOUTH
KOREA
OCEAN
AFGHANISTAN
PEOPLE'S REPUBLIC OF CHINA
NEPAL
BHUTAN
PAKISTAN
MYANMAR (BURMA)
TAIWAN
Tropic of Cancer
INDIA
LAOS
BANGLADESH
VIETNAM
THAILAND
PHILIPPINES
MARSHALL
ISLANDS
SRI LANKA
MICRONESIA
MALDIVES
BRUNEI
MALAYSIA
Equator
KIRIBATI
SINGAPORE
NAURU
SEYCHELLES
INDONESIA
PAPUA
NEW GUINEA
SOLOMON
ISLANDS
TUVALU
INDIAN
OCEAN
VANUATU
FIJI
MAURITIUS
Tropic of Capricorn
NEW CALEDONIA
(FRANCE)
AUSTRALIA

NEW ZEALAND

Antarctic Circle

0   1,000   2,000 Miles
0   1,000   2,000   3,000 Kilometers